STATISTICS IN CORPUS LINGUISTICS RESEARCH

Traditional approaches focused on significance tests have often been difficult for linguistics researchers to visualise. *Statistics in Corpus Linguistics Research: A New Approach* breaks significance tests down for researchers in corpus linguistics and linguistic analysis, promoting a visual approach to understanding the performance of tests with real data, and demonstrating how to derive new confidence intervals and tests.

This fully revised second edition includes a brand-new chapter describing a novel extended 'MOVER' method to derive accurate confidence intervals for numerous properties. With sample datasets and easy-to-read visuals, this book focuses on practical issues, such as how to

- pose meaningful research questions in terms of choice and constraint;
- employ confidence intervals correctly (including in graph plots);
- select a significance test (and interpret its results);
- construct confidence intervals for functions of independent proportions;
- measure the size of the effect of one variable on another or the similarity between two distributions; and
- evaluate whether the results of two experiments significantly differ.

Appropriate for anyone from the student just beginning their career to the seasoned researcher, this book is both a practical overview and valuable resource.

A website with downloadable resources for the calculations in this book is published at https://corplingstats.wordpress.com/siclr

Sean Wallis is Principal Research Fellow and Deputy Director of the Survey of English Usage at UCL.

STATISTICS IN CORPUS LINGUISTICS RESEARCH

A New Approach

Second Edition

Sean Wallis

Routledge
Taylor & Francis Group
NEW YORK AND LONDON

Cover image: 'Wilson distribution, $p = 0.3$, $n = 10$, with half-Normal distributions at tails, $\alpha = 0.05$.' © Sean Wallis 2025

Second edition published 2026
by Routledge
605 Third Avenue, New York, NY 10158

and by Routledge
4 Park Square, Milton Park, Abingdon, Oxon, OX14 4RN

Routledge is an imprint of the Taylor & Francis Group, an informa business

First edition published by Routledge 2021

Library of Congress Cataloging-in-Publication Data
Names: Wallis, Sean author
Title: Statistics in corpus linguistics research : a new approach / Sean Wallis.
Description: Second edition. | New York, NY : Routledge, 2026. | Includes bibliographical references and index.
Identifiers: LCCN 2025038840 (print) | LCCN 2025038841 (ebook) | ISBN 9781041031871 hardback | ISBN 9781041031864 paperback | ISBN 9781003622697 ebook
Subjects: LCSH: Corpora (Linguistics)—Data processing | Linguistics—Statistical methods | Computational linguistics
Classification: LCC P128.C68 .W35 2026 (print) | LCC P128.C68 (ebook)
LC record available at https://lccn.loc.gov/2025038840
LC ebook record available at https://lccn.loc.gov/2025038841

ISBN: 978-1-041-03187-1 (hbk)
ISBN: 978-1-041-03186-4 (pbk)
ISBN: 978-1-003-62269-7 (ebk)

DOI: 10.4324/9781003622697

Typeset in Times New Roman
by Apex CoVantage, LLC

CONTENTS

PART 3
Confidence Intervals and Significance Tests 123

PART 4
Effect Sizes and Meta-Tests 297

PREFACE

1 Why Do We Need Another Book on Statistics?

This book arose from the realisation that conventional approaches to the teaching and discussion of statistics – in the field of linguistics at least – are not working.

'Statistics' is central to modern science, but students and researchers – even experienced professional scientists – find statistics extremely difficult to rationalise. *Inferential statistics* is an extremely powerful branch of mathematics, but one with counter-intuitive elements that require care to explain and effort to grasp.

Researchers commonly play safe: find a textbook or academic paper, reproduce the method, replace one set of data with another and duplicate the statistical procedure. Medical statistical analysis is outsourced to specialist units. Statistics and research methods are divorced. Researchers are instructed how to collect data. Analysts are permitted certain statistical methods. Research methods stop innovating.

Traditional books encourage the same approach. Copy the method. Do not worry *how* it works: it just works. If you want your work published, you need 'statistics'. Turn the handle. Report the results.

What seems missing is a clear explanation as to how a test procedure works from the ground up. By this I do not mean that tests are not sufficiently described to the mathematically initiated. I mean that teachers and textbook writers need to recognise that, fundamentally, *statistical reasoning is often counter-intuitive*, and successful understanding requires a mental effort by the student. Absent is a patient explanation of the intermediate steps from first principles of probability and chance to distributions and basic tests.

Yet whenever we apply *any* method in science, we must ask if it is appropriate for our data and if we can draw the type of conclusions we intend. If one merely copies a method, errors and misunderstandings are likely to propagate. Weaknesses are frequently exposed in essay conclusions. But problems of method are not limited to students!

I never expected to be writing this book. But around 2008, my work in artificial intelligence and corpus linguistics forced me to recognise that I was as confused as everyone else. Instructions in textbooks, and common practices, were clearly wrong. But it was in the conclusions of papers, commonly in student work, but sometimes in that of peers, where it became obvious that, as a community, we did not understand the logic of the methods we were using or the types of claim we were making.

I am a product of statistics teaching, and my own reading and research. I was taught statistics formally twice: at advanced level at school and at university. I have also engaged in a certain amount of pure mathematics over the years, so derivations and proofs are familiar.

I write this book fully conscious that any criticism I might level against others I recognise in my own research practice. In machine learning research 30 years ago, I used a log-likelihood statistic I have since discovered is less than optimal. I too have compared '*p* values', or slipped into this type of reasoning.

The core of this book, Part 3, is concerned with the fundamentals of the statistical analysis of observed *Binomial proportions* from first principles. These are some of the simplest statistical methods in existence. This might seem a narrow focus, but this type of analysis has wide utility. Once we understand the underlying mathematics, we can create new tests and intervals.

My principal area of current research is *corpus linguistics*. Corpora are volumes of linguistic data ('texts') that have been collected to obtain volumes of raw material for analysis. A corpus linguistics researcher comes to this data 'post hoc', after the collection decisions have been made.

It is an observational science. Researchers can select texts and samples, but cannot retrospectively manipulate the conditions under which data were originally collected! True, it is conceivable that one might design a corpus to answer a specific research question, but a corpus usually contains numerous confounding variables. One reason is that corpora are typically 'ecological' data collections. Data come from real-world sources rather than controlled laboratory conditions. Participants in an experiment may be given the same task. But corpus compilers typically collect texts produced by speakers or writers performing *different* tasks, each motivated by their communicative goals at the time.

Linguistics has its own particular issues to deal with. Crucially, thanks to the structured nature of language, many phenomena are most meaningfully analysed in terms of *choice*. A speaker utters expression A or B – or A or nothing. A writer uses a particular word or grammatical construction out of a set of potential alternatives. Sequences of decisions are chained. Choices, once made, permit or exclude others.

In Chapter 1, I argue that to study linguistic choices, we need spontaneously produced data. In spontaneous speech, the majority of choices are unconscious and autonomous. But in non-spontaneous contexts, choices may be conscious, artfully crafted, mannered acts of self-presentation – like the act of writing this book, edited and re-edited over time.

Binomial proportions represent the proportion of occasions a particular option is selected. As we shall see, this type of statistics is particularly relevant to (corpus) linguistics.

The book is organised in the following way. After Part 1 on motivations, I address issues of experimental design and data collection in corpus linguistics in Part 2, discuss statistical methods in Parts 3 and 4, and return to corpus linguistics in Part 5 to address particular problems of this discipline. In Part 6, I show how to calculate distribution curves and conclude the book.

This book is intended to supplement, not replace, other textbooks in statistics or linguistics. We are primarily concerned with understanding the fundamentals of statistical reasoning. What exactly are we doing when we use a statistical procedure?

2 Statistics and Scientific Rigour

Complex models must be built on solid foundations. And researchers who use them are obliged to understand them.

In the past, many researchers were encouraged to focus on the process of selecting and performing tests with their data, and to be rarely concerned about the underlying mathematical models on which their tests were based. 'Statistics' became little more than magic pixie dust sprinkled on hard-won experimental data to make papers publishable.

Yet statistics is a branch of *mathematics* governing the logic of experimental research. It is rooted in logic, set and number theory. It should be possible to understand how common tests are derived from first principles, reason logically about the results of tests and derive new test procedures.

I believe the fundamentals of inferential statistics can be properly conveyed to anyone prepared to persevere. I think the hardest part is not the mathematical notation and algebra – which are quite simple – but the slightly peculiar, occasionally counter-intuitive, way of thinking one must adopt to understand how it works.

One of the most pervasive mistakes concerns the quoting and comparing of error levels of tests, so-called 'p values'. Academic papers quote test scores to as many as four decimal places (e.g., '$\chi^2 = 53.4386$') or convert them to p values and cite them ('$p < 0.0001$'). Once reported, comparisons are inevitably made, implying that 'my p value is smaller than yours, so my data/paper is more significant than yours'. Such a comparison is entirely fallacious.

I suspect the first reason why this type of citation is popular is that it aligns with our natural positivist inclinations. We all want to be right. Thanks to SPSS™ or Excel™, a test procedure can retrospectively compute an error level to many decimal places, so why not quote it? The practice provides a stamp of scientific conclusiveness to experimental conjecture. But a smaller error level merely means that our results are less likely to be a one-off and more likely to be replicated should we perform our experiment again.

Indeed, herein lies a dangerous misdirection. Scientific reasoning requires a dispassionate self-critical mind. The strength of scientific conclusions comes from the scientific procedure and research journey. Strong conclusions rely on the theoretical basis of the experiment, the justification for the variables selected, the care taken in obtaining relevant data, and most of all, *the elimination of alternative explanations*.

There may be multiple possible reasons why we see a correlation in our data. The proper role of 'statistics' is to impartially evaluate data and allow us to eliminate these other potential explanations. A close 'fit' of existing data is insufficient. We must test alternative explanations, perhaps collect new data or annotate existing data before deciding to reject them.

Statistical analysis is only as good as the underlying method. A statistically 'significant' result may be an artifact of a weak experimental method, the result of an underlying process the researcher failed to account for, or the application of a mistaken mathematical model.

Every student is taught that correlation does not equal cause. But causal thinking is *so* seductive!

The correct way to think about statistical significance is that it is based on two connected aspects:

- It is a *binary judgement representing a prediction about replication.*
- This judgement is based on a *particular mathematical model of expected behaviour*, that is, the mathematics of the underlying test.

Imagine we repeated an experiment many times, acquiring new data and analysing them. So-called 'p values' are *error levels* of a mathematical model that predicts the likely range of results of future potential experimental repetitions. With an error level of 0.05, we predict that 19 times out of 20, we would obtain a similar result. With an error level of 0.001, this becomes 999 times out of 1,000.

But if the experiment is flawed, or the mathematical model is incorrect, all bets are off! Indeed, tests may involve mathematical approximations that dwarf 1-in-100 error levels (Wallis, 2013a). The test is not 'wrong', but ultra-citation is ridiculous. The procedure must be properly understood as a binary one. Once a result is deemed significant, the p value is irrelevant.

Second, despite protests by statisticians, *p* values are inevitably compared. Nieuwenhuis et al. (2011) found that, of 513 papers in prestigious neuroscience journals that made the comparison, almost half made the following erroneous claim. Since their experiment was significant, and an earlier experiment was not, researchers argued *their second result was significantly different from the first.* The correct approach is discussed in Chapter 14.

The question of properly comparing experimental results is not an obscure side issue. It is how we empirically compare different datasets, versions of experiments and replication attempts.

It hardly seems fair to criticise students if published scientists make basic mistakes. But scientists were students once, and their errors stem from misunderstandings in the statistical literature, reproduced in textbooks and propagated in papers because they appear common sense. Technology has also played its role. The ease of computing *p* values to many decimal places and the ability to collect large amounts of data have made small *p* values trivial to obtain.

What is going wrong? I hope most scientists will agree with my depiction of science as a self-consciously rigorous exercise. The fault must lie in the practice. Reluctantly, I have to conclude that most researchers do not fully understand what they are doing when they apply significance tests.

3 Why Is Statistics Difficult?

Most presentations of statistics skate over its mathematical and philosophical core. Inferential statistics is not intuitive, and getting to grips with it is a necessary conceptual struggle. The distribution of randomly sampled observed means, an idea at the heart of every statistical model, is difficult to conceive of. Common errors are the result of intuitive misconceptions about this underlying conceptual framework.

Ultimately, I believe the core of the problem is cognitive, not mathematical. I think the reason we find statistics difficult is that *it does not model our direct experience, but the sum of many experiences.*

A well-known concept in child developmental psychology is ‘naïve physics’ (Baillargeon, 1994): a world model children acquire by interacting with their surroundings. Their journey starts in the crib, focusing vision and hand-eye coordination, and learning to recognise faces and sounds. Three-month-old children acquire the concept of ‘object constancy’ (objects exist despite being hidden). Learning about the physical properties of the world accelerates once a child becomes active, mobile and dexterous. Crawling teaches three-dimensional space, length, area and volume. Edges, hard and soft, become tangible through experience! Walking teaches balance and orientation, focuses vertical coordination, frees up hands, and so forth.

By contrast, statistics is concerned with the distribution and probability of *many* events. We cannot acquire this knowledge by absorbing life’s experiences, but by systematic observation and counting. If naïve physics is first order, immediately experienced knowledge, statistics is second order, requiring attention, reflection and memory. Hence, we are, as a species, really rather incompetent at estimating risk. Young children who have never had a major accident are invincible – but ultra-cautious after a fall. Elderly people overestimate risks of mugging, being – rightly – fearful of the consequences. We rely on physics, not probability, when crossing the road. We are led by our biases and preferences, and we rely on intuitions for decisions.[1]

Our brains tend to identify patterns based on perceptually salient variables easy to detect and recall, like young birds avoiding red berries, or children, sour tastes. Recognition involves memory, but frequently overgeneralises stereotypes and forms misleading associations. Pattern recognition has enabled us to survive and learn, but easily misleads us.

Memory plays other tricks on us. As we view the world, our memories are simultaneously recalled and projected onto our perceptions. Agreed mechanisms differ (see, e.g., Harth, 1995), but it is an axiom of cognitive science that *perception* is distinct from *conception*. Perception might inductively teach us concepts, but conception frequently leads and frames perception. We tend to perceive what we expect to see, like shapes in the fog. In this world of apparently continuous sensory perception, we chance on optical illusions. Walking in the mist, a suspicious figure becomes a harmless bush as we draw near.

In the statistical world of abstraction from multiple events, events are historic, and we only have our recorded data to inspect. We ascribe causality to a remembered sequence of events: I was sick after eating some berries, therefore all similar-looking berries are toxic.

Yet the scientific method requires *care and restraint*. It requires us to 'play devil's advocate': to be ruthlessly self-critical and enumerate alternative hypotheses, some of which may require new data. Our natural tendency to rely on intuition and pattern recognition must be tamed with careful reasoning and procedure.

4 Looking Down the Observer's End of the Telescope

Statistics concerns fundamentally intangible concepts, such as probabilities and distributions. Our task is to make the intangible tangible. In this book, we rely on a trick that has aided many a mathematician down the years: we prioritise visualisation over tables of data and mathematical formulae.

In science and mathematics, there is a long and noble tradition of diagrams, rather than symbols, proving central to scientific discovery, from Euclid's geometry to Newton's *Principia* (1687). George Polya's famous book *How to solve it* (1945) teaches diagrammatic reasoning. Briggs (2016, p. 31) calls this Eureka moment 'induction-intellection': identifying truths by intellectual leaps from data.

But diagrams risk being too specific, misleading the researcher. The astronomer Johannes Kepler adduced that the orbits he saw through his telescope were elliptical rather than circular. But he did not consider the possibility of parabolic or hyperbolic orbits, which Isaac Newton inferred.

A tendency to occasionally overgeneralise has led diagrammatic reasoning to periodically fall from fashion. Nonetheless, it is worth considering why visualisation is powerful. Visualisation allows a problem system to be viewed as a whole, rather than a series of component parts. Giardino (2017) is a useful review of this mathematical tradition.

In statistics, Braithwaite and Goldstone (2013) report that overall, competent graphs improve the performance of researchers' comprehension of their data compared to tables, but may bias certain perspectives over others.

'Visualising significance' means replacing significance testing procedures – where tables of numbers output yet more numbers – by graph plots with *confidence intervals*. On these graphs, we can see *significant differences*. Visualisation has just taught us a key concept: 'significance' only makes sense when applied to differences between values.

A confidence interval about an observed value is the range of values statistically consistent with it.[2] Whereas traditional statistical testing assumes an expected population value (or set of values), and compares our observations with this target projection; we look down the other end of the telescope. We start with our observation and ask, *where is the true value in the population?*

Consider the following problem.

> Suppose, for the sake of argument, we ask 20 random people whether they had ever had the common illness chicken pox (varicella). Five say yes, 15 no. Our task is to try to work out *the range of values consistent with our observation* for the true incidence of chicken pox exposure in the population we sampled.

This is an incredibly useful procedure, but it is not a test. The 'range of values' is a confidence interval. We decide on an acceptable level of error and compute a range.

One of the best methods for calculating confidence intervals on proportions like this (termed 'Binomial proportions') is due to Edwin Bidwell Wilson (1927), who in the process of explaining his formula, demolished a common statistical fallacy. This is to assume *that expected random variation of the true population proportion around an observed sample proportion will be Normally distributed*, that is, symmetrically distributed according to the iconic 'bell curve'. Wilson explained that even if we assume that *observations about the true population value* are Normally distributed, *the reverse cannot be true*. We discuss this in Chapter 6.

We can calculate Wilson's *score interval* with our thought experiment for p(chicken pox) = 5/20 = 25%, using a 5% error level. Do not worry about how we do this, let us just accept it can be done.[3]

Wilson's formula calculates a confidence interval for p(chicken pox). This can be thought of as an expected range for the true value in the population.

The Wilson score interval for $p = 0.25$, $n = 20$ and $\alpha = 0.05$ is approximately 11% to 47%. Employing Frank Yates's (1934) compensation for smoothing, this becomes a slightly wider and more conservative 9.5% to 49.5%.[4]

> In summary, we can conclude that, on meeting only 20 random people and finding five ex-sufferers of chicken pox among their number, *we are able to predict that the incidence of chicken pox in the population at large is probably less than half (but more than 9%).*

This 'probably' claim is based on an error level, which we set at 5% (or '0.05', if you prefer). The interval is typically quoted as having a '95% confidence' because we are predicting that 19 out of 20, or 95%, of repetitions fall within it. The error level is *the acceptable level of risk* that the true value is outside the range. Thus, if we reduce the allowable error level to 1%, the range of projected values widens (with Yates's correction, to 7.5% to 56%).[5]

This method gave us a range of values. But if we are interested only in the *maximum* rate in the population, we could perform a 'one-tailed' evaluation. A 95% one-tailed evaluation would employ a 90% interval on the upper bound: 43.2%, or 45.8% with the smoothing correction. Now we can report that the true incidence of chicken pox in the population is likely to be less than 46%.

At this point, you may wonder how on earth could we draw *any* inference about the population from a mere 20 random people? This question caused many 19th-century scientists much heartache. But this little thought experiment reveals the great strength of statistical models. 'Statistics' is largely irrelevant with thousands of observations: sampled results will be close to true population values anyway. Confidence intervals, estimates of uncertainty, become infinitesimal.

The strength of inferential statistics lies in *small samples*. With very limited data, we can infer characteristics of an infinitely large population, *provided that the sample is randomly drawn from the population.* This fundamental but counter-intuitive observation deserves its own chapter, Chapter 6, which takes us from observing simple randomness to projecting Wilson intervals on observations. In my experience, it is this leap of imagination that students find the most difficult, hence it deserves a chapter of its own.

Confidence intervals are not the only way to express statistical uncertainty. However, we can plot them on the same scale as our observations. Plotting data with intervals allows us to gain an appreciation of the uncertainty of our results. We begin to make the intangible, tangible. In Chapter 7, we show how, armed with this type of plot, we may compare observations by eye, being compelled to carry out an actual test procedure only when intervals partly overlap.

In this book, I will show that it is possible to explain the mathematical fundamentals of simple significance tests by first relating them to confidence intervals. More complex tests can be derived from these simple tests. Finally, novel tests – original tests absent from the literature – can be derived.

This book sits at the intersection between linguistics and statistics. As a researcher who has worked with academic linguists over many years, my focus is practical. I aim to explain how to approach statistics for linguistics research in a new, and hopefully more meaningful, way.

I also trust that non-linguists will gain insights from this book. But as a result of focusing on linguistics, my focus is narrow. I focus on Binomial and Multinomial (discrete choice) testing rather than, say, comparing Real, Ratio or Ordinal data. Confidence interval computation may be extended in this direction, but it is not central to *this* book.

There are other books on statistics, including those aimed at corpus linguists, which describe new innovations and complex analysis methods. But if you do not understand the mathematics and underlying reasoning of simple tests, you are likely to misread more complex ones.

Simple tests with a single degree of freedom are usually *more conclusive* – a significant result has only one interpretation – than tests with many degrees of freedom. Model fitting depends on getting the underlying mathematical model of the expected distribution of the data correct. It is easy to apply a powerful method only for results to be dominated by artifacts of sampling or experimental design.

Computational methods have been developed for exploratory research with corpora, which perform tasks like identifying collocations or part-of-speech tagging. This book is not concerned with computational tools, although I should perhaps comment that many of these algorithms, while using statistical *formulae*, are not necessarily statistically *sound*.[6]

Increasing numbers of linguists are using corpora, some alongside laboratory experiments. Not all consider themselves 'corpus' linguists. The arguments, methods and tests in this book, particularly in Parts 3 and 4, are equally applicable to experimental and corpus data. I hope this book has something to say to linguists of every stripe.

Before you reach for your data, reach for this book.

5 What Do Linguists Need to Know About Statistics?

Although this book is a statistics book, it is written for an audience of linguists, and corpus linguists in particular.

Some questions are of general interest. Researchers typically want answers to basic questions:

- Which test should I use for this problem?
- What is the difference between chi-square and log-likelihood?
- Can I use the chi-square test when cell values are small?
- What does it mean to say that *this* test is significant?
- Can we plot confidence intervals on this data?
- How might I compare my results to those in the literature?
- Can we compare '*p* values'?

I have focused on central issues that students and researchers struggle with. These include the following:

- how to pose meaningful research questions in terms of choice and constraint;
- how to employ confidence intervals correctly (including in graph plots);
- how to select a significance test (and how to interpret results);
- how to construct confidence intervals for functions of independent proportions;
- how to measure the size of the effect of one variable on another or the similarity between two distributions; and
- how to evaluate whether the results of two experiments significantly differ.

Significance testing is discussed and explained, but it is one topic on this list.

My programme was developed independently from the emerging 'New Statistics' movement, which I briefly discuss in Chapter 11. It shares many similarities with it, including an emphasis on visualisation, confidence intervals and effect size estimation. Where we differ is that I do not reject null hypothesis significance testing (sometimes shortened to 'NHST'). Rather, I explain how this procedure can be explained from first principles. Others may disagree and wish to reject NHST altogether. The debate is important for all of us.

In linguistics, researchers face a range of methodological research questions, both empirical and epistemological. Empirical questions are practical ones. Which methods may be applied to *this* type of data? Which are optimal? Given a particular phenomenon of interest, what meaningful baselines for studying it might there be – and what might different baselines tell us? What kinds of research can be undertaken within a particular linguistic framework?

Epistemological questions are deeper, but equally necessary. Epistemology is the philosophy of knowledge. A crucial question at the heart of the scientific method in linguistics concerns the role of 'frameworks'. A framework could be simply the typological classification of linguistic data, such as the identification of lemmas, parts of speech (wordclasses), phrases or speech acts. But it could also include structural relationships: *this* is the head of *that* phrase, *this* clause turns *that* speech act into a question, and so on. All but the crudest linguistics research programme employs some kind of linguistic framework. But if we use a framework to get our data, *how can we argue that our results are not merely artifacts of the framework?*

This is not a new problem. In science, necessary assumptions required to obtain data are usually called 'auxiliary assumptions': the optics of the microscope, the measurement accuracy of the equipment, the speed of light in a vacuum, and so on. These are scientifically justified but outside the hypothesis under test.

I have long taken the view that linguistics has its own auxiliary assumptions, expressed as frameworks. Suppose we wish to identify particular grammatical elements. We have no choice but to apply relevant grammatical constructions to raw plain text to identify them. Either we make use of a framework that has already been applied to a corpus and apply queries to this annotated corpus to get our data, or we apply queries to unannotated text to find the same instances by other means, *and in the process, apply our own framework*. Whether we like it or not, as soon as we distinguish nouns from verbs, adjectives from adverbs, and so on, we are employing a framework!

Linguists often debate and uphold alternative frameworks. This bothers many. When we perform data collection, *are we imprisoned by our framework* in a 'hermeneutic trap'? Are we engaged in circular reasoning?

What kinds of empirical evidence might help us decide between frameworks? Are there objective means by which we might be able to show that one framework is 'superior' to another, and if so, what might 'superior' mean? In the first chapter, I suggest the solution lies in the concept of *explanatory power*, that a more powerful theory provides more predictions and explanations of novel phenomena, or explains phenomena more simply and efficiently. In the meantime we should avoid over-committing to a particular framework and consider whether employing alternatives might make a difference to our results.

In Part 2 of this book, we spend some considerable time discussing problems of baselines and frameworks because they are central contemporary concerns in corpus linguistics, and students and researchers frequently find these issues as difficult as correctly employing statistical methods. Researchers in other areas of linguistics or other scientific disciplines may find this largely irrelevant to them. Feel free to skim Part 2 and move on to Parts 3 and 4. Part 5 examines two problems found in corpus linguistics. The methods are, however, primarily mathematical rather than linguistic, and may be useful for researchers of other disciplines. Part 6 reveals how I plotted the distribution of confidence intervals so we could view them in this book, hopefully offering new insight into these intervals and tests before concluding.

6 How Has This Book Changed From the First Edition?

For the most part, this book has been improved incrementally. But it has gained a major new chapter, Chapter 9. This introduces a general method for creating confidence intervals on properties of observed data, provided that these properties can be expressed as mathematical combinations of independent proportions. As the title suggests, we elaborate an 'algebra of intervals', a highly productive method for developing intervals on ratios, effect sizes and other scores. This work draws heavily on Zou and Donner's (2008) generalisation of the difference interval, ably assisted by Newcombe's (2020) book, which was published while the First Edition was in press.

Including this chapter has allowed me to streamline explanations elsewhere. For example, the idea of a generalised difference interval formula, $\theta_1 - \theta_2 \in$ **difference**(θ_1, θ_2) is very powerful. If the interval includes zero, θ_1 and θ_2 are not significantly different. The only requirement is that the parameters are independently sampled properties each with robust confidence intervals. Newcombe's Wilson-based interval about $d = p_2 - p_1$ becomes **difference**(p_2, p_1), where both parameters have Wilson score intervals. But the parameters can in principle be any property with a confidence interval.

A notable impact is on my treatment of intervals for *effect sizes*, discussed in Chapter 13. Adding a good quality confidence interval to an effect size like Yule's Q or Cramér's ϕ transforms these properties, often sidelined as approximate and merely descriptive, into citable research results: output parameters capable of evaluation and comparison.

Previously, we might at most carry out a related significance test (implying that the property is significantly different from zero). For ϕ, this is the χ^2 test for independence. But when we used to cite a ϕ score, all we could report was the number. We might say it was found to be in a particular range of numbers (a 'medium' effect from 0.3 to 0.5, say). But we could not say whether *the true value in the population* was likely to be a 'medium' effect.

Now, a confidence interval on ϕ tells us the range of values in which the true value is likely to be found. We can compare the lower bound (or, for signed scores, the bound closest to zero) with a threshold, or make comparisons between experimental scores with **difference**(ϕ_1, ϕ_2). In the First Edition, I demonstrated how this could be employed in priming experiments. But the same approach can be applied to other properties, like entropy or mutual information, once an interval has been derived.

One aspect of the methods developed in Chapter 9 concerns Multinomial sums, sums of functions of proportions in Multinomial competition. This allows us to derive confidence intervals for effect sizes expressing categorical 'goodness of fit', that is, the closeness of one ordered series of frequencies to another. The formula is found in Chapter 13.

Other additions to this book include the 'mid-p' interval and bootstrap intervals discussed in Chapter 8. Experimenting with bootstrap intervals, I was disappointed with their performance, at least for Binomial proportions. But perhaps more concerning was they incorporate an error of circular thinking noted by Edwin Wilson a century ago, namely, to assume that a confidence interval is a kind of sampling interval. Fortunately, we have better methods.

7 Caution and Average Error

At the heart of this book is the idea that confidence intervals, conceived of as ranges of values not significantly different from observations, allow us to visualise and conceive of otherwise unknowable random sampling variation applied to our experimental results. This idea is core to the 'New Statistics' movement (see Chapter 11), but as you would expect with any new development, it is generating ongoing debates about which intervals should be recommended. I touch on this question briefly discussing the Clopper–Pearson and 'mid-p' intervals in Chapter 8, but I should explain how this debate has affected my thinking in this book.

I advance a position that confidence intervals should be consistent with significance tests. In other words, if and only if something is deemed to be significantly different according to a confidence interval, it should also be significantly different according to a corresponding significance test.

This stance allows students taught null hypothesis significance testing ('NHST') to grasp confidence intervals intuitively. An interval outlines just how far a population value would have to be from an observed one to be significantly different from it.

Indeed, compared to previous 'confidence interval methods' like the Wald, delta methods or bootstrap, not defined by the interval equality principle, this represents a tremendous advance. It lays the foundations for an algebra of intervals that can produce multiple new confidence intervals and tests.

From this perspective, every single cited interval independently specifies the boundary of significant difference. But it creates a new issue. Erring on the side of caution, as we must in significance testing, means guaranteeing that the chance of falsely claiming a difference as significant is *at least* our target error level α, in every single case. A generation of students have been instructed 'use the Fisher test when you can, and Yates's χ^2 test when you can't'.

This is not a universally agreed position among confidence interval afficionados. How so? Well, researchers found that despite setting a target α to compute an interval, the actual average tail error found by exhaustively evaluating the interval is rather smaller (and the interval coverage rather larger than the desired $1 - \alpha$). The reason is obvious with Yates's continuity-correction smoothing. Columns of data at the edge may be over-zealously moved inside the interval. But this is also true for other intervals. See Newcombe (2020, p. 107).

The result is that if you plot a lot of data with confidence intervals, or fit your data to a function with intervals, all these little anxious deviations on the side of caution add up! You want the true *overall* error rate to be α (or perhaps only a little less). That 'at least' can add up to a lot of false negatives! Like fitting points to a line, we are seeking the best model *on average*.

Intervals which are robust for citing individually, like the continuity-corrected Wilson or the 'exact' Clopper-Pearson interval are overcautious for plotting trends. This is an argument for the 'mid-p' interval and against continuity corrections when applying the Wilson interval.

Fortunately, thanks to a discovery I made while writing the First Edition, we can be flexible. Adding a continuity correction to a Wilson score interval is easy once the interval formula is expressed as a pair of functions, WilsonLower and WilsonUpper.

Indeed, isolating the continuity correction term from the rest of the formula means it can be *scaled*. Back with my precautionary 'hat' on, I evaluated the **difference** function on several number scales (difference, ratio, log, odds ratio), testing the inner interval against the Fisher 'exact' test, and varying a correction scale factor, γ. A trade-off graph is included in Chapter 9, and the study (Wallis, 2024b) is documented on my blog, **corp.ling.stats**.

Applying a difference interval on these scales at conventional NHST levels of $\alpha = 0.05$ or 0.01 increases the risk of Type I errors. But we can reduce these errors for functions of Wilson score intervals by manipulating this factor. Indeed, slightly increasing Yates's famous correction, $\frac{1}{2n}$, by a factor of $\gamma = 1.5$ eliminates almost all Type I (false positive) errors. If you are of the 'exact' test persuasion, you can use Wilson score intervals with this amplified adjustment. Alternatively, if you seek an average error of α, but wish to suppress additional errors, a correction of $0.5 \times \frac{1}{2n}$ across number scales will outperform uncorrected 2×2 χ^2.

If you are plotting a lot of data, you don't need to pick sides. Reader, you can plot both!

ACKNOWLEDGMENTS

The first edition was written in stages over ten years or so. Some early versions of chapters were first published on my blog, **corp.ling.stats** (https://corplingstats.wordpress.com), from 2011 onwards. I took the risk of self-publication to encourage application, evaluation, debate and feedback. The result was overwhelmingly positive, and the book was stronger as a result. The vast majority of the book had never been published before, being drawn from my own research, collaborations with colleagues and lectures I had given.

An earlier version of Chapter 1 first appeared in the proceedings of the *Olinco* conference in 2014. Other chapters draw on work in published papers, documented as they are introduced. Work published in two chapters – Chapters 8 and 14 – were first published as articles in the *Journal of Quantitative Linguistics*, but were extensively revised for this book. Figure 6.9 is reproduced from another *Journal of Quantitative Linguistics* article (Wallis, 2013a) and Figure 12.3 was first published in an article in the *International Journal of Corpus Linguistics* (Wallis, 2019b). I am grateful to all my publishers for their prompt agreement to republish.

Thanks are due to Evgenii Neumerzhitckii for his permission to use the three-body orbit figure in Chapter 10. His demonstration program is highly recommended.

Although this book has a single author, it could not have been written without many years of active collaboration with numerous linguist colleagues. I owe many thanks to Bas Aarts, Sylvia Adamson, Jill Bowie, Joanne Close, Rachele De Felice, Stefan Th. Gries, Gunther Kaltenböck, Evelien Keizer, Geoff Leech, Magnus Levin, Christian Mair, Seth Mehl, Gerald Nelson, Terttu Nevalainen, Gabriel Ozón, Nicholas Smith and Sali Tagliamonte. A number of reviewers, including Seth Mehl and Valentin Werner, gave me detailed feedback on chapters. Responsibility for errors is of course my own.

I must particularly thank Robert Newcombe for his forbearance in explaining the Wilson score interval to me. Hopefully, I got there in the end! Without him, this book would simply not have been possible. Arguments in the pub with my good friends Dorothy Wright and Geoff Williams improved my ability to communicate some of these concepts. (Well, mostly.)

My wife, Yota Kondopoulou, has given me more support than I could possibly dare to ask. Not only did she put up with my long stints in front of the computer, she tolerated me trying to explain some of these ideas to her! Without her love and support, this book would not exist.

This book is also a product of my research environment. The Survey of English Usage was set up by Randolph Quirk in 1959, inspired by the Brown University team led by W. Nelson Francis and Henry Kučera. The Survey was the first European research centre in corpus linguistics. From the outset, the Quirk team – whose alumni and collaborators represent a veritable 'Who's Who' of English language linguistics – prioritised the collection of spoken data over writing. The Survey corpus eventually grew into the famous *London Lund Corpus* (LLC).

Another decision was perhaps even more fortuitous for the path that led to this book. In the early 1990s, Quirk's successor, Sidney Greenbaum, decided to parse the Survey's second corpus, the *British Component of the International Corpus of English* (ICE-GB). I have been extremely fortunate, as a researcher from cognitive psychology, artificial intelligence and computing, to work with a substantial database of richly grammatically annotated speech for nearly three decades. Once parsed, the Survey had a rich source, with huge potential for research in natural language – but little in the way of research techniques and technologies to make the most of it.

I joined the Survey in 1995 and was immediately involved in the building of ICE-GB, followed by the *Diachronic Corpus of Present-day Spoken English* (DCPSE) some eight years later. My first contribution was by turns technically demanding, necessary and yet outwardly mundane: overseeing the construction of these corpora and writing software to support the process. The software platform I built, ICECUP, was first published in 1998 and turned over to the community to perform research with these corpora.

This book is not about these linguistic resources, projects or software. Readers are directed to Nelson et al. (2002) and the Survey of English Usage website, www.ucl.ac.uk/english/english-usage, for more information. Sample corpora and software are freely available.

However, nearly three decades after ICE-GB was first published, if you wish to carry out empirical research into the grammar of English, ICE-GB and DCPSE are still world-leading – if only because the effort involved in collecting and parsing spoken natural language to a high standard is very substantial!

But the very fact that databases of this kind are difficult to construct also means that we need to exploit them to the fullest. My association with the Survey placed me in the midst of an international long-term effort to make the most we can out of such a rich and important resource. It is for this reason that, in this book, I make no apology for drawing the majority of examples and data from these corpora.

Building a substantial parsed corpus such as ICE-GB or DCPSE is necessarily a team effort, and this book stands on the shoulders of giants. Hopefully, Part 2 convincingly demonstrates that the efforts of a generation of researchers who painstakingly applied linguistic knowledge to the corpus remain worthwhile!

We are still scratching the surface of what these corpora might tell us. In this book, I suggest that the path to deeper knowledge about the complex world we inhabit, including our linguistic world, is through reliable data, creative experimental design and sound statistics.

A NOTE ON TERMINOLOGY AND NOTATION

Since this book overlaps linguistics and statistics, I have had to adopt a strategy for dealing with terminology. In the case of ambiguity, and unless otherwise noted, the meaning of a term should be understood as the mathematical rather than the linguistic one.

Three words, *distribution, function* and *mode*, have distinctive meanings in both domains. In linguistics, 'distribution' means the tendency of a word form to appear alongside others, but in mathematics, it simply means a continuous or discrete ordered set of numbers. In this book, I avoid using the word in a context where it might imply the first meaning. Similarly, 'function' is used here in its mathematical sense, meaning a relationship between two or more variables, but it also has a grammatical meaning. 'Mode' has a mathematical sense (a peak value), so where 'mode of delivery' is meant, this is stated. There is a reasonably comprehensive glossary at the end of the book, where I have attempted to give a brief synopsis of terms I have used.

Many words in common usage also have a precise mathematical meaning, notably *significance*. Where these are used in this book, the mathematical meaning is to be understood. That said, *form* is invariably used in the linguistic sense, but *function* in its mathematical one. Hopefully, the context should make the intended meaning clear!

Despite what might otherwise be the impression to anyone unfamiliar with mathematics, I have made a serious effort to minimise the symbols used in this book.

First, as far as it was possible to do so, I limited my use of the symbols and twiddles that typically adorn mathematics books. I could not avoid using α, χ or ϕ because these have a specific common use. Other Greek letters are used for occasional variables. Twiddles are mostly restricted to $\hat{p}$, means (e.g. $\bar{a}$) and primes (like t'). Second, I have adopted a practice of using lowercase letters to refer to attributes of observed samples, and uppercase letters for populations. So p is used for an observed proportion, whereas P is an expected population probability. Third, I have tried to be as consistent as possible and use different symbols for different concepts.

Some familiarity with basic high school (in the UK, 'GCSE-level') mathematics notation is assumed. But if you are a little rusty, here are a few tips to get you started.

Variables are written X and Y, with discrete values x_1, y_2, and so on, and related concepts are labelled simply X and Y. Sets are written in bold capitals (e.g., **X**). We may define a discrete Binomial variable X as a member of the set $\mathbf{X} = \{x_1, x_2\}$. The usual shorthand applies: '$\in$' means 'is a member of' (e.g., $X \in \mathbf{X}$), '$\equiv$' means equivalence, '$\sum$' means sum, and '$\surd$' means square root. I have occasionally used '$\neq_s$' to mean 'not significantly different'. Logical entailment ('$\rightarrow$') and set union ('$\cup$') are also sparingly used.

Number scales and distributions are a special type of set, marked by italic bold. Thus $\boldsymbol{P}$ represents the probability scale, $\boldsymbol{P} = [0, 1]$. This is the continuous set of all numbers between 0 and 1, *including* 0 and 1 (a square bracket means 'including', whereas a round bracket means 'excluding'). You may also occasionally see square brackets marking out arrays or ordered sequences, such as $[[a, b], [c, d]]$ and $[a, b, c, d]$. This is slightly ambiguous, but the text should help, and in any case, continuous number sets always have precisely two bounds.

An interval is a set of all points between defined bounds, so it is common to see expressions like $p \in (w^-, w^+)$ representing the Wilson score interval for proportion p. Where intervals are centred on zero, we will be explicit about this, e.g. $0 \in (w_{\bar{d}}, w_{\dot{d}})$ is a zero-based difference interval.

Named functions are written in plain text with bracketed parameters, so in Chapter 6 we will see WilsonLower(p, n, $\alpha/2$) return the lower bound of the Wilson score interval with these parameters. A function returning a set or interval is written in bold, hence $d \in$ **difference**(p_2, p_1) returns the set of points between the lower and upper bound of the Newcombe-Wilson interval for $d = p_2 - p_1$.

Occasionally parameters are omitted for simplicity. For example, the function **difference**(θ_1, θ_2) operates on the *intervals* for θ_1 and θ_2 rather than just the scores. We could write **difference**(θ_1, θ_1^-, θ_1^+, θ_2, θ_2^-, θ_2^+), but for ease of reading, these parameters are implied!

One symbol that can cause trouble is the vertical bar '|'. This means 'given' in expressions like '$p(y_1 \mid \{y_1, y_2\})$', glossed as 'the probability of selecting an instance with value y_1 given that its value belongs to the set $\{y_1, y_2\}$'. But bars around an expression (e.g., '$| o - e |$' or '$| \phi |$') mean the unsigned absolute value.

Since we are dealing with sets, series, distributions and tables, it is often necessary to specify members by their index position. These are written as, for example, $o_{i,j}$, and – a little more unusually – o_{i+} to represent the sum of all items on that index, $o_{i,1} + o_{i,2} + \ldots$

Subscripts and superscripts are also used. Subscripts index items or specify critical values. Superscript symbols are limited to '+' and '–' for upper and lower bounds of intervals (thus w_1^+ is 'the Wilson upper bound of observation 1'), but you will also see powers (x^2) and inverse functions (Lower^{-1}).

At all times, I have done my best to explain in plain English what each symbol and formula means. I am sure that occasionally I failed. Please bear with me, read on and read back. Statistical reasoning is not about learning equations but understanding principles. The formulae are presented to allow you to perform calculations of your own, and occasionally, to help you make sense of the argument.

Contingency Tests for Different Purposes

The following test frameworks are the main ones discussed in this book:

- Single-table tests are standard evaluations for analysing data in a single contingency table.
- Meta-tests compare experimental results from two tables. Subset versions of the same three test classes are also discussed.

Single-table tests (Chapter 8)

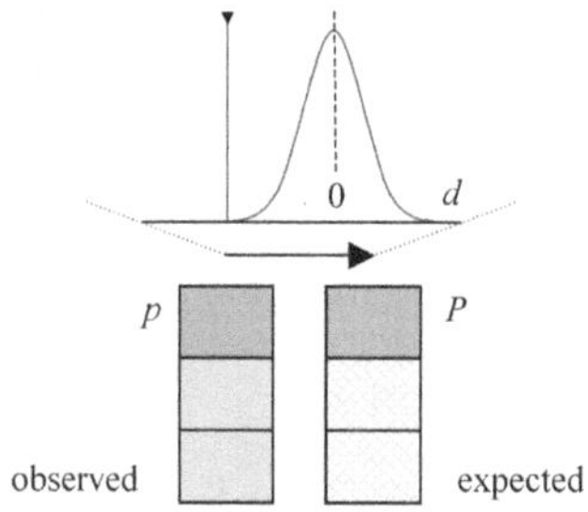

Goodness of fit test: evaluates fitness of proportions or distributions

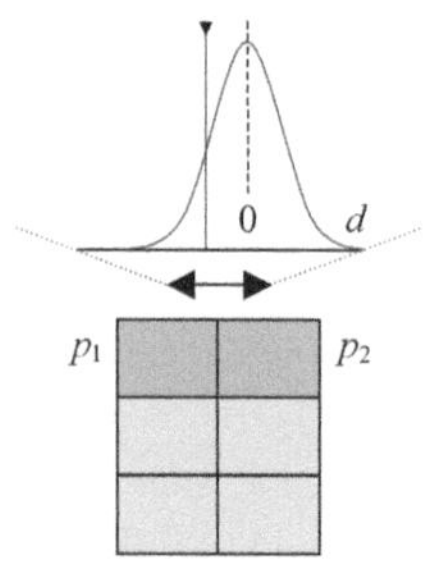

Independence (homogeneity) test: compares differences in proportions or distributions

Two-table meta-tests (Chapter 14)

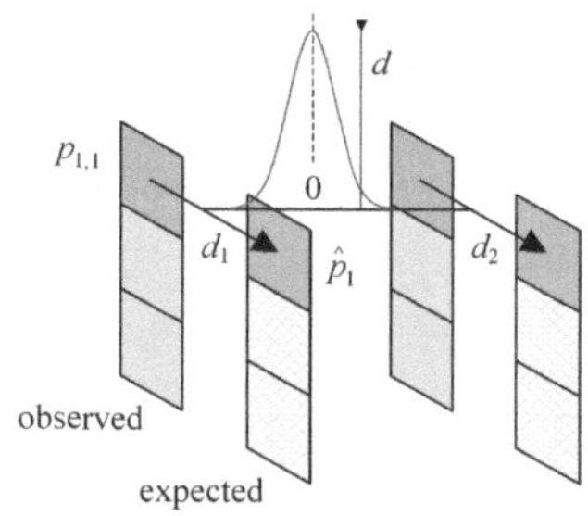

Separability of fit test: evaluates fitness of proportions or distributions between tables

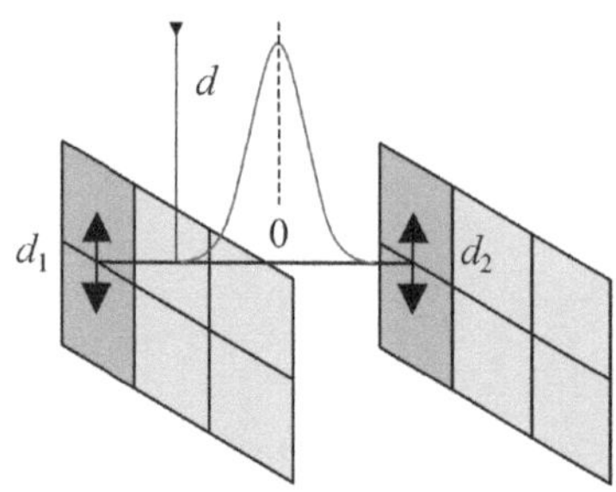

Separability of independence (gradient) test: compares differences in proportions or distributions between tables

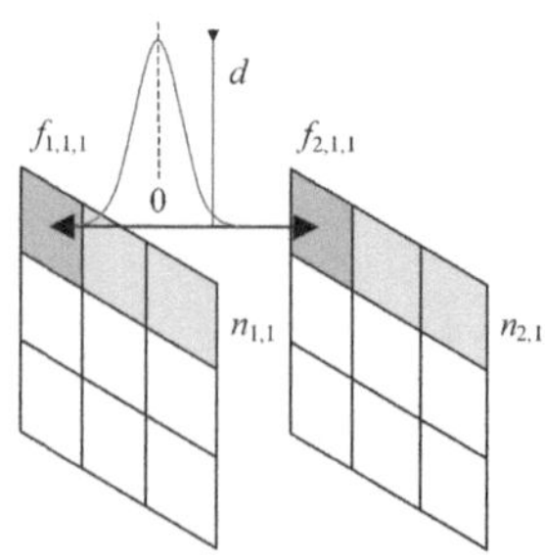

Separability point test: compares matching cell proportions or distributions between tables

Notes

1. I wrote these words in February 2020 before the Covid-19 pandemic became an international catastrophe. Tragically, the ability of humans to accurately estimate risk has become a key problem of public health and politics.
2. Or 'not significantly different from it'. We commonly think of a confidence interval as 'the range of values where the true population value is most likely to be found', although as we note in Chapter 18, that formulation is not quite right.
3. I have deliberately avoided a visualisation at this point to encourage readers to try to imagine how this might work. Interested readers may turn to https://corplingstats.wordpress.com/2019/02/24/the-other-end-of-the-telescope for a discussion with pictures. See also Chapter 18.
4. The equivalent 'exact' 95% Clopper-Pearson interval (see Chapter 8) is from 8.66% to 49.1%, and the equivalent one-tailed upper bound is 45.6%.
5. The 99% Clopper-Pearson interval is (5.83%, 55.97%). The one-tailed maximum is 53.21%.
6. For example, *GraphColl* (Brezina et al., 2015, p. 161) cites an error level of $\alpha = 0.0001$ with a log-likelihood statistic. This is not to single out this excellent tool for criticism – exploration tools often use statistical models as engineering, so what matters is that they obtain useful and interesting results that can be taken further (see e.g., Wallis, 2020a). Exploration tools may be considered *annotation* or *abstraction* algorithms (see Chapter 1). They are not *analysis* algorithms however, and it is necessary to warn students not to uncritically cite a tool's output, however tempting this may be.

PART 1
Motivations

1

WHAT MIGHT CORPORA TELL US ABOUT LANGUAGE?

1.1 Introduction

Corpus linguistics has become popular. Many linguists who would not otherwise consider themselves to be *corpus* linguists have started to apply corpus linguistics *methods* to their linguistic problems, in part due to the increasing availability of corpora and tools. In this chapter, we consider some kinds of research that can be done with corpora, and the types of corpora and methods that might yield useful results.[1] Corpora are also found outside of linguistics, in social sciences and digital humanities.

In this book, we argue against a simplistic 'bigger is best' approach to data analysis and for the centrality of *underlying models*, theories of what might be happening linguistically 'behind the scenes', when we carry out research. More data is an advantage, but there is a trade-off between large corpora with limited annotation and small ones with rich annotation. Our perspective relates theory-rich linguistics with corpus linguistics, implying that we need corpora with rich annotation.

Yet as corpus linguistics has developed as a discipline, the dominant trend has been to build ever larger lexical corpora with very limited annotation: typically, structural annotation (speaker turns, overlaps, sentence breaks in spoken data and formatting in writing), *wordclass* or 'part-of-speech' tagging (identifying nouns, verbs and so on) and *lemmas*. Crucially, with large 'mega' corpora, annotation must be automatically produced without human intervention. The multi-billion-word *iWeb* corpus built by Mark Davies from 22 million web pages (at the time of writing) is at the frontier of this trend.

Not every linguist is in favour of a methodological 'turn to corpora'. Some theoretical linguists, including Noam Chomsky, have argued that, at best,

DOI: 10.4324/9781003622697-2

collections of language data merely provide researchers with examples of actual external linguistic performance of human beings in a given context (see, e.g., Aarts, 2001). We refer to this type of evidence as 'factual evidence' (see Section 1.2). From this perspective, corpora do not provide insight into internal language or how it is produced in the human mind. However, Chomsky's position raises questions about *what* data, if any, could be used to evaluate 'deep' theories.[2]

Nevertheless, this contrary position represents a serious challenge to corpus researchers. Is corpus research doomed to investigate surface phenomena? At the end of this chapter, and as a motivation for what follows, we will return to the question of the potential relevance of corpus linguistics for the study of language production by reporting on a recent study.

Indeed, in recent years this 'turn to corpora' has begun to influence generative linguists. Take language change: a systematic evaluation of how language has changed over time must rely on data. An old antipathy is replaced by engagement. Large historical corpora such as the *Penn-Helsinki Parsed Corpus of Early Modern English* (PPCEME, Kroch et al., 2004) are inspiring a new generation of linguistics researchers to approach corpora in new and more sophisticated ways. Similarly, it is our contention that corpora can benefit psycholinguistics, not as a substitute for laboratory experiments, but as a complementary source of evidence.

What do we mean by 'a corpus'? In the most general sense, corpora are simply collections of language data processed to make them accessible for research purposes. In contrast to experimental datasets, sampled to answer a specific research question, corpora are sampled in a manner that – as far as possible – permits many different types of research question to be posed. Datasets extracted from corpora are not obtained under controlled conditions but under 'naturalistic' or 'ecological' ones. We discuss some implications of this statement in Part 2.

Corpora also typically contain substantive passages of text, rather than, say, a series of random sentences produced by random speakers or writers.[3]

However, the majority of corpora available today have one major drawback for the study of language production. Most data are *written*. Texts are generated by authors at keyboards, on paper or on screens. Writing is rarely spontaneously produced, may be edited by others, but is often included in databases due to easy availability. Like this book, texts are usually written for an imagined audience, in contrast to spoken utterances that are typically produced – scripted performances and monologues aside – on-the-spot for a present and interacting audience.

In the era of the internet, written data are easy to obtain, so large corpora of writing may be rapidly compiled. But if 'language' is sampled from writing (inevitable in historical corpora), we can only draw inferences about written language. Far better to be able to test hypotheses against spontaneously produced linguistic utterances that are *unmediated*, or, to be more precise, that are minimally affected by processes of articulation and transmission.

Not all corpora are drawn from written sources, and it is not a necessary characteristic of corpus linguistics that limits it to the study of written data. If we had no option but to use written sources, this would still be preferable to relying on intuition.

But a better option is a corpus of spoken data, ideally in the form of recordings aligned with orthographic transcriptions. Transcriptions of this kind should record the output word-for-word, including false starts and self-correction, overlapping speech, speaker turns, and so on. The transcription should be a coded record of the audio stream. Faithfully transcribed speech data from an uncued and unrehearsed context is arguably the closest source to genuinely 'spontaneous' naturalistic language output as is possible to find.

A transcription can be richer than a written text. It may be time-aligned with the original audio or video recording, contain prosodic and meta-linguistic information, gestural signals, and so on. The value of these additional layers of annotation will depend on the research aims of users. Researchers interested in language production and syntax are probably less concerned whether transcriptions are time-aligned than whether they are accurate. But if pause duration or words per minute is considered a proxy for mental processing, then timing data are essential.

Although we refer to 'speech' here, we are really referring to *unmediated spontaneously produced language*, the majority of which will be speech. For example, we might justifiably include sign language corpora under the category of 'speech corpora'. It may be attractive to stretch this definition to include conversational text data (e.g., online 'chat'), but usually, a user interface will allow the language producer to edit utterances as they type. If we wish to study unmediated language production, authentic data from spoken sources seems the best option.

Prioritising speech over writing in linguistics research has other justifications aside from mere spontaneity. The most obvious is historical primacy. Hunter-gatherer societies had an oral tradition long before writing was systematised. When writing developed, it was first limited to scribes, and gradually spread through social development and education. In 1820, around 12% of the world's population could read and write. Even today that figure is around 83% (Roser & Ortiz-Ospina, 2018). So the first reason for studying speech is its near-universality. By contrast, historical corpus linguistics – which of necessity can only study written texts prior to the invention of the phonograph – is limited to the language of the literate population of the age, and their region, social class and gender distribution.

There are other important motivations. Child development sees children usually express themselves through the spoken word before they master putting words on a page, and many writers are aware that their writing requires a more-or-less internal speech act. Which comes first, speech or writing? The answer is speech.

Then there is the question of representativeness. A corpus of British English speech has approximately 2,000 words spoken by participants every quarter of an hour. The author Stephen King (2002) recommends aspiring writers write 1,000 words a day. Allowing for individual variation – and excepting isolated individuals or those physiologically unable to produce speech – it seems likely that human beings produce, and are exposed to, an order of magnitude more speech than writing.

Of course, not all speech data are the same. Speech data may be collected for a variety of purposes, some more representative and 'natural' than others. One of the first treebanks containing spoken data, the Penn Treebank (Marcus et al., 1993), included parliamentary language, telephone calls and air traffic control data. Other spoken data might be captured in the laboratory: these are controlled conditions, but ones that are unnatural and potentially psychologically stressed.

Scripting and rehearsal are a feature of many text types found in corpora. The *Survey Corpus* (Svartvik, 1990) and *International Corpus of English* (ICE, Greenbaum, 1996b) include 'scripted speech', that is, transcriptions of pre-written talks. But even unscripted TV and radio broadcasts may be rehearsed, or subject to multiple 'takes'. The *Corpus of Contemporary American English* (COCA, Davies, 2009) contains transcriptions of unscripted conversations from TV and radio programmes.

As we noted, historical corpora have a particular problem in this respect. The first known recording of the human voice is that of Thomas Edison on a cylinder phonograph in 1877. The *Corpus of Historical American English* (COHA, 1810–2009, Davies, 2012) contains film and play scripts. The *Old Bailey Corpus* (1720–1913, Huber et al., 2012) captures the speech of trial participants via the court stenographer.

This leads us to one final point. Some transcripts may be produced by non-linguists, such as court and parliamentary transcribers. Court transcripts are expected to be a close record for legal reasons. Parliamentary transcripts are another matter. Cribb and Rochford (2018) describe how the official record was rewritten, glossed, corrected and expanded. Alexander (2023) identifies phases of distinctive transcription standards in the historical British Hansard. Official transcripts should be treated with a degree of caution, and original recordings retranscribed where possible.

For linguistic research purposes, we are primarily concerned with speech in 'ecological' contexts where speech output is spontaneous, uncued and unrehearsed. An important sub-classification concerns whether the audience is present and participating, that is, in a monologic or dialogic setting.

The fact that a corpus ideal may be collected away from a laboratory should not mean that results are incommensurable with laboratory data. On the contrary, corpus data can be a useful complement to controlled 'laboratory' experiments. But to relate results competently requires some methodological adaptation.

The primary distinction between laboratory and corpus data is as follows: corpus linguistics is characterised by the multiple reuse of existing data, and the *ex post facto* ('after the fact') analysis of such data. On the other hand, experimental data are obtained under laboratory conditions, where a researcher can manipulate conditions to reduce the impact of potentially confounding variables, for example, by requiring each participant to perform the same task.

Corpus linguistics is thus better understood as the methodology of linguistics framed as an observational science (like astronomy, evolutionary biology or geology) rather than an experimental one. So when we refer to 'experiments with corpora' in this book, we mean carrying out investigations on previously collected data. We may select subcategories in corpora, but if we wish to control how our data were sampled, obtain data in new contexts or cue particular responses, we must collect new data. In Chapter 2, we return to the question of what these types of natural experiment might tell us.

This 'multiple reuse' perspective shapes corpora in another way. Corpora usually contain whole passages and texts, open to multiple levels of description and evaluation. To analyse the discourse structure of a conversation, you need the entire conversation. On the other hand, if you only wish to construct a representative lexicon, random sentences will do. By contrast, laboratory research collects fresh data for every research question, and therefore tends to record data efficiently, containing relevant components of the output decided in advance.

However, the lines between the controlled experiment and the corpus are increasingly blurred. Where data must be encoded with a rich annotation (see Section 1.4), such as a detailed prosodic transcription or parsing, data reuse maximises the benefits of costly data collection. Indeed, many sciences have begun to take data reuse seriously. Medical science has seen *meta-analysis*, where data from multiple experiments are pooled and reanalysed, become mainstream.

Let us adopt a working definition of a spoken corpus as a database of transcribed spoken data, with or without original audio files. What can such a database tell us about language?

1.2 What Might a Corpus Tell Us?

There are essentially three distinct classes of empirical evidence that may be obtained from any linguistic data source, whether this 'corpus' consists of plain text or is richly annotated (see Section 1.4).[4] These are as follows:

1. **Factual** evidence of a linguistic event, that is, at least one event x is observed, written 'there exists' x, or, in mathematical notation, '$\exists x$'.
2. **Frequency** evidence of a linguistic event, which we can write as '$f(x)$' observed events.

3. **Interaction** evidence between two or more linguistic events, that is, that the presence of event *y* in a given relationship to *x* affects the probability that *x* will occur, which we might write as '$p(x \mid y)$', 'the probability of *x* given *y*'.

We will discuss each in turn. Whereas much theoretical linguistic argument concerns statements that particular expressions are or are not possible, the *factuality* of any theory ultimately depends on real-world data.

For example, dictionaries expand by observing new forms. In contemporary British English, *bare* (conventionally an adjective) has gained an informal, intensifying adverb use equivalent to 'a lot', 'very' or 'really', as in *bare money* or *bare good.* An etymological dictionary might similarly grow by finding earlier attestations of a known word meaning.

More controversially, we would argue that for a theoretical linguist to maintain that a particular construction found in a corpus is 'ungrammatical' or 'impossible' is not sufficient. The errant datum deserves explanation. Such an explanation *might* be that it represents a performance error, but this cannot be assumed *a priori.* It could be a rare but legitimate form. So factual evidence might include evidence that appears to contradict existing theories.

Occasionally, the systematic examination of a corpus, a task required during annotation (see Section 1.3), uncovers a genuinely novel, previously undocumented linguistic phenomenon. Complementation patterns – patterns of possible objects and complements of verbs – are central to traditional grammars of English. Wallis (2020a) relates how the annotators of the *British Component of the International Corpus of English* (ICE-GB, Nelson et al., 2002) found a complementation pattern absent in their source grammar (Quirk et al., 1985). This 'dimonotransitive' pattern (Subject-Verb-Indirect Object, e.g., *he told her*) appears over 200 times in the corpus. The pattern was too regular to be dismissed as an error. It had to be accounted for, either as a permutation of an existing pattern or as a distinct pattern with its own properties.

Corpora are also a rich source of *frequency evidence* for linguistic phenomena. Much corpus research reports frequencies of linguistic events. Frequency evidence is typically compiled into a *frequency distribution,* a set of related observed frequencies that can be compared.

Frequency evidence has value, even if its meaning is less easy to discern. Knowing that one construction, form or meaning is more common than another has proven beneficial for writers of dictionaries and grammar books, helping them prioritise material for learners. Frequency evidence may be counter-intuitive, and theoretical linguists rarely deny corpus data this purpose. But if corpus linguistics only consists of mere counting of words or constructions, how does such evidence relate to the concerns of the theoretician?

One answer involves applying linguistic knowledge to instances (annotation). *Grammaticalization* (Traugott & Heine, 1991) is a process whereby, over time, an erstwhile regular lexical item (or lexical-grammatical form) acquires a new grammatical function and loses lexical meaning as a consequence. Chapter 7 considers data from one such study: the growth of new uses of progressive BE *thinking*. Obviously, distinguishing these new 'grammatical' signifiers requires a careful case-by-case linguistic review.

Frequency data must also be interpreted carefully. A common confusion mixes up *exposure rates*: typically, that an event x appears f times per million words, and *choice rates*: that x is chosen with probability p when the opportunity of using x arises. See Chapter 3.

An exposure rate tells us how often an audience will be exposed to x. Such 'normalised' frequencies are vulnerable to contextual variation (produce a different text and the exposure rate may differ). There are many reasons why a speaker might utter a particular word or construction in a given text, and an elevated or reduced frequency in one context over another may be due to numerous factors. Exposure rates are not easily compared with results from controlled laboratory experiments and (because they can vary for many reasons) are difficult to relate to linguistic theories.

A per word frequency measure is obtained by

$$\textit{the probability of choosing x out of all words, } p(x \mid \text{word}) = f(x) / f(\textbf{words}),$$

where $f(\textbf{words})$ is the number of words in the sample.

For example, *bare* (adjective, all meanings) appears 19 times in the (approximately) million words of ICE-GB. We can report that $p(\textit{bare}+\text{<ADJ>} \mid \text{word}) = 19/1{,}061{,}263 = 0.0000179032$. Since these probabilities are tiny, they tend to be quoted as a proportion of multiple words. The per million word rate for *bare* (adjective) in ICE-GB is 17.9032.

A more productive way to frame frequency evidence is in terms of choice rates, that is, the probability that speakers (or writers) will use a construction when they have the opportunity to do so. The idea is we identify a set of alternative forms, **X**, including the particular form we are interested in, x (so x is a member of $\mathbf{X}$, $x \in \mathbf{X}$). This gives us the simple formula

$$\textit{the probability of choosing x out of the set } \mathbf{X},\ p(x \mid \mathbf{X}) = f(x) / f(\mathbf{X}).$$

In a laboratory experiment, the choice rate method is equivalent to cueing a participant with a stimulus triggering the set of choices, **X**, and then categorising their response (the selection, x). Since language is highly structured, an adjective such as *bare* is unlikely to appear at an arbitrary point in a sentence.

There are some rare examples (e.g., pauses, coughs and swearing) where an expression, x, could conceivably appear before any word in the corpus. In other cases, it is necessary to account for the fact that the potential for the expression is constrained by the rest of the sentence. To study *bare*, we should first identify those locations where *bare* could appear (e.g., in adjective position, possibly constrained by concrete common noun heads). This approach is mathematically more principled and experimentally more revealing. It is compatible with 'the variationist paradigm' or 'alternation studies', which are common practice in sociolinguistics, but less common in corpus linguistics. We return to this question in depth in Chapter 3.

In this book, we use the term 'choice' as a shorthand for *the act of selection from a set of permissible expressions*. Considered in this way, every language production process consists of a string of choices, some dependent on preceding choices, some which constrain subsequent ones (see Section 1.7), whereas others are structurally independent.

The principal difficulty of choice-based research is a practical one. The experimenter is not present at the time of the utterance. The response is not deliberately triggered ('cued'). Inevitably the speaker (if they could be interviewed) will not recall what they were thinking at the time! Instead, the researcher must decide, retrospectively reviewing utterances, when the opportunity would have arisen.

Reliably identifying locations where choices may arise is not always straightforward. Sometimes the choice is between two words or phrases, such as a choice of modal *shall* or *will*, in which case we can simply pool both options. However, sometimes the choice we are interested in is one of omission, such as the choice between relative and zero-relative clauses (*he thought [that]* . . .). Annotation may help identify these 'counterfactual' cases. For example, the ICE-GB parsing scheme contains a 'zrel' feature identifying zero-relative clauses, without which the task would be more difficult.

A further issue concerns whether the overall meaning is allowed to change as a result of the choice being made, or whether it is sufficient to simply determine that the choice is *available*.[5]

Traditionally, corpus linguistics has tended to focus on exposure rates. Many books on corpus linguistics methodology assume that citation of frequencies per million words is the norm. It should not be surprising, therefore, that some corpus linguists have expressed unease at the choice-based paradigm, with perhaps the most common argument being that the baseline set, **X**, appears to be arbitrary.

Intermediate positions between hearer exposure and speaker choice are also possible. It is legitimate to survey, for example, the changing distribution of modal auxiliary lemmas as a comparative exercise, that is, whether *can* or *will* are increasing as a proportion of all modals over time, without claiming that they are mutually substitutable. A crucial skill for a corpus linguist is to recognise these different kinds of frequency or probability evidence, and to properly report their implications.

The final class of evidence that can be gained from a corpus is *interaction evidence*. This is evidence concerning the effect of choosing one word, construction or utterance on other choices in the same linguistic vicinity or in a given relationship. To take a trivial example, if a speaker starts by saying '*I* . . .', a hearer will intuit the most likely next word will be a verb. Interaction evidence is core to computer algorithms such as automatic wordclass taggers and parsers, but is often overlooked as an important method for higher-level linguistic research.

Interaction evidence is best obtained from choice rates. If we can identify the probability of a speaker employing a construction when they have that option, we can also identify the effect of a co-occurring construction on that probability. We will return to this question in Section 1.6.

1.3 The 3A Cycle

1.3.1 Annotation, Abstraction and Analysis

Our second observation about corpus linguistics is that all traditions within corpus linguistics and related fields (e.g., applying corpus methods to sociolinguistic interview data) can be conceived of as consisting of three cyclic processes. These are *Annotation*, *Abstraction* and *Analysis*. Each cycle operates between two distinct levels of knowledge, so there are four levels in all. This way of thinking about corpus linguistics, which we call the '3A perspective' (Wallis & Nelson, 2001), is sketched in Figure 1.1.

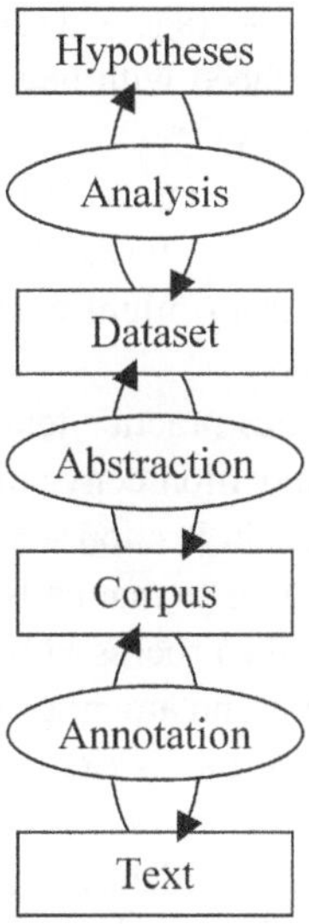

FIGURE 1.1 The 3A perspective in corpus linguistics (after Wallis & Nelson, 2001).

The idea is that each process adds knowledge to one level to transform it into the next, in a cycle of extension and critical reflection. Knowledge is both *necessary* to each stage and *refutable*. It is applied at every level, from sampling decisions to research hypotheses.

For example, when we annotate a text we add information to it – such as sentence boundaries and wordclass tags – and we critically review the annotation scheme we are using. Annotation is sometimes referred to as 'Qualitative Analysis', especially at an early pilot stage as a scheme is developed. But whereas Qualitative Analysis might be applied to a small number of texts or selected sentences, an annotation scheme should be applied systematically across an entire corpus (Wallis, 2007).

Every qualitative annotation decision must be considered carefully. Is it useful to have a concept such as a 'sentence boundary' in spoken data? What set of wordclass tags should we use, and which distinctions should we capture? Does *this* word have that tag? And what should we do if we discover a novel phenomenon while annotating, like the previously undescribed 'dimonotransitive' complementation pattern?

In the case of spoken data, the ultimate source is not text but an audio waveform, and so 'annotation' includes the transcription process. Annotation may be of any conceivable system of linguistic analysis: syntactic, semantic, pragmatic, prosodic or morphological.

Both annotations to the text and the annotation scheme itself may change over the course of annotating an entire corpus. The more initially tentative and experimental the annotation scheme, the more likely it will develop during an annotation phase. Obtaining complete coverage of a scheme across a corpus often raises unanticipated challenges when faced with new phenomena, causing annotators to engage in a retrospective review.

In corpus linguistics, the annotation cycle is typically, although not always, performed by corpus builders. Some research teams have added annotation to data compiled by others, or a team might extend its annotation in a series of phases, each with its own release.[6]

Traditionally, corpus linguistics practice tends to place a sharp line between annotation and abstraction. Annotation conventionally ends with the distributed corpus. However, as we shall see in Section 1.5, during a study, researchers may perform additional annotation steps to manually classify data with new criteria.

That said, abstraction begins the process of 'research proper'. It is the process whereby a linguist takes a corpus and attempts to obtain (to 'abstract') examples of phenomena of interest. If a corpus is richly annotated, they may exploit the annotation.

'Abstraction' can be as simple as identifying single examples for illustrative purposes. However, for empirical research, it must be *systematic*, that is, our task is to find every example of a phenomenon precisely and exhaustively. Abstraction

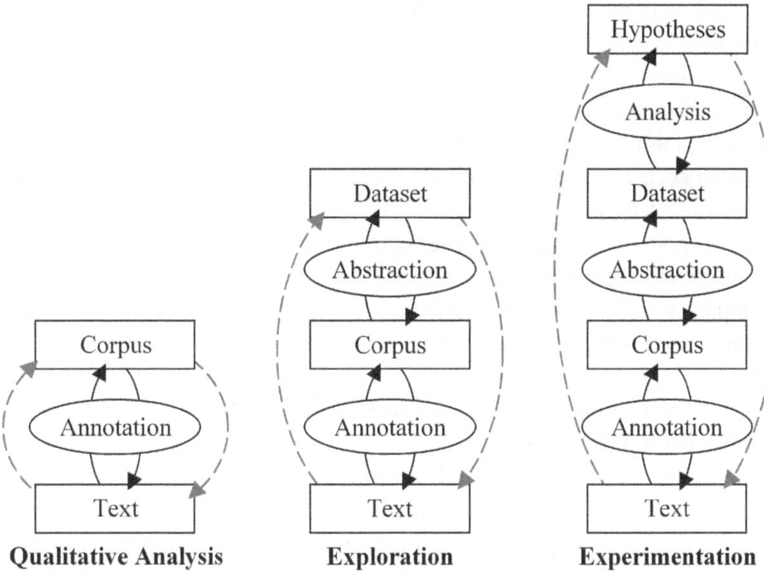

FIGURE 1.2 Qualitative analysis, exploration and experimentation in the 3A model.

can be performed top-down, driven by frameworks and hypotheses in the mind of the researcher. It can also be performed bottom-up, with what are often called 'exploration tools': *collocation* and *colligation* algorithms, *n-grams* and other tools deploying associative statistics on the plain text or existing annotation. See Wallis (2020a) for a review. The combination of abstraction and annotation with research tools may be unified in an 'Exploration' cycle (Figure 1.2).

Exploration can, as the name suggests, be tentative and partial. It allows researchers to gain a greater understanding of viable definitions that might be worth pursuing. However, for a deeper analysis, abstraction must be systematically applied to create a sample dataset consisting of instances classified by multiple *variables*. Systematic abstraction of this kind is sometimes termed 'data transformation' or *re-representation* in the field of Knowledge Discovery, and *operationalisation* in Experimental Design and Statistics textbooks.

At the top of this '3A' series of cycles is the analysis cycle. Analysis consists of working with an abstracted dataset to obtain high-level generalisations, test hypotheses, and so on. It is the principal focus of this book. As we shall see in Chapter 2, when we turn to discussing experimental design, we often work top-down from analysis: starting with hypotheses, we identify the concepts they rely on and try to work out how we might instantiate them from our corpus (i.e., perform abstraction). But it is also possible to work bottom-up, drawing on observations in the corpus data to specify new variables or reformulate existing definitions.

Taken together, all three cycles may be considered as forming a single process: the 'Experimentation' cycle, as shown in Figure 1.2.

Abstraction translates from one framework to another. It selects data from an annotated corpus and maps them to a regular dataset for the purposes of statistical analysis. A corpus query system is the principal tool for this process. When a query is performed, the researcher obtains a set of matching results, including the total frequency count.

Suppose we wished to obtain a set of verb phrases from a corpus. In a corpus already parsed with a phrase structure grammar, the task is simple: verb phrases are part of the annotation scheme, and we perform a query (e.g., 'VP'). However, most corpora are only tagged for wordclass category (noun, verb, auxiliary verb, etc.) plus additional features.

Identifying the verb phrase itself – where it starts and where it ends – in such a corpus is more difficult, but we can obtain a count of main verbs ('V' in ICE-GB). The method is imperfect, and there are exceptions: verb phrases consisting of lone auxiliary verbs (e.g., *Yeah I <u>will</u>* (S1A-002 #137)) and interrogative verbs considered not to be part of a VP (*<u>is</u> it important?* (S1A-003 #18)). However, examining the ratio V:VP across subcategories of speech and writing in ICE-GB finds that counting verbs as a proxy for verb phrases is accurate to within a percentage point.

But if we want to examine complements of the verb, an unparsed corpus creates further challenges. How may we reliably identify indirect objects, for example?

It follows that abstraction is more powerful if the 'heavy lifting' has already been performed in the annotation scheme. But this raises a sensible concern. Are we now *dependent* on the annotation? If another team created and applied a framework, am I, a researcher working in a different framework, now committed to the one embodied in the corpus?

1.3.2 The Problem of Representational Plurality

A crucial problem – and a standard objection to richly annotating a corpus – concerns 'representational plurality'. Every student knows linguistics is full of competing frameworks. But to annotate a corpus systematically, it follows that the annotator must commit to one. The conceptual framework of the linguist researcher 'end user' may be quite distinct from that of the annotation team. Indeed, a researcher taking the given framework as their starting point may find refinements necessary as they work with the corpus.

Whether the original framework matters to the researcher *ultimately depends on the success of abstraction.* If they can reliably obtain examples of the phenomenon of interest, then how the corpus was originally annotated is immaterial. We refer to this perspective as treating annotation as a 'handle on the data' (see Section 1.4), whereby annotation is simply considered in terms of its value for obtaining relevant examples. Abstraction is the key step.

In any given field of research, linguists differ in their ideal representation scheme, and schemes are often in a state of development themselves. Schemes frequently differ terminologically, but much more importantly, they differ in their classification and structuring of linguistic phenomena, what they include and exclude.

In wordclass analysis, CLAWS7 differs from CLAWS5, and both differ from TOSCA/ICE. In parsing, Quirk et al. (1985) exclude objects from verb phrase analysis; Huddleston and Pullum (2002) include them. Constraint grammars represent verb phrases another way, and so on. After two decades of corpus parsing, we have a range of corpora attempting to capture comparable linguistic phenomena with different schemes. Anne Abeillé's book *Treebanks* (2003) contains articles describing at least ten different frameworks applied to substantial corpora.

Any linguist who uses a corpus translates concepts from the annotated corpus to their preferred framework. 'Abstraction' is the elaboration of a researcher-defined set of 'translation rules' that converts terms and structures in these different schemes into concepts relevant to the researcher's framework and hypotheses.

Suppose a researcher is investigating noun phrase (NP) complexity. The definition of a more-or-less 'complex' NP will vary according to theories of complexity and processing. Indeed, the researcher will probably wish to consider multiple definitions. In a parsed corpus, we can identify, for example, NP post-modifying clauses, as in *the car I used to drive*.

Every instance in such a corpus contains considerable detail: the words used, their wordclasses and their grammatical functions and structural relationships. The researcher needs to work out rules and queries that map these structures to their chosen definition of complexity. An NP with no postmodifying clauses might have complexity zero, one with a single postmodifying clause might have a score of 1, and so on. But complexity may be conceptualised differently, focusing on other aspects of the NP, such as the type of head or number of adjectives. See Section 1.6. This does not mean that one definition is 'right' and another 'wrong'. Researchers may merely wish to investigate complexity defined in different ways.

The centrality of abstraction in corpus linguistics is frequently overlooked. But it is a necessary step whereby a researcher reframes the data to their research requirements. Supporting this process is crucial to the design of software tools for working with corpora. Whenever you perform a query against a corpus using software, you need to know that the results you obtain are reliable. Finding examples may be easy. Finding *all relevant examples* can be difficult.

Consequently, the software must let you check queries to determine how it performs. It is not difficult for a query tool to list the cases it finds. The researcher can review these to check whether the cases are correctly included (termed 'true positives') and spot those that should not have been included ('false positives'). But they also need to know that *the search has not omitted cases that should have been included* ('false negatives'). There is, by definition, no simple answer to the latter problem – if we could automatically find falsely omitted cases we would include them!

We can, however, build platforms that allow researchers to explore the corpus with many different queries, and thereby attempt to spot false negatives by other means. Normally, we review examples found and then consider whether cases might have inadvertently been excluded due to variations in the annotation or for other reasons. It is often possible to selectively relax constraints in a query and err on the side of finding more false positives and previously excluded cases, and then eliminate the false positives by review. See Chapter 15.

In summary, the more ambitious the research question, and the richer and more detailed the annotation scheme, the greater the need for researchers to revisit source sentences to ensure that their abstracted dataset is reliable. Tagged corpora offer limited search options, and queries may not require an extensive cyclic process of refinement. But with richly annotated corpora, a researcher may need to try out a range of different queries. Thanks to the diversity of frameworks, it is quite probable that a researcher will wish to use a different conceptual framework from the annotators, even if some labels are the same.

Annotation should never be taken on trust. It may contain errors and biases, particularly if it has been automatically applied but not checked by linguists.

1.3.3 ICECUP: A Platform for Treebank Research

Corpus linguists clearly need effective software tools to engage with annotated corpora. The *International Corpus of English Corpus Utility Program* Version 3 (ICECUP III) research platform (Nelson et al., 2002, see Figure 1.3) was designed around the abstraction cycle to support research with a parsed corpus: initially, the million-word ICE-GB, 60% of which consists of transcribed speech.

The main query system is a diagrammatic query representation that mirrors the visual appearance of grammatical trees in the corpus: *Fuzzy Tree Fragments* or 'FTFs'. An FTF is a tree-like query where nodes, words, and links between nodes and words may be left partially specified. At the top right of Figure 1.3 we have an FTF that searches for structures consisting of subject complement clauses ('CS,CL') containing a subordinator phrase ('SUB,SUBP') followed by an adverbial (adjunct) clause ('A,CL').[7] When a query is applied, the set of matching cases are immediately presented by the interface (middle right). Researchers can review how queries have been matched to the corpus and identify false positives.

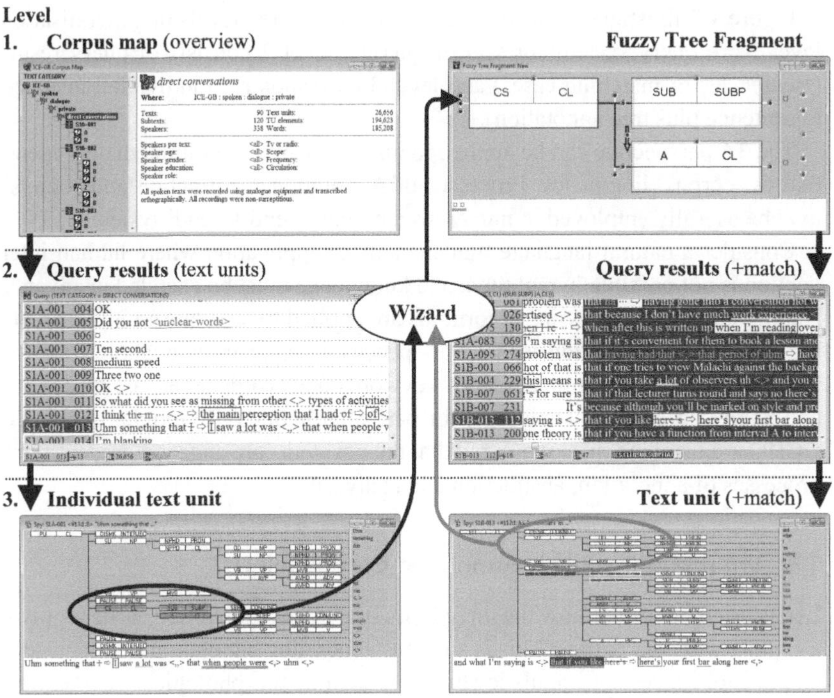

FIGURE 1.3 Exploring the ICE-GB corpus with ICECUP, after Nelson et al. (2002): from the top, down (left), and using the Wizard in an exploration cycle with FTFs (right).†

† For reasons of space, ICECUP defaults to a left-right visualisation of tree structures. The top of the tree is on the left, with sub-elements to the right, and the sentence runs down the right-hand side.

One advantage of a tree-like query system is that it is easy to see how elements of the query map directly onto the tree (bottom right). We can see why and how ICECUP determined that this was a matching example. The reverse – abstracting from an example tree to a query – is also possible. A 'Wizard' tool permits a researcher to select parts of the tree annotation and convert it into an FTF.

The tools are linked by a user interface that sits on top of a specialised database system. Each window in Figure 1.3 depicts a different tool, and the arrows show how corpus exploration is typically carried out. Users may identify a text from the Corpus Map (top left) and, by browsing the text, an individual sentence tree (bottom left). The Wizard tool allows the researcher to select part of this tree and create an FTF query (top right). This query can then be applied to the corpus, and the matching elements in the text unit can be seen in both the query results (middle) and each tree (bottom right).

Figure 1.3 illustrates how tools relate to one of three levels of generalisation: level 1 are query systems or sets of queries, level 2 consists of query results ('sentences' or matching cases) and level 3 corresponds to individual instances (a sentence plus tree annotation).

The 3A perspective can be applied to many processes not immediately identified as 'corpus' linguistics. Processes of Annotation, Abstraction and Analysis may be usefully employed in numerous automatic 'end-to-end' systems.

Consider a natural language 'understanding' application where human intervention is not possible in real time, and knowledge must be encoded in advance. Natural language processing algorithms are applied to annotate an input stream, such as speech recognition and part-of-speech tagging; particular application features, for example, combinations of keywords and wordclasses, are abstracted; and finally processed ('analysed') for particular actions. If Google, Langley or GCHQ are listening in, rest assured that their systems are engaged in identifiable processes of annotation, abstraction and analysis!

1.4 What Might a Richly Annotated Corpus Tell Us?

Let us briefly consider how the three types of evidence identified earlier apply to a *richly annotated* corpus. This is a corpus containing annotation that represents one or more levels of linguistic structure, such as morphological or pragmatic structure. The most common type is a *parsed corpus* (also known as a 'treebank'), that is, a corpus like ICE-GB or its relation, the *Diachronic Corpus of Present-day Spoken English* (DCPSE).

In a parsed corpus, every sentence is given a tree analysis with a chosen scheme. In the case of spoken data, where 'sentences' must be inferred, decisions to split utterances into sentences are integral to the parsing process, that is, they are part of the annotation decisions made in applying the scheme to the data.

The notion of a 'linguistic event' identified in general terms in Section 1.2 is extended to

1. **any single term** in the framework, including the permutation of descriptive features;
2. **any construction** formed of multiple terms in the framework in a given relationship; and
3. **any combination** of the above with elements of the source text.

As multiple levels of annotation are added, this principle applies *between* levels. Thus a corpus consisting of parsed, phonologically and pragmatically annotated text would permit elements to be identified in combination, such as a particular clause structure in a response, a rising tone in a non-interrogative clause and so on.

All three classes of evidence discussed in Section 1.2, that is, factual, frequency and interaction evidence, apply to these linguistic events, which we previously denoted by x and y. Thus, using such a corpus, we can determine whether a particular construction, formed by a combination of annotated terms, is found in the corpus (x exists, i.e., factual evidence), what its distribution might be (frequency evidence, $f(x)$) and whether the presence of a construction increases the likelihood that another, structurally related one is present (interaction evidence, $p(x \mid y)$).

But if we enrich our corpora by parsing, for example, which scheme should we choose, and why? Motivations have included *simplicity* (Penn Treebank I, Marcus et al., 1993), *application potential* (e.g., predicate-argument structure for text mining, Penn Treebank II, Marcus et al., 1994) and *linguistic tradition* (TOSCA/ICE, based on Quirk et al., 1985; Prague Dependency Grammar, Böhmová et al., 2003, etc.).

Let us consider the question from the perspective of a corpus linguist. There are at least two ways of evaluating a rich corpus annotation scheme (including but not limited to parsing).

- **Annotation facilitates abstraction** ('a handle on the data'). This is a theory-neutral position. The premise is that the annotation scheme simply makes useful distinctions between classes of linguistic event (differentiating nouns and verbs, say) and allows us to retrieve cases reliably. From this perspective, it is not necessary for a researcher to 'agree' with the framework employed. Distinctions encoded in the scheme must only be sufficient for research goals. The actual annotation scheme is irrelevant if the researcher can reliably abstract data according to their experimental paradigm.
- **Annotation facilitates analysis**. This is a theory-integral position related to the concept of *explanatory power*. Annotation should be considered according to its potential to progress research goals. For example, models of priming and spreading activation imply that decisions made by speakers and writers are influenced probabilistically by previous decisions. An annotation scheme that enables evidence of this kind to be found reliably is more powerful than one that does not. An ideal annotation scheme for psycholinguistic research could be one that reflected a credible 'trace' of the language production process undergone by the speaker.

In the first perspective, potential annotation schemes are evaluated by their ability to *reliably retrieve* linguistic events (Wallis, 2008).[8] This seems intuitive. We can say that a corpus whose annotation reliably classifies nouns and verbs is better than one with an unreliable classification, and a representation that explicitly denotes subjects of clauses is preferable to one that does not.

However, this criterion is rather circular! Why should we assume, *a priori*, that reliable retrieval of subjects or nouns is important? It also admits redundancy because any representation can improve on another by simply adding levels and becoming more complex.

The second position builds on the atomised linguistic event retrieval perspective of the first. True, it is useful for linguistic events to be reliably identified. However, for psycholinguistic research goals, it is the ability to obtain interaction evidence that has a plausible *linguistic* cause that ultimately justifies decisions regarding annotation scheme design.

If event *y* and event *x* correlate together in their co-occurrence, and we can eliminate trivial explanations of this correlation (e.g., textual topic or contextual artifacts), we are left with explanations that are more likely to be essentially psycholinguistic, such as priming or spreading activation. Of course, other research goals may prioritise other distinctions.

The argument that linguistic annotation schemes should ultimately be evaluated by their explanatory power (i.e., their ability to provide evidence for theoretically motivated goals) is consistent with Lakatos's (1978) epistemology of *research programmes*. This philosophical perspective views science as pluralistic competition between research programmes. Successful research programmes make novel predictions that can be tested. Declining ones are unproductive: for example, they fail to explain phenomena competing programmes address.

Annotation schemes are part of the *auxiliary assumptions* of the research programme (Wallis, 2020a). From this perspective, the annotation scheme cannot be evaluated in the abstract, but should be considered in terms of whether it facilitates the end goals of the research programme – and it is the success or otherwise of the programme that ultimately determines the validity of the scheme. The key question is what linguistic research goals could annotation schemes attempt to further? We will attempt an initial answer in Section 1.6, but first let us consider research of the first kind.

1.5 External Influences: Modal *Shall/Will* Over Time

Many corpus studies investigate external influences on linguistic choices. Aarts et al. (2013) looked at whether the alternation between the modal auxiliaries *shall* and *will* changed with time in first person positive declarative contexts.

The *shall/will* alternation is a striking example of change over two centuries. Two hundred years ago, writers would use *shall* to express future prediction or intention. *Will* was expressly criticised in prescriptive grammars. Yet present day British English finds *shall* rarely used (it is the archaic marked form) and *will* outnumbers *shall*.

Aarts et al. used an alternation methodology that employed grammatical restrictions to focus on a subset of cases. Christian Mair and Geoff Leech (2006) considered *shall* and *will* (including negative *shan't* and *won't* and cliticised *'ll* = *will*) and analysed each modal auxiliary verb in terms of exposure rates (*shall* and *will* per million words). Using their results, it is not possible to refute an alternate hypothesis that one or either trend was due to a varying potential to use either *shall* or *will*. Nor is it possible to infer the true rate over time. Yet it is a relatively simple matter of reframing their data to pose the question in terms of a basic choice rate, *shall* as a proportion of the set {*shall*, *will*}. This is exactly what Aarts et al. proceeded to do.

Mair and Leech had also not evaluated whether *will* was replacing *shall*, although this was an implication of their study. To do this, it is necessary to go back to source texts. Can cases of *shall* or *will* be replaced by the other modal without changing the intended meaning? If the answer is no, these 'non-alternating cases' should be removed. See Chapter 3.

These earlier studies were carried out on tagged corpora. This made it difficult to distinguish between distinct grammatical contexts where alternation is licensed to varying degrees. But for this alternation, the subject matters. By the 1960s, examples of *you shall*... or *they shall*... had become rare. Alternation of *shall* and *will* rarely occurred except with first person subjects. The ideal would be to identify just those cases of *shall* where the speaker has a genuine choice of using *will* instead, and vice versa.

Consider the interrogative form. *Shall we go to the park?* and *Will we go to the park?* are semantically and pragmatically distinct, so do not freely alternate. Aarts and colleagues focused on first person declarative cases and, for similar reasons, decided to eliminate negative cases.

Working with the parsed DCPSE and ICECUP, to reliably extract cases of first person declarative positive *shall* and *will*, one can construct an FTF query like Figure 1.4. Another FTF pattern, where *shall* or *will* is followed by *not*, is applied to identify negative cases, which are then removed from the total.

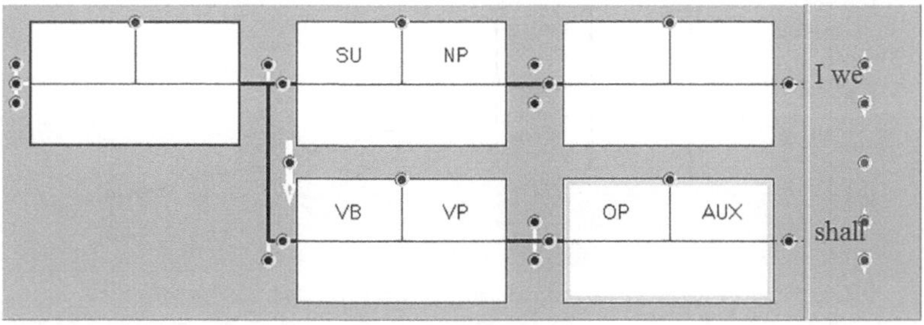

FIGURE 1.4 An FTF for a first person subject (*I* or *we*) followed by auxiliary verb *shall*, after Aarts et al. (2013). To search for *will* and *'ll*, the lexical item *shall* is replaced.[†]

† DCPSE uses the Tosca/ICE scheme (Nelson et al., 2002). Gloss: SU,NP = subject noun phrase; VB,VP = verb phrase; OP,AUX = auxiliary verb acting as an operator. Some links are specified: white down arrow = node follows, but not necessarily immediately; absent up/down links below the SU,NP node insist that the NP has only one child, that is, it consists of the single pronoun *I* or *we*. Both words are directly connected to their associated node.

This FTF works on the annotation scheme by relating individual terms and structure. It is a reliable retrieval mechanism for obtaining relevant cases – as reliable as the annotation is consistently applied, at least. The annotation is a 'handle on the data' allowing researchers to extract instances of linguistic events, in this case, the use of *shall* or *will* in the context required. Graphs such as the one in Figure 1.5 are obtained, showing the tendency to prefer *shall* over *will*, in first person declarative positive contexts, falling over time.

Consider the steps that would be required to obtain these results were DCPSE unparsed. It would be possible to construct queries that searched for patterns of a first person pronoun followed by *shall* or *will*, but researchers would then have to manually review every instance to verify it was part of the same clause. In effect, they would be performing the necessary additional annotation stage during their research. *Annotation is unavoidable.*

In this study, one of the authors manually classified every instance of previously identified cases of *shall* and *will* by their modal semantics (Epistemic, Root and 'other'). This allowed her to conclude that the identified fall in an overall preference for *shall* was due to a sharp decline in Epistemic uses of *shall* (i.e., those with a meaning of intention rather than prediction). This step is also a type of annotation, except one performed by a researcher for a research goal instead of by the corpus compilers prior to distribution.

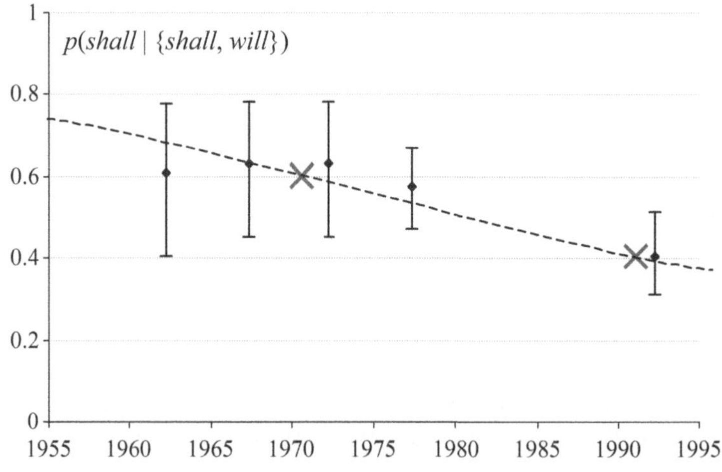

FIGURE 1.5 Declining use of *shall* as a proportion *p* of the set {*shall, will*} with first person subjects, half-decade data ('1960' = 1958–1962 inclusive, etc.) in the spoken DCPSE corpus (after Aarts et al., 2013). The crosses are midpoints of the two DCPSE subcorpora.

1.6 Interacting Grammatical Decisions: NP Premodification

The previous study examined variation in a single linguistic choice over time. Other variables external to the text (commonly called 'sociolinguistic' variables as a shorthand), such as speaker gender, text genre, mode of delivery, monologue versus dialogue, and so on, also fall within this experimental paradigm. The frequency *f*(*shall*) generated a frequency distribution, one frequency count for each value of the independent variable, in this case time subdivided into half-decades. By combining it with the frequency distribution for *will*, we obtain the proportion *p*(*shall* | {*shall*, *will*}) plotted in Figure 1.5.

However, if we are interested in internal influences on language choices, we must extract and attempt to interpret interaction evidence. At its simplest, interaction evidence may consist of a correlation between two grammatical variables. Examples given by Nelson et al. (2002, pp. 273–283) include the interaction between transitivity and mood features of clauses, and the phrasal marking of an adverb and that applying to a following preposition within the same clause. See also Chapter 3.

Suppose we wished to investigate serial repeated additive decisions in language production (Wallis, 2019b). This experimental paradigm considers the decision to add a particular construction to a base construction, and tests whether the speaker or writer is more or less likely to repeat the decision. Here we briefly introduce the idea.

This type of study may be seen as a way of examining *construction complexity* (a static interpretation) or *the interaction between language production decisions* (a dynamic one). The patterns obtained are interesting, occasionally counter-intuitive and certainly worthy of theoretical discussion. An advantage of the dynamic interpretation is that it draws our attention to the process of construction itself rather than merely the outcome of the process.

A simple illustrative example is attributive adjective phrases premodifying an NP head, thus we have *boat*, *green* *boat*, *tall green* *boat*, and so on. Armed with a parsed corpus, we can use FTFs to identify NPs with a head noun, a subset of these NPs with at least one attributive adjective phrase, a subset of those with at least two adjective phrases, and so on.

This model makes no assumptions about the order of decisions a speaker makes. Adjectives might be mentally selected in word order (*tall*, *green*), in reverse order (*green*, *tall*) or in parallel, and then assembled in a subsequent articulation process.

We obtain the data in Table 1.1 by applying a series of FTFs to ICE-GB across both speech and writing. The top line is the frequency of NPs with at least x attributive adjective phrases, $f(x)$, so $f(0)$ is simply all relevant NPs. We can now derive a sequence of probabilities representing the chance that if a speaker or writer has added $x - 1$ adjective phrases, they will add a further one:

additive probability $p(x) \equiv f(x) \,/\, f(x - 1)$.

TABLE 1.1 Frequency and relative additive probability of NPs with *x* attributive adjective phrases before a noun head, in ICE-GB, after Wallis (2019b).

x adjective phrases	0	1	2	3	4
frequency 'at least x' $f(x)$	193,124	37,307	2,946	155	7
probability $p(x)$		0.1932	0.0789	0.0526	0.0452

Slightly less than 20% of all NPs (19.32%) contain at least one attributive adjective, but less than 8% of these contain two.

We plot this additive probability over the number of adjective phrases, x, as in Figure 1.6. This graph includes 95% Wilson intervals (see Chapter 6) and distinguishes spoken and written performance.[9]

The first point to note about this graph is that the null hypothesis would be that decisions at each level do *not* interact. When we toss a coin repeatedly, the probability of obtaining each individual tail or head is constant. If there is no interaction, the graph would be flat.

But this is not what happens. Plotting $p(x)$ reveals that the decision to add a second attributive phrase after a first is less probable than the decision to add the first, and so on. By the fourth adjective phrase, we run out of data and obtain wide confidence intervals, but the overall trend seems reliable. Far from decisions being independent, they interact consistently in a negative feedback loop.

This pattern is not universal. Adverb phrases premodifying a verb phrase (e.g., *quickly, intelligently getting to the point*) result in a much weaker interaction between the probability of deciding to add one or two adverb premodifiers. The chance of adding a postmodifying clause to an NP sequentially (e.g., *a thing* [*called a carvery*] [*which had a vast menu*])) first declines and then increases. See Wallis (2019b).

There are at least three potential sources of an interaction between attributive adjectives:

- **logical-semantic constraints**, including
  - attributive ordering (cf. *long green boat* versus *green long boat*);
  - idioms and compounding (*green long boat*); and
  - avoidance of illogical descriptions (*long short boat*);
- **communicative economy**, avoiding unnecessarily long descriptions, especially on the second and third citation (i.e., on subsequent occasions referring simply to *the boat* rather than, say, *the long green boat over there*); and
- **psycholinguistic attention and memory constraints**, where speakers find it more difficult to produce longer constructions.

Tentatively, the most likely explanation seems to be the first. Communicative economy predicts a rapid drop from $p(1)$ to $p(2)$, but not a subsequent fall.

Psycholinguistic constraints seem implausible because the added constructions themselves are 'light' memory-wise. Indeed, if a speaker forgot they had said a previous adjective phrase, it seems more likely they would act in an unconstrained, rather than a constrained manner.

Figure 1.6 shows that speech and writing do not have exactly the same distribution. For example, we can see that a greater proportion of NPs uttered by speakers have no adjective phrases. When they do employ adjective phrases, speakers tend to use fewer phrases, and so on. There may be other possible additional reasons for this, aside from the difference in mode of delivery. For instance, in a conversation, the audience is present and referents require less elaboration. Nonetheless, both subcorpora obtain a similar overall pattern: one of systematic decline.

This evidence is only obtainable from a corpus. One would not spot this trend by laboratory experiment: we could not acquire enough data. For NP premodification, employing a parsed corpus is not required, and simple sequences of the form <ADJ> <N> obtain similar results, but with a few more errors. On the other hand, to inspect trends generated by serial embedding and postmodification, for example, a parsed corpus is necessary. As soon as we need to examine non-adjacent terms or structure, the reliable representation of that structure is essential.

Finally, comparing spoken and written data is revealing. Most corpora contain little or no spoken data. Figure 1.6 confirms that we are observing a linguistic

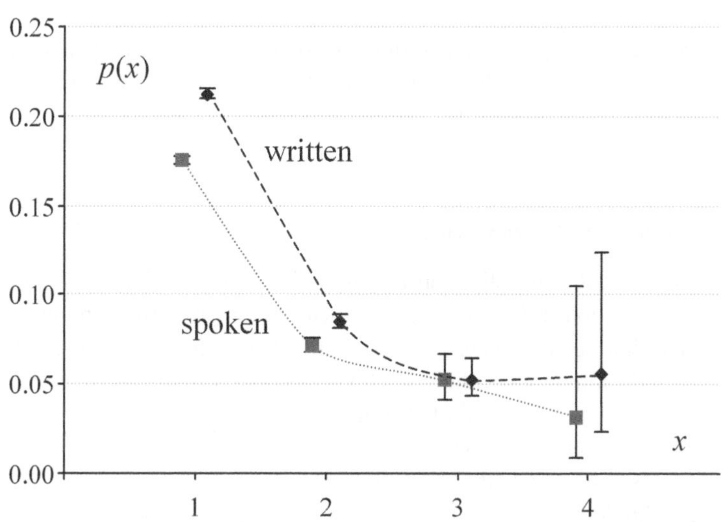

FIGURE 1.6 Declining probability of adding attributive adjective phrases to an NP noun head, data from ICE-GB, patterns for speech and writing.

phenomenon not attributable to a special character of writing or speech, such as a possible tendency for writers to avoid excessive NP length by editing. The presence or otherwise of an audience may affect the rate and starting point of decline, but it does not seem to affect the overall tendency.

1.7 Framing Constraints and Interaction Evidence

This interaction experiment illustrates a principle all linguistic research must contend with. Whenever we carry out research with a corpus, we explore the effect of two different classes of restriction on the choices speakers make.
Choices affect each other in two distinct ways:

1. **framing constraints** that either permit or prevent a potential future choice from occurring; and
2. **interaction evidence**, where one choice *influences* a subsequent choice outcome although the two are structurally independent, that is, we can say these decisions 'interact'.

Framing constraints are extremely important. If a second choice is unavailable, this fact must inform our experimental design. Framing constraints include basic grammar rules, such that violating a constraint can be said to be 'ungrammatical'. This is not to say that these rules are never broken in a corpus. Such violations are indeed potentially worthy of investigation. Rather it means that when they occur, they should be treated as unprincipled 'noise' *for the purposes of the current experiment.*

In other words, framing constraints are part of our 'auxiliary assumptions' like corpus annotation. They are assumed to be true before an experiment commences. They constrain the options available for choices and interactions between them, including those under investigation.[10]

1.7.1 Framing Frequency Evidence

In our experimental investigation into variation in the choice *shall* versus *will* over time (Section 1.5), we justified focusing an investigation on positive, declarative first person contexts. These contexts constrain the choice of modal *shall* and *will*. Importantly, these contexts are ones where both modals share a common meaning. As a result, the writer or speaker's intended meaning is not affected by the choice they make.

We can also decide whether to include the contracted form of *will* (*'ll*), and if so, how it should be incorporated into the experimental design (e.g., as a version of *will*). The process of enumerating available options and grammatical contexts is one of framing the experiment.

These framing constraints are ultimately static. It is extremely important that we are aware of them and maintain them across our data. They should apply to all examples in exactly the same way.

If one choice out of several was affected by a framing constraint – for example, it could only appear in a particular construction, or had a much more restricted meaning – this would bias our experiment. We must compare 'like with like'.

We evaluated the declarative alternation for first person *shall* and *will*. Consider instead the interrogative alternation. Table 1.2 is extracted from the same source as Figure 1.5 – the spoken DCPSE corpus. On the left, we simply have frequencies of *shall* and *will* tagged as 'interrogative operator'. For example:

(1) And how long *will* you be away? [DI-A20 #50]
(2) What *shall* we do? [DL-B10 #798]

The subject of the clause turns out to be a crucial factor in the selection. We can use an FTF like the one in Figure 1.7 to extract interrogative examples followed by a first person pronoun subject *I* or *we*. We can see an obvious difference between how *shall* and *will* tend to be used. See Table 1.2, right.

Almost all the cases of *shall* in DCPSE are followed by *I* or *we*, but very few cases of *will* take a first person pronoun as subject. The previous examples could

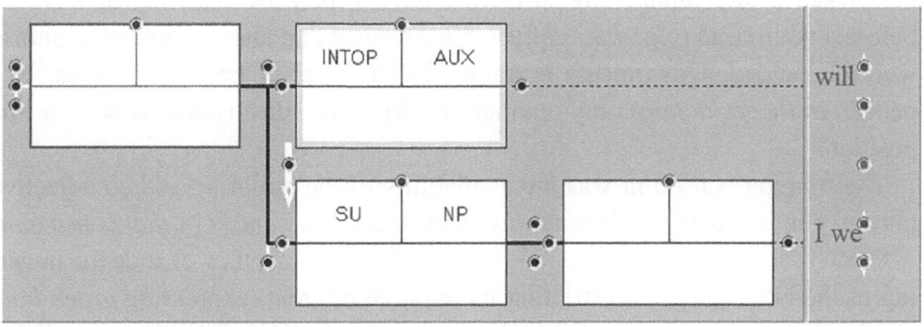

FIGURE 1.7 Fuzzy Tree Fragment for interrogative *will* followed by a first person pronoun subject. As before, we substitute *shall* for *will* to obtain the alternate pattern.

TABLE 1.2 Frequency data for interrogative *shall* versus *will* in DCPSE. Left: all cases. Right: cases followed by a first person pronoun subject.

interrogative	*shall*	*will*	*Total*	*shall I/we*	*will I/we*	*Total*
LLC (1957–1972)	43	71	114	41	3	44
ICE-GB (1990–1992)	39	65	104	38	3	41
Total	82	136	218	79	6	85

conceivably alternate – both *how long shall you be away?* and *what will we do?* are grammatical and plausible – but the meaning changes. A semantic framing constraint applies, and the result is dramatic.

Framing constraints matter in obtaining frequency evidence for two main reasons. First, they affect the population of interrogative clauses we may draw conclusions about. But they also matter because, as far as possible, *meaning should not change with different types of our dependent variable*. See Chapter 3.

Once we know that the type of subject affects the choice in interrogative cases, to perform the study we must control for the subject, that is, we must study first person cases separately from other ones. Failing to do this would conflate two kinds of variation: variation in subject and variation in our target construction, the choice *shall* versus *will*.

1.7.2 Framing Interaction Evidence

Framing constraints are even more important for studies of interaction evidence. This is because we are not simply concerned with the constraints on a single choice, but on multiple choices, and on *the relationship between choices*. Interaction research is best considered as a process of investigating how structurally independent decisions influence each other within a set of framing constraints.

In Section 1.6, we discussed an experiment that measured the degree to which the presence of a number of previous adjective phrases (e.g., *tall* and *green*) before a noun head (e.g., *boat*) affected the chance that another adjective phrase would be added. This process is framed by the rules of English grammar that permit, *in theory at least*, any number of attributive adjectives to appear in this position.

The framing constraint was the availability of the option to add an adjective phrase. The interaction evidence was evaluated *in the context of that constraint*.

Clearly, every time a speaker adds an adjective phrase, they change the meaning of the NP – they are restricting its possible referent (expressing *green boat* eliminates boats of other colours). However, a speaker does not select one choice over another (to add an adjective phrase) because they wish to refer to something else. They are just being more specific.

We discuss the consequences of allowing meaning to change across the dependent variable in more detail in Chapter 3.

1.7.3 Framing and Annotation

The requirement to consider framing constraints has another implication. The richer the annotation scheme applied to the corpus, the greater the number of framing constraints that can be readily employed, and the larger the set of research questions that may be explored.

For instance, in a parsed corpus, it is possible to study the interaction between decisions framed by grammatical constituents. Without reliable means to identify and classify subjects for example, it would be more difficult to distinguish cases of interrogative modals.

Similarly, grammatical annotation allows researchers to reliably identify adjectives in the same NP as a noun head because the NP brackets the query. To take a simple example, a tagged corpus does not distinguish between the following:

- an adjective before a noun, such as *they were young, people said*; and
- an attributive adjective in an NP: *they were young people.*

For obvious reasons, annotation reliability is crucial. This was, if you recall, the minimum condition in Section 1.4. A tagged corpus never manually corrected may contain long strings of words marked as 'adjectives', which turn out to be nothing of the kind when examined (see Wallis, 2019b).

If a corpus is annotated further (e.g., morphologically, prosodically, semantically or pragmatically), then new types of research question become possible. We might characterise these as

- **intra-level research** studying variation and interaction of decisions encapsulated within a level (e.g., within grammar or semantics);
- **inter-level research** studying the impact of decisions between different levels (e.g., the interaction between a grammatical choice and a prosodic one); and
- **integrated research** studying variation and interaction in phenomena that are each identified across multiple levels (e.g., studying variation in NPs that have a particular pragmatic function).

1.7.4 Framing and Sampling

A final aspect concerns sampling. Since decisions made in the same text (particularly if they are adjacent) can interact with each other, this can also affect sampling when, as is common, multiple cases are drawn from the same text. Statistical methods assume by default that instances in a sample are randomly obtained and therefore independent from each other, but in some cases, they may not be. We discuss how we may control for this problem in Chapter 16.

1.8 Conclusions

In this chapter, we summarised two simple corpus linguistics experimental designs to show that corpus linguistics can be commensurate with other approaches to linguistics research, such as theoretical linguistics and psycholinguistics. Corpus linguistics methods can generate linguistically interesting and novel research outcomes that require theoretical explanation and additional experiment.

Science typically proceeds by triangulation rather than refutation, not least because every field of study relies on 'auxiliary assumptions', that is, underpinning assumptions necessary for an experiment to take place. Biological research with optical microscopes relies on optics, slicing and staining techniques; early DNA research relied on electrophoresis; and corpus linguistics relies on standards of linguistic representation, including transcription and annotation standards. Whereas in settled science, auxiliary assumptions infrequently change (although new techniques come to the fore), agreed linguistics frameworks are not universal. We must expect representational plurality and competing frameworks for some time to come.

We have attempted to summarise the different types of evidence that might be obtained from a corpus, and the impact of employing a particular type of rich annotation, a phrase structure parse analysis, on this evidence. We have also shown how different representations in a corpus ('annotation') can be partially separable from research goals by emphasising the need for an explicit mapping between them ('abstraction'). They are *partially* separable: a research question that required the identification of phenomena not annotated at all would require either a fresh annotation effort or the manual extraction of examples.

The three processes of developing and applying annotation schemes, refining queries, and evaluating experimental datasets are each knowledge-rich and cyclic. Annotation is necessarily conditional and subject to revision, either during the compilation of a corpus or in successive post-publication revision cycles.

Similarly, abstraction is cyclic, and – given the plurality of frameworks – necessarily so. We briefly noted how software like ICECUP may accommodate this. Facilitating abstraction in this way has enabled complex novel experiments.[11]

This same cyclic perspective applies to analysis. The overarching perspective of this book is that 'statistical analysis' should be considered a method for evaluating meaningful observations in data.

Analysis is cyclic when it leads to new experimental designs. Researchers should consider not just *that* their data are distributed in a particular way, but what the underlying processes might be that generated this distribution. In other words, they must consider new hypotheses and how they might be tested.

The fact that many of these results are only obtainable from volumes of linguistic data, corpora, demonstrates what corpus linguistics is capable of. Contrary to the dominant paradigm of 'big data' corpus linguistics, these studies emphasise the value of *rich* data. We need annotation to distinguish between linguistic framing constraints and the choices that speakers and writers make within those constraints.

Ignoring framing constraints in research and counting frequencies as if each word was independent from the next (reporting per million word exposure rates) is to ignore the structure of language. However, in the absence of reliable annotation, corpus linguists have tended to overlook this problem – justifying some of Chomsky's criticisms of corpus linguistics.

Corpus linguistics cannot 'prove' the correctness of one internal framework over another. In fact, due to dependence on auxiliary assumptions, no scientific research programme is ultimately capable of refutation merely by observation. Our equipment may be wrong!

Science validates and provokes theories, but theories are not disproved or proved by evidence alone. Indeed, 'evidence', its selection and interpretation, is only obtained by the application of auxiliary assumptions. Without engagement with real-world data, theory rests in the realm of philosophy – however sophisticated and computer literate its adherents.

This, ultimately, is the answer to Noam Chomsky's objection regarding the use of corpora. He is absolutely correct to criticise mere summaries of facts and frequencies without reference to an underlying theory. But to reject corpus evidence *per se* on the grounds that it is an external manifestation of internal processes is ultimately to reject the refutation of linguistic theory. Corpus frequency and interaction evidence provides new evidence for theoretical linguists to engage with.

Notes

1 The research in this chapter was originally published as Wallis, S.A. (2014), What might a corpus of parsed spoken data tell us about language? in L. Veselovská and M. Janebová (eds.) *Complex Visibles Out There: Proceedings of the Olomouc Linguistics Colloquium 2014: Language Use and Linguistic Structure*. Olomouc: Palacký University, 2014. Research introduced in Section 1.6 was published as Wallis, S.A. (2019b), Investigating the additive probability of repeated language production decisions. *International Journal of Corpus Linguistics*, *24*(4), 492–525. www.benjamins.com/catalog/ijcl.

2 Traditional discussions of corpus linguistics methodology have tended to focus on a dichotomy between top-down 'corpus-based' and bottom-up 'corpus-driven' research (Tognini-Bonelli, 2001). In this book, we argue that both positions are better seen as complementary arms of cyclic research. For a detailed discussion, see (Wallis, 2020a).

3 We return to this question in Chapter 16.

4 We could interpret the terms 'corpus' and 'linguistic event' under a still broader definition. Untranscribed tape recordings or handwritten field notes, while not in the digital domain, are 'corpora' for the purposes of this definition. This relaxed definition would allow us to draw parallels with non-linguistic fields such as 'digital humanities', where researchers are engaged in the digitisation and representation of cultural artifacts, from museum exhibits to architectural drawings. The same types of evidence are obtainable by the types of process that we discuss in Section 1.3.

5 Lavandera (1978) argued that alternation research should not involve choices that change referential meaning. See Chapter 3.

6 For example, the *University of Pennsylvania Treebank* was released in two versions: Treebank I (Marcus et al., 1993) and Treebank II (Marcus et al., 1994).

7 See also Nelson et al. (2002) and www.ucl.ac.uk/english/ftfs.

8 The concepts of 'decidability', syntactic gradience (Aarts, 2007) and 'retrievability' (Wallis, 2007) are closely related. See also (Wallis, 2019b).

9 Two points on the same line may be compared visually by checking whether an earlier point is within the interval for a later one. Such cases will not be statistically significant. See Chapter 7.

10 In fact, all quantitative research with language data contains assumptions of this kind (Wallis, 2020a). The most basic auxiliary assumption necessary for a tagger of English to function is that space characters subdivide words. But what about hyphenated forms? Is there a difference between *larger than life* and *larger-than-life*? Is each word grammatically independent or might it be part of a compound? These questions require a decision one way or another. We might further decide to separate out genitive markers (*'s* and *'*), but not possessive markers, and so on.

11 It has also permitted us to develop grammar teaching resources that draw from ICE-GB but may deviate from the parsing scheme such as www.englicious.org.

PART 2

Designing Experiments With Corpora

2

THE IDEA OF CORPUS EXPERIMENTS

2.1 Introduction

In Chapter 1, we introduced the idea of an *experimental cycle* comprising Annotation, Abstraction and Analysis sub-cycles. In this chapter, we discuss how the *scientific method* is applied to corpus research.

Corpus linguistics has been transformed over the last quarter century by the development of large and structurally detailed corpora. Cheap computing power, greater scale, richer annotation and more sophisticated query systems have combined to provide linguists with a myriad of possibilities for research (see, e.g., McEnery & Hardie, 2012; O'Keefe & McCarthy, 2012; Biber & Reppen, 2015).

New researchers are entering the field. Some arrive from scientific disciplines schooled in experimental methods of other sciences, others come from literary disciplines where this kind of thinking is unfamiliar. Corpus linguistics shares features with experimental linguistics and psychology. But it has important differences.

You may be tempted to read an academic paper or two, borrow a method and reproduce it with a slightly different linguistic object of study or a different corpus. This is not wholly unreasonable. But if you follow this path, it stands to reason you will not undergo the same thought process as the original researcher.

Copying a method ultimately means not considering alternatives. It may mean ignoring possible criticisms of that approach. Even if an original method is sound, duplicating it assumes that your research is analogous. Shortcuts can be risky.

When you begin a study, you should immerse yourself in background reading, review other researchers' work, examine previous experiments and only then plan how to take the topic forward. Can results be replicated? What remaining questions might your research address?

DOI: 10.4324/9781003622697-4

It is fair to say that you cannot become a well-rounded researcher by copying methods. You need to understand the logic of the methods available – including alternatives to those you prefer – how they work and what results might imply. Studying systems of method is called *methodology*.

Let us begin from first principles. What is 'the scientific method'? How should it be applied to corpora? How is corpus research different from experimental research? How is it similar?

In Chapter 1, we referred to 'rich' corpus annotation – grammatical tree structures, semantic relations, and so on. How does this affect a scientific approach to corpus research?

In this book, we do not cover the full range of possibly relevant social science methods, any more than we attempt an exhaustive treatise on statistics. Instead, we focus on key problems in the analysis of corpus data every linguist must engage with. As a companion text to Part 2, you may find books on social science methodology useful (e.g., Singleton & Straits, 2017).

2.2 Experimentation and Observation

The purpose of science is to identify underlying processes: to see beyond surface phenomena to deeper causes. Medieval ballistics became a science by eliminating irrelevant variables – the mass of a cannon ball is relevant to its trajectory, its colour less so! How do we determine 'relevance'? Answer: relevant variables predict cannon ball motion. Researchers could set up physical experiments where, for example, mass and colour varied, and then compare the flight paths of balls fired from a cannon.

However, corpus linguistics is an observational science. Data collections – corpora – are usually collected for multiple potential purposes.

Some corpus projects are *case studies*. A case study is an empirical evaluation of a situation where conditions and participants have already been defined. If we study a single text source, such as a document, the investigation is likely to be primarily qualitative, involve close reading and annotation – and its conclusions will only apply to the sample. We can only report what we found in that particular text.

These case studies may use an existing corpus as a *control*, thus a medieval text might be compared to contemporary texts. We might discover that in our text, the author used a particular expression more frequently than other contemporaneous writers. But we are still only investigating a single text. To make claims about comparable data, we need an *experimental sample*.

2.2.1 Obtaining Data

Consider a corpus constituting the available data for a study. It is defined by a *sampling frame* – a set of criteria used by the corpus compilers to decide what to collect and how. To perform research, we abstract data from it to create a dataset, and then we analyse this dataset.

In Chapter 1, we said a corpus is a kind of sample, but it is rarely in the optimum form for analysis. The corpus contains annotated text passages, whereas when we test a hypothesis, we focus exclusively on data relevant to that hypothesis.

Exceptionally, the corpus is the total *population* of data we wish to explain, such as Shakespeare's published works. In this case, facts about the sample are also facts about the population. Usually, however, the corpus is not the population we wish to explain, but a tiny sample of it. *The British Component of the International Corpus of English*, ICE-GB (Nelson et al., 2002), contains 120 informal face-to-face conversations, totalling 185,208 words. The equivalent *population*, 'English informal face-to-face conversations between educated British adults in the years 1990 to 1992', is vast.

In Chapter 1, we commented that most corpora contain data from written sources, but most human language is spoken. To make sound claims about spoken language, we need spoken data. Most historical corpora collect the written performance of a *literate fraction* of a population. Exceptions, like the magnificent *Old Bailey Corpus* (Huber et al., 2012), capture plebian 'speech' via court stenographers.

All experiments, including corpus-based ones, are limited by participants. Thus, to examine the language of women in the legal profession, we cannot rely on male lawyers' speeches! If data are missing, we must find another corpus or create our own. Douglas Biber (1993) argues that research goals should dictate corpus design, and corpora should be compiled in a cyclic manner.

Linguists are often concerned about corpus *representativeness* (see, e.g., Biber, 1993; Wattam, 2015; Wallis, 2020a). A more practical question is simply, *is this data representative of the relevant population for my study?*

As corpus linguistics has matured and more corpora have become available, the challenge for researchers has become one of selection rather than compilation. Nonetheless, the research question must drive data selection.

Although corpora could, in principle, contain data from laboratory experiments, what we will call 'corpus experiments' do not manipulate contexts to obtain controlled data, but instead contrast data taken from different contexts. Many controlled 'laboratory' experiments use stimuli, 'cues' or artificial conditions to encourage particular behaviour. Participants commonly perform *the same task*. For example, in a recall experiment, subjects are told the same story and asked to retell it at a later point. The researcher notes linguistic features lost or gained in the retelling. By contrast, most corpora contain utterances of participants performing very different tasks.

However, in other respects, natural data, sometimes called 'ecological' data, are preferable to controlled laboratory data. One reason concerns the problem of *artificiality*. Manipulating experimental contexts or performing a single task can obtain particular data, but linguists seek to explain everyday language. Laboratory data are likely to be unrepresentative of the linguistic performance of a speech community.

A second reason is related to this. Psychology researchers have long been concerned about the problem of *experimenter bias* (Orne, 1969): in the process of eliciting responses, the experimenter 'leads the subject' in a particular direction. Experimental design in the psychological sciences often involves misdirecting the subject so they are unaware of the researcher's goals! As Orne (1969, p. 143) puts it, '[t]o counteract this problem psychologists have frequently felt it necessary to develop ingenious, sometimes even diabolical, techniques in order to deceive the subject about the true purposes of an investigation'. Medical double-blind trials and placebos attempt a similar feat.

In naturally sampled corpora, the intentions of future experimenters are unknown when language is produced.[1] Even if a specific research question is employed to decide the kinds of texts or recordings to sample, *participants are insulated from the researcher*. Nonetheless, participants may introduce two types of bias. Like laboratory subjects, they may be self-conscious about being recorded. And, if they self-collect data, offering recordings, emails or essays after the fact, they can select or edit them before submission.

A third motivation for corpora concerns rich annotation. Corpora offer the potential for embodying situated linguistic analysis in the form of pragmatic, grammatical or semantic annotation. Performing a full syntactic or pragmatic analysis is costly. The prospect of *multiple reuse* – using the same corpus for many research questions – is compelling.

With some exceptions, corpus linguistics is notable for the publication and sharing of source data. Other researchers can see how a study was carried out. Later in this chapter, we classify pronouns into subjects and objects. You, dear reader, should query if our 'subjects' are indeed subjects. Are *all* subjects included? With corpus in hand, you may reconstruct the experiment, examine supporting sentences, manipulate parameters and see if results change.

We take the view that corpus linguistics is a complementary paradigm to laboratory research. Controlled experiments will probably be necessary. But corpus experiments can be an efficient precursor. We can undertake a rapid evaluation of existing data before carrying out an experiment in controlled laboratory conditions.

In summary, corpus linguistics is the *post hoc* analysis of language data. It is the analysis of text samples obtained without bias towards a particular experimental context. But we have also identified a major potential drawback: natural samples in corpus research do not control for variation by creating artificial contexts. We must compensate for this in analysis.

2.2.2 Research Questions and Hypotheses

A scientific experiment is *an empirical test of a hypothesis*. A hypothesis is *an unverified statement that may be true*. The following are all hypotheses:

H1. The word *whom* is used less frequently in spoken English.
H2. When 1990s British English adults had a choice, speakers used *who* instead of *whom* at a different rate to writers.
H3. Gerunds (*-ing* participle verbs and nouns) used to be considered a discrete category, but in present day English, this distinction has disappeared.
H4. The health benefits of drinking a glass of wine a day outweigh the negative consequences.

In each case, the researcher must devise a study to *test* the hypothesis.

Compare hypotheses H1 and H2. The more general the hypothesis, the more difficult it is to collect evidence to test it, and the more likely it is that this evidence might support other explanations.

- H1 does not specify the *baseline* for the purposes of comparison. When we say '*whom* is used less frequently', what are we comparing it with? Do we mean *whom* is increasingly rare in speech overall, or do we mean it has become less common when the option of using either *who* or *whom* occurs? H1 does not say.
- H1 is also unclear as to what the *control* is. What data should we contrast spoken English with? H2 says we should compare spoken data with writing.
- Finally, H2 specifies that we should draw data from a well-defined *population*. H1 does not.

The path from H1 to H2 illustrates a typical process of specification researchers undergo. Indeed, H1 is so general that it is not really a *testable* hypothesis. We might call it a 'research topic' or perhaps *research question*. It is a starting point. It might be an idea for a research article. To evaluate it, we place additional restrictions on it.

For a hypothesis to be testable, we require three things: a *baseline* against which variation will be considered, a *control* (a contrasting dataset) and a *population* from which participants are drawn. For example, the sample for H2 might be varied by demography (social class, region, age, etc.). Over the course of an investigation, we might vary these parameters.

If we choose an existing corpus to carry out our research, available participants are defined for us. If we collect our own data, we may have greater flexibility – but more work to do!

H3 is a theoretical problem of categorisation. It is an even more general research question than H1. There is no simple empirical test for whether we should maintain this distinction or not. Rather, we might try to arrive at a conclusion by *linguistic argument*, considering a range of evidence.

What might the two alternative models (discrete category or not) predict empirically about the distribution of *-ing* participle verbs and nouns? Consider the following clauses, both subjects of the main clause in which they are found:

(3) But [$_{CL}$ *creating* your own] is a help. $_{[DI-A11\ \#230]}$
(4) No [$_{CL}$ what they're *having*] is the school play you see. $_{[DL-B07\ \#401]}$

The bracketed clause in Example (3) has no subject, unlike (4). It is possible, if clumsy, to reformulate the clause in (3) as a noun phrase headed by the gerund *creating*: *the creating of your own.* In (4), the existing subject, *what*, makes this reformulation impossible.

If H3 were true, we would expect to see *-ing* verbs increasingly taking subjects like other verbs. Aarts et al. (2018) examined the *Diachronic Corpus of Present Day Spoken English* (DCPSE) and discovered that over a 30-year period, *-ing* clauses do increasingly contain a subject. They conclude that this observation supports the claim that gerunds are indeed becoming more like regular verbs, and less capable of alternation with nominal forms.

Finally, an entire industry has benefited from headlines claiming the health benefits of a glass of wine a day! Nonetheless, H4 may be operationalised as a series of testable sub-hypotheses. Importantly, legitimate hypotheses include statements you might believe are false. Preconceptions of truth must not cloud our judgement of the testability of hypotheses.

2.2.3 From Hypothesis to Experiment

Whenever we commence research, our aim is to convert research questions (general hypotheses) into a *programme* of experiments, each evaluating (or seeking to refute) a testable hypothesis.

The simplest experimental design consists of the following:

1. a **dependent variable** (DV), say, X, which may or may not depend on
2. an **independent variable** (IV), Y, which varies over the normal course of events.

This is a *bivariate* (two-variable) design. A *multivariate* experiment contains multiple independent variables and considers their combination.

Dependent and independent variables X and Y may be of different numerical types or *scales*, which we can define with set notation, $X \in \mathbf{X}$, $Y \in \mathbf{Y}$, and so on.[2] The following number scales are commonly used:

- **Binomial** – a set of two categories, $\mathbf{X} = \{x_1, x_2\}$ or $\mathbf{X} = \{x_1, \neg x_1\}$, sometimes called 'Boolean' (true/false) or 'binary' categories.

- **Multinomial** – a set of any number of categories, $\mathbf{X} = \{x_1, x_2, x_3\}$, also called a 'categorical' scale.
- **Ordinal** – an ordered set or sequence of categories: first, second, third, and so on. For a set $\mathbf{X} = \{x_1, x_2, x_3\}$, all terms in the sequence are ordered (e.g., $x_1 < x_2 < x_3$). An example might be a time variable divided into 'early', 'middle' and 'late'.
- **Interval** – an ordered set of categories where the difference between category pairs in the sequence is constant. We can write $\mathbf{X} = \{x_1, x_2, x_3\}$, where $x_2 - x_1 = x_3 - x_2$. Natural numbers (1, 2, 3 . . .) are an interval set.
- **Real** – a continuous set of numbers (e.g., $\mathbf{X} = [l, h]$), where $l \leq X \leq h$, and l and h are low and high *bounds*. The variable X can have any value within this range, including the bounds.[3] The Real set, $\mathfrak{R}$, may be defined as the set $[-\infty, \infty]$ (any number from minus to plus infinity).

Different statistical methods and tests are used for each scale. A traditional book on statistics (e.g., Sheskin, 2011) explains these scales and enumerates tests for combinations of dependent and independent variables. If both variables are Multinomial or Binomial, use chi-square; if both Real, use regression techniques; and so on. See Chapter 12.

The most useful tests are those with the greatest explanatory power. Finding a mathematical relationship between variables, like Newton's Second Law ($F = ma$), is very powerful! However, few *linguistic* variables are Real or Interval, and most relationships are not straightforward. Few variables are even Ordinal (e.g., we might consider 'linguistic complexity' or 'weight' as Ordinal). Most are discrete categories, so we are really left with a choice between Multinomial and Binomial scales, and their associated statistics.

The simplest variable type, Binomial, has a small number of fundamental tests to apply, each with a single degree of freedom, which means the test only evaluates a single simple hypothesis, and the results are straightforward to interpret. See Chapter 8.

The more expressive the variable, the greater the number of possible patterns in the data may be detected with a test. For example, two Real variables can be fit to a mathematical function, in this case – because X is our dependent variable – written $X = fn(Y)$. This function could be a straight line (e.g., $X = mY + c$), but it may also match a more complex function. Straight lines are rare in nature, but simple to fit to. The same reasoning applies to *logistic regression* (fitting to the logistic function), discussed in Chapter 11.

More complex multivariate experiments collect data with several independent variables. Analysis consists of a series of tests and regression methods. Multivariate statistical methods allow researchers to evaluate whether two or more variables *working together* might affect the dependent variable, and can also factor out, or 'account for' interaction between variables.

However, complex designs are difficult to interpret. If you see a computer-selected 'optimal' result, you do not see the other possible rejected explanations. If you do not understand how the algorithm drew its conclusions, you are taking it on trust – like risking being short-changed at a till without an itemised receipt. Moreover, the first task for a linguist is to get the *linguistic analysis* correct.

In this book, we adopt a cautious stance. We must understand the simplest types of experiment thoroughly before venturing towards more complex ones. We focus on two-variable tests in this book, and mostly consider Binomial dependent variables. If you find yourself employing multivariate or regression methods later on, you should be able to do so critically.

2.3 Evaluating a Hypothesis

Let us return to Hypothesis H2:

H2. When 1990s British English adults had a choice, speakers used *who* instead of *whom* at a different rate to writers.

To test this, we could draw data from a single corpus of speech and writing, or two corpora, one of each. We will use the ICE-GB corpus (see Chapter 1).

The independent variable (IV) is the mode of delivery, spoken versus written, and the dependent variable (DV) is the choice *who* versus *whom*, that is, whether *who* was used instead of *whom* when the speaker had the choice (see Section 2.4.1). Both IV and DV consist of alternative categories. They are Binomial variables.

The traditional method for evaluating this data is to carry out a *contingency correlation test*, commonly known as a 2 × 2 'chi-square test' (written 'χ^2 test'). We discuss this test at length in Part 3. Here we introduce the basic procedure.

The test obtains a score representing the 'strength of evidence' that there is a correlation between the two variables in the population. This score is calculated from the data using a formula and compared against a threshold 'critical' value, obtained from a mathematical model of the type of variation we are studying: in this case, the Binomial model.

a) If the score is greater than this critical value, the data pass the test. The variables 'correlate significantly'. We are allowed to say that, if we know the value of the independent variable, the dependent variable will tend to vary accordingly. For a 2 × 2 test, this variation will be in the same direction as that observed in the sample.[4]
b) If the score is smaller than the critical value, we cannot draw this conclusion.

A classical approach calls outcome (b) – no change – the *null hypothesis*. The null hypothesis for H2 might be:

¬H2. When 1990s British English adults had a choice, speakers used *who* instead of *whom* at the same rate as writers.

The entire method is termed *null hypothesis significance testing* (NHST). The null hypothesis is the obverse of the hypothesis under test, representing 'no interaction between variables'. A significant result allows us to reject the null hypothesis.

The null hypothesis is that the variables are independent – like cannon ball colour and trajectory. Knowing the value of one variable (that the ball is red), does not help us predict the other (how far it will fly).

Correlations are not causes. A significant result only tells us that change in one variable *co-occurs* with change in another. See Section 2.5. First, how do we perform the test?

2.3.1 The Chi-Square Test

The most common version of the chi-square test, the 'χ^2 test for independence' (sometimes referred to as the 'χ^2 test for homogeneity') is given in Equation (1):

$$\textit{chi-square } \chi^2 = \sum \frac{(o-e)^2}{e}. \tag{1}$$

The large sigma ('Σ') means 'sum' (i.e., 'add up'). This formula is applied to every cell in a frequency table of r rows and c columns, so we could write it in full like this:

$$\textit{chi-square } \chi^2 = \sum_{i=1..r} \sum_{j=1..c} \frac{(o_{i,j} - e_{i,j})^2}{e_{i,j}}, \tag{1'}$$

where $o_{i,j}$ is the *observed frequency* and $e_{i,j}$ the *expected frequency* in row i, column j in the table. It is also common to use f to denote observed frequencies and n for totals.

The observed frequency is simply the number of cases found in each cell. Table 2.1 depicts a two-dimensional contingency table of arbitrary size, sometimes called an '$r \times c$' table. This test may be employed with two Multinomial variables. If r and $c = 2$, this is called a '2 × 2' test, and both variables are Binomial.

TABLE 2.1 An arbitrary-size two-variable contingency table, with notation for each cell.

		dependent variable (DV)				
		column 1	*column 2*		*column c*	*Total*
independent variable (IV)	row 1	$o_{1,1}$	$o_{1,2}$	...	$o_{1,c}$	$n_1 = o_{1+}$
	row 2	$o_{2,1}$	$o_{2,2}$	...	$o_{2,c}$	$n_2 = o_{2+}$
		...	...	...	...	...
	row r	$o_{r,1}$	$o_{r,2}$	...	$o_{r,c}$	$n_r = o_{r+}$
	Total	o_{+1}	o_{+2}	...	o_{+c}	$n = o_{++}$

The expected distribution models 'no change', scaled by the sample size. Expected frequencies are calculated from row and column totals:

$$\textit{expected cell value } e_{i,j} = o_{i+} \times o_{+j} / o_{++}, \quad (2)$$

where

$$\textit{row total for row } i, \quad n_i = o_{i+} = \sum_{j=1..c} o_{i,j},$$

$$\textit{column total for column } j, \; o_{+j} = \sum_{i=1..r} o_{i,j}, \text{ and}$$

$$\textit{overall total} \quad n = o_{++} = \sum_{i=1..r} o_{i+}.$$

Row and column totals are calculated by adding up cell frequencies in that row or column. The notation 'o_{i+}' refers to an index that has been added up (i.e., a total). The total frequency for each value of the IV (often called the 'experimental condition') on the right of the table is also labelled n_i.

2.3.2 Extracting Data

A lexical 'text fragment' search for '*who*+<PRON>' and '*whom*+<PRON>' (*who*/*whom* tagged as pronouns) in spoken and written subcorpora of ICE-GB with ICECUP (Nelson et al., 2002, see Chapter 1) obtains Table 2.2.

Given the choice, is *whom* more or less likely to be found in speech than writing? There are similar numbers of instances of *whom* in the spoken and written sections of the corpus. But there are nearly twice as many instances of the pronoun *who* in the spoken subcorpus (1,452) as in the written (735). If you picked a random case of *who* or *whom* from the corpus, not knowing whether it

TABLE 2.2 Completing Table 2.1 with frequency counts for pronoun *who* and *whom* from ICE-GB. The bold cells are obtained with corpus queries; the others are calculated by simple addition.

		dependent variable DV (*who* or *whom*)		
		who	*whom*	*Total*
independent variable IV	spoken	**1,452**	**41**	1,493
(spoken or written)	written	**735**	**43**	778
	Total	2,187	84	2,271

TABLE 2.3 Performing the χ^2 test with data from Table 2.2.

	observed **O**			*expected* **E**		*chi-square* χ^2		*probability*	
	who	*whom*	*Total*	*who*	*whom*	*who*	*whom*	*p*(*who*)	*p*(*whom*)
spoken	**1,452**	**41**	1,493	1,438	55	0.14	3.66	0.97	0.03
written	**735**	**43**	778	749	29	0.27	7.03	0.94	0.06
Total	2,187	84	2,271			s	**11.10**		

was written or spoken, the odds that it was *who* would increase if you then discovered it had been spoken.

The statistical test takes this variation in total frequency into account. Expected frequencies are calculated with Equation (2). For the first cell, $e_{1,1}$ = 1,493 × 2,187 / 2,271 ≈ 1,438 (quoted to the nearest whole number). We repeat for the other cells in Table 2.3.

We can now calculate the χ^2 score. We calculate scores for each cell pair, according to the inner part of Equation (1). The top left cell is $(1{,}452 - 1{,}438)^2$ / 1,438 ≈ 0.14 (to two decimal places). Finally, we sum these scores. The total χ^2 score is 11.10, which we compare with the *critical value* for χ^2.

The critical value is the threshold score for us to say the result is 'significant'. It is determined by two factors: the number of *degrees of freedom*, that is, the number of ways table cell frequencies can change independently (one for 2 × 2 tables, but a greater number for larger and more complex tables), and the *error level* at which we apply the test. The error level, which we will label α, is an agreed 'allowable error rate'. A typical error level is 1 in 20 (0.05), but some researchers prefer 1 in 100 (0.01).

Probably the most difficult concept to comprehend is *statistical significance*. The idea is deceptively easy to summarise, but counter-intuitive for reasons discussed in the Preface.

This particular test examines the distribution in our data and asks, 'what is the chance that this pattern would arise if there were no underlying relationship between the variables in the population?' A notable result may arise by blind luck, like tossing a coin five times and getting five heads. (We can calculate the chance of this happening: for a fair coin, $p(\text{error}) = 1/32$ or 0.0313, approximately.)

We want to know if there is a relationship between our variables. The test calculates a score ($\chi^2 = 11.10$) that may be converted into the probability that the observed pattern of cell frequencies, or an even more skewed pattern, occurred by sheer luck, *despite there being no relationship between the variables* ($p(\text{error}) = 0.0015$). However, for reasons we discuss in Part 3, it is unwise to quote χ^2 or '*p* values'. Instead, we ask, is the χ^2 score greater than the critical value? If so, the result is deemed 'significant'.

A smaller test error level is, in principle, more cautious. Using a more cautious error level reduces the chance we will accept hypotheses that may ultimately turn out to be false, called 'Type I errors'. But it also means that overall, we will reject some hypotheses that turn out to be true, which is another type of error (a 'Type II error' in statistical jargon). This reasoning comes with a cost-benefit analysis. In medicine, rejecting a drug that might cure a patient could be very costly, as could accepting one with dangerous side effects. Depending on the risk of erring on either side, we might adjust error levels.

In linguistics and other social sciences, researchers do not have this dilemma, and setting error levels is more a matter of choice. As a rule, we recommend deciding on an error level and sticking to it. In the book, we take the standard error level of 0.05 (1 in 20) unless otherwise stated.

The number of degrees of freedom is a measure of 'independent dimensions'. For the χ^2 test for independence with an arbitrary-sized table, it is straightforward to calculate:

$$\textit{degrees of freedom}, df = (r - 1)(c - 1). \qquad (3)$$

With a 2 × 2 table, $df = 1$. The critical value of χ^2 for a 2 × 2 table at an error level of 1 in 20 ('$\alpha = 0.05$') is 3.8415.

The χ^2 score we obtained (11.10) is greater than this number. We may therefore reject the null hypothesis, ¬H2, that the mode of delivery (speech or writing) does not affect the likelihood that you will hear *who* rather than *whom.*

2.3.3 Visualising Proportions, Probabilities and Significance

Table 2.3 is not very clear. The test tells us that the rate of participants using *who* rather than *whom* significantly differs between speech and writing. The test does not tell us in which direction or to what extent this change is occurring. However, we can examine *observed proportions* of the dependent variable. We can carry out two calculations, one simple, one less so, to plot a graph like Figure 2.1. This plots the proportion of cases that are *who* out of the set {*who*, *whom*}, for speech and writing.

We may extract proportions of cases from Table 2.3:

$$proportion\ p_{i,j} = o_{i,j} / o_{i+} = o_{i,j} / n_{i}. \tag{4}$$

Proportions in each row are *exhaustive* and sum to 1:

$$\sum_{j=1..c} p_{i,j} = p_{i,1} + p_{i,2} + \ldots p_{i,c} \equiv \Sigma p(x_j \mid \mathbf{X}) \equiv 1. \tag{5}$$

Here, proportions are expressed out of the set {*who*, *whom*}, so $c = 2$.

In this book, we will mostly use the notation $f(x)$ to refer to the frequency of an item $x \in \mathbf{X}$. For transparency we might simply write

$$proportion\ p(who \mid \{who, whom\}) = f(who) / (f(who) + f(whom)),$$

where $f(x)$ represents the frequency count for item $x \in \mathbf{X} = \{who, whom\}$ in a given row. We then plot $p(x \mid \mathbf{X})$ for each value of the independent variable (the row $i \in$ {spoken, written}).[5]

The sample proportion, $p(who)$, is the fraction of pronoun cases in a subsample that are *who*. It can also be considered a *probability* by the following reasoning:

Imagine we randomly sampled a single instance from the sample, like pulling a name from a hat. The chance that the instance was *who* is a probability. Before we pulled it out, the probability of it being *who* was the same as the proportion of cases of *who* in the sample.

We are not really interested in the probability of drawing a random instance from the *sample*. We have already obtained our sample. We are, however, interested in the probability of observing instances in the *population* from which our sample is drawn.

The 'probability' columns in Table 2.3 show proportions of the dependent variable for each row. With only two values of the dependent variable, we do not actually need to quote the proportion for *whom* as well. We only need plot one line in Figure 2.1 – the bottom line mirrors the top one.

The more complex calculation concerns the 'I'-shaped error bars (properly called 'confidence intervals') in Figure 2.1. We will not give the formula yet, although you can turn to Chapter 6 if you are keen! It is more useful to get an appreciation of how they work.

In simple terms, confidence intervals tell *us the region where we expect the true value in the population to be found.* If the true value were outside this range (e.g., $p(who$, spoken$) \in (0.9630, 0.9797)$) our result would be anomalous. The

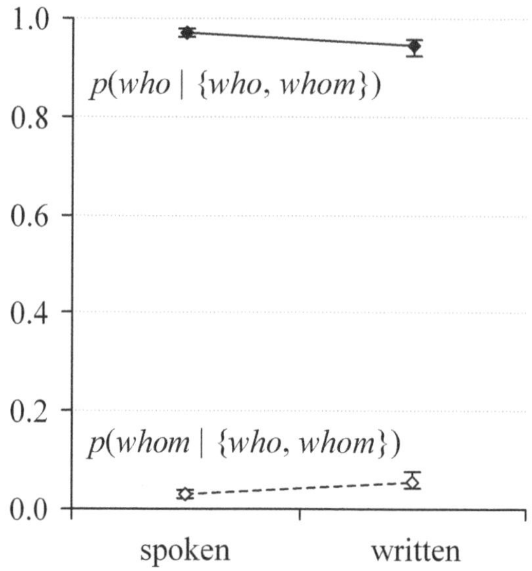

FIGURE 2.1 Binomial proportion difference graph from Table 2.3, showing that writers have a lower propensity to use *who* rather than *whom* than speakers (top line). The dashed bottom line for *whom* mirrors the upper line, and so is redundant. Proportions of the DV are expressed as probabilities and plotted with 95% Wilson score intervals.

true value would be 'significantly different from' the observed proportion *p*, allowing for random chance.

These 'Wilson' intervals estimate the upper and lower probability just significantly different from our observed proportion. They are computed at the same error level (0.05) as the χ^2 test. They are *95% confidence intervals*, that is, we are 95% confident that the true value in the population is within this range. Confidence intervals are like camera blur: the smaller a confidence interval, the more certain ('in focus') the observation.

The saying 'a picture is worth a thousand words' is occasionally appropriate. It should be immediately apparent that, although the proportion of cases that are *who* is very high in both subcorpora, it is lower in the written data than in the spoken.

The confidence intervals are small, so the true value is expected to be close to the observation. They do not overlap, so the difference between them must also be significant. This 'non-overlap' rule is explained in Chapter 7.

2.4 Refining the Experiment

This experiment has one obvious flaw, however. We want to examine the alternation *where participants have a choice*. But if they are using the pronoun in subject position, *who* is mandatory and the choice is made for them. Although we might be interested in exceptions to the grammar rule, we should refine the experimental design to eliminate subjective cases.

This kind of experiment refinement process is common. We must be self-disciplined and consider alternative hypotheses that might explain our results. We are similarly obliged to be transparent about how we obtained our data. If we formulated the experiment poorly or drew unwarranted conclusions, others should be able to spot the error.

In our experiment, failure to remove instances of subjective *who* means Figure 2.1 could be a by-product of a higher ratio of subjects to objects in speech. Perhaps there are fewer transitive verbs in the spoken data, fewer objects and thus a more limited opportunity for speakers to say *whom*.

How may we remove subjective cases of *who* (and *whom*) from our dataset?

- We could review every case of *who* and *whom* manually and decide, one-by-one, whether they were subjects. Reviewing over 2,000 cases will be a lot of work! In Chapter 15, we discuss possible shortcuts.
- In a tagged corpus, *who* and *whom* are marked as pronouns, but are not identified as subjects or objects. We can try to identify them 'by the company they keep', their *linguistic distribution*.[6] We can examine the pronoun's position relative to the main verb:
    - The patterns '*who*+PRON V' and '*whom*+PRON V' (the sequence pronoun *who* immediately followed by a verb, and *whom*, verb, respectively) will identify many subjects.
    - The same applies to the patterns '*who*+PRON AUX V' (pronoun *who*, auxiliary verb, main verb), '*who*+PRON ADV V' (pronoun *who*, adverb, main verb). These sets will not overlap, so the total found can be simply subtracted from the total number of cases of '*who*+PRON'. We repeat the process for *whom*.[7]

      We must review cases found by this technique to check they are actually subjects. But this method is unlikely to be exhaustive. We may fail to catch all the examples, so we must manually review the remainder. Chapter 15 discusses some short cuts.
- In ICE-GB, subjects are explicitly labelled in the phrase structure tree analysis. We can identify pronouns functioning as subjects with a single *Fuzzy Tree Fragment* (FTF, Nelson et al., 2002, see Chapter 1). The FTF for *who* as a subject is shown in Figure 2.2.

ICECUP finds matching examples like Figure 2.3 in ICE-GB. (For reasons of space, trees and FTFs are presented left-to-right, with the 'top' of the tree at top left.) The phrase structure grammar of ICE-GB is *fully instantiated*, so pronouns are the head of a noun phrase, even if the noun phrase consists of a single word.[8]

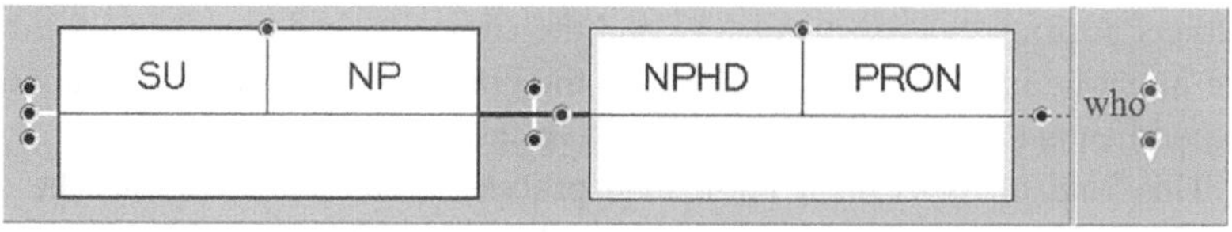

FIGURE 2.2 Fuzzy Tree Fragment for *who* (PRON, pronoun) as the head (NPHD) of a noun phrase (NP) functioning as a subject (SU).

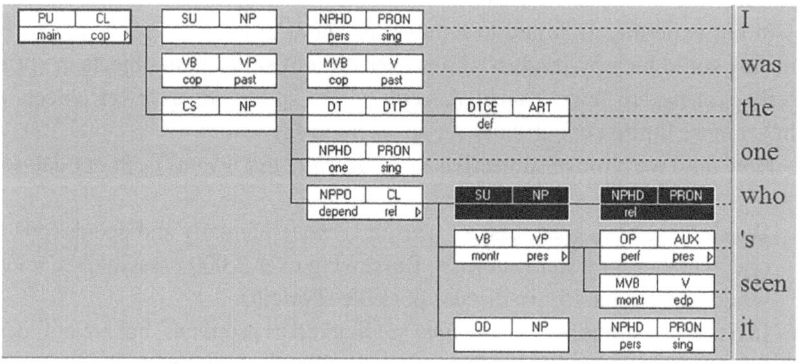

FIGURE 2.3 Matching case for the FTF in Figure 2.2 in ICE-GB, *I was the one* who*'s seen it* (S1A-006 #71). The tree is drawn left-to-right here for reasons of space.[†]

[†] Gloss: PU = parsing unit, CL = clause, main = main clause, SU = subject, NP = noun phrase, NPHD = noun phrase head, PRON = pronoun, pers = personal, VB = verbal, VP = verb phrase, cop = copular, MVB = main verb, V = verb, CS = subject complement, DT = determiner, DTP = determiner phrase, DTCE = central determiner, ART = article, def = definite, one = pronoun 'one', NPPO = noun phrase postmodifier, depend = dependent clause, rel = relative, montr = monotransitive, OP = operator, AUX = auxiliary verb, perf = perfect, OD = direct object.

TABLE 2.4 Subtracting *who* and *whom* subjects identified with an FTF (Figure 2.2). The test is significant.

	who		*whom*		*observed* **O**			*expected* **E**		*chi-square* χ^2		*probability*
	all	*SU*	*all*	*SU*	*who*	*whom*	*Total*	*who*	*whom*	*who*	*whom*	*p(who)*
spoken	**1,452**	**1,317**	**41**	**0**	135	41	176	116	60	3.25	6.22	0.77
written	**735**	**713**	**43**	**2**	22	41	63	41	22	9.08	17.38	0.35
Total	2,187	2,030	84	2	157	82	239			s	**35.94**	

Applying this subjective *who* FTF and an equivalent *whom* FTF, we obtain subject ('SU') frequency counts in Table 2.4. Almost all cases of written *who* (713 out of 735) are subjects. Nearly two-thirds of the remaining written cases (41 out of 63) are *whom*, whereas more than three quarters of spoken cases are *who*.

We found two cases of *whom* as a subject. These seem suspect. We could inspect these cases to decide whether they were genuine examples of 'grammatically incorrect' usage, or they were incorrectly labelled by the corpus annotators. However, the numbers are tiny. Irrespective of their labelling, we will see a significant difference between speech and writing.[9]

Importantly, by removing subject cases, we have eliminated the possibility that a varying proportion of subjects could explain our results. We have refined our hypothesis and focused only on contexts where participants had a genuine choice: object pronouns.

2.5 Correlations and Causes

A significant result identifies a *reproducible correlation.* A correlation is not a cause.

We cannot conclude, for example,

1 that the act of speaking 'caused' 1990s speakers to say *who* instead of *whom* in object position more frequently than when they wrote;
2 that speakers pay less attention to the grammatical rule that *whom* must be used in object position; or
3 that both writers and speakers intuitively say *who*, but correct themselves when they spot the error (usually in writing).

These may be *possible* causal explanations for the observed phenomenon, each with different underlying mechanisms. A correlation between an independent variable *Y* and a dependent variable *X* does not mean that *Y* causes *X*. 'A correlation between *Y* and *X*' simply means that a change in one variable *coincides* with a change in the other. The pattern could be due to a particular underlying cause. But it might be a symptom of something else.

The χ^2 contingency correlation test is *bidirectional.* A correlation between *Y* and *X* is also a correlation between *X* and *Y*. In this example, *Y*, mode of delivery, subdivides participants as well as data, so there is no plausible mechanism for *X* to 'cause' *Y*. It seems absurd to argue that a desire to express objective *who* caused a writer to speak rather than write!

However, as we will see, it is possible to carry out studies where both *X* and *Y* are text-internal variables describing different aspects of the same event. We may well be interested in whether influence flows from one event to another. A linguistic argument is required to conclude, for example, that decision *Y* was made before *X*.

A poorly designed experiment might even correlate two aspects of the same phenomenon, demonstrating a relationship between *Y* and itself! If we concluded that the transitivity feature of a verb predicted the presence of a direct object, we would be engaging in *circular reasoning*, since this is precisely how transitivity is defined.

It is sometimes claimed that *controlled* experiments allow causal claims to be made because we can manipulate independent variables and hold all other variables constant, like opening a tap causing water to flow. But strictly speaking, we cannot be sure that an observed correlation represents a causal relationship because the set of 'all other variables' is infinite. The tap might be faulty.

2.6 A Linguistic Interaction Experiment

We may conduct an experiment to investigate local in-text factors possibly influencing the objective *who* or *whom* choice. This evaluates *interaction evidence* (see Chapter 1), hence it is a 'linguistic interaction experiment'.

Does the *subject of the relative clause* introduced by *who* or *whom* – by definition, another word – affect this choice? Examples of relative clauses are bracketed in (5) and (6). The subjects are underlined. There are some 51 in total:

(5) 'The magicians, [$_{CL}$ *whom* <u>*he*</u> often repelled in confusion and defeat]'. $_{[W1A\text{-}002\ \#68]}$
(6) I had to meet this girl [$_{CL}$ *who* <u>*I*</u> haven't seen for ten years] from my school $_{[S1A\text{-}062\ \#193]}$

We need to classify subjects in some way. We might distinguish between pronouns, nouns and longer ('expanded') noun phrases, or between singular and plural subjects. Let's consider *self-referential* subjects – the first person pronoun *I* or *we* – versus other types.[10] In almost all cases, the subject immediately follows the relative pronoun. Our new hypothesis, H5, could be expressed as

H5. When 1990s British English adults have a choice, speakers and writers use *who* instead of *whom* more frequently if the subject of the relative clause is a first person pronoun (*I* or *we*) rather than something else.

The FTFs in Figures 2.4 and 2.5 are two of the four queries we must apply to the parsed ICE-GB corpus to obtain Table 2.5. In this configuration, the pronoun *who* or *whom* cannot be the subject of the clause.

We apply both FTFs with *who* and *whom* in the 'relative pronoun' slot. The FTF in Figure 2.5 obtains baseline frequency data in the 'Total' row. It will find any subject in this position, including cases identified by Figure 2.4. We subtract the '*I* or *we*' frequency from the total to obtain 'other'.

In Table 2.5, both variables are local, text-internal ones. The test is significant, meaning that the type of subject correlates with the choice *who* versus *whom*. In

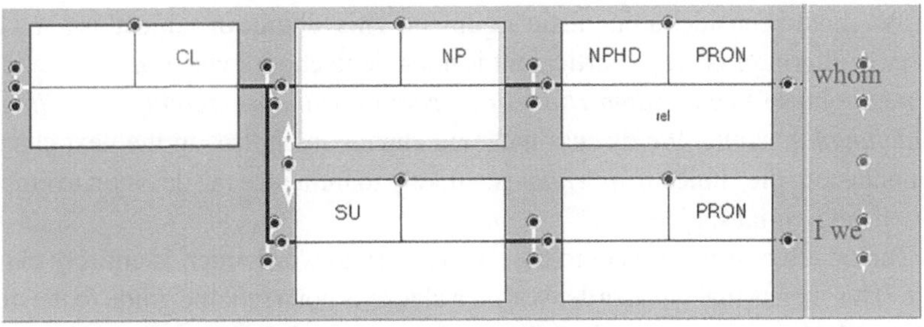

FIGURE 2.4 FTF for *whom* in a clause (CL) with a first person subject (pronoun *I* or *we*). The double-headed white arrow means that the subject may appear before or after *whom* in the same clause. (We expect it will follow, but we relaxed this requirement.) The words 'I we' represent the set {*I*, *we*}.

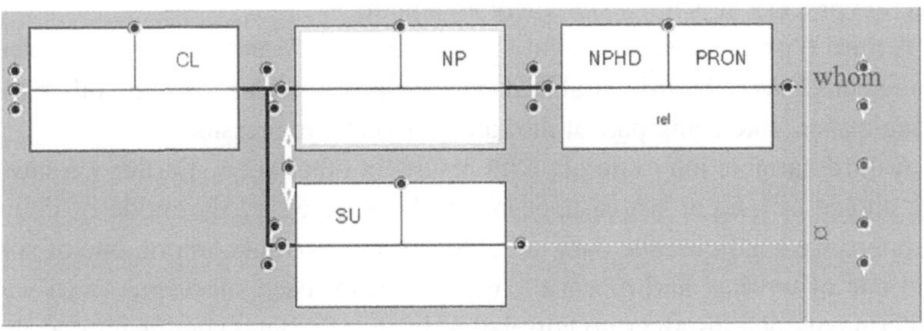

FIGURE 2.5 FTF for *whom* with an unspecified subject of the relative clause.

TABLE 2.5 Performing the χ^2 test with data obtained from ICE-GB using the FTF patterns in Figure 2.4 (top line) and Figure 2.5 ('Total'). The result is significant.

all data	*observed* **O**			*expected* **E**		*chi-square* χ^2		*probability*
	who	*whom*	*Total*	*who*	*whom*	*who*	*whom*	*p*(*who*)
I or *we*	**20**	**4**	24	16	8	1.29	2.36	0.83
other	13	14	27	17	10	1.14	2.10	0.48
Total	**33**	**18**	51			s	**6.89**	

particular, we can report that the pattern *who I/we* is more likely than *whom I/we* (0.83 > 0.17), but other cases are about 50:50.

What can we say about possible causation? Does this mean that we can say that the choice of subject (first person pronoun or not) affects the choice of *who* or *whom*, or could the choice affect the choice of subject?

We should consider a linguistic argument. This 'choice of subject' is not a free one. In uttering *I* or *we*, a participant is not able to choose *you* or *they* instead (or a noun phrase like *Saddam Hussein's tyranny*), *without referring to a different individual or entity*. We discuss meaning change in choices in the next chapter. Conclusion: the choice *who/whom* is unlikely to influence the decision to employ a self-referential subject.

But an effect from subject to object, contrary to word order, is entirely plausible. This means that word order within a clause is not a reliable guide to the order in which decisions are made by a speaker as the clause is composed. Indeed, selecting *who* over *whom* might be a performance choice made during articulation, whereas the choice of a self-referential subject is likely to be an earlier planning decision.

Note how this reasoning relies on a theoretical framework of linguistic meaning and optionality, alongside some assumptions about a plausible language production process. It is not a *statistical* argument!

A third type of causality might take place. Both *X* and *Y* may be affected by some undiscovered third variable *Z*. They might co-occur for some other underlying reason, like being part of the same idiomatic expression.[11]

A third variable may interact with results in other ways. Earlier we saw that the choice of *who* or *whom* appeared to be affected by the mode of delivery. Suppose we subdivide the data in Table 2.5 into two subcorpora, one of speech and one of writing, and repeat the evaluation for each subcorpus (a tri-variate experiment). We discover no correlation in speech, but a significant correlation in writing. See Table 2.6.

TABLE 2.6 Performing χ^2 tests for spoken and written data separately. The result is distinct: in speech, no correlation is found, whereas in writing, a significant correlation is found.†

spoken	*observed* **O**			*expected* **E**		*chi-square* χ^2		*probability*
	who	*whom*	Total	*who*	*whom*	*who*	*whom*	*p*(*who*)
I or *we*	**18**	**3**	24	18	3	0.01	0.05	0.86
other	13	3	27	13	3	0.01	0.06	0.81
Total	**31**	**6**	51			ns	0.13	
written	*who*	*whom*	*Total*	*who*	*whom*	*who*	*whom*	*p*(*who*)
I or *we*	**2**	**1**	3	0	3	5.76	0.96	0.67
other	0	11	11	2	9	1.57	0.26	0.00
Total	**2**	**12**	14			s	**8.56**	

† Some statistics books will tell you not to carry out a χ^2 test where any cell has a frequency count of less than 5. To put your mind at ease, an 'exact' Fisher test is significant at a threshold of 0.05. See Chapter 8.

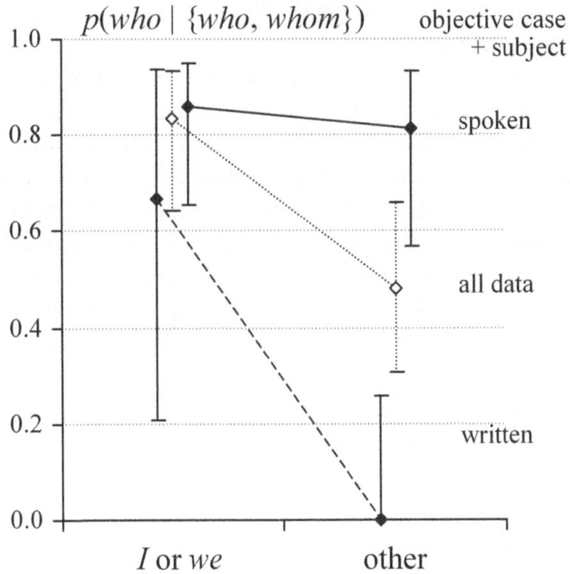

FIGURE 2.6 Binomial proportion difference graphs illustrating correlations between choice of subject (*I* or *we* vs. other) and choice of preceding objective relative pronoun. Data in Tables 2.5 (all data) and 2.6 (spoken, written) are expressed as probabilities of the dependent variable (DV) and plotted.

We plot the three Binomial proportion difference patterns in Figure 2.6. The Binomial proportion difference graph for ICE-GB speech and writing pooled together ('all data') lies between the two subcorpora graphs (it is an average, so this fact should be unsurprising). The graphs differ. The spoken data plot is flat and non-significant. Each proportion is within the other's confidence interval. By contrast, the written proportion reveals a significant difference.

The 'all data' Table 2.5 adds up results from a corpus of 60% spoken, 40% written data. But as we noted in Chapter 1, the vast majority of British English words uttered in the 1990s are likely to be spoken. The true ratio is unlikely to be 60:40! If results differ, it is wise to make separate claims about writing and speech than cite a pooled average from a corpus. See Chapter 5.

2.7 Experiments and Disproof

A significant result does not 'prove' a hypothesis. It merely identifies a statistical correlation between two or more variables in the data. But if an experiment yields a non-significant result, does it *disprove* the hypothesis?

The conventional language of experiments is couched in double negatives. The default is the *null hypothesis*: the negation of the hypothesis under test. For

Hypothesis 2, this was ¬H2, 'British English 1990s speakers used *who* instead of *whom* at the same rate as writers'.

If a test does not find significant variation, the researcher reports that the null hypothesis cannot be rejected. This is not the same as saying the original hypothesis is false, rather, *the data do not allow us to reject the proposition that nothing is happening in the population.* Collecting more data, revising linguistic categories and redefining variables might obtain significant results in the future.

The philosopher Hilary Putnam (1981) emphasised that scientific theories are not assumption-free, but are built on auxiliary assumptions – assumptions external to a theory necessary for research to be performed. See Chapter 1.

In the physical sciences, auxiliary assumptions include estimates of constants and the correct functioning of equipment. In linguistics research, a crucial set of auxiliary assumptions concern the *linguistic frameworks* employed by researchers and annotators. H2 requires researchers to identify pronouns; H5, subjects, objects and clauses. Whenever we report experiments, we must clearly state the assumptions we have made.

Even the apparently simple matter of counting instances requires principled methodological decisions, like when we eliminated subjective *who*. Spoken corpora often contain examples where participants repeat words to correct themselves.

(7) designed by an architect ~~*who*~~ *who* himself was ~~a~~ a paraplegic [S1A-003 #56]

Both utterances of *who* are legitimate data (they were both produced by the speaker), but unless we are interested in the phenomenon of self-correction itself, we should exclude the first instance. There are two reasons why. First, if speakers correct themselves, we assume they did not intend to express *who* twice. The first *who* is a 'performance error'. Consciously or not, the speaker overruled it by expressing it again. Second, repeat instances are not independent. Since our ideal is a random sample of *independent* utterances, we ignore the first case to avoid double-counting. A related problem arises with repeated phrases in coordination or lists.[12]

Irrespective of the corpus, to carry out an experiment we must identify each and every independent case of the phenomenon of interest in the corpus.

A parsed corpus like ICE-GB can offer an efficient route to obtaining initial results. We may trust the grammar and search tool to find cases, at least initially. However, researchers should always review matching sentences to be sure that what they found was *sound* (instances are genuine examples of the phenomenon) and *complete* (they are all the relevant examples). See Chapter 15.

If we employ a tagged corpus, we are compelled to use approximate methods to spot subjects, increasing the risk of missing legitimate cases or including illegitimate ones. We rely on a human linguist to discriminate them. Whether specified in the annotation or a researcher's framework, auxiliary assumptions are unavoidable.

2.8 What Is the Point of an Experiment?

Experiments gather evidence and permit researchers to advance a position. If independent evidence points to the same general conclusion, the research programme may be on the right track. This is termed 'triangulation'.

Classical 'Popperian' views of science place an exclusive emphasis on *falsification* – testing (null) hypotheses and rejecting them when contradicted by experimental data. But definitive falsification is difficult because an auxiliary assumption may be incorrect. We may have measured or counted data incorrectly.

Scientific research is better viewed as a cycle. Research effort may be expended bottom-up, generalising hypotheses from data, termed *induction*. Induction is controversial but necessary, at least in its simplest form of researchers identifying interesting phenomena in data and formulating hypotheses to test.

Much more controversial is the automation of this process, *machine learning* and *model fitting*. Why is this controversial? Science is more than finding the closest fit to data from a pre-defined set of potential variables and equations. It requires critical thinking, including reframing and redefining auxiliary assumptions, variables and hypotheses.

The philosopher Imre Lakatos (1978) considered research as a *social process*. An effective research programme makes novel predictions one can evaluate experimentally. Competing bodies of theory, according to Lakatos, are not 'falsified' and disappear overnight. They progress or regress depending on whether they are productive and so generate novel predictions, or degenerate into a patchwork of exceptions, local explanations and arbitrary assumptions.

Within a community of researchers, provided experimental methods are transparent, others can reproduce experiments with the same or alternative data. A shared corpus becomes a *locus of discussion* within the research community, as well as a testbed for theories.

2.9 Conclusions

Scientific theories can be characterised in terms of four components:

- **Variables** – measurable/classifiable aspects of observed phenomena that vary;
- **Hypotheses** – statements predicting behaviour of phenomena that may be tested;
- **Assumptions** – statements external to the theory but necessary for it; and
- **Axioms** – principles and rules (e.g., logic and mathematics) that are agreed to be true.

In this chapter, we discussed the first three elements. The fourth includes the statistical methods that we use. This is the principal focus of this book.

We saw how to perform robust natural scientific experiments on corpora. The richer the annotation in the corpus, the easier it is to extract meaningful data and perform reproducible experiments. However, researchers must *critically engage* with any given annotation framework. The researcher must check how consistently the framework was applied to the data, *at least with respect to the relevant conceptual terms of their research study*. Are all true cases of the phenomenon found? Are all irrelevant ones excluded?

Second, in reporting results, researchers must consider compatibility with alternative frameworks. Our ambition, *pace* Lakatos, is that over time we should be able to compare frameworks in terms of their predictive and explanatory power (see Wallis, 2019b).

The dominant trend in corpus linguistics is to build ever-larger 'flat' tagged corpora and employ greater reliance on computation. Some, such as Mark Davies (2012) claim that larger corpora generate 'more accurate' results. This may be true for certain research questions. Discovering lexical novelty requires a large corpus. But it is far from a universal principle! We saw how extracting subjective pronouns was difficult in tagged corpora. Losing precision undermines statements of 'accuracy', especially once we turn from lexis to syntax, semantics or pragmatics. Corpus linguistics risks becoming limited to 'the statistical analysis of automatically-identifiable language phenomena in corpora'.

In this book, we argue for the primacy of *linguistic knowledge*, incorporating rich, verifiable annotation and critical cyclic research. Indeed, we may employ a pluralistic strategy, and combine small parsed and large lexical corpora in research. Bowie and Wallis (2016) used FTFs in ICE-GB to estimate the error rate for lexical-tagged queries on a large tagged corpus, the *Corpus of Historical American English* (COHA). This 450 million-word megacorpus could produce far more data than ICE-GB. The researchers estimated that fewer than 10% of cases in the larger corpus were not found.

Some grammatical or semantic distinctions are easy to make, and wordclass tagging has become ubiquitous as a result. Counting tags or sequences may be a sufficient 'proxy' for some phrase types (cf. the verb versus verb phrase counting discussion in Chapter 1). But other distinctions are considerably more subtle or complex to determine, and – until such time as they are systematically annotated – are likely to require manual intervention by the researcher, making large-scale research difficult.

This problem does not simply concern the representation of *individual* terms. It will be difficult to reliably extract two linguistic terms *in a given relationship* (say, 'X premodifies Y') if that relationship is not reliably represented in the corpus.

This brings us to a final issue. Even with the richest annotation, *researchers should always question their data.* Re-examine corpus examples after analysis! Did a speaker or writer really have a choice at every point? Is each case in the same text independently produced from the others? These are the questions to which we must continually return. We must ask ourselves: *are our conclusions justified by our evidence, or might alternative hypotheses explain our results?*

Notes

1 Corpus data is not immune from experimenter bias. David Crystal recounts how, in the 1960s Survey of English Usage, researchers competed to slip in natural-sounding perfect progressive passive verb phrases into casual conversation in Randolph Quirk's office, knowing that Quirk surreptitiously recorded them.
2 This means 'the variable X is a member of the set $\mathbf{X}$'.
3 If bounds are excluded from the possible values of X, we use round brackets, so if $\mathbf{X} = (l, h)$, $l < X < h$.
4 The test does not tell us the direction of the change (increase or decrease), but we can examine the data to answer this question.
5 For brevity, we will leave out the 'given the set' expression ('| {*who, whom*}') unless we need to make a clear distinction between different baselines or data sources. Briggs (2016, p. 40) points out that all probabilities depend on something. In our case, observed probabilities, p, are conditional on the sample, **s**. But again, for brevity, we do not write, for instance $p(who \mid \{who, whom\} \wedge \mathbf{s})$. Population probabilities may be based on a test assumption – $P = 0.5$, say – or a prior probability estimate.
6 The term 'distribution' is used in linguistics to describe how words tend to co-occur, but it means something very different in mathematics. In this book, we use terms like 'distribution' and 'significance' only in their precise mathematical senses. See the Preface.
7 Some researchers use programming languages, like Python, to attempt to automate this process.
8 Grammatical schemes differ greatly, so whenever you obtain data from a grammatically annotated corpus, you must ensure your query is correct. There is little point in extracting data blindly 'on a hunch', guessing your results are 'about right' – and then employing sophisticated statistics! You must be *sure* that your data represent *precisely* what you think they do – that they capture instances of the phenomenon in question and only these. See Chapter 15.
9 This *worst-case analysis* approach to reviewing data is discussed in Chapter 15.
10 Participants could refer to themselves in the third person, but these cases are rare, difficult to identify and represent a 'marked' (conscious, mannered) case irrelevant to the main argument.
11 The biologist Stephen J. Gould (1996a) gives the example of a dataset where the price of petroleum and age of petrol pump assistants correlate. The price of petrol does not increase *because* petrol pump attendants age, or vice versa! Both correlate with a third variable Z, *time*. To eliminate this effect, we should change the experimental design and sampling frame. Longitudinal data from a small number of garages with low staff turnover might contain time-dependent effects. But a synchronic snapshot over many garages should not.
12 In ICE-GB instructional texts, modal *must* appears before a coordinated set of bullets, as in *The AG 3 must be: • dated within 14 days of your sight test, and • the refund*

claimed within three months of the sight test (W2D-001 #92). It also appears individually within clauses, such as *Readers must not lean on books, etc, or handle them roughly: they must not put them on the floor; they must not bend them back, lay them face downwards when open, or do anything else which might damage the binding* (W2D-006 #42–44). A writer's decision to include *must* in a list like this is stylistic (they could have written *Readers must not lean on books, put them on the floor, bend them back, lay them face downwards when open . . .*). Nonetheless, the data raises an important theoretical question: is each instance of *must* in a list truly independent? Should we count each one as if it were drawn from a random sample of English, or should we treat them as a single instance?

3

THAT VEXED PROBLEM OF CHOICE

3.1 Introduction

Many research questions we might wish to use a corpus to investigate are properly formulated in terms of the *linguistic choices* of participants. A variable that encodes the distinction *who/whom* represents a decision by speakers or writers. In the previous chapter, we did not just count up both forms. We eliminated subjective cases where the choice should have been unavailable.

A choice-based approach is sometimes termed *variationism* or (to use the Latin) *onomasiology*, based on the 'variationist model' or 'alternation model'. The idea is simple: in forming utterances, speakers and writers make conscious and unconscious decisions. The linguist's task is to study influences on these decisions, identifying factors that affect the selection of one option over another.

An underlying model of choice is axiomatic in sociolinguistics (Labov, 1972; Lavandera, 1978) and cognitive linguistics research. But it is less common in corpus linguistics. Indeed, the dominant model relies on *per word* frequency rates, often expressed as per thousand or per million words (commonly shortened to *pmw*). These *exposure rates* tell us the chance a hearer or reader will come across the word or construction.

In this book, we argue that studies of language variation and change should *primarily* be conceived as changes in rates of selecting one form out of a set of alternative forms, rather than rates per word. Exposure rates are the consequences of rates at which language elements are produced.

We can thereby ask linguistically meaningful research questions otherwise impossible with per word rates (Schegloff, 1993; Ball, 1994). In the last chapter, a simple study of *who* versus *whom* in speech and writing developed into an

DOI: 10.4324/9781003622697-5

investigation of the *interaction* between *who/whom* and a semantic aspect of the clausal subject that followed. A study of serially repeating choices in Chapter 1 used the same approach. Questions of choice and baseline are central to experimental design, and take precedence over statistical analysis.

3.1.1 The Traditional 'Per Million Words' Approach

Aarts et al. (2013) presented data on the rate of progressive verb phrases (VPs) per million words in the *Diachronic Corpus of Present Day English* (DCPSE), reproduced as Table 3.1.

This corpus contains fully parsed orthographically transcribed speech data from the late 1950s to the early 1990s. The time period can be split into two subcorpora – an early section (the 'LLC subcorpus') is nominally dated '1960s' but runs until the mid 1970s, and a late section drawn from ICE-GB is limited to the years 1990–1992. The data are not sampled annually, and there is a large gap in the middle, but it is sufficient to identify general trends over time.

Table 3.1 reports the cited item ('VP(prog)'), baseline (words) and rate for each time period. The unscaled rate is simply

$$\textit{observed proportion } p = p(\text{VP(prog)} \mid \text{word}) = f(\text{VP(prog)}) \,/\, f(\textbf{words}). \qquad (6)$$

A *per million* word rate (often abbreviated to 'pmw') is calculated by multiplying p by 1,000,000.

The *null hypothesis* is that p (or $p \times 1{,}000{,}000$) is constant when the independent variable ('time') varies. The null hypothesis for our study is

¬H6. The ratio of progressive VPs to the number of words in spoken British English does not vary between the 1960s and 1990s.

TABLE 3.1 A word-based baseline. Change over time of 'VP(prog)' expressed as a proportion of the number of words in DCPSE ('baseline'). After Aarts et al. (2013).

	item	*baseline*	*rate*	*effect size*
	VP(prog)	*words*	*per million words*	*percentage difference*
LLC (1960s)	2,973	464,063	6,406 (0.64%)	
ICE-GB (1990s)	3,294	420,986	7,824 (0.78%)	+22.13% ±5.48%†
Total	6,267	885,049	7,081 (0.71%)	

† Quoted in Aarts et al. (2013). Equation (28) obtains $d^{\%} = 22.13\% \in (16.25, 28.32)$. See Chapter 7.

Table 3.1 reveals a higher rate of p in ICE-GB than LLC, relative to the chosen baseline (words). This difference is presented as *percentage difference*, which uses the simple formula

$$\textit{percentage difference } d^{\%} = (p_2 - p_1) / p_1, \tag{7}$$

where p_1 and p_2 represent rates for LLC and ICE-GB subcorpora, respectively.

Percentage difference is a common way of expressing change. In news reports, we read that 'food prices have risen by 3% in the past year' or 'this drug reduces incidents of heart attacks by 30%'. See Chapter 7.

But our concern right now is not Equation (7), but the *baseline* for the purposes of comparison, *f*(**words**).

3.1.2 How Did Per Million Word Statistics Become Dominant?

There are many problems with relying on word-based baselines in linguistic research. First and foremost, *language is not a sequence of random words!* Language is not 'just one damn word after another'.

If language is constructed by choices, quantitative language change should be considered as *change in tendencies of speakers and writers to choose one form over another*. Bauer (1994, p. 19) comments that 'change is impossible without some variation'. As we saw in the last chapter, language data captures many other sources of variation apart from speaker choice: arbitrary variation in topic, context, participants and so on. Bauer's point is that if speakers had no choice about the words or constructions they used, language would be incapable of change.

Yet from the start, mainstream 'common sense' corpus linguistics trod a different path. Generations of researchers learned to quote so-called 'normalised frequencies': rates per word. Early researchers, working with paper-based collections, had limited opportunity to consider questions of choice.

The first corpus in Europe (second after the US Brown University Corpus), was the *Survey of English Usage Corpus*, constructed by Randolph Quirk and his colleagues. It was hand-transcribed from audio recordings, typed onto card files and duplicated. Cards were manually annotated, one annotation marker per card, creating card indexes for numerous phenomena from rising tones to noun phrases. To obtain a single frequency statistic from such a corpus, a researcher would manually examine cards, classify and count them. The effort was immense. Obtaining *two* frequencies – one for the item and one for a baseline or an alternate form – appeared impossible.

Annotation is still a problem with computerised corpora. In Chapter 1, we noted that most large corpora have shallow grammatical annotation. They are *tagged*, where every word is allocated a *wordclass* label (sometimes termed a 'part-of-speech' or POS tag): singular proper noun, copular verb, and so on. Algorithms for assigning these labels, 'taggers', are fairly reliable (over 95% accuracy rate is typical) so very large corpora can be rapidly constructed.

However, this annotation level is limited, especially when it comes to reliably identifying linguistic choices. In the last chapter, we saw how obtaining instances of subjective *who* or *whom* was more difficult with a tagged corpus than a parsed one. Ball (1994) proposed subtypes of *clause* as baselines for certain grammatical research questions. But to reliably identify clauses, we need a parsed corpus.

Theoretical linguists place a premium on meaningful linguistic concepts and relationships in texts. To see if a detailed annotation scheme is viable, we might use Qualitative Analysis to apply it to selected texts. 'Annotation' proper begins when we scale the framework to larger volumes. Whereas many corpus compilers have concentrated on building bigger corpora, others have prioritised richer ones: parsed corpora with full grammatical analysis, pragmatically annotated corpora containing speech acts, semantically annotated corpora with predicate-argument relations, and so on.

The corpora the author has developed and worked with for more than two decades, ICE-GB (Nelson et al., 2002) and DCPSE, are fully parsed treebanks. They have one phrase structure tree for every utterance in the corpus based on a standard reference grammar framework, Quirk et al. (1985).

This tree analysis does not solve all the problems of identifying choices. At best, it helps us determine candidate 'choice points', where choices might arise. It does not guarantee that every candidate instance is free to vary. Some constructions may be idiomatic and inflexible. Grammatical permutations are not *meaning-preserving choices*, and one grammatical construction may cover multiple meanings. This is the subject of this chapter.

The absence of a parse analysis is not necessarily an impediment to *thinking* about research in terms of choice. But some choices are time-consuming and error-prone to study without parsing.

3.1.3 Choice Models and Linguistic Theory

A model of choice is fundamentally a *linguistic* model. It starts with the observation that a study of language must be cognisant of structure, even as we debate what that structure might be.

We must distinguish two things:

1. variation in the **opportunity** to use an expression; and
2. variation in the **choice** of a particular form of that expression when that opportunity arises.

Choices may have local impact (choosing a word; selecting a progressive verb over simple present or past; adding an optional construction, etc.) or trigger a wholesale grammatical transformation, such as the decision to express a question as a full interrogative clause rather than a question tag. A choice-based framework is extremely powerful, and can address criticisms of corpus linguistics as mere 'counting of surface phenomena'. But the interpretation of variation for different kinds of choice requires care.

In Chapter 1, we observed that choices may affect each other in two distinct ways:

1. **Framing constraints** *enable or prevent* other choices in a binary fashion (excepting the odd innovation), primarily through grammatical rules. Consider a variable encoding the presence or absence of a construction, such as a postmodifying clause. If the clause is present, we can consider choices within this clause; if absent, these choices do not arise. Framing constraints determine opportunities that follow.
2. Operating within these constraints, **one choice may influence another**, increasing or decreasing a tendency to make a second choice. Consider the phenomenon of *syntactic priming*. When a second identical choice arises in a conversation (traditionally, where speaker A primes B), the first decision tends to be replicated. But this type of influence is more ubiquitous than just a tendency to repeat a choice. Apparently diverse decisions can influence each other within an utterance. In the last chapter, we saw evidence suggesting that the type of subject influenced the choice of relative pronoun in ICE-GB writing. Linguistic models of *spreading activation* (Anderson, 1983) imply influence between unlike terms.

Posing questions of choice brings the *language producer* into focus. Speakers and writers 'do' language: it is *their* choices we study when we perform linguistic research. Receivers are dependent, utterance by utterance, on the decisions of producers. Hence, choice rates are primary to exposure rates.

This does not mean, however, that only research conducted in this paradigm is legitimate! Exposure rates ultimately arise from speaker or writer choices, and have their own value. Likewise, research into meaning change – *semasiology* to use the Latin term – also relies on opportunities to use studied expressions. See Chapter 4.

Conceptualising linguistic hypotheses in terms of choice has one final advantage. It allows us to evaluate corpus data in a manner maximally commensurable with other types of linguistic research (see Schönefeld, 2011). Thus, Gries (2011) could compare results obtained from a corpus with those from laboratory experiments. Conventional statistics used for laboratory-based research can also be used with corpus data – subject to an important caveat discussed in Chapter 16.

3.1.4 The Vexed Problem of Choice

If language production consists of choices, it follows that one of the first tasks of a researcher is to formulate hypotheses about linguistic variables representing a set of alternative forms (a 'choice set' or 'set of alternates').

In the laboratory, it is straightforward to constrain choices in advance: give participants a stimulus and ask them to press button A or B. The experimenter *designs in* the choice. But corpus research is different. Researchers carry out analyses of data collected without any such constraint, after the fact (termed 'ex post facto' or 'post hoc' research). This has numerous advantages (see Chapter 2), but one big disadvantage.

Linguistic choice corpus research requires *the inference of the counterfactual*. Alongside what participants wrote or said, the researcher must infer what they could have written or spoken instead. Identifying alternatives is sometimes straightforward, as in *who* versus *whom*, but it can be difficult. To take a simple example, consider a study of *that*-omission in relative clauses, as in *The man [that] I saw*. We must be able to reliably identify 'zero-relative' clauses.

New methodological questions arise. If there are multiple alternative forms, should each be included in the baseline? What if an alternative form is not a simple replacement, but conveys an additional or particular meaning?

Consider an appropriate baseline for evaluating changes in the employment of *progressive verb phrases* (VPs). We could take all VPs as a baseline, so 'non-progressive verb phrases' would be the alternate form. But not all VPs can be made progressive. Smitterberg (2005) identifies simple exclamatives (*sit down!*) and fixed constructions. Any context that prevents alternation, termed a 'knock-out factor' by Smitterberg, should be removed. We are left with what we might call 'progressivisable' VPs: VPs that could plausibly be replaced with a progressive form.

Some cases are borderline ones, like stative verbs, of which there are a large number. Historically, statives were considered incapable of rendering in the progressive, but are beginning to appear, as in *I'm loving it*. How should these be treated? Although the speaker is free to choose *I love it* or *I'm loving it* in principle, the novel progressive form is more 'marked': more unusual, and possibly more artfully conscious than the other.

The best solution is to partition the data into two sets: stative and dynamic verbs, and study each separately. In a multivariate model, we might encode the additional variable.

But whether an alternate form is unavailable or likely influenced by different rules, one point should be clear. Reframing hypotheses in terms of choice means more work for the researcher! On the other hand, this work is *linguistic work*, arguably just as important as linguistic annotation and classification.

This practical difficulty has produced a number of objections from corpus researchers. In Section 3.4, we explore three principal objections, what they imply and how they can be overcome to the limits of any given dataset.[1]

3.1.5 Exposure Rates and Other Experimental Models

Not all corpus research concerns choice rates. Corpora are exceptional resources for estimating the overall likelihood of readers or hearers encountering a form.

One of the first corpus datasets ever published, the *Brown Wordlist* (Kučera & Francis, 1967), is a comprehensive frequency list (a frequency distribution) of words ordered by their frequency in the corpus. Obtaining data of this kind is straightforward with a computer. Since comparisons inevitably involve unequal size datasets, researchers cited frequencies divided by the number of words in the corpus – obtaining a per (million) word exposure rate.

Ranking forms by exposure rate helps lexicographers design dictionaries and language teachers prioritise lessons. If learners are frequently exposed to certain forms and rarely others, exposure rates are likely relevant to theories of learning and language change.

Exposure rate observations can reveal trends worthy of further investigation. David Denison (2018, p. 78) noted an increase per million words since the 1970s for certain verbs in 'V *that*' constructions in the *Corpus of Historical American English* (COHA). Faced with this finding, we cannot rule out the possibility that ACCEPT *that*, the most rapidly increasing pattern, increased its frequency because ACCEPT (with or without a following *that*) also grew in popularity! But this alternative hypothesis can be tested using a baseline of all cases of ACCEPT, that is, a choice rate.

Exposure rates and choice rates are different measures:

$$\textit{exposure rate} \quad p(x \mid \text{word}) = f(x) \,/\, f(\textbf{words}), \tag{8}$$
$$\textit{choice rate} \quad p(x \mid \mathbf{X}) = f(x) \,/\, f(\mathbf{X}), \tag{9}$$

where f represents frequency counts, and **X** is a set of alternate forms including x.[2] The chance a hearer or reader will be *exposed* to a form is not the same as the chance that a speaker or writer will *use* a form when they have the option to do so.[3]

Choice rates obtain different results from exposure rates. The exposure rate for progressive VPs in LLC is 0.64% (see Table 3.1), but the choice rate per VP is 4.70%, rising to 4.73% after 'knockout factors' are taken into account (Aarts et al., 2013). Few, if any, exposure rates reach a maximum of 100%,[4] a fact that can negatively impact on the performance of statistical methods.

The chance that a choice is available at any point in a sentence (the opportunity) is highly likely to vary from location to location. Any analysis method based on exposure rates cannot but conflate opportunity and choice. The good news is that by reformulating the analysis in terms of choice, as in the ACCEPT example, we may eliminate alternative hypotheses.

We might identify a third proportion, the *opportunity rate*:

$$\textit{opportunity rate}\ p(\mathbf{X} \mid \text{words}) = f(\mathbf{X}) \,/\, f(\textbf{words}). \tag{10}$$

This represents the chance that *the choice is available* at any word. Opportunities – locations where a choice may be made – are likely to vary widely between texts. The opportunity rate is a confounding variable in our analysis. Selecting a meaningful choice rate allows us to factor it out.

Choice rates *contain twice as much information* as exposure rates: they consist of the ratio of two distributions, $f(x)$ and $f(\mathbf{X})$. The distribution $f(\mathbf{X})$ captures data from the source corpus and is conditioned by the framework. It is part of the auxiliary assumptions of the theory (e.g., 'this variable is meaningfully considered as a proportion of VPs'). See Chapter 2. No mathematical method can add this information for us. Consequently, we can make the following strong claim: *a statistical analysis based on exposure rates is less powerful than one based on meaningful choice rates*.

A second type of research, termed 'semasiological research', is discussed in more detail in Chapter 4. Whereas the idea of an onomasiological choice is that the core referential meaning is stable while the speaker makes a choice (see Section 3.2.4), semasiological research studies how words change their meaning.

Finally, there are experimental designs where the target dependent variable is not linguistic. In attribution studies, the dependent variable is *the author*. Independent variables could be single linguistic features typical of the author's prose, or statistics aggregated from multiple features. However, since an author's use of an expression must be a choice, choice-based predictors (independent variables) are likely to be more reliable than per word ones.

3.1.6 What Do We Mean by 'Choice'?

So far, we have used the term 'choice' liberally. For our purposes, 'choices' may be unconscious. Indeed, many sciences employ what we might term 'ecological models of choice', that is, alternative outcomes selected by organisms in a natural context.

Examples of this type of 'choice' include the following:

- **Market research.** Researchers are tasked with finding out why shoppers tend to buy product A rather than product B. This choice is the focus of the research (the dependent variable). Other variables, such as whether they purchased other items at the same time, locations of products in the store, and so on, may be independent variables.

- **Plant morphology**. Consider the 'choice' of a flower, such as a cherry flower, to bud from a node: not all nodes, where leaves appear, contain a flower. Environmental factors and genetic variation cause the numbers of flowers produced by a plant to vary. The meaningful baseline for flower growth would be the number of nodes capable of producing a flower.

The second example illustrates the very broad sense in which we employ the term 'choice' in this book. Although we have referred to living organisms, the principle applies to *the unavoidable process of selection from any set of alternative outcomes in a process*. You could use the term 'potential' rather than 'opportunity', if you prefer, but the same principle applies. The capacity for conscious decision-making is not a precondition for selection to take place.

These examples present similar challenges to the linguist attempting to extract choices from naturalistic data. If you wish to study why shoppers and cherry trees do what they do, you pose the research question in terms of a *model of choice* that identifies where a choice can be made. Shoppers and plant nodes incapable of making a selection are discounted. This basic choice model can then be applied to more complex models of co-occurring outcomes – such as repression of budding when a plant has more than a threshold number on a stem, or when other flowers have been fertilised.

Note that we need an explicit framework of opportunity that predicts the counterfactual: where a flower failed to appear, or where a shopper made no purchase. Structural (framing) constraints are all-important. Different plants produce flowers at different points. Cherry blossoms flower alongside leaves, but roses flower only at shoot ends ('axiliary buds', Bendahmane et al., 2013).

3.2 Parameters of Choice

3.2.1 Types of Mutual Substitution

An *alternation experiment* may be defined as one where a dependent variable consists of two or more alternate forms, where each form can be replaced by any one of the others. Alternation depends on *mutual substitution*, which we might define formally as follows:

> **Mutual substitution:** The dataset consists of events of type A and B drawn from a corpus, where events A and B are mutually replaceable.

We identify all points in the text where a participant could plausibly substitute B for A and A for B, limited by grammatical constraints. The baseline for the experiment, which we define more formally in the following section, is simply the total number of items in the dataset, and the dependent variable (DV) is the choice A or B:

$$\textit{dependent variable}\ (\text{DV})\ X \in \mathbf{X} = \{\text{A}, \text{B}\}. \quad (11)$$

This mathematical notation says 'X is a member of the set $\mathbf{X}$ of items of Type A and Type B'.

A stricter definition of mutual substitution we will term *independent* mutual substitution, where meaning is held to be constant across the choice:

> **Independent mutual substitution:** The dataset consists of events of type A and B drawn from a corpus, where events A and B are mutually replaceable *without altering the meaning of the utterance.*

If the choice does not alter the meaning of the utterance, then it is essentially self-contained, hence 'independent'. It is unlikely to be semantically affected by, or affect, its context. It is reasonable to assume *a priori* that the decision to choose A or B has no other effect on the sentence. If the experiment then finds an effect, it could be worth reporting.

Semantic independence is not an essential prerequisite for research, but it is to be preferred as far as possible.

Let us revisit an experiment we saw in Chapter 1 to see how this might work. Using the spoken DCPSE corpus, Aarts et al. (2013) studied how time (the independent variable, IV) affected the modal *will/shall* alternation (the dependent variable, DV).

Modal *shall* versus *will* may be considered a simple choice:

(8) I *shall* try to get to know you [DI-B13 #267]
~ I *will* try to get to know you

Type A represents the modal verb *shall* and B *will*. Whereas almost all cases of *shall* may legitimately be replaced by *will* without changing the meaning of the utterance (a mere eight are formulaic in DCPSE), the reverse does not apply. Not all cases of modal *will* can be readily changed to *shall*.

To ensure mutual substitution was possible, first, Aarts et al. limited cases of *will* and *shall* to those with first person subjects. Second and third person *shall* (e.g., *you shall* and *they shall*) has become archaic, implying a greater meaning change when alternating with *will*.

This does not mean that we should never consider data concerning second or third person *shall/will*. This alternation pattern was much more common in the 19th century. Rather, the transition from *shall* to *will* with second or third person subjects was effectively complete by the period of our sample. These data are removed, not because alternation is impossible, but *because we have reason to believe this would represent a distinct trend* from first person *shall/will*, and merging data prevents us seeing these distinctions.

The meaning is also likely to change with alternation of interrogative (*shall I/we?* vs. *will I/we?*) and negative forms (*shall not/shan't* vs. *will not/won't*). These were also eliminated from the data.

The binary choice A versus B is exclusive, so observed change may be characterised as *replacement*. The proportions of cases of Type A and B are inversely related. When one proportion increases, the other must decline.

The variable could cover cases with more than two alternates, for example, including semi-modal present BE *going to*. Type A still replaces B_1, B_2 and so on, but we cannot be sure which alternate form was replaced. We discuss options for analysing multiway choices next.

Suppose we violate the principle of mutual substitution by including a *non-substitutable* form within our dataset, which we will call Type C. The most common way such cases are introduced in corpus data is when word-based baselines are used. In an exposure rate, Type C represents every other word in the corpus *except* first person declarative *will* or *shall*, for example:

dependent variable $X \in \{A, B, C\} = \{$*shall*, *will*, (every other word)$\}$.

If we do not characterise dependent variables as the choice of mutually substitutable terms A or B, we cannot distinguish variation due to *choice* (A vs. B) or *opportunity* (A + B vs. C).[5]

Type C cases are not only found in word-based baselines. They are *any* non-substitutable case introduced into a dependent variable, such as non-progressivisable statives, or modal verbs with a different meaning from *shall* or *will*. Variation in Type C cases, whatever they may be, will be *confounding noise* that obscures the relationship between Types A and B. So if such cases cannot be eliminated altogether, their number (and thus their effect) should be minimised. As a general principle, we should focus on a clean choice as far as possible.

3.2.2 Multiway Choices and Decision Trees

Focusing on choice allows researchers to be more precise and subtle. Isolating first person positive declarative *will/shall* allowed Aarts et al. to examine freely varying instances. They could then consider further patterns, including the contraction ('clitic') *'ll* and semi-modal BE *going to*.

A multiway choice may be a simple set of alternates $\{A, B_1, B_2 \ldots\}$. Provided that in each case in the corpus, one type may be substituted for any other, we can treat the choice as the outcome of a single decision, for example, *shall* versus *will* versus *'ll* versus BE *going to* (Figure 3.1, left). At every point where *shall* is employed, we allow that it be replaced by any other member of the set; similarly for *will*, *'ll* and semi-modal present tense BE *going to*:

(9) we *'ll* move on $_{\text{[DI-A03 \#38]}}$
(10) I *will* modify it $_{\text{[DI-A11 \#233]}}$
(11) I *shall* never come home again $_{\text{[DI-B52 \#130]}}$
(12) I *'m going to* give you a prescription $_{\text{[DI-A18 \#196]}}$

Past tense BE *going to* has a different meaning than *will* or *shall*, and does not alternate with them:

(13) I *was going to* say $_{\text{[DI-B03 \#275]}}$

Nonetheless, following a review of cases we might define the dependent variable as follows:

dependent variable $X \in$ {*shall*, *will*, *'ll*, BE *going to* (present)}.

However, we have another option. We can also order decisions into a *decision tree* and study each decision separately. This involves auxiliary assumptions regarding a plausible order of decisions in which the meaning preservation principle is crucial.

First, *'ll* is a contraction of *will*, so grouping these two into a set makes sense. Meaning is entirely preserved – *'ll* just means *will*. Second, as well as being lexically more complex, BE *going to* (present) is a separate modal class altogether (a 'semi-modal'). It is arguably related to progressive BE *going* (a parsed corpus should distinguish between these forms).

Consequently, we may hypothesise that this 'four-way' choice is actually the outcome of three ordered choices forming a decision tree (Figure 3.1, right):[6]

overall choice (DV) $X \in \mathbf{X} = \{\mathbf{X}_1,$ BE *going to* (present)$\}$,
modal choice $\mathbf{X}_1 = \{$*shall*, $\mathbf{X}_2\}$,
forms of will choice $\mathbf{X}_2 = \{$*will*, *'ll*$\}$.

Consider data where speakers express prediction or volition with a modal or semi-modal verb form. First, they opt to use a modal or semi-modal verb. If they use a modal verb, the choice of *shall* or *will* becomes available; if they choose *will*, they may contract it.

Employing this approach, the authors could examine three distinct and potentially independent trends (Figure 3.1, right, from top to bottom): the ratios modal versus semi-modal, *shall* versus forms of *will*, and the rate of contraction of *will*.

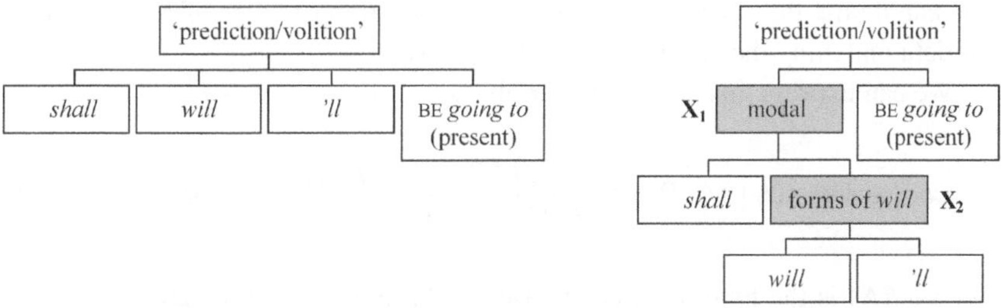

FIGURE 3.1 Considering the alternation of {*shall*, *will*, *'ll* and BE *going to* (present)}) as a single integrated decision (left) and one composed of ordered choices (right).

This decision tree implies that a comparison between BE *going to* and *'ll* (say) is less linguistically meaningful than the choice between semi-modal BE *going to* and the set of modal forms.

Principles of mutual substitution apply to constructing decision trees:

1. **Semi-substitution**. Suppose all cases of *shall*, *will* and *'ll* in our data are mutually substitutable with each other, but some cases are not mutually substitutable with a third type, such as be *going to*. The solution is to perform the comparison separately ('at a higher level' in the tree or in parallel), omitting cases from the dataset that do not plausibly alternate.
2. **Differences in meaning**. With care, we may relax the constraint of allowing meaning to change across a contrast. See Section 3.2.4. We should group 'performative' choices where meaning does not change (like *will/'ll*) below a higher-level decision involving a meaning change. The semi-substitution principle is an empirical consequence of this: some cases may not alternate if meaning changes.

Constructing a decision tree is an experimental design option. If all types are mutually substitutable with each other at the same 'level' or *we have no good reason to order the decisions*, we should retain the multiway choice.

If a decision contains two or more independent sub-choices these may be better evaluated as *parallel decisions* (separate variables). For example, verb complementation patterns may be modelled as independent decisions to add direct and indirect objects.

3.2.3 Binomial Statistics, Tests and Time Series

The most applicable set of statistics to choice rates are Binomial and Multinomial statistics, which we discuss in Part 3. Given a pair of alternates, A and B, we can define the *choice rate* of A as the proportion of cases of A observed out of data matching the alternation set **X** = {A, B}.

We can express this extremely simply as

$$\textit{choice rate}\ p(\mathrm{A} \mid \{\mathrm{A}, \mathrm{B}\}) = \frac{f(\mathrm{A})}{f(\mathrm{A}) + f(\mathrm{B})} = \frac{f(\mathrm{A})}{n} \in \boldsymbol{P} = [0, 1], \tag{12}$$

where $f(\mathrm{A})$ is the total number of cases of Type A, and so on, and [0, 1] is the *probabilistic range*, ***P***, the set of numbers from 0 to 1 inclusive. In Chapter 2, we saw that an observed proportion may also be conceived of as a *probability*: in this case, the chance that a randomly selected item in the sample was of Type A.

An important consequence of the Binomial model is that *an observed proportion can, in principle, be 100%*. If a genuine choice exists, all cases could, in principle, be of either type. In mathematical terms, we say that the rate is *free to vary* from 0 to 1. This requirement is rarely met in the case of exposure rates.

Formalising variables in terms of choice rates permits some simple statistical methods. We can estimate a *confidence interval* on this rate (see Figures 3.2 and 3.3). We discuss confidence intervals at length in Part 3.

Consider the 2 × 2 contingency table in Table 3.2. The frequency $f_1(\mathrm{A})$ represents the observed frequency for A under independent variable condition 1. The baseline is $n_1 = f_1(\mathrm{A}) + f_1(\mathrm{B})$, and the observed proportion (or probability) is $f_1(\mathrm{A}) / n_1$. The same principle applies to the other rows.

Table 3.2 can be used to calculate a χ^2 test:

- the dependent variable is the choice between two types of event, A and B;
- the independent variable is simply conditions 1 and 2; and
- the baseline for this evaluation is the Total column (n_1, n_2, etc.).

The null hypothesis of this test is simply that the proportion of Type A events out of the set {A, B} (final column) does not change under different conditions (values) of the independent variable in the population. The corresponding rates in the population are expected to be equal, $P_1 = P_2$.

TABLE 3.2 Left: a 2 × 2 contingency table for a χ^2 test to determine if the true rate of A, as a proportion of A + B, varies between two values of an independent variable IV (conditions 1 and 2). Right: observed proportions p_1 and p_2.

	DV	A	B	*Total*	*probability*
IV	condition 1	$f_1(\mathrm{A})$	$f_1(\mathrm{B})$	n_1	$p_1 = f_1(\mathrm{A}) / n_1$
	condition 2	$f_2(\mathrm{A})$	$f_2(\mathrm{B})$	n_2	$p_2 = f_2(\mathrm{A}) / n_2$
	Total	$f(\mathrm{A})$	$f(\mathrm{B})$	n	$f(\mathrm{A}) / n$

TABLE 3.3 Contingency table for *shall* and *will* between ICE-GB and LLC (spoken, first person subject, declarative), excluding *'ll* and negative cases (after Aarts et al., 2013).

	shall	*will*	*Total*	*p*(*shall* | {*shall, will*})
LLC (1960s)	110	78	188	0.59
ICE-GB (1990s)	40	58	98	0.41
Total	150	136	286	0.52

An example should make this clearer. Aarts et al. (2013) initially applied 2 × 2 χ^2 contingency tests over a 'time' variable, comparing rates between two subcorpora in DCPSE. When evaluated, the test is deemed significant at an error level of 0.05, meaning that we can report a difference in the rate of *p*(*shall* | {*shall, will*}) between subcorpora collected in different time periods at this error level.

Table 3.3 shows the probability of selecting *shall*. In LLC, this is 110/188 = 0.59.

Once we can justify a choice rate as a meaningful and freely varying choice in the data, other statistical techniques may be applied. In the previous chapter, we plotted a simple Binomial proportion difference graph.

We can go further. By subdividing the samples by year collected, we can analyse data as a *time series*. Aarts et al. plotted *p*(*shall* | {*shall, will*}) over time, estimating a *logistic curve* where *will* can be seen to replace *shall* (Figure 3.2). See also Chapter 10.

The researchers then considered what happens if clitic *'ll* was included within the alternation (i.e., *shall* vs. *will*+ *'ll*). The introduction of *'ll* alters the curve in Figure 3.3 and any inferences we might make. It depresses the data: *shall* becomes a smaller proportion overall. Despite this, we also know that *shall* was the historically required form (i.e., we can hypothesise that in the past, *p*(*shall* | {*shall, will, 'll*}) = 1).

We can legitimately select either baseline for the same frequency and report the results.

Figure 3.3 implies that a shift in majority usage from explicit, fully enunciated, *shall* to *will* occurred in the middle of the 1970s. This is the choice without the cliticised form. The comparison is legitimate enough – one might argue this is the choice speakers made after opting not to shorten it.

But once we include the contracted form in Figure 3.3, the transition point at 50% of cases moves back in time. Although we do not have data from that period, we may project the curve back in time. We may predict that *will*+ *'ll* became dominant rather earlier, that is, at some point in the first half of the 20th century. (Of course, to confirm this prediction, we would need to collect appropriate data.)

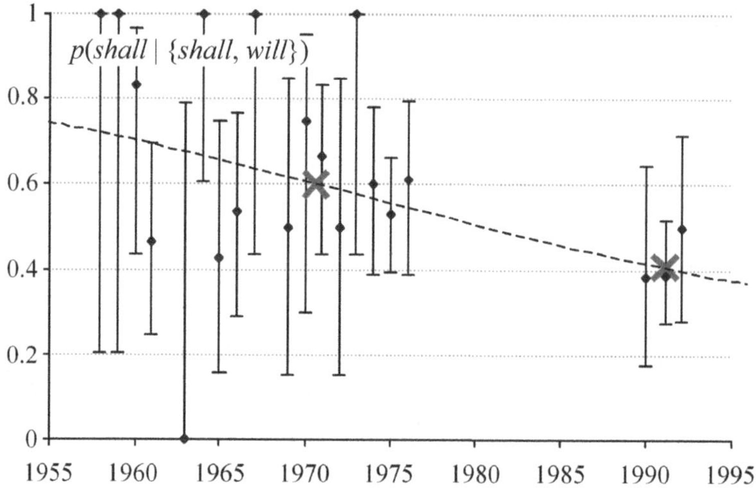

FIGURE 3.2 Declining rate *p*(*shall* | {*shall*, *will*}) over time. The graph depicts evidence of a decline in use of first person declarative *shall* as a proportion of the set {*shall*, *will*}, data from DCPSE (after Aarts et al., 2013).

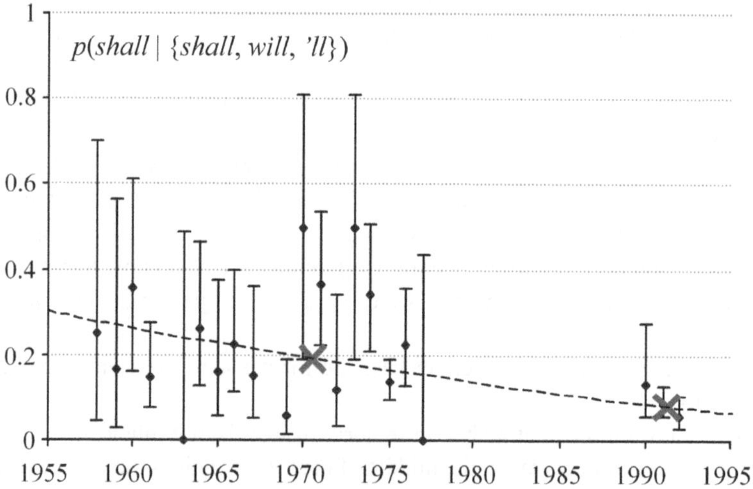

FIGURE 3.3 Plotting first person declarative positive *p*(*shall* | {*shall*, *will*, *'ll*}) over time.

It is entirely legitimate, and often very effective, to employ more than one baseline for the same variable. Both observations may be correct. Indeed, the replacement of *shall* by explicit *will* may be considered a delayed reaction to the first change.

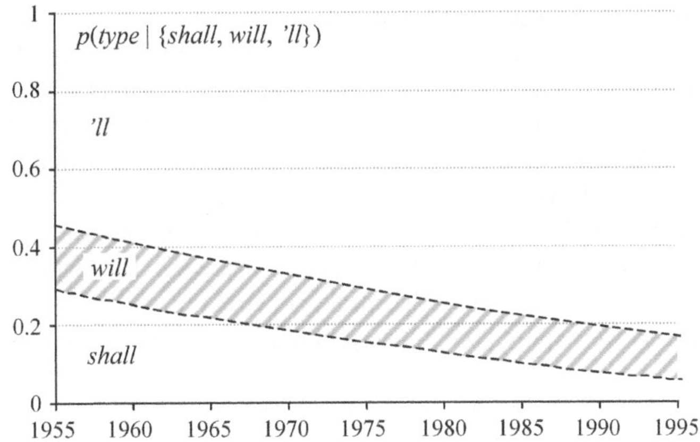

FIGURE 3.4 Plotting three values in competition, *shall, will, 'll*, same data.

Note that baselines are a crucial element of the experimental hypothesis. If you change the baseline, you change the hypothesis.

Another way of visualising these hypothetical trends is in the stacked graph sketch in Figure 3.4. All probabilities are proportions out of the baseline, the total probability is 1, and there are two degrees of freedom. Note how this sketch shows that the proportion of *shall* falls against the baseline over time (cf. Figure 3.3) but also as a proportion of *will+shall* (Figure 3.2). The plot shows that *will* also falls 'in real terms', that is, there is a tendency towards contraction.

Figure 3.4 also indicates another consequence of conflating opportunity and use. Imagine for a moment that cases marked ' *'ll*' in the graph did not substitute for *shall* or *will* but were Type C cases included in error. Now *p*(*shall*) could never rise above the dotted line above *will*.

Methods for estimating a logistic curve assume that trends level out at probabilistic extremes, 0 and 1. See Chapter 10. Non-alternating data points are not merely 'noise'. If 'Type C' forms are a sizeable proportion of the data (as 'other words' are in exposure rates) they *suppress the maximum*. Worse, if the proportion of Type C cases also varies over the IV (time) – as *'ll* does here – they *shape the envelope of possible variation* for the alternation. Not only is the choice unable to reach a maximum of 1 (100%), it does not tend towards a constant!

This issue matters most when the proportion of non-alternating Type C cases is high. The solution is to reduce, and ideally eliminate, Type C cases.

3.2.4 Lavandera's Dangerous Hypothesis

We defined 'independent mutual substitution' as a requirement for meaning to be constant across the dependent variable choice. If a speaker wishes to express a meaning only available with option B, they are not free to choose A!

Linguists have long debated whether a variationist perspective is compatible with situations where making a choice also changes the meaning of the utterance, even subtly. In an influential paper, Beatriz Lavandera (1978) argued that phonological variation such as stress patterns have no ostensible meaning, and therefore upholding meaning preservation is straightforward. Grammatical and lexical variation she considered much more difficult.

A contrarian might argue that every word and construction conveys a constellation of unique meanings to be determined by the receiver in context. See Section 3.5.5. We never know what the speaker or writer meant!

But should we require a complete prohibition on meaning change between A and B? Suppose a speaker chooses between a progressive and non-progressive VP. If progressive aspect cannot be implied in (some) non-progressive examples, the non-progressive option is not an independent alternate form. Where does this leave a study of the changing use of the progressive?

An absolute prohibition on meaning change may be unnecessarily restrictive. But conclusions must be explicit about any relaxation.

At this point, we might usefully distinguish between two types of 'meaning':

- **referential meaning** (the core concept, event, thing or process referred to); and
- **performative meaning** (e.g., level of formality, explicitness or emphasis).

These are gradient categories. There are arguably different types of referential meaning. Compare the core semantics of particular verbs versus their tense and aspect.

Lavandera considers a 'dangerous hypothesis' where referential meaning is allowed to change. She echoes our requirement for checking cases for genuine alternation, calling for a 'strategy of setting aside more and more contexts where both alternants occur but do not say exactly the same thing' (1978, p. 178). But how may we then study linguistic expressions that *uniquely* convey an explicit meaning, like the progressive aspect? *Continuity of action*, explicitly encoded by progressive aspect, is at most implied in non-progressive cases.

We know that progressive aspect has increased in use over time. Hundt (2004) cites exposure rate evidence from the written historical ARCHER corpus (Yáñez-Bouza, 2011), which indicates that progressive verbs are around five times more frequent in 20th century than 17th century writing. But if it has increased over time, did past writers convey continuity of action in other ways, or is *the expression of continuity itself* – the opportunity – more frequent in modern writing?

We might model a process of replacement by saying that progressive verbs replace the simple verb form (whether past or present), but add an *explicit* meaning of ongoing action.

Logically, if the act referred to is completed, a progressive construction is unlikely, but if not, the alternation will be possible. The researcher has a practical problem: reading corpus examples, *how do we know which acts are completed?* We might examine cases and 'guess the counterfactual'. Consider the following examples:

(14) I*'m graduating* in June $_{\text{[DI-A02 \#138]}}$
~ I *graduate* in June
(15) This detail *was coming* out $_{\text{[DI-D18 \#65]}}$
~ This detail *came* out
(16) I*'m rambling* $_{\text{[DI-A01 \#83]}}$
~? I *ramble*

Consider the effect of the temporal adjunct (*in June*) or past tense. Applying or removing progressive aspect does not seem to substantively alter this temporal meaning. In our replacement test, our speaker can select freely between the two and convey more-or-less the same underlying meaning. Example (16), *I ramble*, being unspecified in time, is more uncertain. One might argue that progressive aspect locates the utterance *I'm rambling* within the present conversation (*I am currently rambling*), whereas *I ramble* is less explicit, opening up interpretations of ellipsis.

This observation identifies a potential methodological refinement. As in all alternation experiments, we should review examples to validate the potential for alternation. But we might exploit our insight to review clauses containing a temporal adjunct, object, and so on, separately.

The first relaxation of Lavandera's 'dangerous hypothesis' is that we can potentially accept a difference in meaning between alternants provided that the speaker is still referring to the same event, thing or process.

> **Mutual substitution under consistent meaning change:** The dataset consists of events of type A and B drawn from a corpus, where events A and B are mutually replaceable without altering the core referential meaning of the utterance, *and where performing the substitution changes the meaning in the same way for every instance in the dataset.*

This relaxation must be carefully applied. We should still try to eliminate exceptions where core referential meaning is affected, such as when a progressive verb has a different idiomatic or phrasal meaning than its simple counterpart. We may also decide to partition data, for example, to evaluate past and present cases separately.

The mutual substitution principle is maintained. Even where selecting a choice modified the meaning, the counterfactual form must have been a plausible option at that point. For example, it must be possible to replace present tense progressive instances with simple present ones.

Instances in a dataset must not be fixed (e.g., slogans like *I'm loving it* or idiomatic cases of *shall*) and should be free to vary in a like manner to all other instances. The same alternate forms should be available for all cases.

This restriction is not one of logic, but of linguistics. Logically, alternation studies do not require meaning to be identical for a choice to be available. In Chapter 1, we introduced an experiment concerning the repeated decision to add premodifying adjective phrases in a noun phrase. Adding an adjective refines or adds to the meaning of the noun phrase, presumably without changing the referent in the speaker's mind.

However, if two meanings *do not* refer to the same concept – *I* versus *you*, modal *can* versus *will*, or present versus past, for example – then the choice will surely be predetermined by the speaker's intention, topic or context. Even if an experiment that evaluated such 'alternations' made sense, we would have to eliminate contextual explanations before considering others. This is what we mean by 'changing referential meaning': it is still a 'choice', but one at the level of speaker intention rather than articulation.

This leads us to one final brief comment regarding meaning. It is entirely feasible that, during the process of articulation, the speaker or writer is unaware of their choices. Just as a proficient cyclist does not continually ponder the act of balancing, the articulate speaker does not continually consider the cascade of choices they make. If a choice is 'unconscious', in the sense that a speaker is unaware of making it at the time, then conscious explanations of that choice may be set aside.

Unconscious or 'autonomous' choices are likely to be routine, involve unmarked forms, have little semantic impact on the surrounding utterance, and – most likely – be found in unplanned spoken data.[7] As we noted in Chapter 1, corpora containing spontaneous speech are a more reliable source of unconscious choices than those containing writing or scripted speech. We can observe variation of conscious choices, but if all we are doing is observing writers 'crafting' non-spontaneously, our ability to make deeper claims about language is limited. More interesting hypotheses are likely to concern the unconscious choices we make.

3.3 A Methodological Progression?

We have seen that observations on the basis of per million words are not meaningless, but they conflate opportunity and choice.

Rather than viewing variationist and exposure rate approaches as diametrically opposed, they may be helpfully viewed as points on a *methodological continuum*. In doing so, we recognise that we are often forced to compromise our ideal experimental practice according to the data and tools at our disposal.

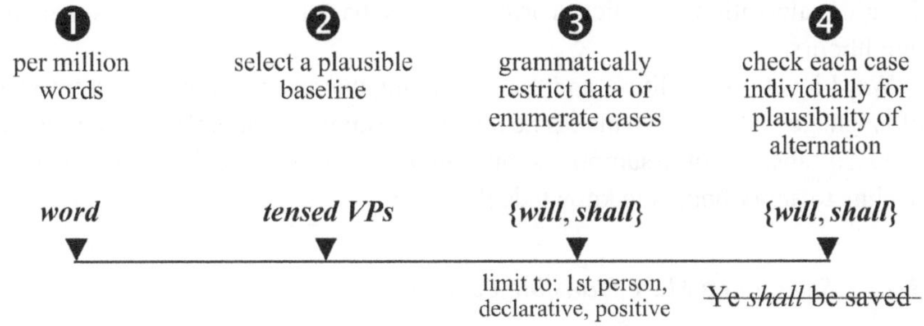

FIGURE 3.5 A methodological progression: baselines for the modal auxiliary *shall*, from normalised word frequencies to verified alternation.

Viewing approaches on a continuum may also allow us to reconcile apparently contradictory results. We may consider the potential of further annotation, and where such an annotation effort would be best focused. By mapping others' research methods onto this continuum and considering their assumptions, we can also identify how that research may be extended.

The idea is sketched in Figure 3.5. The progression consists of four stages each defining a baseline:

1. the words in a subcorpus;
2. a superset in which the item may be found;
3. a set of alternate forms which could vary; and
4. a validated alternation set where every instance is tested for variation.

3.3.1 Per Million Words

Exposure rates estimate the chance that a hearer or reader will be exposed to a particular word if they are presented with similar types of texts to those in the corpus. For a learner dictionary, an exposure rate may be exactly what you need.

Many methods make use of these so-called 'normalised frequencies'. Biber's multidimensional (MD) analysis method (1988) combines them with factor analysis to identify dimensions of register variation. Church (2000) developed a 'topic detector' algorithm by comparing the probability of a word appearing at random in a corpus, $p(w)$, and the probability of the same word appearing twice in the same text, $p(w_2 \mid w_1)$. Thus the word *Noriega* is low frequency in a typical corpus, but likely to appear several times in texts about General Manuel Noriega and Panama in the 1980s.

Collocational tools and wordclass taggers use similar word-level adjacent-probability principles (Wallis, 2020a). Collocational tools exploit the tendency for words to co-occur in potentially linguistically interesting ways.

Tagging algorithms predict wordclass tags based on each word's nearest neighbours.

Word-level probabilities, and the algorithms that use them, rely on a 'model' of language that ignores ('makes no *a priori* assumptions about') language structure. An 'absence of assumptions' appears positive, but it really means that we decline to apply linguistic knowledge!

3.3.2 Selecting a More Plausible Baseline

Today, few corpora are limited to plain text. Tagged corpora differentiate words by wordclass (cf. *will* as a noun vs. auxiliary verb vs. main verb, etc.). With such a corpus, it is usually possible to improve on a word-based baseline.

The modal verb *shall* is an auxiliary to a main verb, so a better baseline than words for examining changes in the proportion *p*(*shall*) would be main verbs or – better still – *tensed* main verbs. This baseline is less susceptible to arbitrary variation by text than words.

Indeed, once we accept the premise of moving away from words, it is legitimate to explore multiple baselines. The baseline is a crucial element of the dependent variable, the research hypothesis and the experimental design.

As we noted, if we move from a general baseline towards an alternation pattern, we reduce the potential for random variation in the *opportunity rate* to affect the outcome. Legal cross-examinations and news reports are characterised by dialogue concerning past events. By contrast, two friends planning a trip are more likely to use *will* or *shall*.

A common myth is that with larger data volumes, variation in opportunity rate tends to 'average out', the implication being that meaningful baselines are less important with large corpora. This is mistaken. True, some sources of variation, like local topic, will tend to average over large numbers of texts, but particularities in purpose and context of text genres (like the degree of future orientation of a text) will remain.

Bowie et al. (2014) examined the impact of spoken text categories in DCPSE on changing modal use over time. Modals can only appear in tensed verb phrases ('tVPs'), that is, a VP where either the main or auxiliary verb has a present or past tense feature. They then plotted the per million word frequency of tVPs in DCPSE (Figure 3.6).

Across the entire corpus, the ratio of tVPs to words ('tVP density') is almost constant (Total column). However, once data are subdivided into text categories, this statement no longer holds true, as other columns illustrate. First, there is large *synchronic variation* between text categories: some categories have more tVPs per word than others. This variation is likely to persist with larger data sizes. Second, tVPs increase over time in some categories; in others they decrease. This variation may be arbitrary, the result of uncontrolled sampling,

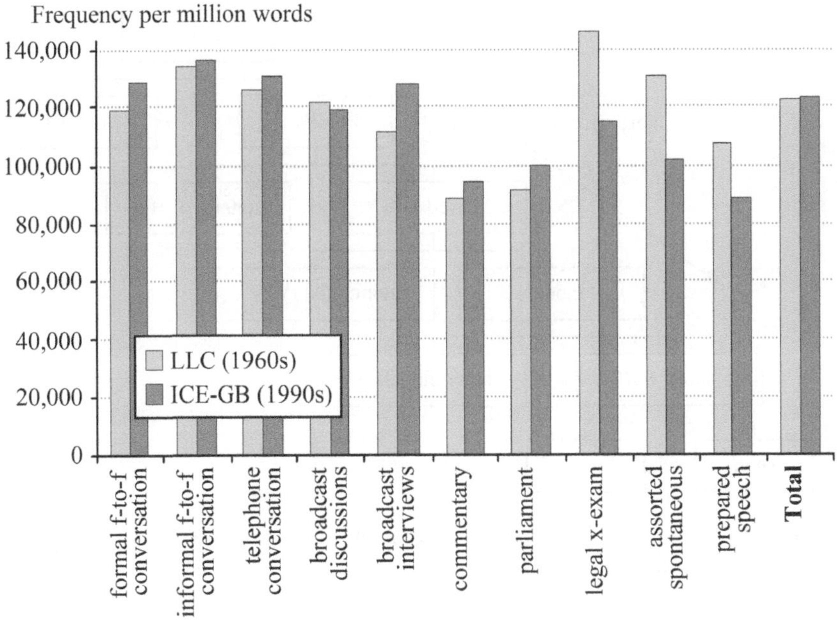

FIGURE 3.6 Tensed verb phrases per million words for each text category (horizontal axis) across the two 'time' subcorpora of DCPSE, after Bowie et al. (2014).

and so tend to average out. Or it may reflect an actual underlying change worth reporting.

Every intersecting subset, *text category* × *time period*, displays variation in the rate of tVP per word. Since tVPs license a modal auxiliary verb, this unevenness represents a source of variation in the opportunity to employ a core modal. Such widespread variation in opportunity would therefore also confound any study that wished to examine the ratio between, say, core modals and words.

We should expect similar variation in differently sampled corpora compiled by multiple teams. Factoring out this varying opportunity can only improve the robustness of comparisons between text categories and corpora, and increase the likelihood that results are replicated.

But this is only one step, and we can often go further.

We can improve a baseline through a *process of elimination*. We pick a higher-level or more general structure, such as all VPs, and then eliminate cases that do not plausibly alternate. Consider the decision tree sketch in Figure 3.7. Each term on the left represents a set of linguistic events that may be counted to obtain a baseline frequency. As in Figure 3.1, there is a strict subset relationship in operation as we descend.

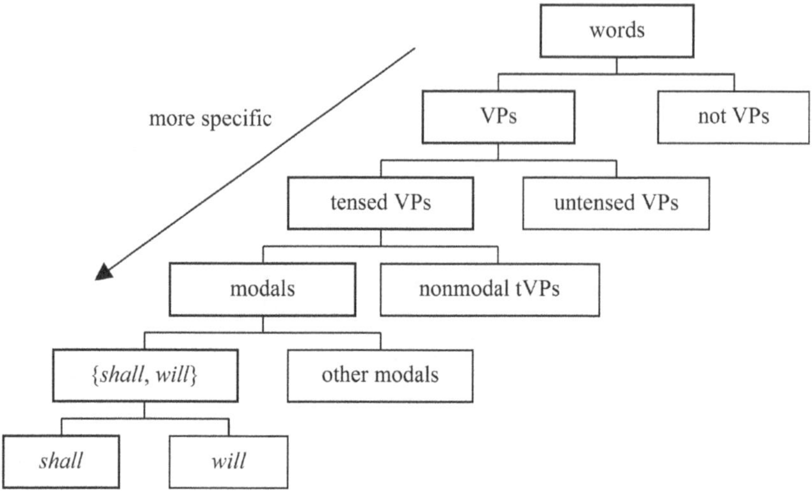

FIGURE 3.7 Conceptual decision tree, from the utterance of a word to that word being modal *shall*.

Tense marking is a precondition for a modal verb to appear in a VP, but the modal is optional. The alternation set {*shall*, *will*} is a subset of all modals (or 'VPs that contain modals'). In short, we subdivide corpus data conceptually into elements on the path from words to the studied phenomenon (here the choice *shall* vs. *will*).

One consequence of changing baselines is shown in Figure 3.8. This is a bar chart of the proportion of DCPSE data in LLC, $f_{LLC}(x) / f(x)$ for each observed frequency x. If data were sampled in a controlled manner, this proportion would be constant (ideally 0.5).

Reading from top to bottom, around 52% of all words in DCPSE are found in the earlier (LLC) subcorpus, whereas there are almost identical numbers of tensed VPs in LLC and ICE-GB subcorpora.

The proportion of modals found in the earlier 1960s data is around 54%. The number of modals as a proportion of words has slightly declined over time in the corpus. Finally, the proportion of all cases of modal *will* or *shall* in the LLC data is around 51.5% (black dot, upper bar) – almost the same proportion as all words. But this baseline has a tremendous advantage over these more general ones: *it eliminates the possibility that an observed difference is due to varying opportunity*. We gain explanatory power.

Furthermore, if we restrict examples grammatically (see Section 3.3.5), the picture changes. The proportion of first person declarative positive *will* or *shall* in the LLC data leaps to 66% of the total (193 out of 291, white dot, lower bar).

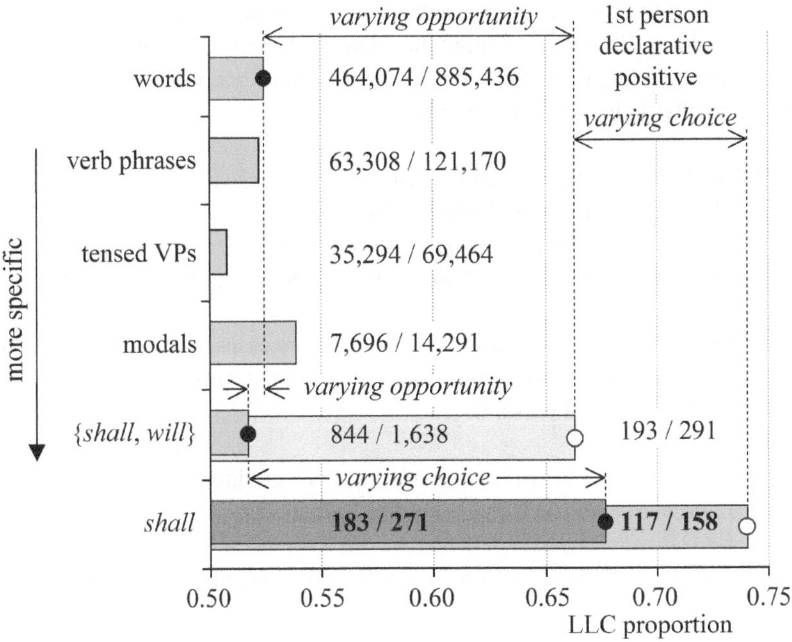

FIGURE 3.8 A bar chart representing the proportion of a range of forms, including the target concept (*shall*) and several potential baseline forms, that are found in the earlier LLC component of the DCPSE corpus. If the baseline did not matter, these proportions would be identical. In this case, 74% of all cases of first person declarative positive *shall* are found in the earlier subcorpus.

Most of the cases eliminated are second or third person *will*, which, as we noted, rarely alternate with *shall*. The choice baseline {*shall*, *will*} reduces the size of the apparent change in choosing *shall* (labelled 'varying choice'), but the result is more precise and more reliable.

3.3.3 Enumerating Alternates

Another approach to identifying a baseline is to start with the target concept and enumerate alternates. Thus, in studying the core modal auxiliary verb *shall*, we might ask 'what could we utter instead of modal *shall* without changing our intended meaning?'

The tVP baseline includes a wide range of VPs where the expression of modal *shall* is unlikely. Where a VP expresses a meaning other than intention or prediction (a past orientation, a different modal meaning, etc.), the speaker's intended referential meaning probably rules out the use of *shall*.

Working top-down, we thought the optimum baseline was the set of modal verbs {*will*, *shall*}, with or without the contracted form *'ll*. But we may have narrowed the field too much. Other expressions of futurity could be included within the same alternation set, for example:

(17) I *will* go abroad and teach English [DL-B16 #621]
~ I *shall* go abroad and teach English
~ I *am going to* go abroad and teach English
~ I *intend/expect/plan/wish to* go abroad and teach English

A further possible step is to consider present tense cases with adjuncts (adverbials) expressing future time. This seems natural with present progressive cases but less so with simple present:

~ I *am going* abroad *to* teach English [after I graduate]
~? I go abroad *to* teach English [after I graduate]

Crucially, we are trying to ensure core referential meaning is retained across the alternation.

3.3.4 Linguistically Restricting the Sample

As we have discussed, a further possibility is to grammatically restrict the set.

Interrogative cases like Example (18) can invoke a referential meaning change from an offer to a prediction. Second and third person cases of *shall* are very rare.

(18) *Shall* we turn this off? [DI-B15 #196] (interrogative)
~? *Will* we turn this off?
(19) some way that they *shall* enjoy it [DL-D02 #151] (third person)
~? some way that they *will* enjoy it

To study *shall*, Aarts et al. (2013) decided it is more meaningful to eliminate all but first person *shall/will* alternation. If we are interested in second and third person expressions of future intention or prediction, we should study these separately (on the semi-substitution principle, see Section 3.2.4).

With a parsed corpus such as ICE-GB or DCPSE, it is possible to construct a grammatical query (a Fuzzy Tree Fragment – see Chapter 2) and restrict cases using the parse annotation. In a tagged corpus, we must rely on word-sequence patterns, which may be inaccurate and incomplete.

However, all annotation schemes have their limits. They make certain distinctions but not others. ICE-GB does not annotate modal auxiliary verbs by modal meaning. It does not distinguish adjuncts into time, manner and place adverbs, nor does it identify future-time expressions.

The limits of pre-given annotation are not necessarily where research has to stop, if the researcher is prepared to manually review cases. As we noted in Chapter 1, the annotation cycle is always available to a researcher. In Aarts et al.'s study, Jo Close classified cases into Root and Epistemic meanings and considered their alternation separately, allowing her to conclude that the decline in *shall* was almost completely due to a collapse in Epistemic *shall.*

3.3.5 Eliminating Non-Alternating Cases

The final level of baseline improvement consists of *verification*, that is, examining corpus examples and eliminating those that do not alternate. Cases will be of a primary form under study (here, *shall*, 'Type A' forms) and alternates (e.g., *will*, 'Type B'). Formulaic or idiomatic instances of either type (or those wrongly classified) should be discarded. We can also think of this step as a kind of 'additional annotation' by working bottom-up from the text.

A key aspect of applying any annotation scheme (or Qualitative Analysis, see Chapter 1) concerns *decidability* (Wallis, 2007). Do we have a reliable, justified method for deciding which cases to include or exclude? The researcher should set down their criteria first, and then attempt to systematically apply them to each case. Where cases are hard to classify, they should review them against these criteria. Sometimes – particularly when dealing with an experimental sample rather than a whole corpus, we might accept a small minority of undecided cases.

Chapter 15 shows how statistical reasoning can assist this process.

3.3.6 A Methodological Progression

Recognising that experimental approaches may be found on a continuum does not imply that one method is 'as good as' another. This continuum represents a trade-off between the ease of obtaining results and the reliability of conclusions. Some steps are straightforward to carry out, however, and benefits far outweigh the cost. By successively eliminating irrelevant data or sets of non-alternating cases from our sample we 'clean our data' and make our research more precise and reproducible. This is a *progression*, and we are making progress!

The final step, reviewing cases in the corpus, may be impossible to perform exhaustively in large corpora, but we can examine a random subsample to estimate the reliability of our sampling. At the very least, we should always perform a 'sanity check' and examine cases in the corpus to confirm that our results mean what we think they do.

3.4 Objections to Variationism

There are three main lines of objection that have been made to the variationist paradigm in corpus linguistics. These are as follows:

- **Feasibility**. Alternates are not reliably identifiable, and the high cost outweighs the benefit.
- **Arbitrariness**. Researchers can arbitrarily select baselines, an exercise which is subjective and unscientific.
- **Over-simplification**. Multiple ecological pressures apply to different elements, so by selecting a baseline we are engaging in a kind of 'reductionism', implying that variation can only happen in this one direction. In any corpus, there are simultaneously many sources of variation.

These objections require a careful discussion.

3.4.1 Feasibility

The original reason for resisting a move towards alternation studies was one of feasibility. We noted that early corpora were not computerised, and that the majority of corpora today have no structural grammatical annotation, only word-class tags.

For some simple lexical alternations unrestricted by grammatical context, such as modal *shall/will* irrespective of subject or clause mood, the absence of parsing may not be fatal. It is still possible to perform an alternation study. Manually checking some 1,600 or so examples in DCPSE would still be feasible.

However, many of the steps we have undertaken are greatly facilitated with a parsed corpus. Parsing allows us to restrict queries grammatically and make identifying 'choice points' easier and thus more precise. In the absence of a parsed corpus, one must be motivated to enumerate tag sequence queries, perform what we might term 'pseudo-parsing' and live with the fact that some cases may be missed.

Let us consider a difficult baseline to determine, identifying Latinate alternates of phrasal verbs. Earlier studies such as Biber et al. (1999) and Gardner and Davies (2007) rely on per million word frequencies to support claims of change over time. We have learned that VP density is a potentially confounding factor in any study of verbs. An easy step forward would be to employ a main verb (or VP) baseline.

Can we improve on this? After all, not all verbs are phrasal verbs or their Latinate alternates. And (at the risk of stating the obvious) *not all verbs mean the same thing!* Let us consider two potential approaches: working bottom-up and working top-down. In the ICE-GB corpus we can generalise the FTF in

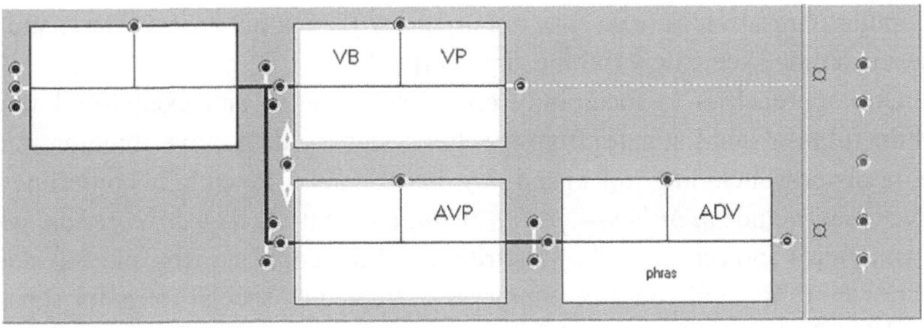

FIGURE 3.9 Fuzzy Tree Fragment for VPs followed or preceded by phrasal adverbs.

Figure 3.9. This FTF obtains some 7,000 cases in ICE-GB and can be treated as a template for further restriction.

To work bottom-up, we must serially identify alternate forms. Phrasal verbs often have many meanings, thus *put up* can mean 'tolerate' (*put up with it*),[8] 'build' (*put up a shack*), 'display' (*put up on the screen*), 'sell' and so on. Latinate alternates of *put up* will differ for each meaning, and these may have other phrasal alternates. Consider Example (20):

(20) *put* the plant *up* for sale
~ *offer* the plant for sale
~ *put* the plant on the market
~ *sell* the plant

If *offer [up]* is considered an alternate form for *put up*, we need to consider all instances of *offer* that could also conceivably be replaced by *put up* or another phrasal verb. We should also decide the degree to which the structure of the clause could legitimately change and still be considered an 'alternate' form.

The effort involved in classifying each phrasal verb instance and finding alternates is extremely high. A bottom-up approach is probably best suited for narrow-focus studies, such as verbs expressing a particular meaning or set of meanings, particular phrasal verbs or those in a limited domain (e.g., legal prose).

What about a top-down approach? Even if we cannot obtain a strict set of alternates for every case, we can improve on a baseline of 'all main verbs'. Our FTF in Figure 3.9 is 'Type A'. 'Type C' forms are verbs with no phrasal alternate. This creates a three-way sorting problem: identify verb forms where potential alternation may be classed as 'yes', 'no' or 'maybe' – the latter requiring us to examine specific corpus examples.

Copular and stative verbs are likely to be excluded. Greenbaum (1996a, p. 152) notes that phrasal adverbs tend to have 'spatial meaning, literal or metaphorical', so dynamic verbs are more likely to have phrasal alternates than stative ones.

Copular phrasal verbs (e.g., *turn out* or *end up*)[9] exist but are very rare, and are best examined separately (with a large corpus).

One approach is to focus only on dynamic verbs, and exclude all stative verbs (phrasal and Latinate) from the study. This would remove common stative phrasal verbs including *stay in* and *stay on* ('remain'). Potentially borderline stative cases include *fit in [with]*, *put up [with]* ('tolerate'), *keep on, carry on, go on* ('continue') and *put down [to]* ('attribute'). Like copular verbs, phrasal stative verbs are finite, and could be enumerated, treated as special cases for separate study, and removed from our dataset.

There are two approaches we can employ for this task.

Option one is to try to identify stative verbs lexically. This can be performed to a fair degree of accuracy. We simply enumerate an exclusion set. But can we be sure that all allegedly 'stative' verbs are actually stative *in context*? Second, do all 'dynamic' verbs have phrasal alternates? At some point we must review a putative dataset to decide whether alternation is possible.

The corpus data are likely to generate so many cases that manually reviewing cases exhaustively is simply unfeasible. This lies behind the criticism that an alternation approach might be a nice idea but it is simply not practical.

This is not an objection of principle. There are 106,770 cases of main verbs (excluding copular verbs) in ICE-GB. This is far too many to examine manually!

However, we can employ some statistical mathematics to assist us. In Chapter 15, we discuss this question at length. The idea is that we manually review a smaller *random subsample*. We can then either simply analyse this subsample or extrapolate the results to a larger sample (or the entire corpus). As a pilot exercise, we drew a 1% random subsample of the spoken data (comprising 63,867 cases). This contained 633 main verb tokens, which we reviewed manually in their context, identifying 361 (57%) as either dynamic with a phrasal alternate, or phrasal with a dynamic alternate. The entire exercise took two person hours at most.

Crucially, we can attack apparently unfeasible alternation studies top-down or bottom-up. Which approach you choose depends on your study. The aim of an alternation as an *ideal*, even if it is not an obtainable one, should not be dismissed due to mere difficulty of execution. Linguistic principles must come first.

3.4.2 Arbitrariness

Many readers may have a different doubt. The option to employ different baselines implies that there is no single 'objective' baseline (e.g., per million words) to compare a term against. Does the experimenter have a free hand in choosing a baseline?

Worse, is there a risk of an experimenter selecting a baseline *to present results as significant?* How do we avoid '*p*-hacking' (see Chapter 11) in selecting baselines? Answer: linguistic principles must come first! Do not report hypotheses merely because we perceive statistically observable (significant) differences.

Our baselines are the opposite of arbitrary. Schegloff (1993) emphasises that *baselines are integral components of research hypotheses*. Change a baseline and we change the hypothesis under test.

The baseline for a Type A item will typically depend on both:

1 the *conceptualisation* of the choice A versus B (and thus the contrast B; or B_1, B_2, etc.); and
2 the *practical ability* to reliably retrieve the baseline.

Whereas the distribution of any given term may be contrasted with another, *the point of an experiment is to test a plausible linguistic hypothesis*. If A cannot plausibly replace B, the hypothesis will be absurd, like modelling for *shall* being replaced with any other random word.

An awareness of the importance of baselines requires greater care in experimental design and reporting conclusions. It does not make the choice of baseline arbitrary. Indeed, where baselines include numbers of non-alternating 'Type C' cases, they are open to further refinement.

The ability to specify a baseline in a principled manner vastly increases the range of potentially valid hypotheses that may be investigated. It is common to compare multiple terms against the same baseline, for example, *shall*, *will*, *may* against all modals. But it can also be valid to compare correlations of the same term against *multiple* baselines.

Bowie et al. (2013) investigated the incidence of present perfect constructions over time using DCPSE. Consider Examples (21) to (23):

(21) I *have done* a bit of writing (before now)	(present perfect)
(22) I *am writing* (now)	(present progressive)
(23) I *was writing* (before now)	(past progressive)

The present perfect construction is somewhat anomalous, in that it relates both to a previous completed action *and* the present context. But it does not directly refer to the present. Example (21) logically entails (23) but not (22). At most, Example (22) is a possible pragmatic implicature of (21).

Consequently, these examples are not independent mutually substitutable alternates. The meaning changes, and the present perfect has a particular temporal aspect not easily expressed any other way. At best, to study alternation we would need to limit the expression to semantically close alternates, such as the simple past (cf. *I <u>did</u> a bit of writing before*).

In Chapter 13, we report that present perfect constructions correlate more closely with present-marked constructions (Example (22)), than those marked for past tense such as (23), across multiple contrasts in DCPSE.

What does this mean? Present tense cases *are not an alternation pattern for the present perfect.*

The most plausible hypothesis for this closer correlation concerns *co-occurrence*. In other words, it is the pattern we would expect to see if the present perfect tended to occur in present-oriented passages in the corpus (i.e., ones with a higher proportion of verbs oriented to the present) more often than in past-oriented ones. There is a correlation, but it may not be due to alternation. This is an example of the 'third variable *Z*' problem we mentioned in the last chapter.

The best way to guard against arbitrary selection of baselines and '*p*-hacking' (see Chapter 11) is to focus on the *linguistic* logic of the research hypothesis itself. The aim of experimental refinement is to try to eliminate alternative hypotheses – not to obtain 'significance', which is a fool's errand.

3.4.3 Oversimplification

A third set of objections concerns the fact that there may be multiple pressures on a particular linguistic term being used. Speakers make numerous choices, each influenced by multiple pressures. To talk about there being a single 'choice' is misleading.

Smith and Leech (2013, p. 75) argue 'it is commonplace in linguistics that there is no such thing as free variation', and so multiple differing constraints apply to each instance. They propose an 'ecological' approach, although this is not well defined.

This objection seems to conflate two distinct arguments: one relating to lexical meaning and another relating to multiple pressures on choices.

3.4.4 The Problem of Polysemy

The first issue concerns *polysemy* (the fact that words may have multiple lexical meanings). Recall the problem of finding alternates for particular phrasal verbs.

The critique goes like this. Finding semantic alternates to polysemous words is a Herculean task, so obtaining *'semantic alternates' is an idealisation.* Even were we to employ state-of-the-art semantic tagging, the results are likely to be at best approximate, and – thanks to the 'black box' dependency on an algorithm and database – difficult to replicate and explain. At best, we can approximate a general baseline and pooled results.

This argument is clearly correct. It is why we describe the problem of choice as 'vexed'! Being mindful of this, we discussed a *methodological continuum* of approaches, from refining the baseline to limiting a choice to verified strict alternates. Alternation studies can be divided into three types: those that maintain constant meaning, those that maintain constant referential meaning and those that permit a limited type of consistent meaning change:

1 **Constant meaning.** Types A and B simply replace one another without any meaning change. There is a small set of heavily studied alternations of this type: the genitive/*of* alternation, the dative alternation, and so on. Here is another:

(24) the people *living* in France
~ the people *who were living* in France

2 **Constant *referential* meaning.** A and B refer to the same underlying concept, although the surface meaning has changed. Consider:

(25) a centre for *predicting* climate change
~ a centre for *the prediction of* climate change

3 ***Consistent* meaning change.** Replacement of A by B adds explicit meaning in some way, as in the gain of an explicit progressive aspect, addition of an object, adjective, and so on. Yet *the writer or speaker's intended referential meaning* (the concept they had in mind) has not changed, so it still qualifies as an 'alternation study'.

We are flirting with Lavandera's 'dangerous hypothesis'. A change in sentence structure conveys a corresponding change in underlying meaning, and hypotheses about one cannot exclude possible explanations concerning the other. Consider the following:

(26) People always *ask me this* about my novels $_{\text{[S1B-048 \#8]}}$ (ditransitive)
~ People always *ask this* about my novels (monotransitive)

The loss of the indirect object in the second monotransitive case loses meaning, as the 'undergoer' of the asking, *me*, is unspecified (it may be implied from the context). However, the speaker or writer is still likely to be referring to the same individuals, capacities, events, and so on. Replacement is conceivable.

This, we suggest, represents the limit of alternation studies. Once meaning can change *inconsistently*, we lose the ability to claim that the dataset constitutes a consistent set of choices. (This is particularly important when we consider the fact that the corpus is an uncontrolled language source. See Chapter 2.)

Were we to permit inconsistent meaning change, we may still have a better baseline than words, and obtain interesting exploratory results. But the experiment is no longer an alternation study.

3.4.5 A Complex Ecology?

A second argument goes something like this: *multiple pressures apply to every choice*. Therefore the kind of narrow experimental research perspective we have outlined oversimplifies patterns found in rich, 'ecological' corpora.

Dylan Glynn writes (in Arppe et al., 2010, p. 12), 'when a speaker chooses a concept, he or she chooses between a wide inventory of lexemes, each of which profiles different elements of that concept. Moreover, the speaker profiles that lexeme in combination with a wide range of grammatical forms, each also contributing to how the speaker wishes to depict the concept'. This is true. But it is not a valid objection to variationist studies with corpora.

Statistical methods *anticipate variation*, and natural language is no exception. We know speakers have personal preferences, may adopt particular uses with genre and register, be affected by context and audience and so on. We do not require that at every single choice point exactly the same influences, biases and constraints apply. This is what we meant by saying that corpus data were 'uncontrolled'.

Nor are we attempting to explain why, precisely, an individual speaker or writer chose to perform a *particular* utterance at a given point! Rather, we are attempting to *generalise* across the entire set of such choices to identify statistically sound patterns, correlations and trends.[10]

The critical question for a researcher is whether one or more of these multiple influences represent a *systematic bias* on the rate of selecting A rather than B. Such a bias should be detectable by experiment – provided we have sufficient data and pose the question correctly.

If the 'ecological objection' is understood in this second sense, it is really an objection to corpus linguistics. No model will be sufficiently complex to address the myriad of potential influences on each utterance.

Most of all, this is not a good argument for a word-based baseline! Variation of opportunity will *also* be affected by this surrounding ecology!

3.4.6 Necessary Reductionism Versus Complex Statistical Models

Glynn says that the study of binary alternations in linguistics is the result of 'two methodological errors':

- a theoretical inheritance from generative grammar and
- the methodological convenience of employing simple statistics (e.g., chi-square).

He argues that more complex statistical methods, such as multivariate analysis (exploring multiple independent variables in combination), are more appropriate.[11]

Logically, this argument is not an objection to an alternation methodology *per se*. Gaëtanelle Gilquin points out in the same article that alternation studies, including binary alternation studies, remain a starting point for linguistic research. Multivariate analyses are built on 'bivariate' ones. Each variable proportion or rate, $p = f / n$, requires us to decide how both f and n are counted. The baseline count, n, is part of the variable. Competent multivariate analyses also rely on the ability of instances in datasets to alternate, and that observed proportions p can vary from 0 to 1.

So-called 'ecological' or 'holistic' arguments are not objections to linguistically restricting samples or eliminating non-alternating cases by reviewing them. On the contrary, many of these points are best addressed by such methods.

One might partition data and carry out separate studies, or perform a single multivariate study incorporating multiple coded variables. However – and this is the crucial point – *the latter must still be premised on the possibility of alternation.*

This issue is not statistical but linguistic. Refining the experimental design, categorising types and extracting baseline data for each hypothesised alternation is motivated by linguistic analysis.

There are some statistical modelling algorithms that inductively model variation in data. Since they examine actual variation, p need not be able to reach 1. They can work with per word exposure rates. However, we know that variation in such rates combine two distinct elements: *variation in opportunity and variation in choice*. Suppose that against a baseline of words, a proportion p increased, but declined against a meaningful choice baseline. No amount of clever statistics will detect this! We need data on how the baseline behaves.

We cannot avoid the vexed question of choice by computation. There are legitimate criticisms of χ^2-type tests in corpus linguistics, which we address in Chapter 16. But *this* argument is misconceived. Neither multivariate nor modelling methods solve the problem of defining a meaningful baseline.[12]

3.4.7 Discussion

The most obvious problem with these objections is they do not offer a real alternative. Arguing against alternation studies on the grounds that they are difficult is defeatist. We have hit the limits of corpus linguistics research. We are stuck with counting words.

Yet many types of alternation experiments are feasible with limited additional work. We can generalise from those experiments to explore how much effort might be expended in applying a variationist method to less tractable problems. Once we recognise the desirability of *that* goal, we can choose to review data, or employ more annotation and computation, to try to achieve it.

Recall the 3A cycle introduced in Chapter 1. We argue for richer annotation, not for decorative purposes, but *to improve our ability to perform abstraction to test relevant research hypotheses*. We distinguish between *annotation* as a 'general good', a process of enrichment for multiple purposes, and *abstraction* as a method of translating an annotated corpus into a relevant corpus dataset.

The objection that baselines are arbitrary is also incorrect. Schegloff (1993) points out that baselines are an intrinsic component of the act of quantification itself, that is, they are part of the research hypothesis.

Finally, we addressed the objection that by adopting a variationist paradigm we 'over-simplified' our explanations. In the case of lexical polysemy, this objection reprises the feasibility objection – adding semantic annotation to a corpus is laborious.

However, a second version of the same 'ecological' argument requires a more substantive response. If true, it would undermine the feasibility of studying variation within naturally occurring corpus data altogether. But this argument conflates *random variation* and *systematic bias*. The first is expected and can be factored out; the second may be detected by changing baselines and variables. Moreover, to the extent to which the same variables may be encoded in a corpus study and a controlled 'laboratory' experiment, results from corpora may be disambiguated by controlled experiments.

TABLE 3.4 Four questions for corpus data analysis, in order of increasing restriction. Mutual substitution guarantees freedom to vary, which is the minimum condition for Binomial and Multinomial statistics. See Chapter 6.

1. **Freedom to vary**
   - Can each value of the dependent variable conceivably reach 100% in the population?
2. **Mutual substitution**
   - Are all values of the dependent variable capable of replacement by all others for all instances in the population? Have we eliminated 'Type C' cases from any putative comparison?
3. **Mutual substitution with consistent meaning change**
   - If meaning change occurs as a result of mutual substitution, is it the same meaning change for each member of the dataset? Does the underlying concept still refer to the same concept, process or thing? Where a loss of meaning occurs, is it plausible to believe that the speaker or writer still had this meaning in mind, even if they did not convey it explicitly?
4. **Independent mutual substitution**
   - Do values of the dependent variable refer to the same concept, process or thing, such that replacement does not affect the meaning at all, and the choice is entirely free in principle?

For those inclined to consider a multivariate approach, variationism represents an optimal starting point. A multivariate, multilevel analysis will only be as good as the data it is given. If we have not identified the baseline of the dependent variable, the algorithm will not do it for us! If we use an exposure rate, variation of opportunity will confound the statistical method.

It follows that our starting point must be one framed in terms of linguistically meaningful questions of choice, defined by the researcher, related to previous research and investigated thoroughly in research papers.

Along the way, the ability to test alternate hypotheses by changing baselines is central to any research argument. In the next chapter, we will show how this perspective can be applied in research into meaning change.

3.5 Conclusions

Every researcher must pay attention to questions of choice and baselines. Selecting a baseline is necessary to construct a hypothesis and carry out an experiment to test it. All baselines specify the *expected distribution* over the independent variable contrast. Recall that the core *null hypothesis* is that the term we are interested in ('Type A') does not change in proportion to the baseline.

The alternative to selecting a linguistically motivated baseline *does not avoid selecting a baseline*. It selects a baseline that is the least optimal for most research purposes – the word.

Word-based baselines do not distinguish opportunity and choice, and are vulnerable to arbitrary variation. We cannot then distinguish between changes in opportunity and variation in a particular choice. This additional uncontrolled opportunity variation also reduces the chance that results will be replicated in future experiments.

It is a truism that sheer randomness, arbitrary selection, speaker preferences, changing topic and other 'ecological' local influences all conspire to cause random variation in any observed linguistic act. As we descend a hierarchy of baselines from words to *will/shall*, say, each intermediate baseline is potentially affected by all such influences. For most purposes, we select a baseline that is closest to the item under study and represents the most meaningful choice.

In alternation research, we require that the baseline represents the *opportunity* for the speaker to choose a Type A item. We identify those occasions at which the speaker was 'on the threshold of choosing' A or B (or A, B_1, B_2, etc.). Our ideal dataset consists of a set of 'choice points' or opportunities.

Alternation can be interpreted *strictly*, that is, where mutual substitution must occur between all cases of Types A and B, or more generously, where we risk allowing a small number of additional non-alternating 'Type C' terms into a baseline. A strict interpretation would require that the researcher check each case for the plausibility of their alternation.

We build on Lavandera (1978), who argues for ensuring that referential meaning remains constant across an alternation. We believe this is desirable, but 'constancy of referential meaning' is a relatively elusive concept in lexis and grammar. We argue instead for the minimum condition that if meaning changes across the alternation, it should change consistently in a single dimension and the underlying core meaning should not change. We must also address the question as to whether we are witnessing a change in meaning over the contrast (say, an increase in strong obligation or progressive aspect) or a change in its explicit representation (use of modal *must* or progressive VPs).

Consistent meaning change implies a binary alternation: where A differs from B_1, B_2, and so on, a decision tree may be constructed and the A versus $\{B_1, B_2 \ldots\}$ alternation can be studied separately from B_1 versus B_2, etc.

Tangential core meanings, such as those of all verbs, may be pooled. The requirement is that between Types A and B, if one type conveys an additional meaning (e.g., explicit progressive aspect), it does so consistently.

Our approach has multiple benefits, including:

- **It identifies where options are genuinely possible.** The dataset consists of 'choice points' abstracted from a corpus, where the potential for choosing Type A and B (or B_1, B_2, etc.) was genuinely *available* at every point. A, B, and so on must be capable of selection.
- **It views language production as primary.** Speakers and writers make their selection as they speak or write. Hearer or reader statistics, termed *exposure rates*, are the consequence of many different choices made by language producers, that is, they are secondary. Such rates may be useful, but are theoretically and mathematically distinguishable from the original choice.
- **It focuses research.** We employ a clearly stated experimental hypothesis and its null hypothesis counterpart. A principled baseline of choice *adds information* to the experimental design.
- **It increases the robustness of analysis.** Factoring out varying opportunity and minimising the number of non-alternating 'Type C' terms increases the likelihood that results will be replicated. The ideal is to remove Type C cases altogether, so that $p(C) = 0$, but a *graceful degradation* principle applies: the fewer such cases, the more robust the results.[13]

Our perspective is pluralistic. Exposure rates and semasiological uses are valid but secondary to a primary question of choice. Understanding these as 'secondary models of variation' is helpful for two reasons. It allows us to recognise the different kinds of claim one can make from different types of experiment. And it indicates alternative hypotheses and baselines for any notable observation we may wish to explain.

Focusing on alternation allows corpus linguists to obtain evidence commensurable with those obtained in other linguistic fields and with other research methods (see Schönefeld, 2011), such as those concerned with investigating the process of language production.

Notes

1 The process of obtaining an optimum experimental design is occasionally referred to as one of 'formulation and operationalisation of hypotheses' (Gries, 2009, p. 176), where *formulation* refers to the definition of variables and cases, and *operationalisation* the definition of corpus queries. Our argument, developed from Nelson et al. (2002, pp. 258–262) is simply that this process of formulation must take into account a relevant baseline.

2 The vertical bar means 'given', so the notation $p(x \mid \mathbf{X})$ means 'the probability of x given a superset $\mathbf{X}$ containing x'. A pmw exposure rate also contains a scale constant, $k = 1{,}000{,}000$.

3 It is worth noting that a word baseline may be a valid choice rate in a limited number of cases. Consider an experiment to find factors that predict when speakers pause, self-correct or stop sentences abruptly. With no prior knowledge of the structure of English, the default assumption would be that these events could take place at or following any word. *Any* variation from this is considered remarkable and worth examining.

4 Some empirical data might be useful. The mean exposure rate of the most common word in English, *the*, across ICE-GB, $p(the \mid \text{word}) = 0.055$ (5.5%). The highest rate for a single text category is 0.080 (8%), in a single 2,000-word text, slightly over 10%. Wordclasses obtain higher rates. The mean rate of nouns in ICE-GB reaches a maximum of just below 33% in a text category and 47% in a single text.

5 The opportunity rate for employing *will* or *shall* is not the same in earlier and later DCPSE subcorpora. See Figure 3.8.

6 Four alternates entails three 'degrees of freedom', that is, that the data can be explained by three patterns of binary alternation.

7 Not all written texts are the same. We might hypothesise that handwritten texts are less likely to contain as many 'crafted' sentences as, say, typed texts. A similar argument might apply in the case of rapidly typed electronic 'chat' communications (Skype™, WhatsApp™, etc.).

8 Some grammarians might consider the first form a 'phrasal prepositional verb' to be distinguished from phrasal verbs *per se*.

9 ICE-GB has *which has <u>turned out</u> extremely fruitful* (S2A-027 #40). Huddleston and Pullum (2002, p. 288) cite some eight examples including *she <u>ended up</u> as captain.* Both alternate with BECOME.

10 The concept of 'free variation' employed in this book concerns grammatical and semantic *possibility* – the choice becomes available to the speaker (so they could hypothetically replace *who* with *whom* in every case). We distinguish this from the mere possibility of utterance (speakers could, in theory, repeat the word *whom*, say, *ad nauseam*) but we do not expect them plausibly to do so.

11 Glynn's argument partly concerns 'reductionism'. This is the idea that it is possible to treat a complex system as if it were a simpler one. The experimental method is *necessarily reductionist*. It is inevitably necessary to simplify (e.g., to focus on a single change and control other variables) to carry out an experiment. An important distinction lies between reductionist *methods*, which are necessary, and reductionist *explanations*, which are likely mechanistic and wrong. A bivariate method is reductionist,

exploring the relationship between two and only two variables, X and Y. But we do not claim that changes in Y cause changes in X. Indeed, a common critique of multivariate models is that they fall into the trap of 'explaining' the data by the particular combination of pre-given variables presented to the algorithm. Overfitting is a reductionist *explanation* as well as a reductionist method.

12 This is not a new debate. Artificial intelligence has been dominated for half a century by an argument between proponents of greater *processing* effort and those advocating greater *knowledge*.

13 Some mathematical models are fragile and fall apart if you break a rule. To take a trivial example, if *and only if* $x + y = z$, then $x = z - y$. By contrast, statistical models weaken gradually the more assumptions are broken. This principle of *graceful degradation* (or improvement, if you proceed in the opposite direction) means that even if you can never guarantee that every case in the dataset can freely alternate, every step that systematically subtracts Type C cases will improve plausibility, focus and robustness. Note 'systematically': processes of elimination must be applied to the whole dataset.

4

CHOICE VERSUS MEANING

4.1 Introduction

Linguistic researchers are often interested in *semasiological* variation, that is, how meanings of words and expressions vary over time or between varieties. How do new meanings come about? Why do others decline? Do old meanings die or retain a specialist use?

In the previous chapter, we considered *onomasiological* variation in the choice of words or constructions expressing the same meaning. In an alternation study, meaning is held to be stable if not constant. We might express a choice rate as follows:

> Given that a speaker or writer wishes to express some thought, T, what is the probability that they will choose expression E_1 out of a set of alternate forms $\{E_1, E_2 \ldots\}$ available to express it?

We classed these alternate forms, E_1, E_2 as 'Type A', 'Type B', and so on, to emphasise their capacity for mutual substitution. The probability of choosing E_1 is meaningful in the language production process: the baseline is the set of options to express T available to the speaker at the point of utterance.

Semasiological researchers are concerned with a different probability:

> Given that a speaker or writer used an expression E, what is the probability that their meaning corresponded to thought T_1 out of a set of possible thoughts $\{T_1, T_2 \ldots\}$?

DOI: 10.4324/9781003622697-6

For the hearer, this measure can also be thought of as a special kind of *exposure rate*: how often should a hearer/reader expect to interpret E as expressing T_1? From the speaker's perspective, onomasiological variation is variation in *choice rates*, and semasiological variation is variation in *meaning rates*.

Since most corpora are not annotated for sense disambiguation, researchers have two options. They may systematically annotate the corpus for the different senses in their study, and then abstract their data from it. Usually they abstract data first and then classify the resulting dataset according to those senses. For example, Levin (2013) examined changes in the proportion of meanings of progressive BE *thinking*, including formulaic and 'grammaticalised' ones. See Chapter 7. He extracted cases and then sorted them by hand.

This second approach is quicker, but it has a major drawback. We have not captured alternative ways of expressing each meaning, E_2, E_3, etc. In this chapter, we argue that this step should be an essential component of semasiological studies.

For illustrative purposes, we will examine a phenomenon for which data are straightforward to extract. Existing grammatical annotation in most corpora will readily identify different senses of *very*.

4.2 The Meanings of *Very*

Historically there have been three principal uses of *very* in British English, which are easily grammatically distinguished, and have distinct meanings or senses:

1 *Very* as a particularising adjective: '*very* N', for example, *the very person*$_{N}$. Historically it is the dominant form, but it is rare in contemporary English.
2 *Very* as an intensifying adverb modifying an adjective: '*very* ADJ', for example, *the very tall*$_{ADJ}$ *person*. This seems to have been the first alternative use of *very* to arise. It is the dominant form in contemporary English.
3 *Very* as an intensifying adverb modifying another adverb: '*very* ADV', for example, *very slightly*$_{ADV}$ *moving*. This is also a frequent case today.

This is not a complete set of possible constructions. There are 12 instances of *very* modifying a preposition in DCPSE, as in *very near Astor College* (DI-B10 #227), and *very like Franz* (DL-C01 #158).

We can see how these three broad uses of *very* have changed in their relative proportion over time. The meanings of *very* one might be exposed to have consequently also changed.

Even within the limited three-decade period covered by the DCPSE corpus, it is possible to find changes in proportions of the meanings of *very*.

We use Fuzzy Tree Fragments (FTFs, Chapter 1) to ensure that *very* refers to a particular head noun, adjective or adverb. (Since patterns are simple and intervening elements are disallowed, a lexical tagged query, '*very* <N>', and so on, while slightly less precise, is probably sufficient for experiments with a tagged corpus.) In the FTFs, the premodifier consists only of the single word *very*.

Table 4.1 summarises data extracted from DCPSE.

TABLE 4.1 Data for the use of *very* modifying a noun, adjective and adverb, drawn from DCPSE using the FTFs in Figure 4.1.

	very N	*very* ADJ	*very* ADV	*Total*
LLC (1960s)	**27**	**1,194**	**415**	1,636
ICE-GB (1990s)	**23**	**950**	**248**	1,221
Total	50	2,144	663	2,857

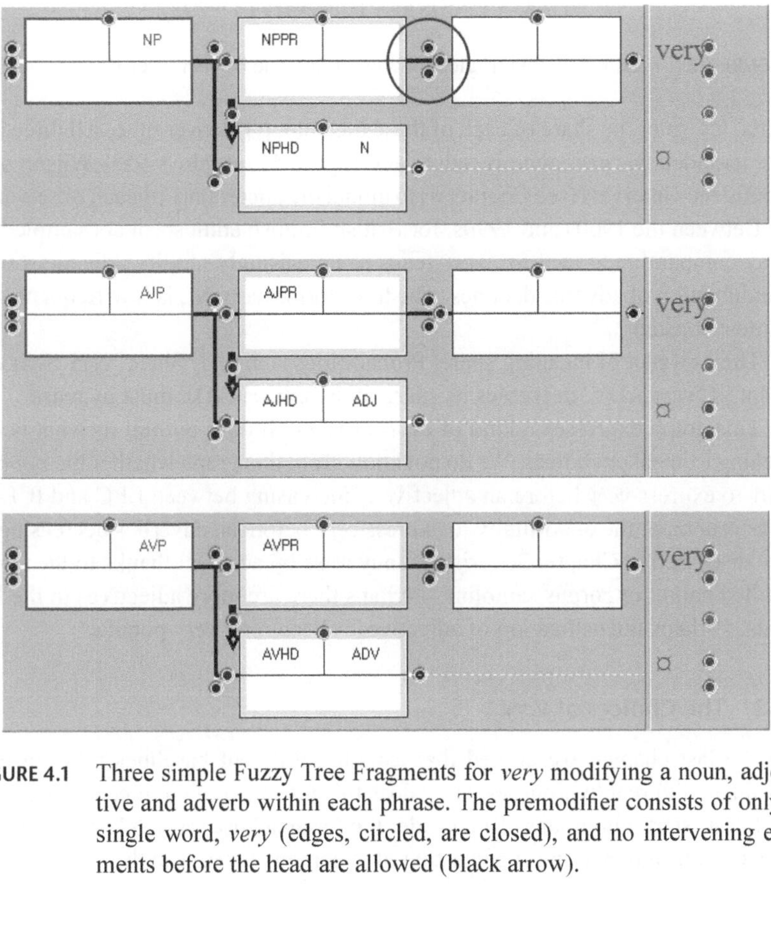

FIGURE 4.1 Three simple Fuzzy Tree Fragments for *very* modifying a noun, adjective and adverb within each phrase. The premodifier consists of only a single word, *very* (edges, circled, are closed), and no intervening elements before the head are allowed (black arrow).

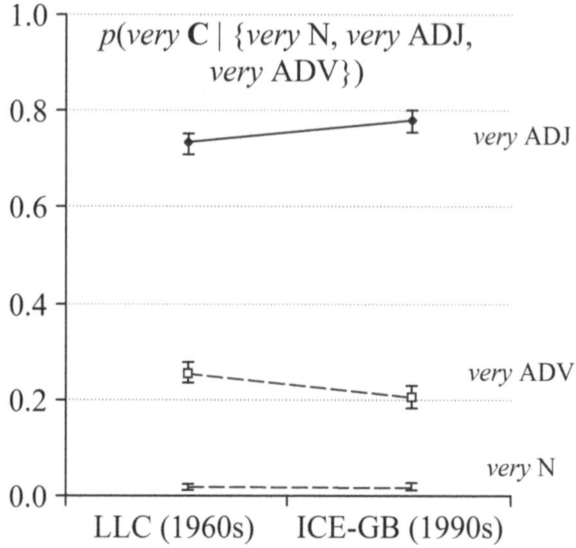

FIGURE 4.2 Plotting semasiological change in the use of *very* over time in DCPSE.

First, let's plot the share of each of these meaning types over time. All three lines are included because none is redundant. Figure 4.2 employs 95% Wilson score confidence intervals (see Chapter 6) to model the uncertainty of each observation.

Between the 1960s and 1990s, for British English adult speakers sampled in a way comparable to DCPSE, *very* tends to increasingly modify adjectives while modification of adverbs declines. The third form, '*very* N', is low frequency and almost constant.

This is a plot of meaning share. Probabilities sum to 1. Since '*very* N' is constant, if '*very* ADV' decreases its share of uses, '*very* ADJ' must increase.

This graph expresses a kind of *exposure rate*. It does not tell us what is happening to speaker choices. We do not know from this graph whether the *opportunity* to express *very* before an adjective is increasing between LLC and ICE-GB subcorpora, or the opportunity to express *very* before an adverb is decreasing. As we discussed in Chapter 3, variation may arise by accident thanks to the uncontrolled nature of corpus sampling. Perhaps there are more adjectives in the later data. Perhaps intensification of adjectives is becoming very popular!

4.3 The Choices of *Very*

In the last chapter, we argued that isolating different baselines allowed us to evaluate different hypotheses. How does this insight apply to meaning types?

Let us start with nouns. To consider the 'archaic' use '*very* N', we might create a simple alternation set consisting of synonyms for *very* in this position (e.g., '{*very*, *exact*, *precise*} N'). We modify the noun FTF in Figure 4.1 to substitute the set {*very*, *exact*, *precise*} in the slot for *very* and apply it to the corpus. We obtain examples such as:

(27) I couldn't give you the *exact* date $_{\text{[DI-D09 \#179]}}$
(28) At this *precise* moment she's being taken in hand $_{\text{[DI-B84 \#19]}}$

Alternation with *very* is possible (*very date*, *very moment*), although it sounds archaic to modern ears. We should not rule out such cases on this intuition, however, because we are exploring an archaic target construction! The numbers are quite small, and we could eliminate cases that do not appear to alternate, although for illustration we do not do this here.

Plotting '*very* N' against this alternation set obtains the graph in Figure 4.3, alongside a plot with an even more expanded baseline. However, neither baseline suggests a significant variation in use between the two 'time' subcorpora.

Similar results are obtained for '*very* N' in this data against other 'choice' baselines (all NPs with a noun head, all such NPs with a premodifying adverb, etc.). The null hypothesis that '*very* N' is unchanging is not overturned. The form seems archaic and to have reached a plateau.

We turn next to the intensification of adjectives. If we compare '*very* ADJ' against a baseline of adjectives with a premodifying adverb of any type (i.e., 'ADV ADJ'), we see no significant change over time (Figure 4.4, lower line). However, not all adverbs alternate with *very*.

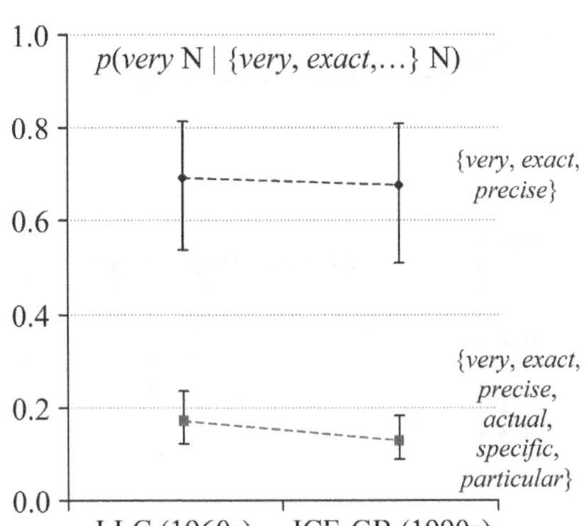

FIGURE 4.3 Plot of *very* N against two baselines of particularising adjectives before a noun, over two time periods in DCPSE. Against both baselines the changes are non-significant.

A sensible first step to improving the baseline is to consider existing annotation. In the TOSCA/ICE scheme, *very* is generally classed as a plain intensifying adverb with no other features. We could evaluate *very* against a baseline of intensifying adverbs in this 'slot' by modifying the appropriate FTF in Figure 4.1.

We use the same FTF structure with the '*very*' node replaced by 'ADV(inten, ¬comp, ¬sup)', that is, 'an intensifying, but not a comparative or superlative, adverb'. See Figure 4.6. This eliminates non-intensifying *wh*-adverbs and superlatives such as *most*. Examples of this restricted set include

(29) I was <u>*really*</u> *interested* in that $_{\text{[DI-A07 \#96]}}$
(30) I'm <u>*a bit*</u> *confused* really $_{\text{[DI-A08 \#3]}}$
(31) I was getting <u>*quite*</u> *fond* of him $_{\text{[DI-B41 \#25]}}$

This set includes 'downtoners' (de-intensifiers) like *quite* and *a bit*, which we might remove as not being a plausible alternate for *very*. In the last chapter, we discussed improving a baseline by subsampling and reviewing cases. We consider an alternative approach in the next section.

Consider what happens with this 'plain intensifier' baseline. When plotted against the revised baseline, '*very* ADJ' (upper line in Figure 4.4) declines from around 44% of cases to 34% (both 95% confidence intervals are around plus or minus 2%). This contrasts with Figure 4.2, which reported that '*very* ADJ' is increasing its *share* of all uses of *very*.

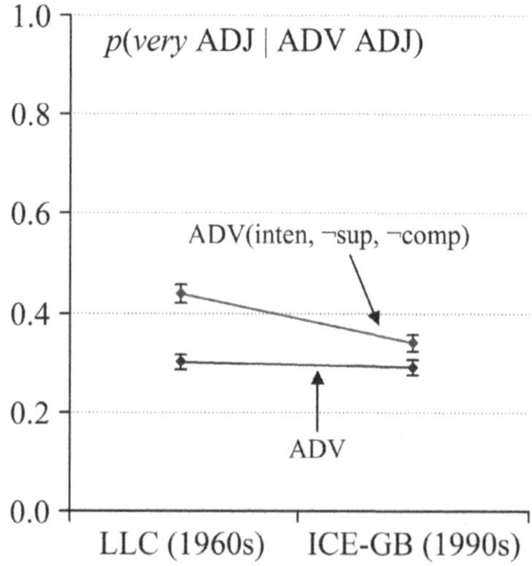

FIGURE 4.4 Plot of *very* ADJ against two baselines of adverbs before a head adjective: all adverbs (lower), restricted set (upper).

The same approach may be applied to adverbs. First, we evaluate '*very* ADV' against a baseline of comparable adverbs. This reveals a significant and quite steep fall in our data (Figure 4.5). The lower line in the graph shows the changing proportion of uses of *very* given that the speaker used an adverb in that position. The upper line shows the changing proportion against a baseline of intensifying (and not comparative or superlative) adverbs in this position.

This baseline also contains downtoners. The FTF for intensifying, non-superlative or comparative adverbs obtains examples such as the following:

(32) <u>*quite*</u> *possibly* Imola $_{\text{[DL-B02 \#259]}}$
(33) it's <u>*much*</u> *more* recently than that $_{\text{[DL-B02 \#53]}}$
(34) we leave it <u>*so*</u> *late* preparing it $_{\text{[DL-B04 \#365]}}$

Subjecting this output to a mutual substitution test again reveals that we should remove adverbs such as *fairly* and *quite*. *Much* is an 'uptoner' and might be considered to alternate with *very*, but replacement often involves the addition of *more*.

Where does this leave us with interpreting patterns of semasiological change in the data? Whereas '*very* N' does not change significantly in either direction, both '*very* ADJ' and '*very* ADV' decline over time when compared with other intensifying adverbs in the same positions. This might be due to the rise of another popular form, or an increasing diversity of forms.

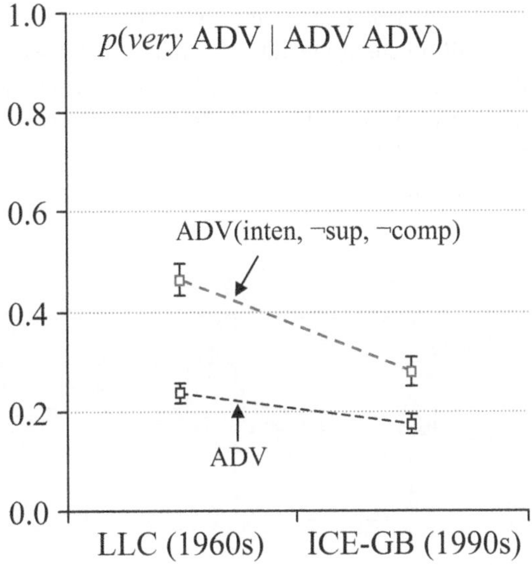

FIGURE 4.5 Plot of *very* ADV against two baselines of adverbs before the head adverb.

Whatever the reason, we can see that the changing semasiological distribution ('shares') of *very* in Figure 4.2 is taking place within an overall decline in favour of other intensifying adverbs. But we needed to identify alternates and plot Figures 4.4 and 4.5 to identify this.

4.4 Refining Baselines by Type

Our previous baseline classes were not very satisfactory from a meaning-preservation perspective. Not all intensifying, non-comparative and non-superlative adverbs are uptoners like *very*. When we study alternation within a 'closed class', like pronouns or modal verbs, we can simply enumerate the category to identify potential alternates. But this task is more difficult with open class items like nouns, verbs, adjectives and adverbs.

In Chapter 3, we briefly discussed refining a baseline for phrasal verbs by reviewing *tokens* (i.e., instances). We reviewed Latinate verbs by examining every utterance in which the construction occurs and deciding whether the verb was capable of alternation with a phrasal verb. Random subsampling was used to make the process tractable.

Here we briefly consider an alternative approach. This is to review adverb alternates for *very* by reviewing *types* (distinct patterns or words) rather than tokens. This builds on the '*very* N' example where we identified a small set of particularising adverbs that might alternate with *very*.

Adverbs are a large set, but they are relatively closed compared to nouns and verbs. Suppose we are interested in finding an alternation baseline for *very* that is more plausible than all 'intensifying' adverbs. In particular, we wish to eliminate downtoners and other modifiers that do not plausibly alternate with *very*.

First, we will restrict data slightly, employing the generic FTF pattern in Figure 4.6. Applying this FTF to DCPSE finds 2,616 cases in the LLC part of 'DCPSE' and 2,680 in the later 'ICE-GB' part (see Table 4.3). This defines the

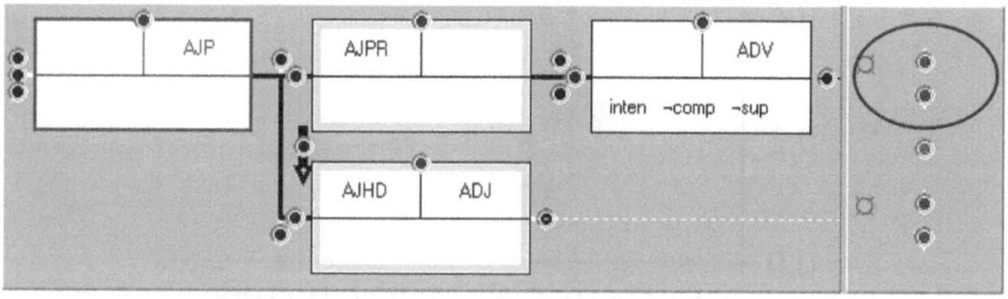

FIGURE 4.6 Generic FTF for adjective premodification (cf. '*very* ADJ'), restricting premodifying adverbs to those that are intensifying, but not comparative or superlative.

total set of all possible cases. All subsequent steps modify the word tagged by the adverb (circled upper right).

Lexical types tend to exhibit an exponential frequency distribution (Zipf, 1949), with a small number of high-frequency types covering many cases. If a single high-frequency type can be reliably classified as 'a downtoner' or 'an uptoner', we can save ourselves a lot of work. We only need review individual tokens (cases) for words like *quite* that have both potential meanings.

Software programs may extract data in different ways. ICECUP's lexicon tool can be limited to 'ADV(inten, ¬comp, ¬sup)', data exported to Excel™, sorted by frequency and then reviewed. The idea is to extract 'the top 95 percentile' (or a lower proportion, if you prefer), and classify these.

Excluding compounds, this method obtains some 40 intensifying (non-superlative or comparative) regular adverbs, accounting for 95% of all cases. The list leaves out compounds like *a lot, a bit, sort of* or *round about*, which account for another 1,481 adverb tokens (cases). Adding these to the list makes the set more diverse, and obtains the 54 types in Table 4.2. Words like *how* and *the* also arise as part of compound adverbs.

The table gives us two things: an ordering, and a cut-off point for deciding when to stop. Five types {*very, quite, so, just, much*} represent over half the tokens. Of these, *just* and *much* can be eliminated in this 'first pass'. A mere 14 types cover three quarters of all tokens, and so on. We can work down this list and categorise tokens according to whether they have any meaning that might alternate with *very*.

Elimination by type assumes it is possible to make this decision without context, which may be difficult for *quite*. If we are in doubt – as we are for *quite* and possibly *much* – we simply review cases in the corpus. Close synonyms of *very* in this list include *so, really, terribly* and *extremely*. Reviewing examples of these suggests that alternation with *very* is generally possible.

Having obtained a list, we first reinsert *very*, and then the set of potential alternates, into Figure 4.6, and obtain frequency data for each category of the independent variable (1960s, 1990s).

We have now classified about 95% of cases. Suppose we perform a χ^2 test or observe a significant difference in a Binomial difference graph. We have not exhaustively evaluated all our data. How can we be sure that the 'long tail' of unseen diverse types does not undermine the result?

If we have not got a significant result at this stage, we cannot perform the following step.

First, we search for cases absent from the 54-word list. We replace *very* in Figure 4.6 with the list, and subtract the total from the generic FTF search result. Few remaining instances are found in practice: 49 in the older corpus and only 1 in the 1990s data. It seems the remaining 5% are rarely found before an adjective. We could review these 50 cases manually, but we will take a different tack.

We adjust the contingency table. Note we did not employ random sampling to sort types, but frequency prioritisation. We cannot therefore assume that the remaining '5% of types' (50 tokens) have the same tendency to alternate with *very* as the preceding 95%. Instead we use a simple logical argument.

Consider two extreme possible scenarios:

a) the remaining 5% are *all* Type B (uptoners) in LLC and *all* Type C (downtoners) in ICE-GB; or
b) the 5% tail are all of Type C in LLC and Type B in ICE-GB.

TABLE 4.2 The top 95 percentile of intensifying adverb types in DCPSE: 54 types ordered by decreasing frequency constitute the top cumulative proportion, Cum(p), summed from the top. Coding: '✓' = uptoner, '?' = probable superlative.

	ADV(inten)	f	p	Cum(p)		ADV(inten)	f	p	Cum(p)
✓	***very***	3,052	0.2481	0.2481	✓	***perfectly***	78	0.0063	0.8733
	quite	1,234	0.1003	0.3484	?	***absolutely***	77	0.0063	0.8795
✓	***so***	788	0.0640	0.4124		*a little*	72	0.0059	0.8854
	just	622	0.0506	0.4630	✓	***a lot***	70	0.0057	0.8911
✓	***much***	622	0.0506	0.5135	✓	***enough***	68	0.0055	0.8966
	sort of	614	0.0499	0.5634		*that*	64	0.0052	0.9018
	rather	416	0.0338	0.5973		*more than*	58	0.0047	0.9065
✓	***too***	400	0.0325	0.6298	?	***entirely***	53	0.0043	0.9108
	about	357	0.0290	0.6588		*kind of*	50	0.0041	0.9149
	a bit	259	0.0211	0.6798		*over*	43	0.0035	0.9143
✓	***really***	249	0.0202	0.7001	✓	***awfully***	37	0.0030	0.9173
	as	231	0.0188	0.7188		*partly*	35	0.0028	0.9202
	almost	215	0.0175	0.7363	✓	***straight***	33	0.0027	0.9229
✓	***well***	173	0.0141	0.7504	✓	***highly***	33	0.0027	0.9255
	fairly	156	0.0127	0.7631	✓	***indeed***	29	0.0024	0.9279
	pretty	145	0.0118	0.7749		*the*	29	0.0024	0.9303
	slightly	134	0.0109	0.7857	✓	***jolly***	27	0.0022	0.9325
	a little bit	125	0.0102	0.7959	?	***fully***	26	0.0021	0.9346
✓	***terribly***	117	0.0095	0.8054		*practically*	26	0.0021	0.9367
?	*completely*	110	0.0089	0.8144		*virtually*	25	0.0020	0.9387
✓	***far***	106	0.0086	0.8230		*how*	24	0.0020	0.9407
	nearly	95	0.0077	0.8307	✓	***badly***	22	0.0018	0.9425
?	***totally***	94	0.0076	0.8383	?	***utterly***	22	0.0018	0.9442
?	***all***	91	0.0074	0.8457		*reasonably*	21	0.0017	0.9459
✓	***extremely***	91	0.0074	0.8531		*somewhat*	21	0.0017	0.9477
✓	***right***	88	0.0072	0.8603	✓	***incredibly***	20	0.0016	0.9493
	more or less	82	0.0067	0.8669		*hardly*	18	0.0015	0.9507

The idea is we select the scenario that has the potential to undermine our observed significant change, the 'worst-case scenario'. We reclassify cases and reapply the significance test. If the decline is still significant, we need not review the remaining 5%.

Consider the onomasiological analysis of '*very* ADJ'. Against the 95% refined set we find a fall in '*very* ADJ' from p = 65.6% to 58.4%, with 95% intervals of ±2.4% (see Table 4.3, left, and upper line, Figure 4.7).

This means the worst case is scenario (a), where the unclassified 5% are all Type B in LLC (reducing the larger proportion) and all Type C in ICE-GB (eliminated, so not changing the baseline). We adjust n by assuming that all 49 cases in the tail alternated with *very*, which reduces p to around 63.9% (see Table 4.3). The fall is still significant.

TABLE 4.3 Applying a worst-case adjustment to an observed fall in p(*very* ADJ). The column 'tail' is the number of tokens of the FTF pattern in Figure 4.1 with a word not listed in Table 4.2.

very ADJ	*f*	*n*	*p*	*all cases*	*reviewed*	*tail*	*worst-case n*	*p*
LLC (1960s)	1,167	1,778	0.6564	2,616	2,567	49	→ **1,827**	0.6388
ICE-GB (1990s)	949	1,625	0.5840	2,680	2,679	1	1,625	0.5840

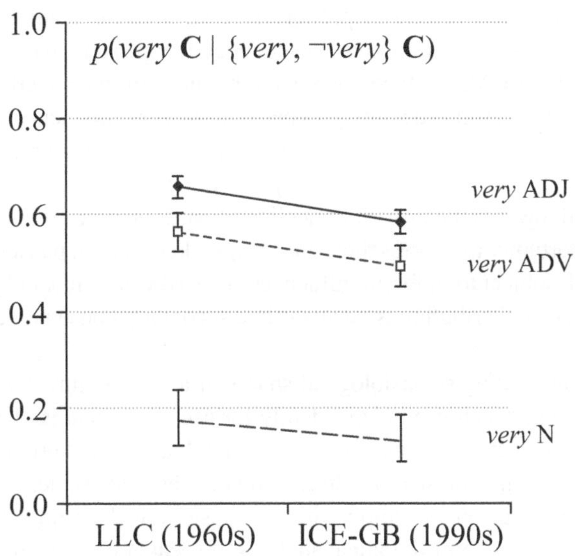

FIGURE 4.7 Independent onomasiological trends for '*very* N', '*very* ADJ', and so on, against members of an optimal set of particularisers or intensifiers.

The worst-case scenario is that the unseen data ('tail' column) distributes in such a way as to potentially undermine the result for the 95 percentile list we reviewed. If the result is still significant *in the same direction* after applying this adjustment, we can uphold the result. We are erring on the side of caution, and can cite our data according to this worst-case analysis. The idea of combining worst-case logic and statistical modelling to improve the robustness of research is discussed further in Chapter 15.

4.5 Conclusions

Observing semasiological change is not as straightforward as may first appear.

The semasiological *share* of different meanings in Figure 4.2 represents a kind of 'exposure rate': the chance a hearer or reader will be exposed to that meaning rather than another. This experimental model is based on a heterogeneous collection of choices.

Results of this kind may not be robust, as this heterogeneity means data come from uncontrolled sources. When we employ choice baselines we factor out variation by identifying opportunities to use an expression. But when we plot proportions of non-alternating cases we pool data from different opportunities. This variable is free to vary – '*very* N' might be 100% in a historic population – but it is not undergoing mutual substitution with the other forms in the study. See Table 3.4, Chapter 3.

An apparent change in the relative proportion of one sense within a set of different senses (e.g., the increasing proportion of *very* before an adjective) does not necessarily represent a variation in the tendency for speakers to prefer it. Indeed, we found that '*very* ADJ' fell compared to other intensifying adverb premodifiers of adjectives. (It was also declining in per million word frequency.)

Within a semasiological distribution or graph, diverse meanings of a word or construction should be considered independent, even if we observe an overall general trend towards the growth or decline of particular meanings. The motivation and opportunity to express those meanings takes place in particular locations in texts, each subject to different influences. This is what is meant by saying that a semasiological distribution is necessarily a secondary consequence of primary choices.

Rather than plotting semasiological shares of a type, Figure 4.7 simply plots the onomasiological choice independently for each type, that is, the tendency to employ *very* against an alternate token baseline. Independent proportions do not sum to 1, but we may present the three trends on the same scale.

The key conclusion is simply this. Semasiological arguments should be underpinned by an onomasiological analysis of speaker choices for each distinct meaning. These analyses are tangential – and complementary.

5

BALANCED SAMPLES AND IMAGINED POPULATIONS

5.1 Introduction

What does it mean to say that a corpus is 'representative'?

There are at least three possible answers. A corpus might be said to be representative of the *language as a whole*, because every text is randomly drawn from it. It might be representative of certain kinds of *text* known to be present in the population. Or it might be representative of types of *participant* – literally, of 'the population' of speakers and writers of a language.

Unlike experimental samples, where *instances* are sampled at random from a population, corpora are conventionally sampled as series of whole *texts* or part-texts (including transcribed recordings). If instances were sampled randomly, we can assume that they are, for all intents and purposes, independent from each other. See Chapter 2. But this would require us to collect a random sample of instances for every research task. We discuss this issue in Section 5.5. In Chapter 16, we discuss a mathematical compensation for this problem.

Most corpora are collected according to the idea of a *balanced sample*, that is, the distribution of material has similar proportions in each category, or is in rough proportion with the perceived availability of material, identified in proportions or numbers of words by a *sampling frame*. The sampling frame may also specify a fixed number of words per text. In corpora consisting of *text categories* or 'genres', it will specify the number of texts in each category. It may also specify the proportion of genders, age ranges and other attributes of participants.

A true *random sample of texts*, on the other hand, would populate the corpus purely at random.

DOI: 10.4324/9781003622697-7

There are two advantages of the balanced approach. The corpus collector can concentrate on 'completeness', obtaining texts in any sub-subcategory of the corpus to permit research in this subdomain. A random sample does not guarantee to be equal in its distribution of text types, but a balanced sample can ensure this.

Adopting a balanced sample does not mean we should not ignore the main selection bias corpus compilers have to deal with – *availability*. Whether we actually sample randomly from a population or construct a balanced sample, if we wish to make claims about the language of any sizable populace, we should not rely on the most readily available material, but make every effort to take texts from random, potentially distant, sources. Should we throw a dart at a map like an explorer in Victorian fiction, or blindly thumb a name in a telephone directory to find locations and participants? Or may we record our friends, colleagues and students, and hope that the language sample produced is 'representative' of a larger and more diverse population? The former is preferable; the latter, while common, should really be avoided.

However we obtain recordings and texts, it is difficult to control this sampling process for other variables, such as attributes of speakers. If we select texts from an archive of 18th century legal cross-examination, say, how can we ensure we have equal numbers of words from men and women in both prosecutor and defendant roles?

Sociolinguists have tended to follow Labov (1966) in going further than balanced sampling to recommend *stratified samples* (sometimes called *quota samples*). The aim is to address two issues: including wide variation and sufficient numbers of participants falling into specific subcategories, and avoiding important variables being 'entangled' (e.g., if male participants tend to be younger than female ones). The aim is to attempt to sample the population of speakers proportionately, but also to maintain the independence of variables describing them.

A stratified sample need not have *equal* numbers of cases in each stratum, but they should be in *consistent* proportions. A corpus with one third words uttered by women, for example, should ideally have the same proportion in every text category and age group.

However, the aim of a stratified sample may place unfeasible requirements on compilers. The *International Corpus of English* (ICE) project (Greenbaum, 1996b) collected equal-sized text categories in varieties of English worldwide. It is stratified by text category and variety. But some ICE teams found it difficult to obtain telephone calls. Similarly, how might one collect representative data for men and women from societies that severely limit women's opportunities? As we noted in Chapter 1, a written corpus is necessarily a sample of the *literate* portion of the population, with all the demographic limitations this might entail.

Maintaining strict independent partitions helps the researcher differentiate variables and potential correlations. We want to eliminate the risk of a third variable *Z* predicting both *X* and *Y* (see Chapter 2). However, the more variables we include, the greater the number of combinations of variables to be found and sampled, with the result that 'full' stratification is rarely attainable.

This difficulty raises another obvious question, namely: what if there are no data in a given intersection? Or what if cases are extremely rare, and to include them would make the corpus unrepresentative? It turns out that desirable principles of 'representativeness' and 'inclusion' often pull in opposite directions (Wattam, 2015).

Inevitably corpora embody a compromise because *different research questions impose different requirements on experimental samples*. When we collect a corpus, we cannot envisage the many research purposes to which it may be applied.

A simple example will suffice. Suppose we compile a corpus neatly stratified into subcorpora of the same numbers of words for men and women, for different age groups, in each category. But this corpus may still generate a skewed sample *for a given research question*: say, examining *shall* versus *will*. The opportunity {*shall*, *will*} is not certain to be in proportion to the number of words. It may be that in our sample, women happen to be communicating more in texts where future planning and prediction is more common than average. Our careful stratification efforts are thereby undermined!

Ultimately, as Gries (2015) rightly observes, we must accept that sampling is likely to be uneven and try to address this in our analysis methods.

5.2 A Study in Genre Variation

A study in the sensitivity of modal variation across genres (text categories) nicely demonstrates why we should be careful in explaining results and making statements about sampling. Bowie et al. (2014) examined changes in the frequency of modal verbs over time in the spoken genres of the *Diachronic Corpus of Present-day Spoken English* (DCPSE).

Table 5.1 summarises statistically significant percentage decreases and increases of individual modal verbs against a tensed verb phrase baseline ('tVP', see Chapter 3) over time. Data are drawn from LLC and ICE-GB subcorpora (broadly, '1960s' and '1990s') of DCPSE.

The table summarises independent change from the 1960s to 1990s for individual core modals in each spoken 'genre' category, and presents percentage changes if they are statistically significant. Thus a highlighted figure of '−42%' means that the item concerned (*may* in 'informal face-to-face conversation', say) declines significantly, at a best estimate of 42% from its earlier level (calculated with a Newcombe-Wilson test, see Chapter 7).

For our purposes, the percentages do not matter, but the direction of travel, indicated by the font in the cell, is relevant. Bold font represents a significant fall over time, italic, an increase.

TABLE 5.1 Significant changes in the proportion of individual core modals out of tensed VPs from LLC (1960s) to ICE-GB (1990s), expressed as percentage difference from LLC (bold = fall, italic = rise, 'ns' = non-significant at α = 0.05). After Bowie et al. (2014).

	can	*may*	*could*	*might*	*shall*	*will*	*should*	*would*	*must*	*All*
formal face-to-face	ns	ns	ns	ns	ns	ns	**−60%**	ns	**−75%**	ns
informal face-to-face	*27%*	**−42%**	ns	*47%*	**−32%**	ns	ns	ns	**−53%**	ns
telephone conversations	**−37%**	ns	**−44%**	ns	**−56%**	**−30%**	ns	**−44%**	ns	**−35%**
broadcast discussions	**−41%**	**−59%**	ns	ns	**−83%**	ns	ns	ns	**−54%**	**−20%**
broadcast interviews	ns	**−61%**	ns	**−59%**	ns	**−41%**	**−55%**	**−32%**	**−57%**	**−35%**
spont. commentary	ns	ns	ns	ns	**−93%**	*58%*	ns	ns	**−64%**	ns
parliament language	ns	ns	ns	ns	ns	**−39%**	ns	**−30%**	ns	**−20%**
legal cross-exam	*304%*	ns	ns	ns	ns	ns	*1,265%*	*254%*	ns	*157%*
assorted spontaneous	ns	ns	ns	ns	ns	ns	ns	ns	ns	ns
prepared speech	ns	**−63%**	ns	ns	ns	*327%*	ns	**−32%**	**−48%**	ns
All genres	ns	**−40%**	**−11%**	ns	**−48%**	*13%*	**−14%**	**−7%**	**−54%**	**−6%**

Taking all genres together (see bottom row in the table), apart from *will*, most forms decline significantly as a proportion of tVPs. But in the (large) category of 'informal face-to-face conversation' (second row from top), *can* and *might* significantly increase. Out of the text types, 'legal cross-examination' is an outlier. However, this is the smallest category, a mere 885 text units and nine recorded participants. An increase of 1,265% (12 times) for *should* should therefore be treated with a pinch of proverbial salt!

This table models variation against the potential to employ a modal auxiliary verb, assuming all tensed VPs can take each modal. The paper goes on to evaluate modal verbs as a proportion of a *pooled set* of core modals (i.e., given that a speaker employs a modal verb, which do they use?). This is not an alternation study, even if proportions are free to vary. Speakers do not choose between modal verbs freely in all situations! Opportunity is conflated with choice.

Nonetheless, a 'core modal set' baseline focuses on the question: how does each modal verb vary in relation to the others? Bowie and colleagues recalculated a table for the modal set baseline and clustered text categories together into a category tree (or 'dendrogram') using a simple nearest-neighbour clustering technique. The method, *repertory grid analysis* (RGA, Kelly, 1955), is a descriptive or *exploratory* method.

Text genres were clustered as shown in Figure 5.1. The tree shows 'broadcast discussion' to be closest to the category of prepared speech in their behaviour over

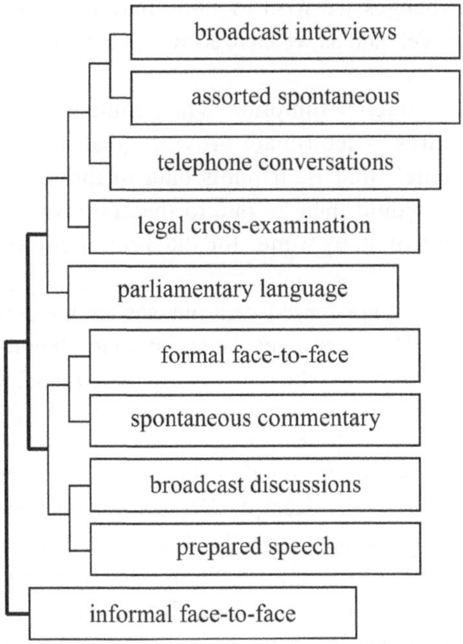

FIGURE 5.1 Repertory grid analysis (RGA) 'dendrogram' tree of text genres, clustered by similarity of within-modal set diachronic change in DCPSE, after Bowie et al. (2014).

time, whereas 'spontaneous commentary' and 'formal face-to-face conversation' are also similar. 'Informal face-to-face conversation' appears as an outlier in this analysis.

The authors also clustered modal verbs by genres, finding, for instance that the set {*shall*, *must*, *may*, *can*} are distinct from the remainder of the core modals in their patterns of change. This tells us how similar each lexical item is to others *in their patterns of changing share of the set of core modals in the data*, not how 'semantically similar' they are!

5.3 Imagining Populations

This study indicates that observed changes in the modal system appear to be more sensitive to genre than is often thought. Even if modal verbs were unusual in this respect, this result should cause us reflection. In short: genre effects are likely to be present in samples.

The claim that changes we wish to study may be sensitive to genre is not itself particularly novel, and as we have seen, lies behind the idea of a 'balanced corpus'.

But a common unstated assumption is that comparing results between corpora of pooled genres is legitimate provided that each corpus 'adopts the same sampling frame', that is, it pools data in the same proportions. Significant differences would then be due to the contrast between the corpora: 'variety' in the case of ICE, 'time' for diachronic corpora such as COHA, and so on.

Neither the modal set nor tensed verb phrases are meaning-preserving baselines (see Chapter 3). However, once we accept that a linguistic phenomenon is sensitive to the type of text in which it is likely to be found, this recognition has profound implications:

1. **Representativeness**. The average, or *mean*, is in proportion to the relevant data in each subsample. For example, ICE corpora contain 60% of speech and 40% of writing. An average across the data will tend to be weighted accordingly. But the proportion of spoken words *actually* produced is probably an order of magnitude greater than writing. See Chapter 1.
2. **Averages conceal variation**. Often it is simpler and far more informative to draw data from particular subtypes (genres). Table 5.1 reveals that parliamentary language and legal cross-examination in DCPSE differ quite markedly – in different ways – from the average trends.

An observed change in a given corpus cannot be extrapolated to, say, 'English' in general. At most, a significant result is one likely to be seen *in similar texts to those found in our corpus, collected in similar conditions and proportions*. We call this extrapolated infinite superset an 'imagined population'.

As a first step, researchers must always be explicit about the process of corpus sampling, and not mistake simulacra for the real thing. TV scripts are not spontaneous speech. Eighteenth century writing might tell us how the literate part of the population wrote, but they do not record daily speech, even when they quote directly.

A good example of a written approximation to speech is the *Old Bailey Corpus* (Huber et al., 2012), a historical corpus that collects 18th and 19th century court statements. But the combination of the court context and uncertain transcription standards should caution us from making strong claims about contemporaneous everyday speech of the period. Far better to refer to an imagined population of 'officially transcribed speech in court contexts like the Old Bailey during that period'.

5.4 Multivariate and Multilevel Modelling

Pooling data affects comparisons. If we pool data from multiple genres – as we might when comparing results from 'balanced corpora' like the *British National Corpus* (BNC), ICE-GB or DCPSE as a whole – *we must compare like-for-like.* It is not enough to say we have 'spoken' data in both corpora. We must ensure that we have the same *proportions* of comparable spoken sub-genres in each corpus. Failing this we are obliged to compare sub-genres separately.

Ultimately the best solution is likely to involve more complex modelling calculations than we have space to discuss in this book. *Multilevel statistical modelling* (Gries, 2015) and 'Q-level' *hierarchical linear modelling* (HLM: Shin & Raudenbush, 2013) are types of multivariate (multi-variable) analysis. Instead of a researcher worrying about which datasets to pool, the computer considers many permutations at a time. A 'multilevel model' codes each instance with group variables (e.g., genre), text variables (date and location), speaker variables (gender, age, education level, etc.) and instance variables (including the dependent variable, e.g., the modal verb).

In this book, we have avoided discussion of multivariate modelling for two reasons. The first is that most people have difficulty grasping fundamental statistical principles. Before a researcher even considers using multivariate methods, they must understand the simple bivariate statistical methods on which they are based.

Sheskin (2011, p. 1431) comments that 'certain assumptions (e.g., normality, homogeneity of variance-covariance and linearity) most of which are also associated with parametric bivariate procedures must not be violated'. Yet sometimes, multivariate algorithms are employed with 'per million word' data that violate the most elementary freedom to vary assumption, conflating opportunity and choice. Glynn's argument in Chapter 3 that multivariate modelling is an 'ecological' substitute for baseline analysis illustrates this confusion. Multilevel modelling, however sophisticated, risks being undermined unless the dependent variable is properly considered in terms of freely varying, ideally meaning-preserving, choices. To be fair, Gries's (2015) alternation example avoids this error.

However, the second problem is that this class of computer algorithms employs processing choices – which model to select, which variables to discard, and so on – that are not transparent, and likely to be taken on trust. Alternative parameters and algorithms obtain apparently different results with the same data! Attempting to find out why this occurs can be extremely difficult and time-consuming.

These methods require considerable care. Multivariate algorithms *build on* the methods described in this book and are not a substitute for them. In the meantime, researchers need to pay much more attention to the potential for diverse results from different text categories and genres.

5.5 More Texts – or Longer Ones?

A sample of utterances drawn from a corpus of a finite number of *texts* is not the same as a genuine random sample of *utterances*. Indeed, two instances of any language event drawn from different texts are more likely to differ than if they were drawn from the same text.

This principle has the characteristic of 'graceful degradation' depending on how instances are distributed within texts. If few instances are drawn from any one text, the dataset is a good approximation to a true random sample. But if a study focuses on a linguistic event that happens to be concentrated in only a few texts, results may be misleading.

We can expect participants and topics to bias repeated choices within a text. Speakers may have conscious and unconscious preferences, and may 'prime' themselves or each other. See Chapter 13. Interesting linguistic phenomena, from text cohesion to templating, count against us if we wish to draw multiple instances from the same text.

Improving the baseline to factor out varying opportunities helps, but it cannot eliminate the problem, because random sampling and random-*text* sampling are distinct. We return to this question in Chapter 16.

Just as with optimising baselines, we cannot fix a weak experimental design with clever statistics. We should consider how best to collect data to generalise to a population, and what kinds of claims can be made on the basis of available corpora.

If we are building a corpus, as well as sourcing texts from wide-ranging participants, we can make another design decision that can help. *A corpus containing many short texts is usually preferable to one with a few long texts*. Apart from the additional compilation effort involved, the only disadvantage of such an approach is it makes it harder to investigate phenomena over the length of a text that require entire texts to be sampled, such as in research into narrative structure. The benefit is in the number of independent participants and contexts.

Planning his *Survey of English Usage* corpus, Randolph Quirk (1960, p. 50) wrote that 'the basis must be copious materials, made up of continuous stretches or "texts" taken from the full range of co-existing varieties and strata of educated English, spoken as well as written, at the present time'. He did not say how long such 'continuous stretches' should be. Eventually, Quirk and colleagues opted for texts of 5,000 words, some spliced together from subtexts. Thirty years later, Greenbaum's ICE-GB corpus consisted of 2,000-word texts.

Aston and Burnard (1997) report that the British National Corpus contains texts of up to 45,000 words with a mean text length slightly less than 25,000 words. The Spoken BNC 2014 contains recordings of an hour and 50 minutes – around 15,000 words for a native speaker. But if our argument is correct, corpus compilers should aim to collect smaller texts, and many more of them!

5.6 Conclusions

Bowie et al.'s results should sound a note of caution against the common assumption that a 'balanced corpus' of numerous types is somehow guaranteed to be 'representative' of English more generally.

We propose the following approaches:

- **Single-genre samples.** If the sample (corpus) is a single type of text, then claims must be couched in terms of *that type of text*. Thus, a corpus drawn from Shakespeare's works does not inform us about 'Elizabethan English' but about a particular type of English found in his works. A corpus of 1990s British English telephone conversations is a source of evidence about British English spoken on the telephone in the 1990s, and so on.
- **Multi-genre samples.** If the sample (corpus) is drawn from multiple text types, it does not give us license to claim that averaged results are generalisable to 'English as a whole', but at most to *an imagined population of an infinite number of comparable corpora.* A statistically significant result in a multi-genre corpus like ICE-GB can be said to generalise to an infinite collection of British English of the same period *obtained in the same proportions and with the same collection method* as the genre categories of ICE-GB.

Lest this seems overly restrictive, it is helpful to distinguish two types of statement: (a) *claims* about what our data show, and (b) *arguments* about what we might predict future research could tell us about other data.

For example, we might *argue* that telephone conversations, being drawn from speakers of the period, will share many characteristics of spoken English of the same period, and we might *predict* some expected behaviour in other text categories as a result. This is a statement of type (b). But we should limit research *claims* (type (a)) to imagined populations of similar data.

An imagined population is easy to misrepresent when converted to shorthand. To take an example we have discussed, British English in the 1990s was – as in all time periods – overwhelmingly expressed through speech. ICE-GB is 60% spoken, but this is almost certainly a tiny fraction of the true proportion in the population of utterances of that period. An imagined population of British English in which 60% is spoken is therefore *heavily weighted towards writing!* But until this is spelled out, it may not be obvious that ICE-GB could not really be representative of 'British English' in that sense.

A better approach is to subdivide data into sub-genres and report results separately where possible. In Chapter 2, we performed a simple interaction experiment (interaction between relative pronoun object *who/whom* and following subject) using all ICE-GB data, then speech and writing separately. A significant result was found in ICE-GB as a whole and in writing, but not in the speech data. Once we know this, it is wise to make separate claims for speech and writing.

With separated claims, any difference in proportions of speech and writing between sample and population become immaterial. We can go further. In ICE-GB, both speech and writing are subdivided, and we may then turn to sub-genres, such as dialogues and monologues.

Multilevel modelling can automate this process and combine multiple variables. It may be used to find the closest fit at different levels of a genre hierarchy for the most salient combination of variables out of a particular set. However, we would raise a different note of caution. The more the researcher cedes control of their research to an algorithm, the more they become dependent on it. We advise performing research carefully and manually first, getting to grips with variable definitions, cleaning up data, and so on, and trying simpler analyses before turning to automatic 'black box' methods.

In conclusion, we might note the following. Researchers should report claims in terms of an 'imagined population of sampled corpora' rather than language in general. And provided sufficient data are available, researchers should avoid pooling data across genres, instead examining phenomena in distinct genres separately.

PART 3

Confidence Intervals and Significance Tests

6

INTRODUCING INFERENTIAL STATISTICS

6.1 Why Is Statistics Difficult?

Imagine you are walking on a country road. It is peaceful and calm. You hear a car coming down a side road. As it rounds the corner and comes into view, the driver loses control and the car crashes into a wall. The driver is fine, but cannot recall exactly what happened.

Let us think about what you experienced. The car crash involves a number of variables that would interest an investigator.

- How fast was the car going? Where were the brakes applied?
- Get out a tape measure. How long was the skid before the car finally stopped?
- How heavy was the car? How loud was the bang when the car crashed? How much damage did the car sustain?

These are *physical variables*. We are used to thinking about the world in terms of these variables: velocity, position, length, volume and mass. They are tangible: we can see and touch them, and we have physical equipment that can measure them.

To this list we might add variables we cannot see, such as how loud the collision was. We might not be able to see it, but we can appreciate that loudness ranges from 'very quiet' to 'extremely loud'! With a decibel meter, we might get an accurate reading, but if you were trying to recall how loud something was to a police officer, you might only give a rough assessment. Some variables, such as time, velocity, acceleration, temperature and colour, are tangible to varying degrees, but require equipment to measure accurately.

DOI: 10.4324/9781003622697-9

We are used to thinking about other variables that might be relevant to a crash investigation. If we were investigating on behalf of the insurance company, we might wish to know about some less tangible variables. What was the value of the car before the accident? How wealthy is the driver? How dangerous is that stretch of road?

We think about the physical world in terms of variables, but we also live in a social world of economic value: the value of the car and the wealth of the driver. These *social variables* may be less absolute or objective. 'Value' can be subjective: the car might be 'vintage'. Different buyers might place a different value on it. Nonetheless, we appreciate the idea that a car can be sold, and in that process, a price attached to it. Likewise, 'wealth' might be measured in different ways or in different currencies. Although not physical variables, they are tangible to us.

But what about that last variable? We asked, *how dangerous is that stretch of road?* This variable is a risk value. It is a *probability*. We could rephrase the question as 'what is the probability that a car would crash on this road?' If we can measure this, we might make useful comparisons. Perhaps we have discovered an accident 'black spot' where there is a greater chance of a road accident than normal.

However, a probability cannot be calculated on the strength of a single event. It can only be measured through a process of systematic observation. We must observe *many* cars driving down the road, count those that crash and build up a set of observations. Probability is not a tangible variable, and it takes imagination to think about it.

The first thing that makes the subject of statistics difficult, compared to, say, engineering, is that even the most elementary variable we use, observed probability, is *not physically tangible*. Cognitive psychologists refer to children learning 'naïve physics', where they learn rules of the physical world through experience. What we might call 'naïve statistics' is much more difficult to acquire. It is also more likely to mislead.

Let us think about our car crash for a minute.

We said that you have never been on this road before. You have no data on the probability of a crash on that road. It would be easy to assume from the simple fact that you saw a crash that, if the road surface seemed poor, or if it was wet from rain, these factors contributed to the accident and made it more likely.

But you have only one data point to draw from. This kind of inference is not valid. It is an over-extrapolation. It is a guess.

Our natural instinct is to form explanations in our mind and to look for patterns and causes in the world. Our brains are wired for pattern recognition.

An important aspect of scientific training is to be suspicious of this inclination. Our intuitions *might* be right, but we must be relentlessly careful and self-critical before we conclude they are.

To evaluate if this location was an accident black spot, we could set up equipment and monitor the corner of the road for accidents. If the chance of an actual accident per vehicle is small, we would need to observe the road for a substantial period of time to get the data we need. This would be a 'natural experiment' (see Chapter 2) observing driver behaviour and crashes.

Alternatively, we might conduct a 'laboratory' experiment and recruit volunteers to drive cars past our corner. Either way, we may need to observe many cars before we could make a realistic estimate of the chance of a crash.

If probability is difficult to observe directly, this must have an effect on our ability to reason about it. Probability is not conceived of like length, say. We all vary in our spatial reasoning abilities, but we experience reinforcement learning from daily observations, tape measures and practice. Probability is much more elusive *because it is only observed from many observations*. This makes it difficult to reliably estimate probabilities in advance and to reason with probabilities.

The psychologists Tversky and Kahneman (1971) reported findings from a questionnaire they gave professional psychologists. Their questions concerned decisions one would make in research based on statements about probability. Not only were these experts unreliable, they exhibited persistent biases, including the one we mentioned earlier – a belief in the reliability of their own observations, even when they had limited data on which to base their conclusions.

So if you are struggling with statistical concepts, do not worry. You are not alone. Indeed, *it is necessary to struggle with probability*. One of our criticisms of traditional statistics teaching is that most treatments skate over the core concepts and dive into statistical tests and methods that the student experimenter, with no conceptual grounding in statistics, must take on faith. Worse, if results fail to replicate (see Chapter 11), they may conclude 'statistics' should be treated with cynicism.

Probability is difficult to observe. It is an abstract mathematical concept that can only be measured indirectly *from many observations*. And a simple observed probability is just the beginning. In discussing inferential statistics, we will need to keep in mind three distinct types of probability, and we will use a simple labelling system:

- the observed probability (or proportion), labelled with lower case p;
- the 'true' population probability, capital P; and
- the probability that an observation is unreliable, error level α.

6.2 The Idea of Inferential Statistics

In Chapter 2, we discussed an experiment exploring the objective case *who/whom* alternation. We observed the proportions $p = p(who \mid \{who, whom\}) = 135/176$ in the spoken part of ICE-GB and $p = 22/63$ in the written subcorpus.

These are statements of *fact* about ICE-GB. We could, if we so wished, cite the fraction 135/176 to any number of decimal places – 0.77, 0.7670, 0.76704545, and so on. We can be as precise as we wish. Similarly, we can cite the ten most frequent words in Shakespeare's *First Folio* with complete certainty – allowing for variant spelling. Such statements would be facts about the text. Statements about a sample are sometimes called *descriptive statistics* (the word *statistic* here being used in its most general sense, i.e., a number).

But our data are collected as a sample of a much larger population, one we could consider effectively infinite: 'objective *who/whom* in early-1990s British English sampled like ICE-GB'. Our dataset is interesting if it tells us something about the wider population from which it is sampled.

The basic idea of *inferential statistics* is to draw an *inference* from our sample to this population. This inference is not a fact. It is a *best guess*, informed by two things: our knowledge of the structure of the data and mathematical laws of randomness.

We can expect our observation to be 'robust' up to a point. That is, we can anticipate that if we repeated our experiment, we would probably get a similar result to the one we found – not an exact replica, but a 'similar' result.

But if a result is 'similar', can we justify quoting p to two, four or eight decimal places? Suppose that instead of seeing 135 cases, we saw 136, something that could happen by chance very easily. Now, p would become 136/176 = 0.77272727. Even four decimal places would be inaccurate. Citing p to two decimal places would still give us $p = 0.77$, but even two decimal places may be an example of overstated precision. How reliable is our sample? How precise are our observations?

Inferential statistics is a method of *extrapolation* from data. It rests on a mathematical model that allows us to predict values in the population based on observations in a sample drawn from that population.

Central to this method is the reporting of not just the observation itself but also the *certainty* of that observation. There is more than one way to express this 'confidence', but a useful approach is to consider the range of plausible values for the true value in the population, P.

Suppose we were to collect, annotate and extract data on objective *who* and *whom* from 100 new corpora of the same size as ICE-GB Release 2, under exactly the same sampling regime. What values of p would we expect to see?

6.3 The Randomness of Life

Life is random because we cannot control it. Conjurers might fix the order of cards they supposedly shuffled, but for most people, the act of shuffling is an act of randomisation. Many games involve an initial randomising stage, shuffling playing cards, throwing dice or performing a snooker break, to create new scenarios to challenge the skill of players or give a weaker player a chance. Randomness is typically generated from either *uncontrolled* processes, like shuffling decks of cards, or *chaotic* processes (Gleick, 1977) where multiple bodies interact non-linearly (see also Chapter 10).

When we sample data from the world, we try to do so without cheating or 'biasing' the sample. We allow these processes to influence our data. We expect randomness.

6.3.1 The Binomial Distribution

The Binomial distribution is a type of *sampling distribution*, a distribution of the total frequency of repeated runs of a *Binomial sampling procedure*, called a 'Bernoulli trial'.

Let us try to do this in practice. It is well worth trying it for yourself with a group of friends. If you are a teacher, you can do this in class. The procedure is as follows:

1. Hand out a coin to each participant, and ask them to decide which side is 'heads'.
2. Ask participants to toss the coin ten times and write down the total number of heads they got on a score sheet. Give them time to complete the exercise. (Expect laughter. Someone will lose their coin.)
3. Then, starting with zero and counting up to ten, ask participants to raise their hands if they got no heads, one head, two heads, and so on. Each time, write down on the board the number of hands raised. Finally, plot a bar chart ('histogram') of these totals.

A pattern I obtained with $t = 20$ students and $n = 10$ coin tosses is shown in Figure 6.1. On this occasion, no students reported getting all tails (no heads) or all heads (no tails).

The number of *heads*, r, is the 'observed frequency', which we previously denoted with f. $\psi(r)$ is 'the frequency of the frequency'. Figure 6.1 plots the number of student participants who observed r heads.

This last point takes some thinking about: it is the number of students who raised their hands saying they got two, three, four heads, and so on. We obtained 20 answers for r, each different because the selection process (coin tossing) was random.

The result is irregular, typical of the patterns you will get if you only perform this sampling process 20 or so times. Randomness is like this: it does not usually produce those nice, neat, smooth distributions we tend to see in books (and we will see later ourselves) except by averaging over *very* many repetitions! What is that peak doing at eight heads?

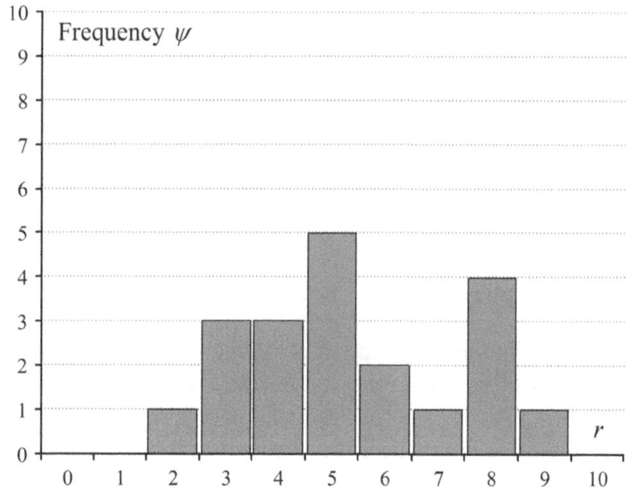

FIGURE 6.1 An observed Binomial distribution for $\psi(r)$, $n = 10$ from $t = 20$ samples, unbiased coins.

As a frequency count, ψ is an integer, and it is not very portable as a result. We can express this distribution in terms of *the chance* that a particular experimental result was r. To do this, we divide by t, the number of 'trials' (samples, students, 'coin toss runs', corpora, etc.):

observed Binomial probability $b(r) = \psi(r) / t$, (13)

In this case, $b(r)$ represents the chance that, should you pick up a score sheet at random, you will find one belonging to a student who threw r heads. So on this occasion, one student had got nine out of ten heads. The probability of picking up the student's score sheet was $b(9) = 1/20 = 0.05$.

Let us recap.

- Every student performed the same 'experiment'. We ran the experiment 20 times (or sampled 20 different datasets). Each student represents a single sample, 'trial' or 'corpus'.
- Crucially (and this is the part that requires thinking about) the graph plots *the distribution of the results of 20 experiments*, not 'the distribution of an experiment' (whatever that might be). Each student had an independent experimental result.
- Suppose we asked each student to repeat the experiment another 19 times as homework (including the student who had 9/10 heads) and write down

the number of times they got each outcome. We can expect them *all* to each obtain a similar result to Figure 6.1 because we think the true rate P for all of them was the same: 0.5. No one was given a 'trick coin'.

This last point is extremely important. Armed with a model of the likely distribution of experimental samples, we can employ it to predict the likely result of *future* runs of the same experiment.

Although we tossed a coin, exactly the same principle applies to any other sampling procedure. The more samples we take, the more accurate our overall estimate of the true rate will be. The best estimate is obtained by averaging the samples. But the *actual* rate for each sample is likely to vary between samples, as we saw here.

We plotted data with a horizontal axis of r out of ten 'heads' observed in each sample. But we could also turn this frequency count into a proportion, p:

$$\textit{observed proportion } p = r \mathbin{/} n, \qquad (14)$$

where n = number of coin tosses in each sample (i.e., 10). Note that this probability is still discrete, so if n is 10, $r \in \{0, 1, 2 \ldots 10\}$, and therefore, $p \in \{0, 0.1, 0.2 \ldots 1\}$.

What happens if we increase n? It is unfair to ask students to toss coins forever, so we will allow a computer to take over.[1] For $n = 20$, we might get the distribution in Figure 6.2.

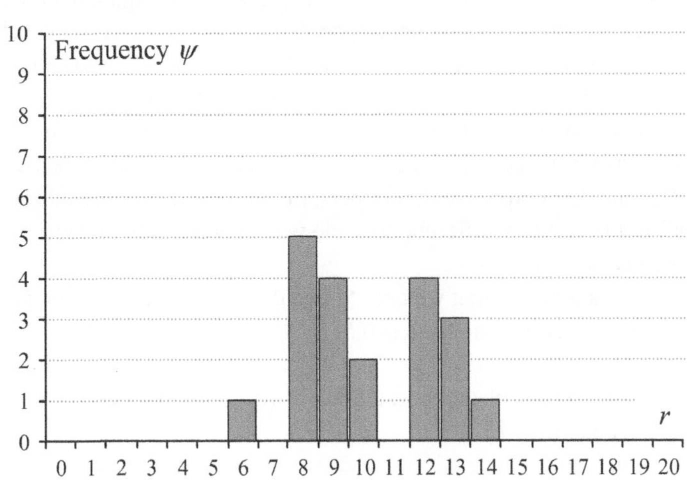

FIGURE 6.2 Results of a randomly sampled simulation of the classroom experiment with $P = 0.5$ and $n = 20$.

As n increases, the distribution tends to 'bunch' closer to P (which *we think* is 0.5). On a frequency axis $\{0, 1 \ldots n\}$, the distribution tends towards $P \times n$, in this case, 10.

This principle is called *The Central Limit Theorem*. If you increase sample size n, the observed proportion p tends to be more reliable (it tends to be closer to the true value, P). In algebra we might write this:

The Central Limit Theorem:

At the limit where $n \rightarrow \infty, p \rightarrow P$. (15)

With our simulator, we can apply and reapply the same random sampling several times. Randomness is still revealed: we get different results each time. We are only repeating our sampling exercise $t = 20$ times. There is still potential for random variation to upset our distribution. Why, for example, in Figure 6.2 are there no examples of 11 out of 20 ($p = 0.55$)?

We can smooth out this randomness if we allow the number of sample trials t to tend to infinity, or, in algebra, $t \rightarrow \infty$. We turn to this next.

6.3.2 The Ideal Binomial Distribution

The graph in Figure 6.3 is the expected distribution of the probability function $B(r)$ after *infinite* sampling, $t = \infty$, assuming that the probability of throwing a head, $P = 0.5$ and $n = 10$. This mathematically ideal Binomial distribution is much more regular than one obtained from 20 random samples ($t = 20$, Figure 6.1). We get no 'twin peaks' or sudden dips.[2]

Like all the graphs we have seen in this chapter thus far, Figure 6.3 is a distribution of observed sample means about a population mean, in this case, the chance of throwing a head of an unbiased coin, $P = 0.5$. If we toss an unbiased coin ten times, the most likely result would be five out of ten heads, but it is not the only possible outcome. It is also possible that there would be four out of ten, six out of ten, and so on. The chance of each outcome is represented by the height of the column.

To calculate this graph, we do not perform an infinite number of coin tosses! We work out how many different possible ways you can obtain zero heads, one head, two heads, and so on.

Imagine for a moment that we only tossed the coin twice. Our coin is fair, that is, the chance of getting one head is 0.5.

- What is the chance of getting zero heads (or two tails, i.e., $r = 0$)? We can write this pattern as TT.
- Now, what is the chance of obtaining two heads (zero tails, $r = 2$) or HH?
- Finally, what is the chance of obtaining *one head* (one tail, $r = 1$)? We can obtain this outcome in two distinct ways – either by throwing one head, then a tail; or by one tail, then one head. We can get HT or TH.

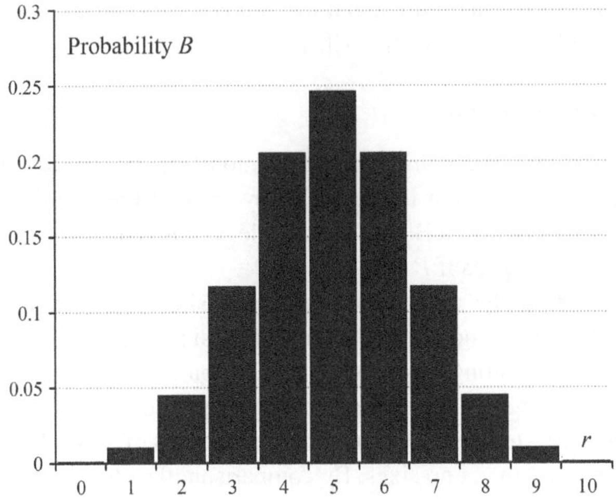

FIGURE 6.3 The ideal Binomial distribution $B(r)$ for $P = 0.5$ and $n = 10$.

Here are the frequency and probability distributions for $n = 2$ and $P = 0.5$:

ideal Binomial frequency distribution $\boldsymbol{\Psi} = \{1, 2, 1\}$,

ideal Binomial probability distribution $\mathbf{B} = \{1/4, 1/2, 1/4\}$.

This is obviously a trivial example. What if the expected probability is not 0.5? What about sample sizes greater than $n = 2$?

The full Binomial formula is more complicated:

$$\textit{Binomial probability } B(r; n, P) \equiv nCr.\ P^r (1 - P)^{(n-r)}, \tag{16}$$

where $P \in [0, 1]$.[3]

This formula simulates the process of sampling. It calculates the probability of observing a particular frequency r, out of a sample size of n, when the true population probability is P.

- The first part of the equation, nCr, is called 'the combinatorial function', which calculates the total number of ways (combinations) you can obtain r heads out of n throws.
- The second part of the function is the chance of throwing each combination. If $P = 0.5$, then this part simply becomes $P^n = 0.5^n$ (or $1/2^n$, if you prefer).

If you would like to read more about the Binomial formula, see Sheskin (2011, p. 311). We will discuss it again in Chapter 8.

6.3.3 Skewed Distributions

One problem with using coin tossing to demonstrate the Binomial distribution is that many people stop at this point. They assume Figure 6.3 is simply 'the expected distribution' for a Binomial variable. But it is the expected distribution if $P = 0.5$. What happens if P is not 0.5?

We could repeat the class experiment with six-sided dice, ask students to throw them ten times and count the number of sixes. Now, $P = 1/6$. Figure 6.4 shows what the resulting ideal expected distribution B looks like. It predicts there is about a 16% chance that a student will get no sixes at all in ten throws (first column), or – to put it another way – in our class of 20 students, on average we would expect 3 to get no sixes. By comparison, the chance of obtaining zero heads for $P = 0.5$ is $1/2^{10}$, slightly less than 0.1%.

Indeed, using Equation (16) with different values of P, we can produce the ideal Binomial distributions in Figure 6.5. We see that as P becomes closer to zero, the distribution becomes increasingly lopsided.

6.3.4 From Binomial to Normal

The Binomial function is quite difficult to calculate and generalise. The first problem is the effort involved in calculating the Binomial distribution for an arbitrary sample size n.

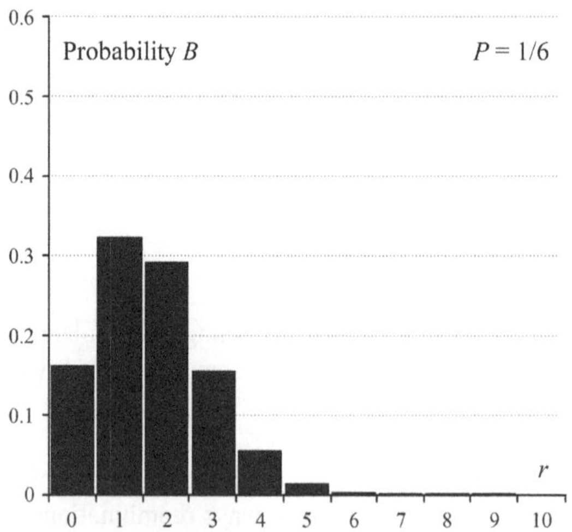

FIGURE 6.4 The ideal Binomial distribution of the probability of throwing r sixes with a die, $n = 10$.

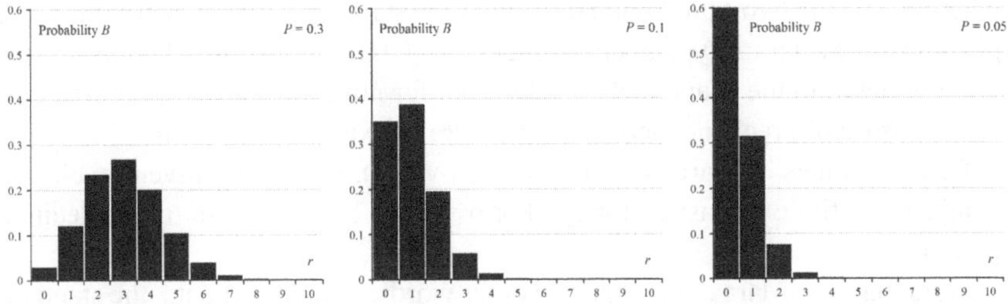

FIGURE 6.5 The effect of varying P on the ideal Binomial distribution B: from left to right: $P = 0.3$, 0.1 and 0.05. If $P = 0$, 100% of the distribution is found in the '0' column.

Historically, this had to be done by hand, and it was pretty heroic to calculate! It is not too difficult to do for small values of n, like $n = 10$. The combinatorial function, nCr, is obtained by multiplying and dividing three factorials, which are very large numbers. The factorial of 10, written 10!, is $1 \times 2 \times 3 \times \ldots 10 =$ 3,628,800. Computers can precalculate factorials, but there are limits.[4]

Second, to carry out a Binomial test (see Chapter 8) or calculate a Binomial sampling interval about P, we must calculate a *cumulative* value of B. We add up a total across a series of values of B.

Realising that the Binomial function is difficult to work with, statisticians performed a trick. They said, *let us assume that the Binomial distribution is approximately the same as the Normal distribution.* This works surprisingly well, but it can obtain slightly different results in certain circumstances.

Stahl (2006) describes some of the lengths that mathematicians used in order to work around this problem before the Normal approximation was discovered. (Indeed, some of the early 'error curves' he shows look very different to either the Normal or Binomial! They are like maps of the world made by medieval navigators.)

The *Gaussian distribution* (renamed 'the Normal distribution' by Karl Pearson) is due to Carl Friedrich Gauss. Gauss derived it by generalising a method of 'least squares' that he had used to predict the position of the moon Ceres, making his name as a young mathematician.

Gauss's equation was originally expressed in a slightly more complex manner, but it can be simplified to a formula with two parameters: the *mean*, in this case, P, and the *standard deviation*, which we will label simply as S:[5]

$$\begin{aligned}
&\textit{population mean } P = F / n, \\
&\textit{standard deviation } S \equiv \sqrt{P(1-P)/n}, \qquad (17) \\
&\textit{Gaussian interval about } P, (E^-, E^+) = P \pm z_{\alpha/2}.S,
\end{aligned}$$

where $z_{\alpha/2}$ is 'the two-tailed critical value of the standard Normal distribution at a given error level α'. A typical error level is $\alpha = 0.05$. We discuss what this means in more detail in the chapters that follow, but for now, you can simply think of α as a measure of precision, and S as a measure of expected variation.

Critical values of z are constant (a fixed value), so for any given level, you can just substitute a constant for $z_{\alpha/2}$. For $\alpha = 0.05$, $z_{\alpha/2} = 1.95996$ to five decimal places.

Note that if n is large, S is small. In other words, with lots of data, the standard deviation – a measure of the width or 'spread' of the distribution – will be smaller than if we have very little data. Like the Binomial, S conforms to the Central Limit Theorem (Equation (15)). This sampling interval identifies the two-tailed expected range of resampled observations p of size n allowing for an error α. A proportion observed outside this range is *significantly different from P*.

It is much easier to perform calculations using the Normal distribution than the Binomial, but it is an *approximation* to the Binomial, and this approximation introduces a small error. If n is large, then the Binomial and Normal tend to match closely, provided P is not very close to zero (or one). For smaller values of n, or if P is close to zero, then it may not match it every single time.

Consider where $P = 0.3$ and $P = 0.05$. In Figure 6.6, the Normal distribution is continuous and symmetric. It follows the Binomial distribution fairly well, but there are some errors.

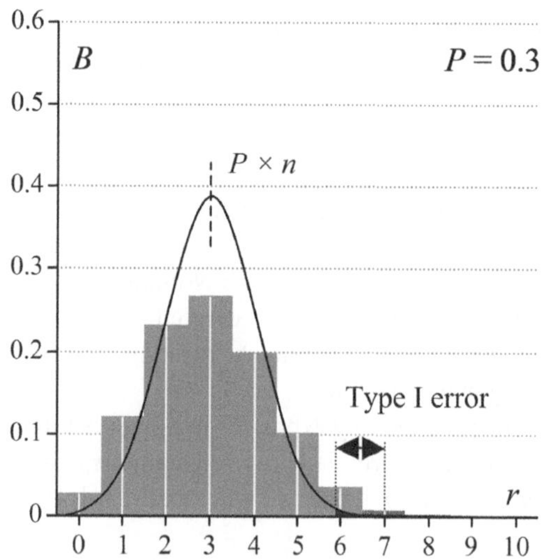

FIGURE 6.6 Binomial and Normal distributions for a random event (e.g., tosses of a trick 'weighted' coin), where the chance of an event (head), the population probability, P, is 0.3 and $n = 10$.

So far, we have drawn the discrete Binomial distribution on an Interval scale, where it looks 'chunky', like a series of tall tower blocks clustered together. But in fact, the Binomial frequency for $r = 1.1$ or 1.5, for example, is undefined. We are comparing the Binomial with a continuous distribution, the Normal, plotted on a Real scale. On this scale, we only compare the *centre point* of the 'chunk', where $r = 0, 1$ (and $p = 0.0, 0.1$) and so on.

As you might expect when substituting one formula for another, there is some disagreement between the two resulting distributions. Many discrepancies are interesting, but have little practical effect. As we shall see, significance tests and confidence intervals concern the *tails* of the distributions in Figure 6.6 (where the area under the curve $\alpha/2 = 0.025$, say). Discrepancies here could lead to a different result in a test.

Using Equation (17) with $P = 0.3$, $n = 10$ and $\alpha = 0.05$, the Normal upper bound of P is $E^+ = 0.5840$. If we observe $p > E^+$ (e.g. $p = 0.6, 0.7 \ldots$), then we say p is significantly different from P.

To calculate the Binomial upper bound for $\alpha = 0.05$, we add up the Binomial column in Table 6.1, working backwards from 1 until the total exceeds $\alpha/2$. We then pick the previous point visited, because the total must be less than $\alpha/2$. For $P = 0.3$ (left columns), we obtain a tail area of 0.0106 and threshold $p = 0.7$.

This method obtains a 'conservative' sampling interval, erring on the side of caution. Had we chosen $p = 0.6$, the tail area would be 0.0473, nearly twice the target of 0.025.

The result is an excess 'Type I' error: the Normal distribution predicts a narrower interval than the Binomial. A significance test comparing $P = 0.3$ and

TABLE 6.1 Binomial and upper cumulative Binomial distributions for $p = r / n$ and $n = 10$ used to add up the upper tail (bold).

	$P = 0.3$		$P = 0.05$	
p	*Binomial column*	*Cumulative area*	*Binomial column*	*Cumulative area*
0.0	0.0282	1.0000	0.5987	1.0000
0.1	0.1211	0.9718	0.3151	0.4013
0.2	0.2335	0.8507	0.0746	0.0861
0.3	0.2668	0.6172	0.0105	**0.0115**
0.4	0.2001	0.3504	0.0010	**0.0010**
0.5	0.1029	0.1503	0.0001	**0.0001**
0.6	0.0368	0.0473	0.0000	**0.0000**
0.7	0.0090	**0.0106**	0.0000	**0.0000**
0.8	0.0014	**0.0016**	0.0000	**0.0000**
0.9	0.0001	**0.0001**	0.0000	**0.0000**
1.0	0.0000	**0.0000**	0.0000	**0.0000**

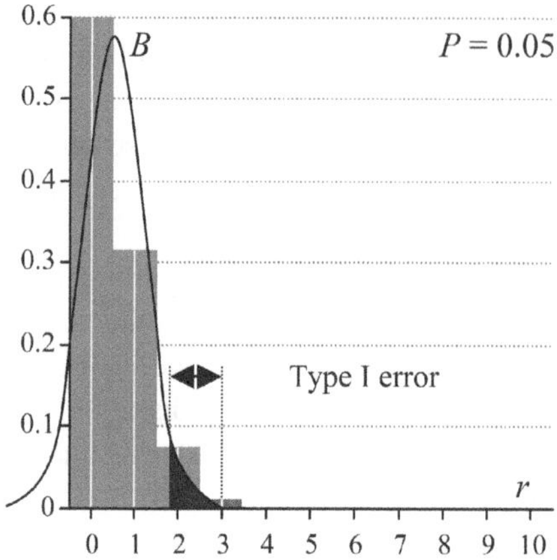

FIGURE 6.7 Binomial and Normal distributions for a random event with low probability, $P = 0.05$.

$p = 0.6$ is significant with the Normal interval but is non-significant with the Binomial.

What happens if $P = 0.05$, as in Figure 6.7? The curve below zero is impossible. As we saw, the Binomial distribution is concentrated at zero heads.

We have another example of this kind of error. The Normal upper bound is 0.1851 (so $p = 0.2$ is significantly different from $P = 0.05$) but the Binomial one is 0.3 (tail area 0.0115, see Table 6.1). Employing the Normal distribution with skewed P and small sample sizes may lead to additional Type I errors compared to the exact Binomial test.

Yates's continuity correction (Yates, 1934) attempts to address these discrepancies by expanding the Normal line outwards from the mean by 0.5 units on the frequency scale. See Figure 6.8. This reduces the number of Type I errors that arise out of the approximation of the Binomial to the Normal, but it makes the test more conservative, increasing the chance of 'Type II' errors.[6]

On a probability scale, the correction is divided by n (i.e., $0.5/n = \frac{1}{2n}$). The sampling interval about P becomes

$$\text{Yates's interval about } P, (E^-_{cc}, E^+_{cc}) = P \pm (z_{\alpha/2} \cdot S + \tfrac{1}{2n}), \tag{18}$$

and the upper bounds for $P = 0.3$ and 0.05 become 0.6340 and 0.2351, respectively. The test performs comparably to the Binomial calculation because it rounds 'out', away from P.

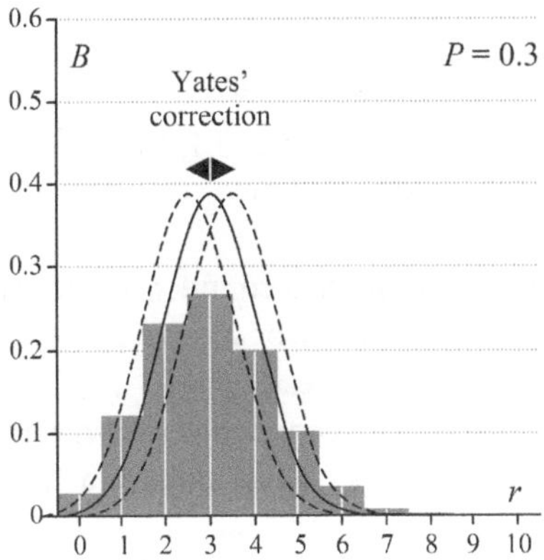

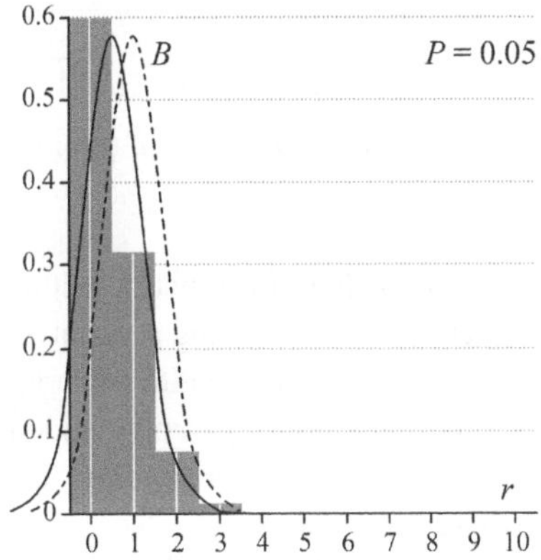

FIGURE 6.8 Visualising Yates's correction applied to Figures 6.6 and 6.7. We add 0.5 to either side of the mean, that is, selecting the dotted line curve on the outside of the figure. The area under this 'combined curve' is now greater than 1.

6.3.5 From Gauss to Wilson

We computed Binomial and Normal distributions about an expected population probability, *P*. We used these to calculate *sampling* intervals about *P*, like Equation (17) and Equation (18). We can employ these intervals in a significance test where we assume a particular value of *P* and test against it. See Chapter 8.

But most of the time, we do not know what *P* is! When we sampled relative pronouns in Chapter 2, we did not know their actual proportions, *P*, in each case. We only had observed proportions, *p*, to go on. Our task is to calculate a *confidence* interval about an *observed* proportion, *p*.

How should we do this? A common mistake is to simply insert *p* in place of *P* in Equation (17). If you see someone quote a 'standard error' for a proportion or cite a 'Wald interval', you are seeing this kind of error. Swapping *P* and *p* leads to all kinds of conceptual confusion. It is in part to avoid this error that in this book, rather than use other symbols, we use capital letters for population values and small letters for sample values.

The correct approach was pointed out by Edwin Bidwell Wilson in 1927, in a paper that appears to have been read by few at the time. His paper was rediscovered in the late 1990s by medical statisticians keen to accurately estimate confidence intervals for skewed observations, that is, where *p* is close to zero or one.

Let us briefly see what happens if we follow the incorrect 'Wald' method for $p = 0.05$, $n = 10$ and $\alpha = 0.05$. This is what we would get:

mean $p = 0.05$,

standard deviation $s \equiv \sqrt{p(1-p)/n} = \sqrt{0.0475/10} = 0.0689$,

Wald Gaussian interval about p, $(e^-, e^+) = p \pm z_{\alpha/2}.s = 0.05 \pm 0.1351$
$= (-0.0851, 0.1581)$.

The true value of P must be within the range [0, 1]. But this confidence interval 'overshoots', modelling a variation of P *that cannot exist*. Worse, where $p = 0$ or 1, the interval has a width of zero. The observation becomes *certain*!

Common advice given to students is 'do not calculate confidence intervals for highly skewed data or small n'. The maths does not work, so just avoid situations where it goes wrong![7]

However, there is a third problem. The Wald interval obtains results that are inconsistent with significance testing, even when it is approximately of the right order of magnitude. Confidence intervals become approximate, not 'proper statistics'. They merit a page or two in textbooks before a veil is hastily drawn over the proceedings.[8]

The source of the problem lies in the careless swapping of p and P in Equation (17). Wilson points out that the correct approach to calculating a confidence interval about p involves an *inversion* of Equation (17). His paper uses mathematical language ('finding the roots of an equation') that may put off the uninitiated. But the simplest way to summarise his argument is this:

> Whenever p is at either the lower or upper sampling interval bound for P (i.e., if p were equal to E^- or E^+), then P must be at the corresponding opposite confidence interval bound for p.

Or to put it another way, if p is significantly different from P, P is also significantly different from p.

We call this axiom the 'interval equality principle' and visualise it with Figure 6.9. It can be written as follows, where w^- and w^+ are the desired lower and upper bounds of a Wilson confidence interval for any error level α:

The interval equality principle:

$$w^- = P_1 \quad \leftrightarrow \quad E_1^+ = p, \text{ where } P_1 < p, \text{ and} \qquad (19)$$
$$w^+ = P_2 \quad \leftrightarrow \quad E_2^- = p, \text{ where } P_2 > p.$$

The first line says 'if the lower confidence bound for p (labelled w^-) equals a possible population mean P_1, then the upper sampling bound for P_1 must be p'. This is pictured in Figure 6.9. The second line does the same for w^+. This approach has general application. See Appendix A.

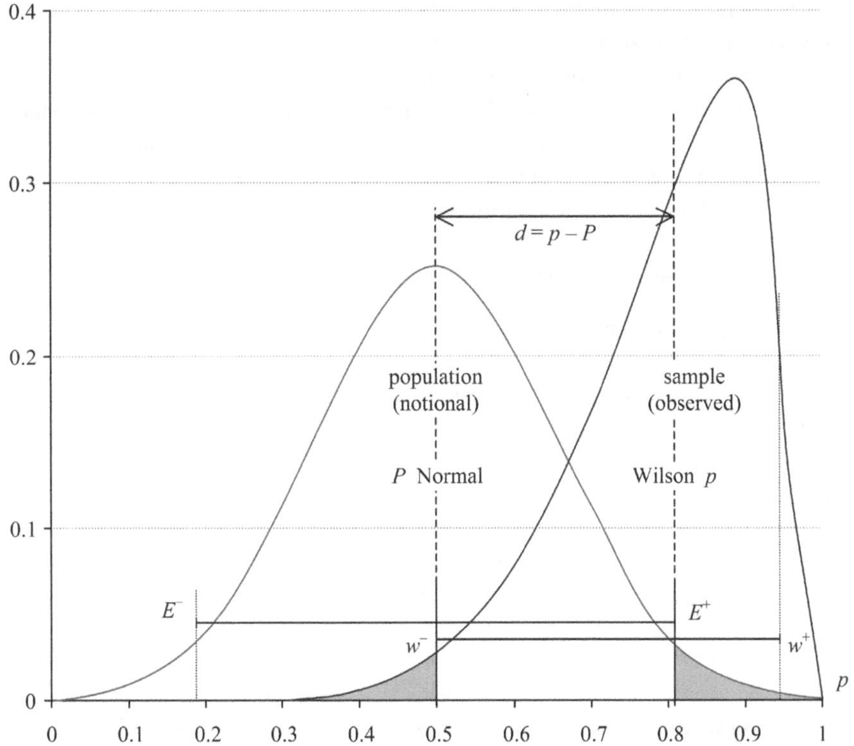

FIGURE 6.9 The interval equality principle with Normal and Wilson intervals (Wallis, 2013a). In this case, the lower bound for p, $w^- = P$. The bounds of the Normal interval about P are E^- and E^+ (which equals p), and the bounds of the Wilson interval about p are w^- and w^+. Distributions for $P = 0.5$ and $n = 10$ are plotted, with two tail areas for $\alpha = 0.05$. These curved 'triangles' have an equal area.†

† Note how the Wilson area is bisected at $p = E^+$, but, due to being squeezed by the boundary at 1, the peak continues to rise, so the mean, median and mode are not equal. The distribution curve is calculated by varying α for $p = E^+$. See Chapter 17. It is possible for $E^+ > 1$, in which case the distribution is not computed.

Let us define two mathematical functions[9] from Equation (17), one for each bound of the Normal distribution:

$$\text{GaussLower}(P; n, \alpha/2) \equiv P - z_{\alpha/2}\sqrt{P(1-P)/n}, \text{ and}$$

$$\text{GaussUpper}(P; n, \alpha/2) \equiv P + z_{\alpha/2}\sqrt{P(1-P)/n}. \qquad (17')$$

You may recall from high school that the inverse of a function, written $x = fn^{-1}(y)$, reverses the effect of a function $y = fn(x)$.[10]

We need to find bounds on p instead of P.

Note that as well as inverting the function, the interval equality principle states that the upper bound for p must translate into *the lower bound* of the corresponding sampling interval on P and vice versa. See Figure 6.9.

We must find values for the following functions:

$$w^- = P_1 = \text{GaussUpper}^{-1}(p;\, n,\, \alpha/2), \text{ and}$$

$$w^+ = P_2 = \text{GaussLower}^{-1}(p;\, n,\, \alpha/2).$$

The semicolon distinguishes the parameter (P or p) being inverted; n and α do not change.

How do we invert a function like Equation (17')? One method is to use a computer *search procedure*. The computer tries values of p until $P - p$ is just significant. See Appendix A.

Fortunately, there is a simpler way. Wilson (1927) derived a formula for directly calculating w^- and w^+. This is the *Wilson score interval*:[11]

$$\textit{Wilson score interval } (w^-, w^+) \equiv \frac{p + \dfrac{z_{\alpha/2}^2}{2n} \pm z_{\alpha/2}\sqrt{\dfrac{p(1-p)}{n} + \dfrac{z_{\alpha/2}^2}{4n^2}}}{1 + \dfrac{z_{\alpha/2}^2}{n}}. \quad (20)$$

The formula looks complicated, but it can be broken down into two components: an adjusted centre, p', and error, e'. We can also precalculate $z_{\alpha/2}^2/n$ to make life easier:

$$\textit{Wilson centre } p' \equiv \left(p + \frac{z_{\alpha/2}^2}{2n}\right) \Big/ \left(1 + \frac{z_{\alpha/2}^2}{n}\right),$$

$$\textit{Wilson error } e' \equiv z_{\alpha/2}\sqrt{\frac{p(1-p)}{n} + \frac{z_{\alpha/2}^2}{4n^2}} \Big/ \left(1 + \frac{z_{\alpha/2}^2}{n}\right), \quad (20')$$

$$\textit{Wilson score interval } (w^-, w^+) \equiv p' \pm e'.$$

The confidence interval is asymmetric (except where $p = 0.5$) and tends towards the middle of the distribution (as Figure 6.9 reveals). The centre, p', is the weighted mean of p and 0.5 (weighted by 1 and $z_{\alpha/2}^2/n$, respectively).

The Wilson interval cannot exceed the probability range [0, 1]. For example, applying $p = 0.05$, $n = 10$ and $\alpha = 0.05$ to Equation (20') obtains an interval of (0.0052, 0.3445).

We can write functions for this interval using the following notation:

$$\text{WilsonLower}(p, n, \alpha/2) \equiv w^- = p' - e', \text{ and}$$

$$\text{WilsonUpper}(p, n, \alpha/2) \equiv w^+ = p' + e'. \qquad (20'')$$

The Wilson interval identifies all points that are not significantly different from p according to the single-sample z test (Equation (17)). The following are equivalent:

$$\text{WilsonLower}(p, n, \alpha/2) \equiv \text{GaussUpper}^{-1}(p; n, \alpha/2), \text{ and}$$

$$\text{WilsonUpper}(p, n, \alpha/2) \equiv \text{GaussLower}^{-1}(p; n, \alpha/2).$$

This confidence interval is usually *two-tailed.* It is possible for P to be less than or greater than p. But if p is 0 or 1, this is no longer true. P cannot be less than 0 or greater than 1! The interval becomes one-tailed. We write $p \in [0, w^+)$ or $p \in (w^-, 1]$. The square brackets mean that the value 0 or 1 is *within* the range.

The Wilson interval calculation has a weakness because it employs the Normal approximation to the Binomial (see Section 6.3.3). But we can create a 'continuity-corrected' version of the Wilson interval that echoes Equation (18). See Chapter 8.[12]

Let us return to our example of objective case relative pronouns *who* versus *whom* from Chapter 2. See Section 6.2. We had the following data: $f = 135$, $n = 176$ and $p = 135/176 = 0.7670$. Employing Equation (20') with an error level $\alpha = 0.05$ gives us

Wilson centre $p' = 0.7613$,

Wilson error $e' = 0.0620$,

Wilson score interval $(w^-, w^+) = 0.7613 \pm 0.0620 = (0.6993, 0.8234)$.

We can predict, *solely on the basis of observed f and n, and a Binomial model of variation,* that the proportion of relative pronouns that are *who* rather than *whom* in an infinite imagined population of British English spoken data, collected according to the proportions in ICE-GB's sampling frame, will range from 0.6993 to 0.8234, or from just under 70% to a little over 82%.

Let us think about this. It is an astonishing claim. It seems counter-intuitive that we can be this specific with such limited data.

In his brief history, Stahl (2006) comments that, for centuries, mathematical models of inference were hotly debated.

The dominant idea for a long period – one with more than a grain of truth in it – was that experimenters should simply be *careful* to minimise randomness (noise) in data collection rather than estimate the effect of randomness. Since we cannot 'see' random variation, the idea we might attempt to predict and account for it appeared to be more sorcery than science!

But predict we may, thanks to the mathematical law of permutations expressed by Equation (16). It was *this* formula that gave us the Binomial distribution, which we approximated to with the Normal distribution and ultimately used to derive the Wilson score interval.

We can now apply confidence intervals on any freely varying observed proportion. We demonstrate the power of this method to help us understand research data in the next chapter.

6.3.6 Scatter and Confidence

Before we end this chapter, we should briefly address one last common misconception. This concerns two very different concepts:

- **scatter**: relating to the observed distribution of a sample; and
- **confidence**: relating to the projected distribution of resampled means (proportions are a type of mean).

If you see 'error bars' based on the spread of an observed distribution (sometimes including 'notches' or percentiles of the same), you are looking at scatter, not confidence. Projections of scatter can summarise data, but they are not confidence intervals.

Consider the following thought experiment. Suppose we wanted to know the average age of people in UK households. We sampled a large household and obtained ages $\mathbf{A} = \{3, 4, 11, 31, 34, 65\}$.

The following are descriptive statistics about this sample:

$$\begin{aligned} &\textit{sample mean (average age)}\ \bar{a} = \frac{\sum a_i}{n} = 24.6667, \\ &\textit{sample variance (spread of ages)}\ s^2 = \frac{\sum(a_i - \bar{a})}{n-1} = 567.4667, \qquad (21) \\ &\textit{sample standard deviation}\ s = \sqrt{s^2} = 23.8216. \end{aligned}$$

This standard deviation is huge. We have six data points, broadly dispersed. Ages are spread across the generations.

However, if we used this *sample* standard deviation to estimate a 95% Gaussian interval, we would have an error of $z_{\alpha/2}.s = 46.6893$ and a '95% interval' of (−22.0227, 93.3786)! Leaving aside the absurdity of negative ages, the distribution of *sample data* is not the same as the predicted distribution of *sampled means*.[13]

The latter would be the likely range of values in which we would expect to find the *average age* of households in the population. This standard deviation of sampled means, or 'standard error' of the population, S, may be calculated by dividing the standard deviation of the sample, s, by $\sqrt{n}$.

As we learned in this chapter, inferential statistics is concerned with making predictions about the population. The type of variation we are concerned with is variation of a sample mean due to the process of sampling from the population, not the spread of a sample. The confidence interval relates to this estimate of the *population mean variance*, S^2, rather than the observed sample variance, s^2.

Aarts and Wallis (2014) investigated the distribution of simple noun phrases (NPs) by ICE-GB text category. They plotted the scattergraph in Figure 6.10. This has two dimensions: the proportion of NPs consisting only of a single word ('simple' NPs) and, *of those simple NPs*, the proportion that consisted only of a personal pronoun (*I*, *you*, *we*, etc.).

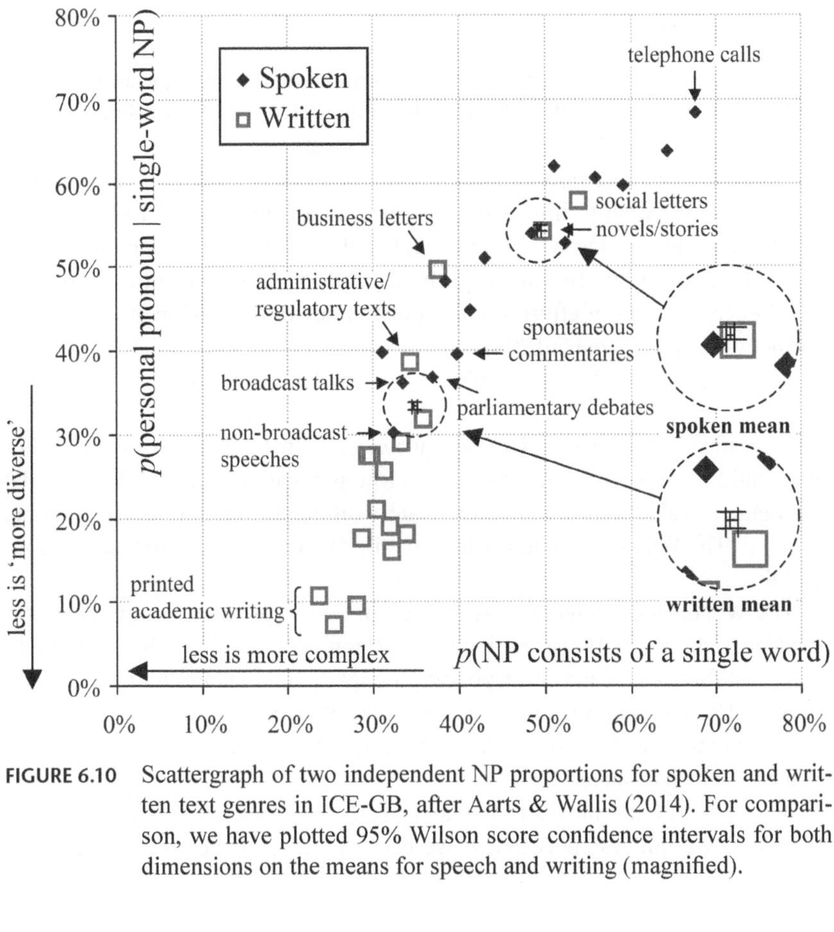

FIGURE 6.10 Scattergraph of two independent NP proportions for spoken and written text genres in ICE-GB, after Aarts & Wallis (2014). For comparison, we have plotted 95% Wilson score confidence intervals for both dimensions on the means for speech and writing (magnified).

To their graph, we have added confidence intervals to the means for speech and writing. Indeed, to make them visible on the same scale, we have magnified them at the lower right. What should be immediately obvious is that – as with our example of household member ages – *the likely range of a resampled average is very different from the spread of an observed sample!*

The variance of sample data is like observing *the size* of the moon. The confidence interval for an observed mean expresses uncertainty about the probable position of the mean (or 'centre') of the observation. It concerns *the accuracy of the location* of the moon.

Inferential statistics relies on mathematical models that predict the certainty of observations based on what the model tells us we should expect about an infinite number of possible future observations! This process of extrapolation can seem counter-intuitive and intangible. It should be no surprise that the uncertainty associated with an observed proportion or mean is sometimes confused for a more tangible distribution of the sample itself.

6.4 Conclusions

In Part 2, we discussed the importance of formulating research questions in terms of freely varying, mutually substitutable choices. This obtains observed proportions of Binomial or Multinomial dependent variables.

But once obtained, how reliable are our observations? We have only got a sample, but we wish to infer what the true value is most likely to be based on available evidence. Had we world enough and time, we might keep on sampling to estimate reliability. But this is prohibitively expensive (imagine reproducing the 25-person years of effort to collect and annotate ICE-GB many times), and further data may be unavailable.

To extrapolate from our sample to the population of data from which it is drawn, we need to engage in a type of mathematical reasoning known as inferential statistics. We need a *high-quality best guess* for the range of values where we would be most likely to observe the true population value, P. We calculate the range of values that are not significantly different from our observed proportion, p.[14] The Wilson score interval is an efficient and accurate method for doing just this.

The Wilson score interval was derived in two steps: first, by approximating the Gaussian (Normal) distribution to the Binomial, and second, by inverting the Gaussian formula for the corresponding sampling interval around P.

Actual resampling reveals *the randomness of arbitrary selection.* Faced with this variation, the idea we might derive a reliable prediction of future performance seems like sorcery!

It is easy to both underestimate and overestimate the effect of genuine randomness. We might expect that if we had, say, 20 students in a class, tossing a coin ten times, most students would get five out of ten heads. The fact that such expectations are wrong reflects the psychological difficulty we began with – probability is not directly perceived, but calculated from many experiences.

On the other hand, many students are encouraged to believe that most distributions are Normal. We might call this ideological predisposition the 'Normal fallacy' or 'bell curve expectation', a predisposition not helped by Karl Pearson's rebranding of the Gaussian distribution.

Indeed, with a large n and semi-central observation p, the Normal 'Wald' approximation *almost* works. But it rests on a fundamental logical error. A confidence interval requires us to invert the model of the sampling procedure. Once this is done, we obtain far more credible intervals, ones that are robust even where data are skewed or sample sizes small.

There are many good reasons why we might wish to work with small samples.

Consider a clinical trial for a new heart drug for patients vulnerable to heart attacks. We have an expected rate of heart attacks for this group based on previous clinical data. For sound ethical reasons, we do not wish to recruit more subjects than necessary, so we must work with small n. The expected chance of a heart attack, P, over a set period is likely to be close to zero, but it will not be zero.

A responsible clinical trial manager must then contend with two questions:

1. How many heart attack incidents are significantly greater than would be expected by chance? In other words, does the lower bound, w^-, of p, the observed rate of heart attacks in the trial group, exceed P? This would cause us to stop the trial immediately because the drug appeared to be having a negative effect on survival.
2. Following a set trial period, is the drug working so well that further trials may be accelerated, more subjects recruited and so on? To decide this, we must examine the upper bound of p.

Either way, we are concerned with probabilities that are likely to be close to, but not equal to, zero, by observing proportions of events found in small samples. Clinical trial managers need an accurate method for identifying when either stopping condition is reached. This is what the Wilson class of intervals obtains.

Thankfully, linguists are not concerned with such life-and-death decisions, but they can borrow from medical statistics.

The remainder of this part develops the ideas of this chapter. In Chapter 7, we exploit Wilson's formula in practical work with data. We discuss the relationship between confidence intervals and significance tests in Chapter 8 and develop new intervals in Chapter 9. In subsequent chapters, we discuss some useful consequences of rethinking statistics in terms of confidence intervals before reviewing the thought processes that go into the selection of statistical tests.

If you got this far, congratulations! Ultimately, we are grappling with a concept of possible random variation that *by definition* we can not see in any single observation or dataset! We try to imagine how resampling our data might obtain different results, even while we examine a single set. But we do not experience 'randomness' in a single event.

Notes

1 We can create a random sampling coin-tossing program in Excel™, which 'tosses coins' virtually using a pseudo-random number generator. For this and other resources see https://corplingstats.wordpress.com/siclr.

2 In this book, we use the convention of employing capital letters for population statistics and lower case for sample statistics. See the Preface. We use capital P and B to remind ourselves that these are expected distributions.

3 To apply this function at $P = 0$ or 1, we need to substitute $0^0 \rightarrow 1$.

4 Standard 'C' programming libraries can calculate factorials up to $n = 1{,}500$.

5 The standard deviation of a Normal distribution is the *square root of the variance*; the latter often labelled simply as S^2 or s^2.

6 A 'Type II' error is to incorrectly reject a result as 'non-significant', whereas a 'Type I' error is to accept a result as 'significant' when we should not.

7 It used to be common to read that you *can* employ Equation (17) for calculating confidence intervals on p, but only if p was three standard deviations away from zero, that is, $p - 3s > 0$ or $p + 3s < 1$ (called 'the rule of three' or '3-sigma rule'). In Normally distributed data, 99.7% of the distribution is within three standard deviations of the mean.

8 Thus, for example, Zar (2010, p. 85) uncritically presents the Wald interval. Sheskin (2011, p. 286) proposes the Wald interval for cells in a contingency table, and (2011, p. 661) discusses the Wald-based z independent-population difference interval (see Chapter 8), with caveats that both should be applied for large samples. Sheskin also introduces intervals for Student's t (see Chapter 12). These are fleeting references in works of many hundreds of pages.

9 In linguistics, the term 'function' means the structural relationship of a wordclass or phrasal term to a higher-order element, such as the subject of a clause or a head of a noun phrase. Often contrasted with *form*. Unless otherwise specified, in this book, we use the mathematical concept: a defined formula with parameters. See the Preface.

10 We can write this as the axiom $x \equiv fn^{-1}(fn(x))$. To take a trivial example, adding 5 to a number reverses the effect of subtracting 5 (i.e., $x \equiv (x - 5) + 5$). Many functions have known inverses, such as squaring a square root.

11 Wilson and other mathematicians may use alternative notation, and occasionally express intervals on the frequency scale $[0, n]$ rather than the probability scale, $\mathbf{P} = [0, 1]$. Thus, for example, Wilson (1927, p. 209) writes

'If $\lambda^2/n = t$, the solution is $p = \dfrac{p_0 + t/2}{1+t} \pm \dfrac{\lambda\sqrt{p_0 q_0 t + t^2/4}}{1+t}$.'

Here, λ is Wilson's symbol for $z_{\alpha/2}$, p_0 is the observed proportion, $q_0 = 1 - p_0$ and p is the interval bound. (Wilson's typesetter left out the λ before the square root.)

12 This method for defining confidence intervals by inverting a statistical test was first set out by Wilson (1927), followed by Clopper and Pearson (1934) for the Binomial, and Neyman (1937) as a general principle. However, not everyone defines a 'confidence interval' in this way. See Gilliland & Melfi (2010). Some researchers

have argued that confidence intervals defined by interval equality should be termed 'compatibility intervals' since they are compatible with a known test. But this seems unhelpful. Intervals should be well-defined so we can draw meaningful conclusions. Indeed, one of the themes of this book is that they may help us comprehend the tests from which they are derived.

13 Strictly speaking, this interval should be based on the critical value of Student's t with five degrees of freedom, which would be about a third wider. See p. 290.

14 These two statements are not quite the same, as we discuss in Chapter 17. When we calculate significant difference, we do so for each bound (where $P < p$ and where $P > p$) separately. See also Chapter 8.

7

PLOTTING WITH CONFIDENCE

7.1 Introduction

In Chapter 2, we were introduced to *Binomial proportion difference graphs*. These are simple plots of pairs of observed Binomial proportions of the dependent variable, each with confidence intervals. In the last chapter, we finally discovered how to calculate these confidence intervals.

An observed proportion p can also be considered as a probability. It may be extracted from a 2×2 contingency table: one cell as a proportion of the dependent variable column or row total (depending on how the table is laid out). This approach is extensible to larger '$r \times c$' contingency tables and Multinomial dependent variables.

Magnus Levin (2013) examined the changing meaning of the verb *think* in progressive contexts (i.e., BE *thinking*) in the TIME Magazine corpus over three decades: 1920s, 1960s and 2000s. His study is a semasiological one (see Chapter 4) because it distinguishes four different senses of BE *thinking*. He called these meanings 'cogitate', 'intend', quotative and interpretative.

Levin extracted examples from each of the three decades and manually classified them into these categories. The most common are 'cogitate': literal uses of *think*, as in Example (35), and 'intend': reporting an intention, as in (36). He identifies two further types: quotative, where the verb phrase is followed by reported speech, as in (37), and interpretative, where the clause containing the verb phrase comments on the interpretation of a subordinate clause, as in (38).

(35) Stephens, aggrieved, *had been thinking* the same thing. $_{\text{[TIME: 1929/12/23]}}$
(36) Mom, *I'm thinking of* joining a cult and want to leave it everything in my will. $_{\text{[2000/01/15]}}$

DOI: 10.4324/9781003622697-10

(37) 'I *was thinking*, Man, this is normal?' says Danielle. [2000/09/04]

(38) When he said that stringent water-pollution standards would hinder industry, he *was* again *thinking* of Alaska and its abundance of clear rivers. [1969/01/24]

Levin's data are shown in Table 7.1, presented as in the original article.

This is not an atypical presentation of data in corpus linguistics articles. We only need the raw frequencies in brackets to create the semasiological contingency table, Table 7.2.

We extract the raw frequencies in brackets from Table 7.1 and (for consistency) swap columns and rows to distribute values of the dependent variable horizontally.

Conventionally a statistics book will advise computing a χ^2 test (see Chapter 2) and then laboriously carrying out subtests (Sheskin, 2011, p. 666) or examining partial scores that make up the χ^2 test (Sheskin, 2011, p. 671). We could also try a different test – we might argue that 'time' was an Ordinal variable (1920s < 1960s < 2000s), if not exactly an Interval one. In this chapter, we demonstrate an alternative approach.

In Chapter 2, we explained how to carry out a χ^2 test. Although this test is less powerful than one optimised for Ordinal data, it obtains a significant result ($\chi^2 = 29.1682 > 12.5916$, the χ^2 critical value with six degrees of freedom and $\alpha = 0.05$).

TABLE 7.1 Four meanings of progressive *think* per million words, with raw frequencies in brackets: three time periods in the TIME corpus (after Levin, 2013).

BE *thinking*	*1920s*	*change %*	*1960s*	*change %*	*2000s*
'cogitate'	6.7 (51)	0%	6.7 (108)	178%	18.6 (119)
'intend'	2.0 (15)	100%	4.0 (65)	123%	8.9 (57)
quotative	0.0 (0)	-	0.4 (6)	925%	4.1 (26)
interpretative	0.0 (0)	-	0.1 (2)	904%	1.3 (8)
Total	8.7 (66)	29%	11.2 (181)	193%	32.8 (210)

TABLE 7.2 A 4 × 3 contingency table extracted from Table 7.1 (bold = copied).

		dependent variable (meaning of progressive *think*)				
		'cogitate'	*'intend'*	*quotative*	*interpretative*	*Total*
independent	1920s	**51**	**15**	**0**	**0**	66
variable	1960s	**108**	**65**	**6**	**2**	181
(time)	2000s	**119**	**57**	**26**	**8**	210
	Total	278	137	32	10	457

TABLE 7.3 Performing a 4 × 3 χ^2 test for homogeneity (independence) with data from Table 7.2. The resulting score is in bold at the bottom right.†

	observed **O**					*expected* **E**				*chi-square* χ^2			
	cog	*intd*	*quot*	*intp*	*Total*	*cog*	*intd*	*quot*	*intp*	*cog*	*intd*	*quot*	*intp*
1920s	**51**	**15**	**0**	**0**	66	40	20	5	1	2.93	1.16	4.62	1.44
1960s	**108**	**65**	**6**	**2**	181	110	54	13	4	0.04	2.13	3.51	0.97
2000s	**119**	**57**	**26**	**8**	210	128	63	15	5	0.60	0.56	8.68	2.52
Total	278	137	32	10	457							s	**29.17**

† In a conventional chi-square treatment, we would be instructed to either remove interpretative uses of *think* entirely or otherwise collapse cells. In this case, the interpretative 'intp' column falls foul of Cochran's rule ('no expected cell should have a frequency below 5'). We do not need to do this, not because the rule is excessively conservative (see Chapter 8), but because we do not place any particular weight on the total χ^2 score.

But this merely tells us that the dependent variable is not independent from the independent variable (time). It says 'something is happening' in the data. It does not tell us *which* values are changing, over which time periods.

Some statisticians propose you examine individual χ^2 scores in the right-hand section of Table 7.3. We might remark on the higher values in the quotative column ('quot', second from the right). Sure enough, this column alone contributes nearly 60% of the total score. But this does not tell us what this fact means! Is quotative change a more 'important' change, or *more distinct from* the other types? Is it increasing or decreasing?

χ^2 cell scores measure the degree to which that cell differs from the expected value assuming no interaction between the variables, scaled by the available data. But once we know that there *is* an interaction, they do not tell us much more.

7.1.1 Visualising Data

Let us plot the data with confidence intervals.

Before we do, remember this is a *semasiological graph.* See Chapter 4. The baseline of choice for the four different forms differs for each form, but we do not have this baseline data in our table. The outward verb forms may be the same (e.g., *consider, contemplate* or *wonder* might alternate with both Examples (35) and (36)), but the referential meaning of each expression would be different. Alternate verbs for the interpretative form (38) might include *recall* or *refer [to]*, whereas the quotative (37) is grammaticalised, with no obvious alternate (possibly *remember*). The data allows us to estimate a reader's chance of coming across different meanings of BE *thinking* in data like the *TIME* Magazine corpus: a type of 'exposure rate'.

Figure 7.1 tracks the *share* of each of the four senses of progressive *think*, p(meaning | BE *thinking*), over the three time periods. We plot the data in Table 7.2 as proportions p with Wilson score intervals using Equation (20). For each time period, the proportion of each type adds up to 1:

$$p(\text{'cogitate'} \mid \text{BE } thinking) + p(\text{'intend'} \mid \text{BE } thinking) + p(\text{quotative} \mid \text{BE } thinking) + p(\text{interpretative} \mid \text{BE } thinking) = 1.$$

When we plot a two-valued (Binomial) dependent variable we usually plot a single line because as one proportion increases, the other declines by the same amount. Plot lines mirror each other.

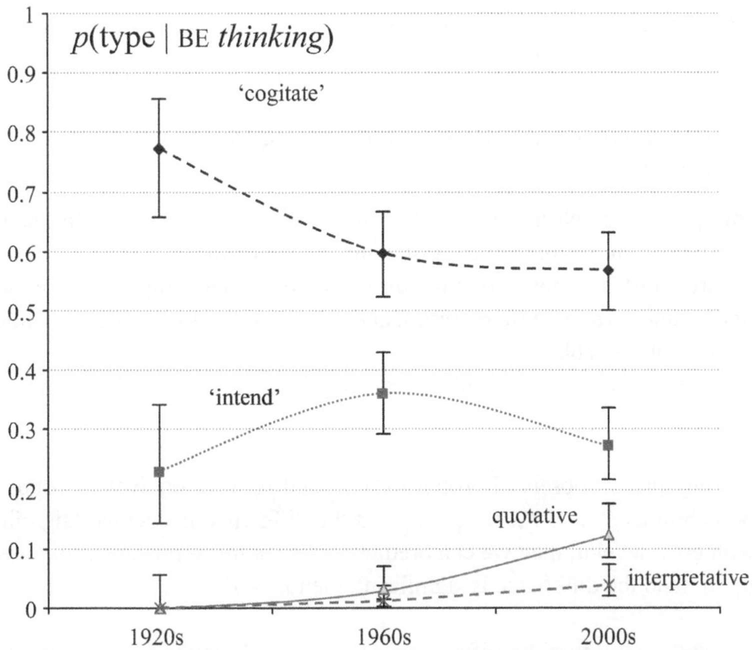

FIGURE 7.1 A graph plot of Table 7.2 showing changing proportions of meanings of progressive *think* over time in the US TIME Magazine Corpus, with 95% Wilson score intervals, after Levin (2013).†

† This graph connects points like a necklace, with a smoothed line to make points of each type easier to identify. No inference should be drawn about values between the points.

For Multinomial dependent variables, we should plot each line. Each proportion can change to a different degree. They are not completely independent, the total still sums to 1, but each proportion is worthy of separate examination.

What does Figure 7.1 tell us?

The graph depicts a changing distribution whereby two synchronically distinct uses ('cogitate' and 'intend') become four over time. In the 1920s data, there are no observed cases of what are later termed quotative and interpretative uses of BE *thinking*. This does not mean they do not *exist* – the confidence interval here is [0, 0.055), meaning we estimate the true value in the population as between 0% and 5.5% (at a 95% level of confidence). These cases increase in number to the 2000s, by which time interpretative cases represent an estimated 1.9% to 7.3% of instances and quotative cases have a share of between 8.6% and 17.5%.

Meanwhile we can see that this growth has been at the expense (in terms of *share*) of literal 'cogitate' cases, and, to a lesser extent, 'intend' cases. (Remember that a decline in *proportion* does not mean that 'cogitate' uses are necessarily declining overall. See Table 7.1.)

7.1.2 Comparing Observations and Identifying Significant Differences

To interpret the graph in Figure 7.1 more closely, let us note a useful heuristic that derives from the mathematics of confidence intervals.

We are entitled to compare any pair of points: horizontally, across values of the independent variable (here, time); and vertically, across competing values of the dependent variable.

When we say that two points are 'significantly different' we mean the following:

> For any pair of observed proportions, p_1 and p_2, with equivalent population probabilities P_1 and P_2, if $p_1 > p_2$ and the difference is deemed 'significant' with error level α, then we can predict $P_1 > P_2$ at this error level. Likewise, if $p_1 < p_2$ and the difference is significant, then $P_1 < P_2$.

This is *not* saying that the differences in scores will be the same. A difference $d = p_2 - p_1$ is not predicted to *equal* $D = P_2 - P_1$. The population difference D is predicted to be non-zero and *have the same sign* (plus or minus) as d.

Statistical tests for comparing two independent Binomial proportions are reviewed in Chapter 8. We have already seen one: the 2×2 χ^2 test (Chapter 2). However, there is a short cut for analysing graph plots containing Wilson score intervals that means we often do not need to perform a significance test at all.

Wilson interval comparison heuristic: (22)

For any pair of points representing observed proportions:

1. if two points' confidence intervals **do not overlap**, the points *must* be significantly different;
2. if one point is **inside the interval** of the other, the points *cannot* be significantly different;
3. **otherwise**, carry out a statistical test to decide whether they are significantly different.

This heuristic follows from the logic of confidence intervals plotted on the same scale.[1] In algebra we can write:

$$\max(u_1, u_2) < w_d < (u_1 + u_2),$$

where u_1 and u_2 represent the *inner interval widths* for p_1 and p_2, and w_d is the correct combined interval width for d, however this is calculated. Only if intervals overlap, but points are excluded, do we need a statistical test. Figure 7.2 illustrates the principle.

Let us look at Figure 7.1 again. Using this Wilson interval comparison heuristic, we can immediately see, for example, that quotative and interpretative shares of progressive *think* in 2000 are significantly different. There is a gap between the intervals. We can say that we are at least 95% confident that interpretative cases are more numerous than quotative ones in a population of data drawn from texts like the TIME magazine data of the 2000s.

The same cannot be said for the 1960s data. We cannot significantly distinguish rates for quotative and interpretative uses of BE *thinking* because the

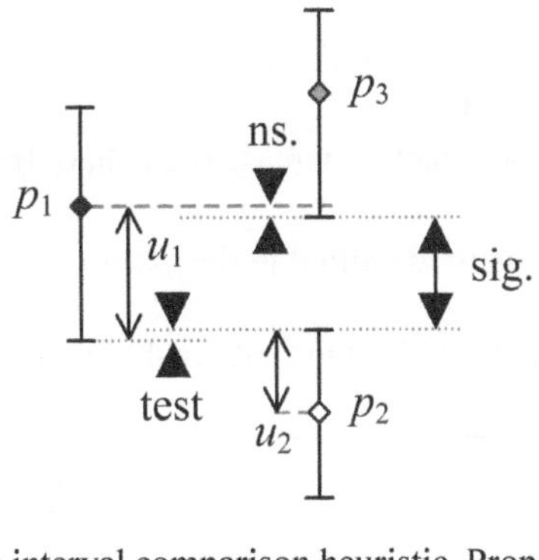

FIGURE 7.2 The Wilson interval comparison heuristic. Proportions p_2 and p_3 *must* be significantly different; p_1 and p_3 *cannot* be significantly different (p_1 is inside the confidence interval for p_3); and p_1 and p_2 *might* be significant, so test it! Inner intervals for p_1 and p_2 are also indicated.

proportion of the quotative use is within the interval for the interpretative. (This is more difficult to spot, as intervals are presented on top of each other here.)

'Cogitate' uses reduced their share between the 1920s and 2000s. These intervals overlap, so we cannot quite conclude anything about their apparent decline between the 1920s and 1960s without a significance test.

We do not need to apply a test comparing 'cogitate' rates between the 1960s and 2000s. The observed point for one is inside the 'I'-shaped error bar for the other. They are not significantly different.

We only need apply a test if condition 3 applies, as in the 1920s–1960s 'cogitate' comparison. (We might say the intervals are 'holding hands' if it helps you remember the rule.)

Which test you use depends on the contrast being considered:

- **Across an independent variable** (IV): use Yates's 2 × 2 χ^2 or the Newcombe-Wilson test with continuity correction. See Chapter 8. Newcombe's test is introduced next.
- **Across the dependent variable** (DV): use Yates's single-sample z test for two competing proportions or an equivalent continuity-corrected Wilson interval test. We introduce these 'more' tests in Section 7.4.

An Excel™ spreadsheet for carrying out 2 × 2 tests is available online.[2] This lets us perform a quick check for any two points across the IV. We input frequency data from Table 7.2 into the spreadsheet.

For example, to compare 1920s and 1960s 'cogitate' share we may extract data, as in Table 7.4. We delete the 2000s data and sum the cells that are not cogitate (marked '¬cog').

With this heuristic-and-test method we find, for instance, that

- the initial fall (from 1920s to 1960s) for 'cogitate' uses is significant ($\chi^2 = 6.54$);
- 'intend' uses do *not* change significantly over time (the curved 'interpolation line' is misleading); and
- quotative uses do significantly increase their share from the 1960s to 2000s.

Other changes can be easily identified in the graph.

TABLE 7.4 Carrying out a 2 × 2 χ^2 test to compare the fall in 'cogitate' share from 1920s to 1960s.

	observed **O**			*expected* **E**		*chi-square* χ^2	
	cog	*¬cog*	*Total*	*cog*	*¬cog*	*cog*	*¬cog*
1920s	**51**	**15 + 0 + 0 = 15**	66	42	24	1.71	3.08
1960s	**108**	**65 + 6 + 2 = 73**	181	117	64	0.62	1.12
Total	159	181	247			s	**6.54**

As we report data, we should again remember that Figure 7.1 is a semasiological share graph, so we need to avoid making statements that imply, for example, that 'writers in later periods increasingly preferred to employ BE *thinking* in a quotative way'. To make this kind of claim, we would need to compare the proportions of quotative BE *thinking* against a baseline including other ways of expressing the same meaning (quotative BE *wondering*, for example). See Chapter 4.

Finally, before we move on, let us compare our observations to the χ^2 table (Table 7.3, right). Traditional statistical treatments suggest the way to analyse a table like this is to examine χ^2 cell scores and investigate those with the highest absolute value greater than the one degree of freedom critical value (3.8415 for $\alpha = 0.05$).[3]

The χ^2 table gave the highest individual χ^2 score (8.6766) to quotative BE *thinking* in the 2000s, and a fairly high score for other values of quotative. The quotative meaning cases seem to be doing something distinctive in this table. Similarly, the next highest χ^2 cell score, 'cogitate' in the 1920s, seems rather higher than in later periods. Higher cell scores pick out *relative* peaks or troughs in any given series, but do not tell us if a peak or trough is *statistically significantly different* from other values in the series.[4]

Confidence intervals are easier to interpret and more decisive: many can be 'eyeballed' and evaluated, and if intervals overlap, they can be compared with a robust test. As long as the comparison is meaningful, any pair of Binomial proportions may be contrasted in this way.

7.2 Plotting the Graph

In Figure 7.1, we plotted values of observed proportions, p, with Wilson score interval error bars.

Wilson intervals can also be calculated using a 'continuity correction'. This adjusts for the fact that Binomial frequency data are discrete rather than continuous (see Chapter 6) and makes the intervals slightly wider. In the following example, we will use the uncorrected interval, but the method outlined here can also be used with the continuity-corrected Wilson interval.[5]

7.2.1 Step 1. Gather Raw Data

First we gather the raw data. We need to identify the raw frequencies, f, and the relationship between the different data series. Does it make *sense* to take proportions out of the total frequency, n? What should the baseline be for any change?

In this particular exercise, we have chosen to plot *semasiological share* (see Chapter 4), so n is the total number of cases of BE *thinking*, the 'Total' column in Table 7.3.

This might appear a trivial step, but many researchers struggle at this point – should we be plotting proportions of the 'Total' *column* or *row* in Table 7.3?

What do proportions in the Total row represent? They correspond to the proportion of an item falling in a particular decade. But we are not trying to predict the decade in which we are most likely to find a particular item (say, 'interpretative')! Our dependent variable is the semasiological share, and thus n is the column total. Time is the *independent* variable.

We extract a set of observed semasiological proportions for each cell frequency, $p = f / n$.

7.2.2 Step 2. Calculate Basic Wilson Score Interval Terms

The Wilson score interval can be broken down into two components.

In Chapter 6, we introduced Equation (20'), which calculates the Wilson interval in two parts: an adjusted probability p' representing the midpoint of the confidence interval, and an error term e':

$$\textit{Wilson centre } p' \equiv \left(p + \frac{z_{\alpha/2}^{2}}{2n}\right) \Big/ \left(1 + \frac{z_{\alpha/2}^{2}}{2n}\right),$$

$$\textit{Wilson error } e' \equiv z_{\alpha/2}\sqrt{\frac{p(1-p)}{n} + \frac{z_{\alpha/2}^{2}}{4n^{2}}} \Big/ \left(1 + \frac{z_{\alpha/2}^{2}}{n}\right), \qquad (20')$$

$$\textit{Wilson score interval } (w^{-}, w^{+}) \equiv p' \pm e'.$$

Some of this is unnecessarily forbidding. For an error level α of 0.05 (i.e., a confidence level of 95%), $z_{\alpha/2} = 1.95996$.

We can also precalculate the *Wilson denominator*, $(1 + z_{\alpha/2}^{2}/n)$, for each time period.[6]

Performing the first two calculations in Equation (20'), we obtain the values in Table 7.6. Normally, we would not present these – they are intermediate components. At most we might present p and its interval bounds. But this step helps us understand what the equation is doing.

TABLE 7.5 Converting data in Table 7.2 to Binomial proportions of all cases of *think* (baseline n = 'Total' column).

	observed frequency f					*observed proportion p*			
	cog	*intd*	*quot*	*intp*	*Total n*	*cog*	*intd*	*quot*	*intp*
1920s	**51**	**15**	**0**	**0**	66	0.7727	0.2273	0.0000	0.0000
1960s	**108**	**65**	**6**	**2**	181	0.5967	0.3591	0.0331	0.0110
2000s	**119**	**57**	**26**	**8**	210	0.5667	0.2714	0.1238	0.0381
Total	278	137	32	10	457				

TABLE 7.6 Applying Equation (20') to the data in Table 7.5 to compute intermediate values of the score interval, $\alpha = 0.05$.

	Wilson centre p'				*Wilson error e'*			
	cog	*intd*	*quot*	*intp*	*cog*	*intd*	*quot*	*intp*
1920s	0.7577	0.2423	0.0275	0.0275	0.0994	0.0994	0.0275	0.0275
1960s	0.5947	0.3620	0.0429	0.0212	0.0707	0.0692	0.0276	0.0182
2000s	0.5655	0.2755	0.1306	0.0464	0.0664	0.0597	0.0447	0.0270

Let us look at the first row. In the 1920s data, there are two cells with an observed frequency $f > 0$: 'cogitate' ('cog' for brevity) and 'intend' ('intd'). The other two are zero. The proportions in this row behave as if they are the only two values in competition: p('cogitate') = 0.7727, p('intend') = 0.2273. They obey the 'mirror' rule: p('intend') = 1 – p('cogitate').

The Wilson centre for all observations, p', involves an adjustment that moves the interval midpoint towards the centre of the probability range (0.5). In other words, if $p < 0.5$, $p' > p$; if $p > 0.5$, the opposite is true. In the case of the 1920s data, the adjustment for 'cogitate' and 'intend' is the same, but applied in opposite directions. So p'('cogitate') = 0.7577, p'('intend') = 0.2423, and the equality p'('intend') = 1 – p'('cogitate') also holds. Note, however, that the sum of all four Wilson centres is not 1: we also apply an adjustment of 0.0275 to the zero-frequency cells.

If we examine the corresponding Wilson error values on the right-hand side of the table, we see that e'('cogitate') = e'('intend') = 0.0994. This fact should also not be surprising. In simple Binomial competition, not only do observed proportions mirror each other ($q = 1 - p$), but *the range of extrapolated expected values in the population* will do the same.

Finally, consider the Wilson error for the zero-frequency quotative and interpretative cells. The error is identical to the Wilson centre. Or to put it another way, when $p = 0$, $p' = e'$.

As we see in Table 7.7, since the lower bound $w^- = p' - e'$, when we observe a value of $p = 0$ the confidence interval lower bound, w^-, is also zero. The interval is one-tailed, $p \in [0, 0.0550)$. The square bracket means that $P = 0$ is included in the interval. If $P = p$, P cannot be significantly different from p!

7.2.3 Step 3. Calculate the Wilson Interval

We have performed the hard work. We apply the last step in Equation (20'):

Wilson lower bound $w^- = p' - e'$, and

Wilson upper bound $w^+ = p' + e'$.

TABLE 7.7 Completing the calculation of Equation (20') to obtain lower and upper bounds of the Wilson score interval (w^-, w^+). Data from Table 7.5.

	Wilson lower bound w^-				*Wilson upper bound* w^+			
	cog	*intd*	*quot*	*intp*	*cog*	*intd*	*quot*	*intp*
1920s	0.6583	0.1429	0.0000	0.0000	0.8571	0.3417	0.0550	0.0550
1960s	0.5239	0.2928	0.0153	0.0030	0.6654	0.4313	0.0704	0.0394
2000s	0.4990	0.2158	0.0859	0.0194	0.6319	0.3353	0.1752	0.0734

This gives us Table 7.7. These figures could be cited in articles or used to plot graphs like Figure 7.1. They tell us, for example, that it is predicted that, were we to resample appropriately, it is 95% likely that the 'cogitate' share of *think* in the 1920s is between 0.6583 and 0.8571.

7.2.4 Step 4. Plot Intervals on Graphs

Finally, to produce graphs like Figure 7.1, we plot the best estimate p and specify confidence interval *widths* relative to p. Wilson bounds are absolute – they are points on the probability scale. But Excel™ needs positive relative widths for its 'custom error bars'. We calculate these easily:

$$\textit{Wilson relative error interval widths } (u^-, u^+) = (p - w^-, w^+ - p). \qquad (23)$$

The result is a graph like Figure 7.1 that we can inspect and use to compare intervals.

7.3 Comparing and Plotting Change

So far, we have seen how to plot a series of single observed proportions with confidence intervals. We can also plot *differences*, such as $p_2 - p_1$, with confidence intervals. A 'change over time' is a difference in the same Binomial proportion at different time points (e.g., p('cogitate', 2000s) – p('cogitate', 1960s)).

7.3.1 The Zero-Based Newcombe-Wilson Interval and Test

Robert Newcombe (1998b) proposed a new interval, based on the Wilson score interval, for the difference between two Binomial proportions $d = p_2 - p_1$. We refer to this interval as the *Newcombe-Wilson interval*.[7] It can also be used in a test; see Figure 7.3.

As before, indices 1 and 2 refer to the first and second proportions and any statistics derived from them, thus w_1^- and w_1^+ refer to the lower and upper

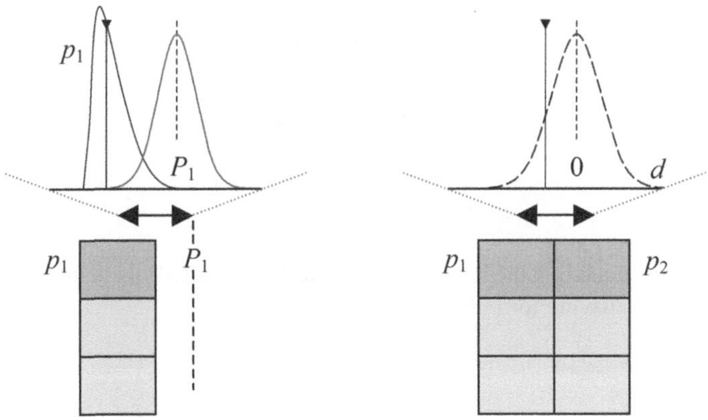

FIGURE 7.3 Visualising tests. Left: the Wilson score interval for p_1 and 2×1 test (see Chapter 6). Right: the Newcombe-Wilson test, where we compare $d = p_2 - p_1$ with an interval about zero (dashed).

bound of the Wilson score interval for p_1, and w_2^- and w_2^+ refer to the same bounds for p_2.

We will perform this calculation in two steps. First, we will calculate a zero-based interval which we can use in a test. If d is outside this interval, the test is significant. Then, we will convert this into an interval about d.

We employ a formula owing to the French mathematician Irénée-Jules Bienaymé. Bienaymé generalised Gauss's method of summing squares to summing independent *variances* (squared standard deviations). Two independent observations are said to have *tangential variation* at right angles in a two-factor probability space, $\boldsymbol{P} \times \boldsymbol{P}$ (where $\boldsymbol{P} = [0, 1]$). The combined inner interval width should be Pythagoras's hypotenuse, the sum of the two squared inner interval widths.[8]

The formula can be applied as follows:

$$\textit{Bienaymé interval width} = z_{\alpha/2}\sqrt{S_1^2 + S_2^2} = \sqrt{u_1^2 + u_2^2}$$
$$= \sqrt{(P_1 - p_1)^2 + (P_2 - p_2)^2}, \quad (24)$$

where P_1 and P_2 represent the values of P at the 'just-significant' ends of the *inner* ('mesial') interval. In Figure 7.4, with a declining $d = p_2 - p_1$, we use $P_1 = w_1^-$ and $P_2 = w_2^+$.

Whereas Bienaymé's rule is classically expressed in terms of summing independent variances, we can employ the *squared Wilson score interval widths* instead. This shortcut is permitted by the interval equality principle and the fact that $z_{\alpha/2}$ is a constant, unaffected by Bienaymé's formula.

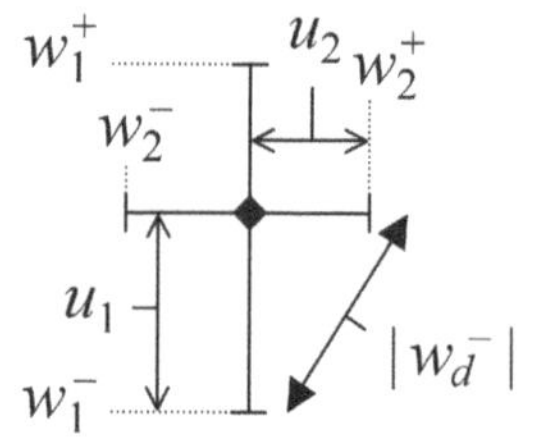

FIGURE 7.4 Calculating the lower bound of the Newcombe-Wilson interval using the Bienaymé formula. See also Figure 7.5.

Consider where $p_2 < p_1$, so $d < 0$. We need to calculate the interval lower bound: the largest fall that would be considered 'non-significant'. The sketch in Figure 7.4 illustrates the idea. Observed proportions p_1 and p_2 are independently sampled, so their standard deviations are at right angles to each other. The hypotenuse, $| w_d^- |$, is the square root of the sum of the squares of the other two sides.

We can employ the two inner values of the Wilson score interval to calculate a *zero-based Newcombe-Wilson difference interval* (w_d^-, w_d^+) for the difference $d = p_2 - p_1$:

$$0 \in (w_d^-, w_d^+) = (-\sqrt{(p_1 - w_1^-)^2 + (w_2^+ - p_2)^2},$$
$$\sqrt{(w_1^+ - p_1)^2 + (p_2 - w_2^-)^2}). \quad (25)$$

Note how the lower bound width, w_d^-, is composed of the lower interval width of p_1 and the *upper* interval width of p_2; the upper bound is composed of the opposite pair. We will see why shortly. The interval may be expressed as a significance test, *the Newcombe-Wilson test for the difference between two Binomial proportions*. This can be simply stated.

Newcombe-Wilson test:

If $w_d^- < p_2 - p_1 < w_d^+$, there is no significant difference between p_1 and p_2. (26)

Any point outside the interval represents a significant difference between the two proportions. (The consequent on the right, 'there is no significant difference . . .' is the *null hypothesis* of the test.)

The test asks 'does the observed difference, *d*, deviate from zero far enough for us to argue that this is not a chance effect, and, therefore, can we predict that an equivalent difference in the true population values, $D = P_2 - P_1$, *will be other than zero in the same direction as d*?'

7.3.2 Comparing Proportions: An Illustration

Consider the two 'cogitate' points for the 1920s and 1960s in Figure 7.1. These intervals overlap slightly. We tested them with a χ^2 test in Table 7.4. Now we will use the Newcombe-Wilson method.

The relevant raw data are in Table 7.8. The first row, '1920s', we will refer to as p_1, w_1^- and w_1^+, the second p_2, and so on. The observed difference $d = 0.5967 - 0.7727 = -0.1760$.

We can see that the probability of observing BE *thinking* with a 'cogitate' meaning in the 1920s was $0.7727 \in (0.6583, 0.8571)$ or, in percentages, between 65.83% and 85.71%, but by the 1960s it had declined to $0.5967 \in (0.5239, 0.6654)$. All three variables are on a probabilistic scale (i.e., p, w^-, $w^+ \in \boldsymbol{P} = [0, 1]$).

Figure 7.5 is a close-up of part of Figure 7.1 showing the same data pictorially. The 'width' terms are shown as arrows. The left arrow, for example, has width $u_1 = p_1 - w_1^-$.

TABLE 7.8 Single intervals for 'cogitate' in the 1920s and 1960s, with squared interval width terms for calculating the Newcombe-Wilson difference interval. The numbers in bold are the inner intervals (squared) in Figure 7.5.

	probabilities			*squared widths*	
cogitate	p	w^-	w^+	$(p - w^-)^2$	$(w^+ - p)^2$
1920s	0.7727	0.6583	0.8571	**0.0131** ↓	0.0071
1960s	0.5967	0.5239	0.6654	0.0053	↑ **0.0047**

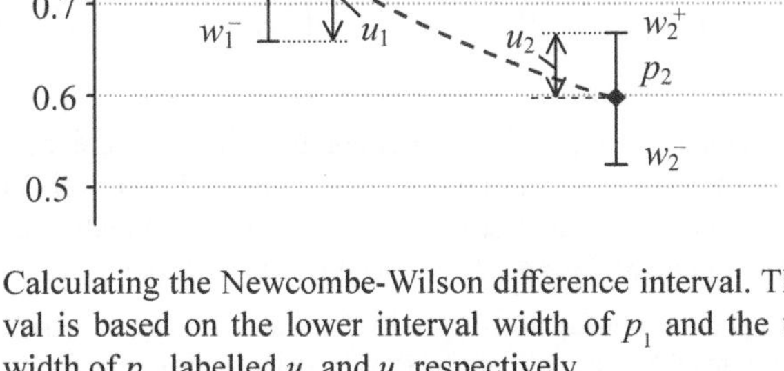

FIGURE 7.5 Calculating the Newcombe-Wilson difference interval. The inner interval is based on the lower interval width of p_1 and the upper interval width of p_2, labelled u_1 and u_2 respectively.

Applying Equation (25) with this data gives us

$$w_d^- = -\sqrt{0.0131 + 0.0047} = -0.1335,$$

$$w_d^+ = \sqrt{0.0071 + 0.0053} = 0.1114.$$

As d is less than the lower bound ($-0.1760 < -0.1335$), the difference between points p_1 and p_2 is greater than is likely to occur by chance at a 95% confidence level, and we can report that their difference is statistically significant.

7.3.3 A Newcombe-Wilson Interval for Difference d

The interval (w_d^-, w_d^+) is zero-based, that is, it has an origin of zero, and we may perform a significance test by examining whether d lies inside or outside it (Equation (26)).

Now we will construct a confidence interval for the difference, d. We simply subtract the zero-based interval from d. See Figure 7.6.

Subtracting the interval swaps the bounds, putting the lower number first:

$$d \in (d^-, d^+) = \textbf{difference}(p_2, p_1) = d - (w_d^-, w_d^+) = (d - w_d^+, d - w_d^-). \tag{27}$$

The function **difference**(p_2, p_1) returns the confidence interval (two bounds and the set of points between them) not significantly different from $p_2 - p_1$.

An interval about d has further applications. To test for significant difference from zero, we test the inner interval to see if (d^-, d^+) includes 0. But now we can also test if (d^-, d^+) includes any chosen difference, D, potentially evaluating the *outer* interval to test the *steepest* gradient.

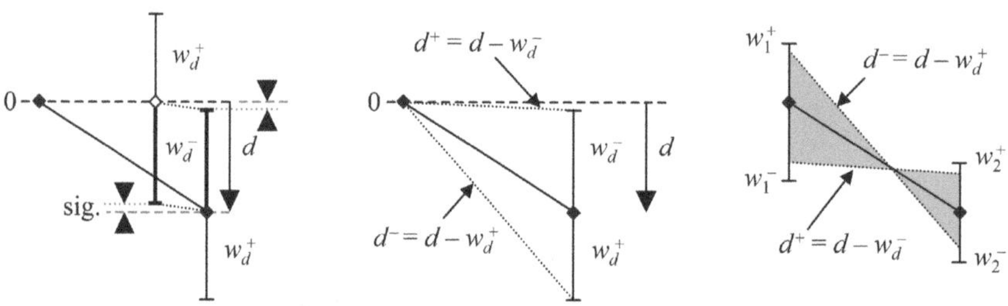

FIGURE 7.6 Geometry of repositioned Newcombe-Wilson difference intervals, for a significant fall $d < 0$. Left: the Newcombe-Wilson lower bound w_d^- repositioned at d. We can test if $d < w_d^-$ or $d - w_d^- < 0$. Middle: repositioned gradient interval for $d \in (d^-, d^+)$. Right: with Wilson intervals for p_1 and p_2.†

† The gradient lines do not join up the score interval bounds – the Bienaymé sum (hypotenuse) is shorter than the sum of the other intervals (other sides of the triangle). See Figure 7.4.

For $d < 0$, the steepest gradient is the lower bound of the difference, $d^- = d - w_d^+$. Naturally, where $d > 0$, the steepest gradient is the upper bound.

We can quote differences with confidence intervals. In our worked example, $(d^-, d^+) = (-0.2874, -0.0425)$. We can report that d is between -0.2874 and -0.0425 with a 95% confidence. This excludes zero, so the fall is significant.

7.3.4 Comparing Multiple Points

We can perform a Newcombe-Wilson test for every horizontal comparison, that is, any pair of points in each series. With three dates ('data points', or values of the independent variable), this means three sets of comparisons, but if you have more than three, it may make sense to limit comparisons to adjacent points.

The number of different possible pairs for k values (e.g., time periods) is the *triangle number*, $k(k - 1) / 2$. For $k = 10$ data points, there are 9 *adjacent* comparisons but 45 possible comparisons in total.

We also know that time samples are *ordered* (Ordinal) at the very least. They form a well-defined sequence. Arbitrarily comparing time points is unprincipled if we want to describe *trends* over time.[9] A better approach may be to estimate a curve. See Chapter 10.

At present we only have three time points to consider. So in Table 7.9, we perform pairwise comparisons for each of the three pairs. In this table, 'ns' means non-significant, 's–' refers to a significant decline and 's+' means a significant increase.

Apart from 'cogitate', the only other significant difference by time is to be found in the 2000s for quotative uses of *think*. Although the 'intend' share fluctuates, there is insufficient data for us to conclude that the observed change is significant.

At first sight, this table might appear disappointing. Although this summary is more exhaustive and precise than applying a visual heuristic to Figure 7.1, it has not revealed anything new. Figure 7.1 plus some selected 'overlap tests' told us all we needed to know!

These additional steps confirmed our initial reading of the graph a little more systematically.

7.3.5 Plotting Percentage Difference

Change is commonly expressed in newspapers in terms of *percentage difference*. We often read statements like 'our student numbers rose by 30%' or 'the rate of infection fell by 10%'. Percentage difference is commonplace so deserves a brief mention. However, it has some defects as a measure of change.

TABLE 7.9 Pairwise comparison tables for three time points.

	1920s–1960s				1960s–2000s				1920s–2000s			
	d	w_d^-	w_d^+		d	w_d^-	w_d^+		d	w_d^-	w_d^+	
'cogitate'	−0.1760	−0.1335	0.1114	s−	−0.0300	−0.0977	0.0964	ns	−0.2061	−0.1317	0.1082	s−
'intend'	0.1318	−0.1111	0.1322	ns	−0.0877	−0.0920	0.0911	ns	0.0442	−0.1059	0.1272	ns
quotative	0.0331	−0.0373	0.0578	ns	0.0907	−0.0544	0.0532	s+	0.1238	−0.0514	0.0668	s+
interpretative	0.0110	−0.0283	0.0556	ns	0.0270	−0.0362	0.0339	ns	0.0381	−0.0353	0.0581	ns

We first mentioned percentage difference in Chapter 3:

$$\textit{percentage difference } d^{\%} = (p_2 - p_1) / p_1 = d / p_1 = p_2 / p_1 - 1. \qquad (7)$$

To create a confidence interval for percentage difference, the best method is to use the last expression, $d^{\%} = p_2 / p_1 - 1$, as a basis. In Chapter 9, alongside **difference**, we define a **ratio** interval function which returns an interval for the ratio of the two parameters. This gives us a simple expression:

$$d^{\%} \in \mathbf{ratio}(p_2, p_1) - 1, \qquad (28)$$

where **ratio**(p_2, p_1) returns the set of points not significantly different from p_2 / p_1.

With this formula, we might plot graphs of percentage difference like those in Figure 7.7, comparing the 1920s data with 2000s (cf. Table 7.9, right).

Figure 7.7 shows how confidence intervals for the percentage difference are derived from intervals for the ratio of two proportions.

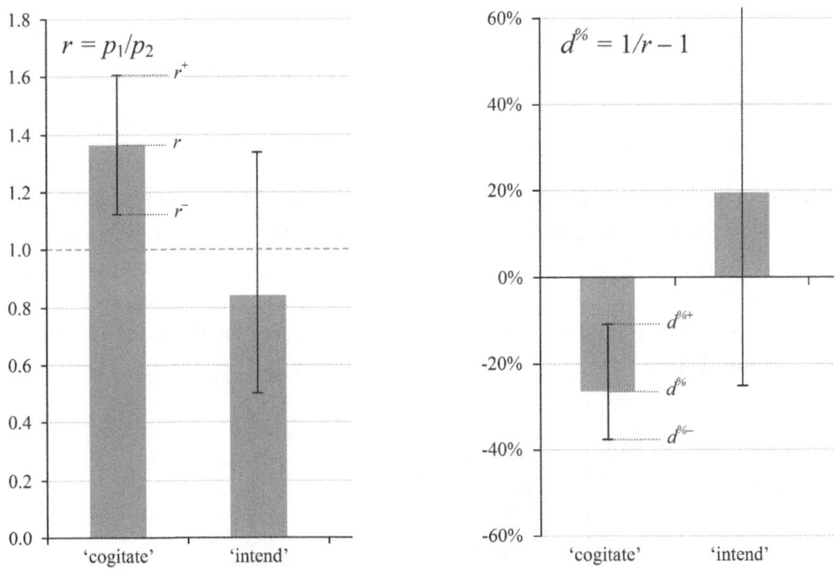

FIGURE 7.7 Deriving confidence intervals for percentage difference, $d^{\%} = (p_2 - p_1) / p_1 = p_2 / p_1 - 1$, for comparing change from the 1920s to 2000s in Levin's BE *thinking* data, 'cogitate' and 'intend' bars (the other two types, quotative and interpretative, have $p_1 = 0$, and cannot be drawn). Left: confidence intervals for the ratio $r = p_1 / p_2$. Right: intervals for $d^{\%} = p_2 / p_1 - 1$.

In the right-hand graph, we see that our data supports a prediction at 95% confidence that for a comparable population, 'cogitate' forms fell over the period 1920s to 2000s by between 11% and 38%. The interval excludes zero. We can see that 'cogitate' uses of BE *thinking* significantly fell over the period.[10]

However, percentage difference presents us with problems:

1. If the starting point p_1 is zero, we cannot compute a result. Notice that we could not report changes in quotative and interpretative shares, because $p_1 = 0$ in the 1920s data.
2. Each observation of $d^{\%}$ is scaled by a *different* factor, p_1, so observations are difficult to compare. It is tempting to consider whether, for example, change in the 'cogitate' share might be significantly different to that for 'intend'. But a difference between differences $d_2 - d_1$ (see Chapter 14) is not the same as a difference between *percentage* differences, $d_2^{\%} - d_1^{\%}$. We need to be sure that comparisons are meaningful. If not, we should not compare observed rates and intervals, and even their visual juxtaposition in a graph could be misleading.
3. Finally, despite its popularity, the measure has a major counter-intuitive defect. *Positive and negative percentage differences are not equivalent*: +100% means doubling, whereas the inverse (halving) is −50%. Suppose you read in a newspaper that crime rates declined by 10% in the first year and rose by 10% in the second. What has happened to the crime rate compared to its starting point? What if it went down by 50% and then up by the same percentage?[11]

7.3.6 Floating Bar Charts

Bowie et al. (2014) proposed the idea of *floating bar charts* as an alternative visualisation for examining multiple simple changes over time. The idea is to plot a range from p_1 to p_2 as a floating column between 0 and 1. Newcombe-Wilson intervals are drawn on the end point of the bar (p_2), and the bar, representing the difference between the two points, is shaded to indicate the direction of change. See Figure 7.8.

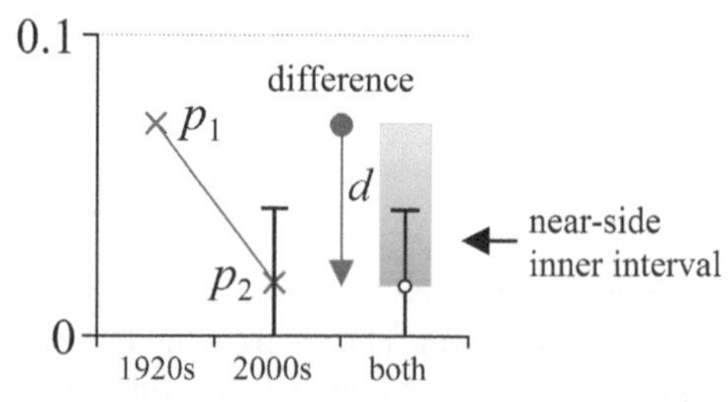

FIGURE 7.8 From line plots to floating bars. Conventional two-point plot of p_1, p_2 and so on (cf. Figure 7.1) and the same plot as a floating bar.

Levin's data for the 1920s–2000s differences are plotted as two floating bar charts in Figure 7.9. Note how the direction of change is expressed by shading. The graph includes repositioned Newcombe-Wilson intervals.

We can now see that quotative change has a statistically significant increase, something we could not see with percentage difference in Figure 7.7 because p_1 (1920s) was zero.

Like our first graph (Figure 7.1), the floating bar chart shows start and end points. It conveys more information than percentage difference graphs. We could add Wilson score intervals on either end. But here we just include an interval for their difference (length).

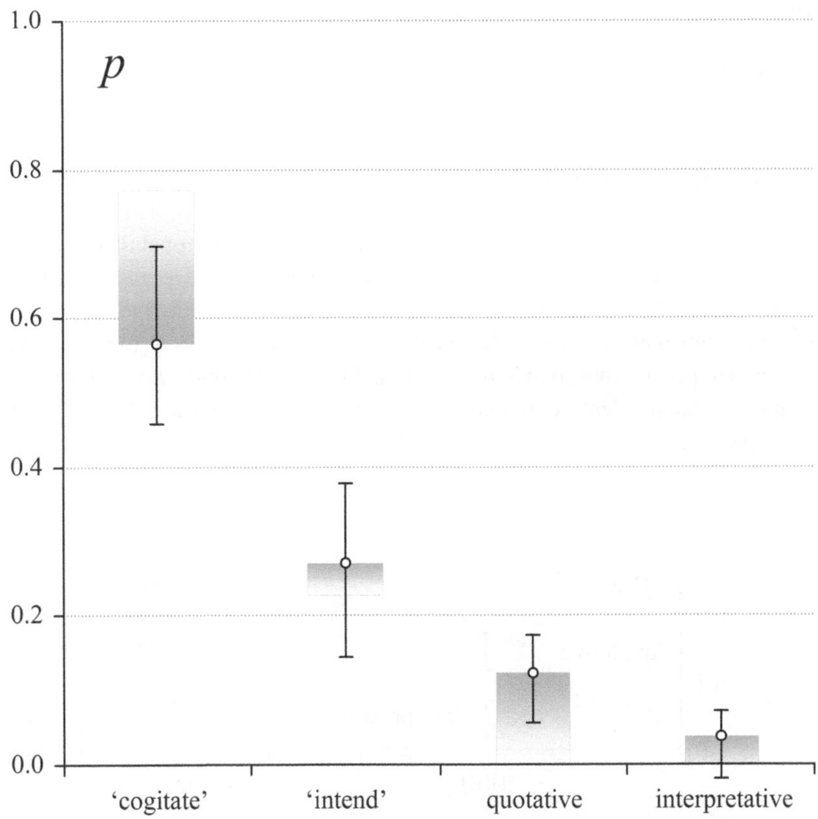

FIGURE 7.9 Floating bar charts of changing meanings of BE *thinking*, 1920s–2000s. Shading indicates direction (from light to dark), with repositioned Newcombe-Wilson intervals at the end point (2000s).

In Figure 7.1, we could visually compare intervals vertically and horizontally for their overlap. But in this plot, we only evaluate one difference – that concerning the bar itself. The graph shows 'cogitate' declining from a majority form, and quotative instances growing significantly between the time periods.

7.3.7 An Apparent Paradox

Consider the confidence intervals in Figure 7.10, taken from two figures in this chapter. Look closely at the interval for the 'interpretative' data for 2000s (left) and the difference interval (right).

The first interval for *p*(interpretative | 2000s) (left, from Figure 7.1) excludes zero, that is, it is significantly different from zero. The second interval (reproduced right, excerpted from Figure 7.9) for difference d = *p*(interpretative | 2000s) – *p*(interpretative | 1920s) *includes* zero. But the 1920s probability is zero. This interval exceeds the observed change, that is, we cannot report that d is significantly different from zero. How can this be possible?

The answer is that these intervals and tests are different (see Figure 7.3):

- **The single-observation confidence interval** allows for the possibility that the true value in the population for the 2000s data (P_2, say) is near-zero, but the sample is large enough to report that the observed probability is significantly different from it. In other words, *on the basis of observation* p_2, *we do not expect* P_2 *to be zero.*
- **The difference confidence interval** compares two samples drawn from independent populations, one in the 1920s and one in the 2000s. *Each* observation has an independent confidence interval to be accounted for. The difference interval records that *on the basis of both observations,* p_1 *and* p_2 *are not significantly different.*

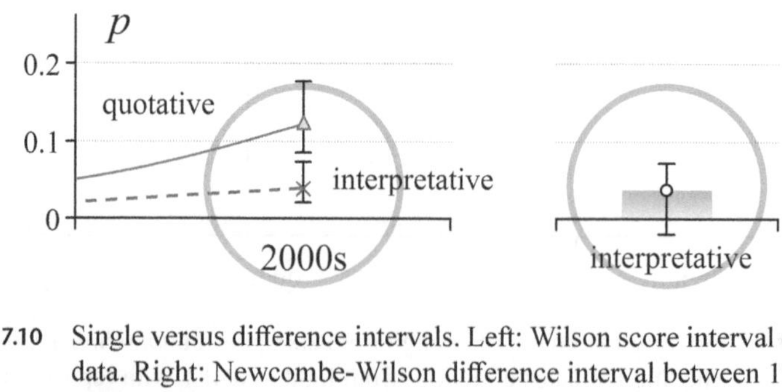

FIGURE 7.10 Single versus difference intervals. Left: Wilson score interval on 2000s data. Right: Newcombe-Wilson difference interval between 1920s and 2000s data.

In Section 7.3.3, we said we can think about significant difference in more than one way. If we say a difference is 'significant' we usually mean it is *significantly different from zero*, hence the difference is either positive or negative, and we can predict the direction of change to be found in the population.

Single observation intervals and difference intervals answer different questions, just as different χ^2 tests are applied to different hypotheses. We discuss this in the next chapter.

Whenever you are plotting graphs and intervals, you need to remind yourself what they mean – and *make sure you explain this to your readers*!

7.4 Comparing Competing Proportions

How might we decide whether *competing* proportions across an independent variable are significantly different? For example, suppose we wished to report that 'cogitate' was the most frequent form in each time period in Levin's data. It seems obviously true, but how do we test it? The answer turns out to be simple but rarely discussed.

We have already explained how to compare *independent* proportions using a Newcombe-Wilson test or 2 × 2 chi-square test. But competing proportions are not independent: each is dependent, or partially dependent, on the other.

Consider Figure 7.1. For each time period, we have four proportions, each representing a competing type, adding up to 100%. The frequency distribution for the 1960s column is $\mathbf{F} = \{108, 65, 6, 2\}$. The set may be converted into a probability distribution by dividing by the baseline frequency, $n = 181$: $\mathbf{P} = \{0.60, 0.36, 0.03, 0.01\}$ (approximately). There are $k - 1$ degrees of freedom, where $k = 4$ is the number of types.

7.4.1 A 'More' Test for Competing Frequencies and Proportions

The following test compares proportions p or frequencies $f = p \times n$. Multiplying proportions by a constant does not change the logic of a test.

Let's see if there are significantly **more** 'cogitate' instances than the next largest group, 'intend'.

In the 1960s data, the respective frequencies are $f_1 = 108$ and $f_2 = 65$. We ignore all other cell frequencies in the data to focus solely on this pair, and convert frequencies into competing Binomial proportions.

Let the new sample size $n' = f_1 + f_2 = 173$, of which proportions p_1' and p_2' are simple fractions.

$$\textit{adjusted } p_1' = p(\text{'cogitate'} \mid \{\text{'cogitate', 'intend'}\}, \text{1960s}) = f_1 / n' = 0.6243,$$
$$\textit{adjusted } p_2' = p(\text{'intend'} \mid \{\text{'cogitate', 'intend'}\}, \text{1960s}) = 1 - p_1' = 0.3757.$$

These two observed proportions are mirror-image ('alternate') Binomial proportions (see Figure 2.1 in Chapter 2). They are significantly different if, *and only if*, their Wilson score intervals exclude 0.5, due to the following trivial axiom:

Axiom (unequal alternate proportions):

Where $P_2 = 1 - P_1$, $P_1 \neq 0.5 \leftrightarrow P_1 \neq P_2$. (29)

This is another way of saying that any pair of competing proportions P_1 and P_2 can only equal each other if they both equal 0.5! So if the Wilson interval for p_1' excludes 0.5, so must its mirror for p_2', and the intervals do not overlap. There is no possible P which falls within both intervals, so they must be significantly different.

Wilson 'more' test:

Assign cell frequencies f_1 and f_2 such that $f_1 > f_2$, $n' = f_1 + f_2$ and $p_1' = f_1/n'$, and obtain the Wilson score interval for $p_1' \in (w_1^-, w_1^+)$.

Where $w_1^- > 0.5$, f_1 is significantly greater than f_2. (30)

The following alternative methods conduct the same test. See also Chapter 6.

- **The Wilson score interval** for p_1' and n' may be calculated using Equation (20'). For $\alpha = 0.05$, this gives us the interval $p_1' \in (0.5501, 0.6930)$, which excludes 0.5, as in Equation (30). Therefore p_1' must be significantly different from p_2', f_1 is significantly different from f_2, and, since $f_1 > f_2$, significantly *more* than f_2.
- **The single-sample *z* test** checks if the Normal interval centred on $P = 0.5$ excludes p_1', in which case we report p_1' is significantly different from P, and therefore p_1' is significantly different from p_2'. Equation (17) obtains a 95% Gaussian sampling interval $P = 0.5 \in (0.4255, 0.5745)$. This does not include p_1', so p_1' and p_2' are significantly different.
- **The 2 × 1 goodness of fit χ^2 test** compares $\mathbf{O} = \{f_1, f_2\}$ against $\mathbf{E} = \{n/2, n/2\}$. This obtains $\chi^2 = 10.6879$, which is greater than $\chi^2(0.05, 1) = 3.8415$, and therefore f_1 and f_2 are significantly different.

A more test can be adjusted for the discreteness of the Binomial distribution. A *continuity correction* may be applied to the single-sample *z* test (Equation (18), Chapter 6). In Chapter 8 we see how the same adjustment may be made to the χ^2 test and Wilson interval (Equations (32) and (33)). We can also employ an 'exact' Binomial test with $P = 0.5$.[12]

7.4.2 The Wilson Interval Comparison Heuristic, Revisited

Is the more test consistent with Equation (22), the Wilson interval comparison heuristic? Can we compare the original Wilson score intervals in Figure 7.1 visually as a shortcut?

The answer is yes. If there were only two original Binomial proportions, this is true by definition. But what if, as in our example data, there were $k > 2$ Multinomial proportions? Well, as k increases, each proportion becomes increasingly more independent from the others. Since the (fully) independent proportion test abides by the heuristic, the same must be true for confidence intervals on competing Multinomial proportions.

The interval comparison heuristic is applicable to competing proportions 'vertically' in Figure 7.1, and you can check intervals by eye before applying a more test.

In Chapter 8 we discuss some other interval formulae. If you intend to compare proportions using one of these other intervals, you should plot data with these intervals in the first place.

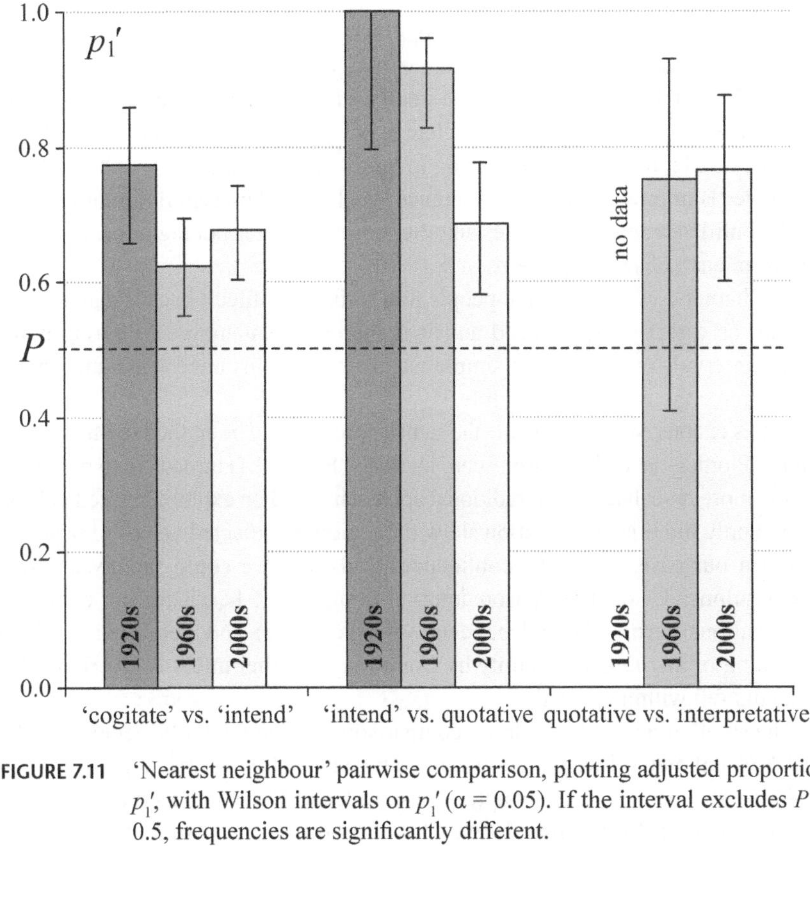

FIGURE 7.11 'Nearest neighbour' pairwise comparison, plotting adjusted proportion p_1', with Wilson intervals on p_1' ($\alpha = 0.05$). If the interval excludes $P =$ 0.5, frequencies are significantly different.

7.4.3 Visualising This Test

Normally when evaluating a graph, we can save ourselves a lot of work by employing the interval comparison heuristic and selectively extracting part-overlapping pairs to test.

But for purposes of demonstration, we will evaluate Magnus Levin's data in Table 7.1 by comparing 'nearest neighbours' by frequency, reading from the top of our graph in Figure 7.1 down each column. (If multiple intervals overlapped, or lines crossed, we might wish to perform other comparisons.)

To visualise the test in Figure 7.11, for each pair of values we plot a histogram of adjusted proportion p_1' with Wilson score intervals. As we know, the test is significant if the Wilson interval crosses the $P = 0.5$ line. This step confirms what we have observed so far, but it allows us to draw definitive conclusions and cite an appropriate test.

7.5 Conclusions

In this chapter, we took a practical approach to analysing a Multinomial 4 × 3 contingency table by plotting data in a variety of ways.

In a 2 × 2 table, there is only one degree of freedom, so a result can only be 'significant' due to a single type of change. Nevertheless, even the simplest contingency table may be worth plotting in this way. In Chapter 2, we showed how a simple 'Binomial proportion difference graph' could present different patterns, with confidence intervals expressing the range of values not significantly different from each observed proportion p.

In Chapter 6, we argued that people find statistics difficult because uncertainty cannot be directly experienced and it is therefore 'intangible'. Plotting confidence intervals on graphs is a simple way to picture this uncertainty and (hopefully) make the intangible tangible.

In this chapter, we showed how the same approach may be applied to Multinomial tables. Plotting data with Wilson score intervals (Figure 7.1) turned out to be considerably more revealing than a traditional approach based on exploring χ^2 cell values.

Not only did this visualisation show the region of expected values of observed data (in our case, to a 95% confidence level), but we could rapidly compare observations. Using the Wilson interval comparison heuristic, we compared observations across the independent variable (time) and dependent variable (meaning of BE *thinking*), simply by examining whether intervals overlapped or if points fell within intervals.

The small number of remaining comparisons that could not be decided by this quick visual method were then examined by a pairwise significance test.

In the second part of the chapter, we introduced Newcombe's difference confidence interval (Newcombe, 1998b), based on Bienaymé's 'sum of independent variances' rule. Since we have already calculated Wilson score intervals to plot the graph, obtaining a Newcombe-Wilson interval for the difference between any two independent proportions is straightforward.

Newcombe's method gives us two things: an interval we can plot alongside difference measures (with upper and lower bounds on the observed difference), and a statistical test to compare two Binomial proportions. It offers a slightly different way of calculating a 2 × 2 chi-square test, focusing on proportions of the dependent variable.

We briefly considered a commonly quoted statistic: percentage difference. However, this turns out to be a difficult measure to use for a number of reasons. We also introduced a confidence interval for the ratio of two properties, which we will revisit in Chapter 9.

This led us back to plotting simple difference (i.e., $p_2 - p_1$). We showed how we could present data as 'floating bars' with difference intervals on the end point.

Finally, we discussed a simple 'more' test to check if one frequency count was significantly more than another, for example to claim that 'cogitate' forms were more frequent than 'intend', and 'intend' forms more common than the remainder.

The process of plotting and visualising data is often overlooked as a statistical method in its own right. Even if you think you are comfortable with statistical reasoning and you are sure you understand what your results mean, this does not mean that your audience is equally clear. Diagrammatic reasoning offers you insight and helps your audience understand your results.

The usual guidance for presenting data apply: plot all data on the same scale to compare observations, and do not shorten an axis to exaggerate change. On a computer you can 'zoom in' on a pair of intervals to check if they overlap temporarily. However, when presenting your data in articles, you should avoid foreshortening axes. At the very least, keep a continuous p axis from 0 to the observation, even if the entire range [0, 1] is not visible.

Whenever you write experimental reports, whether for a specialist or general audience, it is essential to explain what you can conclude from your results. Often, a well-chosen graph can assist you. Sometimes a picture *is* worth a thousand words.

Notes

1 This heuristic is also valid for any difference interval or test that carries out a 'MOVER' Bienaymé variance-sum evaluation including the Newcombe-Wilson difference, ratio, odds ratio and log intervals, and effect size difference intervals (Chapter 9).

2 The 2 × 2 χ^2 spreadsheet and others are available from https://corplingstats.wordpress.com/siclr. Note that in this spreadsheet the IV and DV are transposed.

3 Or their signed square root, termed 'standardised residuals' (Sheskin, 2011, p. 671).

4 In any case, we should be careful not to make strong claims about one-off peaks and troughs. See Chapter 11.

5 The calculations in this chapter are documented and performed in a spreadsheet available from https://corplingstats.wordpress.com/siclr.

6 You can also use the continuity-corrected score interval discussed in Chapter 8. This confidence interval corresponds to Yates's 2 × 1 χ^2 test. For most plotting purposes, however, the standard Wilson interval is perfectly adequate.

7 'Method 10' in Newcombe (1998b, p. 876) is the difference interval based on the single proportion Wilson score interval without continuity correction. Newcombe's 'Method 11' employs a continuity correction.

8 Strictly speaking, probability space is logistic (curved) rather than Cartesian (flat), so this step involves a conservative approximation. See also Chapter 10. Zou and Donner (2008) argue that unless interval widths are large, the error thereby introduced is small.

9 We should not 'cherry-pick' pairs to perform comparisons, that is, spot the most distant pairs and then make a big fuss out of their significant difference! See Chapter 11. But we may compare neighbours and examine overall trends – again, something that is much easier to do using graphs with intervals.

10 In the left-hand graph, the ratio interval excludes 1, which also indicates a significant result.

11 The answers are 99% and 75%, respectively.

12 The following tests are also significant. The 95% Wilson interval with continuity correction for p_1' is (0.5472, 0.6957), which excludes 0.5. Yates's corrected sampling interval about $P = 0.5$ is (0.4226, 0.5774), which excludes $p_1' = 0.6243$. Yates's 2 × 1 $\chi^2 = 10.1965$, which is greater than 3.8415. The Binomial tail sum for $P = 0.5$ from 0 to $f_2 = 65$ ('intend') is 0.000669, which is less than $\alpha/2 = 0.025$.

8

FROM INTERVALS TO TESTS

8.1 Introduction

Our focus thus far has been on Binomial observations, sampling distributions and confidence intervals.[1] However, most treatments of statistics, and most courses, approach the subject in a different way – through the medium of *null hypothesis significance testing* (sometimes abbreviated to 'NHST'), using significance tests. See Chapter 2.

As we discussed, researchers are expected to carry out experiments to test null hypotheses. In the process, they apply a statistical analysis of results, interpret those results and construct new experiments to eliminate possible alternate hypotheses and refine their understanding.

A core theme of this book is that the main difficulty most of us have in reasoning about statistics is that probability, and distributions of probability, are intangible and invisible. Since we literally cannot see what is going on, statistical reasoning is often confusing. Intuitions mislead us. Mistakes are made, incorrect advice abounds and errors propagate in textbooks and the experimental literature.

One of the most common errors concerns the claim that one test result is 'more significant' than another. At the heart of this mistake is a misconception about the meaning of test scores like χ^2 and error levels (commonly termed 'p values'). Viewing the world of statistics via confidence intervals, we can see that a smaller error level just generates a higher critical value and a wider interval.

The usual way that significance tests are presented is an equation to compute a test score and a generic statement of the null hypothesis the test is meant to evaluate. An example calculation is given with some relevant example data. This

DOI: 10.4324/9781003622697-11

type of presentation is useful, but unsatisfactory. We cannot see how the test works, or how it relates to any other test or evaluation.

We have focused on confidence intervals and distributions because they help us visualise the uncertainty inherent in our sample. They allow us to robustly 'read' and communicate our results, predicting a range of likely values for the population score. These intervals define a set of values for a population probability P that are *not significantly different from* an observed proportion p according to a test. The same principle applies to confidence intervals for difference d, ratio r or percentage difference $d^{\%}$, all of which we introduced, albeit briefly, in the previous chapter.

Along the way, we saw how different statistical models behave. In Chapter 6, we found that, in certain circumstances, a symmetric Wald interval 'overshoots' (escapes the bounds of probability) and collapses to zero width (certainty)! See also Wallis (2013a). This model is *wrong*, and obtains a poor test.[2]

In this chapter, we discuss the relationship between confidence intervals and significance tests in more detail.

8.1.1 Binomial Intervals and Tests

We met Karl Pearson's chi-square (χ^2) contingency test in Chapter 2. χ^2 is derived from the z statistic, which, as we now know, is based on the Normal distribution.

In fact, χ^2 with one degree of freedom can be shown to be *mathematically identical* to equivalent z tests. The tests produce the same result in all circumstances, and it does not matter which method you use.

Indeed, for all intents and purposes, 'chi-squared' with a single degree of freedom could be called 'z-squared'. The critical values of χ^2 with one degree of freedom are the square of the corresponding critical values of z.

- The standard '2×2 χ^2 test for independence' (sometimes called the test for 'homogeneity') is another way of calculating the z test for two independent proportions drawn from the same population (Sheskin, 2011, p. 655).
- This test is based on an even simpler test. The '2×1 goodness of fit χ^2 test' (or 1×2 test) may be implemented as a Binomial test or single proportion z test (Sheskin, 2011, p. 314). This test compares a sampled proportion against a predicted probability that is assumed to be Binomially distributed.

If this is true, why might we need chi-square? Pearson's principal innovation in developing chi-square was a test of a larger array with *more than two rows or columns*, extending the Binomial 2×2 test to a more general Multinomial test with r rows and c columns. Such a test has more than one degree of freedom. Similarly, the z test can be extended to a Multinomial $r \times 1$ χ^2 test to evaluate the 'fitness' of a discrete series of r observedfrequencies or probabilities to a given distribution.

Such a procedure permits us to detect significant variation spread across multiple values instead of relying on two-way comparisons. However, further analysis is then needed, in the form of 2 × 2 or 2 × 1 χ^2 tests, to identify *which* values are undergoing significant variation (see Chapter 7).

The fundamental assumption of these tests can be stated in simple terms as follows:

> An observed dataset is a random sample drawn from a much larger population. Were we to obtain multiple samples, we might get slightly different results. In reporting results, therefore, we need a measure of their *reliability*. Stating that the result of a χ^2 test is significant at a certain level of error (e.g., $\alpha = 0.05$) is another way of stating that, were we to repeat the experiment many times, the chance of obtaining a result inconsistent with the reported result would be below this error level.

8.1.2 Sampling Assumptions

To estimate this idea of 'reliability', we must make some mathematical assumptions about data in the population and our sample. We have discussed these in some detail already, but they are worth recapitulating briefly from the perspective of significance testing.

The concept of 'the population' is an *idealisation*. See Chapter 5. An example population for corpus research might be 'all texts sampled in the same way as the corpus'. In a laboratory experiment, it might be 'all participants given the same task under the same experimental conditions'. Generalisations from a corpus of English speech and writing, such as ICE-GB (Nelson et al., 2002), would apply to 'all similarly sampled texts *in the same proportion* of speech and writing and their subcategories' – not 'all English sentences from the same period'.

Deductively rationalising beyond this well-defined population to a wider 'super-population' is common. Indeed, laboratory researchers are expected to argue that their results would be replicated in non-laboratory conditions. After all, results *only* found in a laboratory but not replicated in the real world would be of little use! The argument they must make is that the difference between laboratory and non-laboratory conditions is not relevant to the issue under investigation ('does not bias the results'), so the results are not merely an artifact of laboratory conditions. (See Chapter 5 on the distinction between a claim and an argument.)

This kind of argument is generally easier to make in the biological sciences than the social. Subjects in linguistics and psychology experiments are frequently aware of the artificiality of their treatment (see Orne, 1969). In medicine, bacteria are unaware, but humans are susceptible to placebo effects!

Considerable thought goes into experimental design to address this. If we cannot make laboratory conditions unrealistic, we can at least try to ensure they do not explain a result. Typical methods include minimising differences between groups of subjects (e.g., giving control group patients a placebo) or misdirecting subjects about the true purposes of an experiment.

In the case of corpus linguistics, we may wish to argue why a particular sampling method used to construct the corpus or a subsample, is, *at least in the respect under consideration*, 'representative of' the wider population.

Important as the question of representativeness is, this type of deductive argument is external to the statistical method. At most, it concerns the design of a corpus and its sampling frame. See Chapter 5. In this chapter, we are concerned with making sense of the underlying statistical model that allows us to report a result as 'significantly different' in the first place.

Assumption 1. Randomness and Independence

The first assumption we need to make is that the sample is *a random sample* drawn from the population, that is,

- each observation is *taken from the population at random*; and
- *each member of the sample is independently sampled* from the next.

A classical analogy concerns a procedure of sampling a fixed number of mixed single-colour billiard balls (say, red or white) from a large bag of many balls, where we do not know how many balls of each colour are in the bag in the first place (the true proportion). Every ball in the population has an equal chance of being sampled in the first place.

However, in corpus linguistics, instances are often not drawn independently from the population. Instead, we draw cases from groups of adjoining cases – texts – in a process sometimes called 'cluster sampling'. As a minimum safeguard, we must consider whether adjacent cases could plausibly be independent (see Nelson et al., 2002, p. 273 and Section 8.5.3). Ideally, we should attempt to measure and factor out the impact of this clustering. We return to this question in Chapter 16.

Assumption 2. Every Sampled Instance Is Free to Vary

The second assumption is that every case in our sample is free to vary. For a Binomial choice, A versus B, each case may be of Type A or B. This also means that any sample could, in theory, consist exclusively of Type A (observed $p = 1$) or Type B cases ($p = 0$).

It is common in linguistic data for an observed rate to be very small and conceivably zero. For example, a rare word or construction may not be found in a corpus. But as we saw in Chapter 3, it is quite common for baselines to be defined that include invariant 'Type C' cases that can never be replaced by either A or B. This happens when (per million) words are used as a baseline, but there are many other examples, such as studying the progressive (Type A) with all clauses as a baseline. Clauses incapable of alternating with the progressive are Type C. What this means is that the maximum, $p = 1$, is not theoretically plausible for at least one of the types A or B.

Accepting Type C cases into a sample breaches Assumption 2. It introduces uncontrolled variation and undermines the statistical model.

Assumption 3. The Sample Is Very Small Relative to the Size of the Population

The third assumption is that the population is much larger than the sample, potentially infinite. If the sample from which we derived our observed proportion was, say, half the size of a finite population (the balls in our imaginary bag), we would have a *greater* confidence in our estimate of the true value than if it were drawn from a much bigger or infinite population.

In such circumstances, using a z or χ^2 test tends to underestimate the reliability of our results. In linguistics, this assumption may be broken when generalising from a large subset of the population – such as treating Shakespeare's *First Folio* as a subset of his plays. We return to this question in Section 8.5.5.

These assumptions are not all-or-nothing. They can be breached without giving up on the entire model. The statistical model can be said to 'gracefully degrade', although this does not mean that anything goes!

It is possible to accept a small number of 'Type C' cases into a baseline (Assumption 2) or to employ Binomial models with data drawn from a collection of texts (Assumption 1). In some cases, we can adjust the model to compensate for the fact that we are, strictly speaking, unable to comply precisely with these assumptions. However, where possible, we should improve the experimental design to obtain cleaner and more reliable data rather than try to fix the problem by a mathematical adjustment.

8.1.3 Deriving a Binomial Distribution

The central principle of Binomial tests is quite difficult to grasp on first reading. We discussed it at some length in Chapter 6 and suggested a classroom simulation exercise you can try yourself. It can be stated as follows:

> After very many repetitions, the sampling of a frequency obtained by drawing a fixed number of instances, each consisting of one of two potential alternatives, from the population, builds up into a Binomial frequency distribution centred on the population mean, and this distribution may be approximated by the Normal distribution.

Suppose we carry out a simple experiment as follows: We sample 45 cases over two binary[3] variables, $X = \{x_1, x_2\}$ and $Y = \{y_1, y_2\}$. As in Chapter 2, Y is our *independent variable* and X our *dependent variable*. This means that we try to see if Y affects the value of X; schematically, $Y \rightarrow X$.

This kind of table might summarise the results of an experiment measuring a speaker's tendency to employ, say, modal *shall* rather than *will* in first person singular cases (so x_1 stands for *shall* and x_2 for *will*) in a spoken rather than written English sample (y_1 = spoken, y_2 = written).

Now imagine that we repeated our experiment, say, 10,000 times, to obtain a 'sample of samples'. The more repetitions we perform, the greater will be our confidence that the average result will be close to the 'correct' mean of the population – if we could measure it.

The statistician David Sheskin (2011, p. 153) explains that 'the standard error of the population mean represents a standard deviation of a sampling distribution of means'. If you followed Chapter 6, you should have an inkling of what he is saying. The Binomial distribution is *a distribution of sampled means*, and it is the standard deviation of *this* distribution that we might term 'the standard error of the population mean'.

The Binomial model states that the result for any given cell in our table is expected to be distributed in a Binomial distribution centred on the population mean P. This pattern is represented by the columns in Figure 8.1. The frequency axis, Ψ, represents the frequency of samples at a particular point, that is, the number of times a sample obtains a particular outcome on the x-axis, assuming that each sample is randomly drawn from the population.[4]

The Binomial distribution is a discrete distribution, hence the columns in Figure 8.1. Cell frequencies must be whole numbers. For reasons of ease of calculation and generalisation, we may approximate the Binomial distribution to a *continuous* distribution: the Normal or 'Gaussian' distribution, depicted by the curve in Figure 8.1.[5]

In inferring this distribution, we are not assuming that the *sample* of a variable is Binomially or Normally distributed, but rather that this distribution of the mean of the variable would be arrived at after *very many samples* were taken from the population, randomly and independently from each other, and their observations plotted as a distribution. The height of each column represents the chance that a particular rate would be observed in the future.

A Normal distribution can be specified by two parameters. The expected distribution $\mathbf{E}[P, S]$ has a *mean*, P (the centre point), and *standard deviation*, S (the degree of spread). The Normal distribution is *symmetric*, with the mean, median and mode coinciding.

Recall from Chapter 6 that

$$\textit{population standard deviation } S = \sqrt{P(1-P)/n}, \qquad (17)$$

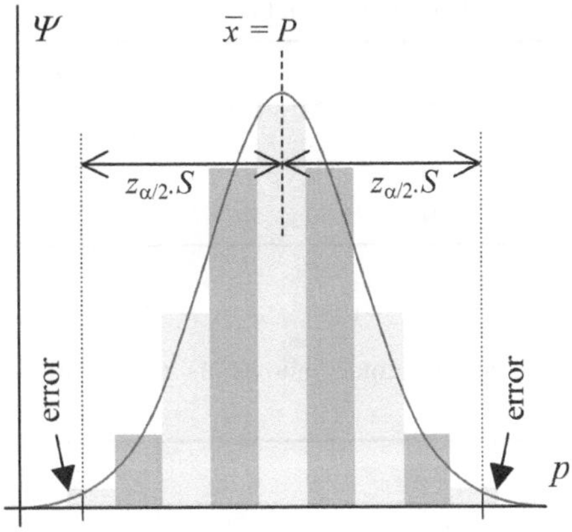

FIGURE 8.1 Normal approximation to a Binomial frequency distribution plotted over a probabilistic range $p \in [0, 1]$.

where P is the expected value of the Binomial distribution we are approximating, and n is the size of the sample.

These distributions are *expected sampling models*, that is, mathematical models of how future samples are likely to be distributed. They are based on a particular sample size and expected mean. The heart of *inferential* statistics is attempting to predict how future experimental results would behave allowing for chance variation.

We can now use the Normal distribution model to 'peek into the future' and estimate the reliability of a single observed sample.

A sampling interval on a population proportion P is the range of values that an observation is expected to take at a particular probability of error (say, $\alpha = 0.05$). This error level can also be expressed as a degree of confidence: '95%'. What we are interested in is *how far an observation must deviate from the expected value to be deemed statistically significantly different from it* at a given error level. This 'significant difference' is simply the difference that is so large that it is unlikely to have occurred by chance.

Consider Figure 8.1. The total area under the curve adds up to 100%. The two tail areas under the curve marked 'error' represent extreme values. Suppose we find the tail areas that each cover 2.5% of the total area ($\alpha/2$ for $\alpha = 0.05$). We then have a range between them, inside which 95%, or 19 in 20 experimental runs, should fall if our expected P is correct. The chance of an experimental result falling above the upper bound or below the lower bound is 1 in 20.

We might insist on a smaller error (e.g., $\alpha = 0.01$). In this case, these tails would be smaller (0.005) and the interval wider. Our tolerance for random variation would increase, and any result found outside the range would be likely to occur only 1 in 100 times – *if the given value for P was correct.*

This gives us a simple significance test.

TABLE 8.1 An example 2 × 2 contingency table, containing frequencies *f*.

f	*speech* y_1	*writing* y_2	*Total*
shall x_1	20	5	25
will x_2	10	10	20
Total	30	15	45

TABLE 8.2 Dividing by column totals allows us to rewrite Table 8.1 in terms of probabilities *p*.

p	*speech* y_1	*writing* y_2	*Total*
shall x_1	2/3	1/3	5/9
will x_2	1/3	2/3	4/9

8.1.4 Some Example Data

Suppose we obtained a table of frequencies for modal *shall* versus *will* in speech and writing in a corpus. We will use fictional results for the purposes of this demonstration, and these are given in Table 8.1: [[20, 5], [10, 10]].[6]

Consider the first column, y_1 = {20, 10}, which in our experiment represents spoken data. Out of $n = 30$ observations, 20 are of type x_1 (*shall*) and 10, x_2 (*will*). The probability of picking type x_1 at random from this set is equal to the proportion of cases of type x_1, so $p = 2/3$. The probability of choosing type x_2 given y_1 is the remaining probability, $q = 1 - p = 1/3$. In Table 8.2, we have listed these probabilities.

8.2 Tests for a Single Binomial Proportion

Confidence intervals and tests have a straightforward relationship. See Table 8.3. If we can construct a confidence interval, we can use it to perform a test. Test calculations can be simpler, but intervals are more flexible. We need an interval to plot upper and lower bounds on data.

The tests on the right of Table 8.3 assume we know the population value *P* and test against it. The intervals on *p* obtain an identical result to the equivalent test via the interval equality principle.

8.2.1 The Single-Sample z Test

The single-sample z test for a Binomial proportion (Sheskin, 2011, p. 149) performs the evaluation procedure outlined here.

Suppose we wished to test if results matched an expected proportion P. For example, we might want to test if a coin was unbiased, that is, the true value of P was 0.5. Our null hypothesis would be that $P = 0.5$, and our test would evaluate whether this null hypothesis could be rejected based on an observed proportion p obtained by tossing the coin n times.

One way we can do this is calculate the Normal sampling interval about P, and test if p is far enough away from P to be considered *significantly* different from it. If it is, we may reject the null hypothesis.

Most of the time, we will employ a 'two-tailed' test, that is, we envisage that p could be less than or greater than P. The test can be converted to a 'one-tailed' test very simply.

The test simply compares an observed value, p, with a Normal sampling interval about a given P (see Figure 8.2). If p is within the sampling interval, we conclude that we are unable to reject the null hypothesis that there is no difference

TABLE 8.3 Confidence intervals and test equivalents.

Confidence intervals on p	*Significance tests with P*
Wilson score interval	2 × 1 'goodness of fit' χ^2 test
Wilson interval with continuity correction	2 × 1 'goodness of fit' Yates's χ^2 test
Clopper-Pearson interval (by search)	2 × 1 Binomial B test
'mid-p' interval (by search)	2 × 1 mid-p Binomial test
log-likelihood interval (by search)	2 × 1 log-likelihood G^2 test

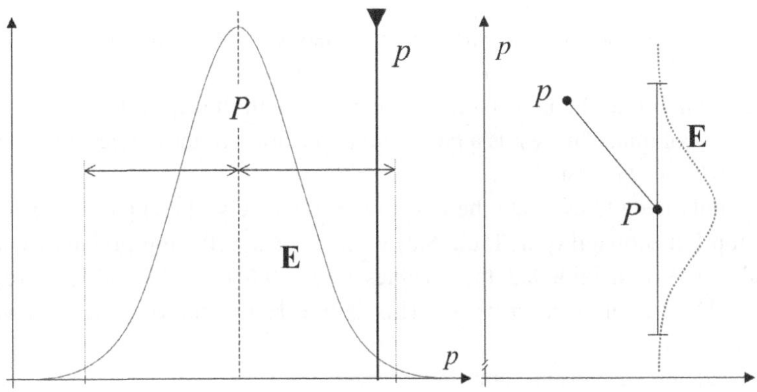

FIGURE 8.2 The single-sample population z test: comparing an observed $p = 0.6667$ with the sampling interval about the population mean (0.3777, 0.7334) (left). The sampling interval (arrows) may be plotted as an 'I' shaped error bar in an equivalent graph (right).

between the predicted result P and the sample. Those values of p outside the range are significant at the chosen error level.

The null hypothesis of a two-tailed z test is that an observation p is not significantly different from a particular value of P.

P could be any legitimate probability. If you want to know whether your observed probability is significantly different from 0, 0.5 or 0.9, say, you can put these values into P and apply the test.

Single-sample *z* test (two-tailed):

If $P - z_{\alpha/2}.S < p < P + z_{\alpha/2}.S$ there is no significant difference between p and P. (31)

S represents the standard deviation for the population value P calculated with Equation (17), and $z_{\alpha/2}$ the critical value of z for a two-tailed interval for a given error level α. The two-tailed critical value $z_{\alpha/2}$ where $\alpha = 0.05$ is 1.95996. The consequent 'there is no significant difference . . .' is the null hypothesis.

A one-tailed test is used if we want to test only one bound, for example, if p is significantly less than P, and it does not matter if $p > P$. In this case, we substitute z_α into the equation, which can be spelled out as Equation (31'). The corresponding critical value z_α for $\alpha = 0.05$ is 1.64485.

Single-sample *z* test (one-tailed):

If $P - z_\alpha.S < p$ then p is not significantly less than P; alternatively,

If $p < P + z_\alpha.S$ then p is not significantly greater than P; (31')

In this book, we will use the stricter two-tailed test unless otherwise stated.

Let us use Tables 8.1 and 8.2 for our illustration and compare an observation for one column of the independent variable, Y, with the equivalent row value in the Total column. This test is a particular application of the single-sample z test: the *goodness of fit* test.

We only need to evaluate the first row, x_1. So we will compare $p = p(x_1 \mid y_1)$ (the top left probability in Table 8.2) with $P = p(x_1)$ (the top probability in the Total column). In Table 8.2, these values are $p = 0.6667$ and $P = 0.5556$, respectively. The sample size, n, is 30. This is the data supporting the observation $p = p(x_1 \mid y_1)$.

We calculate a Normal sampling interval about P:

$$\textit{population standard deviation } S = \sqrt{P(1-P)/n} = \sqrt{0.5556 \times 0.4444/30} = 0.0907,$$

$$\textit{population interval } P \pm z_{\alpha/2}.S = 0.5556 \pm 0.1778 = (0.3777, 0.7334).$$

To perform the test, we compare the resulting interval about P with $p = p(x_1 \mid y_1) = 0.6667$.

The test is significant if p falls outside the expected interval for P. In this example, $0.6667 < 0.7334$, so the result is not significant. We cannot overturn the null hypothesis that the proportion at y_1 (2/3) is consistent with the expected overall proportion (5/9) at a 1 in 20 error level. There is more than a 1 in 20 risk of falsely claiming that this difference is genuine.

The method described previously creates a sampling interval about P. But the equation can also be rearranged by simple algebra to find the value of z for any given difference, $P - p$:

$$z = (p - P) / S. \tag{32}$$

We might then check if the absolute value $|z|$ is greater than $z_{\alpha/2}$, and if it is, reject the null hypothesis. The sign of z (plus or minus) tells us in which direction the change can be found:

$$z = (0.6667 - 0.5556) / 0.0907 = -1.2247.$$

The absolute score is smaller than $z_{0.025} = 1.95996$, and therefore the difference is not significant.

It bears repeating that all tests are tests for *reproducibility* (see Chapter 11). Scores are not a measure of the size of the result. Saying that results are 'non-significant' is to state *we cannot be sure that our results are not simply due to random chance* (at the error level we set).

8.2.2 The 2 × 1 Goodness of Fit χ^2 Test

Earlier, we said that the square of the critical value of z is equal to the equivalent critical value of χ^2 for one degree of freedom. There is a direct relationship between z tests and chi-square tests.

The goodness of fit χ^2 test compares two discrete frequency distributions with each other. It uses the standard χ^2 formula and compares the result with the critical value of χ^2. The formula is summed over each cell in an observed and expected distribution.

In Chapter 2, we provided a formula for the homogeneity test. This sums rows and columns with indexed terms, $o_{i,j}$, representing the observed cell value in row i, column j. For the $r \times 1$ χ^2 test, we sum only in one dimension, a column or row (depending on the layout):

$$\chi^2 = \sum_{i=1}^{r} \frac{(o_{i,j} - e_{i,j})^2}{e_{i,j}} \tag{1'}$$

In our case $j = 1$, and $r = 2$, the observed distribution is the column, $o \in \mathbf{O}_1 = \{20, 10\}$, and the expected distribution is based on the 'total' column *scaled to the same sample size*, that is, the total column frequency. Consequently, $e \in \mathbf{E} = \{25, 20\}\times 30/45 = \{5/9, 4/9\}\times 30 \approx \{16.6667, 13.3333\}$. See Tables 8.1 and 8.2. We might also use Equation (2) from Chapter 2:

$$\textit{expected cell value } e_{i,j} = o_{i+} \times o_{+j} / o_{++}. \tag{2}$$

The test result obtains $\chi^2 = 0.6667 + 0.8333 = 1.5$, which is below the critical value of χ^2 with one degree of freedom, $\chi^2(0.05, 1) = 3.8415$. Again, the test is not significant. For Multinomial $r \times 1$ tests, $df = r - 1$.

Chi-square test:

If $\chi^2 < \chi^2(\alpha, df)$, the observed distribution does not significantly differ from the expected distribution. (33)

The single-sample z test in the goodness of fit evaluation reported $z = -1.2247$. $z^2 = 1.5 = \chi^2$. The 2×1 χ^2 test is mathematically equivalent to the z test where $P = p(x_1)$.

Note that in the χ^2 test, we sum terms calculated from both cells. That is, we also compare $p(x_2 \mid y_1)$ with $p(x_2) = 0.4444$. We do not need to do this in the z test. It is only necessary to compare the proportions of the first row of cells because the second row is *mathematically determined* by the first. The test has one degree of freedom.[7]

In our evaluation, we compared $p = p(x_1 \mid y_1)$ with the average proportion for the table, $P = p(x_1)$, for both χ^2 and z tests. Only the subset column is free to vary, so the sampling interval on P is calculated using the number of cases n in that column (hence $n = 30$).

Not every variable is binary. The advantage of the χ^2 formula is that it is extensible to larger tables, including Multinomial goodness of fit tests. In Section 8.5, we review the analysis of larger tables.

8.2.3 *The Wilson Score Confidence Interval*

In Chapter 6, we mentioned the Wald interval. This assumes that a confidence interval about an observation p is Normal, an assumption we learned is false.

The correct approach uses the now-familiar Wilson score interval about an observed p (Wilson, 1927):

$$\textit{Wilson score interval } (w^-, w^+) \equiv \frac{p + \frac{z_{\alpha/2}^2}{2n} \pm z_{\alpha/2}\sqrt{\frac{p(1-p)}{n} + \frac{z_{\alpha/2}^2}{4n^2}}}{1 + \frac{z_{\alpha/2}^2}{n}}. \tag{20}$$

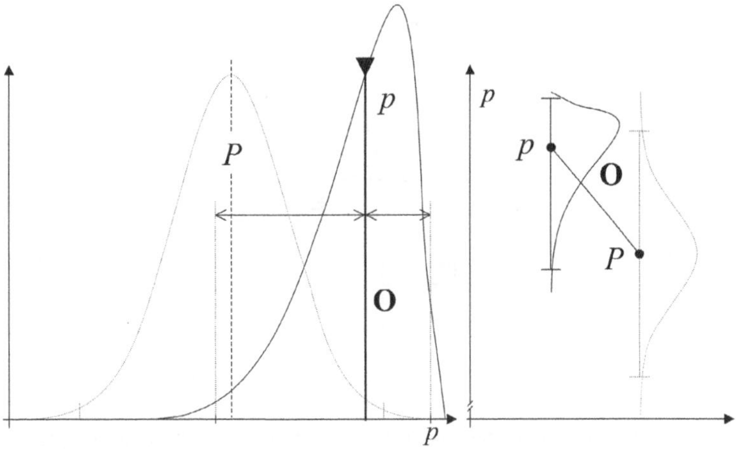

FIGURE 8.3 The Wilson score test: the observed proportion $p = 0.6667$ has an asymmetric Wilson score interval (0.4878, 0.8077) (left). The confidence interval (arrows) may be plotted as an 'I' shaped error bar in the equivalent graph (right). The Normal distribution about an expected proportion P (dotted) is shown for comparison.

Whereas both the z and χ^2 tests relied on P (selecting $P = p(x_1)$ in the case of χ^2), the Wilson interval does not require us to quote P at all. This is why this interval is so useful.

Instead, we use the interval to test if any arbitrary test point, P_i, falls outside an expected range for p, (w^-, w^+). We calculate the confidence interval once and inspect graphs (see Chapter 7). As we discussed, the Wilson score interval about p inverts the Gaussian sampling interval about P. It obtains the same result as the single-sample z test (and the equivalent 2×1 goodness of fit χ^2 test) thanks to the interval equality principle. The difference is the same, $|p - P| = |P - p|$, whether we measure it from P or p. See Figure 8.4.

We can state this interval in the form of a significance test.

Wilson score test:

If $w^- < P < w^+$, there is no significant difference between p and P. (34)

In Chapter 7, we used Wilson's formula to plot confidence intervals on graphs, with error bars extending to w^- and w^+. An example plot for Table 8.2 (a Binomial proportion difference graph for $p(x_1)$) is given in Figure 8.5.

In our example data (Figure 8.5, left point), $p = 0.6667$, $n = 30$ and $z_{\alpha/2} = 1.95996$. We obtain a score interval for the probability of using *shall* in speech, $p(x_1 \mid y_1)$, of (0.4878, 0.8077). Since $P = 0.5556$ is within this range, the result is

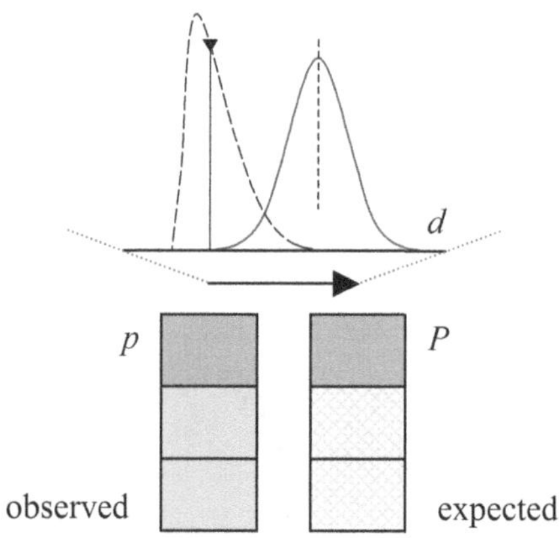

FIGURE 8.4 Two different methods for performing the same test comparison: the single-sample z test employs the Normal sampling interval on either side of the population (expected) proportion P; and the Wilson score test uses the score interval about the observed proportion p.

not significant. We may obtain a similar interval for the second 'writing' column, $p(x_1 \mid y_2)$, Figure 8.5 (right data point).

Wilson's interval is based on an asymmetric distribution restricted to the probability range [0, 1]. Unlike the Wald interval, which breaks down near extreme values, we can compute intervals at $p = 0$ or 1. At the midpoint $p = 0.5$, the Wilson score interval is symmetric, and appears similar to the Wald.[8]

8.2.4 Correcting for Continuity

In Chapter 6, we described how adopting the continuous (smooth) Normal approximation to the discrete (chunky) Binomial distribution introduced an error. The uncorrected Wilson interval and χ^2 test are a little *too* inclined to be considered 'significant' when an exact Binomial test would not. Frank Yates (1934) proposed a simple adjustment, called a continuity correction, c, that separates P and p by an additional 'half-chunk', $\frac{1}{2n}$:

$$\textit{Yates's interval } (E^-_{cc}, E^+_{cc}) = P \pm (z_{\alpha/2} \cdot S + \tfrac{1}{2n}), \tag{18}$$

With our data, $n = 30$ and $P = 25/45 = 0.5556$, $S = 0.0907$, and the continuity correction term, $c = 1/60 = 0.0167$. This obtains an interval about P of (0.3611, 0.7500). Since $p = 0.6667$ is within this range, the test is non-significant.

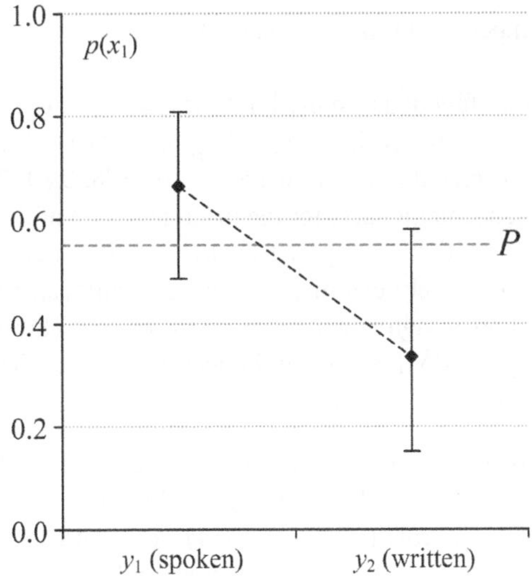

FIGURE 8.5 Plotting Wilson score intervals on $p(x_1)$: data from Table 8.2, with expected $P = 0.5556$.

To apply the same principle to the χ^2 test, we subtract 0.5 from each squared difference term. This gives us Yates's formula for χ^2:

$$Yates\text{'s } \chi^2 \equiv \sum_{i=1}^{r} \frac{(|\, o_{i,j} - e_{i,j} \,| - 0.5)^2}{e_{i,j}}. \tag{35}$$

Yates's test obtains $\chi^2 = 1.08$, which is compared with the critical value of χ^2 and is also, unsurprisingly, non-significant.

Finally, we need to apply Yates's correction to the Wilson score interval. Commonly, a complicated equation is quoted (Equation (114), see p. 414). However, by far the easiest way to define this is to employ our *Wilson functions* from Chapter 6. This gives us a much more flexible formula, which can be adapted in other ways.

In Chapter 6, we said let us define two Wilson functions, one for each bound, using Equation (20), which for convenience we call WilsonLower and WilsonUpper.

$$\text{WilsonLower}(p, n, \alpha/2) \equiv w^-, \text{ and WilsonUpper}(p, n, \alpha/2) \equiv w^+. \tag{20''}$$

Equation (20) contains a 'plus or minus' ('±') sign. 'WilsonLower' is Equation (20) with a minus sign and 'WilsonUpper' is the equation with a plus sign.

We apply Yates's correction to the observed p first, widening the interval:

$$w^-_{cc} \equiv \text{WilsonLower}(\max(0, p - \tfrac{1}{2n}), n, \alpha/2), \text{ and}$$

$$w^+_{cc} \equiv \text{WilsonUpper}(\min(1, p + \tfrac{1}{2n}), n, \alpha/2). \quad (36)$$

The 'max' and 'min' functions simply limit the parameter to $\mathbf{P} = [0, 1]$. With our data, this gives us a corrected interval of $(w^-_{cc}, w^+_{cc}) = (0.4717, 0.8206)$, slightly wider than the uncorrected interval, $(w^-, w^+) = (0.4878, 0.8077)$.

This adjustment accommodates for the discrete nature of the Binomial by erring on the side of caution. Compared to the 'exact' Binomial, it trades Type I errors (the error of falsely claiming a result as significant) for Type II errors (mistakenly rejecting a significant result). It does not eliminate excess Type I errors completely. To do this, we would need to increase the correction factor further – by 1.5 times to $\frac{1.5}{2n}$ (Wallis, 2024a).

Using this adjustment, the performance of χ^2, z and Wilson tests are such that they can even be used for small $n < 10$ and small $p \approx 0$.[9]

Cochran's much-cited rule (Cochran, 1954) says that where an expected cell in a table has a frequency of less than five it should be collapsed (merged with another), or the χ^2 test abandoned in favour of the Binomial or Fisher's test.[10] This is unnecessary when the '1.5×' continuity correction is employed.

8.2.5 The 'Exact' Binomial Test

For small samples, 'exact' tests are generally preferred over Yates's χ^2. These are the Binomial test for 2 × 1 goodness of fit test conditions, which we discuss here, and Fisher's exact test for 2 × 2 tests, which we discuss in Section 8.3.5. These methods avoid the Normal approximation to the Binomial, so are termed 'exact'.

To recap from Chapter 6, the *ideal Binomial probability distribution* is the distribution of the chance of selecting r heads out of n tosses of a coin with 'weight' (a prior chance of occurring) P. In our case, we will use our test value $P = 0.5556$.

The distribution is defined in terms of a series of discrete probabilities for r, where the height of each column is calculated by the following expression (Sheskin, 2011, p. 311):

$$\textit{Binomial probability } B(r; n, P) \equiv nCr \,.\, P^r(1 - P)^{(n-r)}, \quad (16)$$

where $P \in (0, 1)$, and for $P = 0$ or 1, we substitute 1 for 0^0. The function nCr is the *combinatorial function*, the number of ways that r heads out of n tosses can be achieved.

Like the z test, the Binomial test requires us to know P and test p. Equation (16) tells us the height of each column r for a given P and n. To apply the test, we simply add up the 'columns' beyond our observed p. A worked example is in Table 6.1, Chapter 6.

The following formula simply adds up a range of columns from r_1 to r_2 inclusive:

$$\textit{Cumulative Binomial probability } B(r_1, r_2; n, P) \equiv \sum_{r=r_1}^{r_2} nCr.P^r(1-P)^{(n-r)}. \quad (37)$$

To calculate the 'tail area' from 0 to f (where $p < P$, $p = f / n$), we set $r_1 = 0$ and $r_2 = f$. If that tail is smaller than $\alpha/2$, the test is significant. A similar substitution applies for the other tail from f to 1. Table 6.1 in Chapter 6 offers two worked examples.

Binomial test:

Where $p < P$, if $B(0, f; n, P) \geq \alpha/2$, the difference $p - P$ is non-significant; or

where $p > P$, if $B(f, n; n, P) \geq \alpha/2$, the difference $p - P$ is non-significant. (38)

This test takes more effort than the equivalent z test. We have to calculate the combinatorial function nCr for every integer value of r within the designated range. A one-tailed test employing the threshold α can be calculated if we know if $p > P$ or $p < P$ (see Section 8.2.1).

We can save some effort by sequencing. Since any sum of terms will always increase as we add them together, we can take the largest term first, then the next largest, and so on. At each stage, we test if the total is greater than $\alpha/2$. For $p < P$, this means summing from 0 to f in reverse order.

If, at any point during this process, the partially completed tail area sum exceeds the threshold, we can stop and report a non-significant result. However, if the result is significant, we will need to add up every term. With our data, $p > P$. The Binomial tail area is 0.1488, which, for a two-tailed test, is greater than $\alpha/2 = 0.025$. The difference is not significant.

8.2.6 The Clopper-Pearson Confidence Interval

The Binomial formula may be converted into an 'exact' Binomial confidence interval (b^-, b^+) using a computer search procedure. This interval is known as the 'Clopper-Pearson' (CP) interval (Clopper & Pearson, 1934). First, let us consider the lower bound of p, that is, where $P < p$ (as in Figure 8.3). Thanks to interval equality, this is the upper bound of P at a 'just-significant' difference.

Equation (37) assumes we know P. But we want to find the lower bound for $p = f / n$ at an error level α. For a two-tailed interval, we search for the value of P whose upper Binomial tail is $\alpha/2$:

Find $b^- = P$ where $B(f, n; n, P) = \alpha/2$. (39)

A computer searches for P by trying a number of possible values of P until it converges on the best answer satisfying Equation (39).[11] This method tends to an exact result for any integer f. See Appendices A and B.

This method is often labelled 'exact' because it avoids the Normal approximation to the Binomial. However, it has two disadvantages. It involves significant computation that can be difficult to carry out for large sample sizes, and it is difficult to generalise.

To obtain an upper bound for p, we can use the equality $b^+(p) \equiv 1 - b^-(1 - p)$, that is, calculate the lower bound formula for $(1 - p)$ and subtract it from 1. Alternatively, we can find P using the lower tail cumulative Binomial formula for P:

Find $b^+ = P$ where $B(0, f; n, P) = \alpha/2$. (39')

We obtain $(b^-, b^+) = (0.4719, 0.8271)$ by search. In this case the interval has a lower bound close to the continuity-corrected one ($w^-_{cc} = 0.4717$), but a higher upper bound.

The CP interval may be used as a 'gold standard' for evaluating the performance of other intervals (Wallis, 2013a). However, the idea that the Clopper-Pearson interval is optimal or even 'exact' has been criticised recently.[12] It is widely agreed that the interval is excessively conservative (it has a higher coverage in practice than the desired $1 - \alpha$) because the Binomial evaluation guarantees an interval contains the population proportion at an error level of *at least* α. This 'at least' hides fluctuation due to the discrete Binomial distribution.

Sometimes the error rate will be smaller than this, and the effect is greatest with small n. If you plot a lot of data with CP intervals, the overall (average) Type I error rate will be smaller than the target value. The same objection applies to the use of continuity corrections.

This makes sense if you have *many* datapoints. For example, if you model a curve with upper and lower bounds and wish to draw conclusions about the data overall. The aim should probably be an interval method (like the uncorrected Wilson) which has an average coverage of $1 - \alpha$.

However, if you wish to make a claim from an interval about a *particular* datapoint, averaging is risky. You want to know that the actual error rate of a chosen interval is no greater than α. A precautionary approach using a CP or continuity-corrected interval is appropriate for the same reason that the equivalent test is recommended.

8.2.7 The 'Mid-p' Confidence Interval

A variant of the CP interval that accommodates for this 'excessive conservatism' objection is the 'mid-p' confidence interval (Berry & Armitage, 1995;

Newcombe, 1998a, 2020, p. 65). This method allocates half the Binomial column at $p = f / n$ to the tail area, leaving half inside the interval (see Figure 8.6).

We alter the search procedure in Equation (36) slightly.

$$\text{Find } b_m^- = P \text{ where } B(f; n, P)/2 + B(f+1, n; n, P) = \alpha/2. \quad (40)$$

As before, the upper bound may be calculated from $b_m^+(p) \equiv 1 - b_m^-(1-p)$, or by search:

$$\text{Find } b_m^+ = P \text{ where } B(f; n, P)/2 + B(0, f-1; n, P) = \alpha/2. \quad (40')$$

For an observed proportion $p = 20/30$ with $n = 30$, we obtain $(b_m^-, b_m^+) = (0.4858, 0.8167)$. This interval is narrower than the CP interval and can be thought of as the Binomial equivalent to the Wilson score interval without a continuity adjustment. It is slightly wider in this case: $(w^-, w^+) = (0.4878, 0.8077)$. For large sample sizes, the Wilson interval may be substituted.

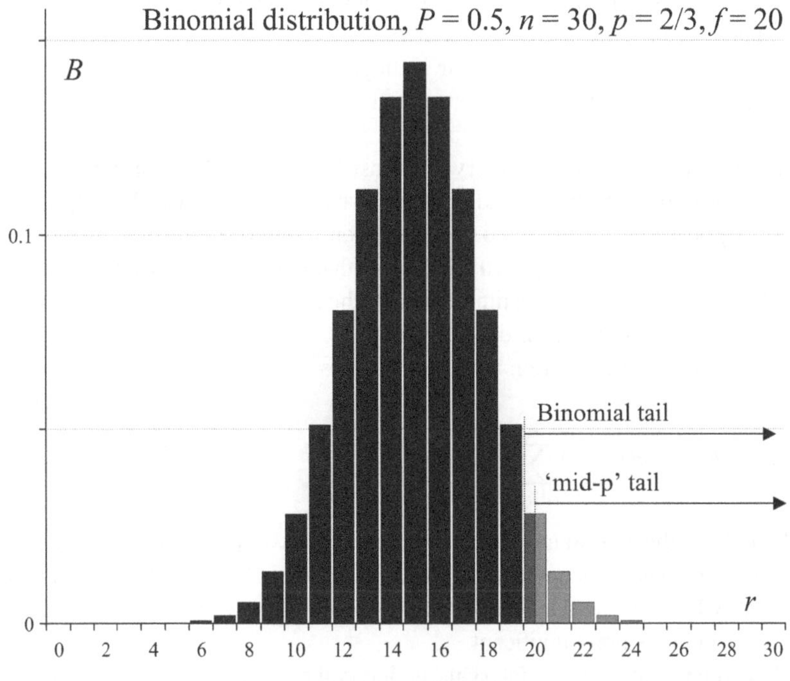

FIGURE 8.6 Calculating Binomial and 'mid-p' tail areas for $p = 2/3$, $n = 30$, in this case selecting $P = 0.5$. To calculate the lower bound of p, we must find P where the shaded area is $\alpha/2$.

The main drawback of the mid-p interval is that the test from which it is derived is little known in the literature. We may set it out simply:

Mid-p Binomial test (38')

Where $p < P$, if $B(f; n, P)/2 + B(0, f - 1; n, P) \geq \alpha/2$, the difference $p - P$ is non-significant; or

where $p > P$, if $B(f; n, P)/2 + B(f + 1, n; n, P) \geq \alpha/2$, the difference $p - P$ is non-significant.

If you use a 'mid-p' interval you must explain this. Whereas the Wilson score interval is the inverse of an extremely well-known, indeed 'foundational' significance test, the 'mid-p' confidence interval is not. Claims about 'significant difference' should be made carefully, and the method used stated (e.g., 'by a two-tailed mid-p evaluation with $\alpha = 0.05$').

8.2.8 The Log-Likelihood Test and Confidence Interval

The log-likelihood test is occasionally proposed as an alternative to χ^2. It is summed in a similar manner (although some cell scores may be negative) and compared against the critical value of χ^2.

The test has found some favour in linguistics due to Dunning (1993), who found it appeared to perform better than uncorrected χ^2 when testing for significant difference when p was small (as in per million word rates). However, evaluating a log-likelihood interval against the Clopper-Pearson interval, Wallis (2013a) observed that it had poor performance in other conditions, and that Yates's χ^2 (or the continuity-corrected Wilson interval) performed better in any case. Newcombe (1998a, p. 870) comments that it may be 'regarded as leading to a different kind of interval estimate, which should be called "likelihood interval" to distinguish it from a confidence interval'.

Nevertheless, the function may be written as

$$\textit{log-likelihood}\ G^2 \equiv 2 \sum_{i=1, j=1}^{r,c} o_{i,j} \ln(o_{i,j} / e_{i,j}), \qquad (41)$$

where 'ln' is the natural logarithm function, and any term where o or $e = 0$ simply returns zero. Using our example data, this obtains $G^2 = 7.2929 + (-5.7536) = 1.5392$, which is less than the critical value we have been using ($\chi^2(0.05, 1) = 3.8415$) and thus non-significant.

Like the CP and 'mid-p' intervals, an interval may be computed by search (see Appendix B).[13]

8.2.9 Bootstrap Intervals

The 'bootstrap' method (Hesterberg et al., 2010) has found favour in some textbooks recently. This method is distinct from those discussed so far. It makes three assumptions: that the sample is a good approximation of the population, that a confidence interval may be estimated via a standard error obtained by resampling with replacement, and – in the case of the single proportion at least – the resulting interval will be a (symmetric) 'Normal' interval.

For our Binomial proportion $p = 20/30$, we would create a series of new random samples each of size $n = 30$, each drawn from our original sample with replacement. Imagine drawing 30 coloured balls from a bag containing just 20 red and 10 white balls, noting their colour *and putting them back in the bag each time* (hence 'replacement'). The new sample will not necessarily have the same number of red balls as there are in the bag. The idea is that the observed variance of the mean rate of many such new samples ($p_1, p_2, p_3 \ldots$) gives us an estimate of the uncertainty of that rate, termed the 'standard error'.

We discussed a version of this idea in Chapter 6. Repeated sampling of a known proportion P obtains a Binomial distribution about P. Over many iterations, the result tends towards the ideal Binomial distribution.

Now, if we derive a Normal 'standard error' interval from this resampled distribution, $p = P$, we find ourselves with the 'Wald' interval for p. But as we discovered, that interval overshoots the range $\boldsymbol{P} = [0, 1]$, collapses to zero when $p = 0$ or 1, and is not consistent with significance tests! The bootstrap method represents a step backwards, for the single Binomial proportion at least.

A bootstrap method *could* be applied to the problem of finding intervals for properties without a known formula (see Chapter 9), but it must be unreliable for small samples because we *expect* them to vary from the population! Since bootstrap intervals are based on resampling rather than significance testing, it makes sense not to call them 'confidence intervals'.

This method makes the same fundamental error Wilson (1927) noted: it confuses the distribution of p about P (a sampling distribution) with the distribution of P about p (the distribution that forms the basis of a confidence interval). It does not follow the interval equality principle introduced in Chapter 6, and we cannot use them to make reliable claims about significance or confidence, even for large samples.

8.2.10 A Simple Performance Comparison

With several alternative calculations for a single Binomial proportion test and confidence interval available, how should you choose between them? We will discount the Wald (or bootstrap) interval because it is mathematically incorrect.

Performance differences between the other methods described previously are more subtle and require some effort to identify.

Detailed evaluations have been published. Newcombe (1998a, 2020) evaluated average and minimum *coverage probabilities*, whereas Wallis (2013a, 2020b) compared their performance against the CP interval. Newcombe comments that CP is always conservative, whereas both Wilson and mid-p methods have slightly conservative coverage probabilities *on average* but are not guaranteed to be conservative in every case. Every CP interval has an effective Type I error rate of at most α, but Wilson and mid-p intervals may produce a higher error rate in some cases, that is, they incorrectly class some differences as significant. Wallis (2020b) notes these excess errors are greatest for small *n*.[14]

A simple way to see the difference in the performance of these intervals is in Figure 8.7, which plots lower bounds for integer values $p = f / n$. We use a small sample size because this makes differences easy to see.

Upper bounds mirror the curve in a way indicated by the shaded upper CP bound. The guaranteed-conservative line is the lower CP bound.

- Uncorrected '$\chi^2(P)$' is equal to the Wilson lower bound of *p*. This allows the most excess 'Type I errors' ('excessive generosity'), that is, deciding that a

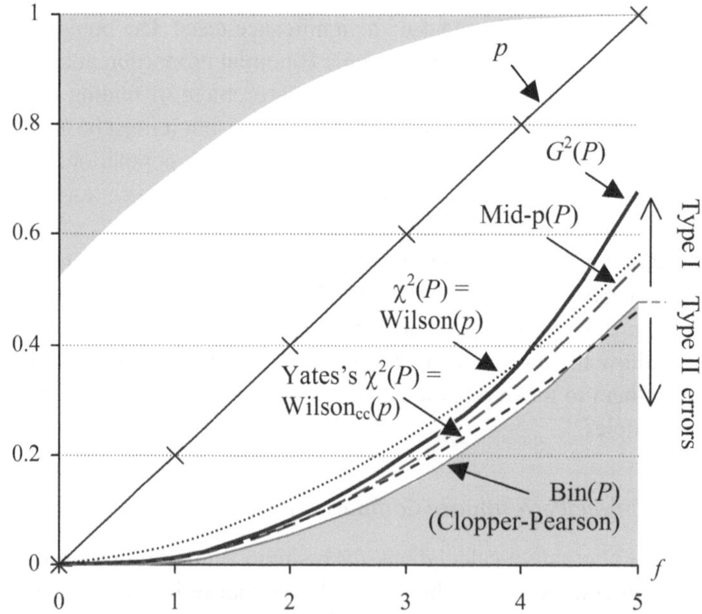

FIGURE 8.7 Estimates for the lower confidence interval bound of p, $p = f / n$, $n = 5$, $\alpha = 0.05$.

value is significantly different when it should not be according to the Binomial test.

- The mid-p lower bound, 'Mid-p(P)', is generally more conservative than the Wilson, so it has fewer Type I errors. It tends to be closer to the Wilson at f= 5. In fact, for larger samples, as p tends to 1 it is less conservative than the Wilson. It is necessarily less conservative than the Clopper-Pearson.
- The line marked '$G^2(P)$' shows the performance of the log-likelihood interval, which performs well for small p, but then diverges from the optimum line as $p \rightarrow 1$, accepting more errors and underestimating the interval width.
- Finally, 'Yates's $\chi^2(P)$', plotted by the continuity-corrected Wilson lower bound for p, has the closest fit to the Binomial CP line of these methods. It even occasionally exhibits 'Type II errors' ('excess conservatism').

Note that the distance on this graph between bounds – between the lower bounds for $G^2(P)$ and Bin(P), say – is not proportional to *the number of times* an error might occur. The actual additional risk of error is *the Binomial tail area* between the $G^2(P)$ and Bin(P) bounds (see Wallis, 2020b).

8.3 Tests for Comparing Two Observed Proportions

8.3.1 *The 2 × 2 χ^2 and z Test for Two Independent Proportions*

The *z test for two independent proportions* (Sheskin, 2011, p. 655) compares two proportions to see if they are significantly different. We will use this test to compare columns y_1 and y_2 in Table 8.1 as we did with a 2 × 2 χ^2 test. Both observations are free to vary independently (Figure 8.8).

Suppose we use $\mathbf{O}_1$ to represent a Wald distribution for p_1 in the first column of the corresponding probability table, Table 8.2 (i.e., $p_1 = p(x_1 \mid y_1)$, the proportion of *shall* in spoken data). Similarly, $\mathbf{O}_2$ will represent the corresponding distribution for written data, and $p_2 = p(x_1 \mid y_2)$ the written proportion.

This z test combines distributions $\mathbf{O}_1$ and $\mathbf{O}_2$ into a single *difference* distribution $\mathbf{D}[0, S_d]$ centred on zero (a difference of zero is no change in either direction). $\mathbf{D}$ represents the sampling distribution of the difference, d, between observed probabilities, $d = p_2 - p_1$.

To carry out this test, we calculate the standard deviation of the difference, S_d, which depends on *the pooled probability estimate*, $\hat{p}$. In our contingency table this is simply the row total over the grand total, $n = n_1 + n_2$, that is, the mean probability of x_1, $\hat{p} = p(x_1)$:[15]

probability estimate $\hat{p} \equiv (n_1 p_1 + n_2 p_2) / n$, and

standard deviation $S_d \equiv \sqrt{\hat{p}(1-\hat{p})(\frac{1}{n_1}+\frac{1}{n_2})}$, thus (42) *difference interval width* $e_d = z_{\alpha/2}.S_d.$

The confidence interval is then simply $\pm e_d$. See Figure 8.9. Once S_d has been estimated, carrying out the test becomes extremely simple. Since the distribution is symmetric and centred on zero, the test can ignore the sign (direction) of the difference.[16] We can simply test if $|d| > e_d$, where $d = p_2 - p_1 = p(x_1 \mid y_2) - p(x_1 \mid y_1)$. Our data in Table 8.1 gives us the following:

$$\hat{p} = (20 + 5)/45 = 0.5556,\ S_d = 0.1571,\ e_d = 0.3080.$$

This gives us a confidence interval of ± 0.3080 at the $\alpha = 0.05$ level.

The difference in the observed probabilities $d = p_2 - p_1 = 1/3 - 2/3 = -0.3333$. Since $|d|$ exceeds 0.3080, we report this result as significant. See Figure 8.9.

Two-proportion *z* test:

If $-e_d < p_2 - p_1 < e_d$, there is no significant difference between p_1 and p_2. (43)

This is a two-tailed test. As before, it is possible to demonstrate that the result obtained from this test is the same as that obtained from the 2×2 χ^2 test for independence. We may obtain a z score by simply rearranging the formula:

$$z = (p_2 - p_1) / S_d. \quad (44)$$

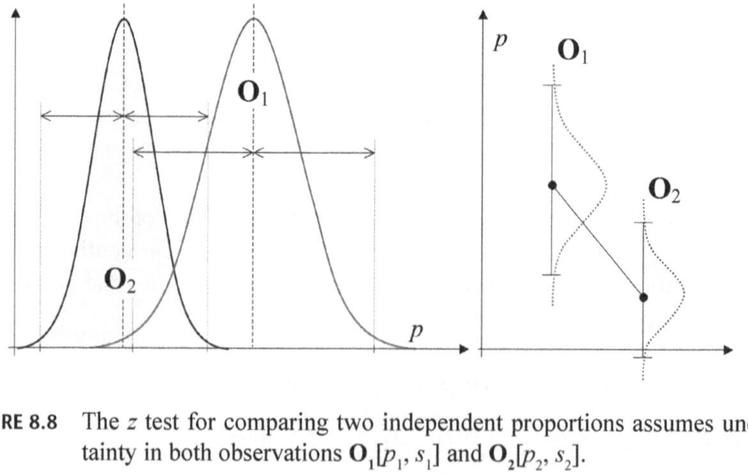

FIGURE 8.8 The z test for comparing two independent proportions assumes uncertainty in both observations $\mathbf{O}_1[p_1, s_1]$ and $\mathbf{O}_2[p_2, s_2]$.

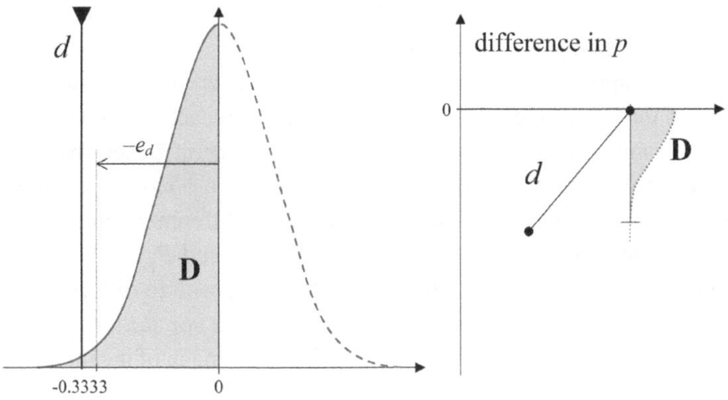

FIGURE 8.9 The new *difference* confidence interval for $d = p_2 - p_1$ is centred on the origin. **D**[0, S_d] is assumed to be Normal and symmetric, and we only need test the difference in the direction of change.

This gives us $z = -2.1213$, which has an absolute value $|z| > z_{0.025} = 1.95996$. The test is significant for $\alpha = 0.05$.

The equivalent χ^2 test for independence (homogeneity) can be calculated for the contingency table, Table 8.1, by applying the χ^2 formula (Equation (1')) to expected values using Equation (2). This is a test we first saw in Chapter 2:

$$\chi^2 = (0.6667 + 1.3333 + 0.8333 + 1.6667) = 4.5.$$

This value is also greater than the critical value of χ^2 and is therefore significant.

In fact, $z = -2.1213$ squared is 4.5. Recall that 'z^2' is the same as χ^2 with one degree of freedom. The two calculations achieve the same result.

The 2×2 χ^2 test has one further useful property. It can be calculated by simply adding together the results of the two goodness of fit χ^2 values for y_1 and y_2. The degrees of freedom and critical value of χ^2 do not change. Consequently, a 2×1 goodness of fit χ^2 test is always stricter than its corresponding 2×2 χ^2, which must be significant if either goodness of fit test is significant.

8.3.2 The z Test for Two Independent Proportions From Independent Populations

In the 2×2 χ^2 test, it is assumed that y_1 and y_2 are drawn from the same population, and proportions are tested for consistency with that assumption. That population has a mean (the pooled probability estimate) and standard deviation estimated with Equation (39).

However, in some cases, it is better to characterise the z test in terms of sampling *different*, independent populations with distinct means, P_1 and P_2. Their average distribution is not Binomial, but potentially a wider 'bimodal' distribution (with two peaks). See Figure 8.10.

Imagine an apparatus where two narrow funnels are fixed close together 10 cm above a desk and fine sand is slowly poured into each of them – possibly in different amounts or at different rates. We would expect to see two small sand dunes with distinct peaks form on the desk. This is a *bimodal* distribution: the data (sand) comes from two different sources with different means.

The same-population z test evaluates whether P_1 and P_2 are likely to be different in one direction or another, that is, that the absolute difference $| d | > 0$, and *therefore the data are in fact drawn from different populations*. This test will reject the null hypothesis according to the Binomial 'mean of means' distribution about $\hat{p} = P$ in Figure 8.10 (lighter columns).

But suppose we need to account for a known difference in population means in the test. For example, we might test whether the difference d is not equal to an expected constant $D = 0.4$. The null hypothesis now would be based on a bimodal distribution like the one shown in Figure 8.10.

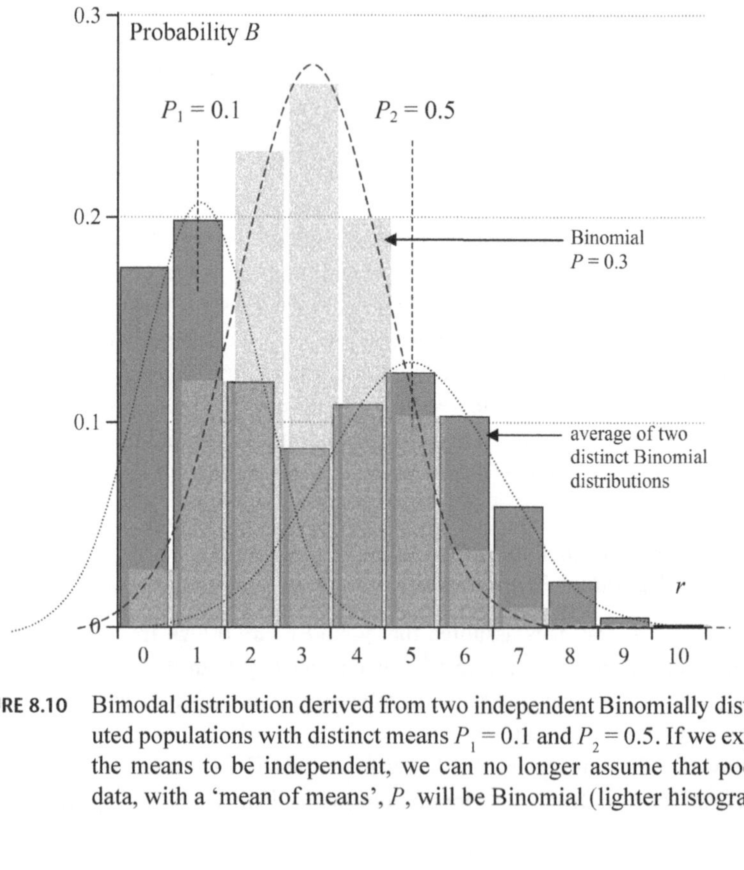

FIGURE 8.10 Bimodal distribution derived from two independent Binomially distributed populations with distinct means $P_1 = 0.1$ and $P_2 = 0.5$. If we expect the means to be independent, we can no longer assume that pooled data, with a 'mean of means', P, will be Binomial (lighter histogram).

The way to address this is to estimate variation about *each observation*, p_1 and p_2, rather than about a pooled probability estimate (the weighted mean $\hat{p}$). Sheskin (2011, p. 658) proposes taking the standard deviation as the Bienaymé sum of the independent variances for each subsample, s_1^2 and s_2^2:

$$\text{standard deviation } S_d = \sqrt{s_1^2 + s_2^2}, \tag{45}$$

in place of the pooled standard deviation formula in Equation (42).

However, this formula performs poorly because s_1 and s_2 are the Gaussian (Wald) standard deviations at p_1 and p_2 (see Chapter 6).

A better approach, owing to Newcombe (1998b), uses the *Wilson score interval* for p_1 and p_2. See Figure 8.11. As we saw in Chapter 7, the idea is to combine the inner interval widths using the Bienaymé formula for summing variances.

To recap, to calculate the lower bound of the difference interval for $d = p_2 - p_1$, we consider negative $d < 0$, where $p_2 < p_1$. The 'inner interval' is then based on the lower bound of p_1 (w_1^-) and the upper bound of p_2 (w_2^+) (see p. 163). For the upper bound, we consider where $p_2 > p_1$, and combine the other pair. This obtains the following zero-based Newcombe-Wilson interval, against which we test the difference d. The simplest formula is Equation (25):

$$0 \in (w_d^-, w_d^+) = (-\sqrt{(p_1 - w_1^-)^2 + (w_2^+ - p_2)^2}, \sqrt{(w_1^+ - p_1)^2 + (p_2 - w_2^-)^2}). \tag{25}$$

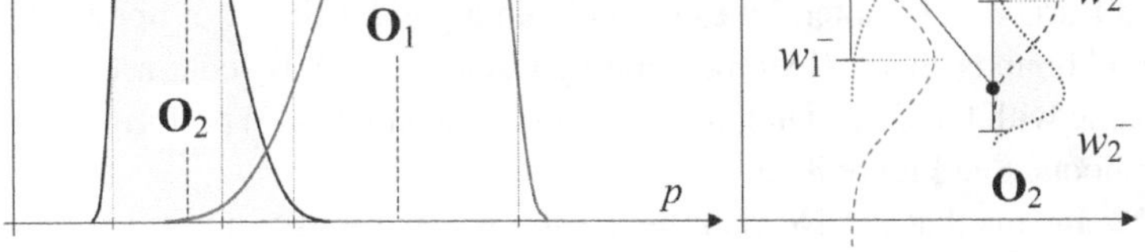

FIGURE 8.11 The Newcombe-Wilson test assumes that uncertainty in each observation, **O**$_1$ and **O**$_2$, is distributed according to the Wilson distribution (see Chapter 17). By the interval equality principle, Gaussian variances may be calculated at the inner Wilson score interval bounds (w_1^-, w_2^+, dashed, right) and combined to form a new difference interval.

An alternative formulation is given in Equation (25'):

$$0 \in (w_d^-, w_d^+) = (-z_{\alpha/2}\sqrt{w_1^-(1-w_1^-)/n_1 + w_2^+(1-w_2^+)/n_2}\,,$$
$$z_{\alpha/2}\sqrt{w_1^+(1-w_1^+)/n_1 + w_2^-(1-w_2^-)/n_2}\,). \qquad (25')$$

For the uncorrected interval, this equation can be shown to be equivalent to Equation (25) by interval equality.[17]

This second formulation reveals how this zero-based interval is derived. The 'Bienaymé Gaussian' formulation mirrors Equation (42). This interval is assumed to have Gaussian variances, not at p_1 and p_2, *but at their inner bounds*. See Figure 8.11, right.

Using the data in Table 8.1, we obtain an interval of $0 \in (-0.3070, 0.2299)$, which is slightly less conservative than the Gaussian interval from the z test for two proportions drawn from the same population (±0.3080).

In Chapter 7, we introduced the Newcombe-Wilson test:

Newcombe-Wilson test:

If $w_d^- < p_2 - p_1 < w_d^+$, there is no significant difference between p_1 and p_2. (26)

As before, the interval is based around zero. It defines all values of difference d, including zero, which would be deemed non-significant. The difference in the observed probabilities $d = p_2 - p_1 = -0.3333$. Since $d < -0.3070$, the result is significant.

8.3.3 *The z Test for Two Independent Proportions With a Given Difference in Population Means*

Wallis (2013a) shows that the Newcombe-Wilson method obtains very similar, but slightly less accurate, results to the same-population method (or 2 × 2 χ^2) in cases where we wish to test if d is significantly different from zero, $d \neq_s 0$.

We learned in Chapter 7 we could obtain a good estimate of upper and lower interval bounds about d by repositioning Equation (25). By contrast, trying to do the same with the Gaussian interval about $\hat{p}$ (Equation (42)) performs poorly and overshoots. See Figure 8.12.

This means that the Newcombe-Wilson test is robust for comparing d to an arbitrary non-zero constant, that is, to test if $d \neq_s \boldsymbol{D}$.

Newcombe-Wilson test for a given difference *D*:

If $w_d^- < p_2 - p_1 - D < w_d^+$, the difference $p_2 - p_1$ is not significantly different from D. (26')

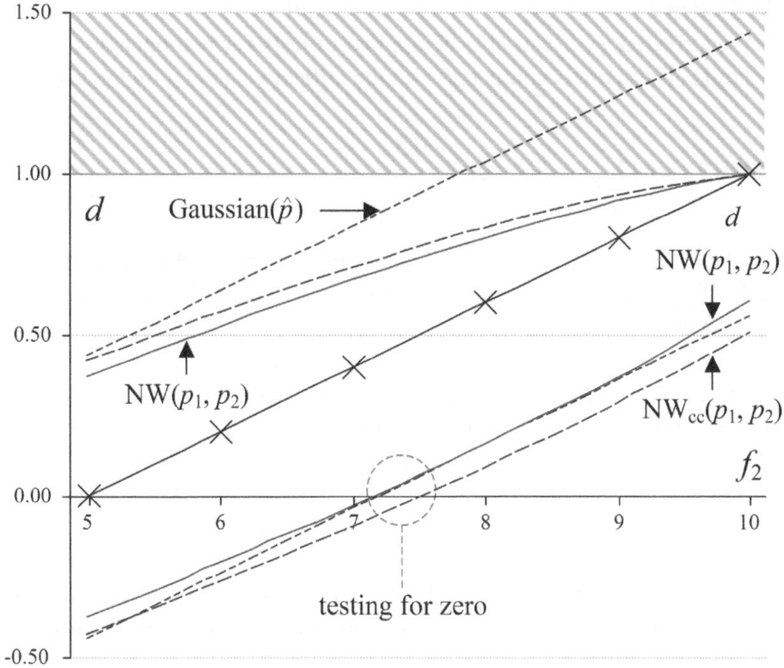

FIGURE 8.12 Plotting Gaussian and Newcombe-Wilson intervals (corrected for continuity and uncorrected) across the diagonal of a contingency table with column totals n_1, n_2 = 10 for positive $d = p_2 - p_1$ with frequencies $f_1 = 10 - f_2$, $f_2 \in (5, 10)$, and $\alpha = 0.05$.

This constant could be any number. For example, it might be used when we have a known difference in population means (e.g., $D = P_2 - P_1$ or $D = \hat{p}_2 - \hat{p}_1$). This is particularly useful for meta-tests, which we will see in Chapter 14.

Therefore, whenever we plot confidence intervals on differences d (as in Chapter 7), the Newcombe-Wilson interval should be used. In the next chapter we will see how Newcombe's method can be extended to create a general difference interval function, $\theta_1 - \theta_2 \in$ **difference**(θ_1, θ_2).

8.3.4 Continuity-Corrected 2 × 2 Tests

Conventional statistics textbooks recommend Yates's correction for 2 × 1 and 2 × 2 tests, but as tests become more complex, correcting for continuity tends to be forgotten.[18] However, there is a good argument that corrections for continuity should be applied to any test or interval that involves a Normal approximation to the Binomial. Briefly, if an underlying source distribution is discrete, we should accommodate that fact in our test or interval.

In Section 8.2.4, we applied Yates's formula to the 2 × 1 goodness of fit test. Like uncorrected χ^2, it can also be applied to tests for homogeneity, including 2 × 2 tests. The score is compared with the critical value of χ^2 in the usual way:

$$\text{Yates's } \chi^2 \equiv \sum_{i=1,j=1}^{r,c} \frac{(|o_{i,j} - e_{i,j}| - 0.5)^2}{e_{i,j}}. \tag{35}$$

This obtains $\chi^2 = 3.2513$ in our 2 × 2 test condition, below the critical two-tailed χ^2 value for $\alpha/2$ (3.8415), that is, a non-significant result. The continuity correction reduces the χ^2 score.

We also discussed how to apply Yates's continuity correction to the Wilson score interval. We substitute continuity-corrected intervals (w^-_{cc}, w^+_{cc}) into Equation (25). This correction is similarly conservative, meaning that in some borderline cases it may cause us to reject hypotheses that would otherwise be accepted (a so-called 'Type II error').

With our example data, continuity-corrected Wilson score intervals for p_1 and p_2 are (0.4714, 0.8206) and (0.1299, 0.6131), respectively. The Newcombe-Wilson interval with continuity correction becomes (−0.3412, 0.2551). This interval is wider and includes $d = -0.3333$. As with Yates's test, the difference is now deemed non-significant.

Figure 8.12 includes a plot of the wider Newcombe-Wilson continuity-corrected interval repositioned about d.

8.3.5 The Fisher 'Exact' Test

First, we define Fisher probability scores for a particular combination:

$$p_{\text{Fisher}}(a, b, c, d) = \frac{(a+c)!(b+d)!(a+b)!(c+d)!}{n!a!b!c!d!} \tag{46}$$

where a, b, c and d represent cell values in a 2 × 2 contingency table, [[a, b], [c, d]], and $n = a + b + c + d$. In our notation, $p_1 = a / (a + c)$ and $p_2 = b / (b + d)$.

The summation is performed by adding up Fisher scores diagonally:

$$p_{\text{FSum}}(a, b, c, d) = \begin{cases} \sum_{i=0}^{\min(b,c)} p_{\text{Fisher}}(a+i, b-i, c-i, d+i) & \text{if } \frac{a}{a+b} > \frac{c}{c+d}, \\ \sum_{i=0}^{\min(a,d)} p_{\text{Fisher}}(a-i, b+i, c+i, d-i) & \text{otherwise.} \end{cases} \tag{47}$$

To perform the test we examine if the tail sum exceeds $\alpha/2$.

Fisher's exact test

If $p_{FSum}(a, b, c, d) > \alpha/2$, there is no significant difference between p_1 and p_2. (48)

where $p_1 = a / (a+c)$ and $p_2 = b / (b+d)$. As with the Binomial test, the summation may be sequenced from the inner cell outwards, which means adding the largest Fisher score first, allowing us to stop early if the threshold is reached. The Fisher score for our data, [[20, 5], [10, 10]], is $p_{Fisher} = 0.0285$, which is greater than 0.025, so this test is non-significant, and we do not need to add further terms. (The total, $p_{FSum} = 0.0285 + 0.0062 + 0.0008 + 0.0001 = 0.0355$.)

In practice, although these tests do not rely on the Normal approximation to the Binomial distribution, and are thus 'exact', they are not so superior to equivalent χ^2 and Wilson-based methods as to require us to insist on them.

Even for small n, employing a continuity-corrected test avoids most false positive (Type I) results. The main reason for choosing a Fisher or Binomial test over a continuity-corrected test is to minimise 'Type II' errors (rejecting null hypotheses unnecessarily) (see Wallis, 2013a).

8.4 Applying Contingency Tests

We have learned about different types of contingency test, how they work and alternative methods of calculating them. What are the practical implications of this understanding? How should these tests be applied in corpus research?

8.4.1 Selecting Tests

A common mistake is to confuse independence tests and goodness of fit tests. A focus on confidence intervals helps us decide when each is appropriate. Consider the Binomial variable $Y \in \{y_1, y_2\}$ illustrated by Figure 8.13, possibly influenced by another Binomial variable X (not shown).

Figures 8.2 and 8.8 illustrate the mathematical distinction between the two types of test we have discussed. Figure 8.13 summarises their different purposes.

1. The 2 × 1 goodness of fit (single-sample) test (Figure 8.13, left) is used to compare an observed proportion, say, $p(x_1 \mid y_1)$, with an expected proportion, P. This has multiple applications, including the 'more' test (see Chapter 7), where $P = 0.5$. A common application is a *subset* test, comparing a proportion with an observed proportion at a superset ($P = p(x_1)$) in a typological hierarchy: the superset value is treated as a constant for the purpose of the test. The test examines if the proportion at a single value, y_1, has a confidence interval excluding the superset proportion. In Chapter 1, this test was used to evaluate

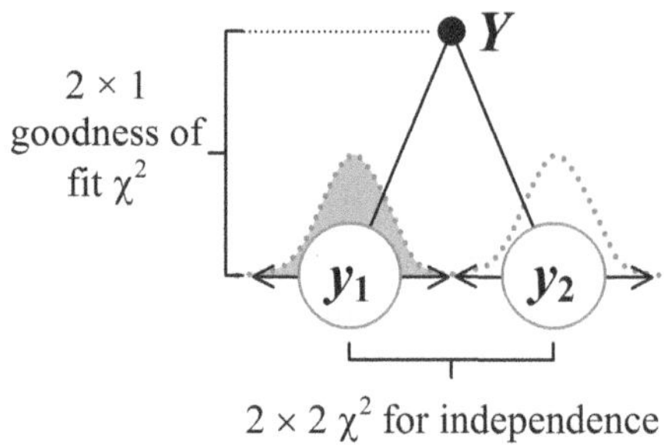

FIGURE 8.13 Employing χ^2 tests for different purposes. The superset Y is considered a known fixed point; y_1 and y_2 are subject to observational error.

the successive addition of attributive adjectives to a noun phrase (each set was a subset of the previous).

2. The 2×2 χ^2 test (Figure 8.13, lower) compares two uncertain proportions, say, $p(x_1 \mid y_1)$ and $p(x_1 \mid y_2)$. It assumes that the expected distribution for their difference is averaged between them. The test takes sampling uncertainty at both values of Y into account. Use this test to evaluate if the values y_1 and y_2 behave differently from each other with respect to X (i.e., to test if $p(x_1 \mid y_1) \neq_s p(x_1 \mid y_2)$).
3. The Newcombe-Wilson test is a more extensible alternative to the 2×2 χ^2 test. It can be used for more complex comparisons between uncertain proportions, for example, to compare their difference against a constant (test if $p(x_1 \mid y_2) - p(x_1 \mid y_1) \neq_s D$).

In Chapter 12, we discuss the selection of significance tests more generally.

8.4.2 *Analysing Larger Tables*

In some experiments, we may begin with a larger, multi-valued $r \times c$ contingency table. We discussed a semasiological example, Levin's BE *thinking*, in Chapter 7.

Consider Table 8.4, a contingency table to investigate if the mood of a clause predicts its transitivity. As we noted in Chapter 7, the usual starting point is to carry out an initial $r \times c$ χ^2 test to determine if variation is being observed at all. However, a general $r \times c$ or $r \times 1$ test merely tells us that there appears to be significant variation *somewhere*!

The number of degrees of freedom is greater than one, which means that a significant result could be due to a specific pattern buried within the table, or simply represent a generalised difference spread over several values which may not easily be pinpointed. To identify what is going on, we need to analyse the table more

TABLE 8.4 Mood versus transitivity in ICE-GB clauses (sampled from Release 2, after Nelson et al., 2002).

	montr	*ditr*	*dimontr*	*cxtr*	*trans*	*intr*	*cop*	*0*	*Total*
exclamative	**6**	**0**	**0**	**0**	**0**	**2**	**14**	1	**23**
interrogative	**2,199**	**72**	**17**	**132**	**90**	**1,350**	**1,869**	64	**5,793**
subjunctive	**61**	**2**	**1**	**10**	**3**	**85**	**70**	1	**233**
imperative	**1,139**	**62**	**25**	**128**	**112**	**697**	**54**	4	**2,221**
declarative	**58,502**	**1,589**	**199**	**3,803**	**2,373**	**30,281**	**29,867**	10,295	**136,909**
Total	61,907	1,725	242	4,073	2,578	32,415	31,874	10,365	145,179

TABLE 8.5 Testing the interaction between mood and the monotransitive/intransitive choice.

	montr	*intr*	*Total*
exclamative	**6**	**2**	8
interrogative	**2,199**	**1,350**	3,549
subjunctive	**61**	**85**	146
imperative	**1,139**	**697**	1,836
declarative	**58,502**	**30,281**	88,783
Total	61,907	32,415	94,322

closely. In other words, it is necessary to 'drill down' using more focused tests, each with a single degree of freedom.

Table 8.4 has $(r-1) \times (c-1) = 4 \times 7 = 28$ degrees of freedom. Applying the χ^2 test for independence (Equation (29)), $\chi^2 = 1{,}771$, which corresponds to a critical value with an infinitesimal error level! The result is significant. But this does not really tell us much except 'the variables interact'. Something is happening, but we do not know what it is.

A more meaningful evaluation might break down the transitivity patterns into speaker or writer *decisions*. In this case, we can consider the decision to include an object, which assumes that the option of adding an object is always available. We return to this assumption next.

We can re-analyse the intransitive versus monotransitive data, which corresponds to the decision to include a direct object in complementation patterns without an indirect object. This gives us the reduced table, Table 8.5.

The result is a 5×2 χ^2 for independence, $\chi^2 > 71$. It has four degrees of freedom, and corresponds to a tiny error level according to the model. Again, we can report that this result is significant.

The actual χ^2 scores are irrelevant, as are error levels derived from them. What matters is that the test was significant, that is, the difference in distributions was greater than would be expected by chance at a given error level, say $\alpha = 0.05$.

The output score is high, and a derived error level ('p value') would be small because we have a sample of almost 100,000 cases! But *the test* is still uninformative. It only tells us that the mood of a clause in ICE-GB and the decision to add a direct object are not independent variables *but correlate to some extent*.

What should we do next? Well, we could carry out pairwise tests on different values of mood. But in Chapter 7, we discovered a more revealing method of analysis: to plot probabilities like p(montr | {montr, intr}) with Wilson score intervals. This gives us another kind of evaluation procedure.

We can perform a similar pairwise test for dimonotransitive versus ditransitive cases, that is, the choice of adding a direct object when an indirect object is expressed. This is also significant ($\chi^2 > 29$). Plotting the probability of adding this direct object alongside the first obtains Figure 8.14.

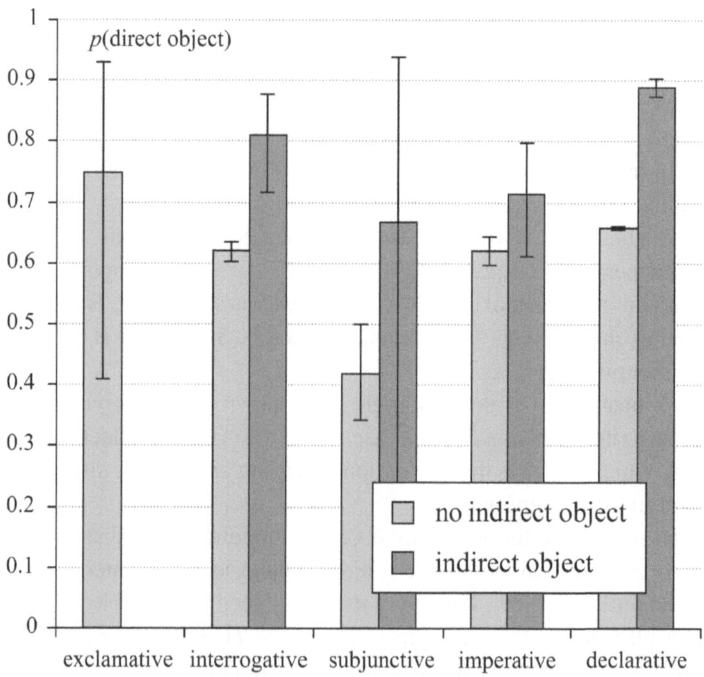

FIGURE 8.14 Plotting the probability that a complementation pattern contains a direct object for cases of intransitive, monotransitive, dimonotransitive and ditransitive patterns with and without an indirect object. Data from Table 8.4 (from ICE-GB Release 2).

The plot is more revealing than the table because we can perform pairwise sub-evaluations visually by comparing confidence intervals rather than by carrying out tests one-by-one. Some intervals are small due to the large quantity of data available, even after focusing in on subsets of clauses.

The visualisation also permits us to make observations that we had not considered. For example, perhaps the most striking result is that, for declarative and interrogative cases at least, *the chance of a clause containing a direct object increases when an indirect object is present.*

The confidence intervals either do not overlap (a significant difference) or include an end-point of the bar (a non-significant one), so we need not actually perform a pairwise test comparison. See Chapter 7.

However, we should not get carried away. The crucial question is, *what do these results mean?* A significant difference simply tells us that we have found a correlation between two variables across a sample. It does not tell us what the source of that correlation might be.

In this case, the data are all clauses drawn from ICE-GB. These clauses contain different lexical verbs. The verbs used in different moods are likely to vary – do speakers or writers use all of the same verbs for exclamative clauses, for example, as in declarative clauses?

A verb such as *ask* may be used in all four complementation patterns, but these cases are rare. We would need to eliminate the alternate hypothesis that what we are seeing is a byproduct of *different verbs* limiting the selection of objects. We have taken some steps towards this goal. We analysed clauses with and without indirect objects separately. Whereas many verbs can take direct objects (so the choice is available), many do not take indirect objects.

In conclusion, to learn what is really going on, we need to refine our experimental design – in this case, by limiting lexical verbs in our dataset – rather than by applying further tests or intervals to this data.

Recall the 3A model of corpus linguistics in Chapter 1. The 'analysis' arc in the 3A model is cyclic, and connected to the abstraction cycle. It is often necessary to change our experimental design to sample data differently and test alternate hypotheses. We may even need to put our corpus aside and collect laboratory data.

8.4.3 Linguistic Choice

One of the assumptions of Binomial and z tests and their derived intervals (Assumption 2, p. 180) is that every instance in the sample is free to vary. They assume that, for every single case sampled, the speaker or writer was free to choose either construction (e.g., *shall* or *will*). This means that observed values of p can range from 0 to 1. The same assumption holds for goodness of fit tests. With a Multinomial dependent variable $\{A, B_1, B_2 \ldots\}$, all instances should, in principle, be capable of alternating with all other values of the variable, so, for example, $p(B_2)$ should also be capable of reaching 1. There should be no 'Type C' instances. The dependent variable (DV) may then be said to be free to vary for all of its values.

With two-variable χ^2 tests for homogeneity, we can allow that one variable may not be free to vary. For example, if we sampled an equal number of instances of *shall* or *will* produced by men and women, the overall rate for the independent variable (gender) would be fixed at 0.5. But the rate for *p*(*shall*) might be any number from 0 to 1 for either gender. This type of situation is common in experimental settings, where equal proportions of an independent variable are designed into the experiment. Nonetheless, every participant was free to choose *shall* or *will*.[19]

Recall that in Chapter 1 we limited our example of *shall* and *will* to first person singular cases, where contemporary alternation in English is possible. Speakers can, with a few formulaic exceptions, freely choose to say *I* <u>*shall*</u> *go to the pictures* or *I* <u>*will*</u> *go to the pictures* without violence to the semantic context (cf. Lavandera, 1978). See Chapter 3.

Unfortunately, this requirement of the test is not always upheld. As we have seen, corpus linguists have frequently cited rates per million words and used log-likelihood tests (see Rayson, 2003)[20] to evaluate whether change in such rates are significant.

But once we understand how the statistic works, it should be clear that this type of approach *undermines the mathematics of the test* – irrespective of how it is calculated (χ^2, log-likelihood or Binomial). Not every word in a sentence could be *shall* or *will*, and therefore if we wish to investigate how *shall* behaves, these non-alternating words should be excluded from our data for the purposes of our analysis.

In Chapter 3, we demonstrated that the introduction of Type C non-alternating terms, first, introduces unwanted noise into the experiment (it varies the envelope of variation), and second, depresses observed proportions of the phenomena we wish to investigate.

However, there is a further problem that is rarely discussed. The inclusion of large numbers of non-alternating terms, *even if they do not vary in number*, also causes the test to overestimate confidence intervals, exaggerate the range of predicted variation and cause the test to lose power. See Wallis (2012c).

The solution, quite simply, is to work to eliminate Type C cases from the data-set, and focus exclusively on cases where the choice of a target item (or items) arises.

If observed proportions of the dependent variable are free to range from 0 to 1, we can employ the Wilson and Newcombe-Wilson tests comfortably. The χ^2 test for homogeneity is associative, which means it works in both directions. It can be safely employed where the dependent variable is not free to vary, *provided that the independent variable is free to do so.*

This means, reassuringly, that tests and intervals are applicable to linguistic research into meaning change ('semasiology'), *if we interpret the outcome correctly.* We must remember that the observed proportion is not a single series of comparable choices, but rather, the pooled result of different choices. See Chapter 4.

8.4.4 Are Instances Independent?

Assumption 1 was that the sample was randomly drawn from a population. Each case in the sample should be independent from the next.

However, in corpus linguistics, it is common to derive samples from a database consisting of substantive texts. Corpora are collected for multiple purposes. Researchers might examine narrative structure and turn-taking spanning multiple utterances; pragmatic and discourse phenomena; macro and micro-syntactic structure; semantics at multiple levels; and local lexis, morphology and prosody.

This creates a conundrum: if a corpus is constructed out of whole texts, then drawing multiple instances from the same text breaches Assumption 1. On the other hand, randomly selecting a single instance and disposing of the rest wastes data. If sampled data are only possible from rich annotation (e.g., where identifying grammatical phenomena relies on accurate parse analyses), then the inefficiency of this procedure cannot be understated!

Suppose we adopted the one-instance per text restriction. Even if we had enough data sampled corpus-wide to draw statistically sound conclusions, what happens if we restrict our investigation to a subcategory, or impose some other restriction? We will rapidly run out of data.

The alternative is to adjust the Binomial model. We expect that speakers or writers may produce the sampled construction or constructions (*shall* or *will* in our example) multiple times in the same text. If we maximise the use of our data, and include every case found, then we are not strictly engaging in random sampling – even if the texts themselves are effectively randomly obtained.

In Chapter 16, we discuss how to adjust the statistical model to account for what we might term 'random-text sampling', that is, the drawing of instances from a random sample of texts.

8.4.5 Large Samples and Small Populations

Assumption 3 (see p. 137) was that *the population was infinite*, or so much larger than the sample (say 20 times larger or more) that it was effectively infinite.

Imagine for a minute that the sample was identical to the population. Uncertainty and confidence intervals would shrink to zero. *Every difference becomes*

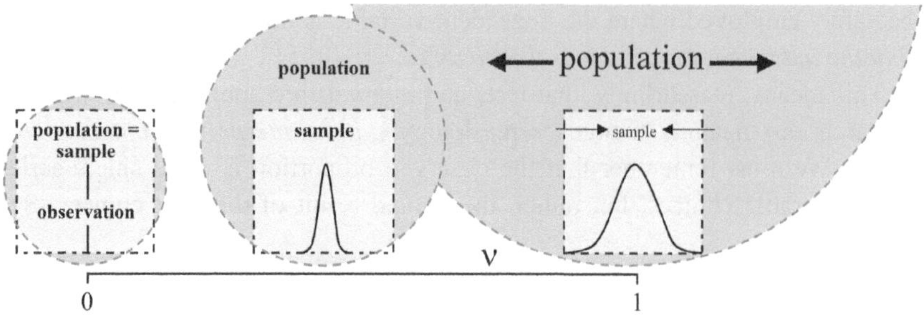

FIGURE 8.15 From descriptive to inferential statistics. Descriptive statistics (left) considers the sample as if it were the entire population, whereas inferential statistics, (right) assumes the population is infinite. If the sample is a large part of a (finite) population the standard deviation may be multiplied by a finite population correction factor $\nu \in [0, 1)$ (middle).

'significant' because every difference in the sample is a difference in the population. Every statement about the sample is a statement of fact about the population. We only need descriptive statistics.

However, what about an intermediate situation? Suppose the sample is a *large fraction* of the population. For example, imagine we are studying the grammar of William Shakespeare's plays. The *First Folio*, published in 1623, is a very large sample of Shakespeare's published plays.

It is not, however, the population of 'Shakespeare's play text'. Shakespeare may have written other undiscovered plays, drafts or versions. The *Second Folio*, published in 1632, includes over 1,700 changes. This sounds a lot, but it is a tiny proportion of the total words. Let us conservatively estimate that the *First Folio* represents half of his entire playwriting output.[21]

If a sample is a proportion of a finite population, estimates of uncertainty will decline according to a *finite population correction* (usually abbreviated to 'f.p.c.'). Figure 8.14 illustrates this principle of moving from descriptive to inferential statistics as the f.p.c., labelled ν, increases.

The following formula is commonly employed:

$$\textit{Finite population correction } \nu \equiv \sqrt{(N-n)/(N-1)}\,, \qquad (49)$$

where n is the size of the sample and N the size of the population. Note that ν is less than 1, and as n approaches N it will tend to zero, that is, certainty. This correction is not particularly informative on its own, but it may be introduced into other formulae.

A corrected population standard deviation may be obtained by multiplying Equation (17) by ν. This produces a smaller Gaussian interval for P:

$$\textit{Standard deviation (f.p.c.)}\ S \equiv \nu\sqrt{P(1-P)/n}. \tag{50}$$

For the Wilson score interval, the easiest way to introduce a finite population correction is by adjusting Wilson functions. We substitute n / ν^2 for n in Wilson score interval functions (Equation (20'')):

$w^- = \text{WilsonLower}(p, n / \nu^2, \alpha/2)$, and
$w^+ = \text{WilsonUpper}(p, n / \nu^2, \alpha/2)$. (20''')

This is a highly 'decomposable' method – any time that a Wilson score interval is used, we can also employ a finite population correction.

In the case of χ^2 tests, the simplest method is to perform the test in the normal way, and then divide the result by ν^2 before comparing it to the critical value.

Chi-square test (f.p.c.):

If $\chi^2 / \nu^2 < \chi^2(\alpha, df)$, the observed distribution does not significantly differ from the expected distribution. (51)

This method is appropriate for standard χ^2 and the continuity-corrected Yates's χ^2 test. (It can also be used for log-likelihood tests by the same logic.)

We can apply the finite population correction to continuity-corrected intervals. Obviously, the observed sample size does not change when we adjust for a small *population*. The sample size n in the continuity correction term, $\frac{1}{2n}$, should therefore *not* be adjusted by the finite population correction.

To apply the finite population correction to Yates's population interval, we calculate S using Equation (50) and substitute it into Equation (18). We do not adjust the continuity correction term:

$$\textit{Yates's population interval}\ (E^-_{cc}, E^+_{cc}) = P \pm (z_{\alpha/2}.S + \tfrac{1}{2n}), \tag{18}$$

Wilson functions make the inclusion of both adjustments straightforward. Recall that without the finite population correction interval, two-tailed bounds are as follows:

$w^-_{cc} = \text{WilsonLower}(\max(0, p - \frac{1}{2n}), n, \alpha/2)$, and

$w^+_{cc} = \text{WilsonUpper}(\min(1, p + \frac{1}{2n}), n, \alpha/2)$. (36)

Now we can introduce a finite population correction very easily:

$$w_{cc}^{-} = \text{WilsonLower}(\max(0, p - \tfrac{1}{2n}), n/\nu^2, \alpha/2), \text{ and}$$

$$w_{cc}^{+} = \text{WilsonUpper}(\min(1, p + \tfrac{1}{2n}), n/\nu^2, \alpha/2). \quad (36')$$

The finite population correction alters confidence intervals, test scores and significant difference calculations. *Effect sizes* (see Chapter 13) are not adjusted for a finite population or discrete sample (continuity), but their intervals may be.

A useful application of this correction is in calculating error intervals of manually reviewed *subsamples*. In this case, the 'population' is the initial sample, which is then subsampled and reviewed. See Chapter 15.

8.5 Comparing the Results of Experiments

A frequent question asked by researchers is whether they can argue that the result of one experiment is in some sense 'stronger' or 'more conclusive' than another. As we observed, it is a common fallacy to state that if one χ^2 test is significant at $\alpha = 0.01$ and another is significant at $\alpha = 0.05$ that the first is a 'better' result than the second. Now that we understand how these tests work, we can see why this reasoning is false.

First, we saw how variance, standard deviation and the threshold for a difference to be significant, all *fall with increased sample size*. Different experiments will typically be based on different sample sizes. Significance tests combine two distinct elements with a standardised model of expected variation. Consider the two-proportion z test (another way of calculating the 2×2 χ^2 test). It extracts a *size of effect* (the difference, d) and tests this value against a *threshold* (the Gaussian confidence interval width) based on the sample size n.

Second, if we inspect the tails of this interval we can see why we should not treat error levels this way. Reducing the chance of one type of error increases the chance of another. As α is decreased, the interval widens and the tails shrink, we increase our confidence that, were the experiment to be repeated many times, we would reach the same conclusion. In other words, our results are expected to be more 'robust'. But we will also tend to prematurely eliminate promising results (increasing the chance of so-called 'Type II' errors). Researchers should select different error levels to control this trade-off, and not confuse this question with the 'size' of the result.

Third, correlations are not causes. Numerical assessment is secondary to experimental design. The test is part of the entire experimental process, from the specification of hypotheses and variables to the design of corpora from which data are sampled. Comparing two tests carried out in different processes may obtain different results for a variety of reasons. A 'better' experiment is one that *develops our understanding* because it is framed to eliminate alternate hypotheses or because it independently verifies an observation ('triangulation'). Thus, for instance, accurately identifying linguistic events and restricting the experiment to genuine choices (e.g., limiting our transitivity experiment by verb forms) is much more important than the test score. See also Chapter 2.

Fourth, the fact that two test results are *significant* does not imply that they are statistically *separable*, that is, we cannot say that the results are *significantly different from each other*. They could be significant, but consistently so!

This leads us to the final problem with this misconception about 'p values' or χ^2 scores. It means that researchers fail to recognise they have a problem to solve, namely, *how do we test whether two otherwise comparable results are significantly different?*

It turns out that there are solutions to this problem that may be derived from the methods we have discussed in this chapter. We discuss these 'meta-tests' in Chapter 14.

8.6 Conclusions

Inferential statistics is a field of mathematics that models the likely outcome of repeated runs of an experiment, predicted by an underpinning mathematical model of expected variation, from the observation of a single experiment. The ability to make this type of prediction is extraordinarily powerful, but it is counter-intuitive. The underlying mathematical model also relies on certain assumptions, which, if broken, can undermine the model and test.

For types of linguistic experiments where the dependent variable represents a single binary alternative, the Binomial model is appropriate. A related model, termed the Multinomial model, applies for more than two outcomes.

We concentrated on the simplest Binomial versions of these tests because a single degree of freedom implies only one potential conclusion, and therefore the test is more straightforward to interpret. As we saw when working with a larger table, to make sense of variation within it, it is usually necessary to subdivide data anyway.

Although it is possible to perform 'exact' Fisher and Binomial tests, these are relatively arduous to calculate and difficult to work with except through computation.

Instead, statisticians from Gauss onwards have approximated the Binomial distribution with the Gaussian (Normal). Once we have assumed that the Binomial is approximately Normal, we can carry out χ^2 tests and compute confidence intervals. Although this involves an approximation, the errors introduced by this step are small, and may be compensated for with Yates's continuity correction.

In this chapter, we explained the relationship between confidence intervals and significance tests for three different experimental designs with Binomial variables. These are the 2 × 1 goodness of fit test, the 2 × 2 test for independence (also known as the homogeneity test) and the 2 × 2 Newcombe-Wilson test. The first compares an observed distribution against a specific given distribution. The second and third compare two sample distributions. The Newcombe-Wilson method should be used for plotting intervals on differences and comparing d to values other than zero. In both cases we gave formulae for confidence intervals and tests, and showed the relationship between them.

A test for one or two Binomial variables has one degree of freedom, which means that it can be expressed in terms of differences in observed proportions. In this form it is a logical statement that, should a difference exceed an interval, the difference is said to be greater than is expected to occur by chance, hence it is significant.

The chi-square computation is more general, and can be extended to a Multinomial $r \times 1$ or $r \times c$ test with arbitrary numbers of rows and columns. In the case of 2 × 1 and 2 × 2 χ^2 tests, we demonstrated that these computations obtained the same result as the square of the equivalent z score.

Section 8.4 concerned the correct application of these tests. We discussed when different tests should be used. We note two common problems, particularly prevalent in *ex post facto* corpus linguistics research, where dependent variables are not free to vary and where cases are not independently sampled.

The first scenario revisits an issue we discussed in Chapter 3. At that point, we considered the question from the perspective of obtaining the most meaningful and reliable results. Our argument against including invariant 'Type C' terms was that if they did not alternate with Types A and B, they would necessarily act as 'noise' in our experiment, reduce probability estimates and potentially distort the results if Type C proportions varied.

In this chapter, we revisited this problem, armed with an understanding of the mathematics of these tests. Crucially, these tests assume an observed proportion is free to vary from 0 to 1 (or at least one variable is free to vary). But if a single Type C case is included, the proportion of Type A or B instances can never equal 1.

Our emphasis on focusing on simple tests is demonstrably powerful, not because the data are simple, but because these methods can be used in the analysis of more complex data. A single degree of freedom means *a single axis of variation*, one that allows us to plot a confidence interval on an observation and perform pairwise tests.

As we saw, this type of visualisation and analysis may also lead to the identification of general principles, such as those relating the presence of direct objects to indirect objects.[22] Figure 8.14 represents a simple multivariate (three variable) model, albeit one built up from first principles. But rather than attempting to derive a general formula to describe this pattern, we are far more interested in encouraging researchers to understand their data and how these variables (and, by revision, permutations of their definitions) affect the distribution. We must open the 'black box'.

Notes

1 A version of this chapter was first published as Wallis, S.A. (2013b), *z*-squared: The origin and application of χ^2. *Journal of Quantitative Linguistics*, *20*(4), 350–378. www.tandfonline.com.
2 Any interval can be employed to perform a simple difference-from-zero significance test. It is also possible to compute a confidence interval for a test with a single degree of freedom using the interval equality principle. See Appendix A. Crucially for us, visualising such a test as a confidence interval permits us to see precisely how each test performs.
3 Variables on a Binomial scale have two mutually exclusive values, and may be referred to as 'binary' (two-valued) or 'Boolean' (true/false). For a proportion to be properly a *Binomial* variable, every sampled instance must, in principle, be able to select either value (be 'free to vary').
4 We use the Greek letter psi (Ψ) to represent this second-order 'count-of-samples' frequency to avoid confusion with first-order observations of frequency in a single experiment denoted by f or F. See Chapter 6.
5 It *is* possible to evaluate significance using only the Binomial test or Fisher's 2 × 2 test (see Sections 8.2.5 and 8.3.5), but these tests require combinatorial calculations, which are onerous without a computer. The Normal approximation has thus proved very attractive. See Chapter 6.
6 Many of the calculations discussed here may be carried out easily in a spreadsheet available online at https://corplingstats.wordpress.com/siclr. You can download this spreadsheet and enter the data in Table 8.1 into it.
7 However, note that comparing $p(x_1 \mid y_2)$ with $p(x_1)$ is a different test (for a different column in Table 8.1) and obtains a *different* result. This considers how closely the distribution for y_2 (e.g., writing) matches that of the total column.
8 Note the simple relationship between the interval and the test. With slightly different labels, Equation (34) can be thought of as a general axiom that converts any interval (o^-, o^+) about an observation o to a test. Where an expected value e is within the interval, the difference between observed and expected values is not significant.
9 As a rule, continuity corrections should not be used when computing *effect sizes* (see Chapter 13). But they may be applied to confidence intervals on those effect size estimates.
10 Roscoe and Byars (1971) improve on Cochran by noting that there is no need to collapse cells provided that $n / k \geq 2$ ($\alpha = 0.05$) or 4 ($\alpha = 0.01$), where k is the number of cells.
11 This method is Newcombe's (1998a) Method 5 using exact Binomial tail areas.
12 See, for example, responses to Brown et al. (2001) and the authors' subsequent discussion. See also the Preface.
13 This method is also used for estimating intervals for other properties, but in this chapter we consider its application to the single proportion p.
14 These additional errors can be substantial. Computing error rates from Binomial tail area of lower bounds and recording each Type I excess separately, Wallis (2024a) notes that with $n = 10$, the effective mean excess Type I error α for the uncorrected Wilson score interval is about 0.03 for a target of 0.05, falling to 0.02 for $n = 20$. Applying a continuity correction of $\frac{1}{2n}$ suppresses most of these errors. Increasing it to $\frac{1.5}{2n}$ eliminates them.

15 Whereas in the single proportion (goodness of fit) test, we compared a sample proportion with a population rate, here we compare two sampled proportions. This test evaluates whether subset means p_1 and p_2 significantly differ from the pooled mean $\hat{p}$, that is, whether they represent the means of significantly different distributions.

16 Of course we may be interested in the direction of the observed change! However, at this point we are simply considering alternative computations for tests, and the equivalent χ^2 test does not output this.

17 Take the formulation for the lower bound, w_d^- (top row). This is the negated Bienaymé sum of two Gaussian intervals ($e_d = z_{\alpha/2}.S_d$) centred on $P_1 = w_1^-$ and $P_2 = w_2^+$. Thanks to the interval equality principle (Appendix A), these distances must be equal to the interval width for the Wilson score interval, $z_{\alpha/2}.S_1 = p_1 - w_1^-$ and $z_{\alpha/2}.S_2 = w_2^+ - p_2$, respectively. The same reasoning applies to the lower bound.

18 Thus, for example, Zar (2010, p. 475) suggests that it is not needed for meta-testing (see Chapter 14).

19 In author attribution research, the dependent variable is the author, and, in this case, the DV might not be free to vary. Nonetheless, if we were attempting to predict an author based on their proclivity for writing *shall*, we would still require that the author was, in principle, free to write *will* otherwise!

20 See also https://ucrel.lancs.ac.uk/llwizard.html.

21 My illustrious Shakespearean colleagues might dispute this estimate, but it suffices for our little thought experiment!

22 By contrast, in multivariate analysis, you must first specify the variables to be included, perform the 'number crunching', and then interpret the resulting equation.

9

AN ALGEBRA OF INTERVALS

9.1 Introduction

In Chapter 6, we learned we may derive confidence intervals by inverting the sampling distribution of a property. Wilson score confidence intervals on Binomial proportions, p, are constructed by inverting the Normal approximation to the Binomial distribution for samples of p. Then in Chapter 7, we introduced an interval derived from the Wilson interval. This was the Newcombe-Wilson interval for the difference between two independent proportions, $d = p_2 - p_1$, which helped us analyse multi-valued data. In Chapter 8, we revisited this relationship between intervals and tests, and discussed how these calculations may be corrected for continuity and finite populations. We also learned about other intervals for p, such as the Clopper-Pearson (CP) and 'mid-p' intervals, both of which are derived from the Binomial distribution without a Normal approximation.

In this chapter we will convert Newcombe's difference interval into a general *closed form*[1] method for calculating confidence intervals for properties derived from Binomial and Multinomial proportions. The method, sometimes known as 'MOVER' ('method of variance estimate recovery', Newcombe, 2020), deserves to be better known because it is flexible and confidence intervals are efficient to calculate. It also appeals to a recurring theme of this book: that we should understand statistics as a type of logical (and mathematical) reasoning.

In Chapter 7 we noted a confidence interval for percentage difference, $d^{\%}$, but did not provide a complete formula. In this chapter we will show how such an interval may be derived.

The chapter is organised as follows. We discuss confidence intervals for functions of proportions in Section 9.2. We generalise Newcombe's method for the

DOI: 10.4324/9781003622697-12

difference of two independent *proportions* to the difference between any two independent *properties* in Section 9.3. In Section 9.4 we consider how to deal with dependent properties, before considering the limits of the method.

9.2 Functions of a Binomial Proportion

Suppose we want an interval for some property that is a function of the simple proportion, which we might write as $fn(p)$. For example,

1. **minus** $-p$
2. **weighting** (e.g., frequency $f = np$, where sample size n is a 'given' constant)
3. **addition of a constant** (e.g., an intercept c, as in $kp + c$)
4. **logarithm** $\log_k(p)$ or $\ln(p)$ ('ln' is the natural logarithm)
5. **odds** $p / (1 - p)$
6. **logit** $\ln(p) - \ln(1 - p)$, also known as 'log odds'
7. **logistic** $1 / (1 + e^{-(mx + c)})$, which can be used to invert the logit[2]
8. **power** p^k (provided $k \neq 0$)
9. **reciprocal** $1 / p$ (this may be employed to obtain *clause length*, see also Chapter 16)
10. **squared difference terms** $(p - P)^2$, where P is 'given' or constant

All points within a confidence interval for $fn(p)$ can be found by finding all points within a confidence interval for p and transforming them onto the new scale.

9.2.1 *Confidence Intervals for Monotonic Functions*

First, let's consider how to calculate confidence intervals for *monotonic* functions of a proportion (Smithson, 2007). These are functions that always either increase or decrease with their parameter (say, p) over the parameter's range. See Figure 9.1. They obtain a unique value when transformed, so the transformation is reversible with no loss of information.

In the list in the previous section, all functions except the last ('squared difference terms') are monotonic. 'Minus' and 'reciprocal' are decreasing functions. The others are increasing. (If in doubt, the easiest way to find out whether a function is monotonic or not is to plot it over the parameter's range.)

Functions 1–9 obey the following principle. If p is significantly different from P, their transformed values are also significantly different ('$\neq_s$') and vice-versa:

$$p \neq_s P \leftrightarrow fn(p) \neq_s fn(P). \tag{52}$$

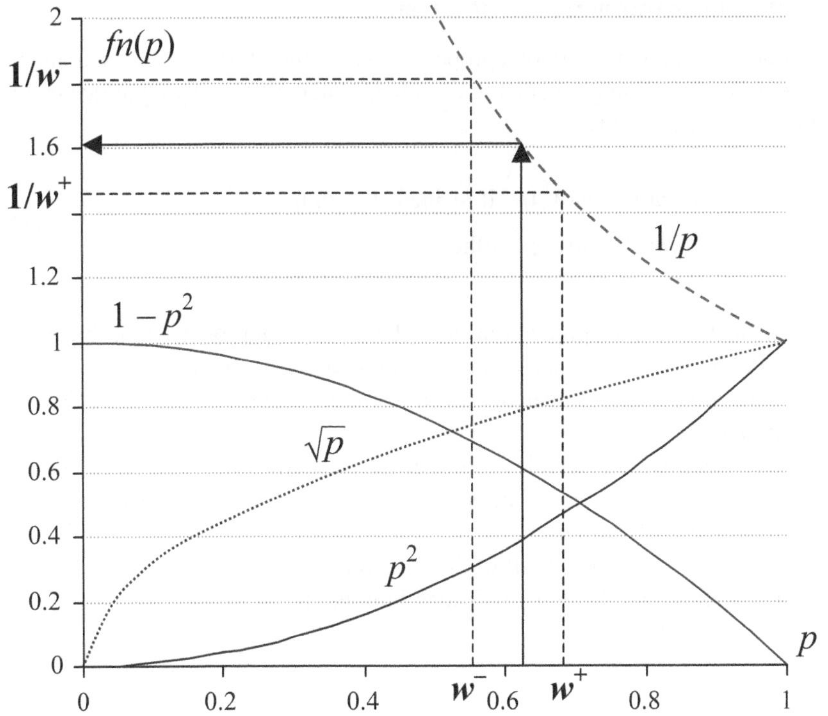

FIGURE 9.1 Example monotonic functions, including p^2 and $1/p$. Any function with a negative gradient, such as $1/p$, will cause the upper and lower bounds to be swapped.

The range of the parameter is important. If the parameter is the proportion $p \in \boldsymbol{P} = [0, 1]$, then

- $fn(p) = p^2$ is monotonic and increasing over this range, but
- $fn(p) = (p - 0.5)^2$ is non-monotonic over the same range. See Figure 9.2.

Alternatively, if the parameter is a difference in proportions $d \in [-1, 1]$,

- $fn(d) = d^2$ is non-monotonic over this range.

With a monotonic function, all points in a transformed interval are guaranteed to be in either ascending or descending order, so to obtain a confidence interval we only need to pay attention to the bounds of the range. This leads us to the following general theorem.

Monotonic transformation theorem:

For any function, $fn(\theta)$, of a property θ with interval (θ^-, θ^+) that is monotonic over its range, we may calculate a confidence interval by applying the same function, fn, to the bounds.

$$fn(\theta) \in \begin{cases} (fn(\theta^-), fn(\theta^+)) & \text{if } fn \text{ increases with } \theta, \\ (fn(\theta^+), fn(\theta^-)) & \text{otherwise.} \end{cases} \quad (53)$$

Note that the original property need not be a Binomial proportion: if the original confidence interval is accurate, the transformed interval will also be comparably accurate. This means we can use this transformation principle for other intervals we derive.[3]

Let's start with a simple example. Suppose we observe $f = 12$ out of a sample of $n = 20$ total instances. A 95% Wilson score interval for $p = 0.6$ is (0.3866, 0.7812). Now suppose we wish to express the same interval in terms of *odds*. The odds for 12 out of 20 is 12:8 (1.5:1) or 0.6/0.4. The odds function is monotonic. We apply the same function to the bounds, odds(p) = 1.5 $\in$ (0.6303, 3.5704).

9.2.2 Confidence Intervals for Non-Monotonic Functions

Not all functions are monotonic. A *non-monotonic* function contains at least one 'turning point' (a local maximum or minimum). See Figure 9.2. Most will contain only one.

One such function is *Binomial entropy*. This has a general formula

$$\textit{Binomial entropy } \eta(p) = -(p.\log_2(p) + (1-p).\log_2(1-p)), \quad (54)$$

and equals 0 for $p = 0$ or 1. This function has a turning point, a maximum, where $p = \hat{m} = 0.5$, and $\eta(p) = 1$. See Figure 9.2.

In order to calculate a confidence interval for $\eta(p)$ based on the Wilson score interval for p, we need to consider two cases:

- If the interval for p does not include the turning point, the function can be said to be monotonic *within the interval*. A conservative interval for $\eta(p)$ may be obtained with Equation (53).[4]
- Alternatively, if the confidence interval $p \in (w^-, w^+)$ includes the turning point, $\hat{m}$, the upper bound of the new interval is simply the transformed maximum value $\eta(\hat{m}) = 1$, and the lower bound is the smaller of the two transformed bounds, $\min(\eta(w^-), \eta(w^+))$. This interval is rather more conservative.[5]

This example illustrates a general principle. Where a transformed interval contains a single turning point, its function will be an included upper or lower bound of the new interval. Thus where $fn(\hat{m})$ is a maximum and $\hat{m} \in (\theta^-, \theta^+)$, the following interval will be cited:

$$fn(\theta) \in (\min(fn(\theta^-), fn(\theta^+)), fn(\hat{m})]. \qquad (53')$$

Note the square bracket, which means that the upper bound is retained within the interval.[6]

Let's calculate a confidence interval for Binomial entropy with $f = 12$ out of $n = 20$ instances. The 95% Wilson score interval for $p = 0.6$ is, as before: (0.3866, 0.7812).

Next, we apply Equation (55) to p and its bounds, w^- and w^+. This gives us the following scores: $\eta(p) = 0.9710$, $\eta(w^-) = 0.9626$ and $\eta(w^+) = 0.7580$.

However, we cannot simply quote $\eta(p) \in (0.7580, 0.9626)$, because $\hat{m} = 0.5$ falls within the score interval. As Figure 9.2 reveals, many points within the

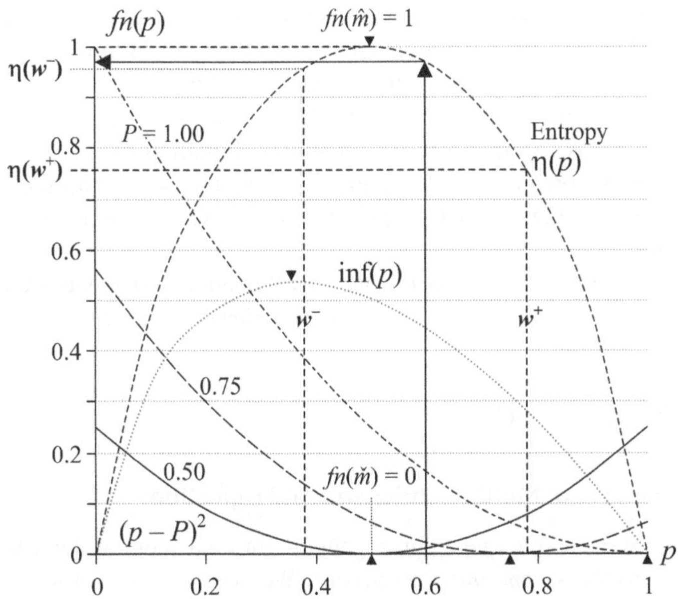

FIGURE 9.2 Example non-monotonic functions, $\eta(p)$ and $(p - P)^2$ for $P = 0.5$, 0.75 and 1, and a projected interval for $\eta(p)$. Where a confidence interval for p includes a turning point, such as $p = 0.6 \in (0.3866, 0.7812)$, which includes $\hat{m} = 0.5$, the transformed interval must include that point, thus $\eta(p) \in (0.7580, 1]$. Although $(p - P)^2$ is monotonic where $P = 0$ or 1, we should treat the function as non-monotonic in general.

interval for p generate entropy scores greater than 0.9626! Instead, we must find the largest possible score and include it. The corrected entropy confidence interval is $\eta(p) \in (0.7580, 1]$.

Another example function is found in *squared difference terms* of the form $(p_i - P_i)^2$, where p_i and P_i are observed and expected proportions respectively. We have a Binomial confidence interval for p_i, but P_i is treated as 'given', certain or constant, so it has no interval. The term has a *minimum* turning point, $\check{m} = P_i$, where $fn(\check{m}) = 0$.

Where an interval includes a minimum, $\check{m}$, the transformed interval becomes

$$fn(\theta) \in [fn(\check{m}), \max(fn(\theta^-), fn(\theta^+))). \qquad (53'')$$

Confidence intervals on non-monotonic functions of a property are sound if the original interval is sound, but they will be more conservative in practice. In other words, the coverage probability of the interval will increase above $1 - \alpha$. In science we generally adopt a cautionary approach, so we are entitled to accept a more conservative interval if necessary. We will return to this question briefly in the conclusions.

What about functions with more than one turning point? These are rare, but the principles set out previously would apply. The aim is to find the smallest and largest values of $fn(p)$ within the interval. We evaluate each turning point within the interval (θ^-, θ^+) to find the interior minimum $\check{m}$ and maximum $\hat{m}$. A simple approach applies Equation (53) as a first pass, and then compares $fn(\check{m})$ with the lower bound and $fn(\hat{m})$ with the upper. If they exceed the transformed interval, we substitute them and mark them for inclusion.

Transformed intervals are sound, but *lossy*. Equation (52) only operates in one direction: if the transformed properties are significantly different, so must be the original properties.

$$p \neq_s P \leftarrow fn(p) \neq_s fn(P). \qquad (52')$$

9.3 Functions of Multiple Independent Proportions

The next step in our quest for a general formula method for calculating intervals involves *combining* properties. We need an interval method for a function of two or more variables. We have already seen one example of such a function: Newcombe's method for calculating the difference between proportions.

Zou and Donner (2008) take Newcombe's method further. They propose an interval for the difference between two independent *parameters*, $d_\theta = \theta_1 - \theta_2$, where $\theta_1 \in (\theta_1^-, \theta_1^+)$, and $\theta_2 \in (\theta_2^-, \theta_2^+)$. Crucially, they argue, *these parameters need not be Binomial proportions*, provided they have good coverage intervals. We create a general difference interval function,

$$d_\theta \in \mathbf{difference}(\theta_1, \theta_2) = (d_\theta^-, d_\theta^+),$$

where

$$d_\theta^- = d_\theta - \sqrt{(\theta_1 - \theta_1^-)^2 + (\theta_2^+ - \theta_2)^2}\text{, and}$$

$$d_\theta^+ = d_\theta + \sqrt{(\theta_1^+ - \theta_1)^2 + (\theta_2 - \theta_2^-)^2}\,. \tag{55}$$

Rather than write **difference**(θ_1, θ_1^-, θ_1^+, θ_2, θ_2^-, θ_2^+), for brevity we will write **difference**(θ_1, θ_2).

This function returns a *set*: an interval with two bounds (d_θ^-, d_θ^+). We can define a Newcombe-Wilson difference interval about $d = p_2 - p_1$ (Equations (25) and (27), see Chapter 7) in these terms. Parameters are reversed, so $\theta_1 = p_2$, $\theta_2 = p_1$, with their corresponding Wilson intervals, that is $(\theta_1^-, \theta_1^+) = (w_2^-, w_2^+)$, and $(\theta_2^-, \theta_2^+) = (w_1^-, w_1^+)$.[7]

Using the interval function, we can write simply:

Newcombe-Wilson interval $d \in (d^-, d^+) =$ **difference**(p_2, p_1).

See Figure 9.3. In the previous chapter, we argued that Newcombe's method (using the Bienaymé sum of variances rule) was justified by the fact that variance at interval bounds was Normal. Zou and Donner (2008, p. 1695) say that Equation (55) may be applied to other properties than Binomial proportions *even if the underlying distribution for each bound is not Normal*, provided that each has 'separate confidence limits that have coverage levels close to nominal'.

Armed with what we have learned about confidence intervals of functions of proportions, we can replace θ_1 and θ_2 with a wide range of functions of p_1 and p_2.

Before we do, however, it is worth making one last observation. Equation (55) also gives us a significance test for comparing two independently obtained properties.

Generalised difference test:

If $0 \in$ **difference**(θ_1, θ_2), there is no significant difference between θ_1 and θ_2. (56)

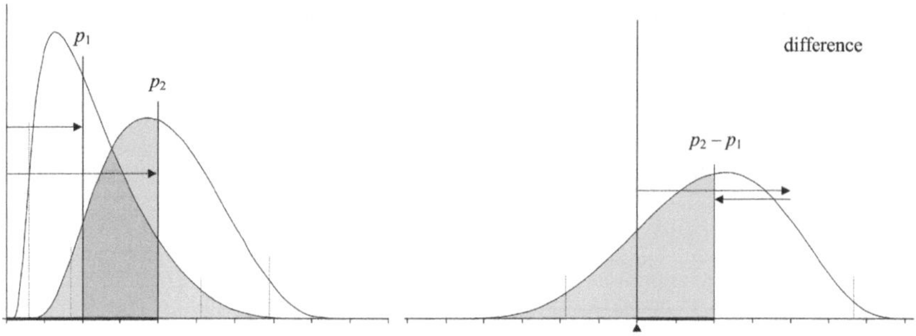

FIGURE 9.3 Creating a Newcombe-Wilson difference interval for $d = p_2 - p_1$ (right) from two Wilson score intervals (left), for $p_1 = 0.2$, $p_2 = 0.4$, and $n = 10$. The inner interval bounds for p_1 and p_2 (greyed) are combined to calculate the bound closest to $d = 0$ (equivalent to a homogeneity χ^2 test). Confidence interval distributions are calculated by delta approximation. See Chapter 17.

9.3.1 Confidence Intervals for Ratios, Odds Ratios and Logarithms of Independent Proportions

Zou and Donner obtain an interval for a *ratio* of two proportions (termed the 'risk ratio'), $r = p_1 / p_2$, by observing that a ratio (a fraction) is a difference on a log scale.

log of ratio $\ln(r) = \ln(p_1) - \ln(p_2)$.

This log of the ratio has a difference interval:

$\ln(r) \in$ **difference**$(\ln(p_1), \ln(p_2))$.

This takes us partway. We need an interval for r, not $\ln(r)$. But logarithms are monotonic, so they have a monotonic inverse function. The inverse of the natural logarithm 'ln' is 'exp', sometimes written e^x. To obtain a confidence interval on the original ratio scale, we apply this function to each bound of the difference interval:

risk ratio $r \in (r^-, r^+) =$ **ratio**$(p_1, p_2) = \exp($**difference**$(\ln(p_1), \ln(p_2)))$. (57)

This process is summarised in Figure 9.4. For convenience, we will define a **ratio** interval function for this interval. This can be used to obtain other formulae.

The *odds ratio* is the ratio of two odds, where odds$(p) = p / (1 - p)$. This is a monotonic function. To obtain a confidence interval for the odds ratio, we write

odds ratio $o \in (o^-, o^+) =$ **ratio**$(\text{odds}(p_1), \text{odds}(p_2))$. (58)

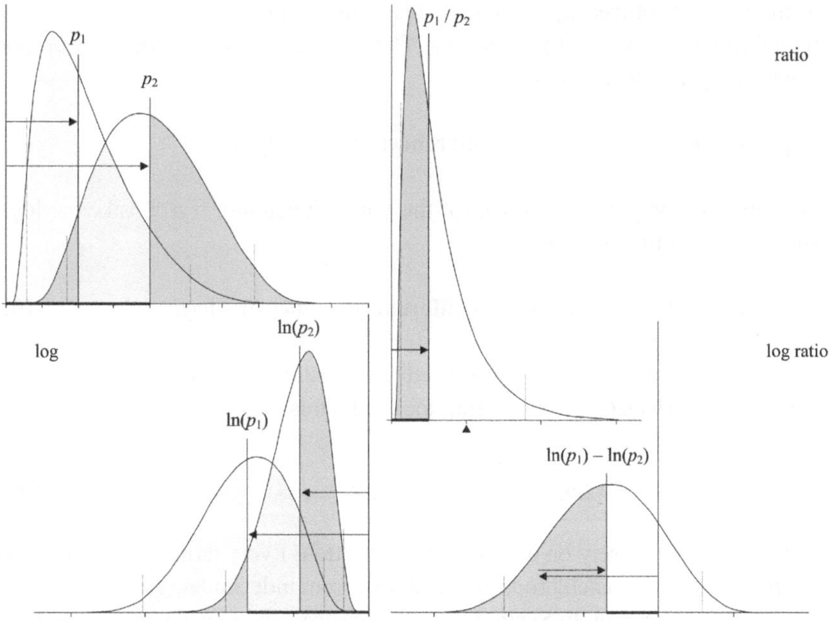

FIGURE 9.4 Creating an interval for the ratio $r = p_1 / p_2$ requires us to take the difference in intervals on a log scale (lower). Upper left: Wilson score intervals; lower, left: intervals transformed by the natural logarithm function; lower, right: their difference interval; upper, right: ratio confidence interval after inverse transformation with the 'exp' function.

This interval can also be used to create an interval for *Yule's Q*. See Chapter 13.

The *logarithm* relationship 'log *a* to base *b*', $\log_b(a)$, is equal to the ratio $\log(a) / \log(b)$, so we can write

$$\textit{logarithm } l \in (l^-, l^+) = \exp(-\exp(\mathbf{ratio}(-\ln(p_1), -\ln(p_2)))). \quad (59)$$

The minus signs are necessary for the **ratio** function to be computable. We transform the result to the original scale with the double exponent 'exp(–exp)'. See Table 9.1.

9.3.2 Confidence Intervals for Sums, Products, and Powers of Independent Proportions

Simple negation is trivially monotonic, so a confidence interval for the *sum* of two independent proportions, $p_1 + p_2$ can be easily obtained:

$$\textit{sum } s \in \mathbf{difference}(p_1, -p_2). \quad (60)$$

Similarly, **difference**($fn(p_1)$, $-fn(p_2)$) gives us an interval for the sum of two transformed independent proportions. The *product* of two independent proportions, $p_1 \times p_2$, is their *joint probability*.

$$product\ m \in (m^-, m^+) = \exp(\textbf{difference}(\ln(p_1), -\ln(p_2))). \quad (61)$$

We can also compute an interval for the *power* function $g = p_1^{p_2}$. Like the logarithm, this is a little trickier.

$$power\ g \in (g^-, g^+) = \exp(-\exp(\textbf{difference}(\ln(-\ln(p_1)), -\ln(p_2))). \quad (62)$$

The sum or product may be generalised to any number of independent terms, θ_i, each with intervals (θ_i^-, θ_i^+). The sum looks like this:

$$sum\ s \in (s^-, s^+) = (\Sigma\theta_i - \sqrt{\Sigma(\theta_i - \theta_i^-)^2}, \Sigma\theta_i + \sqrt{\Sigma(\theta_i^+ - \theta_i)^2}). \quad (60')$$

These formulae all rely on one crucial assumption. Every term must be *independently* obtained, i.e. each proportion is drawn from independent samples. But this is not always the case. In Section 9.4.2 we discuss how to calculate intervals for functions of Multinomial proportions, that is, where proportions sum to 1.

9.3.3 *Summary*

Table 9.1 summarises formulae obtained by substituting parameters θ_1 and θ_2 in Equation (55), with a final transformation to the resulting difference, yielding intervals for the six basic mathematical operators applied to two independent proportions.

TABLE 9.1 Substitutions for θ_1 and θ_2 in Equation (55) for basic operators, with back-transforms to the resulting d_θ and its interval. Thus, for the interval for the ratio p_1 / p_2, we substitute ($\ln(p_1)$, $\ln(p_2)$) for (θ_1, θ_2) and their bounds in Equation (55), and then apply the back-transform to the result, $\exp(d_\theta)$, yielding Equation (57).

		θ_1	θ_2	*back-transform*
difference	$p_2 - p_1$	p_2	p_1	d_θ
sum	$p_1 + p_2$	p_1	$-p_2$	d_θ
ratio	p_1 / p_2	$\ln(p_1)$	$\ln(p_2)$	$\exp(d_\theta)$
product	$p_1 \times p_2$	$\ln(p_1)$	$-\ln(p_2)$	$\exp(d_\theta)$
logarithm	$\log_{p_2}(p_1)$	$\ln(-\ln(p_1))$	$\ln(-\ln(p_2))$	$\exp(-\exp(d_\theta))$
power	$p_1^{p_2}$	$\ln(-\ln(p_1))$	$-\ln(p_2)$	$\exp(d_\theta)$

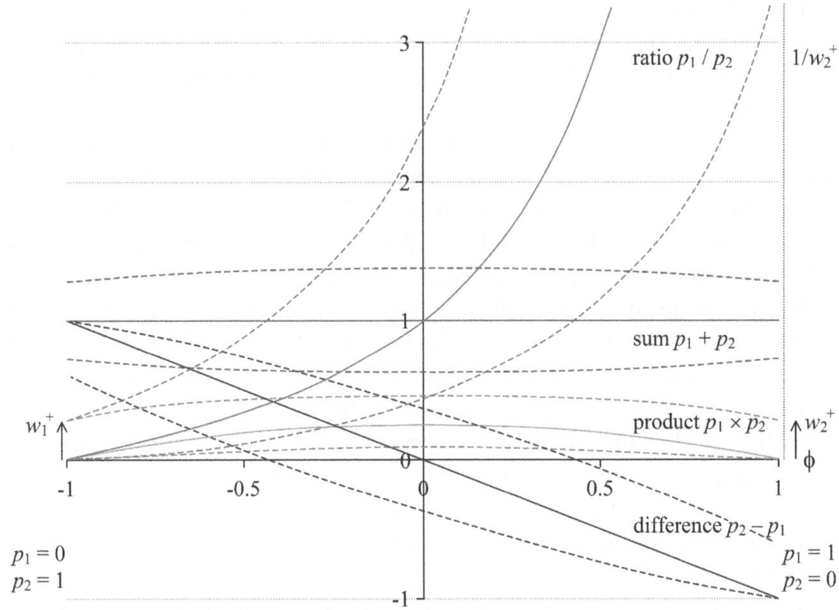

FIGURE 9.5 Confidence intervals for difference, sum, product and ratio of Binomial proportions p_1 and p_2, obtained by combining Wilson score intervals for $\alpha = 0.05$, and sample sizes $n_1 = n_2 = 10$, plotted over the diagonal of a matrix where $\phi = p_1 - p_2$ and $p_1, p_2 \in (0, 1)$.

For ratios, products, powers and logs, if either parameter is 0 or 1, without continuity-correction the interval may not be computable (the logarithm of 0 is $-\infty$). A good general solution may be obtained by deviating inwards very slightly, e.g., by $\delta_p = 10^{-6}$. This allows us to plot Figure 9.5.

By inspection, we find that ratio and product intervals at $p_1 = 0$, $p_2 = 1$ (left) converge to $[0, w_1^+)$. For $p_1 = 1$, $p_2 = 0$ (right), the ratio interval converges to $(1/w_2^+, \infty)$ and product interval $[0, w_2^+)$.

In sum and difference formulae, p_1 and p_2 may be replaced by Real parameters. For products and ratios, both parameters must be positive.

9.3.4 Performance

To see how these formulae behave, we have plotted confidence intervals for the difference, sum, product and ratio of two proportions over the diagonal of a contingency table matrix.[8] On the left of Figure 9.5, $p_1 = 0$ and $p_2 = 1$. We increase p_1 and decrease p_2 in equal amounts until we reach the right, where $p_1 = 1$ and $p_2 = 0$. Along the diagonal, the horizontal axis ϕ is equal to the negated difference $-d = p_1 - p_2$.[9]

Each interval is 'well-behaved'. Not one interval collapses to a zero width or overshoots the range of the property. Although ratios and products cannot be calculated where p_1 or $p_2 = 0$ or 1, employing a small δ_p adjustment has a negligible error cost.

How do these intervals perform? Examining the risk ratio interval (Equation (57)), Zou and Donner (2008) comment that it behaves more consistently with χ^2 than previous 'delta' methods (Altman et al., 2000). However, this is a poor comparison. These methods employ a 'Wald'-type standard error on a logarithmic scale and obtain infinite intervals at extremes.

Newcombe justified his 'Method 10' (Newcombe, 1998b) by assuming variance at interval bounds was Normal. See Section 8.3.2. But ratio, product, power, logarithm, and so on combine bounds on different number scales. See Figure 9.4. The log of the Normal distribution cannot be Normal.

Wallis (2021) proposed a way to examine this issue. Recall that a difference interval becomes comparable to the Fisher or χ^2 test for homogeneity (independence), by checking if the confidence interval $d \in (d^-, d^+)$ contains 0 (Equation (56)). We can do the same for the ratio, odds ratio and log intervals by testing if their intervals include 1.

We can then calculate a mean error rate by the following method. For all possible combinations of each proportion, we carry out the Fisher test and the interval test we wish to evaluate. If our new test is wrongly 'significant', we call it an excess Type I error. If it is wrongly 'non-significant', it is an excess Type II error. These errors are then weighted by the chance of the combination occurring at random, and summed. See (Wallis, 2024b).

This evaluation is an *inner interval* comparison, so only the interval bound nearest to 0 or 1 is tested, and it is only applied to *differences* and *ratios* (not sums, products, etc). But it gives us an insight about how MOVER performs on different number scales.

If we calculate the mean excess Type I error against the Fisher 'exact' test, interval performance may be ranked by ascending error rates ('>' means 'better'):

difference (***P***)
  > risk ratio (ln(***P***))
    > logarithm (ln(–ln(***P***)))
      > odds ratio (ln(odds(***P***))).

These differences in error rates are detectable, but small compared to the impact of *continuity correction*. See Figure 9.6. Evaluating excess errors against Fisher for a declining α from 0.1 to 0.001, Wallis (2024b) found that whereas the number scale (***P***, ln(***P***), etc.) affects the result, adjusting a continuity correction factor can be used to manage excess Type I and II errors, with an optimum trade-off for most number scales at about 1.5 times Yates's correction.[10]

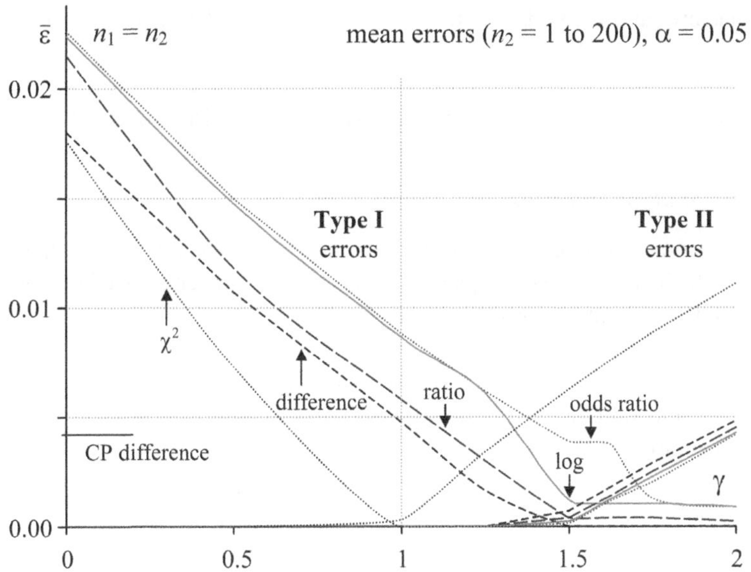

FIGURE 9.6 Mean excess errors of inner intervals for difference, ratio, log and odds ratio formulae, $\bar{\varepsilon}$, evaluated against the Fisher test, for combinations of tables with equal sample sizes $n_1 = n_2$, from 1 to 200, with varying continuity corrections $\gamma \times \frac{1}{2n}$. Yates's correction is where γ = 1 (dotted): this minimises excess Type I errors for χ^2 at a minimum additional Type II error cost. But for ratio, log and odds ratio intervals, γ = 1.5 may be more appropriate.

9.4 Functions of Multiple Non-Independent Properties

If you want to create an interval for a particular formula, how should you go about it?

So far, we have assumed that our formulae consist of independently sampled properties. But equations are not always written in this format. Often they are written to be easy to remember or explain. Cited terms might not be independent.

Consider this trivial example. What is the confidence interval for $p_1 + p_1$? Answer: $p_1 + p_1 = 2p_1 \in (2w_1^-, 2w_1^+)$.

Both terms are 'directly dependent': variation due to random sampling in the first term is duplicated in the second term. The independent sum formula (Equation (60)) assumes that terms are independent and sums *variances* (squared standard deviations). It creates an interval whose width is the Pythagorean hypotenuse of a triangle whose other sides are the independent widths. That interval will be too narrow (interval widths will be $\sqrt{2}$ times, rather than twice, the respective single interval width).

Here's another trivial example: what is the confidence interval for $p_1 - p_1$? Answer: $p_1 - p_1 = 0 \in [0, 0]$. Dependent variation can also cancel out.

9.4.1 Analytic Reduction

If two or more parameters in a formula are not independent, the first step is to try to rewrite the formula as an equation in a *canonical form* comprised of independent parameters that are only cited once.[11]

Consider the interval for the difference between competing Binomial proportions, where $p_2 = 1 - p_1$. We substitute for p_2 into the difference formula and obtain a function of a single parameter, p_1, and a monotonic transformation:

$$d = p_2 - p_1 = 1 - 2p_1 \in (1 - 2w_1^+, 1 - 2w_1^-). \tag{63}$$

This is the corollary of the Wilson 'more' test in Chapter 7.

What about the *percentage difference* between two independent proportions? It is usually written in the following form, because it is easy to explain:

$$d^{\%} = d \,/\, p_1 = (p_2 - p_1) \,/\, p_1.$$

This formula mentions p_1 twice. If we were to apply Zou and Donner's theorem first to the difference $d = p_2 - p_1$, and then to the ratio $d \,/\, p_1$, we would obtain a poor interval. But there is a better method. We can rewrite it so that each independent term appears once only:

$$d^{\%} = p_2 \,/\, p_1 - 1 \in \mathbf{ratio}(p_2, p_1) - 1. \tag{64}$$

In Chapter 8, we distinguished between goodness of fit and independence (homogeneity) interpretations. This distinction is also relevant to deriving intervals.

Wallis (2024c) documents how confidence intervals for the *Dice coefficient* (Dice, 1945), μ (Evert, 2004), *Difference coefficient* (Hofland & Johansson, 1982) and Q (Yule, 1944) may be derived on a homogeneity basis.

The interval for Dice's coefficient is a good example. Dice's formula is conventionally stated as a function of the observed frequency of the first cell in the table, $o_{1,1}$, and row and column totals n_1 and c_1. It may be rewritten as a function of the row proportion $p_1 = o_{1,1}/n_1$ and column proportion $p_1' = o_{1,1}/c_1$.

$$dice = 2o_{1,1} \,/\, (n_1 + c_1) = 2/(1/p_1 + 1/p_1').$$

How does this help? In a homogeneity table, n_1 and c_1 are constant,[12] so p_1 and p'_1 are in an increasing monotonic relationship, that is, $p_1 = \text{fn}(p'_1)$. Although they are not identical, an increase in p_1 must generate an increase in p'_1, and vice versa. It follows that *dice* is also a monotonic transformation of p_1. We can now derive the following formula for the interval:

$$dice \in (2/(1/w_1^- + 1/w_1'^-), 2/(1/w_1^+ + 1/w_1'^+)), \qquad (65)$$

where $p_1 \in (w_1^-, w_1^+)$ and $p'_1 \in (w_1'^-, w_1'^+)$. We don't need to work out the exact relationship between p_1 and p'_1.

In Chapter 13 we obtain an interval for 2×2 ϕ with a similar method.

9.4.2 Confidence Intervals for Sums of Multinomial Terms

For 2×2 tables, this kind of approach may be sufficient. But what about larger tables? In Chapter 7 we noted that competing Multinomial proportions are *partially dependent*, because their sum, $\sum p_i$, must equal 1, and Binomial proportions are *wholly dependent*: $p_2 = 1 - p_1$.

How should we create an interval for a sum of k Multinomial terms? The interval for the sum of *proportions* is trivial (it is exactly $1 \in [1, 1]$). But to obtain an interval for a Multinomial *effect size* (see Chapter 13) we sum a series of a *function* of Multinomial proportions.

To create a confidence interval for such a sum, we can modify Equation (60') by scaling each interval width by a factor, $\kappa = k/(k - 1)$, which accounts for this Multinomial constraint:

$$\textit{Multinomial sum } s_k \in (s_k^-, s_k^+) = (\Sigma\theta_i - \sqrt{\kappa\Sigma(\theta_i - \theta_i^-)^2},$$
$$\Sigma\theta_i + \sqrt{\kappa\Sigma(\theta_i^+ - \theta_i)^2}). \qquad (60'')$$

This method is more conservative than the equivalent Binomial method.

Let us consider an example. In Section 9.2.2, we observed that Binomial entropy $\eta(p)$ is a non-monotonic function (Equation (54)), and an interval may be obtained by examining turning points of that function. We will construct an interval for *Multinomial entropy* for a Multinomial variable with k values, each with a proportion p_i.

First, we write a simple general formula for entropy as the sum of k 'information' terms, $\inf(p_i)$.

$$\inf(p_i) = -p_i.\log_k(p_i),$$
$$\textit{Multinomial entropy } \eta = \Sigma\inf(p_i), \qquad (54')$$

Next, we create intervals for $\text{inf}(p_i) \in (h_i^-, h_i^+)$. Like Binomial entropy, the 'inf' function is non-monotonic, with a maximum at $\hat{m} = 1/e \approx 0.367879$. The maximum value of the 'inf' function where $k = 2$, $\text{inf}(\hat{m}) \approx 0.530738$. See Figure 9.2.

We obtain a transformed interval. The Wilson interval (w_i^-, w_i^+) will occupy one of three regions: below, above or including the maximum:

$$(h_i^-, h_i^+) = \begin{cases} (\text{inf}(w_i^-), \text{inf}(w_i^+)) & \text{if } w_i^+ < \hat{m}, \\ (\text{inf}(w_i^+), \text{inf}(w_i^-)) & \text{if } w_i^- > \hat{m}, \\ (\max(\text{inf}(w_i^+), \text{inf}(w_i^+)), \text{inf}(\hat{m})] & \text{otherwise.} \end{cases} \quad (66)$$

Finally, we perform the Multinomial k-constrained summation. We sum interval terms with Equation (60"), substituting $\text{inf}(p_i)$ for θ_i and (h_i^-, h_i^+) for (θ_i^-, θ_i^+).

$$\eta \in (\eta^-, \eta^+) = (\eta - \sqrt{\kappa\Sigma(\text{inf}(p_i) - h_i^-)^2}, \eta + \sqrt{\kappa\Sigma(h_i^+ - \text{inf}(p_i))^2}). \quad (67)$$

If the resulting upper bound η^+ overshoots the range [0, 1], we close the interval at 1.

The interval performs reasonably well, but for $k = 2$, where a direct comparison is possible, it is more conservative than the transformed Binomial interval (Section 9.1.2). See Wallis (2022).

Let's repeat the task of estimating a 95% confidence interval for $f = 12$, $n = 20$. We obtain Wilson score intervals and then 'inf' scores for each of p_1, w_1^-, etc.

For $p_1 = 0.6$, $\text{inf}(p_1) = 0.4422 \in (0.2783, 0.5301)$, because the maximum $\hat{m} = 1/e$ lies (just) outside the interval (see Figure 9.2). The function declines above the maximum.

On the other hand, for $p_2 = 1 - p_1 = 0.4$, $\hat{m}$ is within the interval, and $\text{inf}(p_2) = 0.5288 \in (0.4325, 0.5307]$.[13] After correcting for overshoot, the Multinomial sum with $k = 2$ (Equation (66)) gives us $\eta = 0.9710 \in (0.7022, 1]$.

This confidence interval is more conservative than the Binomial interval, which had a lower bound of 0.7580, so the Binomial formula is preferred where $k = 2$. Should we incorrectly apply the unconstrained sum formula (Equation (60')), the lower bound would become 0.7809, and the interval too small.

9.4.3 Limitations and Alternatives

The method described in this chapter can be used to derive accurate closed form confidence intervals for properties that can be expressed in terms of independent Binomial proportions, each cited once. Creating an interval becomes an exercise in algebra, attempting to reformulate an expression in these terms.

Sometimes the result comes with a cost of increased conservatism, due to the use of non-monotonic functions or Multinomial sums. Nonetheless, the advantage of a direct method of computation should not be understated. The additional error introduced by carrying out the Pythagorean sum on logarithmic (or higher) number scales turns out to be small, capable of management by boosting a continuity correction.

However, some formulae are resistant to reformulation. Wallis (2024c) summarises an exercise in systematically attempting to create closed form confidence intervals for Anthony's (2023) list of common descriptive statistics used in Corpus Linguistics algorithms. This exercise was mostly successful, but some formulae proved difficult. Thus a single-cell Mutual Information (MI_{11}) homogeneity interval was derived, but one for a variant measure, termed MI^2_{11}, turned out to be more problematic.[14]

What can we do if we wish to create a confidence interval for such properties?

One option is a bootstrap interval (see Chapter 8). This is not ideal, first because it is not a true confidence interval, and second, because it will be inaccurate for small samples or where the observed property is near a boundary. If this is a route you wish to explore, you should also consider whether you should employ a different number scale – for example, by assuming the interval is Normal for $\ln(x)$ rather than x. In Figure 9.4 the distribution of the interval for the log of the ratio appears Normal-like.

A better alternative employs the interval equality principle for the transformed property. The idea is we search for interval bounds by inverting a significance test. A common example is where we are given a sampling interval formula for a property. This method is also used by likelihood-based intervals.

Suppose we have a formula for the sampling standard deviation of a property, θ, which we write $S(\theta)$. Assuming a Normal sampling distribution, we search for θ^- and θ^+, where

$$\theta^- + z_{\alpha/2}.S(\theta^-) = \theta,$$
$$\theta^+ - z_{\alpha/2}.S(\theta^+) = \theta.$$

In Chapter 13 we use this method to calculate an interval for Cramér's ϕ for $r \times c$ tables.

9.5 Conclusions

The MOVER method (Zou & Donner, 2008; Newcombe, 2020) can be thought of as applying Newcombe's (1998b) difference interval method to properties such as monotonic transformations of proportions. Since the log of a ratio is equal to a difference in logs, and the log function is monotonic, a difference interval on the log scale creates an interval for the ratio of two properties. Intervals for sums and products may be obtained by negation. Logarithm and power operators follow a similar path.

Smithson (2007) observed that one can safely employ a monotonic transform to a confidence interval. The idea is a range of values on $\mathbf{P}$ are 'projected' by the function onto a new range of values, fn($\mathbf{P}$). For example, to obtain an interval for p^2 we simply square the bounds of the Wilson score interval for p; for an interval for $1/p$, we cite $(1/w^+, 1/w^-)$. This method relies on the property p being a Binomial proportion that is randomly sampled and free to vary.

More controversially, and in an extension to MOVER, in Section 9.2.2 we demonstrated that intervals on non-monotonic functions of properties were also viable, if 'lossy' and non-invertible. Such transformations require us to examine turning points of the function. Usually there is only one: a maximum or minimum. The resulting interval tends to be conservative, in the worst case, the majority of one tail may fall within the interval, such that the resulting interval has a real-world error rate close to $\alpha/2$ rather than α.

This might be addressed by a search procedure, at a cost: a significant difference in transformed properties would no longer be guaranteed to reflect a significant difference in untransformed ones (Equation (52')). This may be acceptable. Not every comparison or evaluation must obtain identical results. However, this distinction should be noted, as it may not be obvious to the reader.

We also discussed a second innovation, Multinomial summation, where k-valued variables have $k - 1$ degrees of freedom and we reweight the interval width accordingly. As we saw when discussing entropy, we can expect a Multinomial sum to produce more conservative confidence intervals than a Binomial formula, so it is wise to derive both and use the Binomial method if the option arises.

These two extensions to the MOVER method are frequently required when creating intervals for effect sizes. We have already met one such measure. Simple difference d is an effect size: the greater the difference, the bigger the effect. But there are other measures. In Chapter 13 we discuss effect sizes and use what we have learned to create confidence intervals for them. In Chapter 14 we introduce meta-tests which exploit the generalised difference test.

The methods described in this chapter can be employed with other confidence intervals for the single proportion. A Clopper-Pearson or 'mid-p' interval might be substituted. However, the Wilson-based approach allows continuity, finite population and random-text sampling adjustments (see Chapter 16). Continuity corrections are particularly important. Increasing a continuity correction factor slightly can absorb the error introduced by applying MOVER to properties on different measurement scales. It can suppress more errors than the difference between two CP intervals. See Figure 9.6. If we wish to cite confidence intervals on properties cautiously, the Wilson score interval is an excellent starting point.

Notes

1 'Closed form' means that a result can be calculated directly with an algebraic formula. The Clopper-Pearson interval (Chapter 8) is obtained by search, so it is not a closed form.
2 Euler's constant, e = 2.7183 ..., is the base of the natural logarithm. See also Chapter 10.
3 In Equation (57), we apply the function 'exp' to a difference interval calculated on a logarithmic scale.
4 This confidence interval is conservative because some values of P beyond (w^-, w^+) can generate entropy scores which fall within the transformed interval. Non-monotonic functions like entropy (and their intervals) are 'lossy', that is they lose information.
5 Consider Figure 9.2, where $\eta(w^-) > \eta(w^+)$. Setting the lower bound of the transformed interval at $\eta(w^+)$ means that ostensibly non-significant values of P less than w^- (from 0.2188 to w^- = 0.3866) generate scores falling within the confidence interval for η. This includes that part of the tail area of w^- adjacent to the bound where most of the area will be. The result is that the effective overall error level may nearly halve. In Figure 9.2, 99.85% of the lower tail falls within the transformed interval!
6 Recall that in Chapter 6, where p was 0 or 1 the Wilson score interval was one-tailed, and we said that 0 or 1 lay within the interval. Otherwise the bounds are the nearest points significantly different from p, and therefore lie just outside the interval.
7 In Chapter 7 we also defined interval widths $(u^-, u^+) = (p - w^-, w^+ - p)$, and superscripts may be assigned appropriately.
8 Since there are $(n_1 + 1) \times (n_2 + 1)$ contingency table patterns, there are other ways of permuting values. Nonetheless, this 'matrix diagonal' method is a simple way of visualising how different intervals perform. See also Chapter 8.
9 In Chapter 13 we discuss Cramér's 2 × 2 ϕ, which obtains the same values along the diagonal, and is 'associative', that is, it does not matter whether it is calculated with row or column probabilities.
10 The odds ratio fails at extreme values, hence the 'bump' on the right of Figure 9.6. It is *indeterminate* where $p_1 = 0$ and $p_2 = 1$, or vice-versa. The interval becomes infinite or zero-width. This issue also applies to Yule's Q. Power $g = p_1^{p_2}$ also converges to a zero-width interval where $p_1 = 1$ and $p_2 = 0$.
11 By 'independent parameters', we mean variables like observed proportion p, which are subject to sampling variation and are given confidence intervals. Other terms, such as sample size n or population proportion P can be cited multiple times.
12 This is a fundamental assumption of the Fisher test. See Chapter 8.
13 When combining intervals with a mix of open and closed bounds, we propose prioritising closed bounds, that is, the bound is included in the interval. If one component bound is closed, the result should be closed. Here, the upper bound for inf(p_2) is closed, so the upper bound for the sum should be closed. In this case, the resulting interval is closed for a different reason – the overshoot.
14 True at the time of writing (summer 2025). The author continues to experiment with deriving intervals by this method, reporting results on the **corp.ling.stats** blog, https://corplingstats.wordpress.com.

10

COMPETITION BETWEEN CHOICES OVER TIME

10.1 Introduction

So far, we have primarily concerned ourselves with single observations or pairs of observations. In this chapter, we turn to the analysis of a series of observations expressed over time, termed a *time series*.

Evaluating choices over time implies studying competition between alternates. We will discuss the mathematical properties of a competitive Binomial system undergoing simple continuous change over time, before considering more complex systems.

Consider the example of Binomial *shall/will* alternation over time from Aarts et al. (2013) that we met in Chapter 3. In the *Diachronic Corpus of Present-day Spoken English* (DCPSE), speakers were sampled in different time periods. The proportion of first person declarative positive {*shall*, *will*} utterances where *shall* is chosen, *p*(*shall* | {*shall*, *will*}), is in competition with the alternate proportion for *will* (they are subject to mutual substitution, see Chapter 3).

In Chapter 2, we noted some elementary properties of Binomial proportions. The probability of observing a member x_1 of a set of alternates $\mathbf{X} = \{x_i\}$, $p(x_1 \mid \mathbf{X})$, is *bounded* by $\boldsymbol{P} = [0, 1]$, and *exhaustive*, $\sum p(x_i \mid \mathbf{X}) \equiv 1$.

A bounded system behaves differently from an unbounded one. Every child knows that a ball bouncing in an alley behaves differently than in an open playground. The bounds, 'walls', direct motion towards the centre.

In Chapter 6, we commented briefly that a symmetric Gaussian distribution might be a plausible model of variation for an unbounded system. The *t* distribution for comparing means of Real values is not bounded, and tends to the Normal for large samples. However, the same does not apply to sample means of binary choices (Binomial proportions).

DOI: 10.4324/9781003622697-13

10.2 The 'S Curve'

When you hit rock bottom, the only way is up. In an empty pond, a lily plant colonises the pond at an exponential rate. However, the pond has a finite size, which places an upper limit on growth. Once the pond starts to fill, the reduction in available light and space causes growth rates to slow.

The pattern of expected behaviour is the well-known 'S curve' (properly known as the 'sigmoid' or *logistic curve*) shown in Figure 10.1, where P represents the expected proportion of the pond covered by the plant, and t, time.

A simple logistic curve that crosses the midpoint $P = 0.5$ at $t = 0$ can be expressed as

$$P(t) = \text{logistic}(t, m) \equiv 1 / (1 + e^{-mt}), \qquad (68)$$

where t represents time, m is a gradient parameter and e is Euler's constant.

Varying m obtains different gradients or growth rates. See Figure 10.1. The sign of m represents the direction, and the absolute value, $| m |$, the slope. If m is negative, the curve declines at the same rate as the equivalent curve for (positive) $-m$ would increase. Note how, for positive values of m, the line accelerates from the lower edge and decelerates on approaching the top edge.

Our water lily competes with its environment. In other evolutionary models, species may compete for the same niche, or predator and prey species compete.

Two alternate forms performing the same linguistic function (e.g., *shall* and *will*) also compete with each other. All other things being equal, if *shall* is in a

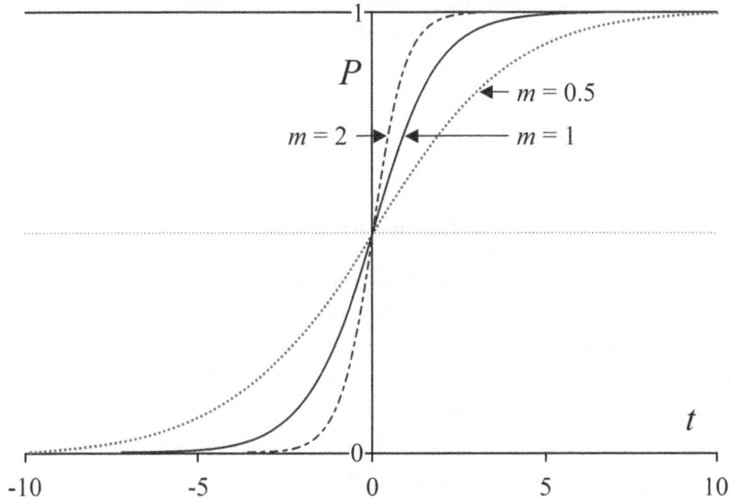

FIGURE 10.1 Example logistic curves with different gradients, m.

small minority, it is unlikely to die out altogether. We say it becomes 'marked in use', which is another way of saying speakers become aware of the form due to its rarity. On the other hand, fashionable neologisms or usages may spread rapidly through the language until they become the norm.

The curve is a default or 'ideal' mathematical model. *All other things being equal*, we expect change under binary competition over time to follow a logistic curve.

This does not mean that observed change will always be logistic. Consider Isaac Newton's famous first law of motion. This states that 'a body will remain at rest or continue in uniform motion in a straight line unless acted on by an external force'.

The default expected motion of an object in Cartesian space is a straight line. Indeed, as we shall see, the logistic curve can be thought of as *a straight line in Real × probability* ($\mathfrak{R} \times \boldsymbol{P}$) *space*. Saying that 'data are expected to fit the logistic curve' is like citing Newton's First Law.

The curve identifies an *expected* pattern of change. We may then investigate when *observed* behaviour deviates from this expected pattern.

The logistic curve is a mathematical model that predicts behaviour in a simplified set of circumstances. It does not determine the actual outcome. Frequently, there are more than two forms interacting at once. Or to paraphrase Newton, there may be external forces acting on the Binomial choice. 'All other things' may not be equal.

Neologisms may die out as fast as they spread, for example, if they are driven out by other, new alternates. If more than two alternate forms are competing, behaviour may be more complex because two forms may be increasing in usage at the same time. The system may oscillate. Minority species may 'bounce back'.

Whereas linear regression is conventionally employed as a starting point for fitting Cartesian observations to data (two Real axes, $\mathfrak{R} \times \mathfrak{R}$), *logistic regression* may be employed for fitting data when one of the axes is probabilistic (a Binomial proportion), that is, $\mathfrak{R} \times \boldsymbol{P}$. See Section 10.5.

10.3 Boundaries and Confidence Intervals

Boundaries do not only impact on how P is predicted to change over time. They affect estimates of the *probable location* of P in a similar way. In Chapter 6, we saw that the Normal distribution fits the Binomial poorly when P is *near* the boundary (0 or 1) or n is small. This is distinct from the issue of *continuity correction* proper, which arises from the fact that the Normal distribution is continuous whereas the Binomial is discrete. However, if you employ Yates's correction, the boundary issue is largely addressed as a by-product.

As a general rule, whenever we see boundary conditions on variation, we can expect asymmetric behaviour. Nature is full of boundaries.[1]

10.3.1 Confidence Intervals for p

Boundaries on the probability range at 0 and 1 apply to population probabilities, P, observed proportions (probabilities), p, and confidence intervals on p.

Since neither p nor P can fall below 0, as p approaches 0, confidence intervals on p become increasingly asymmetric. Hence Wald and other Normal-based interval estimation techniques must fail in bounded systems.

Both the Wilson score confidence interval and its continuity-corrected version have this property of asymmetry, as do 'exact' Clopper-Pearson (CP) intervals obtained by search. See Chapter 8. These intervals tend towards the centre in a similar way to the S curve.

10.3.2 Logistic Curves and Wilson Intervals

Figure 10.2, left, plots the logistic curve for $m = 1$, with 95% Wilson score intervals at $n = 10$ and 100. (Clopper-Pearson and continuity-corrected Wilson intervals are comparable – see Chapters 8 and 17.)

By way of comparison, on the right is the same figure with Wald intervals. This demonstrates both *overshoot* ($p < 0$ or $p > 1$) and *zero-width intervals*. Both these failings create a substantial problem when it comes to line fitting.[2]

The Wilson interval is widest at $p = 0.5$. Against a logistic curve, correct intervals appear almost 'tubular' (Figure 10.2, left). What happens if we flatten the line out?

The 'logit' is the inverse logistic function (see Chapter 9). Substituting $a = mt$, we have the equivalence

$$p = \text{logit}^{-1}(a) \equiv \text{logistic}(a) = 1 / (1 + e^{-a}),$$

and the logit can be expressed as

$$a = \text{logit}(p) \equiv \ln(p / (1 - p)) = \ln(p) - \ln(1 - p), \quad (69)$$

where 'ln' refers to the natural logarithm. See Chapter 9.

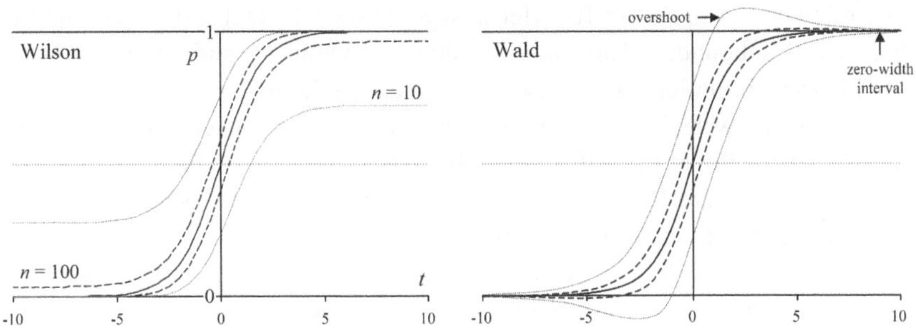

FIGURE 10.2 Left: logistic curve ($m = 1$) with Wilson score intervals for $n = 10$ and 100, and $\alpha = 0.05$. Right: the same curve with (incorrect) Wald intervals.

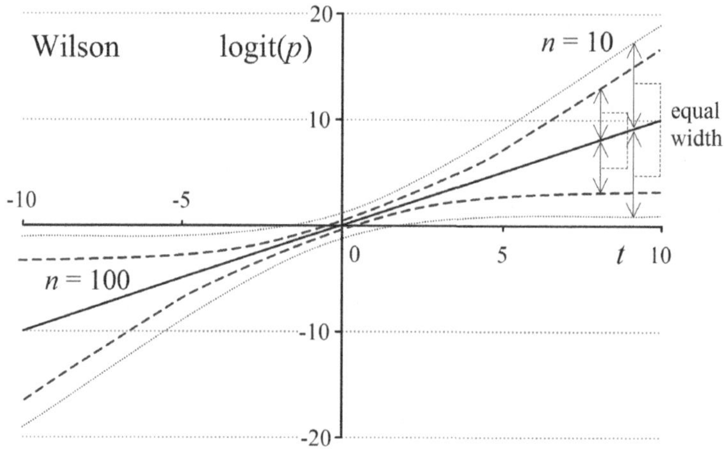

FIGURE 10.3 Graph of Figure 10.2, left, on a logit scale.

The logistic function maps Real values $\mathfrak{R} \equiv [-\infty, \infty]$ to probabilistic ones, $\boldsymbol{P} \equiv [0, 1]$. The logit function is the inverse, flattening the probability dimension into a Cartesian one. On this surface, the logistic curve for p with $m = 1$ becomes the straight line, $y = t$. See Figure 10.3.

Although the Wilson interval is skewed on a probability scale, Newcombe (1998a, p. 870) notes that on a logit scale the Wilson interval is symmetric, that is,

$$\text{logit}(p) - \text{logit}(w^-) = \text{logit}(w^+) - \text{logit}(p), \qquad (70)$$

where $p \in (0, 1)$. At the extreme $p = 0$, $p = w^-$ and $\text{logit}(0) = -\infty$, so this equality breaks down.

Figure 10.3 is plotted by simply applying the logit function to the vertical (p) axis of all curves in Figure 10.2 (left). Now the scale is Real and goes to infinity, that is, it is unbounded. The interval widths are symmetric and fan out from 0.

This transformation can be used to explain the logistic curve. Imagine Figure 10.3 as if it were drawn on the surface of a U-shaped 'trench' curved like Figure 10.4. Time flows along the trench. If we look down from above, Figure 10.3 will look like Figure 10.2, left. We have a system bounded by 'walls' at $p = 0$ and 1, directing motion inwards to $p = 0.5$.[3]

In summary, the logistic scale provides a model of competition over time within a system *as linear change bounded probabilistically*.

These bounds do not simply affect the extremes (like balls bouncing off walls), but curve the space as they are approached. This has two consequences: a steady

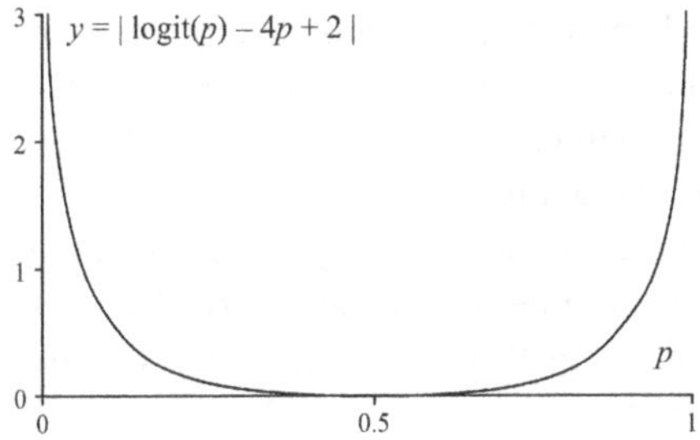

FIGURE 10.4 Absolute logit cross-section folding an infinite plane into a probabilistic trench.†

† The tangent at the intercept $(y, p) = (0, 0.5)$ is $4p$, hence the formula adjusts for time by subtraction. Employing absolute values creates a 'trench'.

change adopts a logistic curve rather than a straight line, and random variation tends towards the centre (0.5), causing intervals and distributions to behave likewise.

10.4 Logistic Regression

By performing the logit transformation (Equation (69)), the logistic curve in $\mathfrak{R} \times \boldsymbol{P}$ ('Real × probability') space becomes a straight line in logit (Cartesian) space. The principal application, for which the model is sound, is where the independent variable Y is Real (e.g., time, $Y = t$) and the dependent variable is an observed Binomial proportion, $p_t = p(x_1 \mid t)$. We want to determine an unknown function to predict the true value, $P(t)$, at time t.

Wilson score intervals for an observed $p \in (0, 1)$ are symmetric in logit space. Variation on either side of p is assumed *equally probable* (equally likely to be above or below) but *differently scaled* (curved by the logit transformation to a probabilistic scale).

The logit function is monotonic and reversible. We can translate a linear function on the logit scale, $y = mt + c$, to the probability scale with Equation (68):

$$P(t) = \text{logistic}(t, m, c) = 1 / (1 + e^{-(mt + c)}), \tag{68'}$$

where m is the gradient of the line in logit space and c a fitting constant (the 'y intercept'). An alternative formulation, which identifies the point in time where $P = 0.5$ (the crossover point in probability space, or the t intercept in logit space), is given by the following:

$$P(t) = \text{logistic}(t, m, k) = 1 / (1 + e^{-m(t - k)}). \tag{68''}$$

Whichever formula is preferred, it is possible to conceive of m as equivalent to an *effect size* measure (see Chapter 13): the steeper the gradient, the more dramatic the effect. The coefficient of fit, r^2, is a kind of *confidence level* for the fit, where $r^2 \approx 1$ means a close fit.

This is the rationale for 'logistic regression', or more accurately, 'logistic linear regression for multiple independent variables'. This is the conventional 'black box' approach to logistic regression. It relies on a number of mathematical assumptions, including:

- **independent variables are Real or Interval**, like time, or can be meaningfully approximated by an Integer, such as 'word length' or 'complexity'; and
- **logit relationships are linear**, that is, the dependent variable can be fit to a model or function, consisting of a series of weighted factors of a subset of supplied independent variables, t, u, v, and so on, thus $y = m_1 t + m_2 u + \ldots c$ (a straight line in n-dimensional logit space).

It is not uncommon to see multiple logistic regression with Binomial independent variables (see, e.g., Sheskin, 2011, p. 1596), but this only makes sense in combination with at least one Real or Interval IV.

However, logistic regression can do more than this. As we shall see, there are good reasons for believing that relationships may frequently *not* be linear on a logit scale. Unbounded motion, like Newton's First Law, is rarely observed in nature.

10.4.1 From Linear to Logistic Regression

Logistic regression attempts to fit data in the $\mathfrak{R} \times \boldsymbol{P}$ space to the logistic curve. There are a number of methods in the literature, many of which employ maximum likelihood estimation (see Hilbe, 2009; Sheskin, 2011, p. 1600). In this chapter, we discuss a simple approach that performs conventional regression in logit Cartesian space ($\mathfrak{R} \times \mathfrak{R}$), minimising least square errors over variance, where 'variance' is approximated by the square of the (suitably transformed) Wilson interval width. The fitting algorithm is thus performed in logit space, and results are transformed to probability space with the monotonic logistic function. An algorithm is given in Appendix B.1.

The simplest function of a relationship between two Real variables is a straight line, which, as we have already seen, maps to a conventional logistic curve. Logistic regression may therefore be implemented as a logistic transform of *linear regression*.

Simple linear regression finds the best straight line, $y = mx + c$ or $y = m(x - k)$, through a series of data points by minimising an error ε, calculated from each point to the line. (Multiple linear regression does the same thing in more dimensions.) The regression score, r^2, estimates the degree to which points deviate from the line: 1 is a perfect fit, 0 a cloud.

We can fit to a logistic function like $P(t)$ (Equation (68)). The computer tries different values for m and c and finds the 'best fit'. Gauss's *method of least squares* is sometimes called 'ordinary least squares' or 'OLS'. We minimise ε where

$$\textit{error}\ \varepsilon = \sum(P(t) - p_t)^2. \quad (71)$$

However, different data points have greater certainty than others (the data are 'heteroscedastic'). A conventional approach is to scale each squared error term by the Gaussian *variance* for the point before summing the results:

$$\textit{variance}\ S(t)^2 = P(t)(1 - P(t)) / n_t,$$
$$\textit{error}\ \varepsilon = \sum(P(t) - p_t)^2 / S(t)^2. \quad (72)$$

This method assumes a Normal distribution about $P(t)$ on the probability scale. This method works after a fashion. All else being equal, this method will prioritise

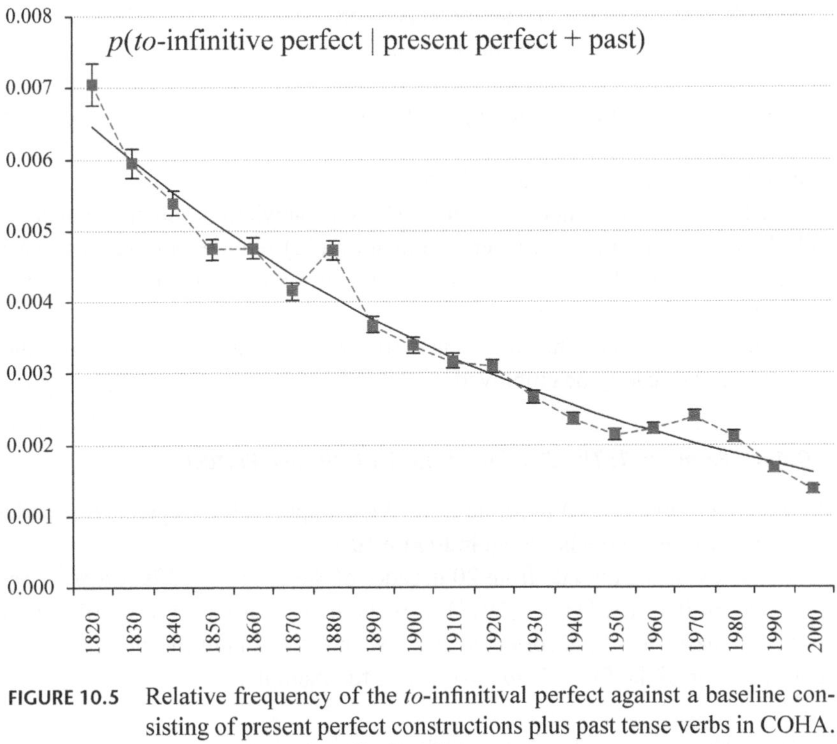

FIGURE 10.5 Relative frequency of the *to*-infinitival perfect against a baseline consisting of present perfect constructions plus past tense verbs in COHA. After Bowie and Wallis (2016).

fitting at extremes, as $P(t)$ tends to 0 and 1. However, we want a fit to be more sensitive to the *crossover point* (where $P(t) = 0.5$) and *gradient*.

10.4.2 Logit-Wilson Regression

The Wilson interval in logit space is symmetric. Can we use it to estimate variance? Bowie and Wallis (2016) used a method that minimised the following error sum:

$$error\ \varepsilon = \sum(\text{logit}(P(t)) - \text{logit}(p_t))^2 / (\text{logit}(p_t) - \text{logit}(w_t^-))^2. \qquad (73)$$

The Wilson interval width can be thought of as an adjusted error for sample probability values. It contains an additional constant, $z_{\alpha/2}$, but this cancels out.[4] Datapoints where $p_t = 0$ or 1 must be removed.[5] To weigh up different evaluations, Pearson's *coefficient of determination* r^2 compares the extent to which different curves 'fit' data:

$$Pearson\text{'s } r^2 = 1 - SS_{\text{err}} / SS_{\text{tot}}, \qquad (74)$$

where $SS_{\text{err}} = \varepsilon$, and the total sum of squares SS_{tot} is obtained with the same variance estimate. For our method the appropriate formula would be

$$SS_{\text{tot}} = \sum(\lambda - \text{logit}(p_t))^2 / (\text{logit}(p_t) - \text{logit}(w_t^-))^2, \qquad (75)$$

where λ is the arithmetic mean of $\text{logit}(p_t)$.

The logit-Wilson method is efficient. The Wilson width is calculated once for all observed proportions p_t, whereas Equation (72) requires all Gaussian variances to be recalculated each iteration. Without a moving target, regression is guaranteed to converge to a single minimum error.

Here we fit to a straight line, $\text{logit}(P(t)) = mt + c$, but a polynomial or other function could readily be employed.

10.4.3 Example 1: The Decline of the To-Infinitive Perfect

Bowie and Wallis (2016) used the logit-Wilson approach to regress time series data. A simple example is shown in Figure 10.5.

The study draws on data from 20 decades of the *Corpus of Historical American English* (COHA, Davies, 2012). It plots the proportion of cases of present perfect or past verbs ('past oriented verbs') using the *to*-infinitive perfect, that is, constructions of the form 'V *to have* V-ed', for example,

(39) He *seems <u>to have known</u>* about it.

TABLE 10.1 Raw data for *to*-infinitival perfect against a baseline of past-oriented verb phrases in COHA (1810–2000).

year	*f*	*n*	*p*	w^-	w^+
1810	300	28,750	0.0104	0.0093	0.0117
1820	2,215	314,471	0.0070	0.0068	0.0073
1830	3,512	590,832	0.0059	0.0058	0.0061
1840	3,790	703,768	0.0054	0.0052	0.0056
1850	3,765	794,709	0.0047	0.0046	0.0049
1860	4,008	842,690	0.0048	0.0046	0.0049
1870	4,061	979,250	0.0041	0.0040	0.0043
1880	4,851	1,026,312	0.0047	0.0046	0.0049
1890	4,050	1,103,191	0.0037	0.0036	0.0038
1900	4,094	1,207,914	0.0034	0.0033	0.0035
1910	3,911	1,232,516	0.0032	0.0031	0.0033
1920	4,229	1,366,965	0.0031	0.0030	0.0032
1930	3,704	1,392,658	0.0027	0.0026	0.0027
1940	3,371	1,432,544	0.0024	0.0023	0.0024
1950	3,007	1,403,559	0.0021	0.0021	0.0022
1960	2,902	1,303,701	0.0022	0.0021	0.0023
1970	3,091	1,286,669	0.0024	0.0023	0.0025
1980	2,987	1,414,049	0.0021	0.0020	0.0022
1990	2,459	1,479,291	0.0017	0.0016	0.0017
2000	2,212	1,610,303	0.0014	0.0013	0.0014

Bowie's data show that these constructions have declined as a proportion of past-oriented verb phrases in comparable US English over two centuries. The argument for this baseline is that the construction, which involves introducing a catenative verb such as SEEM, is an option that arises in the context of a past-oriented verb phrase, like the option to make a verb phrase progressive. This alternation is therefore one where meaning is undergoing change. The particular catenative verb (e.g., SEEM and OUGHT) adds a *particular* 'stance meaning'.

It turns out that 95% of catenative verbs (tokens) are constituted by some 30 lemmas (types), which may be grouped into some five 'meaning classes'. These classes are not meaning-preserving alternates, but specify different stances or aspects:

(39)	He *seems to have known* about it.	(V-catenative V-*to*-infinitive perfect)
	~ He *knew* about it.	(V-past)
	~ He *has known* about it.	(V-present perfect)

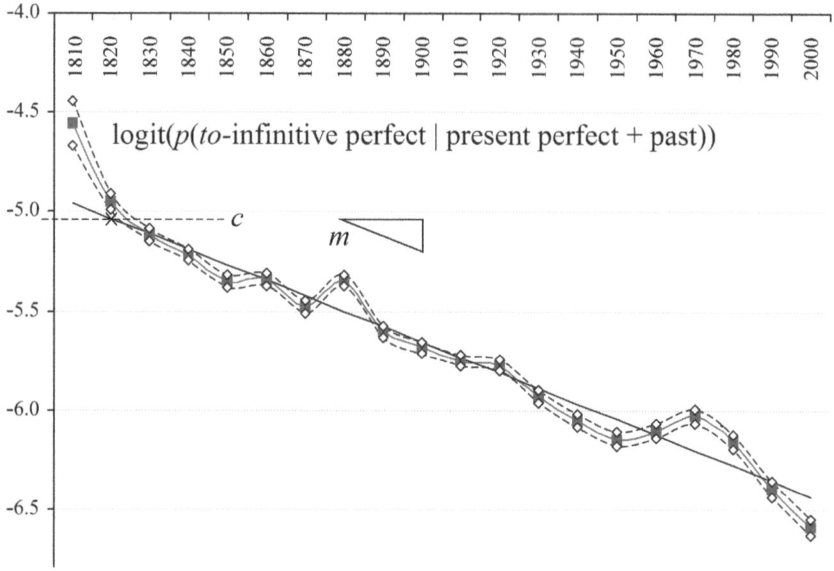

FIGURE 10.6 Figure 10.5 transformed to the logit scale. The dashed lines express the range of the Wilson confidence intervals on this scale. We fit the linear function $y = mt + c$ to this transformed data (excluding 1810 because this data was inconsistently sampled) to obtain values for m and c for the straight line indicated.

This pooled set of meanings implies a possible risk to Lavandera's 'dangerous hypothesis' (Chapter 3). Nonetheless, Bowie's aim was not to obtain a definitive result but to estimate the average rate of decline of the phenomenon itself, that is, the *gradient*.

The logit-Wilson method (Equation (73)) obtains the weighted regression line in Figure 10.6. It has a small negative gradient $m = -0.0778$, and intercept $c = -5.0353$ (1820) with an error $r^2 = 0.9603$.

In this case, intervals on a logit scale are approximately equal in width. Applying an unweighted OLS method to the logit scale, taking no account of the variable uncertainty of observations, obtains a similar result.[6]

The resulting line is transformed back to the probability scale as the logistic curve in Figure 10.5.

10.4.4 Example 2: Catenative Verbs in Competition

A second example is more challenging. Consider the chance of selecting the catenative verb OUGHT out of the top 3 'modality' catenative verbs OUGHT, HAVE and

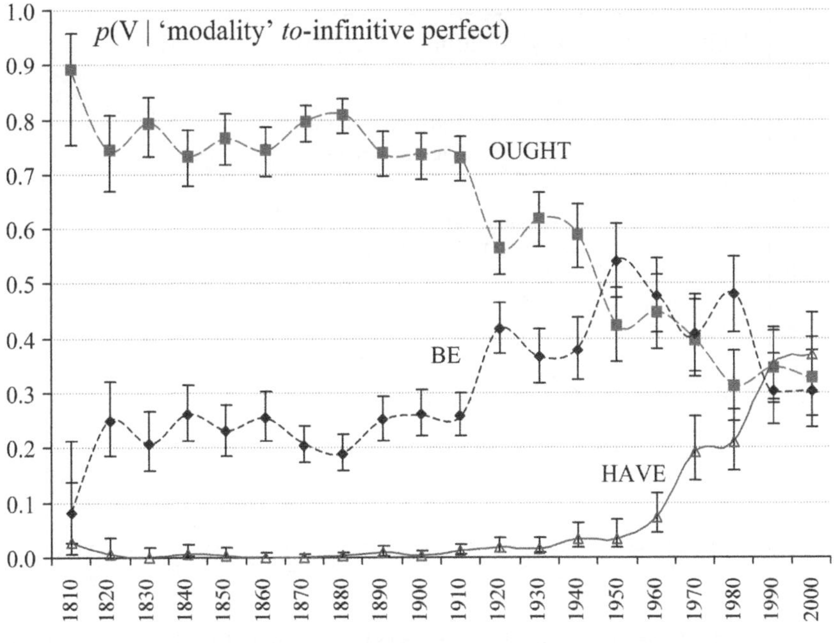

FIGURE 10.7 Changing shares within the top 3 'modality' set of *to*-infinitive perfect constructions, {OUGHT, HAVE, BE}, COHA (1810–2000).

BE. This three-way split is also not an alternation pattern, as they cover distinct meanings:

(40) They <u>ought</u> *to have known* about it.
~? They <u>have</u> *to have known* about it.
~? They <u>are</u> *to have known* about it.

Nonetheless, within this data, we can see a transition that could fit a logistic curve. Confidence intervals are wider and more varied, so it should present a greater challenge to a fitting algorithm. It also includes cases where $p = 0$. See Figure 10.7.

The result is a poorer fit. The logit-Wilson method obtains regression lines for OUGHT and BE similar to OLS regression (for r^2 scores, see Table 10.2).

However, the logit-Wilson method generates a closer fit than OLS for HAVE, thanks to its prioritisation of data with smaller Wilson intervals on the logit scale. See upper right of Figure 10.9.

We are now in a position to present all three regression curves. Figure 10.10 plots the same data with regression lines and Wilson score intervals on a probability scale.

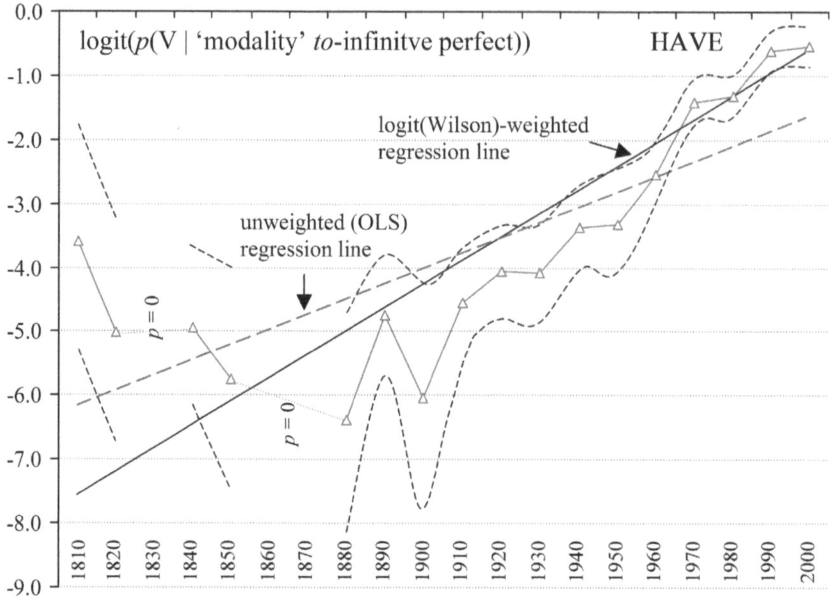

FIGURE 10.8 Linear regression in logit space for HAVE out of {OUGHT, HAVE, BE}, *to*-infinitive perfect, COHA (1810–2000). The fitting algorithm ignores points where $p = 0$ or 1. The unweighted 'OLS' regression line, by failing to account for differing variance, diverges substantially from the weighted line.

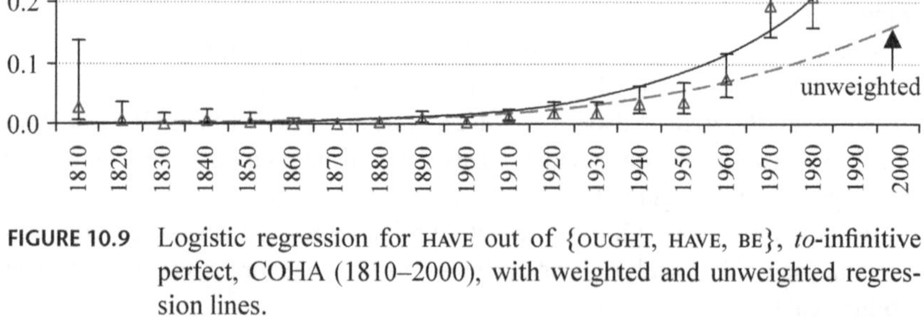

FIGURE 10.9 Logistic regression for HAVE out of {OUGHT, HAVE, BE}, *to*-infinitive perfect, COHA (1810–2000), with weighted and unweighted regression lines.

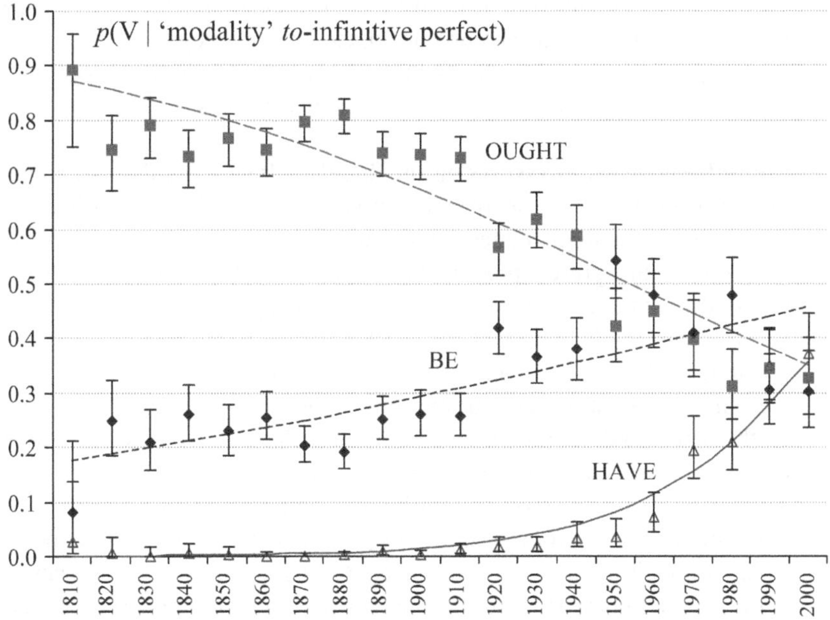

FIGURE 10.10 Logistic regression of Example 2. See also Figure 10.7.

10.4.5 Review

In Example 1, we demonstrated that time series data may follow a simple logistic regression line. Intervals were small, the data followed the curve closely and we computed a close fit. Almost identical performance was obtained for a Gaussian 'OLS' method that took no account of the certainty of observations. In the second example, we had three competing forms, less data and patterns of variation that did not appear logistic. This was more challenging for fitting algorithms, and one dataset, the data for HAVE, performed better using the logit-Wilson method than the unweighted method. See Figures 10.8 and 10.9.

However, this second example bears out our earlier observation that we could conceivably apply functions other than straight lines to these data. The lines for OUGHT and BE may approximate better to a non-linear function. These data are not from an alternation study, and there may be additional random variation in our data because texts collected in different periods are not obtained in a controlled way.

We would advise against overfitting data to regression lines. As a rule, *it is better for researchers to visualise their data first, and treat logistic regression as indicative or exploratory*. Like all correlations, results from regression do not tell us whether there is a causal relationship between variables. It also does not tell us that the correct function (linear, polynomial, etc.) was employed.

Data may converge to a non-linear function on a logit scale (i.e., other than a logistic curve on a probability scale) for at least two reasons:

- **Multiple ecological pressures on the linguistic item** – in this case, proportions of lemmas out of a set of *to*-infinitive perfects in COHA. In Chapter 3, we argued that a single dimension of meaning change (e.g., turning a simple present into a present progressive) *could* be considered a type of alternation study, but the combination of multiple meaning changes means that data becomes vulnerable to context and speaker variation. The relative success of Example 1, despite it pooling catenative verbs, can be considered a single meaning change at a more abstract level. The three-way 'modality' verbs, on the other hand, represent the sum of three distinct opportunities, almost certainly influenced by context and writer intent.
- **The forms may be subject to Multinomial competition**. In Example 2, we have three competing forms, a three-body situation that would not be expected to obtain a logit-linear ('logistic') outcome. For simplicity, we plotted curves, but it is wise to bear in mind that the logistic function implies a model of a simple change along a single degree of freedom, whereas a three-way variable has two degrees of freedom. We discuss this issue in the next section.

For exploratory purposes, we might compare regression scores numerically (all fitting algorithms try to maximise r^2). If we simply wish to establish a direction of change, the threshold for a fit can be low, with scores above 0.75 being citeable. On the other hand, if we have an r^2 of 0.9 or higher we may meaningfully cite the gradient m and crossover point $k = -c / m$ (translated into years).

Generally, however, conventional thresholds for fitting tend to be more relaxed than those applied to confidence intervals and significance tests because the underlying logic of the task is distinct. Several functions may have a close fit to given data. We should not select between them by comparing regression scores, even if we deployed confidence intervals. Consequently, we should cite gradients with caution and treat them as indicative.

Considered as a method for identifying a general correlation with time, logistic regression is an improvement over 'joining the dots'. Compare Figures 10.7 and 10.10. But this does not mean that a particular logistic model or curve is correct.

10.5 Impossible Logistic Multinomials

A number of linguists have questioned the assumption that linguistic change is necessarily logistic. Nevalainen (2015) offers empirical observations that show that whereas data sometimes follow such a curve, this does not always happen. Some data may not represent a freely varying alternation. In this section we note two mathematical reasons why simple logistic regression may not be observed.

The fundamental assumption of logistic regression is that a Binomial proportion representing a true fraction of a quantity undergoes a continuous process of change, which *by default* follows a logistic pattern. This is reasonable in limited circumstances.

Regression methods find the closest match between an observed set of data and a function, such as a straight line, a polynomial, a power curve or, in this case, an S-curve. For *logistic* regression, we say that the logistic curve is the underlying model we expect data to be matched against ('regressed to'). But what are the 'limited circumstances' in which this model is plausible?

- *Change is assumed to be continuous*: the input independent variable is Real and linear, such as time t (and not, e.g., probabilistic).
- Proportions must be *free to vary* from 0 to 1, so the trend can reach a limit of 1.
- The *envelope of variation* must be constant, that is, it must be always possible for an observed proportion to reach the same maximum (1). (See also Chapter 3.)

These conditions together mean that proportions must be Binomial, not Multinomial.

10.5.1 Binomials

As we saw, the logistic curve can be expressed as the function

$$P(t) = \text{logistic}(t, m, k) \equiv 1 / (1 + e^{m(t-k)}), \qquad (68'')$$

where k is the crossover constant (where $P = 0.5$) and m the gradient. In a simple Binomial alternation, we have two probabilities, P and Q, where $Q = 1 - P$. We can write this as

$$P(t) + Q(t) = \text{logistic}(t, m, k) + \text{logistic}(t, -m, k) \equiv 1.$$

One curve goes up, the other goes down, with the same gradient but opposite sign. The logistic model relies on there being a single degree of freedom.

10.5.2 Impossible Multinomials

However, if there are more than two alternating types, *not all forms can follow the logistic curve against the same baseline*. It is mathematically impossible.

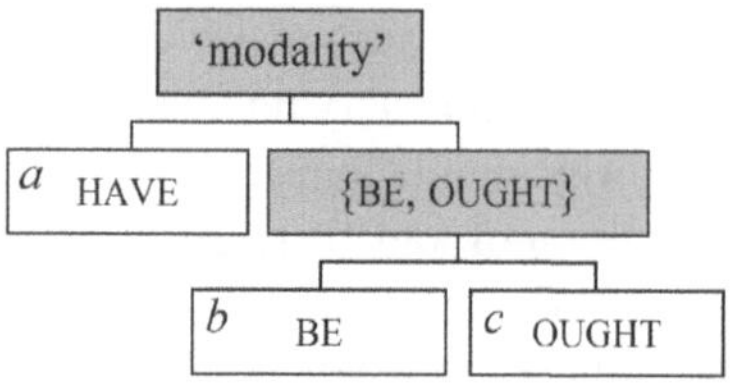

FIGURE 10.11 Potential decision tree representing a hierarchical three-way alternation for {BE, HAVE, OUGHT}.

Take another look at Figure 10.10. We might argue, for example, that HAVE approximates to a logistic curve, but what can we say about BE, which rises to the 1950s (the point at which HAVE takes off) and then falls? (This rise and fall is statistically significant, as the confidence intervals indicate.)

As Nevalainen points out, results like this should not be surprising, and we should not feel obliged to 'explain' them as if they were a defect in the data. The defect is in the model.

10.5.3 Possible Hierarchical Multinomials

Given that Multinomial proportions cannot all follow a logistic curve, this begs a question. What patterns might we expect?

One possibility is *hierarchical alternation*. Consider the decision tree $\{a, \{b, c\}\}$, where a alternates with the set $\{b, c\}$, and b independently alternates with c. Outcome a could be the lemma HAVE, whereas b and c might correspond to BE and OUGHT, respectively. See Figure 10.11.

In this tree, a alternates with $\{b, c\}$ at the top. We can plot $p(a \mid \{a, b, c\})$, and it could follow a logistic curve over, say, time. Second, since b alternates with c at the second level, $p(b \mid \{b, c\})$ is also free to adopt a logistic curve over time.

But what would the change of b look like within our global baseline $\{a, b, c\}$? It is alternating within $\{b, c\}$, *the envelope of variation defined by the remainder after subtraction of a* (i.e., $1 - p(a \mid \{a, b, c\})$). From the perspective of our original data, b does not appear to be undergoing logistic change. The curve is hill-shaped, indicated by $p(b \mid \{a, b, c\})$ in Figure 10.12.

The take home point is this: we might have a genuine logistic alternation taking place in our data, but only by finding the correct hierarchical decomposition of alternates can we reveal it.

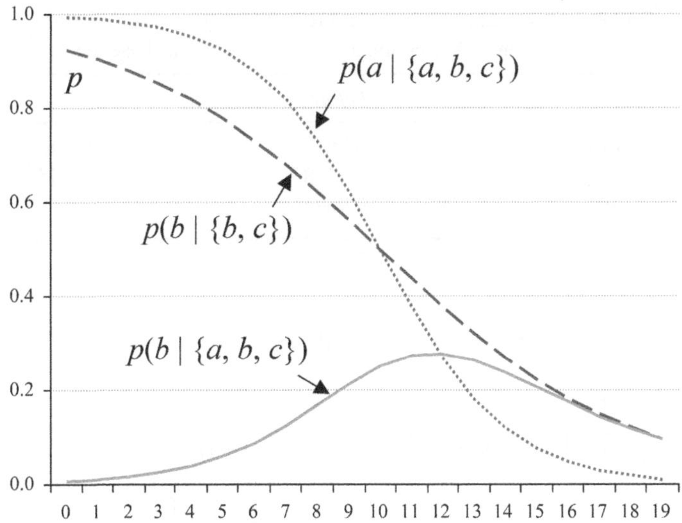

FIGURE 10.12 Strict hierarchical alternation, synchronised turning constant ($k = 10$), $m_a = -0.5$ and $m_b = -0.25$, probability scale.

10.5.4 A Hierarchical Reanalysis of Example 2

Suppose for the purposes of argument, we accept that HAVE maps to a logistic curve against the three-way baseline. It has the highest r^2 fit score of all three (Table 10.2). A stepwise hierarchical approach would remove it from the data, focus on BE versus OUGHT, and perform logistic regression against the resulting baseline.

This recalculation produces the graph in Figure 10.13. Table 10.2 shows that the fit for BE improves, but the fit for OUGHT declines to the same value (the curves mirror each other). However, *the total fit* for the pair increases.

10.5.5 The Three-Body Problem

It is not mathematically possible for three or more types to simultaneously adopt a logistic curve against the same baseline. At least one of the trends will appear non-logistic. If types alternate hierarchically and independently at two or more levels or scales, we *might* see independent alternation patterns. However, with more than two types in competition, there is no reason why *any* particular type will follow a logistic curve.

TABLE 10.2 Pearson's r^2 (measured on the logit scale), before and after elimination of HAVE from the baseline.

r^2	*before*	*after*
OUGHT	0.8077	0.7315
BE	0.5228	0.7315
HAVE	0.9622	

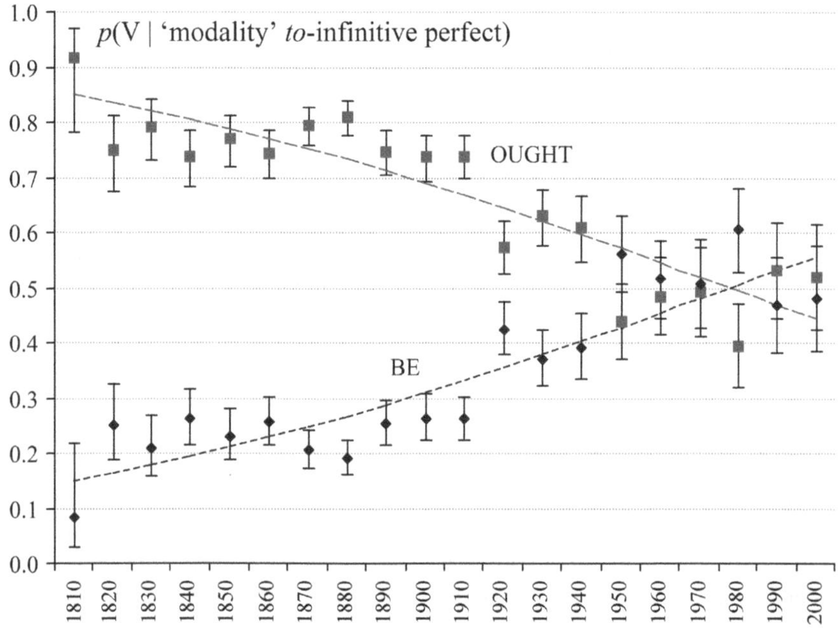

FIGURE 10.13 Reanalysis of Experiment 2 data, OUGHT versus BE *to*-infinitive perfect forms over time, for COHA (1810–2000). Logistic curves are independently estimated.

We inserted the word 'independent' earlier – we assumed that the transition in preferred use from *b* to *c* (e.g., OUGHT and BE) *would occur in isolation from the other substitution* (for *a*, e.g., HAVE).

In practice, however, even this pattern of neat independent alternation is unlikely. Just as a close up of part of a curve might appear a straight line, the fact that a function matches a logistic curve for a brief period does not mean that the *overall* pattern of change is logistic.

The so-called 'three-body problem' is a well-known fundamental problem in studying physical dynamic systems, causing them to generate bounded chaotic

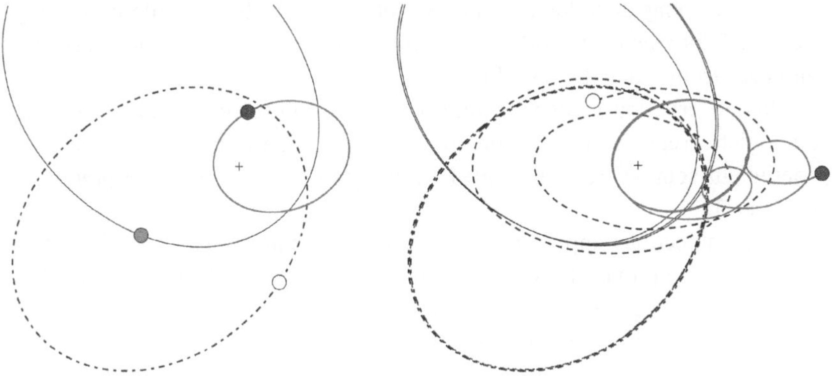

FIGURE 10.14 A sketch of the three-body problem generating unpredictable non-linear behaviour ('chaos') from a computer simulation.[†] The left-hand figure plots initial, apparently stable, orbits of three bodies around a common centre of gravity. Over time, the orbits break down, and this stable state collapses (right). Chaotic systems have the property that infinitesimal differences in initial conditions can lead to different outcomes, rendering medium term prediction impossible.

[†] A number of computer simulators demonstrating the three-body problem are available on the internet. Thanks are due to Evgenii Neumerzhitckii for his simulator and this figure, see https://evgenii.com/blog/three-body-problem-simulator.

outcomes (Gleick, 1977). This book is not the place to discuss chaos theory, except to note that non-linear behaviour ('chaos') arises *when three bodies are continuously influencing each other*, such as two moons orbiting a planet, or a planet orbiting two stars (Figure 10.14).[7] The analogous situation is where three or more alternating types exist.

We should not therefore be surprised if three-way competition does not converge to a neat logistic curve but some other pattern. More worrying, this may even occur in a study that only examines the alternation of two simple types, *if there are other types in the same field of competition*. Independent hierarchical alternation is theoretically possible, but it is not the only plausible pattern of alternation.

Note this is a matter of degree. A third type may have so minor an influence as to make little measurable difference to the alternation of two principal types. Binary stars orbit a common centre of gravity, but their masses are so great as to be relatively unaffected by much smaller and more distant planetary masses.

Our reasoning about logistic curves should be considered similarly. The logistic model, like the Kepler orbit, represents an important default model, such that variation from it may be revealing.

This observation is also a sound 'ecological' objection to an over-reliance on logistic regression. We should not select a baseline on the basis of r^2 coefficient scores! Baselines must be selected by a *linguistic argument*. See Chapter 3.

These objections apply only to the task of fitting to a curve. They do not undermine the proper use of confidence intervals, or the testing for significant differences between observations. We might therefore extend the 'limited circumstances' identified previously:

- *Change is assumed to be continuous and Cartesian*, that is, that the input independent variable (x) is Real and linear, such as time (and not, e.g., probabilistic).
- We assume proportions are *free to vary* from 0 to 1.
- The *envelope of variation* must be constant, that is, it must always be possible for an observed probability to reach the maximum.
- *The alternation is not influenced by other alternating forms*, nor otherwise subject to systematic ecological pressures.

10.6 Conclusions

Whenever we examine variation between groups of speakers, modes of communication, genres of writing, and so on, we examine *differences* between discrete categories. But when we examine change over time, we consider *continuous* change over a Real variable. This allows us to estimate a trajectory of change with the logistic function.

The logistic curve is equivalent to a straight line in Cartesian space where one of the dimensions is 'transformed' (bent, if you will) into the bounded range of probability $\boldsymbol{P} = [0, 1]$. Tellingly, if we unfold this space using the inverse logistic 'logit' function, the logistic curve becomes a straight line, and previously skewed Wilson score intervals become symmetric.

This unfolding, termed the 'logit transform', demonstrates the relationship between the logistic curve and the Wilson interval. Whereas Wilson score intervals estimate uncertainty about an observation, the logistic function can predict continuous motion with time.

This does not mean that the logistic curve should be viewed as a kind of iron law that probabilistic changes are bound to obey. Rather, it is more like a version of Newton's First Law. Newton's law is rarely observed in nature on Earth, simply because there are usually external forces operating on an object as it moves, including gravity.

We also showed that where more than two forms were in competition, it was impossible for all of them to follow a logistic curve against the *same* baseline. This could imply a hierarchical subdivision of forms, pairing off categories and producing neat logistic curves. But it could also plausibly exhibit behaviour that does not fit a logistic curve.

Consequently, we should not try to *overfit* data to a logistic curve. *Do not assume the data fit the model, and that if they fit poorly, the fault lies in the data, rather than the model.*

We would not require that a falling body be obliged to follow Newton's First Law, and 'refuse to recognise' gravity or air resistance! Rather, when we observe that a competing form does not closely follow a logistic trajectory, this observation is probably worthy of further investigation.

Logistic regression on time series is best considered as a kind of exploratory analysis tool, helping researchers *identify correlations*, such as whether there is evidence that two forms in competition are subject to external pressure, as well as *obtaining estimates of rates of change* at different times. Logistic regression may facilitate exploration by applying hierarchical decomposition and changing baselines, or by employing non-linear functions, such as polynomial functions, in logit space.

Our concern in this chapter has not been to explore competing algorithms, or the different ways in which logistic regression has been developed. Rather it was to explain how the mathematical model can explain change over time, how it may be justified in certain circumstances, and the limits of this type of explanation.

Notes

1 See (Wallis, 2020d) for an example from evolutionary theory (Gould, 1996b).
2 As a general rule, if you see a graph plot where an observed interval shrinks to zero at the extremes, the interval formula being used is wrong, even if it exhibits no overshoot.
3 A simple exercise to demystify the logistic curve is as follows. First, draw a straight line diagonally on a sheet of paper (our Cartesian space). Then gently bend the paper along the length of the sheet, cupping it in your hand. Try to emulate the cross-section in Figure 10.4. Finally, look down the 'trench' from above. You should see the classic stretched 'S' of the logistic curve.
4 The Wilson interval also includes $z_{\alpha/2}$. It appears by experimentation that $\alpha \approx 0.5$ is optimum for this purpose. See Chapter 17.
5 In these cases, logit(p_t) and the interval width will both be infinite. Dividing by the square of infinity obtains zero, so we can remove the data point from the fitting algorithm.
6 The COHA data has some defects – the 1810 data in particular is sparse and weighted by genre, and is removed prior to fitting.
7 In pool or snooker breaks, three or more balls are in contact at the point of initial impact. They are, for a moment, caught in a multiway continuous interaction.

11

THE REPLICATION CRISIS AND THE NEW STATISTICS

11.1 Introduction

Over the course of 2016, the field of psychology was rocked by a major public dispute about statistics. This concerned the failure of claims in research papers in prestigious psychological journals to replicate (Gelman, 2016).

Replication is extraordinarily important. If you claim your results are statistically significant, you are stating that another researcher performing the same experiment, or drawing data from a comparable corpus, would obtain findings consistent with yours, at your experimental error rate. Confidence intervals and significance tests depend on this model.

If you employ an error rate of 1 in 20 (0.05), you expect a second researcher to find the same results as you, 19 times in 20. Unfortunately, in a number of papers, 'significant' results failed to replicate on the first attempt!

In this chapter, we explore this 'replication crisis' and what solutions might be available. We also consider the implications for corpus linguistics.

11.2 A Corpus Linguistics Debate

Consider the following controversy. Neil Millar (2009), citing data from the US *TIME Magazine Corpus* (Davies, 2007), reported that modal auxiliary verbs were increasing over time. Geoff Leech (2011), using the *Brown series* of US written English corpora,[1] made the opposite claim. Who is right?

DOI: 10.4324/9781003622697-14

In this book, we have learned that stating that something 'significantly increases over time' can be reformulated as follows:

1. Subject to the caveats of
   - *random sampling* (the sample is, or approximates to, a random sample of utterances drawn from the same population); and
   - *freedom to vary* (proportions are genuinely free to vary from 0 to 1), selecting an error rate (say, 1 in 20), we can calculate a confidence interval on the difference in two observations taken at two time points 1 and 2, $d = p_2 - p_1 \in (d^-, d^+)$.
2. If this difference interval excludes zero, we can say 'd is significantly different from zero'. It also means that
   - on multiple repeated runs of the same experiment we can expect to see observed differences d' fail a gradient replication test (see Chapter 14, Section 14.4) – that is, $d' - d$ will fall outside a difference-of-differences interval – *no more often than the predicted error rate* (here, 1 in 20).

When we say that something 'fails to replicate', we mean that on repetition, results are significantly different from the reported outcome more often than the model predicts.[2] In the cases remarked on in the literature a different result is found *on the very next occasion*!

We also need to attribute variation to *time*. This introduces a further caveat. Can we be sure that data from different periods are not sampled such that some confounding variable Z – age of participants, say – also differs with time, and it is *that* variable, rather than time itself, that correlates?

Cumming (2014) makes an important distinction between exploratory research and 'prespecified' research, where researchers control for confounding variables in selecting participants and controlling responses. See Chapter 2. Corpus linguistics is almost inevitably exploratory, and we must frame our conclusions accordingly.

In the Millar versus Leech debate, Geoff Leech obtained a different result on the first attempted repetition of this experiment. This could be an accident, but it appears to be a failure to replicate. There should only be a 1 in 20 chance of this happening. Observing such a replication failure should cause us to question these studies.

The controversy can be summed up by the bottom 'Total' row in Table 11.1. This appears to show a 23% increase in modal use per million words between the 1920s and 2000s. With a lot of data and a sizeable effect, this increase seems bound to be significant.

TABLE 11.1 Changing modal verb exposure rates in the TIME corpus, expressed as per million word frequencies for each decade (after Millar, 2009).

	1920s	*1930s*	*1940s*	*1950s*	*1960s*	*1970s*	*1980s*	*1990s*	*2000s*	*% diff*
will	2,194.63	1,681.76	1,856.40	1,988.37	1,965.76	2,135.73	2,057.43	2,273.23	2,362.52	+7.7%
would	1,690.70	1,665.01	2,095.76	1,669.18	1,513.30	1,828.92	1,758.44	1,797.03	1,693.19	+0.1%
can	832.91	742.30	955.73	1,093.39	1,233.13	1,305.82	1,231.99	1,475.95	1,777.07	+113.4%
could	661.33	822.72	1,188.24	998.83	950.73	1,106.25	1,156.61	1,378.39	1,342.56	+103.0%
may	583.59	515.12	496.93	502.74	628.13	743.66	775.92	937.08	931.91	+59.7%
should	577.46	450.07	454.87	495.26	441.96	475.50	453.33	521.46	593.27	+2.7%
must	485.31	418.03	456.57	417.62	401.36	390.47	347.02	306.69	250.59	−48.4%
might	374.52	375.40	500.33	408.90	399.80	458.99	416.81	474.23	433.34	+15.7%
shall	212.19	120.79	96.42	70.52	50.48	35.65	25.93	16.09	9.26	−95.6%
ought	50.22	37.94	39.31	40.34	36.91	34.29	28.27	34.90	27.65	−44.9%
Total	7,662.86	6,829.14	8,140.56	7,685.15	7,621.56	8,515.28	8,251.75	9,215.05	9,421.36	+22.9%

Why do Leech and Millar obtain different results? Here are six alternative hypotheses:

AH1. **Population differences explain the results.** Are there characteristics of the TIME data that make the dataset distinct from the more general written data of the Brown corpora? For example, does TIME have a 'house style' enforced by editors, which affects the frequency of modals? Has TIME tended to curate more articles with more modal hedges than one might find in other comparable texts? More generally, are modals sensitive to written 'genre'? Bowie et al. (2014) reported that 'genre' subdivisions in the spoken DCPSE corpus exposed different modal trends (see Chapter 5).[3]

AH2. **The result is an artifact of pooling meaning classes.** Grammatically, modals are a well-defined category of verb: a closed category, especially if one excludes the semi-modals. 'Modal use' is a syntactically legitimate variable, but as we know, selecting a *particular* modal verb changes the referential meaning (from *must* to *ought*, say). In Chapter 3, we argued that where any member of a Multinomial type is employed, it should be replaceable by all other members of the set (Types B_1, B_2, B_3, etc.) without changing the intended meaning. If a writer meant to express a different thought, the context in which each utterance was made will probably be different. But neither Millar nor Leech took this into account directly. Instead, they cited individual modals per million words, as in Table 11.1. Both Millar and Leech note that the largest increases in the TIME corpus are for the possibility modals *can*, *could* and *may*. Millar suggests that this may be evidence of an increased degree of speculation in reporting in the TIME magazine. (Possibility adverbs are also on the increase in his data.) But if this is true, then bundling modals of possibility and necessity together is likely misleading. At best, we can say that the distribution of pooled modals over time is the result of at least two independent trends: variation in the tendency to express necessity (e.g., obligation), and variation in the tendency to express possibility.

AH3. **Selective representation of Millar's trend(s) by comparing start and end points.** On close examination, his data do not support a *consistent* observation of increased modal use over time. Bowie observes that Millar's aggregate data fluctuate over the time period (Table 11.1, bottom row), and some changes in sub-periods appear to be consistent with the trend reported by Leech in an earlier study in 2003. Simply expressing the trend as 'an increase in modal verb use' is misleading.

AH4. **Employing a per million word measure is intrinsically unreliable.** Neither Millar nor Leech considers changing the baseline to, for example, modal use per tensed verb phrase (or tensed main verb). They do not measure when writers *choose* to use modal verbs, but the rate at which the reader is *exposed* to them. If VP density changes over time in either corpus, results may differ.

As we discussed in Chapter 3, conflating opportunity and choice undermines the Binomial model of variation, and increases the risk that results will not replicate. The solution is to focus on identifying each 'choice point' as far as possible.

AH5. **Per million word data do not conform to the Binomial statistical model.** The entire corpus cannot consist of modal verbs. Rates of modal verbs will never be observed to approach 100%. This is true, but it will tend to cause *underreporting* of otherwise significant results. See Wallis (2012c). It cannot be an explanation for obtaining two different 'significant' results in opposite directions!

AH6. **Modal use is affected by speaker and text effects.** Is the tendency to use *might* or *must*, say, affected by local factors (topic, context, speaker preference, etc.)? Samples drawn from the corpus contain numerous instances from the same text, and so estimates of variation that assume every instance of a modal is independent from the next are too generous. The solution is to adjust for 'random-text sampling': see Chapter 16.

Perhaps we should be unsurprised at the fact that Millar's overall finding was not replicated in Leech's data. In fact, many of Millar's *individual* trends are consistent with results found in the Brown corpus. Pooling rates of semantically diverse types per million words seems to be asking for trouble!

As we shall see, the problem of replication is not usually that *all* results in one study are not reproduced in another study, rather it is that some results are not reproduced. But this raises an obvious question: *which results should we cite?* If our most debated finding is not replicated, we have a particular problem.

11.3 Psychology Lessons?

The replication crisis began in the social sciences. In psychology, some published findings have been controversial. Claims that 'Engineers have more sons; nurses have more daughters' (Kanazawa & Vandermassen, 2005) have attracted rapid criticism.

In psychology, it is common to perform studies with small numbers of participants – ten per experimental condition is usually cited as a minimum, so between 20 and 40 participants becomes the norm. Many failures to replicate are due to what statisticians tend to call 'basic errors', such as using an inappropriate statistical test. The alternative hypotheses AH1–6 above illustrate problems we discuss elsewhere in this book.

- A common error is to use a test that relies on assumptions that do not hold in the data. For example, a per million word baseline is employed with a χ^2 test or log-likelihood test, but the upper envelope of variation ranges from 0 to 0.01 or 0.02 (say) instead of, as the Binomial model requires, from 0 to 1. This is patently unsound. No method that makes this assumption will work the way that the Binomial model predicts.

- Corpus linguistics has a particular historical problem due to the ubiquity of studies employing word-based baselines (per million words, per thousand words, etc., denoted as *f*(**words**)). It is not possible to adjust an error level to address this problem because the problem is one of *missing information.* We need additional frequency evidence from the corpus, *f*(**X**), that measures the varying frequency of a meaningful superset **X**, representing the opportunity baseline. See Chapter 3.

In this book we concentrate on these very simple statistical methods and show how they may be built upon. Statistical methods rely on a particular underlying mathematical model (e.g., the Binomial model), which assumes particular characteristics of research data. See Chapters 6 and 12. If those assumptions are not true, results will not replicate as predicted.

Complex methods, such as multivariate analysis, are built on simpler methods, and add assumptions. It follows that before we can move to a more complex method, we must be sure that *our research design is sound*, that is, that the model underpinning the statistical method is compatible with the structure of the data we wish to analyse. Otherwise, we risk 'overfitting' the data and over-claiming from results.

However, the replication problem does not disappear entirely once we have dealt with these so-called 'basic errors'.

11.4 The Road Not Travelled

Andrew Gelman and Eric Loken (2013) raise a more fundamental problem. This concerns a question that goes to the heart of the post hoc analysis of data, the philosophy of statistical claims and the scientific method. Essentially their argument goes like this:

1. **All data contain random noise**. Every dataset (including those extracted from a corpus) will contain random noise. Researchers tend to assume that by employing a significance test we 'control' for this noise. But this is not correct. Faced with a dataset consisting of pure noise, we would mistakenly detect a 'significant' result 1 in 20 times at a 0.05 threshold. Another way of thinking about this is that *statistical methods will occasionally detect correlations even when there are none to be found.*
2. **Many potential analyses could be performed on the data**. Datasets may contain multiple variables and there are numerous potential definitions of these variables. In exploring research questions and working with a corpus, we may modify definitions of variables, perform new queries, change baselines, and so on, to perform new analyses. It follows that there are many

potential hypotheses we could test against the data. As a result, we increase the chance that we will stumble on a 'noise' result.

This is not an argument against exploring the hypothesis space to choose a better baseline on *theoretical* grounds, but it is an argument against sifting through data and *selectively* reporting significant results!

This part of the argument is not very controversial. However, Gelman and Loken's more provocative claim is as follows:

1. Few researchers would admit to running very many tests against data and only reporting 'significant' results. Gelman calls this practice '*p*-hacking'. Some algorithms do this, but most research is not like this.
2. However, Gelman and Loken argue that unless we are very careful, standard post hoc analysis methods – exploring data, graphing results and reporting significant results – *may cause us to do the same thing by manual means*. We dispense with blind alleys (so-called 'forking paths') because we, the human researcher, can see that they are unlikely to produce significant results. Although we do not actually run these dead-end tests, for mathematical purposes, our educated 'eyeballing of data to focus on interesting phenomena' has done the same thing.
3. As a result, we overestimate the robustness of our results, and they may fail to replicate.

Gelman and Loken are not alone in making this criticism. Cumming (2014) objects to 'NHST' (null hypothesis significance testing), characterised as an imperative that

> explains selective publication, motivates data selection and tweaking until the *p* value is sufficiently small, and deludes us into thinking that any finding that meets the criterion of statistical significance is true and does not require replication.

11.5 What Does This Mean for Corpus Linguistics?

Figure 11.1 was constructed while writing Bowie & Wallis (2016). The graph does not appear in the final paper because the authors decided to adopt a different baseline (on linguistic grounds). But it is typical of the kind of graph one might examine. There are two critical questions that follow from Gelman and Loken's critique:

- In plotting this kind of graph with confidence intervals, are we *misrepresenting the level of certainty* found in the graph?
- Are we engaging in, or encouraging, *retrospective cherry-picking* of contrasts between observations and confidence intervals?

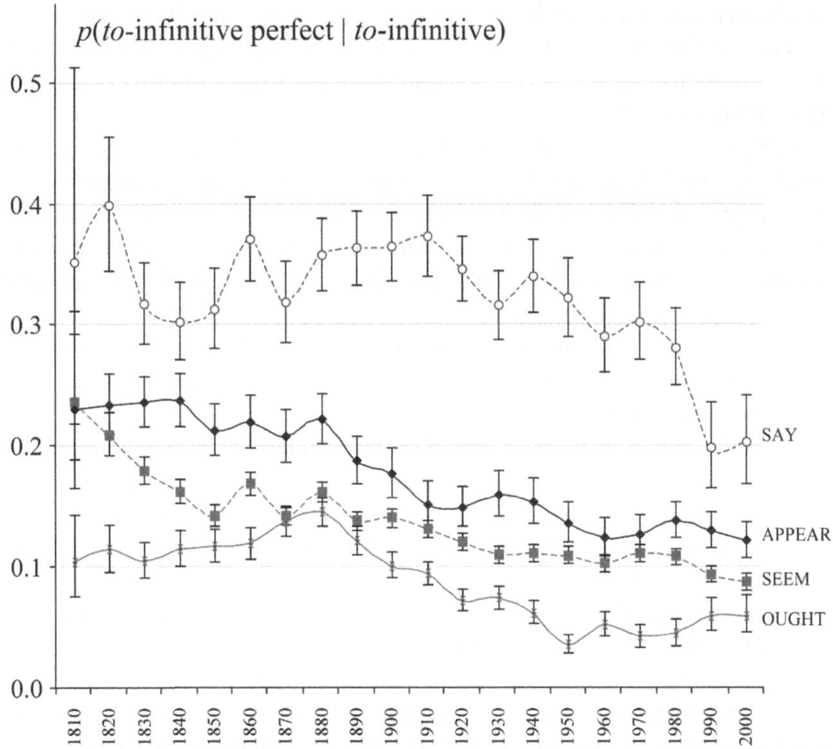

FIGURE 11.1 Independent rates for each catenative verb lemma {SAY, APPEAR, SEEM, OUGHT} of the tendency to employ the *to*-infinitive perfect as a proportion of *to*-infinitive forms (i.e., perfect and non-perfect), plotted over time. Data from COHA, after Bowie & Wallis (2016).

Figure 11.1 is obtained from a large written diachronic corpus, the *Corpus of Historical American English* (COHA, Davies, 2012). The four verb lemmas that most frequently employ the *to*-infinitive perfect construction account for 70% of cases in COHA. The plot is of *p*(perfect | *to*-infinitive), that is, the changing tendency to use a *to*-infinitive perfect construction rather than the plain *to*-infinitive. See also Chapter 10.

This evaluation is performed for each lemma separately, so the line marked SAY plots the rate over time of selecting the perfect form for alternation patterns like Example (41):

(41) She *was said* <u>*to have become*</u> insane on receiving the news [1867:FIC AmbroseFecitThe]
~She *was said* <u>*to become*</u> insane on receiving the news

In Chapter 3, we termed this type of alternation 'mutual substitution under consistent meaning change', in this case, specifying perfect aspect. This should be a robust alternation, as the core referential meaning (encapsulated by the verb BECOME) is constant.

In Figure 11.1, there are 19 decades and four trend lines, in total, 76 confidence intervals. There are 171 × 4 potential pairwise comparisons and 6 × 19 vertical pairwise comparisons. So there are 798 potential statistical pairwise tests that might be carried out with a Newcombe-Wilson test. With a 1 in 20 error rate, we can expect about 798/20 = 39.9 'significant' pairwise comparisons that would not be replicated on repetition.

Gelman, Loken, Cumming and colleagues argue that if we select a few statistically significant claims from this graph, we have committed precisely the 'forking path' error they object to.

However, this is not our method. We should not sift through 800 possible comparisons and then report significant results selectively! We do not encourage this kind of 'cherry-picking'. We are concerned with the *overall patterns* that we see, general trends, regression lines, and so on, which are more likely to be replicable in broad terms.

We are interested in the general pattern. Here it is relevant that not only does SAY decline, but so do other high-frequency verbs.

Similarly, Millar did not select his time period *in order* to report that modals were on the increase – on the contrary, he non-arbitrarily took the start and end point of the entire timeframe sampled. But the conclusion that 'modals increased over the period' was only one statement about the data. Over shorter periods there were significant falls, and individual modal verbs varied differently. Indeed, the complexity of his results is best summed up by the detailed graphs within his paper. It is better to present and discuss the pattern, not an end point or slogan.

Nonetheless, we may still have the sneaking suspicion that we are indulging in a kind of *experimenter bias*. It is easy to report statistically significant results (especially those aligning with our causal preconceptions or anticipated reader interest), and to ignore inconvenient non-significant results (or worse – results that point in the opposite direction).

The fear is that results assumed to be due to chance 1 in 20 times are more likely due to chance 1 in 5 times (say), simply because we have – perhaps inadvertently and unconsciously – already preselected our data and methods to obtain significant results. Far from being objective, we have allowed ourselves to manipulate results by misreporting.

Some researchers have suggested that we correct this problem by adopting tougher error levels – adopt a 1 in 100 level and we might arrive at 1 in 20. But this assumes we know the appropriate multiplier to apply!

It is legitimate to adjust an error level to ensure that multiple independent tests are simultaneously significant, as some fitting algorithms do. But if a statistical model is mathematically inappropriate for the data, the solution must lie in correcting the underlying model, not the error level.

11.6 Some Recommendations

In what follows, we make some recommendations drawn from Gelman and Loken's paper that are particularly relevant to corpus linguistics researchers. Harris et al. (2009) make further recommendations based on an interview study of editors and reviewers in top psychiatry journals.

11.6.1 Recommendation 1: Include a Replication Step

Gelman and Loken suggest that published studies should always involve a replication process. They argue that researchers should publish fewer experiments but include a replication step. Here are two strategies we might use:

- **Random subdivision:** Before you start, create two random subcorpora $\mathbf{C}_1$ and $\mathbf{C}_2$ by randomly drawing texts from the corpus and assigning them to $\mathbf{C}_1$ and $\mathbf{C}_2$ in turn. You may wish to control for balance, for example, to ensure subsampling is drawn equitably from each genre category. Perform the study on $\mathbf{C}_1$ and summarise the results. Apply exactly the same analysis to $\mathbf{C}_2$. Do we get compatible results with the confidence intervals of the first experiment? More precisely, if results are found to be *statistically separable*, we should not report them.[4] See Chapter 14.

We should create a random subsample of independent *texts* or *subtexts*, rather than random *instances* from the same set of texts. Instances drawn from the same source are more likely to share properties than instances drawn from independent sources. See Chapter 16. To perform a replication procedure, data in each replication set must be from independent sources.

A weaker alternative to formal replication is to repeat the experiment with predefined, as distinct from randomly generated, subcorpora:

- **Sampling subcorpora:** Apply your analysis to spoken data and repeat it with written data. Do we get broadly similar results? If we obtain comparable results for subcorpora with a known difference in sampling, it seems probable they would pass a replication test where two subsamples were not sampled differently. On the other hand, if results are different, this would justify further investigation. Thus in a study on repeated choices, Wallis (2019b) compared results between ICE-GB speech and writing (see Chapter 1) and ICE-GB and the BNC. This method is weaker than strict replication, because it is possible that variation in sampling and the difference between populations (speech and writing say) cancel each other out. But it may be a useful complement to replication.

Subsampling by either random or categorical means still subsamples the *original* corpus – ICE-GB, TIME or COHA, for example. If the original corpus was biased in a manner that impacted on the research findings, subsampling the original corpus will not solve this problem. Corpora typically represent a limited demographic, but we often wish to infer the properties of language of people of *all* ages, social classes and regions. Arguably, categorical subsampling may be more informative because categories are representative of different imagined populations. See Chapter 5.

Finally, even where replication is not carried out (for reasons of limited data, perhaps), your research method must be sufficiently clear to allow others to replicate it. Indeed, as a general principle, authors should at least make *raw frequency data* (not just proportions or per million word rates) available to permit a reanalysis by other researchers. Some databases, like IRIS and OSF, actively encourage this practice. Publishing and distributing corpora makes exact reproduction easier: having followed every step with the corpus and reproduced the results, the reader knows exactly what they should do to repeat the study with a new one.

11.6.2 Recommendation 2: Focus on Large Effects – and Clear Visualisations

Another of Gelman and Loken's recommendations is that researchers should spend more time focusing on *sizes of effect* rather than just reporting 'statistical significance'. This is entirely consistent with the central theme of this book, projecting best estimates of proportions, differences and effect sizes onto graphs and plotting intervals about them to estimate our confidence in them. We discuss two classes of effect size estimate appropriate for Binomial and Multinomial data in Chapter 13.

We should be wary of citing just-significant results with a relatively small effect size: indeed, the best option is to calculate confidence intervals on effect sizes. As well as plotting data, this permits us to make claims like 'this effect size is more than 95% likely to represent a medium effect at least', where a 'medium effect' is quoted at some conventional level.

The implication of the 'forking paths' argument is that researchers tend not to report apparent 'dead-end', non-significant results. But well-considered graphs visualise all the data in a given frame – including where confidence intervals overlap and differences are non-significant – rather than selectively reporting significant results.

Graphing data with confidence intervals allows us to see the range of a particular observation, and – providing they are plotted on the same scale – visually compare data points. See Chapter 7. We apply the same criteria to all data points and allow the reader to interpret the graph. Significant and non-significant contrasts alike are available to be viewed, the method duplicated and results compared.

One strength of Millar's paper is in his reporting of trends and graphs. In Figure 11.1, confidence intervals vastly improve our understanding of the overall trends we see. But we should not assume that every 'significant' difference will replicate.

11.6.3 Recommendation 3: Play Devil's Advocate

In Chapter 2, we argued that it is an absolutely essential requirement for an empirical scientist to consider alternative hypotheses to their preferred one, and then systematically and carefully discount them. In simple terms: is there another plausible reason apart from your central hypothesis that can explain what you found?

It is not sufficient to 'find something interesting in data' and publish it. We are trying to detect *meaningful phenomena* in data, or to put it another way, we are trying to find robust evidence of phenomena that have implications for linguistic theory. We are trying to move from an observed correlation to a hypothesised underlying cause.

Inferential statistics is a tool to help us do this. But logic also plays its part.

11.6.4 A Checklist for Empirical Linguistics

The following steps are necessary for empirical linguistics research:

1. **Identify the underlying research question**, framed in general theoretical terms. As far as possible focus on questions of speaker choice. See Chapter 3.
2. **Be clear how your data was sampled.** Do not assume your sample represents 'language in general'. It inevitably represents a particular *restricted type* of language data. Those restrictions define the population. See Chapter 5.
3. **Operationalise the research question as a series of testable hypotheses** or predictions, and evaluate them. Plot graphs! Visualise observations with confidence intervals to understand them and make robust claims. See Chapter 7.
4. **Focus reporting on global patterns across the entire dataset**. If your research identifies an anomalous pattern in part of the data, it may be genuine or it may be an artifact of sampling.
5. **Evaluate whether data are clustered in particular texts**. The best way to do this is to model within-text variation along the lines discussed in Chapter 16, or engage in multilevel modelling. As a first step you can simply check to see if particular constructions are concentrated in a small number of texts.

6. **Critique the results of your evaluation in terms of the original research question**, and play devil's advocate: what other possible underlying explanations might there be for your results? See Chapter 2. Go back to your corpus examples and re-read them!
7. **Consider alternative hypotheses and test them**. Design new experiments to distinguish possible explanations for the observed phenomenon. Consider changing the definition of corpus queries for types and baselines. Does this make a difference?
8. **Plan a replication step prior to publication**. Be prepared to partition the data as described in Recommendation 1, dividing the corpus into different pools of source texts. At the very least examine if major subcategories of the corpus obtain different results. Consider repeating your study on another corpus.

11.7 Conclusions

It is difficult to understate the importance of reporting accuracy and transparency.

If your study does not replicate in the future, possible reasons must be capable of exploration by future researchers. It would not have been possible to explore the differences between Leech and Millar's data had Neil Millar simply summarised a few trends and 'statistically significant' findings.

It is incumbent on us to properly describe the limitations of data and sampling, definitions of variables and abstraction (query) methods for populating them.

This brings us back to a point we made in Chapter 5. A common mistake is to refer to 'British English' (say) as a shorthand for 'data drawn from British English texts sampled according to the sampling frame defined in Section X'. Many failures to replicate in psychology can be attributed to precisely this type of error – the experimental dataset is not representative of the population claimed.

One of the strengths of corpus linguistics research has been that, from filing cabinets to databases, linguists have made their corpora available. Not only can a corpus study be reproduced using the same data as the researcher, but permutations on that research may be performed. You may not carry out a replication step, but others may. Having *reproduced* your study a researcher will likely find it easier to try to replicate it with other corpora or subsets of your data.

However, every silver lining has a cloud. The high cost of collecting, constructing and annotating corpora means that actual replication with a fresh sample can be difficult. In the case of historical corpora, it may be impossible.

Replication is a health check on statistical methods, but it is not a substitute for them. The importance of sound statistics and careful analysis cannot be overstated.

Notes

1 These are the *Brown Corpus of American English* (1960s) and *Frown* (the Freiburg-Brown 1990s resample) written corpora. See www.helsinki.fi/varieng/CoRD/corpora/FROWN for more information.
2 We can evaluate this question with a *separability test* (see Chapter 14).
3 The most likely reason for the non-reproduction of Millar's (2009) TIME result appears to be that at least in certain aspects (e.g., an increase in modals of possibility), his source data turns out to be unrepresentative of written US English of the period.
4 'Replication' does not mean that observed variables, say p_1 drawn from $\mathbf{C}_1$, and p_2 drawn from $\mathbf{C}_2$, will be identical. It means that p_1 and p_2 are not significantly different according to an independent-sample test (Newcombe-Wilson or 2 × 2 χ^2 test for homogeneity). This is called a 'point test' in Chapter 14.

12

CHOOSING THE RIGHT TEST

12.1 Introduction

At this point it seems sensible to review what we have learned and consider how we might apply our new-found knowledge. In this chapter, we address the question every researcher has to deal with:

> What is the right statistical test for my purpose?

Statistics books often provide a list, chart or decision tree to help researchers choose. But this assumes the researcher has already clarified preliminary questions about research design, understood the difference between 'parametric' and 'non-parametric' tests, and so on. In other words, they assume a level of understanding a researcher is unlikely to have on opening the book! The risk is that they dive into the first test they see and get confused.

Conventionally, significance tests are stated in terms of the null hypothesis that a significant result would overturn. But often – because the null hypothesis is a mathematical definition – this statement of the null hypothesis appears so abstract it can be difficult to identify its implications. This does not mean that a statement is *wrong*, but rather that the consequences of the test are unclear.

For example, in his excellent book, Sheskin (2011, p. 532) specifies the null hypothesis of the Mann-Whitney *U* test on *ranked* (Ordinal) data as follows:

> **Null hypothesis:** $\theta_1 = \theta_2$
>
> The median of the population Group 1 represents equals the median of the population Group 2 represents. With respect to the sample data, when both

DOI: 10.4324/9781003622697-15

groups have an equal sample size, this translates into the sum of the ranks of Group 1 being equal to the sum of the ranks of Group 2. A more general way of stating this . . . is that the means of the ranks of the two groups are equal.

Did you follow this? Before we start, note the test works with Ordinal data. So before even attempting to process the previous statement, we need to ensure our data are of the appropriate type. In this case, data should be a sample of independent scores capable of being placed in a ranked order, like scores on a questionnaire 'Lickert' scale (1 = strongly agree, 2 = agree . . . 5 = strongly disagree).

First, we sort data into a sequence.

$$X_1 = [1, 1, 1, 2, 2, 2, 3, 4, 4, 5],$$
$$X_2 = [1, 1, 2, 2, 3, 3, 3, 4, 5, 5].$$

Next, we allocate numbers to ranks. To rank them, number each one and, if there are any tied ranks (duplicate numbers), allocate them the mean of the tied ranks.[1] This obtains the following two series:

$$R_1 = [3, 3, 3, 8, 8, 8, 12.5, 16, 16, 19],$$
$$R_2 = [3, 3, 8, 8, 12.5, 12.5, 12.5, 16, 19, 19].$$

But there is another pitfall in this formulation. The means of *ranks*, $\bar{R}_1$ and $\bar{R}_2$ (9.65 and 11.35) can oh-so-easily be confused with the means of *data*, $\bar{X}_1$ and $\bar{X}_2$ (2.5 and 2.9). This is just one of the potential sources of confusion for the researcher.

In this book, we have approached the problem of understanding significant difference from the perspective of visualising observations and confidence intervals, and then building simple tests using this visualisation. We learned that the same test condition might be calculated with different methods (χ^2, log-likelihood, Fisher, etc.), but that some methods are more precise than others.

To decide which test to use we need to distinguish between:

- different *experimental designs*; and
- optimum *methods* for calculating and testing significance.

The first step in designing an experiment is to select a dependent variable.

12.1.1 Choosing a Dependent Variable and Baseline

In corpus linguistics, as we know, many research questions involve *choice*. See Chapter 3. The speaker can say *shall* or *will*, choose to add a postmodifying clause to a noun phrase or not, and so on. If we wish to predict that choice, the choice will be expressed as values of our dependent variable (DV). Choices are mutually exclusive, that is, a speaker or writer may choose only one option out of a set of alternatives.

Choices might be organised as sub-choices within a hierarchical decision tree, such as {*shall*, {*will*, *'ll*}}, or be structured in other ways. A complementation pattern in grammar is a traditional means for classifying verbs: *this* verb can be found in monotransitive and intransitive patterns; *that* verb also has a ditransitive complementation, and so on. However, in research we are not beholden to this idea. We might view complementation patterns as a consequence of semantic constraints on objects (arguments to predicates). We might treat the decision to employ a direct object as independent from the decision to employ an indirect object. Each would then be recorded by distinct variables. See Chapter 8.

It has been common in corpus linguistics to use Binomial statistical methods with word-based baselines where observed proportions are always close to 0 and reach a maximum at proportions far below 1. This implies that a particular item may be expressed, not just at any arbitrary point in the corpus, but in place of (or after) every word! We identified three objections to this kind of pmw exposure rate study:

1. **The evaluation is not linguistically plausible**. The mathematical model is known to be an unrealistic representation of the way we know language behaves. Sentences are composed by speakers making choices (framing constraints) that exclude or permit other choices. Language is not 'one damn word after another'.
2. **Confounding variation is not addressed**. In a corpus, we can expect that all variables, including the dependent variable, are sampled in such a way that it is inevitable they will be exposed to sources of variation irrelevant to our study. In experimental research, we can try to control experimental conditions, but corpora do not give us that option. A rise or fall might be due to more than one reason. For example, a smaller number of noun phrases than expected might be due to NPs tending to be longer (more lengthy nominalisations, perhaps), or NPs being 'crowded out' by other items (VPs, discourse markers, etc.). Once we allow for alternative baselines we can begin to distinguish alternative explanations.
3. **Potential variation is exaggerated**. The Binomial model presumes that every member of the set is free to vary. If the set consists of all words, the model exaggerates the possible range of variation and renders the test insensitive. See Wallis (2012c). This problem is not unique to per million word studies, but (thanks to the sheer number of words in the corpus), it afflicts this type of study the most.

Consequently, our advice in Chapter 3 remains: you may *begin* with a per million word study – for example, to replicate an existing one – but once performed, you should think how you might improve on a word baseline:

- If you are evaluating a phenomenon within a particular type of phrase, consider a baseline of that phrase type, for example, *shall* as a proportion of all modal verbs. If the phenomenon has an alternate form it is competing with (e.g., modal *will*), can you extract instances of that other form?
- Explore the 'methodological continuum' of Chapter 3. Once you have obtained a baseline or set of alternates, turn to the corpus. Examine instances one-by-one and ask if they properly belong to the set. Is it conceivable that each data point could consist of just one type of the DV, so that $p = 0$ or 1?
- Always bear in mind that corpus queries may be imperfect, either because the annotation is unreliable or because you might have expressed the query incorrectly! Queries may generate 'false positives' that should be excluded and may miss 'false negatives' that should have been found. In Chapter 15, we discuss how to address this issue.

However, some linguistic research topics do not immediately lend themselves to questions of choice. *Semasiological studies* concern variation in the meaning of the same word or phrase. In Chapter 4, we examined how *very* changed its meaning over time. The natural 'dependent variable' appears to be different meanings of the word *very*. But the immediate lexical-grammatical context in which each meaning is expressed is necessarily distinct:

(42) I think that's *very* important [S1A-035 #185]
(43) the *very* day I sat down [S2B-025 #35]
(44) Probably I couldn't do it *very* well [S1A-024 #133]

Examples (42) to (44) are not members of a set of alternate forms. In each case, *very* is chosen from a number of potential intensifiers or specifiers, separately and independently, at different 'choice points'.

Any observed variation of the distribution of meanings of *very* is a *consequence* of these distinct independent choices. How we might identify these independent decisions is discussed at length in Chapter 4. Perhaps unsurprisingly, the solution rests on attempting to identify the alternatives available at each point, and the choices a speaker or writer made. Semasiological variation is then evaluated as an outcome of onomasiological choices, and our studies focus on the chance of a form being used when the option to use it became available.

12.1.2 Choosing Independent Variables

Now that we have settled on our dependent variable, we turn to the question of selecting independent variables (IVs). Many experiments consist of an exploration of the effect of potential factors that influence this choice.

In this book, we have tended to use the broad-brush term 'external' to refer to factors that partition the data by text or participant. Such variables might concern

- the participants themselves (e.g., their gender or age);
- the communicative context of the utterance (e.g., register/genre, interactivity and mode of communication); or
- the domain, purpose and topic of the text.

By contrast, we might use the generic term 'internal' or 'linguistic' to apply to in-text factors, whether they be, for example, pragmatic, semantic, syntactic, lexical, prosodic or morphological. Such factors may be recorded by another 'choice variable' at a location in a defined relationship with the in-text choice DV. What we called *linguistic interaction experiments* are those that investigate whether two or more linguistic choices interact with each other.

What do we mean by 'in a defined relationship'? We mean that there are two co-occurring linguistic events, one represented by the IV and one by the DV, and that this co-occurrence has a particular relationship that allows us to hypothesise that one choice might impact on the other. Events could be aspects of the same expression or, as in the case of priming, distinct and separated in time. Such relationships are as varied as researcher ambition and corpus annotation might allow: the IV might be the semantic class of a verb preceding the DV, the pragmatic class of the clause in which the DV is found, a priming event preceding a second choice in a conversation and so on. Choices may be the occurrence or non-occurrence of an event, provided, of course, that we can detect the latter.

A warning on *directionality* is necessary. Word order is not necessarily a reliable guide to the order in which choices are made by a speaker. We cannot assume that merely because an IV event precedes a DV one in the text, a detected correlation implies the IV 'influences' or 'affects' the DV.

Consider Example (45), from a spontaneously produced spoken text in ICE-GB. We might assume that the head noun, *articles*, is conceived of (chosen) before the adjective phrases *quite big*, *feature* and *illustrated*. Yet in English, by far the most common position for adjectives is attributive, that is, before the noun they modify:

(45) I've done *two quite big feature <u>articles</u> illustrated*, which I published in Bombay but in quite sort of <pause> good quality <pause> uh sort of cultural magazines that have . . . [S1A-066 #162]

In this example, something slightly odd happened in the articulation of *illustrated* that caused it to be placed in postpositive position (after the noun). Perhaps it was an interaction with *feature*. We will never know. The take-home lesson is this: speakers make unconscious decisions, but they do not always articulate them in the sequence they were made! Reordering occurs. Some planning is necessary in language production. Consequently, an IV might relate to a word or construction uttered after the choice recorded by the DV.

Reasoning about decision order is best left to linguistics and logic, not statistics. If two events are not adjacent, for example, the second is in an embedded phrase or clause relative to the first, or they are separated by a sentence or speaker turn, we can be more confident of the order.

When events are (near-) adjacent, it is wise to examine whether referential meaning changes across an alternation. In Section 2.6, Chapter 2 we saw an example where the subject of a subordinate clause was introduced by a relative objective pronoun *who* or *whom*, but the choice of subject (*I/we* or something else) concerns core meaning and so was probably made first. See also Figure 12.2.

Some types of research employ a text-external DV. *Stylistics research* attempts to predict sociolinguistic factors – one author's personal style compared to another's – from lexical, semantic or grammatical features of the text (text-internal variables). IVs are linguistic and the DV is sociolinguistic. Categorical statistical methods discussed next are also viable in such studies. The text is usually assumed to have only one author, and the DV consists of mutually exclusive categories (author A vs. B, or A vs. 'not A'). The writer is not 'free to choose' to be another author(!), but, provided IVs are free to vary, an associative contingency test is legitimate. See next section.

Now that we have framed our research question, we can turn to the appropriate class of tests for our data.

12.2 Tests for Categorical Data

As we have seen, the most common research design in corpus linguistics is when both independent and dependent variables are categorical (Binomial or Multinomial). This is why this book focuses on these types of tests almost exclusively.

12.2.1 Two Types of Contingency Test

The most familiar test of this type is the *contingency test* (Chapters 2 and 8), which comes in two principal versions: 'goodness of fit' tests which compare two distributions, rows or columns in a table (usually where one is assumed to be a subset of the other); and tests for 'homogeneity' or 'independence' which evaluate the association of two variables. χ^2 is one *implementation* of a

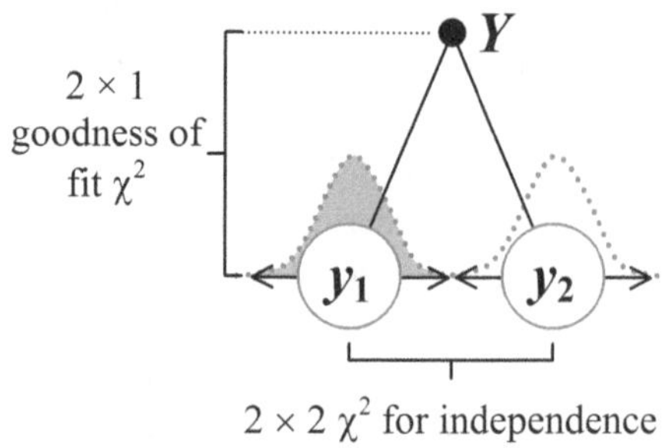

FIGURE 12.1 Goodness of fit and homogeneity tests. See Chapter 8.

contingency test. In Chapter 8, we noted alternative ways of computing these tests (see Section 12.2.7).

Data are collected as a 'contingency table' of frequencies counting up occurrences in each combination, such as $\mathbf{O} = \{o_i\}$ or $\{o_{i,j}\}$, which we compare with an equivalent expected distribution **E**. Test differences concern how the expected distribution is defined.

In a contingency table, the independent variable Y has a discrete set of categories and produces a discrete frequency distribution for each column of the dependent variable X, $\{o_{i,j}\}$. For every value of X and Y (let us call these values x_i and y_j, respectively), there is a cell frequency count $o_{i,j}$ representing the number of times in the sample that $X = x_i$ and $Y = y_j$ at the same time.

- **Goodness of fit tests** compare an observed distribution $\mathbf{O} = \{o_i\}$ which sums to $n = o_+$, with a given expected distribution, $\mathbf{E} = \{e_i\}$ with sum e_+. 'Goodness of fit' means that the proportions $p_i = o_i / n$ in each cell of the distribution closely match ('fits') expected proportions $P_i = e_i / e_+$. It may be implemented as an '$r \times 1$ χ^2 test' with $r - 1$ degrees of freedom.
  - A typical application is where $\{e_i\}$ corresponds to a superset of $\{o_i\}$, as in Figure 12.1, for example, to compare the distribution of X at y_1 with the 'all data' superset at Y.
  - Alternatively, $\{e_i\}$ might be given, as when we performed a *more test* for a pair of competing frequencies (we tested them against $\mathbf{E} = \{n/2, n/2\}$). See Chapter 7.
- **Independence tests** ('homogeneity tests') evaluate whether the value of one variable is independent from the value of the other. We compare a two-dimensional table $\mathbf{O} = \{o_{i,j}\}$ with $\mathbf{E} = \{e_{i,j}\}$ expressing an *average* defined by row and column totals. A significant result means we can reject the null hypothesis that variables are independent.

- We typically use it to test the extent to which, were we to know the value of the IV, *Y*, we could predict the value of the DV, *X*.
- Due to the way the expected distribution is constructed, the test is reversible or *associative*: swapping *X* for *Y* does not change the result. It may also be referred to as an '$r \times c$ test' because it compares distributions of *r* cells across all *c* subvalues of *X*.

Despite their differences, these tests essentially operate by performing two steps: *calculate the size of an effect*, and then *compare this effect size with a threshold*: a confidence interval, critical value or (in the case of Binomial and Fisher tests) error level. Tests for comparing independent tables are explained in Chapter 14.

12.2.2 The Benefits of Simple Tests

Simple 2×1 and 2×2 tests are more conclusive than larger tables ($r \times 1$, $r \times c$). They have one degree of freedom and make few assumptions about the data. They test only one dimension of variation at a time, so if a significant difference is detected, it refers to a correlation along that dimension.

The 2×1 goodness of fit test can be visualised as a single observed proportion *p*, with a Wilson score interval describing the likely range of values that *p* is predicted to take in the population. See Chapter 6.

The 2×2 test of independence can be visualised as a difference between two observed proportions, p_1 and p_2, with Wilson score intervals attached to each observation. Differences may also be plotted with a Newcombe-Wilson interval repositioned at one end of the difference. See Chapter 7.

12.2.3 Visualising Uncertainty

We introduced the idea of a *Binomial proportion difference graph* in Chapter 2 and showed how it can be used. Visualising data like this allows us to put difference in proportion.

Consider the next example, which is grammatically 'incorrect', but not atypical of spoken British English in ICE-GB:

(46) I had to meet this girl [*who I* haven't seen for ten years] from my school [S1A-062 #193]

Figure 12.2 shows that, in 1990s spoken British English comparable to ICE-GB, speakers tend to say *who* rather than *whom* in contexts such as these, termed 'objective *who/whom*'. Yet in the corresponding written English corpus, we find that if the subject that follows *who* or *whom* refers to the writer themselves (they say *I* or *we*) then the writer often 'gets the rule wrong' and adopts the spoken

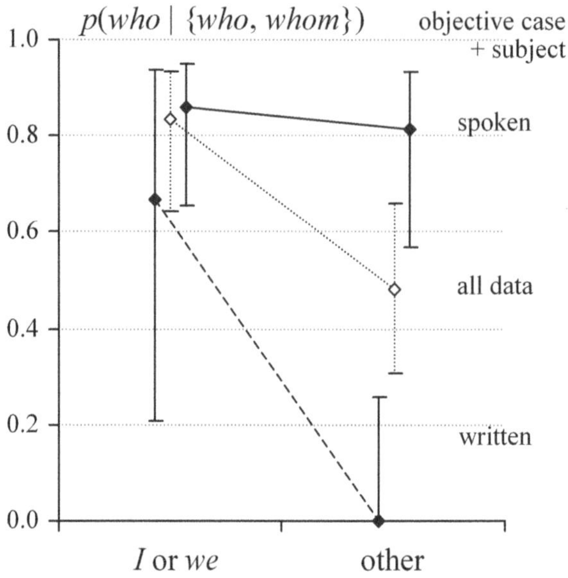

FIGURE 12.2 An example Binomial proportion difference graph, from Chapter 2.

idiom. They seem to be more comfortable with the rule when the subject is not themselves. This effect may be idiomatic, but the result is interesting.

From the perspective of significance testing, confidence intervals tell us about the certainty of observed data points, and help us decide whether points significantly differ. The graph reveals an interaction between the subject and the choice of *who* or *whom* for writing not found in the spoken data. A χ^2 test confirms a significant effect of a following subject on the *who/whom* choice with written data.

A contingency test for independence is reversible. The same result is found irrespective of whether the DV or IV is listed horizontally or vertically in the table. (This is why the test may be used when the IV but not the DV is free to vary.)

But when we *plot* data we should plot proportions of the DV! Figure 12.2 plots $p(who \mid \{who, whom\})$. Our null hypothesis is that this proportion does not change between categories of the IV.

12.2.4 When to Use Goodness of Fit Tests

The 2 × 1 goodness of fit test is the test analogue of a confidence interval of a single proportion, such as the 'written' confidence interval for $p(who)$ for *I* or *we* in Figure 12.2. A goodness of fit test compares observed data against a given expected distribution, considering only the set of observed data to be uncertain.

We then attempt to 'fit' that data against a given distribution. Figure 12.2 tells us that this observed probability is significantly different from $P = 0.2$ or less.

By contrast, tests of independence contrast two or more observed distributions or proportions like $p(who, I$ or $we)$ and $p(who$, other). Both observed proportions are uncertain, both have confidence intervals, and significant difference is evaluated against a difference interval.

A common mistake is to confuse tests of independence and goodness of fit tests. But they are distinct testing régimes, with different assumptions and different purposes. It is essential to state in your essays, articles and project reports which test was used.

Consider an example when a goodness of fit test is appropriate. A common application is to compare an observation p with a known value P. You can either

- calculate a Wilson score confidence interval about p and then compare P with it (as we did with Figure 12.2); or
- calculate a sampling interval about P and compare p with that interval (this is how the chi-square calculation works).

Both methods obtain exactly the same result. See Chapter 8.

Some experiments use goodness of fit tests in less orthodox ways. In Chapter 1, we introduced a study examining serial decisions to add a construction (Wallis, 2019b).

In this experiment, we plot the probability $p(x)$ of adding the x-th term to a sequence of terms (Figure 12.3), so $p(1)$ is the probability of adding the first

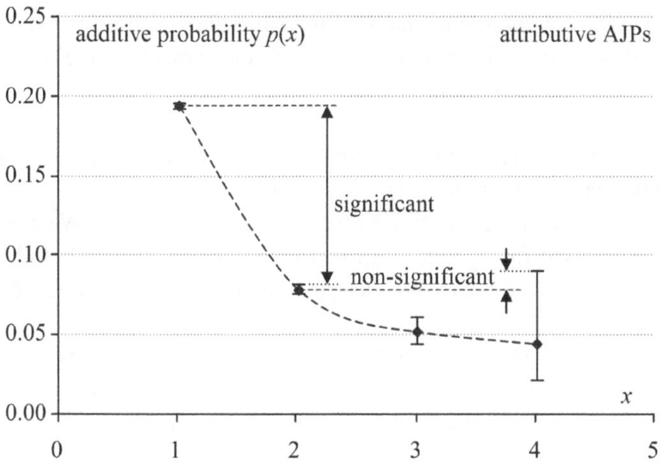

FIGURE 12.3 Additive probability $p(x)$ with 95% Wilson intervals (Wallis, 2019b). See Chapter 1. A goodness of fit test (Wilson score test) compares the previous point with the subsequent Wilson interval.

term, and $p(2)$ the probability of adding the second once the first has been added. Each subsequent decision subdivides the dataset.

The goodness of fit test is appropriate *because we are comparing a subset with its superset*. The test says, in effect: we know that the chance of arriving at the superset may vary (it also has a confidence interval), but *for this evaluation* we are only concerned to see if the chance of adding the subset has varied from the last-observed value.

12.2.5 Tests for Comparing Effect Sizes

In classical null hypothesis significance testing, an 'effect size' is a type of descriptive statistic attached to an experimental analysis.

Such quantities used to be quoted separately from a significance test. You would carry out a test and report the effect size. But all you could do with such a score would be to compare it to a threshold and declare it to be 'large', 'medium' or 'small'. For example, Sheskin (2011, pp. 677–678) describes quoting Cramér's ϕ after a 2 × 2 χ^2 test and comparing the score with a series of ranges: a 'small' effect $\phi \in [0.1, 0.3)$, 'medium' $\phi \in [0.3, 0.5)$ and 'large' $\phi \in [0.5, 1]$.

But in Chapter 9 we learned to create confidence intervals for a range of properties derived by formula from Binomial proportions and contingency tables. We have already seen a number of such measures, although we did not always call them 'effect sizes'. These include the simple difference, d, and percentage difference, $d^{\%}$. Medical studies sometimes quote a risk ratio, r, or odds ratio, o. In Chapter 13 we discuss other effect sizes and intervals.

Once we have a confidence interval for a measure such as ϕ, we can reintegrate this descriptive concept back into inferential statistics. An effect size interval allows us to do three things.

1. We can plot ϕ scores with intervals, so we can visualise the reliability of an estimate, pay attention to the smallest bound, etc.
2. We can test two scores, ϕ_1 and ϕ_2, for significant difference. We create a confidence interval for $d_\phi = \phi_2 - \phi_1$, test whether it includes 0, and conclude that $\phi_2 > \phi_1$ or vice versa. We can go further and identify larger differences between them.
3. We can evaluate intervals against published thresholds. For example, if Cramér's $\phi^- > 0.3$, or (for negative scores) $\phi^+ < -0.3$, we can report that the true population score is deemed likely to be at least a 'medium' effect.

In the case of Cramér's ϕ, the χ^2 test performs the same task as evaluating whether the confidence interval for ϕ contains zero. But with an interval we can do much more.

12.2.6 Tests for Comparing Results

One motivation for comparing effect sizes is to compare runs of the same experiment, evaluate the impact of employing an alternative framework, or perform a replication step. If one evaluation has a significantly larger effect than another, we might report this fact. This is a kind of test-of-tests, or 'meta-test'. In Chapter 14, we explore how it is possible to perform other meta-tests that compare results from two contingency tests.

Data visualisation with confidence intervals helps identify the correct approach to comparing gradients for significant difference. Note how in Figure 12.2, the gradient for spoken data appears shallower than the gradient for written data, but the confidence intervals are smaller. To report that the written gradient is *significantly greater* than for spoken data we must perform a *separability test* to evaluate precisely this question.

12.2.7 Optimum Methods of Calculation

In Chapter 8, we saw how different formulae or methods can be employed to carry out contingency tests. The standard χ^2 calculation has known weaknesses, and several alternatives have been proposed, including 'exact' tests (Binomial, Fisher), employing log-likelihood, and applying Yates's correction. Which should we choose?

A number of authors (in particular, Robert Newcombe (1998a, 1998b) and Wallis (2013a, 2020b)) have evaluated confidence intervals and tests. We can offer some straightforward advice on this topic.

The first question concerns whether you intend to carry out and cite *individual* tests and evaluations, or aim for *average* performance over a series of evaluations, such as to fit a model and average a trend.

If our goal concerns individual evaluations, we should err on the side of caution. Binomial or Fisher tests are preferred, but they are computationally costly. Their additional precision may be valuable in borderline cases. They do not generalise to intervals on other properties in the same way.

A readily available option is to use Wilson-based methods with corrections for continuity when we are performing individual tests.

- The optimum single proportion interval of this kind is the Wilson score interval with continuity correction. The recommended contingency test method ($r \times c$ or $r \times 1$) is Yates's continuity-corrected χ^2 test.
- To compare a difference against an arbitrary difference D, or to plot confidence intervals on differences d, use the Newcombe-Wilson interval with continuity correction.
- In Chapter 9 we identified Wilson-based methods for confidence intervals for the risk ratio and other properties. For difference or ratio intervals, we found

that increasing the continuity correction factor by 1.5 times obtained performance comparable to Fisher.

With multiple degrees of freedom, you can use a $r \times c$ χ^2 test, collapsing cells as necessary (see Chapter 8). But you are likely to learn more about your data by plotting Binomial probability graphs with confidence intervals and experimenting with baselines. Visualisation comes to our rescue.

If on the other hand, we are concerned about the *average* performance of interval calculations, one can use either Wilson or 'mid-p' intervals, or the χ^2 test without an adjustment for continuity. See Chapter 8. When we plot data, we often start with Wilson intervals.

Crucially, as you work with data, bear in mind what we said in the last chapter. Avoid '*p*-hacking', that is, manipulating data or tests until you obtain a significant result. Always remember that correlations do not represent causes, even – especially – when you are *sure* that your hypothesis is correct! Be ruthless in attempting to find alternative explanations. Try to patiently decide between them and your hypothesis. Whenever you are working with significance tests you should always select a method of calculation and an error level, and then stick to it.

As well as accepting a correction for continuity, tests can be adjusted to take account of circumstances where assumptions of random sampling and an infinite population are not followed. If our sample is a credible fraction (say, 5% or more) of a finite population, the *finite population correction* should be used. With corpus data drawn from random texts, we can employ a 'random-text sample correction' explained in Chapter 16.

12.3 Tests for Other Types of Data

The situation becomes more complicated when one of the tested variables is not categorical (Binomial or Multinomial proportions). There are a range of tests for Ranked, Interval or Ratio data. If an independent variable is categorical, you can employ tests for two or more independent samples (Multinomial: χ^2, Ranked: Mann-Whitney U, Real: Student's t test, etc.). The categorical variable then defines the samples: sample 1 is where $Y = y_1$, sample 2, y_2, and so on.

But if a *dependent* variable is categorical, you can also employ the same tests. As a general rule, a significant result from any test is evidence of interaction between the two variables (correlation). It does not mean that one variable causes the other to change, merely that the two variables tend to change together more than would be expected by chance.

In other words, *these tests are reversible.*

12.3.1 t Tests for Comparing Two Independent Samples of Numeric Data

Let us consider a well-known test for comparing two samples where variables are numerical, that is, at least Interval. An example Interval scale is the set of natural numbers {0, 1, 2, 3 . . .}. Other numerical scales include Ratio (true fractions, 'rational numbers') and Real scales ('rational' and 'irrational' numbers). By contrast, when we sampled Binomial variables, each instance was either true or false, yes/no, absent/present, and so on.

The *t* test for two independent samples is commonly stated such that the independent variable (subsample) is Boolean (e.g., speech vs. writing) and the dependent variable is at least on an Interval scale (e.g., clause length). A significant result might tell us, for example, that the mean length of clauses varies according to whether they are found in speech or writing, or that interrogative and declarative clauses tend to have different lengths.

Student's *t* test for two independent samples (Sheskin, 2011, p. 447) is conventionally employed to test the following:

> Null hypothesis: the means of two Normally distributed random samples of Real, Ratio or Interval variables are the same.

The test compares sample means, $\bar{x}_1$, $\bar{x}_2$, for significant difference. A variant of this test might include an expected difference other than zero. It also relies on a number of assumptions. Data are at least on an Interval scale (e.g., integers, like clause length). Samples are assumed to be approximately Normally ('*t*') distributed, so means are not close to a boundary that might affect the distribution. The population variance of both samples should also be about the same, $S_1^2 \approx S_2^2$, an assumption called 'homogeneity of variance' (Sheskin, 2011, p. 454). This assumption, which tends to break down with samples of unequal sizes, can be avoided with Welch's *t* test (Ruxton, 2006). We discuss this text later. First, let us summarise Student's *t* and derive confidence intervals for the mean and difference in means:

$$\textit{Student's t score (two independent samples) } t = d / S_d, \tag{76}$$

where the difference in sample means, $d = \bar{x}_2 - \bar{x}_1$, and

$$\textit{standard deviation of difference } S_d = \sqrt{\frac{df_1 S_1^2 + df_2 S_2^2}{df_d} \times \left(\frac{1}{n_1} + \frac{1}{n_2}\right)}. \tag{77}$$

The size of each sample i is n_i, and its degrees of freedom is $df_i = n_i - 1$. The total degrees of freedom, $df_d = df_1 + df_2 = n_1 + n_2 - 2$.

The mean and estimated population variance are calculated as follows:

$$\textit{mean of sample } \bar{x}_i = \frac{\sum_{j=1..n_i} x_{i,j}}{n_i}, \tag{78}$$

$$\textit{population variance for sample } S_i^2 = \frac{\sum_{j=1..n_i} x_{i,j}^{\ 2} - \left(\sum_{j=1..n_i} x_{i,j}\right)^2 \Big/ n_i}{df_i}. \tag{79}$$

The t test compares the difference in sample means, scaled by the standard deviation of the difference S_d, with a critical value of the t distribution. Equation (76) is very similar in structure to the z test for two independent samples (Equation (44), p. 150). The differences lie in the calculation of variance and the different distribution. See also Equation (42) (p. 199).

Sheskin (2011, p. 180) proposes we can estimate confidence intervals on a sample mean $\bar{x}_i$ using the following:

$$\textit{confidence interval for sample mean } (x_i^-, x_i^+) = \bar{x}_i \pm t_{\alpha/2,} df \,.\, S_i \big/ \sqrt{n_i}, \tag{80}$$

where $t(\alpha/2, df_i)$ is the two-tailed critical value for the t distribution.[2] Sheskin (2011, p. 468) also proposes a difference interval for the two independent sample t test, where $df_d = n_1 + n_2 - 2$:

$$\textit{difference interval } (d^-, d^+) = d \pm t_{\alpha/2,df} \cdot S_d. \tag{81}$$

Both interval estimates assume that samples are t distributed, which also implies that variables x_1 and x_2 are unbounded. However, many scores sampled from nature are in fact bounded. The height of school children, the classic example beloved of teachers the world over, has a lower bound. Clause length $l \geq 1$, that is, a clause must contain at least one word. Even if we allowed absent clauses to be recorded as 'length 0', the variable would still have a lower bound!

In a t test for two independent samples, this fact matters less, because the test is concerned with whether the *difference* between two distributions is significant. If $\bar{x}_1$ and $\bar{x}_2$ measure the same variable in different samples, it is unlikely there will be a boundary (or impossible region) between them. But if we wished to quote confidence intervals, this does matter. The lower bound of Equation (80), x_i^-, might fall below 1, which is obviously impossible.

These intervals are symmetric and based on a 'standard error', rather than a true confidence interval calculated by interval equality. See Chapter 6. An alternative approach to clause length intervals, where length l is considered the reciprocal of a Binomial proportion p ($l = 1/p$, see Chapters 9) accounts for boundaries and can be adjusted for random-text sampling (Chapter 16).

Finally, Welch's test replaces Equation (77) with

$$\textit{standard deviation of difference } S_d = \sqrt{\frac{S_1^2}{n_1} + \frac{S_2^2}{n_2}}. \qquad (77')$$

The degrees of freedom are determined by

$$\textit{degrees of freedom for difference } df_d = \left(\frac{1}{n_1} + \frac{u}{n_2}\right)^2 \Bigg/ \left(\frac{1}{n_1^2 df_1} + \frac{u^2}{n_2^2 df_2}\right), \qquad (82)$$

where $u = S_2^2 / S_1^2$. This standard deviation and these degrees of freedom (rounded down to the nearest integer) may be introduced into Equation (81) to obtain an improved difference interval.[3]

12.3.2 Transposing Tests

The t test is usually applied in the following way:

IV (Boolean) → DV (Numeric).

Like χ^2, the test can be applied in reverse, transposing independent and dependent variables. Given a clause length, we may infer (stylistically) whether it is more likely that the text it is found in comes from speech or writing. Or we might compare different clause types by their length:

IV (Numeric) → DV (Boolean).

The null hypothesis of the test has not really changed. If the independent variable is independent from the dependent variable, the reverse is also true.

This relates to a general point. Tests do not imply direction between variables. A significant correlation can be interpreted from either variable to the other. In Chapter 2, we argued *we cannot infer causality from a correlation between two variables*.

Indeed, arguably, independent and dependent variables are less analytically distinguishable in 'ex post facto' corpus data analysis than in laboratory experiments where independent variables may be controlled or manipulated by the researcher.

12.3.3 Tests for Other Types of Variables

Where both variables are numeric you can employ regression (Spearman's R^2, Pearson's r^2) and ANOVA tests.[4] In Chapter 10, we saw how logistic regression may be employed to relate variables on Real and Binomial scales.

When deciding between tests, bear in mind that analysis often benefits from simplicity. The following steps are all perfectly legitimate:

1. **Use a weaker test**. It is always possible to sacrifice information and employ a test that makes fewer assumptions about the data. This may be an opportunity to review the assumptions made and consider which are more linguistically defensible.
2. **Merge cells and quantise**. Just as we may merge cells in contingency tables, numeric variables may be 'quantised' (see next).

Ages of participants in a corpus may be considered as Interval data (e.g., 15, 23, 30, 45 and 51) or ranked age ranges (e.g., 'child: 0–9', 'teenager: 10–18', 'young adult: 19–29', etc.). A contingency test may be applied to ranked data. The test ignores the ranking when evaluating significant difference.

If these steps are legitimate, why are they not commonly recommended? The answer is that they are conservative and weaken the power of the test. They *underestimate* significant difference (allow more 'Type II' errors). So if it is possible to employ more sophisticated techniques, they are worth considering.

On the other hand, sophisticated regression techniques and parametric tests are powerful, but employ more assumptions.

12.3.4 Quantisation

One final method may be useful. *Quantisation* is a useful technique for the purposes of analysis or visualisation. It converts a continuous variable into one of discrete ordered types ('quanta').

In Chapter 3, we reported DCPSE time series data for first person positive declarative modal *shall* versus *will* alternation. There are few instances of either *shall* or *will* in some annual samples. Confidence intervals for most time periods (particularly in the early 'LLC' portion of the corpus) are correspondingly extremely wide.[5] See Figure 12.4.

With such a large scatter, it is difficult to see whether the trend is indeed downwards. In the paper, Aarts et al. collapsed data into five-year time periods based around the start of a decade. Data for '1960' are obtained by pooling ± 2 years, that is, 1958–1962, and so on. This obtains a series (1958–1962, 1963–1967, 1968–1972, etc.), the data for each were pooled. The proportions obtained could then be plotted as in Figure 12.5.

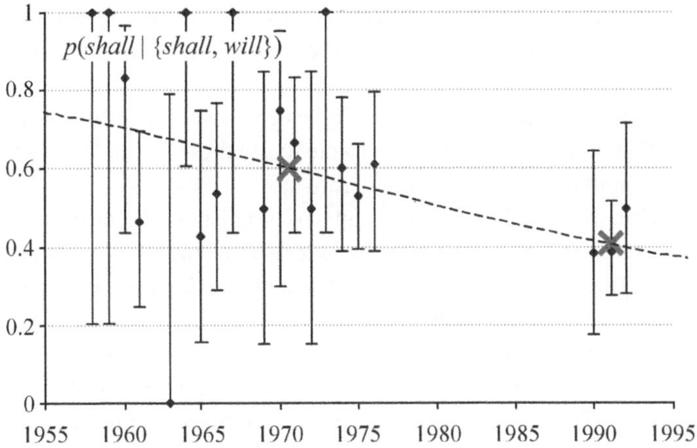

FIGURE 12.4 Declining rate *p*(*shall* | {*shall*, *will*}) for first person positive declarative modal alternation over time, data from DCPSE (after Aarts et al., 2013). The crosses are the centre points of the two subcorpora.

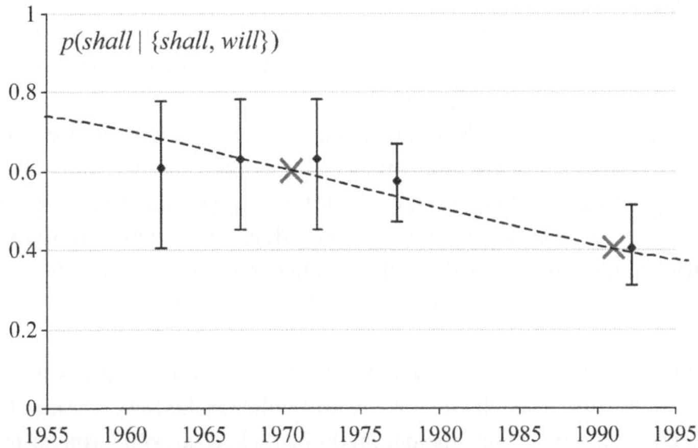

FIGURE 12.5 The same data as Figure 12.4, quantised into five-year time periods.

This plot trades fewer observations for smaller intervals and more certain observations.

12.4 Conclusions

As with all analytical methods, test results must be carefully interpreted and explained. The main pitfalls with complex techniques concern the fact that the method may rely upon mistaken assumptions! Even an intuitive concept like 'simplicity' (parsimony) relies on a choice of variables and how they are expressed.

Recognising that there is a trade-off between power and effort on the part of the researcher, it follows that it is advisable to use these methods last and always be explicit about the assumptions they rely on.

Conventionally, this is not what happens. Statistics platforms like SPSS™ make the exercise of performing multiple tests easy, including tests that are difficult to compute manually. They can follow a processing decision tree, selecting one test if another is significant.

Our concern motivating this book, however, is that *researchers need to understand exactly what their tests are evaluating*. If inferential statistics is counterintuitive and difficult to conceptualise in the first place, the more we automate, the more we risk creating 'black boxes' whose output is taken on faith, making the same mistake as students who misuse generative AI tools. This lack of understanding is ultimately exposed when research is written up.

Once results are obtained and plotted, we should be *more* critical, not less. Correlations do not imply causes. Every researcher is obliged to actively try to debunk their own hypothesis. (If you do not, be sure others will!) Try to think of alternate hypotheses that might explain your results. Do not assume that because you are interested in some underlying phenomenon, that a result that accords with your prediction is 'confirming' it!

The first step of your analysis should be to plot data with confidence intervals, so that you can get an idea of what might be going on. Examine example sentences in the corpus to ensure that you are capturing what you think you are. You must be confident your results are not merely an artifact of the way you designed your variables and queries.[6] Then, depending on the volume of data available, you can consider posing more specific questions and conducting more precise analyses.

In sum, understanding your data and getting the experimental design right is more important than picking the optimum test. Experimental research is cautious: to form robust conclusions we would rather make fewer assumptions and risk rejecting significant results that might be picked up with stronger tests. Statistics is a tool for understanding our data. It should not be rubber-stamping our prejudices.

Notes

1 There are five cases of 1, so the rank position for 1 is the mean, $R(1) = (1+2+3+4+5)/2 = 3$. There are also five cases of 2, so $R(2) = (6+7+8+9+10+11)/2 = 8$, and so on. We end up with a mapping $\mathbf{M} = [3, 8, 12.5, 16, 19]$, which we can use to replace every instance of 1 with 3, every instance of 2 with 8, and so on.

2 In Excel™, use 'TINV(α, *df*)' to calculate $t(\alpha/2, df)$. (Note that this is the two-tailed value.) A table is published at www.itl.nist.gov/div898/handbook/eda/section3/eda3672.htm. For large n, t tends to z, and $t(\alpha/2, df) \approx z_{\alpha/2)}$.

3 This formulation is sometimes called the *Welch Approximate Degrees of Freedom* (APDF) test (Ruxton, 2006).

4 In this book, we do not attempt to reproduce every single test. We have focused on contingency tests (and tests with one degree of freedom) because these are the most useful to linguists. If you are interested in further reading, surveys of standard statistical tests can be found in numerous experimental design and statistics textbooks. Chapter 1 in Oakes (1998) provides a useful (if rather rapid) summary of tests with practical corpus-based examples. If you can persevere with the algebra, Sheskin (2011) is recommended for a comprehensive review (a useful decision table is on pp. 140–146). Gries (2015) is an introduction to multilevel mixed effect models.

5 Thanks to the Wilson score interval, they are constrained within the probability range and are plausible. See Chapter 8. But they are undeniably wide, that is, uncertain.

6 To take one example, Wallis (2019b) considered whether evidence of a serially declining additive probability of embedding postmodifying clauses could be an artifact of annotators breaking the spoken corpus 'stream' into putative sentences before parsing. (Without punctuation, spoken 'sentences' must be identified by annotators.) This was addressed via linguistic argument: it was not possible to split the sentence at the relevant location without changing the utterance by adding words – which was forbidden by the descriptive orthographic transcription standard.

PART 4

Effect Sizes and Meta-Tests

13

THE SIZE OF AN EFFECT

13.1 Introduction

Significance tests may be considered as an assessment combining three elements:

1. a **statistical model of variation**, stating, for example, that observations are expected to be Normally distributed about a population mean P with standard deviation S;
2. an observed **effect size**, for example, the difference $d = p - P$; and
3. the **weight of evidence** supporting the observation, typically based on the sample size, n.

In Chapter 8, we saw two versions of a two-sample z test: the χ^2 homogeneity test and the Newcombe-Wilson independent sample test. These differ only in the first aspect. They have the same difference, $d = p_2 - p_1$ and sample sizes, n_1 and n_2.

In this chapter, we focus on the second aspect: *effect size*. Shorn of test machinery, they are descriptive measures of samples. They can be useful for visualisation and citation purposes. Effect sizes can also gain confidence intervals, allowing them to be used for significance testing or plotted with confidence.

The basic idea is that if two results are significant and therefore likely to represent a reproducible pattern, researchers should pay attention to the result with the larger size of effect. If an exercise regime is likely to have a greater benefit to a patient than a dietary change, which would you recommend?

In this chapter we will discuss two types of effect size: those concerned with two-variable tables, which we call 'independence effect sizes' in Section 13.2

DOI: 10.4324/9781003622697-17

and 13.3, and those concerned with the fit between two columns or rows of data ('goodness of fit effect sizes' in Section 13.4).[1]

13.2 Independence (Homogeneity) Effect Sizes

13.2.1 Simple Difference

Without knowing it, we have already been using an effect size measure for 2 × 2 tables: *simple difference* $d = p_2 - p_1$, which we plotted with confidence intervals in Chapter 7. (We also briefly considered the most commonly cited effect size measure, *percentage* difference, and discussed its disadvantages.)

Table 13.1 consists of two contingency tables, each statistically significant. Their χ^2 scores are similar, but $\mathbf{T}_1$ records a larger (negative) difference d than $\mathbf{T}_2$.

It is insufficient to cite numbers. To compare effect sizes properly, we need to turn the measure back into a significance test. We should apply the same statistical rigour to a comparison of effect sizes as we did to a comparison of proportions. It is rare to find significance tests for comparing effect sizes in the literature, but we will show how to compare tables like $\mathbf{T}_1$ and $\mathbf{T}_2$ in the next chapter.

Statisticians have occasionally proposed effect size measures alongside tests as a kind of 'descriptive analogue' of their test. But for contingency tables, many measures only apply to 2 × 2 tables and cannot be easily generalised to larger tables.

Simple difference d does not obtain a single score in tables of more than two rows or columns. For a larger table we would calculate different d scores for each pair of proportions. This is fine if our task is to analyse results as graphs, as in Chapter 7. But how might we obtain a single composite figure for larger tables with multiple degrees of freedom?

13.2.2 The Problem of Prediction

One way to think about bivariate effect sizes is as a 'prediction problem'. In a contingency test, we are interested in *whether knowing the value of one variable allows us to predict the value of the other.*

TABLE 13.1 Two 2 × 2 tables of illustrative data. $\mathbf{T}_1$: $\chi^2 = 10.67$, $d = -0.6667$. $\mathbf{T}_2$: $\chi^2 = 12.70$, $d = -0.3333$.

$\mathbf{T}_1$	*X Y*	y_1	y_2	*Total*	$\mathbf{T}_2$	*X Y*	y_1	y_2	*Total*
	x_1	10	2	12		x_1	20	10	30
	x_2	2	10	12		x_2	20	50	70
	Total	12	12	24		Total	40	60	100

$\mathbf{T}_1$ has a bigger difference in proportions between rows x_1 and x_2 than $\mathbf{T}_2$. The absolute size of its effect is greater: $|d_1| > |d_2|$.

TABLE 13.2 Two maximally dependent contingency tables, $\mathbf{T}_3$ ($n = 100$, $d = -1$), and $\mathbf{T}_4$.

$\mathbf{T}_3$	*X Y*	y_1	y_2	*Total*	$\mathbf{T}_4$	*X Y*	y_1	y_2	y_3	*Total*
	x_1	50	0	50		x_1	49	0	0	49
	x_2	0	50	50		x_2	0	1	0	1
	Total	50	50	100		x_3	0	0	50	50
						Total	49	1	50	100

Consider Table $\mathbf{T}_2$. If X is the dependent variable (DV), and Y the independent variable (IV), we wish to estimate the extent to which the value of $x \in X$ can be predicted if we know the value of $y \in Y$. Or, to put it another way, what is the 'level of support' for the predictive relationship $Y \rightarrow X$?

We might call this ideal measure the 'dependent probability' of X given Y, $dp(X, Y)$. We do not yet know what that ideal measure is or how it would be calculated, but we can make some general statements about it.

Suppose 100 instances in a sample were arranged as in $\mathbf{T}_3$ (Table 13.2). *In this sample*, the value of X completely depends on the value of Y. The dependent probability would be 1.

For any instance in this sample, the following must be true:

$Y = y_1 \rightarrow X = x_1$; and
$Y = y_2 \rightarrow X = x_2$.

Note that if Y predicts X absolutely, X also predicts Y. The inference is bidirectional.

Unlike simple difference, this reasoning extends to larger tables. $\mathbf{T}_4$ also uniquely maps values of Y to values of X (and vice versa). The actual non-zero cell frequencies are irrelevant. What matters is that all the data in every column and row falls in a single cell, so if Y has that column value (y_3, say), we can identify the value of X in the sample.

For tables with different numbers of columns and rows, if X had fewer values than Y, it would still be possible to predict X from Y with certainty. Some of the values of Y would have no data. Likewise, if X had more values than Y, to be predictable, some values of X must be empty.

13.2.3 Cramér's ϕ

Cramér's ϕ (Cramér, 1946) is a 'probabilistic intercorrelation' for contingency tables based on the χ^2 statistic.[2] An unsigned ϕ score is defined by

$$\textit{Cramér's } \phi \equiv \sqrt{\frac{\chi^2}{n(k-1)}}, \qquad (83)$$

where χ^2 is the $r \times c$ test for homogeneity (independence), n is the total frequency in the table, and k the minimum number of values of X and Y (i.e., $k = \min(r, c)$). For 2 × 2 tables, $k - 1 = 1$, so $\phi = \sqrt{\chi^2 / n}$ is often quoted.

This formula defines a neat relationship between χ^2, ϕ, n and k:

- The sample size n represents the weight of evidence. Dividing χ^2 by n factors out the weight of evidence, allowing tables with different amounts of supporting evidence to be compared.
- The constant k standardises tables with different numbers of rows and columns. The term $k - 1$ is the number of degrees of freedom along the diagonal.
- The square root translates a rescaled χ^2 (units of variance) to a score on the standard Normal scale, z (units of standard deviation).

In the case of $\mathbf{T}_2$ (Table 13.1), we obtain $\chi^2 = 12.70$, sample size $n = 100$, $k = \min(r, c) = 2$, so

$$\textit{Cramér's } \phi = \sqrt{12.7 / 100} = 0.3563.$$

An alternative formula for 2 × 2 tables labelled [[a, b], [c, d]] obtains a *signed* result, where a negative sign implies that the table tends towards the opposite diagonal:

$$\textit{signed } 2 \times 2\ \phi \equiv \frac{ad - bc}{\sqrt{(a+b)(c+d)(a+c)(b+d)}}. \qquad (84)$$

Equation (84) cannot be applied to larger tables.

Wallis (2012a) observes the following properties of ϕ:

1. **Limits.** ϕ has a value of 0 when there is no association between the values of X and Y, that is, when the probability of selecting a value of X is constant for any value of Y, and 1 when it corresponds to a 1:1 mapping. Like simple difference d, signed ϕ has a lower limit of −1 when the mapping between values is flipped.
2. **Interdependence.** ϕ measures *the linear interpolation* from a flat matrix **F** to an identity matrix **I** (see Table 13.3 for the idea). It is 'the best estimate of the population interdependent probability' $p(X \leftrightarrow Y)$. This intercorrelation is robust, and gracefully decays the further it deviates from this ideal. It is related to Pearson's product-moment coefficient r^2 in regression (see Chapter 10).[3]

TABLE 13.3 ϕ measures the degree by which a flat matrix **F** tends to an identity matrix **I**.[†]

$\phi = 0$	**F**	y_1	y_2	$\phi = p$	Φ	y_1	y_2	$\phi = 1$	**I**	y_1	y_2
	x_1	$^1/_2$	$^1/_2$		x_1	$^{(p+1)}/_2$	$^{(1-p)}/_2$		x_1	1	0
	x_2	$^1/_2$	$^1/_2$		x_2	$^{(1-p)}/_2$	$^{(p+1)}/_2$		x_2	0	1

[†] If we use Equation (84), ϕ may be negative. A score of $\phi = -1$ gives us the *backward* identity matrix $\mathbf{J} = [[0, 1], [1, 0]]$. Alternatively, ϕ might be thought of as representing the degree of 'flow of information' between Y and X or vice versa.

3. **Direction**. Dependent probabilities such as $p(x_1 \mid y_1)$ are directional. Interdependent probabilities are not. This is easy to see with Equation (83): $\chi^2(X, Y) = \chi^2(Y, X)$, so $\phi(X, Y) = \phi(Y, X)$. In fact, both formulae for ϕ are non-directional.

This reasoning concerns the sample, not the population from which it is drawn. Effect sizes without confidence intervals are descriptive statistics. If, *in the sample*, knowledge of the value of Y does not affect the chance of X having one value or another, the score is zero. Information does not 'pass through' the matrix. Alternatively, if knowledge about the value of X helps us predict the value of Y, the score should be other than zero. If it tells us the result definitively, the score is 1 (or possibly -1 in the case of signed 2×2 ϕ).

13.2.4 Other Independence Effect Sizes

Other potentially competing measures are proposed in the statistical literature. However, metrics are often developed independently and rarely compared.

Sheskin (2011, pp. 673–691) identifies Pearson's *contingency coefficient* C and C_{adj}, Yule's Q and *odds ratio* o as well as Cramér's ϕ. The odds ratio and Yule's Q are limited to 2×2 tables. The odds ratio is also not probabilistic (it is the proportion between two probabilities), although the logistic function (see Chapter 10) can be applied to it to obtain the probabilistic metric *log odds*. Wallis (2012a) discusses three effect sizes that may be applied to arbitrary-sized $r \times c$ tables: Cramér's ϕ, Pearson's C_{adj} and Bayesian dependency. He concludes that ϕ is the best-justified of these measures.

13.3 Confidence Intervals on Independence Effect Sizes

In Chapter 9, we introduced a general method for calculating confidence intervals on functions of Binomial proportions, which we can use to construct intervals on ϕ, just as we did for simple difference *d*. There are three situations where this might be useful.

1. **To plot or cite the measure with intervals.** The main purpose for calculating confidence intervals is to improve understanding of the reliability of graphs, as with simple difference *d*. See Chapter 7.
2. **To compare scores with thresholds.** We can test if the interval excludes zero, but the standard χ^2 test is simpler and just as effective. But we can also test intervals against other threshold scores.
3. **To compare tables for statistical separability.** We can carry out comparisons between observed scores, ϕ_1 and ϕ_2. Effect size measures for $r \times c$ tables collapse variation along multiple degrees of freedom to a single number. These tables can generate the same effect size score in more than one way, just as rectangles of different dimensions can have the same area.

Next, we discuss an experiment where we compare ϕ scores. We will return to the question of comparing contingency tables in the next chapter.

13.3.1 Confidence Intervals on 2 × 2 ϕ

Wallis (2012a) proves that for signed 2 × 2 ϕ (Equation (84)), the following equivalence holds:

$$\phi(X, Y)^2 \equiv d_x \times d_y, \tag{85}$$

where d_x represents the difference in proportions of y_1 on the *x* axis, $d_x = p(y_1 \mid x_2) - p(y_1 \mid x_1)$ and d_y is the corresponding difference on the *y* axis, $p(x_1 \mid y_2) - p(x_1 \mid y_1)$. ϕ has the absolute value of the *geometric mean* of d_x and d_y.

These differences are positively *monotonically* related (see Chapter 9). If d_x increases, so must d_y, and vice-versa. On the other hand, ϕ and d_x (and ϕ and d_y) are negatively monotonically related.

In Chapter 9 we discovered that a monotonic transformation of an interval is lossless. Equation (85) helps us derive confidence intervals for ϕ from difference intervals.[4]

First, we calculate Newcombe-Wilson intervals across each axis using the difference interval function (Chapter 9).

$$d_x \in (d_x^-, d_x^+) = \textbf{difference}(p(y_1 \mid x_2), p(y_1 \mid x_1)), \text{ and}$$

$$d_y \in (d_y^-, d_y^+) = \textbf{difference}(p(x_1 \mid y_2), p(x_1 \mid y_1)).$$

Equation (85) holds for ϕ and d, but *also for their interval bounds*. We can create a new interval $\phi \in (\phi^-, \phi^+)$ applying this geometric mean rule:

$$\phi^- = \begin{cases} -\text{sign}(d_x^+)\sqrt{d_x^+ \times d_y^+} & \text{if } d_x^+ \times d_y^+ \geq 0 \\ 0 & \text{otherwise} \end{cases}, \text{ and}$$

$$\phi^+ = \begin{cases} -\text{sign}(d_x^-)\sqrt{d_x^- \times d_y^-} & \text{if } d_x^- \times d_y^- \geq 0 \\ 0 & \text{otherwise} \end{cases}, \tag{86}$$

where '$-\text{sign}(d_x^+)$' (etc.) reinstates the sign of ϕ.[5] Since ϕ is negatively monotonic with d_x and d_y, we negate and swap bounds.

This method is easily adapted to include continuity corrections, finite population corrections, and so on. A ϕ interval derived from Newcombe-Wilson intervals (with or without continuity correction) is constrained within ± 1. See Figure 13.1.[6]

13.3.2 Confidence Intervals on $r \times c$ ϕ

The previous method is limited to 2×2 tables. For a more general solution, we may employ the following *best estimate of the population variance* of ϕ for $r \times c$ tables:

$$S^2(\phi) \approx \frac{1}{4\phi^2 n(k-1)} \left\{ 4\sum_{ij} \frac{p_{i,j}^{\,3}}{p_{i+}^2 p_{+j}^2} - 3\sum_i \frac{1}{p_{i+}} \left(\sum_j \frac{p_{i,j}^{\,2}}{p_{i+}p_{+j}} \right)^2 \right.$$
$$- 3\sum_j \frac{1}{p_{+j}} \left(\sum_i \frac{p_{i,j}^{\,2}}{p_{i+}p_{+j}} \right)^2 \tag{87}$$
$$\left. + 2\sum_{ij} \left[\frac{p_{i,j}}{p_{i+}p_{+j}} \left(\sum_k \frac{p_{k,j}^{\,2}}{p_{k+}p_{+j}} \right) \left(\sum_l \frac{p_{i,l}^{\,2}}{p_{i+}p_{+l}} \right) \right] \right\}, \text{for } \phi \neq 0$$

where $p_{i,j} = f_{i,j} / n$ (n is the total frequency for the entire table) and p_{i+}, p_{+j}, (etc.) represent row and column (prior) probabilities (Bishop et al., 1975, p. 386).[7]

We compute a confidence interval by search (see Appendix A). We find (ϕ^-, ϕ^+) by a process that populates a contingency table from ϕ scores (via a version of Table 13.3, see Wallis, 2020c) and we then search for bounds:

$$\phi^- \text{ where } \phi = \phi^- + z_{\alpha/2}.S(\phi^-), \text{ and}$$
$$\phi^+ \text{ where } \phi = \phi^+ - z_{\alpha/2}.S(\phi^+). \tag{88}$$

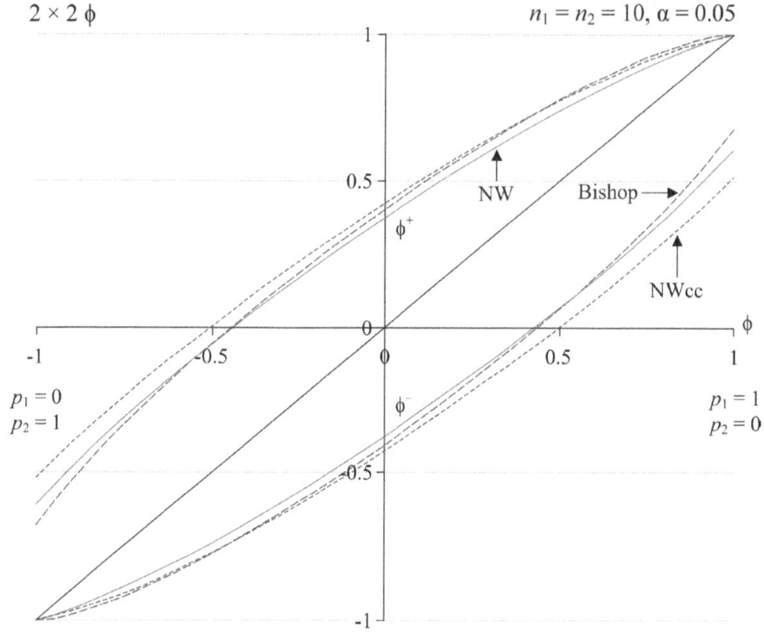

FIGURE 13.1 Newcombe-Wilson and inverted Bishop intervals for 2 × 2 ϕ plotted across the diagonal of a matrix, from $p_1 = 0$ to 1, $p_2 = 1 - p_1$, $n_1 = n_2 =$ 10 and $\alpha = 0.05$.

The disadvantages of this method are that it requires a search procedure, and it is not easily corrected for continuity. With multiple degrees of freedom, there are several ways one can obtain a particular ϕ score, making a search more complicated.

Figure 13.1 plots the performance of these methods for ϕ scores over 2 × 2 tables where $n_1 = n_2 = 10$, across the diagonal of a matrix permuted $p_1 = 0$ to 1, with $p_2 = 1 - p_1$, alongside intervals calculated with Equation (86). Both methods are 'well-behaved' and obtain comparable scores within the range [−1, 1]. Inverting Bishop's standard deviation estimate yields a slightly more 'distal' (less central) interval.

13.3.3 Example: Investigating Grammatical Priming

Figure 13.3 plots the results of an investigation into grammatical priming in ICE-GB, evaluating the effect of Binomial choice interaction measured with 2 × 2 ϕ.

Priming research evaluates whether a choice made by a speaker at one point, which we will call D, affects a second choice at a later point in the same passage,

G. Consider the tendency to reuse a grammatical construction already employed in the same sentence. Event D appears before G in the sentence. Although 'priming' is usually considered in relation to acts of different speakers, the paradigm may also be used to investigate any pair of choices in the same passage, including in the same sentence. Note that although event D precedes G in the sentence, we cannot assume word order is a guide to decision order: G might prime D *in anticipation*, or they might have an idiomatic connection.

Next, we select a linguistic alternation to extract cases from ICE-GB. What we want to know is whether the decision about this choice is 'communicated' from one point to another in the sentence. For the sake of illustration, we will select the relative/non-finite clausal alternation, where either construction could postmodify the same noun phrase head (underlined):

(47) <u>people</u> [*living in France*] (non-finite)
~ <u>people</u> [*who/that/which live in France*] (relative)

This alternation is relatively 'free'. Referential meaning does not change, and either option seems possible at each point. It is also common. ICE-GB contains hundreds of cases with multiple opportunities in the same utterance.

D and G have a shared ancestor node, C. See Figure 13.2. Suppose we are interested in evidence of coordination affecting priming. We will divide the data into two sets by the coordination status of C.

In Examples (48) and (49), C coordinates D and G. Alternatively, C will be a regular phrase or clause, as in (50):

(48) You don't have a single <u>photoreceptor</u> [$_{\text{CL(coordn)}}$ [*going to a single bipolar cell*] [*going to a single photoreceptor*]] $_{\text{[S1B-015 \#153]}}$
(49) For inside the final furlong it's [$_{\text{NP(coordn)}}$ [$_{\text{NP}}$ <u>Filial</u> [*striding clear*]] *and* [$_{\text{NP}}$ <u>Mack the Knife</u> [*trying to raise his gait*]] $_{\text{[S2A-006 \#201]}}$
(50) [$_{\text{CL}}$ Uhm <u>the movement language</u> [*that's being developed*] is <u>one</u> [*which involves different people with different skills*]] $_{\text{[S1A-001 \#39]}}$

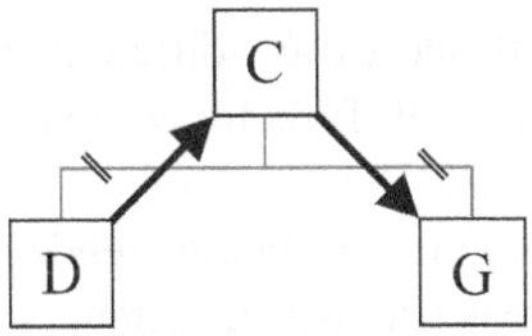

FIGURE 13.2 The transmission model of within-sentence priming. The idea is that a choice made at point D is 'transmitted' to a choice point G via a common ancestor C. In this example, we calculate the distance between D and G by counting the intermediate nodes between D and C and between C and G.

TABLE 13.4 Contingency table for priming between coordinated postmodifying clauses at one level up, one down, like Example (48). Inspect the diagonal cells (bold): 73 out of 85 relative clauses at D are repeated at G, 12 not. Similarly, 38 out of 52 relative clauses are repeated. The 2 × 2 ϕ score is 0.5943 ∈ (0.4329, 0.7107), using Newcombe-Wilson intervals in Equation (86) and $\alpha = 0.05$.†

D *G*	*relative*	*non-finite*	*Total*
relative	**73**	12	85
non-finite	14	**38**	52
Total	87	50	137

† Solving for Bishop et al.'s formula (Equation (87)) obtains the smaller interval (0.4447, 0.7104).

Second, we measure *total path length* λ in parent-child links from D to C and C to G. Where sentences have more than two instances, we evaluate each combination of node pairs once.

Like the additive probability experiment (Wallis, 2019b), this experimental design partly depends on the *particular* grammatical scheme – here, the Quirk-based phrase structure analysis of ICE-GB. It relies on the plausibility of 'grammatical path length' but is more revealing as a result. (From a research perspective, employing auxiliary assumptions is permissible provided you state them clearly. See Chapters 1 and 2.)

Partitioning data in this way (coordinated vs. non-coordinated ancestors; by distance between D and G), we obtain a series of 2 × 2 frequency tables like Table 13.4. We compute ϕ with confidence intervals for each table with Equation (86), and plot Figure 13.3. ϕ is positive when speakers tend to repeat their choice, and negative if they tend to *avoid* repeating themselves. $\phi = 0$ means 'independent', and ± 1 means 'completely determined'.

In Figure 13.3, at path length $\lambda = 0$, non-coordinated clauses modify the same NP head. This negative ϕ score is not significantly different from zero ($\chi^2 = 3.2740$). Mean ϕ scores are also shown. Overall, coordination tends to obtain a higher ϕ score (the mean scores on the left are significantly different). Only at $\lambda = 2$ (one up, one down) does it obtain a significantly greater result *at the same distance*.

The Wilson interval comparison heuristic (see Chapter 7) allows us a quick assessment. We can test if scores are different by simply evaluating if 0 ∈ **difference**(ϕ_2, ϕ_1). See Chapter 9. Tests for comparing tables are discussed in the next chapter.

Even-numbered intervals for coordination tend to be significantly greater than zero. This may be due to patterns where distances D-C and C-G are equal, but we have not tested this.

With a nod to Newton (1730), we term this paradigm a 'linguistic interaction transmission experiment' (LITE). Crucially, ϕ measures the mean *transmission of information* ('priming', repetition, etc.) between choice points.

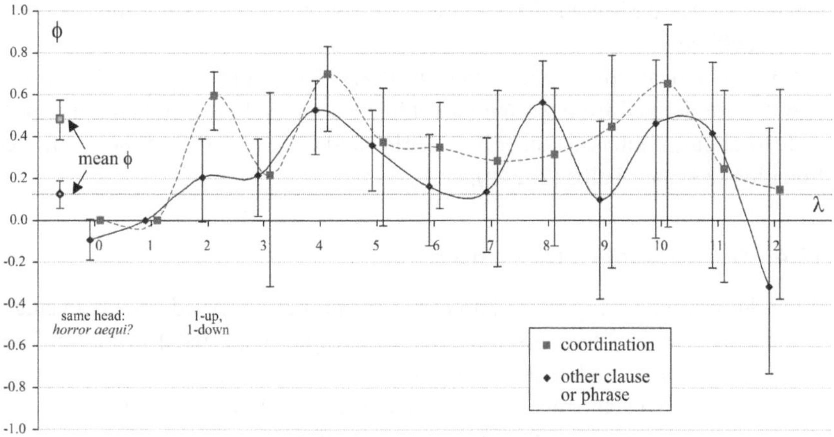

FIGURE 13.3 Plotting the association between two related decisions $\phi(G, D)$ over path length λ. Almost all are positive, that is, there is a tendency to reuse rather than avoid the same construction. Uncertainty is indicated by translated 2×2 Newcombe-Wilson intervals and $\alpha = 0.05$.

The idea of ϕ and similar effect size measures can be very abstract, but in a priming context the concept of 'transmission strength' is effective.

13.3.4 Confidence Intervals on Other Effect Sizes

In Chapter 9 we created an interval for the *risk ratio*, $r \in (r^-, r^+) = \mathbf{ratio}(p_1, p_2)$. We used this to obtain an interval for the *odds ratio* using the function $\text{odds}(p) = p / (1 - p)$:

$$\textit{odds ratio } o \in (o^-, o^+) = \mathbf{ratio}(\text{odds}(p_1), \text{odds}(p_2)). \tag{58}$$

The odds ratio is the basis for another, well-known effect size, *Yule's Q* (Sheskin, 2011, p. 679). To obtain a confidence interval for Q we may employ another monotonic transformation function, $\text{Q}(o) = (o - 1)/(o + 1)$ to the odds ratio bounds:

$$Q \in (\text{Q}(o^-), \text{Q}(o^+)). \tag{89}$$

Q is sometimes seen as a competitor to ϕ. However, it does not have the same equal interdependence property as ϕ. (Yule proposed a variant metric, Y, that does, see Wallis, 2024c). But it has another, less obvious problem. The interval has zero width where $p_1 = 0$ and $p_2 = 1$, and vice versa. At these extremes, the measure cannot be used to decide whether something is or is not significant. See

Chapter 9. David Sheskin also comments that it 'employs less information' than the ϕ coefficient.

Some classical effect sizes, such as Pearson's C and C_{adj} (Sheskin, 2011, p. 675), are derived from χ^2. With a confidence interval for ϕ in hand, it is possible to calculate intervals for χ^2 by squaring and weighting ($\chi^2 = \phi^2\, n(k-1)$). See Equation (83) and Wallis (2024d).

13.4 Goodness of Fit Effect Sizes

A goodness of fit $r \times 1$ χ^2 test (Chapter 8) compares an observed column (a single variable distribution) from a sample of size n with an expected distribution from some other source, such as the equiprobable set $\mathbf{E} = \{n/r, n/r \ldots\}$. It might be used to evaluate whether a subset differs in its distribution from a superset. Does the subset have a significantly different distribution?

In Chapter 8, we saw that the simplest 2×1 test has only two cells. It can be expressed as a z test comparing a difference in observed and expected proportions, $d = p - P$, generalised to a χ^2 test with r cells and $r - 1$ degrees of freedom. With more than one degree of freedom, a single difference d is insufficient. We need a new effect size measure.

This kind of score is not often discussed in the statistical literature, but it can be useful. Wallis (2012b) reviews multiple potential candidate metrics before arriving at the two we briefly document in this section.

Like d, each method scores 0 for a close fit and 1 for divergence, that is, they are 'error scores'. (Pearson's r^2 *coefficient of determination* is quoted as '1 – error'. See Chapter 10.)

To motivate what follows, and to give us some example data, let us consider a real research problem. Bowie et al. (2013) discuss whether the present perfect construction is more properly considered a type of 'present' or 'past' construction.[8]

These constructions appear to bridge the past with the present, for example:

(51) He*'s developed* a sort of a you know a language [S1B-008 #47]
(52) Oh I*'ve written* poetry all my life yes [S1B-048 #2]

The present perfect expresses a kind of continuous relationship between present and past events. In Example (51), the 'development' and in (52), the 'writing', occurred in the past. But the action is potentially still taking place in the present.

Bowie et al. wondered whether these constructions were more common in passages that are more present- or past-referring. This is not an *alternation* question (see Chapter 3). It concerns the extent to which distributions correlate with two different baseline sets ('present' and 'past'). Nor is the present perfect necessarily a subset of both categories.

TABLE 13.5 Distribution of present perfect forms by source corpus, DCPSE. Observed frequency o, proportion p, with 95% Wilson intervals and expected probabilities for present and past tense verb forms, P, $n = 5{,}784$.

	o	p	w^-	w^+	P(present)	P(past)
LLC	2,488	0.4799	0.4664	0.4935	0.4913	0.4456
ICE-GB	2,696	0.5201	0.5065	0.5336	0.5087	0.5546

Using DCPSE (see Chapter 1), they performed a goodness of fit evaluation with two different baseline sets ('present' and 'past', inclusive of their present perfect data). They obtained a smaller ϕ score (a closer fit), that is, a closer correlation for the present tense baseline than the past across the independent variable 'source corpora' (LLC, '1960s' vs. ICE-GB '1990s' data). But they were unable to calculate confidence intervals, so it was not possible to compare scores for significant difference.[9]

Table 13.5 summarises their data, to which we have added 95% Wilson score intervals. We will compare these two target distributions.

13.4.1 Unweighted ϕ_p

The first measure Wallis (2012b) recommends is ϕ_p, which is the *root mean square difference* between an observed series of proportions $\{p_i\}$ and an expected one $\{P_i\}$. It derives from an adjustment to χ^2 that weights each term by the prior chance of selection P_i, hence 'probabilistically weighted'. As this re-weighting cancels out e_i, it may be better thought of as an unweighted metric like the error employed in OLS regression (see Chapter 10):

$$\textit{unweighted}\ \phi_p = \sqrt{\tfrac{1}{2}\sum d_i^2} = \sqrt{\frac{\sum(p_i - P_i)^2}{2}} = \sqrt{\sum\frac{(o_i - e_i)^2}{2n^2}}. \qquad (90)$$

The properties of ϕ_p can be summarised as:

- **Robustness.** Expected proportions P_i or cell values e_i can be 0. However, unlike methods derived from standard χ^2, it does not weight terms by variance.
- **Mutuality.** For a pair of distributions $\mathbf{O}_1$, $\mathbf{O}_2$ with r cells, $\phi_p(\mathbf{O}_1, \mathbf{O}_2) = \phi_p(\mathbf{O}_2, \mathbf{O}_1)$. $\mathbf{O}_1$ need not be a subset of $\mathbf{O}_2$ or vice versa.
- **Convergence.** Where $r = 2$, $\phi_p = |\,d\,|$.

We might say ϕ_p is a *mutual goodness of fit* measure expressed over a discrete variable, rather than a *subset fit* of a distribution to a baseline. (We will see a subset measure in Section 13.4.3.)

Using the data in Table 13.5, we obtain *d*(present) = 0.4799 − 0.4962 = −0.0162 and *d*(past) = 0.4799 − 0.4513 = 0.0287. These have the same absolute value as equivalent ϕ_p scores.[10]

13.4.2 Confidence Intervals on ϕ_p

Signed ϕ_p is equal to difference $d = p_1 - P_1$. A Binomial interval is extremely simple to calculate. Recall from Chapter 9 that P_1 is 'given' (it is invariant and has no interval of its own).

$$signed\ \phi_p = d = p_1 - P_1 \in (w_1^- - P_1, w_1^+ - P_1). \tag{91}$$

Using data in Table 13.5, this gives us intervals for *d*(present) = −0.0162 ∈ (−0.0298, −0.0026) and *d*(past) = 0.0287 ∈ (0.0151, 0.0423). Both exclude zero and are individually significant. The intervals do not overlap, so they must also be significantly different from each other.

Since the *d* interval is negative, *unsigned* ϕ_p(present) = 0.0162 ∈ (0.0026, 0.0298). This overlaps with the interval for ϕ_p(past). We could test their difference with Zou and Donner's generalised difference interval function. We check whether the resulting interval includes zero:

$$\phi_p(\text{past}) - \phi_p(\text{present}) \in \textbf{difference}(\phi_p(\text{past}), \phi_p(\text{present})) = (-0.0067, 0.0317).$$

The unsigned formula has lost information. Now we cannot reject the null hypothesis that scores are equal.

This result was for the LLC/ICE-GB contrast. To draw robust conclusions about the present perfect we should carry out evaluations over several variables, including Multinomial ones. Consider Table 13.6, which enumerates data for the ten *text categories* in DCPSE.

TABLE 13.6 Distribution of present perfect verb forms over DCPSE text categories, with 95% Wilson bounds and the equivalent distributions of present and past tense verbs.

	o	*p*	w^-	w^+	*P*(present)	*P*(past)
formal face-to-face	679	0.1174	0.1094	0.1259	0.1047	0.0985
informal face-to-face	2,502	0.4326	0.4199	0.4454	0.4878	0.4924
telephone conversations	349	0.0603	0.0545	0.0668	0.0580	0.0498
broadcast discussions	628	0.1086	0.1008	0.1169	0.1098	0.0836
broadcast interviews	267	0.0462	0.0410	0.0519	0.0377	0.0698
spontaneous commentary	611	0.1056	0.0980	0.1138	0.1026	0.0563
parliamentary language	173	0.0299	0.0258	0.0346	0.0215	0.0176
legal cross-examination	20	0.0035	0.0022	0.0053	0.0062	0.0203
assorted spontaneous	93	0.0161	0.0131	0.0197	0.0207	0.0270
prepared speech	462	0.0799	0.0732	0.0871	0.0511	0.0847

Where $r > 2$, we obtain an unsigned score. A Multinomial confidence interval for ϕ_p^2 may be calculated by the three-step method we introduced in Chapter 9.

First, we define a function for each term in the sum in Equation (90). We will call this our 'squared difference' function, or 'sqd':

$$\text{sqd}(p_i) = (p_i - P_i)^2/2. \tag{92}$$

This function is non-monotonic, with a minimum where $p_i = P_i$.

Next, we calculate $\text{sqd}(w_i^-)$ and $\text{sqd}(w_i^+)$ for each p_i. Because the function is non-monotonic, we must examine transformed intervals. The transformed bounds, $\text{sqd}(p_i) \in (d_i^-, d_i^+)$, depend on the relationship between the score interval and P_i.

$$(d_i^-, d_i^+) = \begin{cases} (\text{sqd}(w_i^-), \text{sqd}(w_i^+)) & \text{if } w_i^- > P_i, \\ (\text{sqd}(w_i^+), \text{sqd}(w_i^-)) & \text{if } w_i^+ < P_i, \\ [0, \max(\text{sqd}(w_i^-), \text{sqd}(w_i^+))) & \text{otherwise.} \end{cases} \tag{93}$$

This interval includes the lower bound, $d_i^- = 0$, if the score interval includes P_i.

The third step applies the Multinomial sum formula. We obtain bounds for the squared effect size ϕ_p^2 by summing interval widths, adjusted for $r - 1$ degrees of freedom:

$$\phi_p^2 \in (\phi_p^{2-}, \phi_p^{2+}) = (\phi_p^2 - \sqrt{\kappa \sum (\text{sqd}(p_i) - d_i^-)^2},\ \phi_p^2 + \sqrt{\kappa \sum (d_i^+ - \text{sqd}(p_i))^2}). \tag{94}$$

where $\kappa = r/(r - 1)$.

We are almost there. We take the square root of these bounds to obtain a confidence interval for unsigned $|\phi_p|$. This interval is sound but conservative, because Equation (92) is 'lossy' and the interval (d_i^-, d_i^+) can fold back on itself. See Chapter 9.

Let's compute the ϕ_p(present) score and intervals for the text category data. We apply the 'sqd' transform to each term (Table 13.7). Our data for formal face-to-face conversations produce an increasing monotonic transformation over the Wilson interval range, whereas informal face-to-face data yield a decreasing one. The score interval for telephone conversations includes P_i, so we strike out the lower bound and replace it with zero. We repeat for all ten categories, identifying bounds (d_i^-, d_i^+) as we go.

TABLE 13.7 Computing intervals for sqd(p_i) for present verb forms, with 95% confidence intervals for each summed term. Right: '0' includes minimum ($d_i^- = 0$, overruled bound), '›' increasing, '‹' decreasing. Bold: selected upper bound d_i^+

	P	sqd(p)	sqd(w^-)	sqd(w^+)	
formal face-to-face	0.1047	0.000080	0.000011	**0.000225**	›
informal face-to-face	0.4878	0.001526	**0.002310**	0.000901	‹
telephone conversations	0.0580	0.000003	~~0.000006~~	**0.000039**	0 ›
broadcast discussions	0.1098	0.000001	**0.000040**	~~0.000025~~	0 ‹
broadcast interviews	0.0377	0.000036	0.000006	**0.000101**	›
spontaneous commentary	0.1026	0.000005	~~0.000011~~	**0.000063**	0 ›
parliamentary language	0.0215	0.000036	0.000009	**0.000086**	›
legal cross-examination	0.0062	0.000004	**0.000008**	0.000000	‹
assorted spontaneous	0.0207	0.000011	**0.000029**	0.000001	‹
prepared speech	0.0511	0.000415	0.000244	**0.000651**	›
ϕ_p^2		0.002116			

Having identified transformed bounds for each text category term, we are ready to apply the Multinomial sum formula. The weighted lower bound interval width sum is

$$\sqrt{\kappa \sum(\text{sqd}(p_i) - d_i^-)^2} = 0.000689,$$

and the equivalent upper bound is 0.000884. Equation (94) yields an interval for $\phi_p^2 = 0.002116 \in (0.001427, 0.003000)$, to which we apply the square root.

This method obtains non-overlapping 95% intervals. Scores are significantly different.

$$\phi_p(\text{present}) = 0.0460 \in (0.0378, 0.0548),$$

$$\phi_p(\text{past}) = 0.0642 \in (0.0572, 0.0720).$$

Repeating the same exercise over the 280 separate texts in DCPSE also reveals a significantly closer fit (lower score) for the present tense baseline compared to the past.

$$\phi_p(\text{present}) = 0.0184 \in (0.0174, 0.0207),$$

$$\phi_p(\text{past}) = 0.0298 \in (0.0288, 0.0315).$$

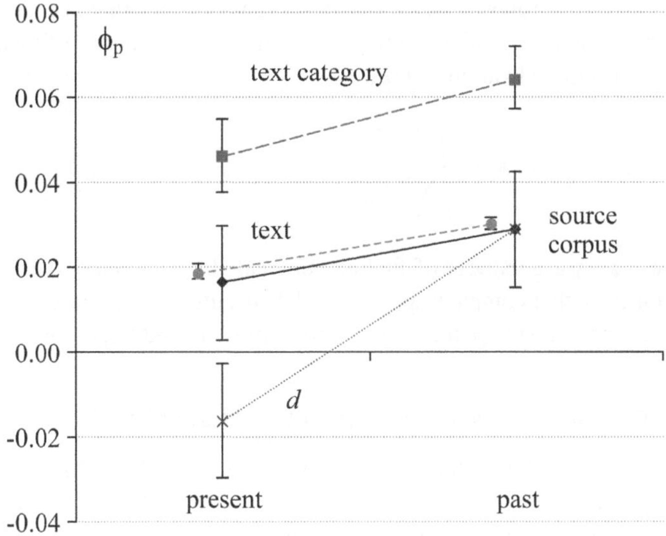

FIGURE 13.4 Root mean square fit ϕ_p with 95% confidence intervals comparing present perfect verbs in DCPSE against 'present' and 'past' oriented baselines over three different categorical variables: Binomial source corpus ($r = 2$), Multinomial text category (10) and text (280). For $r = 2$, signed difference d may be employed. Sample size $n = 6{,}942$. More categories means more information, tending to produce smaller confidence intervals.

These comparisons are plotted in Figure 13.4. As r increases, we gain information and intervals become smaller.

Note how the actual scores might change when different variables (source corpus, text category or text) are used to obtain the categorical distribution. The chosen variable is part of the 'fitness' model. This fact does not invalidate comparisons over the same variable, but comparing ϕ_p scores between different variables is unlikely to be meaningful.

13.4.3 Variance-Weighted ϕ_e

The disadvantage of ϕ_p is it is unweighted by variance or sample size. Look again at the first column in Table 13.6. We have much more data in the informal face-to-face conversations text category (2,502 present perfect examples) than legal cross-examinations (only 20). Although this difference in quantity is factored into the *interval* calculation, it is not accounted for by the metric itself.

Wallis (2012b) proposed two variance-weighted scores that account for this. The simpler one is ϕ_e, which employs a standard χ^2 goodness of fit calculation divided by a summed variance term:

$$\textit{variance-weighted } \phi_e = \sqrt{\frac{\chi^2}{\sum \frac{1}{e_i} n^2}}. \tag{95}$$

Unlike ϕ_p, ϕ_e is a goodness of fit function scaled by variance. It is a 'proper subset' function that compares an observed distribution with a baseline superset. Our present perfect subset should be in both 'present' and 'past' supersets.

13.4.4 Confidence Intervals on ϕ_e (and Goodness of Fit χ^2)

We will create an interval for $r \times 1$ goodness of fit χ^2 and use this to create one for ϕ_e. Equations (93) and (94) can produce confidence intervals for goodness of fit χ^2. We redefine our squared difference function, 'sqd':

$$\text{sqd}(p_i) = n(p_i - P_i)^2/P_i, \tag{92'}$$

where sample size n and expected proportions $\{P_i\}$ are invariant. As with χ^2, if an expected score in any cell is zero, $P_i = 0$, we discount that category and r decreases by 1.

We repeat step two, applying Equation (94) and, finally, create an interval for goodness of fit χ^2:

$$\chi^2 \in (\chi^{2-}, \chi^{2+}) = (\chi^2 - \sqrt{\kappa \sum(\text{sqd}(p_i) - d_i^-)^2}, \; \chi^2 + \sqrt{\kappa \sum(d_i^+ - \text{sqd}(p_i))^2}). \tag{94'}$$

Now we are ready to obtain an interval for ϕ_e. Equation (95) is a monotonic function which divides χ^2 by a constant term before taking the square root, so we apply it to both bounds.

Wallis (2012b) found ϕ_e tended to fall with increasing categories r, so comparisons between tables of substantially different sizes risks being misleading. If in doubt, consider using ϕ_p!

In Figure 13.5, we repeat our examination of the correlation of present perfect verbs, this time using ϕ_e. Note how, with $r = 280$, we have a small ϕ_e score, although the two observations are deemed significantly different.

Both ϕ_p and ϕ_e have their virtues: ϕ_p is robust for comparing independent distributions, whereas ϕ_e is preferred for a more standard subset goodness of fit comparison where only the subset is expected to vary.

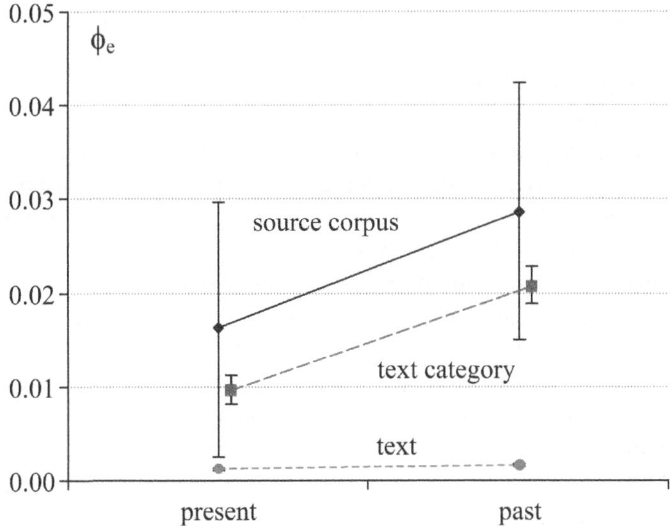

FIGURE 13.5 Evaluating the same present perfect data from DCPSE with variance-weighted goodness of fit ϕ_e. The absolute value of ϕ_e is more sensitive than ϕ_p to the number of categories r across which the evaluation is conducted. See also Figure 13.4.

13.5 Conclusions

Linguistic variables are commonly Binomial proportions, expressing the probability that in a random case drawn from a sample we might find a particular linguistic phenomenon. The same concepts of proportion and probability extend to Multinomial cases where choices are one of several possibilities.

However, sometimes we are interested in effect sizes derived from whole tables, such as the difference between proportions. In this chapter, we considered two types of effect size. The first reflected the degree to which a Binomial or Multinomial variable *reliably predicts* another. In this case, we are not concerned with actual proportions of variables, but *the degree to which outcomes coincide*. An objective measure of this kind can detect patterns of co-occurrence: interaction evidence that can be extremely important in linguistic research.

Cramér's ϕ is a measure of interdependence. It measures the bidirectional association IV ↔ DV. Arguments about direction may be based on a linguistic processing model: the statistical method does not address this.

This measure is well-documented in the statistical literature, and estimates of variance have been developed. We showed how the Newcombe-Wilson interval may be used to derive an accurate interval for 2×2 ϕ. For $r \times c$ ϕ, we can employ Bishop's formula in a search procedure, although this is more difficult.

We applied this score in a priming experiment, where it measured the 'transmission of information' between two binary choice points in the same sentence. A similar experimental design may be used where one speaker primes another, or where a speaker primes themselves in the same passage.

For in-sentence priming, parse analysis allowed us to define 'grammatical distance', whereas conventionally we could only count words or measure time. We showed that a simple grammatical alternation had a greater priming effect within coordinated structures than other types.

Although effect sizes are not commonly discussed in this context, it is also valid to measure categorical correlations or 'fit'. We discussed two measures, unweighted mutual fit ϕ_p, and variance-weighted subset fit ϕ_e. These are similar to the line fitting estimates of r^2 we discussed in Chapter 10. ϕ_e is a scaled goodness of fit χ^2, whereas Cramér's ϕ is a scaled homogeneity χ^2 score.

We showed how it was possible to create confidence intervals for both measures, allowing us to plot scores with intervals, compare scores against threshold values other than zero, and compare scores between tables.

In passing, we noted that ϕ_e scores declined as the number of categories, k, increased, which meant that two tables of substantially different sizes were difficult to compare. Although this is a drawback, we would caution against making claims comparing tables of different sizes.

In practice, since any difference between how tables are sampled allows alternative hypotheses (see Chapter 2), you should minimise other sources of variation across the comparison. In our priming experiment, not only were all tables of the same size (2×2), they were populated by the same variables, arranged identically. Their cell frequency counts were obtained under different conditions. This allows us to claim that ϕ 'is the same variable' in each case.

Cramér's ϕ and interval is robust for low frequency provided no row or column total is zero (any single cell may be zero). Similarly, whereas it is legitimate to delete columns where the expected score was zero from a large goodness of fit table, our advice would be to avoid comparing ϕ_e tables of different sizes and use unweighted ϕ_p instead.

Notes

1 There is a further class of effect size, one which aggregates a score from a single column or row of data, without a fitness comparison. One example of this type of metric is *entropy*, see Chapter 9. Another is *diversity* (Aarts & Wallis, 2014).

2 The metric is occasionally referred to as Cramér's V, although ϕ is now commonly used. Indeed, the first reference was to f. Harald Cramér (1946, p. 443) commented that $f^2 = \chi^2 / N$ and $0 \leq f^2/(k-1) \leq 1$, 'thus $\chi^2 / N(k-1)$ may be regarded as a measure of the degree of association indicated by the sample'.

3 ϕ is in fact a *root mean square* measure of the orthogonal 'distance' from a maximally dependent matrix.

4 See also Wallis (2019c).

5 We check for the rare but possible case where one bound is negative and the other positive. In this case $d_x^+ \times d_y^+$ (say) will be negative and the square root uncomputable. As an alternative to 0, we may substitute the negated arithmetic mean, $-(d_x^+ + d_y^+)/2$.
6 A worked example using Newcombe-Wilson intervals is given in Table 14.7, p. 335.
7 If $\phi = 0$, we must adjust the table by a small delta.
8 Bowie et al. observed that some cases analysed as present perfect *got* with an NP object had a stative meaning, such as *Well, he's got two kids for one thing* (DI-B63 #124). They employed an FTF to find cases in each category and subtracted them from totals.
9 They employed a goodness of fit ϕ' measure which Wallis (2012b) improved on, but the same principle applies.
10 For example, $\phi_p(\text{present}) = \sqrt{((0.4799 - 0.4913)^2 + (0.5201 - 0.5807)^2)/2} = \sqrt{(0.0114^2 + 0.0114^2)/2} = 0.0114$.

14

META-TESTS FOR COMPARING TABLES OF RESULTS

14.1 Introduction

Researchers often wish to compare results of experiments.[1] When we carry out research, it is rarely sufficient to note that a difference is significant. We frequently want to know whether our results are consistent with previous research. There are two main motivations for these evaluations: to compare different *experimental designs* and different *data*.

We might compare different versions of the same experiment to see if a change to the experimental design obtains a significantly different result. We could investigate the effect of modifying an experimental design on reported results. As we have discussed, empirical evidence is not the same as a deductive argument, so we should be careful.

For example, in Chapter 1, we reported on an experiment (Wallis, 2019b) where we examined changes in the probability of applying a construction rule as it was repeated multiple times. To compare patterns obtained by different rules, we need to compare results from separate evaluations. Using the same data, we could compare, for example, whether a decline observed for speech was distinct from the equivalent gradient for writing.

Another motivation for this kind of evaluation arises when we wish to compare results of the same experiment with different data. One use case concerns the *replication problem* introduced in Chapter 11. To recap, if we misanalyse data, replicated samples will not behave the way the underlying mathematical model predicts. Were we to replicate the experiment, we may get significantly different results. This could be due to a number of reasons, including undocumented sampling variation, unstated assumptions or different baselines.

DOI: 10.4324/9781003622697-18

A method for statistically comparing results, which we will term assessing *statistical separability*, allows us to define a 'failure to replicate' on a mathematically sound basis.

> **Replication failure** occurs when subsequent repetitions of the same experiment obtain *statistically separable* results on more occasions than that predicted by the error level, α, used for the experimental test.

Similarly, we can report that one experimental design is statistically separable from another with the same data, and that a change in the design makes a detectable difference to the results.

Consider Table 14.1, taken from Aarts et al. (2013). It summarises data from two independent studies into modal *shall* versus *will* alternation, presented as two contingency tables.

The upper table is compiled by the authors from spoken data drawn from DCPSE. The lower table is from a study by Mair and Leech (2006) that uses written data from the *Lancaster-Oslo-Bergen* (LOB) corpus and the matching *Freiburg-Lancaster-Oslo-Bergen* (FLOB) corpus. Both pairs of subcorpora are sampled over a similar time contrast, with the earlier subcorpora collected in the 1960s and the later in the 1990s.

LOB and FLOB contain one million words each. DCPSE has less than one million words in total. Methods for comparing tables must cope with different sample sizes.

The 2 × 2 tests for each table are both individually significant (χ^2 = 36.58 and 35.65, respectively). However, the tables that generated these scores appear distinct. Consider the effect size measures ϕ and $d^{\%}$. These are numerically

TABLE 14.1 A pair of 2 × 2 χ^2 tables for changing *shall/will* alternation in British English, reproduced from Aarts et al. (2013): upper, spoken; lower, written (with other experimental design differences).

spoken	*shall*	*will*	*Total*	χ^2(*shall*)	χ^2(*will*)	
LLC (1960s)	**124**	**501**	625	**15.28**	2.49	$d^{\%}$ = −60.70% ±19.67%†
ICE-GB (1990s)	**46**	**544**	590	**16.18**	2.63	ϕ = 0.17
Total	170	1,045	1,215	**31.46**	**5.12**	χ^2 = **36.58 s**
written	*shall+*	*will+ 'll*	*Total*	χ^2(*shall+*)	χ^2(*will+ 'll*)	
LOB (1960s)	**355**	**2,798**	3,153	**15.58**	1.57	$d^{\%}$ = −39.23% ±12.88%†
FLOB (1990s)	**200**	**2,723**	2,923	**16.81**	1.69	ϕ = 0.08
Total	555	5,521	6,076	**32.40**	3.26	χ^2 = **35.65 s**

† Figures in the original. Recalculating percentage difference intervals with Equation (64) in Chapter 9 obtains $d\%$ = −60.70% ∈ (−46.07%, −71.44%) and $d\%$ = −39.23% ∈ (−28.29%, −48.52%) respectively.

different. *How might we test if these tables are significantly different from each other?*

Let us visualise our data. Figure 14.1 plots Table 14.1 as two Binomial proportion difference graphs. Binomial proportions, $p = f / n$, are plotted with Wilson score intervals at a 95% confidence level.

We can employ the Wilson interval comparison heuristic (see Chapter 7). Where Wilson intervals do not overlap at all (e.g., LLC vs. LOB, marked '**A**') the difference must be significant; where they overlap such that one point is within the other's interval (FLOB vs. ICE-GB), the difference is non-significant; otherwise, a test must be applied.

In this chapter, we discuss two different analytical comparisons.

A. **Point tests** compare pairs of observations ('points') across the dependent variable, DV (e.g., *shall/will*), and tables. To do this, we compare pairs of points and intervals. We can employ the interval comparison heuristic and, if necessary, carry out a 2 × 2 χ^2 test for homogeneity or a Newcombe-Wilson test (Chapter 8) to compare points. We can compare the initial 1960s data (LLC vs. LOB, indicated) in the same way as we might compare spoken 1960s and 1990s data (e.g., LLC vs. ICE-GB).
B. **Gradient tests** compare differences in 'sizes of effect' (e.g., a change in the ratio *shall/will* over time) between tables. We might ask, is the gradient (rate

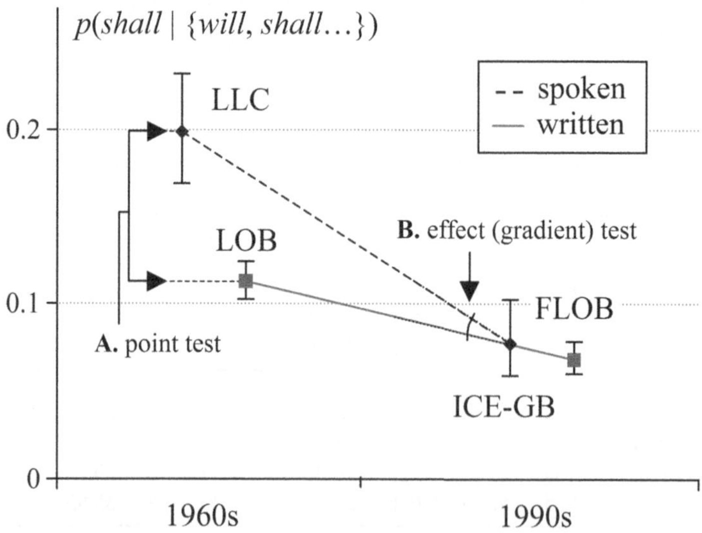

FIGURE 14.1 Example data in Table 14.1, plotted with 95% Wilson score intervals. Points are separated horizontally for clarity.

of change) *significantly steeper* for the spoken data than for the written data? These tests are not commonly discussed in the literature.

Note that these tests evaluate different hypotheses and can have different outcomes. If plot lines are parallel, a gradient test will be non-significant (the gradients are not significantly different), but a point test could still be significant at each pair of points. These tests are complementary analytical tools.

14.1.1 How Not to Compare Test Results

A common, but thoroughly mistaken, approach to comparing experimental results involves quoting the output of significance tests (Goldacre, 2011). Researchers frequently make claims citing t, F or χ^2 scores, 'p values' (error levels), and so on, as evidence for the 'strength of results'. However, this reasoning fundamentally misinterprets the meaning of these measures, and comparisons between such scores are not legitimate.

Consider Table 14.2, which depicts two sub-tables, $\mathbf{T}_1$ and $\mathbf{T}_2$. A moment's glance reveals that $\mathbf{T}_1$ contains exactly ten times the data of $\mathbf{T}_2$, but the data are distributed identically and the gradient is the same. Computing the 2 × 2 χ^2 test for homogeneity (Chapter 2), $\mathbf{T}_1$ is significant (α is very small), whereas $\mathbf{T}_2$, with exactly the same distribution and gradient, is non-significant.

Despite the low error level α, it is incorrect to refer to $\mathbf{T}_1$ as 'highly significant'. χ^2 and α are estimates of the *reliability* of results (the predicted rate of experimental replication), not the *scale* of results.

Similarly, a higher χ^2 score or smaller α does *not* mean that results can be *statistically separated*, that is, that tables of observed data can be said to be significantly different from each other at a given error level.

This type of erroneous reasoning is widespread, and crops up in other ways than comparisons of 'p values' (α error levels) or test scores. A survey of 513 published neuroscience papers in five top-ranking journals (Nieuwenhuis et al., 2011) found that, of those papers that compared results of experiments, almost exactly half asserted that two results were significantly different because one experiment detected a significant effect (cf. $\mathbf{T}_1$) and the other did not ($\mathbf{T}_2$).

TABLE 14.2 Some illustrative data with the results of χ^2 tests for homogeneity in both cases.

$\mathbf{T}_1$	*X Y*	y_1	y_2	*Total*	$\mathbf{T}_2$	*X Y*	y_1	y_2	*Total*
	x_1	290	110	400		x_1	29	11	40
	x_2	220	200	420		x_2	22	20	42
	Total	510	310	820		Total	51	31	82
	$\chi^2 = 35.27$		$\alpha \approx 0.0000$			$\chi^2 = 3.53$		$\alpha = 0.0604$	

14.1.2 Comparing Sizes of Effect

In the last chapter, we introduced 'effect size' statistics. These summarise tables, vectors, etc. as a single score. Unlike test scores, they factor out the quantity of data observed, and so could, in principle, be employed for comparison purposes.

A good example is Cramér's ϕ, based on a two-variable χ^2 test for independence, rescaled by sample size n, which we met in the last chapter. For a 2 × 2 table with cell frequencies [[a, b], [c, d]], a signed score may be computed with Equation (84), ranging from [−1, 1]:

$$\textit{signed } 2 \times 2\ \phi \equiv \frac{ad - bc}{\sqrt{(a+b)(c+d)(a+c)(b+d)}}. \tag{84}$$

With larger $r \times c$ tables, the unsigned score, Equation (83), may be used, where k is the number of cells along the shorter side, that is, min(r, c):

$$\textit{Cramér's } |\phi| \equiv \sqrt{\frac{\chi^2}{n(k-1)}}, \tag{83}$$

Both $\mathbf{T}_1$ and $\mathbf{T}_2$ obtain exactly the same score, $\phi = 0.2074$.

Effect size metrics adjust for the volume of data and measure the pattern of change (the 'gradient') observed. However, traditionally, effect sizes were discussed in surprisingly crude terms, for example, 'small', 'medium' and 'large' effect sizes (see, e.g., Sheskin, 2011, p. 678), and comparisons were limited. This is obviously unsatisfactory.

In the previous chapter we learned that we could calculate confidence intervals on effect sizes. This permits a new type of test evaluating whether effect sizes from experimental 'runs' significantly differ. We provide an example in Section 14.4.3. However, this method has an important weakness (or 'aspect', if you prefer). This concerns *degrees of freedom*.

An effect size summarises variation in a table. If that table has multiple degrees of freedom, independent differences on multiple axes are reduced to a single score in one dimension. If we then compare effect sizes, we will evaluate less information than were we to evaluate these differences independently, just as comparing areas of rectangles does not compare their length or width. For larger tables, such a test will be less sensitive (and more conservative) than one that compares distributions independently.[2]

14.1.3 Other Meta-Tests

The tests we describe here represent the building blocks for 'meta-analysis': they provide a method for comparing experimental results.

Other researchers have proposed tests for comparing experimental runs. The McNemar test (Sheskin, 2011, p. 835) translates cross-tabulated scores to a χ^2 test; Cochran's Q test (2011, p. 1119) generalises this to multiple scores. However, these do not perform the tasks discussed here. The closest method is *heterogeneity analysis* (Zar, 2010, pp. 474, 504), but this is not comprehensive, and in some cases, not robust.

In this chapter, we discuss tests for comparing contingency tables, the primary focus of this book. There is a comparable procedure for comparing multiple runs of *t* tests (or ANOVAs), the 'between-subjects factorial analysis of variance' (Sheskin, 2011, pp. 1139–1140) where one of the factors represents the repeated run.

This chapter is structured as follows: following some preliminaries, in Section 14.3 we introduce the 'point test' and 'multi-point test' for comparing the distribution of data across a dependent variable in homogeneity tables. Section 14.4 introduces 'gradient test' methods for comparing sizes of effect in homogeneity tables, commencing with intervals and tests with a single degree of freedom. It considers a test for Cramér's ϕ effect sizes, and closes with formulae for generalising tests to compare larger tables ($r \times c$ homogeneity tables).

Section 14.5 introduces meta-tests for comparing goodness of fit test results. In Section 14.6 we discuss versions of tests to be used when one table is a subset of another, and Section 14.7 is the conclusion.[3]

14.2 Some Preliminaries

14.2.1 Test Assumptions

All meta-tests in this chapter aim to compare pairs of test results for significant difference from each other ('separability'). These tests build on standard contingency tests, so we first require that these tests have been competently carried out, dependent variables are free to vary and samples are randomly obtained. Tests are expected to conform to a Binomial or Multinomial model of contingent variation. See Chapter 8.

In comparing experimental runs or designs, we further assume that both dependent and independent variables are *matched*, but are not necessarily identical, that is, both tables measure the same quantities by different definitions, methods or samples.

For example, Table 14.1 contains two sets of results that differ in at least two ways: data are drawn from different corpora and a different set of queries were employed. Bas Aarts and his colleagues considered a series of intermediate experimental design changes to identify precisely the point at which a significant difference in results arose. They could then determine whether a difference was due to differences in *data* (speech vs. writing) or *experimental design* (queries). It turned out to be the latter.

Three broad classes of test are summarised in Figure 14.2:

1. comparing goodness of fit tests ('separability of fit');
2. comparing observed proportions (point tests evaluating 'separability of observations'); and
3. comparing homogeneity gradients/patterns ('separability of independence').

We will start by focusing on 2 × 2 and 2 × 1 tests because they have one degree of freedom, so significant differences in size of effect may be explained by a single factor. They also have the advantage of being easy to visualise (as in Figure 14.1).

We will then explain how these tests may be generalised to evaluating larger tables. That said, as we saw in Chapter 7, frequently it is good analytical practice for such tables – which have many degrees of freedom and multiple potential axes of variation – to be subdivided into smaller tables to identify areas of significant difference each with a single degree of freedom. The simplest tests may have the greatest utility.

14.2.2 Correcting for Continuity

The meta-tests discussed in this chapter build on the analysis of Chapter 8. Some simple tests – the point test, for example – may be implemented by repurposing a conventional test.

We advise employing the same statistical model corrections one would normally employ for a standard test. Continuity corrections and finite population

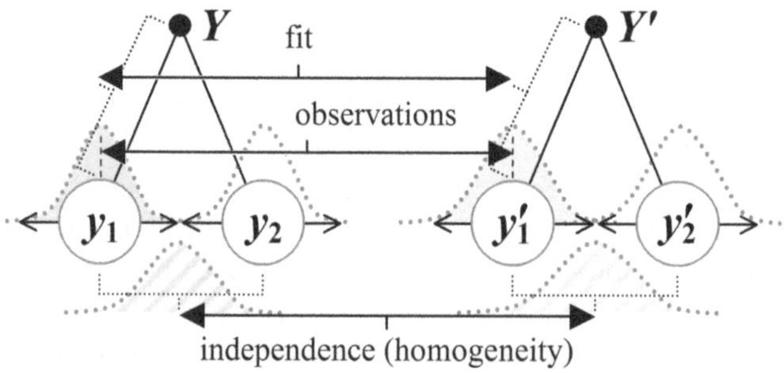

FIGURE 14.2 Visualising separability tests across data subdivisions identified by an independent variable Y. From top: separability of fit compares the fit of y_1 to Y with y_1' to Y'; separability of observations (the 'point test') compares data points y_1 and y_1'; separability of independence compares a homogeneity test for y_1 and y_2 with one for y_1' and y_2'.

corrections are noted in Chapter 8. A correction for random-text sampling, discussed in Chapter 16, may also be applied.

Continuity correction is a little different from the other two adjustments, which modify the variance. It involves introducing a correction term into the formula in the direction of the tested difference.

In the statistical literature, continuity corrections are rarely employed in more complex evaluations, including meta-testing. However, given that continuity corrections improve individual test precision, albeit conservatively, this reasoning appears mistaken. Indeed, if your original tests applied a continuity correction, it makes sense for a meta-test to do likewise.

In this chapter, we employ a method of test generalisation over multiple degrees of freedom using Pearson's χ^2. This creates a new problem with continuity correction.

Yates's $r \times c$ test for independence (see Chapter 8) is commonly expressed as follows:

$$Yates\text{'s } \chi^2 \equiv \sum_{i=1,j=1}^{r,c} \frac{(|o_{i,j} - e_{i,j}| - 0.5)^2}{e_{i,j}}. \tag{35}$$

This subtracts the continuity correction term, 0.5, from absolute differences $|o_{i,j} - e_{i,j}|$. But it can obtain an anomalous result where $|o_{i,j} - e_{i,j}| < 0.5$. Yates's ostensibly more conservative χ^2 score can exceed the standard χ^2 score! In conventional tests, this is immaterial. Such a result will not exceed the critical value of χ^2 for a typical error level such as $\alpha = 0.05$.

However, in this chapter, we use χ^2 to sum *independent* difference terms, and we should be more careful. A zero difference at any point should return zero. See Section 14.4.3.

We employ the following 'DiffCorrect' function. This has two properties: difference $d = 0$ if d is within the range $\pm c$, and the sign of the difference is preserved otherwise:

$$\text{DiffCorrect}(d, c) \equiv \begin{cases} d - c & \text{if } d > c \\ d + c & \text{if } d < -c \\ 0 & \text{otherwise} \end{cases}. \tag{96}$$

We then rewrite Yates's χ^2 as the following. For conventional tests this is not strictly necessary, but serves as an illustration:

$$modified\ Yates\text{'s } \chi^2 \equiv \sum_{i=1,j=1}^{r,c} \frac{(\text{DiffCorrect}(o_{i,j} - e_{i,j}, 0.5))^2}{e_{i,j}}. \tag{35'}$$

TABLE 14.3 Table 14.1, revisited, with notation. The first index refers to the table.

spoken	*shall*	*will*	*Total*	*written*	*shall*	*will*	*Total*
1960s	$f_{1,1,1} = \mathbf{124}$	$f_{1,1,2} = \mathbf{501}$	$n_{1,1} = 625$		$f_{2,1,1} = \mathbf{355}$	$f_{2,1,2} = \mathbf{2{,}798}$	$n_{2,1} = 3{,}153$
1990s	**46**	**544**	590		**200**	**2,723**	2,923
Total	$f_{1,+,1} = 170$	$f_{1,+,2} = 1{,}045$	$n_{1,+} = 1{,}215$		$f_{2,+,1} = 555$	$f_{2,+,2} = 5{,}521$	$n_{2,+} = 6{,}076$

14.2.3 Example Data and Notation

We will use the data in Table 14.1 to exemplify what follows, but first we will introduce some notation. Each table contains a dependent variable X (rows: modal *shall* vs. *will*) and an independent variable Y (columns: time period). In Table 14.3, we reproduce this data with relevant terms. We have three indices identifying a cell: h, representing the table, and i and j representing rows and columns, respectively.

The first column represents frequencies of *shall*. The Binomial DV proportion for *shall*, *p*(*shall* | {*shall*, *will*}) varies by row and sub-table (see Figure 14.1). For row i in table h, $p_{h,i} \equiv f_{h,i,1}/n_{h,i}$. For example, $p_{1,1} = 124/625 = 0.1984$. We will also employ the '+' index notation first seen in Chapter 2 for column totals, so, for example, $n_{1,+}$ represents the total number of cells in the first table, and $f_{1,+,2}$ is the sum of $f_{1,1,2}$ and $f_{1,2,2}$.

Finally, we need to select an error level. In the calculations that follow, we will use a constant error level $\alpha = 0.05$. When applying multiple tests, researchers are often advised to divide the error level α by the number of independent tests to be carried out. We do not do this here for reasons of simplicity.

14.3 Point and Multi-Point Tests for Homogeneity Tables

These tests evaluate tables for the separability of their observations, point by point. The idea may be summarised by Figure 14.3.

The first set of tests compare pairs of *cell proportions* between two tables.

14.3.1 Reorganising Contingency Tables for 2 × 1 Tests

Some methods can be performed very simply by reorganising existing data tables and using the tests we have already seen in Chapter 8. For example, if two independent proportions were plotted with Wilson score intervals, we can compare them using a Newcombe-Wilson difference test, irrespective of whether the proportions were drawn from the same table.

Consider, by way of illustration, the 1960s data in Figure 14.1, drawn from *the first row* in each sub-table in Table 14.3. We arrange data to create a new 2 × 2

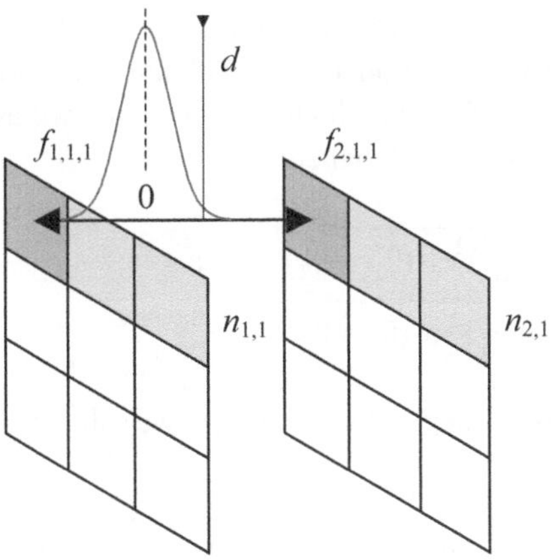

FIGURE 14.3 Carrying out a point test to compare two matching cell proportions $p_{h,i} = f_{h,i,j}/n_{h,i}$ in two tables. We calculate Binomial proportions for each cell and perform a z or Newcombe-Wilson test. In a multi-point test, tests are aggregated across the table by χ^2 summation.

TABLE 14.4 A contingency table for row 1 in Table 14.3 used to carry out a point test.

1960s	*shall*	*will*	*Total*	*p(shall)*
spoken	$f_{1,1,1} = \mathbf{124}$	$f_{1,1,2} = \mathbf{501}$	$n_{1,1} = 625$	0.1984
written	$f_{2,1,1} = \mathbf{355}$	$f_{2,1,2} = \mathbf{2,798}$	$n_{2,1} = 3,153$	0.1126
Total	479	3,299	3,778	0.1268

contingency table, DV × table (Table 14.4). For what follows, we ignore the rest of the table. A separate point test may be carried out for 1990s data (i.e., for other values of the IV).

14.3.2 The Newcombe-Wilson Point Test

We obtain proportions $p_{1,1} = 0.1984$ and $p_{2,1} = 0.1126$ (column *p*(*shall*)), whose difference, *d*, is −0.0858. We test if the difference is significant with a Newcombe-Wilson interval about zero, $(w_d^-, w_d^+) = (-0.0316, 0.0372)$ by Equation (25) (see Chapter 7), which we may test for *d* exceeding.

Newcombe-Wilson test:

$$\text{If } w_d^- < p_2 - p_1 < w_d^+, \text{ there is no significant difference between } p_1 \text{ and } p_2. \quad (26)$$

Alternatively, we may subtract this interval from *d* and check if zero is found in the resulting range, (d^-, d^+).

In Chapter 9 we generalised Newcombe's method to a 'MOVER' interval between any two properties. Equation (55) obtains a confidence interval about a general difference, $d_\theta = \theta_1 - \theta_2$, which may be expressed as an interval function $d_\theta \in$ **difference**$(\theta_1, \theta_2) = (d_\theta^-, d_\theta^+)$ where

$$d_\theta^- = d_\theta - \sqrt{(\theta_1 - \theta_1^-)^2 + (\theta_2^+ - \theta_2)^2}, \text{ and}$$
$$d_\theta^+ = d_\theta + \sqrt{(\theta_1^+ - \theta_1)^2 + (\theta_2 - \theta_2^-)^2}. \quad (55)$$

To create Newcombe's interval for $d = p_2 - p_1$, we substitute $\theta_1 = p_2$ with its interval $(\theta_1^-, \theta_1^+) = (w_2^-, w_2^+)$, and $\theta_2 = p_1$ with its interval $(\theta_2^-, \theta_2^+) = (w_1^-, w_1^+)$. We may calculate interval bounds with the score interval: $(w_i^-, w_i^+) =$ (WilsonLower(p_i, n_i, $\alpha/2$), WilsonUpper(p_i, n_i, $\alpha/2$)) for $i = \{1, 2\}$ creates a Wilson-based difference interval without an adjustment for continuity.[4]

At $\alpha = 0.05$, we obtain $d = -0.0858 \in (-0.1230, -0.0543)$. This interval excludes zero and the difference is significant. Substituting continuity-corrected Wilson intervals for p_1 and p_2 into this test (see Chapter 8) obtains $d = -0.0858 \in (d^-, d^+) = (-0.1214, -0.0535)$, which is also significantly different from zero.

14.3.3 The Gaussian Point Test

The z test for independent proportions or 2×2 χ^2 test performs a similar evaluation. See Chapter 8. These tests assume that both observations are Normally distributed about an intermediate pooled probability estimate, and we can compute a standard deviation using Equation (42). If proportions are significantly different, then the null hypothesis that they are drawn from the same population is rejected.

The estimated population mean is the pooled probability estimate $\hat{p} = f / n$, where f is the total frequency for the row, and n the total sample size, $n_1 + n_2$:

$$\textit{standard deviation } S_d \equiv \sqrt{\hat{p}(1-\hat{p})\left(\tfrac{1}{n_1}+\tfrac{1}{n_2}\right)}. \quad (42)$$

In this case (see the bottom row in Table 14.4), $\hat{p} = 0.1268$ and the standard deviation $S_d = 0.0146$. The Gaussian error $e_d = z_{\alpha/2} . S_d = 0.0286$ obtains an interval $(-0.0286, 0.0286)$ that $d = -0.0858$ exceeds. Again, a continuity correction may be applied to this interval.

Two-proportion z test:

If $-e_d < p_2 - p_1 < e_d$ there is no significant difference between p_1 and p_2. (43)

The standard χ^2 test formula may also be used to carry out the same evaluation (Equation (1), Chapter 2).[5] The point test is carried out by drawing data from the first row of Table 14.5, i.e. **O** = [[124, 501], [355, 2798]], each row of the new table being drawn from different tables.

In the independence (homogeneity) test, expected cells are calculated from row and column totals, $e_{i,j} = (o_{i+} \times o_{+j}) / n$ (Equation (2)), so **E** ≈ [[79, 546], [400, 2753]] (rounded to integers).

The test obtains $\chi^2 = 34.6906$, which exceeds the critical value for one degree of freedom (3.8415).

Chi-square test:

If $\chi^2 < \chi^2(\alpha, df)$, there is no significant difference between table rows. (33)

By extending *i* and *j*, Pearson's χ^2 can be generalised to multiple values of the DV (e.g., a four-way choice {*shall, will, 'll,* BE *going to* (present)}, see Chapter 3) and multiple *tables*.

14.3.4 The Multi-Point Test for r × c Homogeneity Tables

So far, we have simply compared two 'points' (proportions or cells), one from each table. We can also compare an ordered series of points. The Gaussian 'point test' test may be generalised to a 'multi-point test' across all values of the IV by the following simple summation. Suppose the dependent variable is Binomial (a proportion or rate), and the independent variable is Multinomial (e.g., a series of time periods).

We generalise χ^2 by summing scores over the IV:

$$\textit{multi-point}\ \chi^2_{\text{mp}} = \sum_{i=1}^{r} \chi^2(i), \qquad (97)$$

where $\chi^2(i)$ represents the χ^2 point test score for homogeneity for each set of data at position IV = *i* in the distribution. The test has $r \times df(i)$ degrees of freedom, where $df(i)$ is the number of degrees of freedom for each distinct χ^2 score.

χ^2 is generally associative (bidirectional), but χ^2_{mp} is not. The multi-point test factors out variation between summed tables – so if there are a lot more data in one table in a particular time period, say, this does not impact on other expected cell values. But it does not factor out variation over the DV, because this is precisely what we wish to examine.

In brief, the calculation is applied over the dependent variable and table, and summed over the independent variable (here 'time').

Table 14.5 shows the computation for the data in Table 14.3, $\chi^2_{\text{mp}} = 35.3772$. The critical value for χ^2 where $\alpha = 0.05$ and $df = 2$ is 5.9915, which this sum comfortably exceeds.

Since the computation sums independently-calculated χ^2 scores, each may be individually considered for significant difference. We might note the large score for the 1960s data (individually significant) and the small one for 1990s (individually non-significant).[6]

Applying a continuity correction with Equation (35') yields $\chi^2_{mp} = 34.4677$.

This χ^2 method may be extended to Multinomial DVs, for example, X = {*shall*, *will*, BE *going to*} and multiple experimental runs. For DVs with c values over t runs, we create a series of homogeneity tests for $c \times t$ tables and sum them.

Although we lose information, aggregation of this kind may be useful in replication studies. In this application we are less interested in particular differences than if the overall result seems to be different.

14.4 Gradient Tests for Homogeneity Tables

So far, we have compared tables on a point-by-point or proportion-by-proportion basis. This might tell us that *tables* are different, but it does not tell us whether *evidence of change or difference* differs, a concept we generally refer to as differences in 'gradient' or size of effect.

In this section we consider 'separability of independence': whether a difference, effect size or correlation between one variable and another differs between pairs of tables. See Figure 14.4.

TABLE 14.5 Applying a multi-point test to Table 14.1. $\chi^2_{mp} = 35.3772$ is significant with two degrees of freedom and $\alpha = 0.05$.

	shall	*will*	*Total*	*shall*	*will*	*Total*	p_1	p_2	$\hat{p}$	S^2	χ^2
1960s	**124**	**501**	625	**355**	**2798**	3153	0.1984	0.1126	0.1268	0.0002	**34.6906**
1990s	**46**	**544**	590	**200**	**2723**	2923	0.0780	0.0684	0.0700	0.0001	0.6865
Total	170	1045	1215	555	5521	6076					**35.3772**

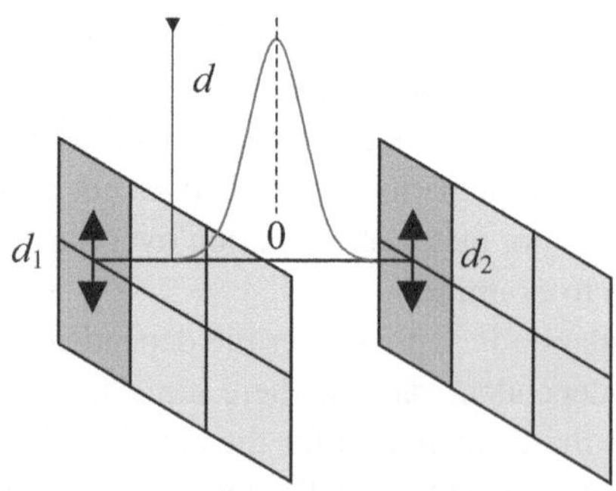

FIGURE 14.4 Carrying out a gradient test to compare differences in proportions, d_1 and d_2, between two tables. In this chapter, we consider tables where one side has two cells, so differences are straightforward to compute.

TABLE 14.6 Table 14.1 revisited to calculate differences in differences, d_1 and d_2.

	shall	*will*	*Total*	*p(shall)*	*shall*	*will*	*Total*	*p(shall)*
1960s	**124**	**501**	625	0.1984	**355**	**2,798**	3,153	0.1126
1990s	**46**	**544**	590	0.0780	**200**	**2,723**	2,923	0.0684
Total	170	1,045	1,215	$d_1 = -0.1204$	555	5,521	6,076	$d_2 = -0.0442$

Suppose we calculate two differences in proportions, d_1 and d_2, which for our example data are $d_1 = -0.1204 = (0.0780 - 0.1984)$ and $d_2 = -0.0442 = (0.0684 - 0.1126)$. See Table 14.6. Differences are negative because both slopes are declining.

These differences represent the gradient decline in Figure 14.1, hence d_1 appears to be a steeper gradient than d_2. But is it significantly steeper? By subtraction, we obtain the *difference of differences*, $d = d_2 - d_1 = 0.0763$. See Figure 14.5.

14.4.1 The 2 × 2 Newcombe-Wilson Gradient Test

Earlier we reminded ourselves of the 'MOVER' method (Chapter 9), at the heart of which is a general difference interval function **difference**(θ_1, θ_2) (Equation (55)).

We can use this to calculate the interval for the difference of differences, $d = d_2 - d_1 \in$ **difference**(d_2, d_1), with Newcombe-Wilson difference intervals for d_1 and d_2, and carry out a generalised difference test.

First, let's calculate intervals for $d_1 = -0.1204$ and $d_2 = -0.0442$. Without continuity correction, 95% confidence intervals are $d_1 = -0.1204 \in (-0.1586, -0.0822)$ and $d_2 = -0.0442 \in (-0.0585, -0.0298)$. Both represent individually significant falls. But are they significantly different from each other?

We compute the difference of differences, $d = d_2 - d_1 = -0.0442 + 0.1204 = 0.0763$. Substituting into Equation (55), we then create a confidence interval for d.

$$d^- = d - \sqrt{(d_1^+ - d_1)^2 + (d_2 - d_2^-)^2} = 0.0763 - \sqrt{0.0382^2 + 0.0144^2} = 0.0354,$$

$$d^+ = d + \sqrt{(d_1 - d_1^-)^2 + (d_2^+ - d_2)^2} = 0.0763 + \sqrt{0.0381^2 + 0.0144^2} = 0.1170.$$

The interval $d \in (0.0354, 0.1170)$ excludes zero and is therefore significantly different from it. See Figure 14.5.

Applying a correction for continuity gives us the following intervals:

$$d_1 = -0.1204 \in (-0.1597, -0.0810), \text{ and } d_2 = -0.0442 \in (-0.0588, -0.0296).$$

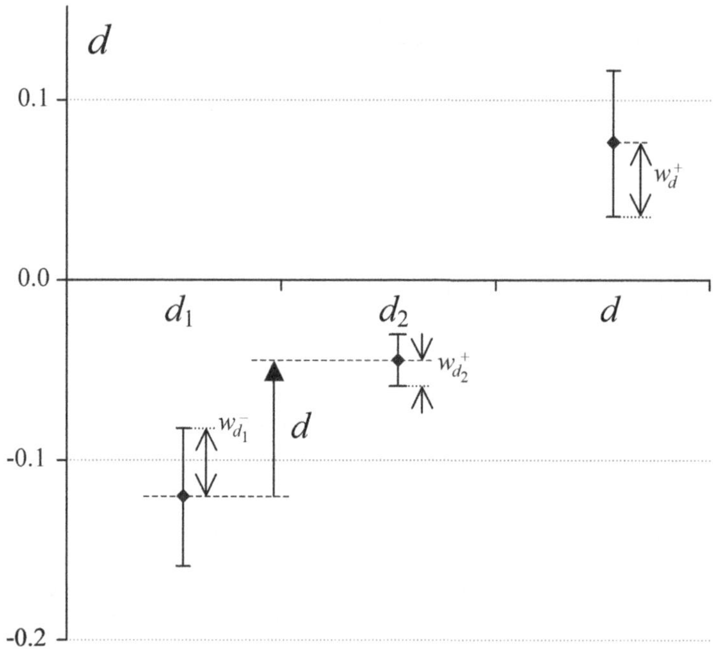

FIGURE 14.5 Newcombe-Wilson difference intervals centred on d_1, d_2 and $d = d_2 - d_1$. d_1 and d_2 are negative, but their difference, d, is positive. All are clearly significantly different from zero.

The resulting interval is $d \in (0.0342, 0.1181)$, which is also significantly different from zero.

14.4.2 Cramér's ϕ Interval and Difference Test

Difference d is a simple effect size. In Chapter 13, we calculated confidence intervals on Cramér's ϕ, an alternative measure. The method described in this section might be replicated for any effect size score with a good quality confidence interval, such as Yule's Q.

For signed 2 × 2 ϕ, this method is closely comparable to the Wilson-based gradient test we have just discussed, thanks to the strict relationship between ϕ and d and its single degree of freedom.

Signed 2 × 2 ϕ captures positive and negative change, and ranges from −1 to +1:

$$\phi \equiv \frac{ad - bc}{\sqrt{(a+b)(c+d)(a+c)(b+d)}} = \frac{f_1(n_2 - f_2) - f_2(n_1 - f_1)}{\sqrt{n_1 n_2 f(n - f)}}. \quad (84')$$

The second formula adopts the notation in Table 14.3, discarding index h for clarity. Using our contingency tables, this formula obtains $\phi_1 = 0.1735$ and $\phi_2 = 0.0766$. Their difference $\phi_2 - \phi_1 = -0.0969$. Since $\phi \in [-1 \text{ to } 1]$, differences in ϕ scores can range from −2 to +2.

In the previous chapter, we introduced two methods for calculating confidence intervals on ϕ. For a signed 2 × 2 ϕ score, Equation (86) may be used:

$$\phi^- = \begin{cases} -\text{sign}(d_x^+)\sqrt{d_x^+ \times d_y^+} & \text{if } d_x^+ \times d_y^+ \geq 0 \\ 0 & \text{otherwise} \end{cases}, \text{ and}$$

$$\phi^+ = \begin{cases} -\text{sign}(d_x^-)\sqrt{d_x^- \times d_y^-} & \text{if } d_x^- \times d_y^- \geq 0 \\ 0 & \text{otherwise} \end{cases}, \tag{86}$$

where (d_x^-, d_x^+) is the interval for the difference in proportions of y_1 out of Y on the x axis, d_x. See Chapter 13.

Table 14.7 provides a step-by-step breakdown of the calculation for the first data table for ϕ_1. Then, applying Equation (86), we calculate the following:

$$\phi_1 = 0.1735 \in (0.1191, 0.2246), \text{ and}$$

$$\phi_2 = 0.0766 \in (0.0518, 0.1009).$$

The Wilson interval comparison heuristic applies. Since the intervals for ϕ_1 and ϕ_2 do not overlap, they must be significantly different.

For completeness, we will perform the full test. The confidence interval for $d_\phi = \phi_2 - \phi_1 = -0.0969 \in$ **difference**$(\phi_2, \phi_1) = (-0.1537, -0.0373)$. It excludes zero, so ϕ_2 and ϕ_1 are significantly different.

We may also compare ϕ scores from larger tables. To perform this task, we compute confidence intervals with Bishop, Fienberg and Holland's standard

TABLE 14.7 Calculating interval bounds relative to difference d on each axis. Using 95% Wilson score intervals without continuity correction obtains an interval for $\phi = 0.1735 \in (0.1191, 0.2246)$.

		x_1	x_2	y_1	y_2
proportion	p	0.1984	0.0780	0.7294	0.4794
difference	d		−0.1204		−0.2500
Wilson bounds	w^-	0.1690	0.0590	0.6581	0.4493
	w^+	0.2315	0.1024	0.7906	0.5097
Wilson width	u^-	0.0294	0.0190	0.0713	0.0302
	u^+	0.0331	0.0245	0.0612	0.0303
Newcombe-Wilson	d^+		−0.0822		−0.1725
relative to d	d^-		−0.1586		−0.3182

deviation estimate (Equation (87)), applying the interval equality principle. See Chapter 13. We obtain the following intervals by search:

$\phi_1 = 0.1735 \in (0.1177, 0.2283)$, and

$\phi_2 = 0.0766 \in (0.0515, 0.1016)$.

Again, they do not overlap. The confidence interval for $d_\phi = \phi_2 - \phi_1$ is slightly larger at $(-0.1572, -0.0358)$, and the observed difference is significant.

In principle, this method is extensible to comparing larger $r \times c$ tables and even tables of different designs. However, in addition to the requirement to use a search procedure, the method has the drawback that it is not easily corrected for continuity.

Effect size measures are 'lossy' because they collapse multiple degrees of freedom into a single variable.[7] Effect size comparisons are like area comparisons: they are *more conservative* than the following tests for larger tables which compare dimensions. But they may also be *more general*, allowing us to compare areas of rectangles and circles.

The tests discussed so far have one degree of freedom only – that concerning the difference between two differences, and are therefore unambiguous in their interpretation. Simply stated, the null hypothesis is that the two tables have the same effect size (ϕ or d).

14.4.3 r × 2 Homogeneity Gradient Tests

Gradient tests can be extended to larger tables with multiple degrees of freedom. Here, this notion of differences in *size* of effect (gradient) might be better conceptualised as differences in '*patterns* of effect', that is, distributions of differences within tables.

For $r \times 2$ tables, we may use Equation (98), which is compared with the critical value of χ^2 with $df = r - 1$ degrees of freedom:

$$\textit{separability of independence } \chi^2_{\text{si}} = \sum_{i=1}^{r} \frac{(d_{2,i} - d_{1,i})^2}{S_{1,i}^{\;2} + S_{2,i}^{\;2}}, \qquad (98)$$

where, to analyse column $j = 1$,

- *difference* $d_{h,i} \equiv p_{h,i,j} - \hat{p}_h$;
- *variance* $S_{h,i}^{\;2} \equiv \hat{p}_h (1 - \hat{p}_h)/n_{h,i}$;
- *probability* $p_{h,i,j} \equiv f_{h,i,j}/n_{h,i}$; and
- *pooled probability* $\hat{p}_h \equiv f_{h,+,j}/n_h$.

The pooled probability estimate, $\hat{p}_h$, is constant for each table column. It is the weighted average proportion, the column total over the sample size of table h. The variance estimate, $S_{h,i}^{\;2}$, is based on this estimate divided by the row total.[8]

To correct for continuity, we employ DiffCorrect (Equation (96)):

$$\textit{separability of independence}\ \chi_{si}^2 = \sum_{i=1}^{r} \frac{\text{DiffCorrect}\,(d_{2,i} - d_{1,i}, c_{1,i} + c_{2,i})^2}{S_{1,i}{}^2 + S_{2,i}{}^2} \quad (98')$$

with corrections $c_{h,i} = 0.5/n_{h,i}$. We perform the test in the usual way.

Chi-square test:

If $\chi^2 < \chi^2(\alpha, df)$, there is no significant difference between table rows. (33)

This test has a particularly useful application. In analysing large $r \times c$ tables, we often plot values of the dependent variable, sometimes over many values of the independent variable.

This test allows us to compare a probability distribution drawn from one data set with a comparable distribution drawn from another.

For example, suppose we wish to plot the probability of selecting a value of the dependent variable, *p*(*shall* | {*shall*, *will*}). As we observed in Chapter 7, Binomial probabilities are mutually exclusive (*p*(*shall*) = 1 – *p*(*will*)). We only need to compare one set of proportions, $\{p_{h,i,1}\}$, because the other set will mirror them. See also Chapter 2.

If there are three or more values of the dependent variable (e.g., {*shall*, *will* and BE *going to*}), we would plot each line *j* and perform comparisons between tables separately.

Consider the example data in Table 14.8. Rows represent values of an independent variable, and columns, those of a dependent variable (e.g., *shall* vs. *will*). We plot the column probability *p*(*shall* | {*shall*, *will*}) with Wilson score intervals in Figure 14.6.

The test is carried out as follows. We calculate $p_{h,i,1} = p(x_1)$ for each row and table, so $p_{1,1,1} = p(x_1 \mid \{x_1, x_2\}) = 20/55 = 0.3636$, etc. as before, and the pooled probability, thus $\hat{p}_1 = 61/138 = 0.4420$.

TABLE 14.8 A pair of 3 × 2 tables with example data. Note that to calculate the test, we calculate probability *p* as a fraction of the longer side, hence *n* and *f* are swapped in this table.

	x_1	x_2	*Total*	x_1	x_2	*Total*
y_1	$f_{1,1,1} = $ **20**	**35**	$n_{1,1} = 55$	$f_{2,1,1} = $ **20**	**35**	$n_{2,1} = 55$
y_2	**40**	**40**	80	**2**	**10**	12
y_3	**1**	**2**	3	**3**	**23**	26
Total	$f_{1,+,1} = 61$	77	$n_1 = 138$	$f_{2,+,1} = 25$	68	$n_2 = 93$

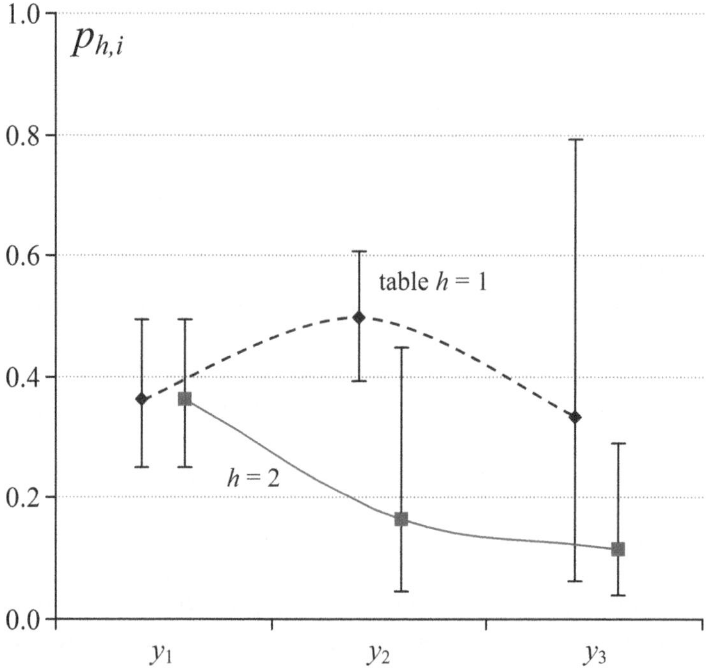

FIGURE 14.6 Plotting data from Table 14.8 with 95% Wilson score intervals. Each line represents column data from tables $h = 1, 2$ plotted against the row total.

We then calculate differences between $p_{h,i,1}$ and $\hat{p}_h$ for each row in each table, $d_{h,i} = p_{h,i,1} - \hat{p}_h$. Finally, we calculate χ^2_{si} using Equation (98). This sums the squared difference of differences, $d_i = d_{2,i} - d_{1,i}$, each divided by the sum of variances obtained using Equation (98).

This meta-test compares the two tables or plot lines against each other, averaging error intervals. In this instance, we obtain $\chi^2_{\text{si}} = 5.0629$ without continuity correction, which is not significant for $\alpha = 0.05$ and two degrees of freedom (the critical value of χ^2 is 5.9915).

Although the observation $p(x_1 \mid y_2)$ significantly differs between tables by a Newcombe-Wilson point test, the overall distribution is not deemed to be significantly different.

To perform the same test with continuity correction, we calculate the correction term for each row and apply Equation (98'). The DiffCorrect function returns 0.1550, −0.1122 and 0, the last zero because the difference is smaller than the correction. The formula obtains $\chi^2_{\text{si}} = 3.6295$, which is (as we would expect) not significant.

A variation of this method generalises the Newcombe-Wilson method of Section 14.4.1 with χ^2. We calculate difference-of-difference intervals for

$d_i \in$ **difference**$(d_{2,i}, d_{1,i})$ and obtain standard deviations $S_{h,i}$ from the resulting inner interval widths. See Section 14.5.3.

14.4.4 Gradient Meta-Tests for Large Tables

Wallis (2019a) proposes a formula for comparing general $r \times c$ tables. Zar's heterogeneity χ^2 method (Zar, 2010, p. 504) can also be used. We sum the χ^2 scores for each independent sample and then subtract the χ^2 score for a pooled table where each cell is the sum of equivalent cells in the samples. (To apply a continuity correction, use Yates's χ^2 for separate tables but not the pooled table.)

This can be useful for a quick replication check. However, a replication assessment should be applied to published claims, not just the overall data.

Earlier in this book, we observed that to be meaningfully analysed, large tables invariably need to be decomposed into sub-tables or plot lines. See Chapter 7. Stating that a large table is 'significant' is almost completely meaningless! We want to know *which aspects* of the table are undergoing significant variation. The same reasoning applies for statements about two large tables, with many degrees of freedom, being significantly different from each other.

As tables increase in degrees of freedom, the meaningful interpretation of a single significant result calculated across many data points is, to put it mildly, rather difficult! A single number has to express the total 'difference' between two tables – a difference that could be due to variation at any point.

Large tables are thus more usefully compared with a series of simpler independent tests. We can divide values of the dependent variable into plot lines and employ the $r \times 2$ test (Section 14.4.3) to consider each value in turn. We may carry out the multi-point test, comprising a series of point-by-point comparisons, each with a single degree of freedom, to explore where differences lie. Plotting data with Wilson score intervals leads us naturally to the Newcombe-Wilson point test (Section 14.3.1) and, if required, the Newcombe-Wilson gradient test (Section 14.4.1).

A crucial assumption in carrying out these meta-tests was that both tables possess an identical structure. They cannot be meaningfully applied if tables are structured differently.

14.5 Gradient Tests for Goodness of Fit Tables

A 2×1 'goodness of fit' chi-square test evaluates whether the distribution of a subset is consistent with ('fits') an overall expected distribution of a superset. It can be calculated in multiple ways (see Chapter 8).

A common application is when we plot the Wilson score interval on proportions and compare that interval with a superset proportion. The 'gradient' in this case is the difference between expected and observed probabilities, $d = p - P$.

Comparing gradients $d_1 = p_1 - P_1$ and $d_2 = p_2 - P_2$ becomes a 'separability of fit' evaluation. See Figure 14.7.

These tests compare whether the difference between expected and observed distributions ('the degree of fit') is significantly different between two tables. Like all these meta-tests, this test is applied to compare repeated evaluations of the type identified.

For example, Wallis (2019b) explored the variation of additive probability, calculated as *successive subset proportions*, testing $p(2) \neq_s p(1)$ with a Wilson score test about the second proportion, $p(2)$. See Chapter 1. A separability of fit test may be used to compare the observed performance in permutations of the experimental design (adjectives vs. adjective phrases) or different data (speech vs. writing).

Another application might be where the same expected distribution **E** or proportion P is used for observed distributions $\mathbf{O}_1$, $\mathbf{O}_2$ or proportions p_1 and p_2, and we wish to compare a series of fitting attempts to that expected distribution. See Chapter 13.

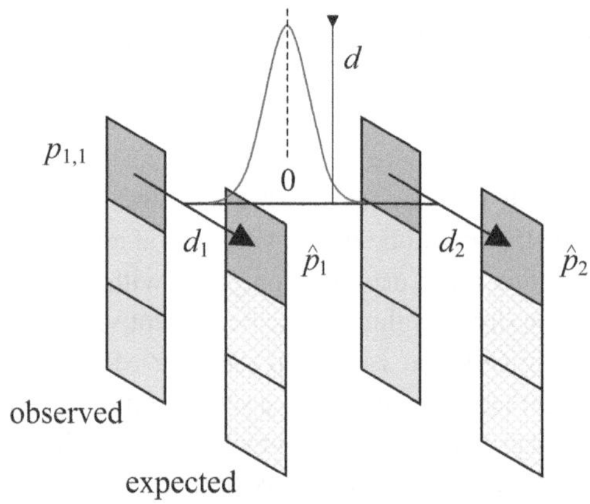

FIGURE 14.7 Carrying out a separability of fit test to compare whether one probability distribution fits its expected distribution to a different extent than another.

TABLE 14.9 Table 14.1 reprised for a goodness of fit test. This time we compare an observed column with the expected total column.

spoken	*shall*	*will*	*Total*	*written*	*shall*	*will*	*Total*
1960s	$f_{1,1,1}$ = **124**	501	$f_{1,1,+}$ = **625**		$f_{2,1,1}$ = **355**	2,798	$f_{2,1,+}$ = **3,153**
1990s	**46**	544	**590**		**200**	2,723	**2,923**
Total	$n_{1,1}$ = 170	1,045	n_1 = 1,215		$n_{2,1}$ = 555	5,521	n_2 = 6,076
	$p_{1,1}$ = 0.7294	0.4794	$\hat{p}_1$ = 0.5144		$p_{2,1}$ = 0.6396	0.5068	$\hat{p}_2$ = 0.5189

By way of illustration, we will evaluate the difference in the distribution of modal *shall* over time from the baseline distribution of *shall* and *will* together over time. Since proportions are drawn from an observed table, on this occasion we will refer to these as prior probabilities $\hat{p}_1$ and $\hat{p}_2$, rather than as population proportions, P_1 and P_2.

Differences are calculated from column 1 (*shall*) and the total (*shall* + *will*). For the spoken data, we have $d_1 = p_{1,1} - \hat{p}_1 = 0.2150$, and for the written data, $d_2 = p_{2,1} - \hat{p}_2 = 0.1207$.

We test whether these differences are significantly different from each other, that is, whether $d = d_2 - d_1$ is non-zero.

14.5.1 The 2 × 1 Wilson Interval Gradient Test

First we will use the Wilson score interval. We compute intervals for each observed probability $p_{1,1}$ and $p_{2,1}$. Priors are 'given' (constant). Confidence intervals for d_1 and d_2 are computed by subtraction, for example, $d_1 \in (w^-_{1,1} - \hat{p}_1, w^+_{1,1} - \hat{p}_1) = (0.1437, 0.2762)$, likewise $d_2 \in (0.0799, 0.1596)$.

Applying Equation (55), the interval function **difference**(d_2, d_1) gives us an interval for $d_2 - d_1 \in (-0.1678, -0.0131)$, which excludes zero. The differences are significantly different.

An even simpler method substitutes $D = \hat{p}_2 - \hat{p}_1 = 0.0045$ into the Newcombe-Wilson test for a given difference D (see Chapter 8). The interval for the difference in proportions, **difference**(p_2, p_1) = (−0.1633, −0.0086), excludes D.

14.5.2 The r × 1 Goodness of Fit Gradient Test

We can generalise a paired $r \times 1$ goodness of fit χ^2 test with $r - 1$ degrees of freedom. This may be used to compare Multinomial distributions against baselines (see Chapter 13).

We use Equation (99). In the following, h and i represent the table and row indices, respectively:

$$\textit{separability of fit } \chi^2_{sf} = \frac{r-1}{r} \sum_{i=1}^{r} \frac{\left(d_{2,i} - d_{1,i}\right)^2}{S_{1,i}^{\ 2} + S_{2,i}^{\ 2}}. \qquad (99)$$

where

- *difference* (observed – expected) $d_{h,i} \equiv p_{h,i} - \hat{p}_{h,i}$;
- *variance* $S_{h,i}^{\ 2} \equiv \hat{p}_{h,i}(1 - \hat{p}_{h,i})/n_{h,i}$;
- *observed probability* $p_{h,i} \equiv f_{h,i}/n_{h,i}$; *and*
- *expected (pooled) probability* $\hat{p}_{h,i} \equiv f_{h,i,+}/n_h$ (or any other pair of baseline distributions).

For each table h, both observed and expected proportions, $\{p_{h,i}\}$ and $\{\hat{p}_{h,i}\}$, are Multinomially constrained over $i = 1 \ldots r$, i.e. are fractions of the column total. We weight the score to account for this constraint. See also Chapter 9.[9]

To apply a continuity correction, we modify the difference with Equation (96):

$$\textit{separability of fit } \chi^2_{\text{sf}} = \frac{r-1}{r}\sum_{i=1}^{r}\frac{\text{DiffCorrect}\,(d_{2,i} - d_{1,i},\, c_{1,i} + c_{2,i})^2}{S_{1,i}{}^2 + S_{2,i}{}^2}, \qquad (99')$$

where $c_{h,i} = 0.5/n_{h,i}$ as before.

The test is evaluated against the critical value of χ^2 with $r - 1$ degrees of freedom. Suppose we take the data in Table 14.8 and compare the first column with the total one. This obtains $\chi^2_{\text{sf}} = 6.9395$. The critical value for 2 degrees of freedom is 5.9915, and the result is significant.[10]

14.5.3 The r × 1 Newcombe-Wilson Goodness of Fit Gradient Test

Equation (99) employs a Gaussian model of variance. But in Chapter 8, we noted that the Newcombe-Wilson interval is preferred to a Gaussian model if non-zero differences, D, must be accounted for. We can do this in the following way.

We calculate Wilson score interval widths $(u^-_{h,i}, u^+_{h,i}) = (p_{h,i} - w^-_{h,i}, w^+_{h,i} - p_{h,i})$ for each table and term i. Next, we *select the inner interval*, that is, we pick the upper bound of the smaller difference and the lower bound of the larger difference. For example, if $d_{2,i} > d_{1,i}$ we would select $S_{1,i} = u^+_{1,i} / z_{\alpha/2}$ and $S_{1,i} = u^-_{2,i} / z_{\alpha/2.}$ Finally, we substitute these standard deviation estimates into Equation (99).[11] A Wilson-based method with the same data obtains $\chi^2_{\text{sf}} = 6.6059$, which is also significant.

A similar method may be applied to χ^2_{si} in Equation (98).

Although superficially similar, these tests and perform different evaluations and yield different results. In the $r \times 2$ separability of independence χ^2_{si} test (Section 14.4.3), we compare differences from the sample mean, whereas in the $r \times 1$ separability of fit test, χ^2_{sf}, we compare differences from a total or superset column.

14.6 Subset Tests

Until now we have assumed that data are drawn from two independent populations, two runs of the same experiment, and so on. Test evaluation assumes that sampling variation in both tables is possible. To perform a point test (Section 14.3), all we needed to do was rearrange data into a new contingency table and carry out a χ^2 test for homogeneity or a Newcombe-Wilson test.

Suppose, however, that we wish to compare two tables where one table represents a *subset* of the other. We observe a superset distribution. We wish to know whether a subset differs from it. Like the goodness of fit, test we assume variation lies wholly in the subset, and consider the superset to be 'given'. Point tests may be implemented as goodness of fit tests, and other tests are adapted accordingly. See Figure 14.8.

One approach to this issue is to substitute zero-width intervals for superset proportions into the equations we have seen thus far. But there are more efficient methods of calculation, which also bear on how we might 'read' graphs.

Let us consider some example data. In Chapter 2, we discussed an experiment that obtained the following data (Table 14.10) from the ICE-GB corpus. We obtained three contingency tables representing speech, writing and 'all data', that is, the pool of both. Considered individually, 'all data' and 'written' show a significant χ^2 effect between the two variables.

To compare speech and writing, we employ the meta-tests we discussed earlier. Spoken and written subcorpora are drawn from independent populations – one

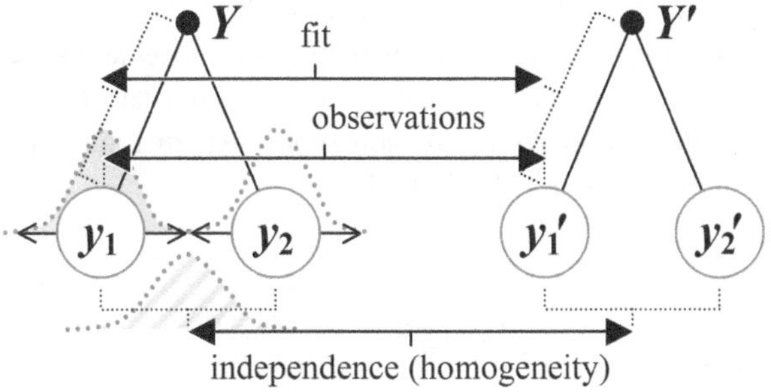

FIGURE 14.8 Visualising separability subset tests, where $Y \subset Y', y_1 \subset y_1'$, etc. For the purposes of the test, supersets have no interval (zero-width intervals, if you prefer). Thus the separability of fit test (Section 14.5) compares the closeness of fit between distributions at value y_1 of variable Y and counterpart distributions at y_1' and Y'. The subset version repeats the exercise, but the difference between y_1' and Y' has no interval.

TABLE 14.10 Contingency tables for objective *who/whom* followed by a subject: all data, plus data subdivided into speech and writing, ICE-GB. See Chapter 2.

	all data			*spoken*			*written*		
	I or we	*other*	*Total*	*I or we*	*other*	*Total*	*I or we*	*other*	*Total*
who	$F_{1,1}$ = **20**	13	$\hat{F}_1$ = **33**	18	13	31	$f_{1,1}$ = **2**	0	$\hat{f}_1$ = **2**
whom	**4**	14	**18**	3	3	6	**1**	11	**12**
Total	N_1 = 24	27	51	21	16	37	n_1 = 3	11	14
	0.8333	0.4815	0.6471				0.6667	0.0000	0.1429

of comparable spoken British English[12] and one of comparable written British English.

Now suppose we wish to compare the written subcorpus, for example, with 'all data', that is, to compare a subset with its superset. Binomial proportion differences are plotted in Figure 14.9.

We do not plot confidence intervals on 'all data' points because *for this purpose*, we assume the distribution is given. We plot 95% Wilson intervals for the 'written' data we intend to compare with this superset.

14.6.1 Point Tests for Subsets

Figure 14.8 immediately reveals that a point test for a self-referential *I* or *we* subject will fail (because P_1 is within the interval for p_1), but a point test for the 'other' category will succeed. The point test has become a goodness of fit test, where observed subset proportions p_i are tested against a given superset proportion, P_i. The principle is sketched in Figure 14.10.

These tests compare cell proportions between a subset and superset table.

Given we have plotted data with Wilson score intervals, the simplest way to perform the evaluation is with a Wilson score test. In Figure 14.9, each point represents a single column in Table 14.10.

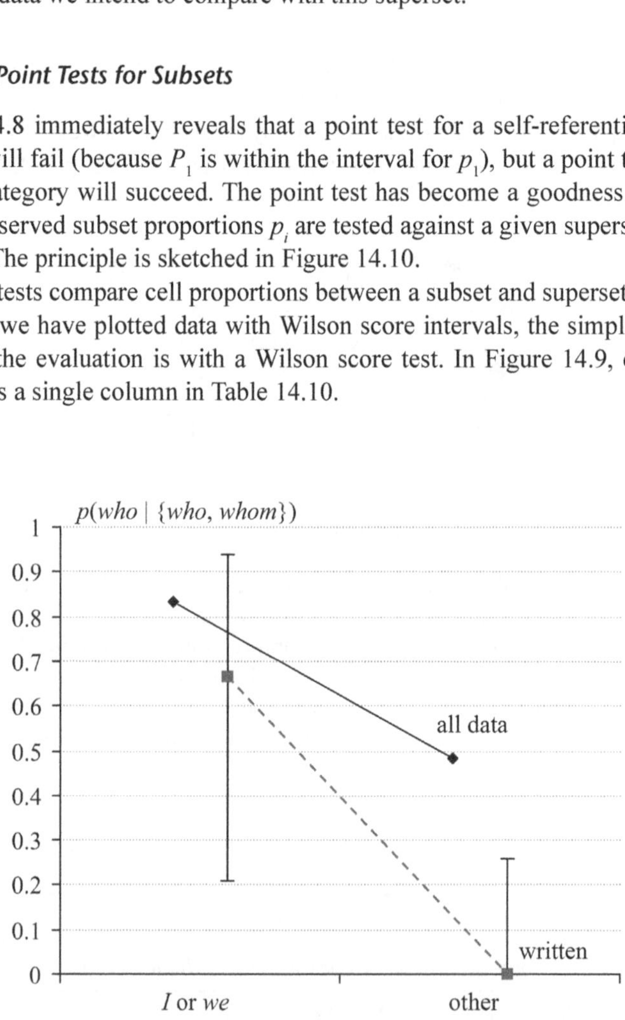

FIGURE 14.9 Example data to illuminate the principle of subset meta-tests. ICE-GB data for objective case *who* versus *whom* followed by a subject: all data plus writing. See Chapter 2.

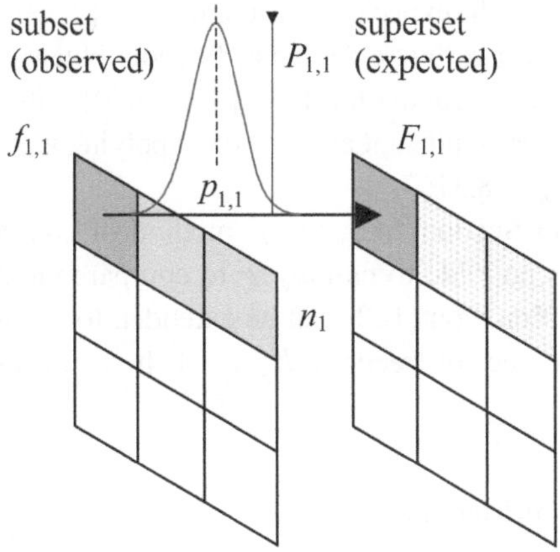

FIGURE 14.10 Carrying out a point test to compare two matching cell proportions $p_i = f_{i,j} / n_i$ and $P_i = F_{i,j} / N_i$ from subset to superset.

Wilson score test:

If $w_i^- < P_i < w_i^+$, there is no significant difference between p and P. (34)

The following are observed proportions from Table 14.10, Wilson intervals (with $\alpha = 0.05$) and superset proportions:

I / we: $p_1 = 0.6667 \in (0.2077, 0.9385)$, $P_1 = 0.8333$: not significant

other: $p_2 = 0.0000 \in [0.0000, 0.2588)$, $P_2 = 0.4815$: significant.

The continuity-corrected interval for p_2 is [0.0000, 0.3214), which also excludes P_2.[13]

The test may be carried out in other ways. The z test for a single sample assumes a Gaussian interval about P. It obtains an identical result.

A useful generalisation involves the 2 × 1 χ^2 goodness of fit test. We rescale the superset to calculate the expected distribution for point i, $\mathbf{E}_i$. We compute $\chi^2(i)$ for each point, comparing $\mathbf{E}_i$ and the subset frequencies, $\mathbf{O}_i$. The expected distribution is based on the superset probability distribution:

$$\textit{expected distribution } \mathbf{E}_i = \{P_{i,j} \times n_i\}, \qquad (100)$$

$$\textit{superset probability } P_{i,j} = F_{i,j} / N_i,$$

where n_i and N_i are the total number of cases in the subsample and superset sample for that point (column totals in Table 14.10), and $F_{i,j}$ represents the cell frequency for the superset table.

In our case, this obtains the expected distribution $\mathbf{E}_1 = \{2.5, 0.5\}$, and $\mathbf{O}_1 = \{2, 1\}$. The goodness of fit χ^2 test with one degree of freedom obtains $\chi^2 = 0.6000$, which is not significant. However, comparing $\mathbf{E}_2 = \{5.30, 5.70\}$ with $\mathbf{O}_2 = \{0, 11\}$ leads to $\chi^2 = 10.2143$, which is significant at $\alpha = 0.05$. Applying a continuity correction, Yates's χ^2 test obtains $\chi^2 = 8.3767$.

As we discussed in Section 14.3, the χ^2 method of computation is extensible in two ways. It is possible to employ χ^2 to compare tables for Multinomial dependent variables. Equation (100) can be extended to r values of the DV ($j = 1 \ldots r$), where the degrees of freedom $df = r - 1$. It can also be used to create a multi-point test.

14.6.2 Multi-Point Subset Tests

As we learned in Section 14.3.3, χ^2 can also be used to sum and average point tests to obtain a multi-point test. In our case, we simply apply Equation (97):

$$\textit{multi-point } \chi^2_{\text{mp}} = \sum_{i=1}^{r} \chi^2(i), \tag{97}$$

where $\chi^2(i)$ represents the point test χ^2 score for point i. This test has $c \times df(i)$ degrees of freedom.

In our example data, $\chi^2_{\text{mp}} = 10.8143$ (or 8.3767 for Yates's test), which is significant with $\alpha = 0.05$ at two degrees of freedom. It is significant because of the large difference at the second point.

14.6.3 Gradient Subset Tests

We can now apply what we have learned to gradient subset tests. As before, the principle is that the superset gradient is 'given', and our test must determine whether an observed difference from this gradient is sufficiently large as to be capable of being deemed 'significant'. The null hypothesis is that the subset gradient is the same as its superset.

These tests compare the gradient, size of effect, or pattern of effect between a subset table and its superset. See Figure 14.11.

Let us consider 2 × 2 subset tests. As we noted in Chapter 8, the Newcombe-Wilson interval should be used when comparing data with a non-zero difference D.

We can compute a 95% Newcombe-Wilson interval for the 'written' subset difference $d = p_2 - p_1 = -0.6667$. This gives us $d \in (d^-, d^+) = \textbf{difference}(p_2, p_1) = (-0.9385, -0.1397)$, or $(-0.9823, -0.0371)$ with a continuity correction. For the superset 'all data', $D = P_2 - P_1 = -0.3519$.

We wish to know whether the subset gradient, d, is different from *the superset gradient*, D. We can apply a test in this form:

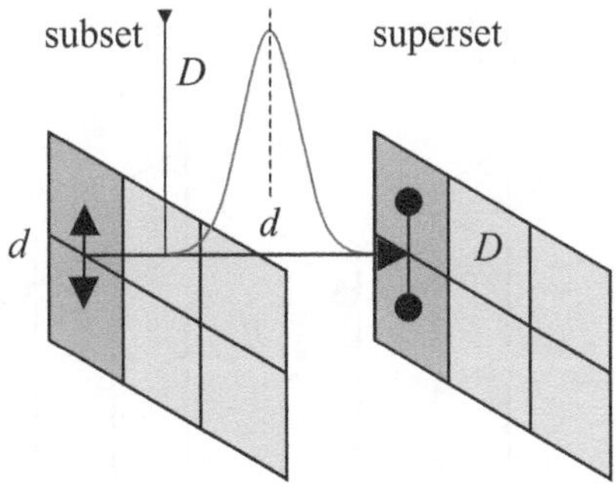

FIGURE 14.11 Carrying out a gradient test to compare differences in proportions, d and D, between a table and its superset.

Gradient subset test (Newcombe-Wilson):

If $d^- < D < d^+$, the subset gradient d is not significantly different from that of its superset, D. (101)

The difference we wish to evaluate, $D = -0.3519$, is within the confidence interval for $d \in (d^-, d^+) = (-0.9385, -0.1397)$. The difference is not significant, even without a continuity adjustment.

Subset tests with other effect sizes, such as Cramer's ϕ, may be carried out in the same way. For a 2 × 2 table, we might compute an interval for $\phi \in (\phi^-, \phi^+)$ with Equation (86) and test if it includes a superset score, Φ.

14.6.4 Goodness of Fit Subset Tests

There is one final evaluation we might wish to consider. This is *the goodness of fit subset test*, the subset version of the test outlined in Section 14.5.

This test compares whether the difference between expected and observed distributions ('the degree of fit') is significantly different between a subset and its superset. See Figure 14.12.

When might such a comparison be useful? Wallis (2019b) used goodness of fit tests to evaluate whether additive probability, $p(x)$, changes as writers or speakers add terms to a sequence. See Chapter 1. Table 14.11 and Figure 14.13 draws data from ICE-GB, 'writing' versus 'all data'.

In this sequence, $p(1)$ represents the probability of adding the first adjective phrase, $p(2)$ the probability of adding the second, and so on. Since the data supporting $p(2)$ are a subset of the data for $p(1)$, we use a goodness of fit test to compare points in the sequence.

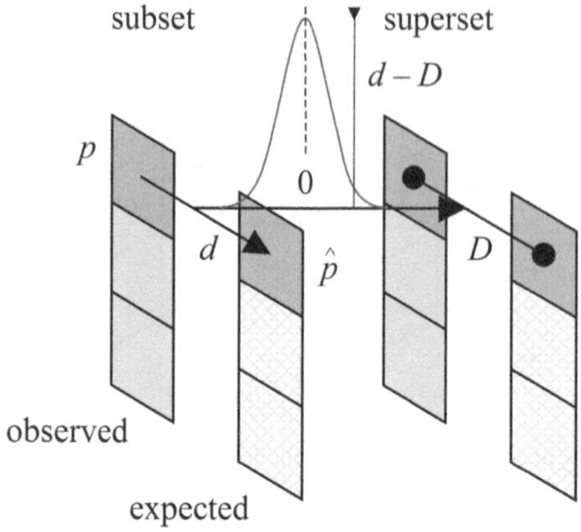

FIGURE 14.12 Carrying out a subset goodness of fit test to compare whether the probability distribution of a subset, $\{p\}$, fits its expected distribution, $\{\hat{p}\}$, to a different extent than its superset.

TABLE 14.11 Additive probability of NPs with x attributive adjective phrases before a noun head in ICE-GB, showing two trends: all data; and written data with confidence intervals (see Wallis, 2019b).

x adjective phrases	1	2	3	4
all data, additive probability $p(x)$	0.1932	0.0789	0.0526	0.0452
written, additive probability $p(x)$	0.2122	0.0850	0.0527	0.0556
Wilson upper bound $w^+(x)$	0.2148	0.0889	0.0644	0.1235
Wilson lower bound $w^-(x)$	0.2096	0.0812	0.0431	0.0240

The paper includes plots of the pattern obtained, with confidence intervals, for spoken and written ICE-GB data. Speech and writing are considered independent samples, so to compare those plots we would employ a meta-test from Section 14.5. But it is also possible to test each additive step to see if the 'written' fall (say) significantly differs from one observed in the entire corpus ('all data'): a superset.

The Wilson approach is the easiest to visualise. In Figure 14.13, looking at the written curve, we can immediately see that the (tiny) Wilson score interval for $p(2)$ does not include the point $p(1)$, the wider interval for $p(3)$ does not include $p(2)$, and so on.

Whether evaluating all the ICE-GB data or only the written subcorpus, Wallis (2019b) observed a significant fall from $p(1)$ to $p(2)$.

Figure 14.13 seems to suggest that for the initial fall at least, $d(2) = p(2) - p(1)$, the gradients are slightly different. But is this difference significant?

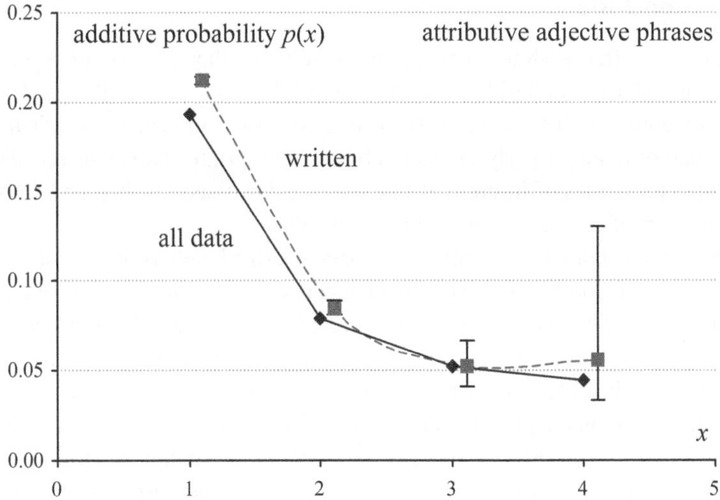

FIGURE 14.13 The decline in additive probability: all data versus a written subset, data from Table 14.11.

To carry out the test we will use the following notation:

freely varying proportion $p = p(2, \text{writing})$, with interval (w^-, w^+),
expected value $\hat{p} = p(1, \text{writing})$,
equivalent superset values $P = p(2, \text{all data})$, $\hat{P} = p(1, \text{all data})$.

Using this notation, this gives us the following:

gradient (writing) $d = p - \hat{p} = 0.0850 - 0.2122 = -0.1273$.
gradient (all data) $D = P - \hat{P} = 0.0789 - 0.1932 = -0.1142$.
difference in gradients $d_D = d - D = -0.0130$.

The only term free to vary is the observed proportion for writing (i.e., $p = p(2)$), which has interval $(w^-, w^+) = (0.0812, 0.0889)$. All other terms are given. The interval for d is obtained by subtraction, $d \in (w^- - \hat{p}, w^+ - \hat{p})$, and the entire evaluation can be expressed as an adjusted Wilson score test:

Goodness of fit subset test (zero-based Wilson interval):

If $w^- - p < d - D < w^+ - p$, the subset goodness of fit for p fitting $\hat{p}$, d, is not significantly different from the equivalent superset fit, D. (102)

14.7 Conclusions

Researchers often wish to compare their results to others. However, as Goldacre (2011) noted, even in highly prestigious journals, researchers fail to perform this analysis correctly. The solution is to recognise that observed numerical differences can only be properly evaluated by an appropriate statistical test. We must bring the principles of inferential statistics we discussed in Chapter 6 to bear on the question of comparing experimental results.

The common practice of citing χ^2 scores or error levels is hopelessly misconceived. First, it combines two distinct concepts: the size of the effect (e.g., ϕ) and the size of the data (n). Second, even if we cite a standardised effect size, such as Cramér's ϕ, we can only say one score is greater than another if we have evaluated whether the difference between the scores is too great to occur by blind luck.

In the previous chapter, we demonstrated this fact by plotting ϕ with confidence intervals (see Figure 13.3). It is worth emphasising the following conclusion. *The correct approach to comparing results, therefore, is to construct a significance test for each of the comparisons we wish to make.*

The solution involves not one test, but many, depending on the hypothesis we wish to evaluate. The **difference** interval function introduced in Chapter 9 can compare any two observed properties with confidence intervals, so it can be used to compare results from comparable experiments.

We can compare proportions for particular values of the independent variable. These 'point tests' allow us to claim that a proportion in one table, sample, or set of results, is significantly different than in another.

A second type of evaluation concerns a 'gradient' test. This has two use cases. The first is comparing experimental claims expressed in terms of change (e.g., 'the DV has increased/decreased in our data') with other similar claims in the literature. The same method may be used for other measures such as Cramér's ϕ.

We also generalised comparisons with Pearson's χ^2 test. This allowed us to extend tests in two ways: to compare an entire distribution of cell frequencies across the DV at one point, or to compare the distribution of points or gradients across multiple values of the IV.

A third type of application concerns goodness of fit. In Chapter 8 we learned that a goodness of fit test evaluates the difference between an observed proportion or distribution and a given one. To compare goodness of fit results we must use a similar gradient-comparison test, but one where the given observation has no interval.

In brief, we have three principal classes of test: point tests ('separability of observations'), homogeneity gradient tests ('separability of independence') and goodness of fit gradient tests ('separability of fit'). When these tests are used, comparisons will mostly be between independent samples. However, there may be occasions where a subset test is appropriate.

We briefly discussed comparing *effect sizes* like ϕ or ϕ_p for significant difference. If we do, we should be aware that the task of comparing effect sizes summarising tables with multiple degrees of freedom is less sensitive than a cell-for-cell or difference-for-difference comparison.

This principle can be seen when comparing values of Cramér's ϕ. As there is only one degree of freedom in comparing 2×2 tables, the ϕ test can be replaced by a Wilson gradient test. But if we wish to make experimental claims in terms of ϕ with more than one degree of freedom, the ϕ interval test may be employed, provided we recognise that it will be 'lossy', and thus more conservative than a gradient comparison between the tables. This is fine provided we remember *we are testing a different hypothesis*.

The method of derivation of tests described in this chapter is original. The issues discussed in this chapter are largely unexplored in the statistics literature. However, there is an existing method that attempts to perform similar evaluations.

Wallis (2019a) compared this 'heterogeneity χ^2 analysis' (Zar, 2010, pp. 474, 504), with our tests. Zar's method is intended for deciding if it is legitimate to pool samples by estimating whether data are likely to have been drawn from the same population.

A comparison of tests and an analysis of their difference reveals that Zar's approach obtains comparable results to an $r \times c$ gradient test (Wallis, 2012a). However, the method is sensitive to the prior expected distribution: it expects distributions to be identical, which will frequently not be appropriate. Second, despite Zar proposing it for goodness of fit tests (see, e.g., Zar, 2010, p. 454), in this context, it can obtain negative χ^2 scores, which do not make sense! Point and subset tests are not considered.

To reliably evaluate significant differences between experimental runs, we need to employ the approach explained in this chapter, starting with the test you wish to compare.

All formulae permit the separate adjustment for finite population (see Chapter 8) and random-text sampling (Chapter 16). However, Bishop et al.'s statistic is not easily corrected for continuity.

Indeed, corrections for continuity are often omitted in more complex analyses. Zar (2010, p. 476) uses uncorrected χ^2 scores in his heterogeneity goodness of fit analysis. But in Chapter 6, we saw how continuity corrections approximate the continuous Normal distribution to the discrete Binomial one. They are equally applicable to meta-tests. Our simplest point test is an application of a Newcombe-Wilson test or – for subsets, a 2×1 goodness of fit test – where a continuity correction is commonly applied.

In the Preface and Chapter 8 we commented in passing that some statisticians are critical of 'overcompensating' for continuity, especially where larger numbers of data points are involved. But irrespective of where you stand on that issue, if original results quote a correction for continuity, it makes sense to employ the same correction when seeking to replicate results. These methods are neutral in that respect.

This chapter underlines the importance of transparency in reporting results. If you wish to compare your study with mine, I must provide you with sufficient information to do so. A quick comparison may be between quoted properties with intervals – the generalised difference test, evaluating if $0 \in$ **difference**(θ_1, θ_2), really comes into its own here – but more detailed evaluations may require raw frequency data in tables.

We end this chapter with a methodological caveat. We discussed the problem of comparing results of two or more contingency tables, representing frequency data from experiments. As a result of performing a test, we might wish to refine our experimental design and resample our data. But we should pause for reflection. Tests and plots might *illuminate* the data we obtain. But a significant result or a narrow interval is not a substitute for scientific thinking!

Statistical methods might assist with experimental refinement, but the refinement itself must be based on underlying theoretical principles. Significance tests cannot 'fix' problems of poor experimental design, but they may draw attention to them. See Chapter 2. They cannot guarantee that the phenomenon measured has real theoretical meaning, that baselines for comparison are meaningful or that observations are genuinely free to vary.

Those questions are matters of careful experimental design. As the old adage goes, a statistic is only as good as the experiment from which it is obtained.

Notes

1 A version of this chapter was first published as Wallis, S.A. (2019a), Comparing χ^2 tables for separability of distribution and effect: Meta-tests for comparing homogeneity and goodness of fit contingency test outcomes. *Journal of Quantitative Linguistics*, *24*(4), 492–525. www.tandfonline.com.
2 In Chapter 13 we saw an example of this principle. In one evaluation, removing the sign of d rendered two unsigned ϕ_p scores indistinguishable.
3 The calculations discussed in this chapter may be carried out with a spreadsheet available online at https://corplingstats.wordpress.com/siclr.
4 If we wished to compare our experiment with one that cited alternative valid intervals (e.g. Clopper-Pearson intervals, see Chapter 8), we could repeat the original CP computation with our data before performing the difference test. We might do this in addition to computing differences in Wilson intervals. It is unwise to take differences between intervals calculated by different methods, for example, to compare results with CP and Wilson intervals!
5 An alternative formulation for 2×2 $\chi^2 = d^2/S_d^2$, where S_d is computed with Equation (42).
6 This is *not* a three dimensional chi-square test (e.g., a $2 \times 2 \times 2$ test) (Zar, 2010, p. 510). That test has three degrees of freedom, one for each dimension, and aggregates differences across all three. In this evaluation we analyse the differences *between* tables, setting aside whether a table is deemed to contain significant differences between columns or rows.

7 Imagine you want to buy flooring for a room. If you are buying carpet, you will need to measure dimensions separately. Carpet comes in rolls of fixed widths. But if you intend to lay polished concrete or parquet, purchases are most accurately estimated by area. Both types of measurement are valid and may be useful.

8 An alternative formula for the 3 × 2 homogeneity chi-square score for table h is $\chi^2 = \sum d_{h,i}{}^2/S_{h,i}{}^2$.

9 Recall that in the Multinomial sum formula, Equation (60"), we multiplied the sum of squared interval widths (equivalent to variance terms S^2) by $\kappa = k / (k - 1)$. In this evaluation, since each χ^2 term is divided by variance, we divide the sum by κ.

10 Applying 'DiffCorrect' to correct for continuity obtains $\chi^2_{sf} = 5.0880$, which is not significant.

11 To apply a continuity correction, we have two potential options: use 'DiffCorrect' or cite corrected Wilson score intervals. Since it cancels out differences within $\pm c$, the former is preferred.

12 This would be something like 'British English speech data sampled in a comparable manner to the method used to obtain the spoken component of ICE-GB'. See Chapter 5 on 'imagined populations.'

13 Note that the Newcombe-Wilson interval for $p_2 - p_1$ simplifies to the Wilson score interval for p_2 if we assert a zero interval width for p_1, that is, set $p_1 = w_1^+ = w_1^-$.

PART 5

Statistical Solutions for Corpus Samples

15

CONDUCTING RESEARCH WITH IMPERFECT DATA

15.1 Introduction

Corpus linguists frequently face a major challenge. Many of the linguistic distinctions we wish to model are either not annotated in a corpus or are inconsistently coded.

When texts are passed through an automatic algorithm (e.g., a part-of-speech tagger, parser or semantic tagger), the program will make classification errors. Some corpus builders review the results of their algorithms for annotation accuracy, although the larger the corpus, the more difficult this task.[1] But whenever we perform a corpus query, we must consider two things: can we improve how our query is formulated using the annotation scheme, and is our corpus accurately annotated for the phenomenon under study? In Chapters 3 and 4, we introduced the idea of reviewing *tokens* (instances) and *types*. A typological review helped us refine queries. But eventually we must examine tokens.

We should *always* build in a cyclic process of manual review of search results. It is not enough to extract frequency counts and extrapolate conclusions. We need to know *which* sentences, *which* examples, justify these counts. In Chapter 1, we called this process of refining queries and reviewing cases *the abstraction cycle*.

Omit this step, and conclusions are suspect. We can never reject the alternate hypothesis that results are evidence of the particular performance of algorithms, annotator biases or queries, rather than the phenomena under investigation. Well-defined corpus queries may obtain incomplete or unsound data on close inspection.

The larger the corpus, the less we should take for granted. But corpora that have been exhaustively manually checked and reanalysed can still contain

DOI: 10.4324/9781003622697-20

important errors. A claimed '1% error rate' is meaningless *if your study concerns that 1%!* Evelien Keizer (2007) studied the noun phrase in ICE-GB, a parsed corpus exhaustively corrected by a team of linguist researchers (see Wallis & Nelson, 1997). She manually reanalysed a minority of interesting and important noun phrases for her monograph. Sometimes the very aspect that made them interesting also made them difficult to correctly parse in the first place.

Whether one is using a simple lexical list query or the most complex grammatical query, we must always hold to the same fundamental principle:

> **The golden rule of data.** We need to know that, as far as possible, our dataset is a *sound* and *complete* set of examples of the linguistic phenomenon in which we are interested.[2]

This rule is even more fundamental than the random sampling principle. It defines the population of linguistic instances we wish to correctly sample. It applies to hand-annotated micro-corpora and auto-annotated mega-corpora alike.

Researchers must review and potentially 'clean' their data in the abstraction cycle. This has the following aspects:

1. **Determine whether the dataset is sound.** Each case in the dataset must be a proper member of its set. Cases may be excluded and sometimes *reclassified* (Type A becomes B, etc.) as a result.
2. **Determine whether the dataset is complete.** Cases incorrectly excluded from the dataset, 'false negatives', must be included. The researcher broadens their search to find potential candidates, and reviews these manually.
3. **Check for alternation.** Items of Type A are checked to see if they may be plausibly replaced by those of Type B, and vice versa. If the alternative construction is semantically implausible, the item should be removed. Naturally, one must decide on *alternation criteria* before starting the review – is meaning preserved or does it consistently change in a single aspect? See Chapter 3.
4. **Perform additional manual subcategorisation.** For example, one might identify meaning subsets, such as 'Epistemic' (intention) modals in the case of *shall* versus *will* (see Aarts et al., 2013). Such annotation is not 'imperfect' but absent. Manual review affords us the opportunity to additionally categorise our data.

Where instances are undecidable, a 'worst-case analysis' should be employed. Exclude them from an initial analysis; if a significant result is found, allocate them to the category that would defeat the result; then re-test. See also Section 15.3.

Data cleaning processes require linguistic decisions about category membership. This is not the same as *removing outliers*, a common, albeit mistaken, process by which researchers selectively remove apparently anomalous results during analysis. Do not be tempted to do this!

Do not use an expected distribution or model (to fit a logistic curve, say) to drive data cleaning. Outliers might be inspected and rejected from the sample on linguistic grounds, but *the same linguistic criteria must be systematically applied to the entire sample.*

Once we accept we must manually review data, we face two practical imperatives. First, researchers must fully document their criteria in experimental reports, so that results may be replicated and methods interrogated. Second, and more troubling, we may have thousands of cases to review. Numbers increase as we eliminate false negatives (point 2).

Now for the good news. Inferential statistics can help.

In this chapter, we consider two common situations and statistical principles that can be used. In the next section, we discuss the task of reviewing random subsamples when the initial distribution of data across the dependent variable is unequal.

In Section 15.3, we consider a different process. This is where a researcher performs an initial analysis with existing annotation, and then checks if significant results may be undermined by a selective review. This is appropriate if initial results are expected to have a small error and are complete (or near-complete). However, if the error turns out to be large, a full review should be conducted.

15.2 Reviewing Subsamples

15.2.1 Example 1: Get Versus Be Passive

Wallis and Mehl (2022) examined cases of GET[3] and BE passive constructions in ICE-GB. The steps they took are instructive.

First, they identified potential cases. They 'cast the net wide' in an initial search, including so-called 'false passives' that must be eliminated. Second, they engaged in a manual review. They confirmed which cases could alternate without changing the referential meaning of the utterance (see Chapter 3).

BE passives include two types of 'passive': *acts* and *the resulting state*, whereas GET passives always refer to acts. States do not alternate, and therefore should be excluded. (This is 'mutual substitution under consistent meaning change': if the change from BE to GET would change the meaning, it must do so *consistently*.) Other cases may be idiomatic and fixed (e.g., *as far as X is concerned*), and again should be eliminated.

Before we commence a review, we must also consider whether there is a potential *reclassification* risk. Here the answer is obviously no. No GET example could be BE or vice versa! Were there such a risk, the review process would need to create a 'transfer list' for each type.

Using FTF searches in ICE-GB, Mehl obtained a set of candidate constructions summarised in Table 15.1, which he planned to manually review for alternation using a number of criteria.

TABLE 15.1 Raw frequencies from applying searches to ICE-GB.

raw unchecked data	*speech*	*writing*	*Total*
GET passives	**166**	**41**	207
BE passives	**4,107**	**5,520**	9,628

TABLE 15.2 Subsampling a contingency table. Independent variable fractions β_1, β_2 may be unequal.

DV	*IV*	y_1	y_2
x_1		$a\,\beta_1$	$b\,\beta_2$
x_2		$c\,\beta_1$	$d\,\beta_2$

15.2.2 Subsampling and Reviewing

Wallis and Mehl took a random subsample of cases. Nine thousand potential BE passives are too large a sample to check manually. On the other hand, the fall from 166 to 41 GET cases seems substantial, so one might not need all this data to obtain a significant result.

Subsampling is perfectly legitimate. It shrinks the amount of data we have to work with, and reduces n. It requires no new mathematics provided we take the same fraction of each proportion, BE and GET. Equal proportion subsampling is defined in the following way:

> **Equal proportion subsampling.** For all values of the *dependent variable*, the same subsample fraction should be drawn.

If we randomly sample 10% of BE cases, we take 10% of GET cases. The simplest approach is to apply the same fraction to the whole table. We subsample a table [[a, b], [c, d]] by a constant fraction β (say 10%) and obtain the table [[$a\beta$, $b\beta$], [$c\beta$, $d\beta$]]. See Table 15.2.

We may apply a different rate of subsampling to different values of the *independent variable.* In historical corpus linguistics, it is quite common for early period subcorpora to be smaller than those of later periods. If we are studying diachronic change, we might not wish to subsample time periods at the same rate. This pattern also conforms to equal proportion subsampling, where $\beta_1 \neq \beta_2$.

However, it should be apparent that Table 15.1 presents a different problem. Suppose we take $\beta = 0.1$. Then, 10% of 166 cases is 17 (rounding to the nearest whole number), and 10% of 41 is 4!

The candidate sets for GET and BE are of such different orders of magnitude that a single high quality and cost-effective trade-off will be difficult. A 10% fraction – even a 20% fraction – for GET disposes of so much data that results become unreliable. Indeed, from a perspective of efficient effort, subsampling GET is unnecessary. We can easily review 200 cases.

We need to subsample the *dependent variable* at unequal rates. This is more complicated, but armed with what we have learned about the Binomial model and Wilson interval, quite possible:

> **Unequal proportion subsampling.** We allow different subsample fractions of the dependent variable to be drawn.

First, Mehl obtained an approximate 10% subsample for BE, but left GET untouched. The subsampling method was inexact, obtaining $\beta_1 = 10.59\%$ of all cases in the spoken part of the corpus and $\beta_2 = 11.51\%$ of cases in the written part.

Next, he checked all 207 GET passives and 1,072 BE passives for alternation. In the paper, he considered a number of alternation tests. Here, we simply consider the simplest – that an example of a GET passive can *conceivably* be swapped for an instance of a BE passive and vice versa:

(53) The time to *get involved* in burden sharing was earlier [W2E-003 #99]
~The time to *be involved* in burden sharing was earlier

(54) the . . . problem of *being isolated* in your wheelchair [S1A-003 #127]
~the . . . problem of *getting isolated* in your wheelchair

Here the test is simply that it is possible to replace the form of GET by the equivalent form for BE. This test tends to eliminate the idiomatic (e.g., GET *carried away* (S1A-042 #266) and *remains to be seen* (S2A-008 #175)) and the odd misanalysed case (e.g., GET *fed up* (S1B-026 #215)).

The results of this review are seen in Table 15.4.

TABLE 15.3 Subsampling BE passives.

raw unchecked data	*speech*	*writing*	*Total*
GET passives	**166**	**41**	207
BE passives	**4,107**	**5,520**	9,627
BE passives ('10%')	437	635	1,072
scale factor β	0.1064	0.1150	

TABLE 15.4 Result of Table 15.3 after the elimination of non-alternating cases.

alternating cases	*speech*	*writing*	*Total*
GET passives *f*(GET)	146	36	182
BE passives ('10%') *f*(BE)	408	614	1,022
Total *n*	554	650	1,204

15.2.3 Estimating the Observed Probability p

We subsampled the DV on an unequal basis. Conceivably, we might still apply an associative χ^2 or Fisher test. These do not distinguish between independent and dependent variables.

However, we cannot reliably estimate the *true proportion*, which undermines plotting graphs and comparing results. The BE passive row cells, f(BE) are based on a random subsample scaled by a factor. But the GET passive row was not subsampled at all. The observed proportion, p(GET | {GET, BE}) has become closer to 0.5 than P is ever likely to be! To make matters worse, BE frequencies were subsampled at slightly different rates.

There is an elegant solution. This is to correct the observed proportion p and then employ the Wilson score interval with subsample size n. As we know, the interval may be calculated with the following functions:

$$w^- = \text{WilsonLower}(p, n, \alpha/2), \text{ and} \quad (20'')$$

$$w^+ = \text{WilsonUpper}(p, n, \alpha/2).$$

Crucially for our purposes, n represents the 'weight of evidence' supporting the observation of p.

Without uneven subsampling, we would employ $p = f(\text{GET}) / n$, where f(GET) is the frequency of GET passives and n the total number of both cases (BE plus GET passives). However, in our example, the best estimate of p is obtained by first dividing the BE passive frequency in the table by the relevant scale factor, β_1, β_2, before substituting it into the previous ratio.

This gives us the following recalibration formula:

$$\textit{best estimate of observed proportion } p = f(\text{GET}) / (f(\text{GET}) + f(\text{BE}) / \beta), \quad (103)$$

$$\textit{sample size } n = f(\text{GET}) + f(\text{BE}).$$

We do not modify the weight of evidence n, even as we expand the baseline denominator for p. We have only our subsample to rely on.

This method is simple, elegant and defensible, consistent with other adjustments (continuity correction, finite population correction, etc.) and capable of deployment in separability tests. Indeed, it is wise to apply a continuity correction whenever we perform unequal proportion sampling:

$$w^-_{cc} \equiv \text{WilsonLower}(\max(0, p - \tfrac{1}{2n}), n, \alpha/2)), \text{ and}$$

$$w^+_{cc} \equiv \text{WilsonUpper}(\min(1, p + \tfrac{1}{2n}), n, \alpha/2)). \quad (36)$$

Applying this approach to Table 15.4 produces Table 15.5. Wilson bounds are computed with n = 554 and 650, respectively. Data are plotted as usual. The intervals do not overlap (w_{cc}^{-}(spoken) > w_{cc}^{+}(written), 0.0242 > 0.0176), which confirms that the two observations are significantly different, despite the rescaling of the BE passive frequency.

15.2.4 Contingency Tests and Multinomial Dependent Variables

If the intervals overlapped, we could use the Newcombe-Wilson test with continuity correction, but we will use Yates's χ^2 test (see Chapter 8). To do this, we reconstruct a new contingency table recalibrated with Equation (103).

The first row is simply $p \times n$, and the second, $q \times n$ (where $q = 1 - p$). Again, n remains the same. The result is significant at $\alpha = 0.05$ and one degree of freedom.

This method is highly extensible. Suppose we consider data with a Multinomial dependent variable (i.e., where $r > 2$), for a recalibrated $r \times c$ chi-square. We simply calculate different probabilities, with different scale factors, for each row. In our example exercise, β for the first row was 1: we did not subsample the GET passives.

TABLE 15.5 Rescaling estimates to obtain the best estimate of the true rate of GET passives out of alternating forms using data from Table 15.4. The continuity-corrected Wilson score interval is recalculated with a rescaled p but the same n ($\alpha = 0.05$).

alternating	*speech*	*writing*
GET passives f(GET)	146.00	36.00
BE passives (rescaled) f(BE) / β	3,853.02	5,329.06
Total	3,999.02	5,365.06
best estimate proportion $p = p$(GET)	0.0365	0.0067
Total n	554.00	650.00
lower bound w_{cc}^{-}	**0.0242**	0.0023
upper bound w_{cc}^{+}	0.0583	**0.0176**

TABLE 15.6 Recalibrated contingency table, using the best estimate p and n, with $q = 1 - p$. Compare with Table 15.4, the same table prior to recalibration. Yates's χ^2 = 12.5819.

alternating	*speech*	*writing*	*Total*
GET passives $p \times n$	20.99	4.39	25.38
BE passives $q \times n$	533.01	645.61	1,178.62
Total n	554.00	650.00	1,204.00

We have the following general solution, where i represents values of the dependent variable (in this layout, the row) and j the independent variable (column). Conforming with the Multinomial model, proportions $p_{i,j}$ sum to 1 over the dependent variable:

$$p_{i,j} = \frac{f_{i,j} / \beta_{i,j}}{n'_j}, \text{ and} \tag{104}$$

$$n'_j = \sum_{i=1}^{r} f_{i,j} / \beta_{i,j}.$$

This method relies on the continuous nature of the Normal distribution (Chapter 6) and Wilson's interval. Fisher's 'exact' test cannot be computed with non-integer cell frequencies, but Yates's χ^2 test has no such problem.

Mehl and Wallis were concerned only with *validating* examples retrieved from the corpus, that is, deciding whether they should be properly considered instances of a phenomenon. There was no question of *reallocating* instances from BE to GET passive cases (within the DV), for example, or from written to spoken subcorpora (within the IV).

If we reallocate data, we must carry it out in proportion, adjusting the contingency table and observed proportion p accordingly. Suppose (suspending disbelief), we decided it were necessary to transfer f(error) cases from BE to GET in Table 15.5. We add f(error) / β to the GET row and subtract it from the BE row. We then recalculate p and intervals. Total n does not change.

15.3 Reviewing Preliminary Analyses

In the last section, we discussed reviewing cases as part of the abstraction process itself, on a 'first pass' through the data. This method is useful when it is strongly suspected that the combination of corpus annotation and queries is insufficient for a first pass.

In some cases, we might have reason to expect initial queries to have a low classification error rate, ideally *complete* if not entirely sound. We might extract data from a corpus using automatic queries, perform an initial analysis, and then pose a different question:

> *Is our initial analysis sufficient to report, or would a review of cases obtain a different result?*

Here the task is different. We are close to publication and erring towards caution. We review initial results by checking corpus examples. Again, this might include deciding that cases of Type A should be reallocated to Type B (or vice versa).

If the error rate turns out to be higher than expected we may revert to the method of Section 15.2, and exhaustively review cases in a sample or subsample. We would certainly need to consider this if we believed our initial sample was incomplete. We broaden our search criteria and review data.

But there is another strategy that is worth considering: *employing the worst-case scenario* and attempting to undermine a preliminary result.

15.3.1 Example 2: Embedded and Sequential Postmodifiers

Wallis (2019b) compared the distribution of sequential decisions of the same type in ICE-GB (see Chapter 1). We might think of this study as a way of mapping the human ability to construct more and more complex utterances by performing the same grammatical operation again and again.

In one experiment, he compared two ways that clauses modifying a noun phrase head may be attached. Example (55) illustrates double-embedding, where the second clause modifies a head within the first postmodifying clause. Example (56) illustrates a different pattern of sequential clauses, where the second clause modifies the original head (*this girl*):

(55) *an optician [who displays a sign [that he or she does NHS sight tests]]* $_{\text{[W2D-001 \#14]}}$
(56) *this girl [called Kate] [who's on my course]* $_{\text{[S1A-038 \#20]}}$

Some cases may be ambiguous. ICE-GB annotates Example (57) as a sequential instance, that is, that it is 'the gentleman', not the unnamed 'anybody', who taught the class. Similarly, but less ambiguously perhaps, in Example (58) 'the series' could have 'followed Cook':

(57) sort of immensely *Christian gentleman [as ever chiselled anybody out of five cents] [who taught his Sunday school class in Cleveland]* $_{\text{[S1B-005 \#176]}}$
(58) *the series [that a navigator [that followed Cook about twenty years after]]* $_{\text{[S1A-013 \#19]}}$

What resolves ambiguity in these examples – tentatively – is *world knowledge*. Automatic parsing programs can find this distinction difficult to make! We happen to know that ICE-GB was automatically parsed and hand-checked by linguists exhaustively. But as researchers, we owe it to ourselves to check, referring back to the source.

Wallis (2019b) describes the process of data extraction, and reports Tables 15.7 and 15.8. He plotted $p(x)$ with Wilson score intervals, obtaining a graph with two plot lines that looks like Figure 15.1. At this point he was interested in the following question. Are we sure all cases designated as 'sequential' and 'embedded'

TABLE 15.7 The additive probability for sequential postmodifying clauses within noun phrases reveals a decline and rise.

x NP postmodifying sequential clauses	0	1	2	3
frequency 'at least *x*' *f*(*x*)	193,135	10,093	166	9
probability *p*(*x*)		0.0523	0.0164	0.0542
significance			s–	s+

TABLE 15.8 The same probability applied to embedded postmodifying clauses exposes only a decline. For embedding, *f*′(*x*) is examined because this avoids double-counting. See Wallis (2019b).

x NP postmodifying embedded clauses	0	1	2	3
frequency 'at least *x*' *f*(*x*)	193,135	10,093	231	4
'at least *x*' unique *f*′(*x*)	183,042	9,862	227	4
probability *p*(*x*)		0.0539	0.0230	0.0176
significance			s–	ns

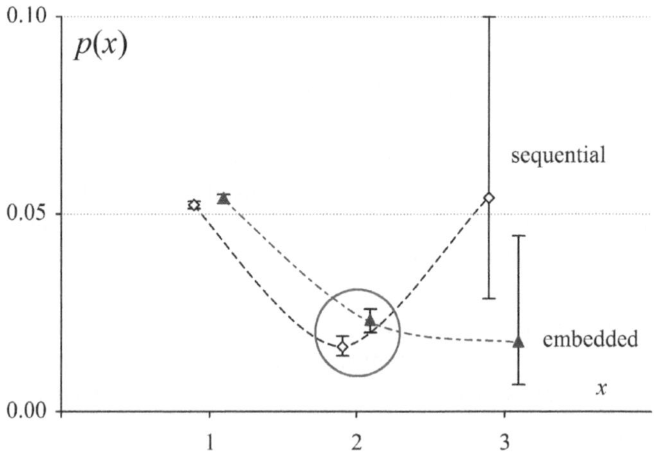

FIGURE 15.1 Sequential versus embedded NP postmodifying clauses, from Wallis (2019b).

are correctly assigned, and that the significant difference identifiable at $x = 2$ (circled) is not an artifact of incorrect classification?

Both embedding and sequential addition fall between $x = 1$ and 2. The graph tells us that the probability of embedding a second postmodifying clause, $p(2)$, is significantly lower than the probability of adding a single postmodifying clause, $p(1)$. The same is clearly true for sequential postmodifying clauses.

What might we report about the two second-stage probabilities, $p(2)$? Raw data from the corpus queries in Tables 15.7 and 15.8 are extracted in Table 15.9.

We can import this data into a 2 × 2 'point' test (see Chapter 14) to confirm that the two observations of $p(2)$ are significantly different. This can be simply tested with a χ^2 or Newcombe-Wilson test.[4]

The data are arranged in a contingency table in Table 15.10. The independent variable becomes 'embedded versus sequential', and the dependent variable is whether or not the additive step is performed.

This test is significant, as Figure 15.1 implies. The intervals do not overlap. But should we rely on the annotation? Are all cases analysed as containing doubly embedded or doubly sequential clauses *correctly analysed*? What about ambiguous cases like Examples (57) and (58)?

15.3.2 Testing the Worst-Case Scenario

Only one type of misclassification could change the outcome of the significance test.[5]

In our case, $p(\text{embed}, 2) > p(\text{sequential}, 2)$, $0.0230 > 0.0164$. Were any 'embedded' cases (like Example (58)) classified as sequential, this will *reduce the difference* between the probabilities, and risk the difference test becoming insignificant. Data move between columns in Table 15.10.

What happens if double-sequential cases are misclassified? Frequencies move in the opposite direction. *An error cannot undermine our initial significant result.* It can only move the two probabilities further apart. Conclusion: first review embedded cases! We only consider sequential cases if the result of the first review was that the significant result became non-significant (see Section 15.3.4).

TABLE 15.9 Comparing the probability of the second decision to embed or sequentially postmodify a noun phrase, a parsing decision that is potentially ambiguous.

	$f(1)$	$f(2)$	$p(2)$
embedded	9,862	227	0.0230
sequential	10,093	166	0.0164

TABLE 15.10 Data from Table 15.9, organised as a contingency table.

		embedded	*sequential*	*Total*
added	$f(2)$	227	166	393
¬added		9,635	9,927	19,562
Total	$f(1)$	9,862	10,093	19,955
probability	$p(2)$	0.0230	0.0164	

TABLE 15.11 Data from Table 15.10, following reallocation of potentially ambiguous embedded cases.

		embedded	*sequential*	*Total*
added	*f*(2)	**220**	→ **173**	393
¬added		9,635	9,927	19,562
Total	*f*(1)	9,855	→ 10,100	19,955
probability	*p*(2)	0.0223	0.0171	

Alongside cases that are incorrectly classified, we should check embedded cases for *ambiguity*. We do not have to definitively decide that an instance is incorrectly annotated, merely that it could be – as in Example (58). If in doubt, reallocate!

Examining all 227 cases, suppose we found that *f*(error) = 7 out of 227 cases were sufficiently ambiguous to suggest that they *could* be analysed as sequential.

We subtract this number from the 'embedded' column, add it to the 'sequential' one and recalculate the significance test. The result (with or without a continuity correction) remains significant.

Our calculation was simple. All we needed to do was consider the impact of misclassification on the experimental design.

In this example, misclassified instances *mutually substitute*. That is, two post-modifying clauses must be analysed as either embedded or sequential. Cases that do not alternate are eliminated.

Note how the method errs on the side of caution. We take a 'worst-case scenario' and transfer both incorrect and ambiguous cases. We apply the same *null hypothesis refutation* logic built into hypothesis testing to this review process. We try to undermine our initial conclusion. If that conclusion is undermined, we may turn to the other cases (sequential ones), to see if the initial conclusions may be restored. But, in this case, we do *not* transfer ambiguous cases (see Section 15.3.4).

This method also presumes that it is feasible to check all cases manually, which is possible for 227 cases, but unrealistic if cases run into the thousands. We turn to this question next.

15.3.3 Combining Subsampling and Worst-Case Analysis

Can we use this approach with subsampling? One option might be to employ the method of resampling and recalibration described in Section 15.2, and reallocate cases using this model.

An alternative method is to *estimate the misclassification rate* by subsampling. Again, we inspect the larger proportion set, so we take a random subsample of it.

Suppose we found that, in a random subsample of 100 out of our 227 cases, 5 were potentially incorrectly included. This factor, $p(\text{error}) = 5/100 = 0.05$, scales to ~11.35 out of 227 cases in error. This is larger than the error rate we identified reviewing every single case (7 out of 227), but maybe in subsampling 100 cases we were unlucky!

We also factor in the additional uncertainty into the inner interval for both observations, $p(\text{embed})$ and $p(\text{sequence})$ – both, since misclassified cases would transfer.

We compute a Wilson interval with a *finite population correction* on $p(\text{error})$. See Chapter 8. The standard Wilson interval assumes the population is infinite. But we obtained our error rate from a subsample, size $n = 100$, from a 'population' of finite size, $N = 227$.

The finite population correction factor ν is obtained from

$$\textit{finite population correction } \nu \equiv \sqrt{(N-n)/(N-1)} = 0.7496.$$

To apply the correction, we modify the interval for $p(\text{error})$ by substituting $n' = n / \nu^2$ for sample size n into Wilson functions (see Chapter 8):

$$\textit{best estimate of error rate } p(\text{error}) = 0.05,$$

$$95\% \textit{ Wilson score interval f.p.c. for } p(\text{error}), (w^-, w^+) = (0.0264, 0.0926).$$

This interval is justified on the basis that a random subsample of 100 cases will have an error, but the subsample is a large finite subset of our original 227-case sample.[6]

We combine this error interval with Wilson intervals for both observations, $p(\text{embed})$ and $p(\text{sequence})$ using the Bienaymé formula. The idea is sketched in Figure 15.2. We apply the scaled transfer frequency $f'(\text{error}) = p(\text{error}) \times N$ to obtain the best estimates of $p(\text{embed})$ and $p(\text{sequence})$ assuming the worst-case scenario, and estimate a new confidence interval for $p(\text{embed})$ and $p(\text{sequence})$. A breakdown of the calculation is provided in Table 15.12.

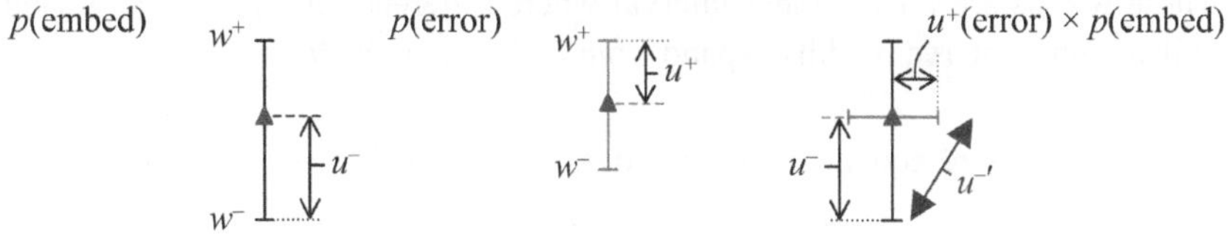

FIGURE 15.2 Bienaymé sum of independent variances rule applied to interval widths for $p(\text{embed})$ (lower bound) and $p(\text{error})$ (upper bound), scaled by $p(\text{embed})$.

TABLE 15.12 Finite population Wilson confidence interval for error, *p*(error), plus Wilson intervals for adjusted embedded and sequential observed rates *p*(embed), *p*(sequence), $\alpha = 0.05$. Inner intervals are indicated (lower right).

		error	*adjustment*	*embedded*	*sequential*
transfer			f'(error)	11.35	11.35
frequency	f	5	$f \pm f'$(error)	**215.65**	→ **177.35**
size	n	100	$N \pm f'$(error)	**9,851.65**	→ **10,104.35**
proportion	p	0.0500	p	0.0219	0.0176
f.p.c.	ν	0.7496			
corrected size	$n' = n / \nu^2$	177.9528			
Wilson score	w^-	0.0264	w^-	**0.0192** ↓	0.0152
intervals	w^+	0.0926	w^+	0.0250	↑ **0.0203**
Wilson widths	u^-	0.0236	u^-	**0.0027** ↓	0.0024
	u^+	0.0426	u^+	0.0031	↑ **0.0027**

Our best estimate of *p*(error) is 0.05 ∈ (0.0264, 0.0926) for $\alpha = 0.05$. Scaled to our $N = 227$ cases, this gives us an estimated range $f'(\text{error}) = 11.35 \in (5.9999, 21.0171)$.

Previously we transferred a fixed frequency ($f(\text{error}) = 7$). We can transfer the mean, but we need to incorporate the additional uncertainty obtained by subsampling.

The solution involves two steps: scale the upper width $u^+(\text{error}) = 0.0426$ by *p*(embed), and then combine it using the Bienaymé formula with the inner interval terms. (Refer to Figure 7.4 in Chapter 7.) We calculate adjustments as follows:

$$\textit{scaled error } u^{+\prime}(\text{error}) = u^+(\text{error}) \times p(\text{embed}) = 0.0010,$$

$$\textit{adjusted lower width, } u^{-\prime}(\text{embed}) = \sqrt{u^-(\text{embed})^2 + u^{+\prime}(\text{error})^2} = 0.0029,$$

$$\textit{adjusted upper width, } u^{+\prime}(\text{sequence}) = \sqrt{u^+(\text{sequence})^2 + u^{+\prime}(\text{error})^2} = 0.0029.$$ [7]

These widths are for the inner interval where difference $d = p_2 - p_1 < 0$. Both Wilson inner interval widths expand from 0.0027 to 0.0029.

$$d = p_2 - p_1 = p(\text{sequence}) - p(\text{embed}) = 0.0176 - 0.0219 = -0.0043,$$

$$\textit{NW lower } w_d^- = -\sqrt{u^{-\prime}(\text{embed})^2 + u^{+\prime}(\text{sequence})^2} = -0.0041.$$

We re-test $d < w_d^-$ and discover the result is still significant.

If misclassified cases were eliminated rather than transferred, we would perform the same process but not add *f*′(error) to the 'sequence' column, adjust *p*(sequence) or modify its upper bound.

We have traded the extra effort involved in checking all 227 cases for a more complex calculation, but a well-constructed spreadsheet can make this exercise simple to perform.

15.3.4 Ambiguity and Error

This method relies on the dataset being complete. The worst possible outcome is merely that we have to read and check every instance in the dataset, reallocating as necessary.

We refined the sample by taking a shortcut. We recognised that the most important question was whether there was evidence that undermined an initially observed significant difference. If we eliminate this possibility, the statement that the two probabilities are different is then safe to report. We do not have to examine the sequential cases to see if they were misclassified.

However, if after examining the larger proportion set, results became non-significant, we could examine the smaller proportion set to see if transferring in the opposite direction alters this result. (Note that, in such circumstances, it may well be preferable to review all cases or a larger subset.)

Any ambiguous member of the dataset must be placed in the smaller proportion set. *Ambiguity favours non-significance!* Err on the side of caution.

The worst-case testing method attempts to make an initial significant observation more robust by reducing the observed difference and increasing the margin of error. The reverse approach is not legitimate. Were our experiment to yield a borderline non-significant result and we were suspicious our data were inaccurate, we might review the dataset, *but we must not eliminate cases just to suit ourselves*.

Thus, if we originally found a non-significant result in Table 15.10, we would need to examine both embedded and sequential cases for classification errors, and the larger set for ambiguous cases.

15.4 Resampling and *p*-Hacking

If the result of reviewing a subsample were non-significant, it is clearly possible – and indeed tempting – to review more cases to see if this obtains a significant result. Here, it is wise to ask the question: is the problem that the subsample is too small – in which case it could legitimately be expanded – or is the perceived difference too small to be significant?

One of the benefits of employing a mathematical approach to inferential statistics is that it allows us to decide whether we have enough data to obtain a significant result. This is sometimes called a 'power calculation'. In this case, it allows us to decide whether it is worth reviewing more cases, and obtain a more accurate error estimate with a smaller confidence interval.

A word of caution is, however, required. Successive reviewing of cases *until* a significant result is found is '*p*-hacking'! See Chapter 11. By examining more cases and refining our estimate, we are gaining more information, but by planning to stop when we reach a significant threshold, we are favouring a significant result over a non-significant one. We should use these methods for the opposite procedure.

A commonly stated solution to this problem is to adjust the error level α by dividing it by the number of resampling operations you have performed. So a 'one in 20 error' becomes a 'one in 40 error' on the second attempt. But this does not really address the problem that by successive resampling, we risk 'selecting for significance'.

In Section 15.2, we subsampled a dataset. Had you drawn 10% in the first instance, you could draw another 10% of data and modify the overall α. Using the method of Section 15.3, it is sufficient to modify the α for p(error) because only this part of the data is being subsampled.

Most of all, however, you must be honest about such successive resampling whenever you write up your experiment!

15.5 Conclusions

Whenever we evaluate linguistic data from a corpus quantitatively, we must never forget that our data must be correctly identified *qualitatively*. 'The golden law of data' says we must be able to defend our data as sound and complete because research is only as good as the data on which it is based.

The process of abstracting data from a corpus and presenting it in a regular dataset is prone to a number of errors. The two principal problems you will need to address are:

- **Validating the dataset**. Candidate cases in the dataset irrelevant to our study ('Type C' cases) should be removed. We may also need to deliberately relax search constraints and obtain more candidates to avoid omitting 'false negatives'.
- **Validating assignment to categories within the dataset**. Misclassified cases must be reallocated across the dependent or independent variable.

If cases should be excluded, we need to consider the effect of excluding them. We review each subset of the dependent variable independently. However, if some cases are misclassified, then the effect of *reclassification* must also be modelled by transferring instances from one cell to another in a contingency table.

Often large samples are too big to be exhaustively checked, which is where the methods we discussed become useful.

Simple equal-proportion subsampling needs little introduction. We take a random subsample with a set proportion, say 10%, for all cells in a contingency table. The data will have the same proportional distribution. The overall weight of evidence has reduced by a factor of ten. We might subsample unevenly across the independent variable.

Where matters become a little more complicated is if we have a highly skewed initial distribution across the DV, as in the GET / BE passive alternation we discussed in Section 15.2. The proportion p is affected, and the resulting analysis may be misleading. We are not simply interested in whether the table 'is significant' (represents a significant difference), but the likely values of P, difference d, and so on.

We showed that we could legitimately apply an uneven subsampling protocol across a dependent variable provided we re-adjust p accordingly. We could even apply different subsampling proportions, β_1, β_2, for different values of p using this method.

Next, we turned to the question of where instances might be misclassified across values of the dependent variable. Preliminary results were significant, but we wished to eliminate the possibility that results were due to misclassification errors.

We applied a 'worst-case scenario' logic to the sample with the higher observed proportion, and demonstrated how this method could be used in conjunction with subsampling.

These methods should be seen as a complement to improving queries and corpus annotation standards. They provide a statistically defensible method in assisting researchers in obtaining the best possible estimate of the true rate of a phenomenon in language data, and determining whether the rate of one phenomenon is greater or lesser than another.

It should go without saying that the minimum requirement of a competent study is to ensure that cited results are not merely an artifact of poor annotation and abstraction methods.

There should be no excuse for not checking your data!

Notes

1 Among English parsed corpora, the *Penn Treebank*, *Susanne*, *Lancaster Treebank*, *DCPSE* and *ICE-GB* corpora were manually checked and corrected, whereas some English Constraint Grammar (ENCG) corpora were not. See Wallis (2020a) for a discussion of the philosophy of manual correction.

2 In commercial 'big data' analysis, this principle is consistently found in a list of consultancies' 'golden rules'! It features as Rule 2 in McKinsey's 'seven rules' for data analytics (Kelly et al., 2017).

3 Small capitals refers to the lemma (i.e., GET = {*get, gets, getting, got, gotten* . . .}).
4 In the paper, a goodness of fit separability test was employed, testing the pair of gradients at $d = p(2) - p(1)$. The same principle applies, but for this illustration we will consider the simpler comparison of the two proportions at $p(2)$.
5 This example considers the misclassification of examples by the independent variable ('embed' vs. 'sequential'), but the same logic applies to a DV.
6 Recall that we divide n by v^2. Arguably, we could use a one-tailed evaluation as we are only concerned with the error upper bound.
7 Although we add f'(error) to p(sequence), the observed error rate is still scaled by *the prior from the superset it was derived from* – the 'embedded' set.

16

ADJUSTING INTERVALS FOR RANDOM-TEXT SAMPLES

16.1 Introduction

In Chapter 8, we documented assumptions of the Binomial model. Two key ones are case independence and the freedom to vary:

- Every sampled case or data point is drawn randomly from an infinite population of instances. Every instance has a value *independent* from that of every other.
- Each instance is *free to vary*, that is, every item could have either value.

However, in many scientific disciplines, true random samples are difficult to obtain. Samples are rarely drawn strictly randomly from the population.

A common sampling bias is *convenience*: we sample the individuals easiest to recruit. This can arise for multiple reasons, such as consent. In a free society, medical researchers sample available volunteers rather than patients called up at random. But consent may bias sampling. Those most likely to give consent (primarily, adults) may not be the target population (children and adults). We must work within ethical constraints. We may turn volunteers away.

Another sampling bias is found in several disciplines, including corpus linguistics. Samples are not usually randomly drawn from a population of independent instances, but from randomly sampled *contiguous subsamples*. In corpus linguistics, these 'contiguous subsamples' are called 'texts'!

In this sampling regime, whereas any pair of instances from different subsamples satisfy the independence requirement, pairs from the same subsample are likely to be more similar to each other. Two clauses in the same text will probably share more characteristics than clauses from distinct texts.

DOI: 10.4324/9781003622697-21

Epidemiological research commonly uses *cluster sampling*, whereby each subsample is drawn from a particular location, family nexus, school, and so on. Just as two clauses from the same text share features, so neighbours or family members are more likely to share characteristics than strangers.

If this sampling assumption is undermined, several questions arise:

1. Are random sample statistical methods *invalid* on data of this type, or do they gracefully degrade?
2. Do we have to employ *different tests* or can existing tests be modified in some way?
3. Can we measure the *degree* to which instances in the same subsample are interdependent?
4. Would revised methods affect the *degree of certainty* of an observed score (variance, confidence intervals, etc.) or might they also affect *the best estimate of the observation* itself (proportions or probabilities)?

Brezina and Meyerhoff (2014) argue that since corpus samples are not 'true' random samples, linguists should dispense with Binomial models entirely. Examining the frequency of particular lexical items (words) per text, they demonstrate that standard Binomial models are unreliable, and propose the Mann-Whitney *U* test (Sheskin, 2011, p. 351, see Chapter 12) in place of χ^2. However, this approach dispenses with information and becomes highly conservative, and the concept of a 'median rank' has limited practical utility. We lose the ability to cite, with confidence, the true rate of an observed proportion.

A more promising approach involves hierarchical model-fitting (Gries, 2015). Q-level *hierarchical linear modelling* (HLM: Shin & Raudenbush, 2013) is a computational method employing maximum likelihood estimation to perform a best fit, a method also commonly employed in logistic regression (see Chapter 10). Cluster samples are defined by levels, so a corpus like ICE-GB might be characterised at three levels: *lexico-grammatical* (per-instance, linguistic alternation), *speaker* (e.g., age and gender) and *text* (text type, date, whether an audience was present, etc.). Variables at one level are assumed to be invariant at the level below (e.g., we assume that speaker age is constant during a conversation).

However, as methods become more complex, they also become more opaque. We have avoided discussing computational statistical methods in this book because they are not our focus. Our principal theme has been that researchers need to gain an understanding of their data.

A possible alternative approach, termed *a posteriori case interaction modelling*, was mooted by Wallis and Aarts (2007). This constructs a model of 'case interaction' by examining the interdependence of instances, and estimates a prior probability score for every instance. Methods based on counting frequencies are adjusted to sum prior probabilities. However, this is a complex exercise, and one that, like HLM, can only be carried by specialised software. It also requires a lot of data to be credible.

In this chapter, we describe a method derived from first principles that makes no assumptions about *why* cases may not be independent. Instead, we observe whether they are distributed *as if* they were independent, and factor this observation into our model of variability. Like HLM, the method is applicable to other research domains.

16.2 Recalibrating Binomial Models

Consider an observation p drawn from a number of texts, t', based on n total instances. We usually assume these n instances are randomly drawn from an infinite population, and employ the Normal approximation to the Binomial distribution. To briefly recap from Chapters 6 and 8, this employs a Gaussian standard deviation and variance:

$$\textit{population standard deviation } S \equiv \sqrt{P(1-P)/n}, \qquad (17)$$

$$\textit{population variance } S^2 = P(1-P)/n,$$

where P is the mean proportion in the population and n is the sample size. We defined Wilson score interval function equivalents $w^- = \text{WilsonLower}(p, n, \alpha/2)$ and $w^+ = \text{WilsonUpper}(p, n, \alpha/2)$, where

$$\textit{Wilson score interval } (w^-, w^+) \equiv \frac{p + \dfrac{z_{\alpha/2}^2}{2n} \pm z_{\alpha/2}\sqrt{\dfrac{p(1-p)}{n} + \dfrac{z_{\alpha/2}^2}{4n^2}}}{1 + \dfrac{z_{\alpha/2}^2}{n}}. \qquad (20)$$

The Binomial model assumes that all n instances are randomly drawn from an infinite (or very large) population. But we know they are actually drawn from clusters ('texts' or 'subtexts'). So, what difference does this make?

First, we measure the variance of observed proportions between text subsamples using two different models: one that assumes each text is a random sample, and another that examines the distribution of *actual* subsample scores.

Figure 16.1 plots a *quantised* frequency distribution of the rate of interrogative clauses per clause, p(inter), in 'direct conversations' in ICE-GB. Every cell count vertically represents a text with mean proportion p(inter) within that range, thus there is one text where $p(\text{inter}) < 0.01$. This graph is remarkably similar to the observed Binomial distribution in Chapter 6.

If subsamples were randomly drawn from a population of non-empty texts with mean $P = \bar{p}$, Equation (17) would estimate the variance as

$$\textit{predicted subsample variance } S_{ss}^2 = \frac{\bar{p}(1-\bar{p})}{t'}. \tag{105}$$

where t' is the number of non-empty texts, and $\bar{p}$ is the mean probability of these texts, $\bar{p} = \sum p_i / t'$. The actual variance of the per-text distribution $\{p_i\}$ is the 'unbiased estimate of the population variance' (Sheskin, 2011, p. 12), calculated by the following:

$$\textit{observed subsample variance } s_{ss}^2 = \frac{\sum (p_i - \bar{p})^2}{t'-1}. \tag{106}$$

Comparing these two variance estimates tells us the extent to which text samples differ from random samples. Equation (105) assumes samples are random. Equation (106) measures the extent of this 'randomness'. The method is reliable unless t' becomes very small (as a rule of thumb, $t' > 5$).

If variance estimates coincide, the entire aggregated sample is (to all intents and purposes) a random sample from the population. No adjustment is necessary.

We expect, however, that often the actual distribution will have a greater spread, $s_{ss}^2 > S_{ss}^2$. We employ the ratio of variances, F_{ss}, as a scale factor for the number of random independent cases, n:

$$\textit{variance ratio } F_{ss} = S_{ss}^2 / s_{ss}^2. \tag{107}$$

Next, we need to adjust n. As a rule, Gaussian variances with the same probability p are inversely proportion to the number of cases supporting them, n, that is, $S^2 \equiv P(1-P)/n$ (Equation (17)). We might estimate a corrected independent sample size n' by multiplying n by F_{ss} and scale the weight of evidence accordingly:

$$\textit{adjusted sample size } n' = n \times F_{ss}.$$

This adjustment substitutes the observed variance (Equation (106)) for the predicted Gaussian variance. However, we already know that t' cases must be independent, so we scale the excess, $n - t'$:

$$\textit{adjusted sample size } n' = (n - t') \times F_{ss} + t'. \tag{108}$$

Thus, if $n = t'$, n' is also equal to t'. If F_{ss} is less than 1, the weight of evidence (sample size) decreases, $n' < n$ and confidence intervals become broader (less certain).

This process adds information about the distribution of $\{p_i\}$ to the final variance estimate. Resulting significance tests should be more accurate and sensitive.

Adjusting n is easily generalised to other methods we have discussed in this book – contingency tests and Newcombe-Wilson intervals, meta-tests, confidence intervals on ϕ, and so on.

For example, we can employ this method with a continuity correction. See Chapter 8. The formula is comparable to the *finite population correction*, and it shares the same relationship with Yates's corrections, applied with the original unadjusted sample size n. Thus, the two-tailed Wilson interval with correction for continuity may be written as

$$w_{cc}^{-} = \text{WilsonLower}(\max(0, p - \tfrac{1}{2n}), n', \alpha/2), \text{ and}$$

$$w_{cc}^{+} = \text{WilsonUpper}(\min(1, p + \tfrac{1}{2n}), n', \alpha/2). \qquad (36')$$

where Wilson functions are defined by Equation (20), and n' is the adjusted sample size.

16.3 Examples With Large Samples

16.3.1 Example 1: Interrogative Clause Proportion, 'Direct Conversations'

Drawing frequency statistics from ICE-GB for interrogative clauses (denoted by 'CL(inter)') and all clauses ('CL'), for each text in ICE-GB, we obtain a large hierarchical table, excerpted in Table 16.1. There are 90 texts within the 'direct conversations' category made up of 120 subtexts. All in all, there are 29,503 clauses in 90 texts (each of approximately 2,000 words).

For now, let us assume each text is approximately the same size, and ignore subtexts. We will return to uneven size subsamples in Section 3.3.

TABLE 16.1 Snippet of data table extracted from ICE-GB.

	CL	CL(inter)	*words*	*p*(inter)
ICE-GB	145,179	5,793	1,061,263	0.0399
spoken	90,422	5,050	637,682	0.0558
dialogue	57,161	4,686	376,689	0.0820
private	32,658	2,901	205,627	0.0888
direct conversation	29,503	2,617	185,208	0.0887
S1A-001	322	20	2,050	0.0621
S1A-002	328	19	2,055	0.0579
S1A-090	326	44	1,968	0.1350

We merely assume that texts are randomly drawn from a population of comparable texts.

Let us consider the probability that a clause is interrogative, $p(\text{CL(inter)} \mid \text{CL})$, which we will label '$p$(inter)' for brevity. For direct conversations we can calculate

$$\textit{observed proportion } p(\text{inter}) = \frac{f(\text{CL(inter)})}{f(\text{CL})} = 0.0887.$$

With a true independent-case random sample, standard deviation and Wilson intervals on the observed proportion p(inter) would be as follows:

sample size $n = f(\text{CL}) = 29{,}503$.

standard deviation $s = 0.001655$.

Wilson interval $(w^-, w^+) = (0.0855, 0.0920)$ at a 95% error level.

This assumes that the 29,503 clauses are drawn at random from an infinite population of English native-speaker direct conversations. They are not. They are drawn from only $t' = 90$ texts (all non-empty). To what degree are these measures an underestimate?

Figure 16.1 plots a frequency histogram of p(inter) across $t' = 90$ texts. As we noted, provided texts are randomly sampled and n is large, this 'frequency distribution of texts' will tend to be Binomial.

We compute a Normal approximation to this observed Binomial distribution of the samples $\{p_i\}$. Mean $\bar{p} = 0.0890$. Equations (105) and (106) obtain

$$S_{ss} = \sqrt{\frac{\bar{p}(1-\bar{p})}{t'}} = 0.0300, \text{ and } s_{ss} = \sqrt{\frac{\sum (p_i - \bar{p})^2}{t' - 1}} = 0.0395.$$

The two Normal distributions, both centred on $\bar{p}$, are plotted in Figure 16.1, alongside the observed Binomial frequency distribution of texts.

The next step is to estimate the degree to which p(inter) does not distribute as random sampling would predict:

ratio $F_{ss} = S_{ss}^2 / s_{ss}^2 = 0.5779$.

The ratio is less than 1, so the observed Normal distribution has a greater spread than the predicted one. We should adjust our confidence intervals for p(inter) drawn from the population accordingly. Employing Equation (108),

adjusted sample size $n' = 17{,}089.02$,

standard deviation $S = 0.002175$,

95% Wilson interval $(w^-, w^+) = (0.0845, 0.0931)$.

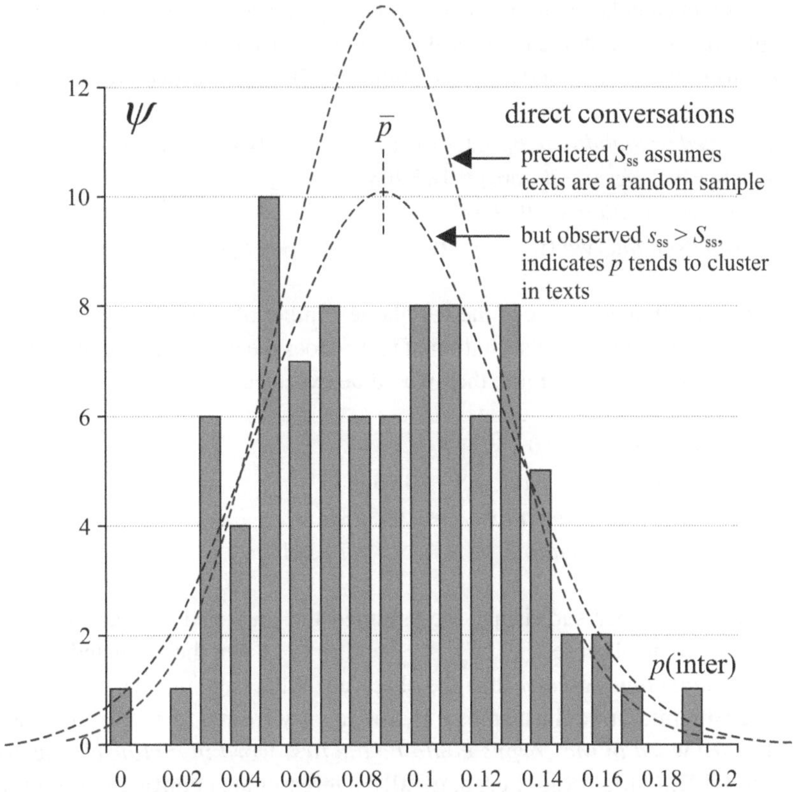

FIGURE 16.1 Observed frequency distribution of subsamples of p(inter), quantised to two decimal places. The two Normal approximations are also shown.

The confidence interval width has increased by a further third. This new sample size might be thought of as a hypothetical random sample supporting the observation, based on our actual corpus sample and its known distribution per text.

16.3.2 Example 2: Clauses Per Word, 'Direct Conversations'

Next, let us consider a word-based baseline or *exposure* rate. This is the probability that a reader or hearer will be exposed to a particular word, sequence or construction. See Chapter 3.

Suppose we wished to study the mean length of clauses, l, that is, the number of words per clause. We might model such a variable as the reciprocal of a Binomial proportion, $l = 1/p$, where p is the probability of any randomly chosen word in the corpus being the first word in a clause, which we might write as 'p(CL | word)'. Like all exposure rates, this probability sets aside what we know about grammatical structure!

We might calculate confidence intervals for p and convert them to intervals on length l by the monotonic reciprocal function. See Chapter 9.

Let us perform our standard calculation for ICE-GB direct conversation data:

observed probability $p = p(\text{CL} \mid \text{word}) = f(\text{CL}) / f(\text{word}) = 0.159297$,
number of cases $n = f(\text{word}) = 185{,}208$,
standard deviation $S = 0.00085$,
95% Wilson interval $(w^-, w^+) = (0.157637, 0.160970)$.

This is a small interval due to the very large number of words, n.

Next, we examine the distribution of texts. Does the distribution of clauses per word over the texts vary more than would be expected by chance?

distribution mean $\bar{p} = 0.159277$,
predicted standard deviation $S_{ss} = 0.038573$,
observed standard deviation $s_{ss} = 0.013781$,
cluster-adjustment ratio $F_{ss} = S_{ss}^2 / S_{ss}^2 = 7.8341$.

This result is rather surprising. We assumed the predicted variance would be smaller than the observed (i.e., $S_{ss}^2 < s_{ss}^2$ and $F_{ss} < 1$). But the predicted variance is nearly *eight times greater* than the observed! What is going on?

The Binomial model assumes p is free to vary from 0 to 1. But this means that *every word in the corpus could be the first word in a clause*! The conventional Binomial model dramatically overestimates confidence intervals for exposure rates (Wallis, 2012c). The dataset contains many 'Type C' cases, max(p) must be less than 1, and Equation (17) overstates the variance of p.

A useful side-effect of our method is we can also compensate for *this* error by observing the *actual* frequency distribution of subsample mean proportions. We are entitled to increase n by F_{ss} and further *reduce* confidence interval widths:

number of cases $n' = 1{,}450{,}317$,
standard deviation $S = 0.000304$,
95% Wilson interval $(w^-, w^+) = (0.158702, 0.159893)$.

We have drawn *more information* from the sample, which we use to improve the precision of tests.

This method does not solve the problem of poorly defined baselines. We merely compensated for the overestimated *variance* of $p(\text{CL} \mid \text{word})$. We did not improve our experimental design. We noted in Chapter 3 that per word rates *conflated opportunity and choice*. We have not separated these. A proportion such as

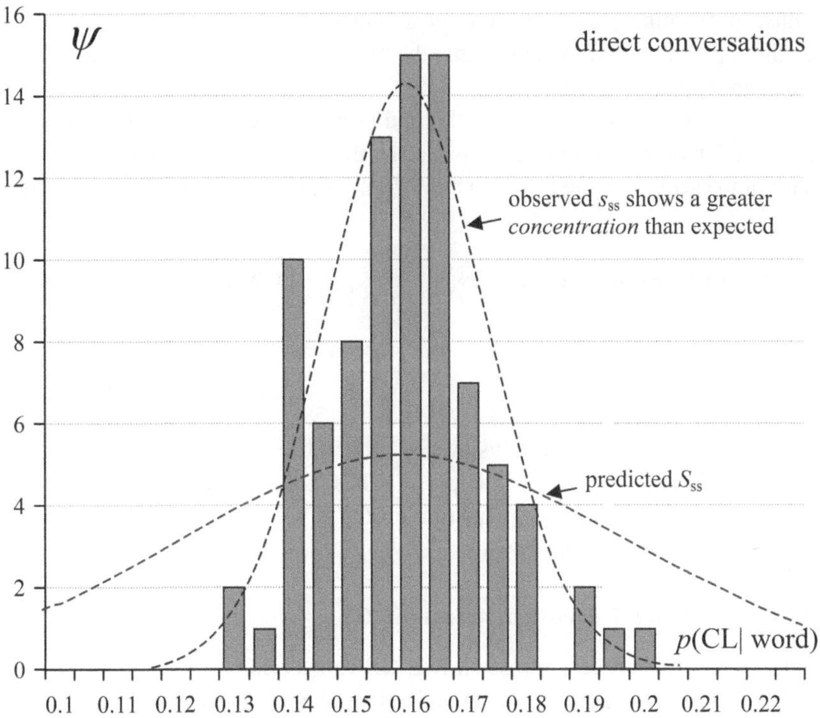

FIGURE 16.2 Frequency distribution per text, $p(\text{CL} \mid \text{word})$, ICE-GB direct conversations, with Gaussian curves based on predicted and observed measures of standard deviation.

$p(\text{CL} \mid \text{word})$ might vary between text types for multiple reasons, and unless we change baselines, we cannot distinguish hypotheses.

16.3.3 Uneven-Size Subsamples

Subsamples can vary in size. This is why the subsample distribution mean $\bar{p}$ and sample-wide mean p may be unequal. However, Equation (106) assumed subsamples were of equal size. We should correct this for two reasons.

- Texts vary in length. In ICE-GB, although texts are nominally 2,000 words in length, some are composed of independent *subtexts*, and we might wish to use these for greater accuracy, especially with smaller samples (see Section 16.4). Other corpora like the BNC contain texts of widely varying lengths.
- The dependent variable may have a different baseline than words! Even if texts had a fixed number of words, the number of *instances* per text, n_i, will likely vary.

Thus, in examining the tendency for a clause to be interrogative, p(inter), we ought to pay attention to the fact that the number of clauses per word also varies between texts.

We can generalise Equations (105) and (106) to uneven-size subsamples. The mean of subsample means, $\bar{p}$, is replaced by the overall mean, p. The internal variance of the set is weighted by $p(x_i) = n_i / n$, and we have $t' - 1$ degrees of freedom:

$$\text{observed subsample variance } s_{ss}^2 = \frac{t'}{t'-1} \sum p(x_i)(p_i - p)^2$$

$$= \frac{t'}{t'-1} \frac{\sum n_i (p_i - p)^2}{n}. \qquad (106')$$

Recalculating our examples using Equation (106'), we obtain $s_{ss} = 0.0397$ (Example 1) and 0.013856 (Example 2). These standard deviations increase by about 0.5%, which is minor. Equation (106') is more robust than (106), so we will use this formula from now on.

16.3.4 Example 1 Revisited, Across ICE-GB

Let us apply this process across all ICE-GB categories.

We anticipate that the probability of a clause being interrogative varies widely between text categories. Written texts and monologues are likely to have fewer than dialogues. Averaging over all 500 ICE-GB texts, we obtain the following:

observed probability $p = p(\text{inter}) = f(\text{CL(inter)}) / f(\text{CL}) = 0.0399$,
number of cases $n = f(\text{CL}) = 145{,}179$,
standard deviation $S = 0.000514$,
95% Wilson interval $(w^-, w^+) = (0.038908, 0.040922)$.

Employing Equation (106') obtains:

$S_{ss} = 0.008753$,
$s_{ss} = 0.044462$,
ratio $F_{ss} = S_{ss}^2 / s_{ss}^2 = 0.0388$.

The variation of p between different texts is much larger than the variation expected by the random sampling assumption. See Figure 16.3. Sample size n has reduced to approximately 4% of the original figure. Following rescaling, we obtain

$p = p(\text{inter}) = 0.0399$,
number of cases $n' = 6{,}107$,

standard deviation $S = 0.002505$,

95% Wilson interval $(w^-, w^+) = (0.035276, 0.045107)$.

This reduction in n amounts to multiplying the interval width by a factor of five. However, the initial interval was tiny, so the new interval is still small.

If we plot this distribution, Figure 16.3 reveals that the observed Binomial distribution does not match the predicted Normal distribution well.

The method merges each set of subsamples into a single set and estimates the variance of the superset. The assumption is that the sum of Binomial distributions is itself a Binomial distribution. The histogram in Figure 16.3 pools the Binomial distributions for every text category in ICE-GB. But instead of matching the ideal Binomial, the result is 'multimodal' with a broad spread.

The distribution is skewed towards zero and 157 texts contain no interrogative clauses.

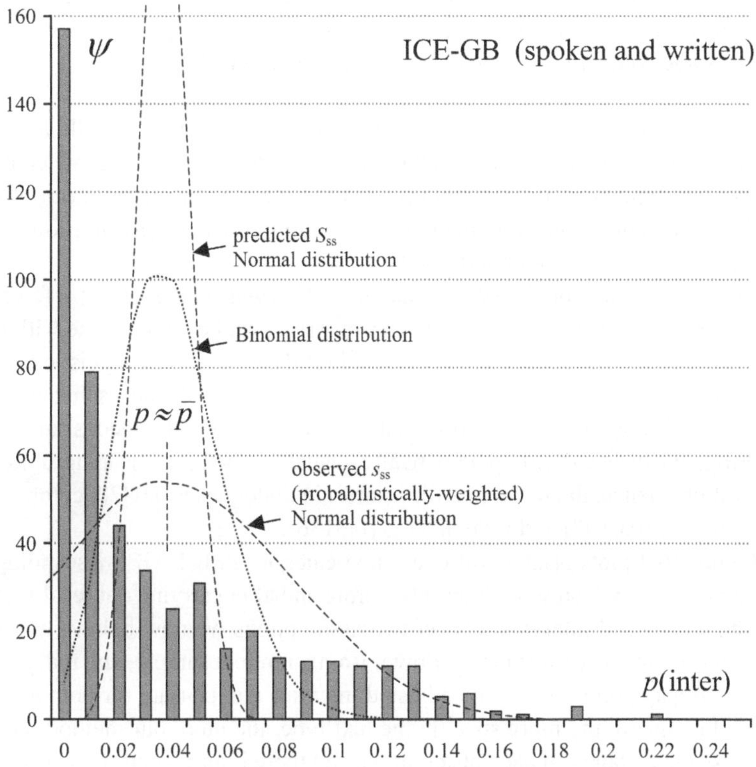

FIGURE 16.3 Frequency distribution for p(inter), all ICE-GB texts, with Gaussian curves for predicted and observed measures of standard deviation.

Let us review our methods. Even if the distribution is not Binomial, the sample is a collection of Binomial random samples. Does this fact undermine our method? Does our method err on the side of caution, or does it allow errors to slip through?

Despite the deviation from the Normal *distribution*, Equation (106') obtains a fair estimate of *variance*, which is what matters in this case. In the next section, we improve on the estimate of p and n using a method of partitioning and pooling.

In Chapter 5, we said the type of claim we can make from a diverse 'balanced' collection of texts like ICE-GB is subject to a cautionary note about the 'imagined population'. When we talk about an average proportion (or probability) calculated across diverse text types, all we can really claim is the following:

- **Multi-genre samples**. If the sample (corpus) is drawn from multiple text types, then this does not give us license to claim that results are generalisable to 'English as a whole', but at most to *an imagined population of an infinite number of comparable corpora.* A statistically significant result in a multi-genre corpus like ICE-GB can be said to generalise to an infinite collection of British English of the same period *obtained in the same proportions and with the same collection method* as the genre categories of ICE-GB.

In other words, were we to repeat the sampling exercise used to build and sample ICE-GB – with texts drawn in the same proportions from the same contexts, genres and time period – we could predict the likely value of the mean p(inter) in that new sample. But were the population subdivided in *different* proportions, that prediction would be undermined.

In Chapter 5, we concluded that, *subject to the limits of data*, it is preferable to rely on results drawn from specific subcategories – and compare 'like with like'.

This question also relates to that of meaningful baselines and linguistic choices. The variable we used in this illustration – the proportion of clauses that are interrogative – is a grammatical option, but it is not semantically unconstrained! An interrogative clause is only pragmatically available when it is meaningful to pose a question. Hence, the mean rate for p(inter) in dialogues is 0.0820, compared to monologues (0.0107) and written texts (0.0136).

Figure 16.4 plots p(inter) for every text category in ICE-GB, descending the hierarchy with Wilson score intervals, before and after carrying out recalibration.

The unadjusted intervals rely on two assumptions we now believe are probably untrue: that each instance is drawn from a random sample, and that p(inter) is free to vary from 0 to 1. The adjusted intervals compensate for both assumptions. In general, the more specific the text type, the more our method tends to increase the certainty of each observation. But there is an exception to every rule. 'Social letters' is less certain. We plot F_{ss} on a logarithmic scale to see where the greatest adjustments are taking place, and in which direction.

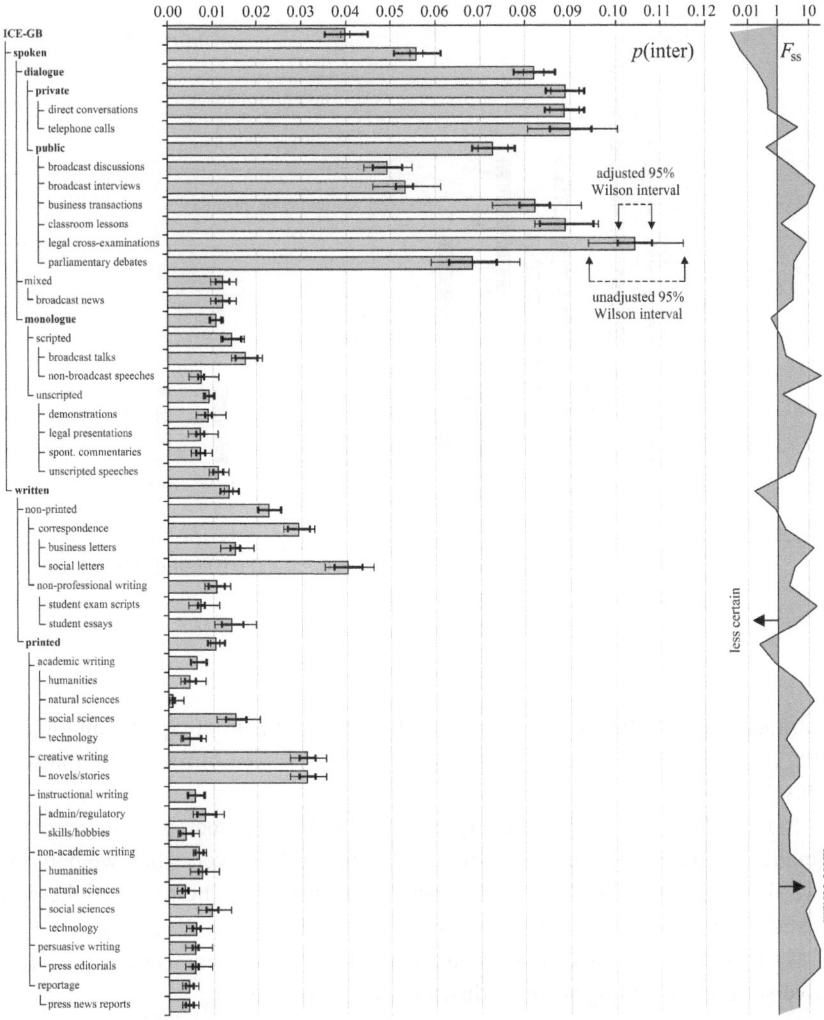

FIGURE 16.4 Proportion of interrogative clauses, p(inter), subdivided by text genre, before and after recalibration. The thick bars represent the adjusted 95% Wilson score interval, the thin bars, the unadjusted interval. F_{ss} is plotted on a logarithmic scale (right). Where $F_{ss} < 1$, recalibration widens the interval, and the observation is considered to be more uncertain.

We commented that pooling distributions tends to increase observed spread. We can see this by inspecting a hierarchical group in Figure 16.4. The category of 'non-printed writing' contains two subcategories: 'correspondence' and 'non-professional writing', each with distinct means. The result is the

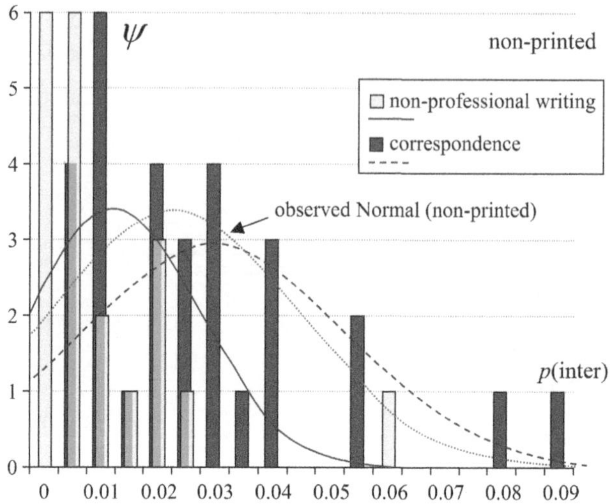

FIGURE 16.5 Observed frequency distributions (histograms) for 'non-professional writing' and 'correspondence', with means 0.0107 and 0.0292, respectively, plus Normal approximations.

'bimodal' distribution in Figure 16.5. The observed Normal approximation to this combined distribution (middle curve) matches none of these distributions closely.

Independently, each subcategory has a ratio $F_{ss} > 1$, that is, p(inter) has a smaller variance than the Binomial model predicts. However, when we pool the two distributions together to form a bimodal distribution, the peaks of the new distribution are quite far apart, contributing to a greater overall spread, and $F_{ss} < 1$ as a result. As we move up the genre hierarchy, we pool data from increasingly diverse sources, ending with the distribution of Figure 16.3.

16.4 Alternation Studies With Small Samples

So far, we have examined datasets with a very large number of cases, where n is large compared to t'. However, many research questions are not like this.

Let us revisit a study we discussed in Chapter 3: Aarts et al.'s (2013) examination of modal *shall/will* alternation, first person declarative positive contexts in DCPSE.

This study has two important attributes. First, data are quite sparse. There are around 100 cases in the entire 1990s subcorpus of 200 texts rather than the average 290 cases per text in the previous example. Second, we know that the dependent variable represents a plausible choice, that is, all cases of *will* could be replaced by *shall* and vice versa. Consequently, we do not expect intervals to contract.

16.4.1 Applying the Large Sample Method

We extract frequency data from DCPSE for LLC (1960s) and ICE-GB (1990s) subcorpora, and for every text within each subcorpus. We repeat the method outlined by Aarts, employing grammatical Fuzzy Tree Fragments for *I/we shall/will*, excluding negative examples followed by *not*.

Let us summarise some basic statistics and calculate the unadjusted interval. Our numbers are slightly higher than those of Aarts et al. because we did not manually review and eliminate a small number of potentially non-alternating cases.

Applying our adjustment, we have $S_{ss} = 0.0639$, $s_{ss} = 0.4247$ and $F_{ss} = 0.0227$ for ICE-GB. This gives us an adjusted n' of 59.95, only just above the number of independent texts, $t' = 59$ (for LLC, $n' = 61.97$).

The corrected intervals are slightly overlapping. Performing a Newcombe-Wilson test, the difference $d = -0.1899$ and interval is $(-0.1722, 0.1613)$. The difference is significant.

Repeating the calculation with subtexts increases t' and reduces the interval width accordingly (Table 16.3). However, F_{ss} appears to be contributing little in excess of t'. Why is this?

16.4.2 Singletons, Partitioning and Pooling

Let us inspect the distributions. Figure 16.6 plots both distributions of *p*(*shall*) per text in DCPSE, quantised to one decimal place. Neither is Binomial. We see two extreme peaks, one at 0 and the other at 1, texts where all cases are uniformly either *will* or *shall*. The peaks are far from the mean and distort the distribution. But the majority are singletons.

A 'singleton' text is one where $n_i = 1$. In our data, 34 texts in ICE-GB and 14 in LLC are singletons. In singleton texts, p_i can only be 0 or 1! Naturally, this distorts the overall frequency distribution of p_i in Figure 16.6. The good news is each singleton case is from an independent source.

TABLE 16.2 Original basic statistics for the alternation modal *shall* versus *will* in DCPSE, $\alpha = 0.05$. This interval assumes that every instance is independently randomly sampled.

	t'	n	*p*(*shall*)	w^-	w^+
LLC	57	193	0.5959	0.5254	0.6626
ICE-GB	59	101	0.4059	0.3153	0.5034

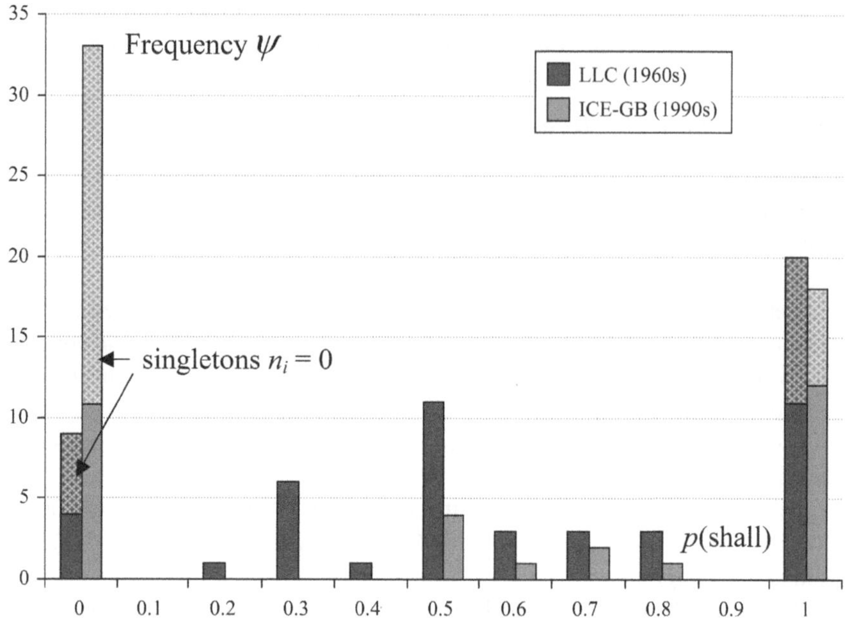

FIGURE 16.6 Distributions of *p*(*shall*) by text, LLC and ICE-GB subcorpora in DCPSE.

TABLE 16.3 Wilson intervals for *p*(*shall*) after re-weighting the evidence.

texts	*t'*	*n'*	*p*(*shall*)	w^-	w^+
LLC	57	61.97	0.5959	0.4716	0.7089
ICE-GB	59	59.95	0.4059	0.2910	0.5322
subtexts	*t'*	*n'*	*p*(*shall*)	w^-	w^+
LLC	78	79.32	0.5959	0.4859	0.6970
ICE-GB	63	63.44	0.4059	0.2939	0.5288

To improve our model, we use a process termed *partitioning and pooling*. We split the data into separate subsets, analyse them separately and then pool the results. For simplicity, we will partition the data into two subsets: the singleton set, **A**, and the remainder, **B**. But we could split **B** into $\mathbf{B}_1$, $\mathbf{B}_2$, and so on. See Figure 16.7.

Subdividing the texts, for ICE-GB we have $t'(\mathbf{A}) = 34$ and $t'(\mathbf{B}) = 25$, that is, there are 34 texts where $n_i = 1$, and 25 where $n_i > 1$. Part A is simple to calculate. Cases are independent, $S_{ss} = s_{ss}$, $F_{ss} = 1$ and $n'(\mathbf{A}) = t'(\mathbf{A})$:

sample size $n(\mathbf{A}) = t'(\mathbf{A}) = 34$,

frequency $f(shall, \mathbf{A}) = n(p_i = 1) = 12$,

proportion $p(shall, \mathbf{A}) = 12/34 = 0.3529$.

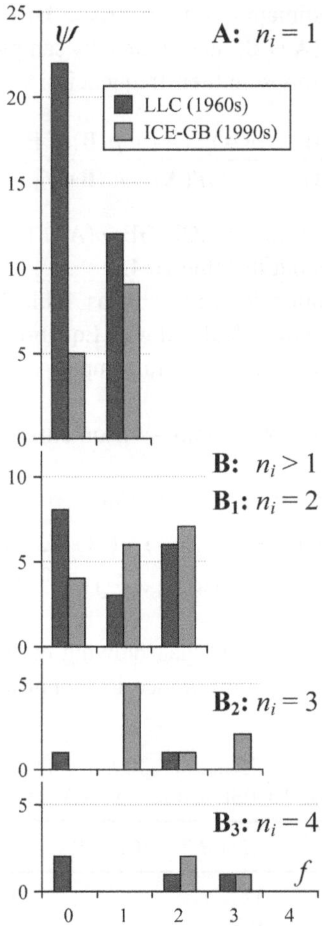

FIGURE 16.7 Distributions of *f*(*shall*) by text in DCPSE, subdivided by total hits n_i. In our example working, we partition the data into **A** and **B**, but further subdivisions are possible.

For part B, the calculation is as follows:

non-empty texts t'(**B**) = 25,
sample size n(**B**) = 67,
frequency f(*shall*, **B**) = 29,
proportion p(*shall*, **B**) = 0.4328.
predicted standard deviation $S_{ss} = 0.0991$,
observed standard deviation $s_{ss} = 0.3943$,
ratio $F_{ss} = S_{ss}^2/s_{ss}^2 = 0.0632$,
adjusted sample size n'(**B**) = 27.6533.

The total sample size estimate is simply $n'(\mathbf{A} \cup \mathbf{B}) = n'(\mathbf{A}) + n'(\mathbf{B}) = 61.6533$. The mean probability, $p(\mathbf{A} \cup \mathbf{B})$, is weighted by sample size. Since these sets do not overlap, we may simply sum their frequencies:

$$p(\mathbf{A} \cup \mathbf{B}) = \frac{f(\mathbf{A} \cup \mathbf{B})}{n'(\mathbf{A} \cup \mathbf{B})} = \frac{p(\mathbf{A})n'(\mathbf{A}) + p(\mathbf{B})n'(\mathbf{B})}{n'(\mathbf{A}) + n'(\mathbf{B})}. \tag{109}$$

The pooled probability of *shall* in ICE-GB, $p(\mathbf{A} \cup \mathbf{B}) = 0.3888$. The calculation for each subcorpus is set out in Table 16.4.

Repeating the calculation for LLC obtains Table 16.5. We have included a continuity-corrected interval calculated with Equation (33) for confirmation. We may perform Newcombe-Wilson tests to compare differences in observed probabilities. See Chapter 7.

We may now carry out a Newcombe-Wilson difference test:

difference $d = 0.3888 - 0.6025 = -0.2138$.
zero-based NW interval $0 \in (w_d^-, w_d^+) = (-0.1720, 0.1550)$,
with continuity correction $0 \in (w_{d\,cc}^-, w_{d\,cc}^+) = (-0.1744, 0.1598)$.

Since $d < w_{d\,cc}^-$, we may conclude that, drawing on the evidence from the per-text distribution, the observed difference in proportion between subcorpora is

TABLE 16.4 Estimating p and evidence weight n' for interval estimation by partitioning distributions per DCPSE text into parts A (singletons) and B (remainder).

LLC	*A*	*B*	*A ∪ B*	*ICE-GB*	*A*	*B*	*A ∪ B*
t'	14	43	57		34	25	59
n	14	179	193		34	67	101
f	9	106	115		12	29	41
p	0.6429	0.5922	0.6025		0.3529	0.4328	0.3888
S_{ss}^2		0.0056				0.0098	
s_{ss}^2		0.0669				0.1554	
F_{ss}		0.0839				0.0632	
n'	14	54.4120	68.4120		34	27.6533	61.6533

TABLE 16.5 Revised Wilson score intervals for *p*(*shall*) achieved by partitioning data, $\alpha = 0.05$.

A ∪ B	p	n'	w^-	w^+	w^-_{cc}	w^+_{cc}
LLC	0.6025	68.4120	0.4841	0.7101	0.4816	0.7124
ICE-GB	0.3888	61.6533	0.2771	0.5135	0.2727	0.5184

significant. Repeating the analysis for subtexts obtains $d = -0.1989$, a zero-based Newcombe-Wilson interval (−0.1609, 0.1467) and, with a continuity correction, (−0.1663, 0.1516), which also represents a significant difference.

Partitioning and pooling exploits our knowledge that the observed distribution per text is drawn from multiple distributions. Notably, pooling also adjusts the best estimate of *p*(*shall*) and hence differences, and this seems to have a greater impact than interval width adjustments.

16.4.3 Review

Figure 16.8 summarises the steps we took in this section. We began with a conventional unadjusted Wilson score interval, which assumes that every choice point is independent. However, we knew that many cases are drawn from the same text, so we took this into account.

The first adjustment applies the probabilistically weighted recalibration method to both subcorpora. We assume the per-text distribution is Binomial and reweight the evidence.

There is a flaw in this method, which becomes more serious with small samples. This 'Binomial' per-text distribution is really *the sum of multiple* Binomial distributions, one for each sample size n_i. Our data included a substantial proportion of texts which had a small number of cases per text. These could only output whole fractions.

In our data, over 40% of DCPSE texts were singletons, in which $n_i = 1$, and $p_i = 0$ or 1. Partitioning data into a singleton set and the remainder, we recalibrated each partition separately. We then pooled proportions p and summed n'.

There is no particular reason why we should stop at two partitions. We could continue subdividing for $n_i = 2$, 3, and so on. See Figure 16.7. However, a law of diminishing returns will apply.

We propose a similar heuristic to Cochran's rule for χ^2 tests:

> Do not partition data such that $t' < 5$. Instead, merge the partition with the smaller of the two adjacent partitions or stop partitioning altogether.

In our data, we opted to partition the data into two parts, and applied our method to DCPSE *texts* of regular lengths (LLC: 5,000 and ICE-GB: 2,000 words), and *subtexts* of variable lengths. Analysing distributions by subtext allowed us to improve sampling accuracy further, especially benefiting the LLC data. But the overall improvement was relatively minor. See Figure 16.8.

At the start of this chapter, we asked whether, by performing a reanalysis, the best estimate of p might change. With partitioning and pooling it does.

Indeed, the key difference between the 'adjusted' and 'partitioned' intervals in Figure 16.8 is that in the case of partitioning and pooling we use local means,

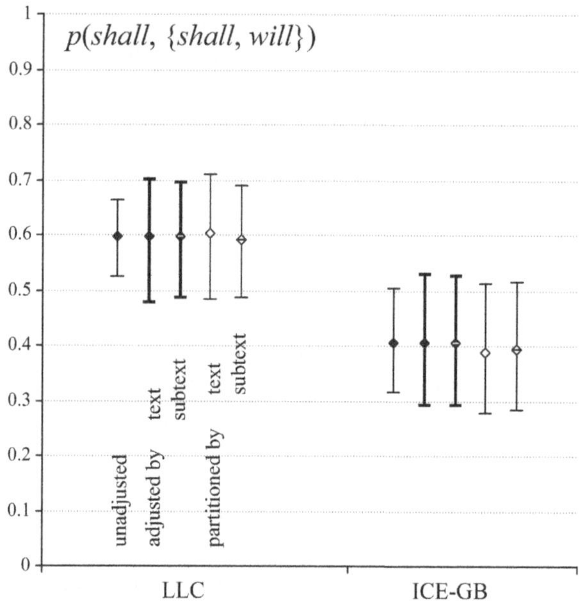

FIGURE 16.8 A range of best estimates and intervals for *p*(*shall*) in DCPSE subcorpora. Continuity-corrected intervals are not shown.

p(**A**) and *p*(**B**), to estimate variance and n', whereas in the standard method we employ a global mean, *p*.

16.5 Conclusions

In this chapter, we demonstrated a method for adjusting the estimated variance of a sample of *cluster samples*. In corpus linguistics, these are drawn from *texts*, but the method is extensible to any discipline where cluster sampling is carried out.

Crucially, as the method adjusts the Normal approximation to the Binomial distribution, it can be combined with other techniques, such as variance-weighted regression (Chapter 10) and meta-analysis (Chapter 14). We applied it to Newcombe-Wilson difference intervals and continuity corrections.

We inadvertently compensated for another issue, namely that many 'probabilistic' variables conventionally measured by linguists cannot plausibly reach 100%. Without this compensation, the Binomial model tends to overestimate the range of values for *p*. Correcting for it increases the power of tests.

In the case of small samples, however, one of our assumptions breaks down. Our working assumption was that the per-text distribution was approximately Binomial, which is reasonable for large samples. With small samples, a partitioning and pooling method was more accurate, but did not substantially change the ultimate result.

Performing the calculations involved described in this chapter is quite involved. For practical purposes, it might be worth noting that the minimum weight of evidence is simply the number of non-empty texts, t'. For small samples, a quick first-pass evaluation may therefore be performed by substituting t' for n in Wilson interval functions (Equation (20'')).

In this chapter, we have shown that a criticism occasionally levelled at corpus linguistics statistics may be resolved without abandoning the Binomial model. Researchers may apply a Binomial model of variation to data drawn from randomly sampled texts by factoring out between-text variance. The resulting method retains the power and flexibility that the Binomial model provides.

PART 6
Concluding Remarks

17

PLOTTING THE WILSON DISTRIBUTION

17.1 Introduction

We have discussed the Wilson score interval at length. But we have not plotted its distribution.

Traditional approaches to statistics focus primarily on theoretical, imaginary and often immeasurable *population* probabilities. Yet thanks to uncertainty, what the true value might be is often little more than a mathematically motivated guess. On the other hand, anyone dealing with data is necessarily contending with actual *observed* proportions.

Our approach to inferential statistics has therefore involved two steps. First, we refocused statistical reasoning onto the sample, away from the population. Second, we pictured sample uncertainty using confidence intervals. We consider two specific putative values of the population probability: the upper and lower bounds of a confidence interval.

The Wilson score interval has been the main vehicle for this approach. We might employ more precise 'Clopper-Pearson' inverted Binomial calculations, but since the Wilson interval aligns closely with the Clopper-Pearson, and is easier to calculate, the benefits of the approximation outweigh small costs of ultimate precision. It is also capable of accepting continuity corrections and other adjustments.

Wallis (2013a) shows that the interval provides a robust method for directly estimating confidence intervals on simple observations of Binomial proportions. Over the course of this book, we have shown how this interval can be applied to plotting data, comparing proportions and analysing larger tables, mathematical transformations and combinations of proportions, and logistic regression.

DOI: 10.4324/9781003622697-23

The Wilson score interval is the inverted Normal sampling interval, based on the famous 'bell curve' of the Normal *probability density function* ('p.d.f.') distribution. See Chapter 6 and Figure 17.1. However, so far, we have not learned how to plot the equivalent *Wilson* distribution. We have shown a curve or two in chapters, but we have not examined how this distribution behaves in different circumstances. As we shall see, it turns out to have some interesting properties of its own.

Given an observed Binomial proportion $p = f / n$ observations and error level α, the Wilson score interval represents the two-tailed range of values where a real value P would be considered to be not significantly different from p. (Note that f and n are normally integers, so whereas P is a probability that can be any value from 0 to 1, p is a proper fraction: a rational number.)

In this chapter, we compute and plot *Wilson p.d.f. distributions*. Our main purpose is to understand the performance of the Wilson formula, distribution and interval itself. When we plot an *interval* we select a single error level α. Visualising a *distribution*, on the other hand, exposes how the function behaves over all possible values of α, for different values of p and n. It reveals some surprises.

A second motivation is to counteract the *Normal fallacy*. This is the tendency to view the Normal distribution as if it were some kind of 'universal law of data'. This is obviously unwise in the case of observations of Binomial proportions, strictly bounded at 0 and 1.

In Chapter 6, we defined *Wilson functions* to compute the Wilson score interval (Wilson, 1927):

$$w^-(\alpha) = \text{WilsonLower}(p, n, \alpha/2),$$

$$w^+(\alpha) = \text{WilsonUpper}(p, n, \alpha/2). \qquad (20'')$$

At the lower bound of this interval (where $P = w^-$), the upper bound for the Gaussian interval for P, E^+, must equal p. We called this the 'interval equality principle'. A practical implication of this principle is that we can carry out a test for significant difference by either

1. calculating a Gaussian interval at P and testing if p is greater than the upper bound; or
2. calculating a Wilson interval at p and testing if P is less than the lower bound.

Where P is greater than p, we reverse this logic. We test if p is smaller than the lower bound of a Gaussian interval for P, or if P is greater than the upper bound of the Wilson interval for p. See also Appendix A.

Yet from the perspective of human experience, P and p are utterly different. Except on very rare occasions, *we never know what P is!* It is an imagined number, possibly given to us by some external standard ('no more than 5% of these light bulbs are permitted to fail after 10,000 hours of use': $P = 0.05$) or belief ('this coin is fair': $P = 0.5$). In a goodness of fit test, we usually compare p with the observed proportion of a superset ('the prior proportion'), so we might assign $P = p(x)$ or $\hat{p}$. But when we are considering variation about an observation, $p = f / n$, the only information we *actually* have is our observed p, and the weight of evidence sustaining that observation, n.

17.2 Plotting the Probability Density Function Distribution

We can define the Wilson *probability density function distribution* as the distribution of the values of this intangible, imagined P that are different from p, predicted by the Wilson score interval formula, Equation (20).

We must consider it as the sum of two distinct p.d.f. distributions:

- the distribution of the Wilson score interval lower bound w^-, based on an observed proportion p; and
- the distribution of the Wilson score interval upper bound w^+, based on p.

In this section, we explain how to plot Wilson score distributions from first principles.

This requires a little mathematical diversion. Fortunately, once we have done this, the same approach may be used to plot other distributions from any interval generating function. In Section 17.4, we use the same method to compute logit-Wilson, continuity-corrected Wilson and Clopper-Pearson distributions.[1]

Other p.d.f. distributions can be found on my blog, **corp.ling.stats**, including for the 'mid-p' interval (Chapter 8), the Newcombe-Wilson difference interval (Chapter 7), and intervals for mathematical operators like the sum and ratio of proportions (Chapter 9) and Cramér's ϕ (Chapter 13). These distributions can teach us interesting things about these relationships and properties. See also Figures 9.3 and 9.4 in Chapter 9.

17.2.1 *Calculating $w^-(\alpha)$ From the Standard Normal Distribution*

The first step is to calculate the lower bound, $w^-(\alpha)$, from Equation (20'''), for a series of values of α. The formula gives us the lower bound for any value of $\alpha \in (0, 1]$ (i.e., excluding zero). Previously we varied p and n. Now we vary α. Let us inspect the equation:

$$w^-(\alpha) = \text{WilsonLower}(p, n, \alpha/2) = \frac{p + \dfrac{z_{\alpha/2}^2}{2n} - z_{\alpha/2}\sqrt{\dfrac{p(1-p)}{n} + \dfrac{z_{\alpha/2}^2}{4n^2}}}{1 + \dfrac{z_{\alpha/2}^2}{n}} \qquad (20''')$$

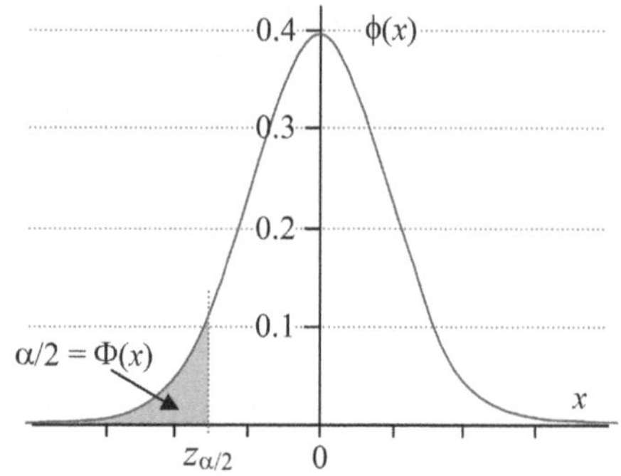

FIGURE 17.1 The standard Normal distribution probability density function $\phi(x)$ plots the Normal 'bell curve' with a standard deviation of 1 and a mean of 0. The cumulative density function $\Phi(x)$ calculates the area under the curve for all points less than or equal to x.

What does $z_{\alpha/2}$ represent? It is the two-tailed critical value of the *standard Normal distribution*. This is a Gaussian distribution with a mean of 0 and standard deviation of 1 (Figure 17.1). Its formula is quite complex, and statistics books traditionally present it in the form of a table. But crucially, it may be *scaled* by changing the standard deviation, and *repositioned* by altering the mean.

If $\alpha = 0.05$, we expect two tail areas, each representing 0.025 of the total area under the curve, at either end of a standard Normal distribution. Since the function of a constant is also a constant (1.95996), we have not worried about how it works! If we prefer $\alpha = 0.01$ or wish to employ a one-tailed test, we use a different constant.

Figure 17.1 plots the standard Normal distribution probability density function, $\phi(x)$. The function defining the area under the curve starting at $-\infty$ (minus *infinity*) and running up to x is called the *cumulative density function*, 'c.d.f.', $\Phi(x)$, the integral of $\phi(x)$.

Where x is equal to $z_{\alpha/2}$, $\Phi(x)$, the c.d.f. for x representing the tail area, is $\alpha/2$. How may we calculate $z_{\alpha/2}$? We employ the inverse function $\Phi^{-1}(x)$. We can write

$$\textit{two-tailed critical value for } \alpha,\ z_{\alpha/2} \equiv \Phi^{-1}(\alpha/2), \qquad (110)$$

where Φ^{-1} is the *inverse c.d.f.* for the standard Normal distribution. $z_{\alpha/2}$ is the position on the x-axis under the standard Normal distribution where *the area under the curve up to that point* is $\alpha/2$. This is the shaded area in Figure 17.1 from $-\infty$ to $z_{\alpha/2}$.

We can now obtain values for $z_{\alpha/2}$ for varying α. For the Normal distribution, we divide α by 2 because we are concerned with both ends of the distribution at the same time. To compute Wilson distributions, we consider each bound and tail separately.

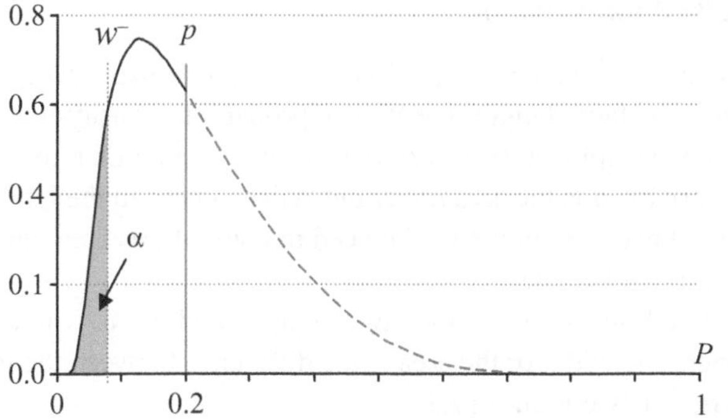

FIGURE 17.2 Sketch of the Wilson lower bound probability density function distribution of P showing the relationship between p, w^- and α.

For the lower bound Wilson distribution, we will refer to the area under the curve less than p as 'half unit area'. Among other things, a unit area is a useful way to compare distributions.

Equation (20''') obtains a position on a horizontal probability scale, w^-, computed for a given cumulative probability α. For $w^- < p$, the formula tells us that there is a probability of α that the true value P is below w^-. See Figure 17.2. The peak represents the most likely value of P less than p.[2]

17.2.2 Plotting Points

To plot an accurate curve, we should ideally plot every point in the range. This is impossible in practice. Experimenting with Excel™, we can obtain reasonably accurate plots by computing $z_{\alpha/2}$ and thus w^-, for $\alpha \in \mathbf{A}$ where

$$\mathbf{A} = \{0.0002, 1/640, 1/320 \ldots 1/40, 0.05, 0.1, 0.15 \ldots 0.95, 1\}.$$

This set excludes zero, but adds a tiny amount to it. It contains a series of fractions up to $1/20 = 0.05$ because we expect the tail area shape to curve, and finally it increases in steps of 0.05 to 1. At the maximum, $\alpha = 1$, $z_{\alpha/2} = 0$ and $p = P$ (the centre of the Normal distribution in Figure 17.1).

Equation (20''') permits one last shortcut. Due to the symmetry of the Normal distribution, the position of equal tail areas are equal, $z_{\alpha/2} \equiv -z_{(1-\alpha/2)}$. Indeed, for $\alpha > 1$, $w^+(\alpha) \equiv w^-(2-\alpha)$. We can plot w^+ using Equation (20''') by merely extending $\mathbf{A}$ to nearly 2:

$$\mathbf{A} = \{0.0002, 1/640, 1/320 \ldots 1/40, 0.05, 0.1 \ldots 0.95, 1,$$
$$1.05 \ldots 1.9, 1.95, 2 - 1/40, 2 - 1/80 \ldots 2 - 1/640, 1.9998\}.$$

17.2.3 Delta Approximation

The next stage is to convert Equation (20'''), the Wilson cumulative density function, into a column height (the Wilson probability density function).

To do this, we employ a *delta approximation*, a step familiar to students of calculus. The variable α is the area under the Wilson curve to the left of the Wilson score interval lower bound $w^-(\alpha)$. We need to convert this area (an integral) to a vertical position (a height).

We calculate Equation (20''') for two areas, α and $\alpha - \delta$, where δ (delta) is a small number. The width of the area is the difference between the two positions, $w^-(\alpha) - w^-(\alpha - \delta)$. See Figure 17.3.

We know that this area is not really a rectangle, but we can approximate it to a column of δ area and h high, and compute $h = width\ /\ area$. We can then plot h over x. There is an unknown error, ε, which we can expect to shrink as the width δ gets smaller.

For areas below p, $\alpha < 1$, we can use the following formula:

$$h(\alpha) = \begin{cases} 0 & \text{if } w^-(\alpha) = w^-(\alpha - \delta) \\ \dfrac{\delta}{w^-(\alpha) - w^-(\alpha - \delta)} & \text{otherwise.} \end{cases} \tag{111}$$

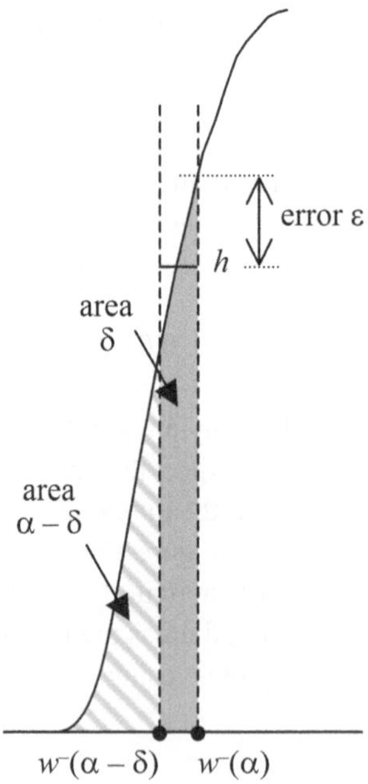

FIGURE 17.3 Estimating the height of $w^-(\alpha)$, $h(\alpha)$, using a one-sided delta approximation. As $\delta \to 0$, error $\varepsilon \to 0$.

The first condition addresses cases where $p = 0$, and all values of $w^-(\alpha) = 0$ (see Figure 17.7).

We can continue this approximation for $\alpha \geq 1$. For symmetric results, we can take a delta above α where $\alpha \geq 1$ (i.e., for w^+):

$$h(\alpha) = \begin{cases} 0 & \text{if } w^-(\alpha) = w^-(\alpha+\delta) \\ \dfrac{\delta}{w^-(\alpha+\delta) - w^-(\alpha)} & \text{otherwise.} \end{cases} \qquad (111')$$

Finally, we set $h(1) = 0$ when $p = 0$ or 1.

Equations (111) and (111') converge as $\delta \to 0$. Ideally, δ should be infinitesimally small – this is how *differentiation* works. But we are approximating with computer software, and this imposes limits. By experimentation, if $\delta < 0.0001$, results are unreliable in our version of Excel™! Rounding errors appear to be the culprit.

This leaves us with a small error in the calculation, as much as 0.003. To minimise this error, we can average heights estimated using delta approximations above and below α. This improves the estimate over the slope for any monotonic region $(\alpha - \delta, \alpha + \delta)$, and does not substantially worsen if α represents a peak value:

$$h(\alpha) = \left(\frac{\delta}{w^-(\alpha) - w^-(\alpha-\delta)} + \frac{\delta}{w^-(\alpha+\delta) - w^-(\alpha)}\right) / 2. \qquad (111'')$$

The Wilson distribution curve may be computed with Equations (20''') for $\alpha \in (0, 2)$, giving us the upper and lower curve. Nonetheless, the Wilson distribution is really the sum of two distributions, each with a unit area of 0.5. The first of these is the distribution for the upper bound w^+, the second, the distribution for the lower bound w^-. In the plots we scale each 'half-distribution' to the same scale as half the Normal distribution above and below p.

17.3 Example Wilson Distributions

17.3.1 Sample Size n = 10, Observed Proportion p = 0.5

First, let us explore natural fractions of $n = 10$. Ten is a small sample size, but not *so* small as to present particular issues. First, we will consider $p = 5/10$. We obtain a distribution that appears approximately Normal (Figure 17.4).

For comparison, we have included half-Normal distributions centred on $P = w^-(0.05)$ and $w^+(0.05)$, divided by $n/2$. Scaled like this, the area on the inner side of the mean of each Normal distribution is equal to the complementary Wilson area.

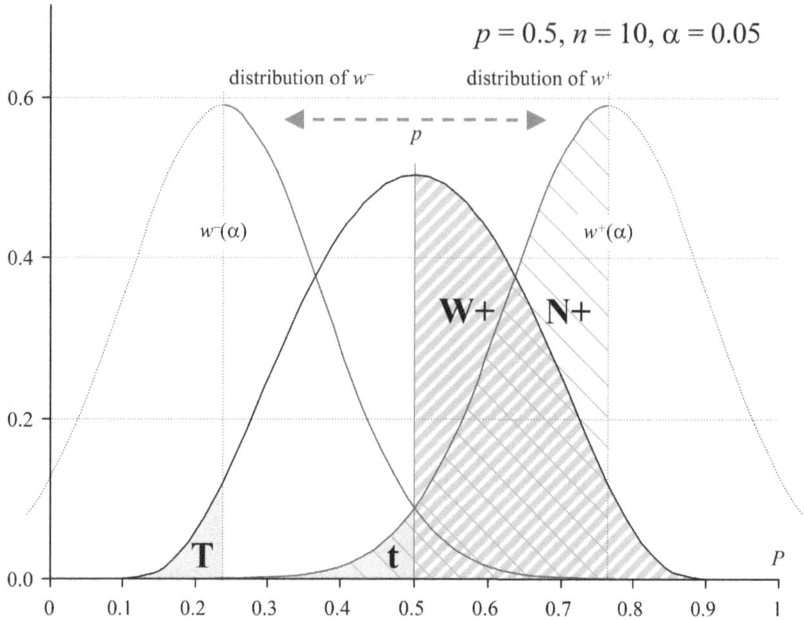

FIGURE 17.4 Plot of Wilson distribution (centre), with tail areas highlighted for α = 0.05, plotted p = 0.5, n = 10; with Normal distributions centred on w^- and w^+.

Were we to continue the Normal distribution beyond w^- and w^+, the other half would be 'clipped' by the boundaries at 0 and 1. However, the outer half is not inverted. *That* curve represents the situation where p is on the other side of w^- or w^+ – which it is not!

17.3.2 Properties of Wilson Areas

In Figure 17.4, the area under the Wilson distribution for w^+ (where $P > p$), **W+**, has the same area as the area under the complementary half-Normal distribution, **N+**. In this case, area(**W+**) = area(**N+**) = $1/n$. We refer to this as 'half unit area'. It has the same area as the Wilson distribution for w^-.

Provided that $p \in (0, 1)$ (i.e., it is not at the extremes), the interval will be two-sided, area(**W+**) = area(**W–**), and the total area under the curve is 2 × area(**W+**) = $2/n$ or 'unit area'.

The *tail areas* of the Wilson distributions, area(**T**), represent α = 0.05 of the area under the curve above and below p, respectively, in the same way as the equivalent tail area, area(**t**), of the Normal distribution represent 0.05 of the area under that curve.

Each tail area for the Normal, area(**t**) = area(**N+**) × α. Each tail area for the Wilson interval, below $w^-(\alpha)$ and above $w^+(\alpha)$, are α = 0.05 of each separate distribution. Thus, in Figure 17.4, area(**T**) = area(**W–**) × α (i.e., α/2 of unit area). This interval corresponds to a two-tailed test when p is not at the extremes, becoming one-tailed when p is at 0 or 1.

17.3.3 The Effect of p Tending to Extremes

As p tends to 0, we obtain increasingly skewed distributions. The interval cannot be easily approximated by a Normal interval, and the result is decidedly not Gaussian ('Normal').

In Figures 17.5 and 17.6, note how the mean p is no longer the most likely value (the mode). Unequal mode, median and mean are characteristics of skewed distributions like this.

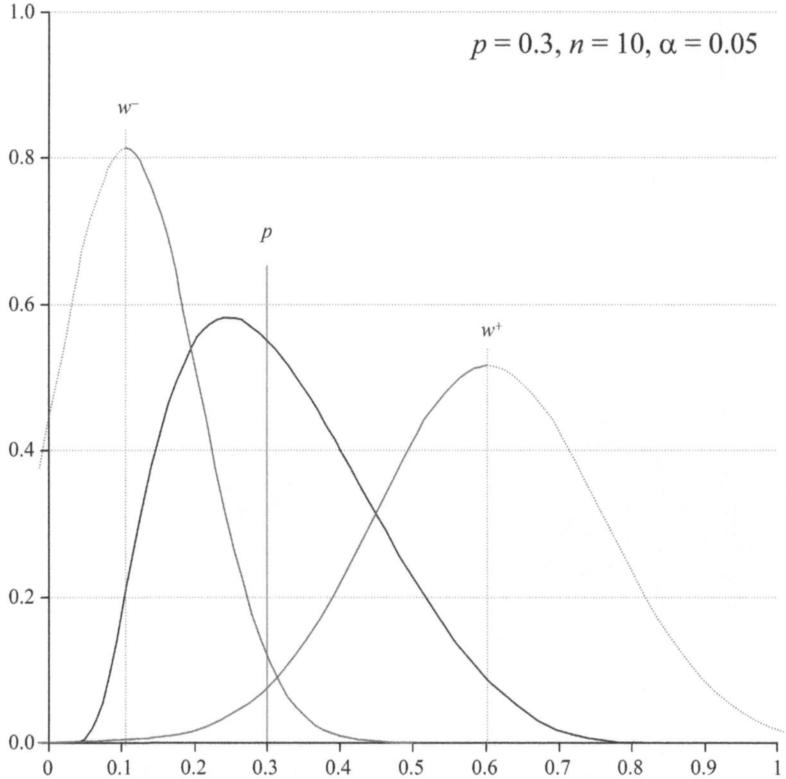

FIGURE 17.5 Plot of Wilson and Normal distributions, for $p = 0.3$, $n = 10$ and $\alpha = 0.05$.

In plotting this distribution pair, the areas on either side of p are projected to be of equal size, that is, we assume the true value P is equally likely to be above and below p. This is not necessarily true (and at $p = 0$ or 1, impossible), but this should not cause us to change the plot. We are exploring the impact of the Wilson distribution and the interval equality principle. In a test we evaluate interval bounds separately.

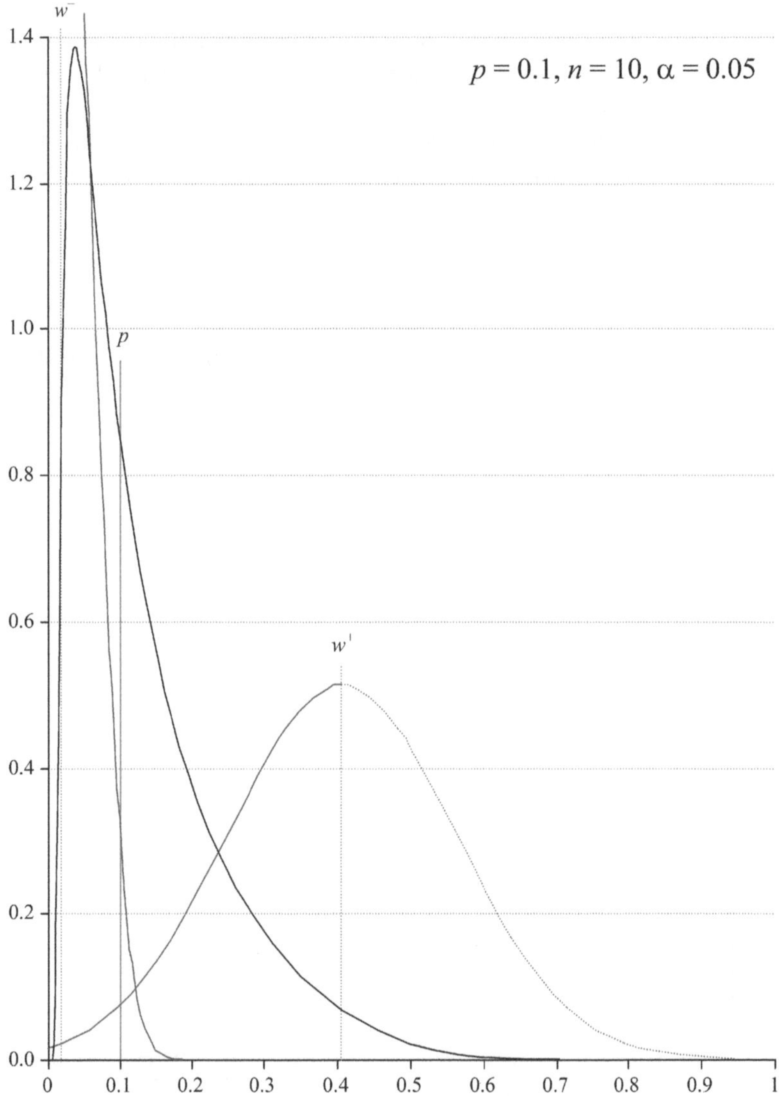

FIGURE 17.6 Wilson and Normal distributions plot, as Figure 17.5, but with $p = 0.1$.

Note how, thanks to the proximity to the boundary at zero, the interval for w^- becomes increasingly compressed between 0 and p, reflected by the increased height of the curve.

The tendency to express the distribution like an exponential decline on the least bounded side reaches its limit when $p = 0$ or 1. The 'squeezed interval' is uncomputable and simply disappears.

17.3.4 The Effect of Very Small n

What happens if we reduce n? All else being equal we should expect that *the smaller the sample size, the larger the confidence interval.*

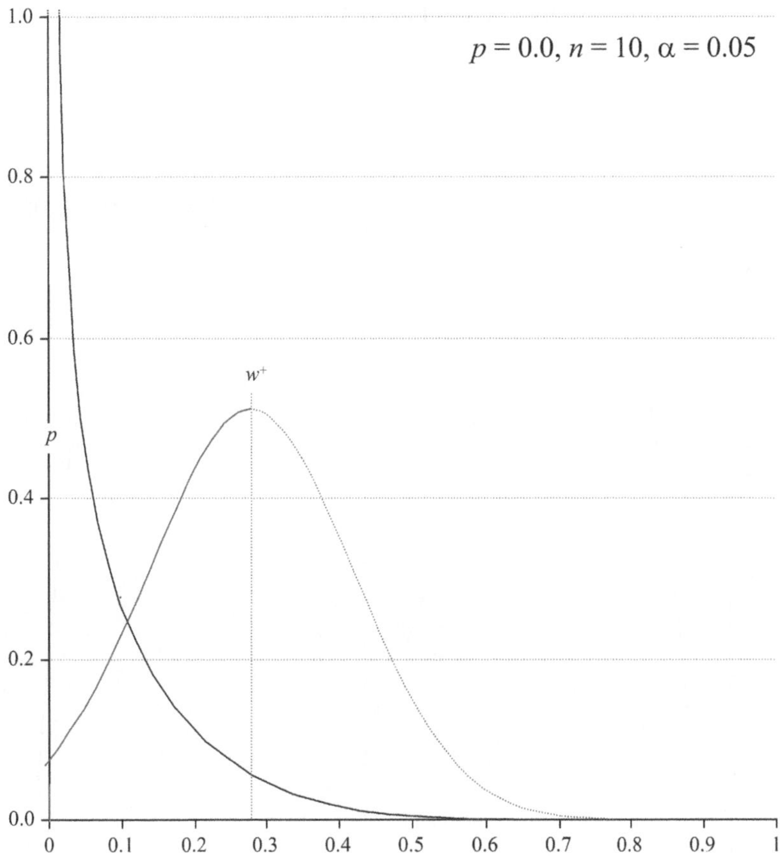

FIGURE 17.7 Plot of Wilson distributions for $p = 0.0$ and $n = 10$. The lower Wilson distribution is uncomputable. (The peak is not shown for reasons of space.)

We may plot Wilson distributions for $p = 0$ and $p = 0.5$ for $n = 2$. (Recall that p must be a true fraction of n, so, e.g., $p = 0.2$ is not possible in practice.)

The interval for $\alpha = 0.05$ now spans most of the range between 0 and 1. The boundaries 'squeeze' it inwards. We obtain the 'wisdom-tooth' shape in Figure 17.8 and an undulating curve in Figure 17.9. (The areas are larger because we are now scaling by 2/2 = 1 instead of 2/10 = 1/5.)

If we look at Figure 17.8 first, we see the gradient undulates as it descends to the right. Compare Figure 17.9 with 17.7. Both plot the distribution when $p = 0$, but Figure 17.7 has $n = 10$, and the curve declines before it is close to the boundary.

Nonetheless, this curve is quite conventional compared to the 'wisdom tooth' distribution for $p = 0.5$! Here the interval is so wide that the boundaries at 0 and 1 cause the area to 'bulge' so much that it is pushed up on either side above the mean. The distribution has become bimodal.

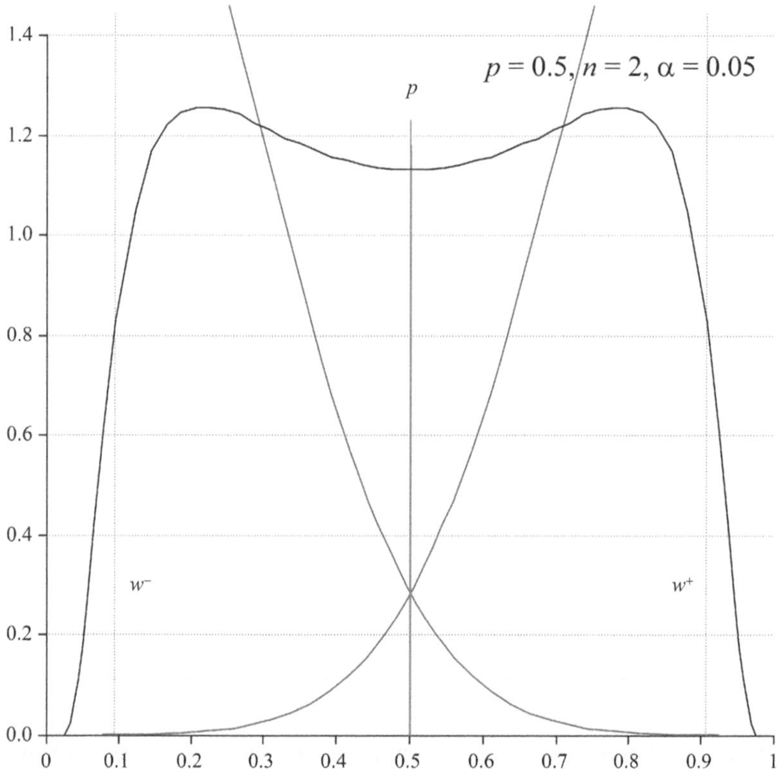

FIGURE 17.8 'Wisdom tooth' plot of Wilson distributions for $p = 0.5$ and $n = 2$.

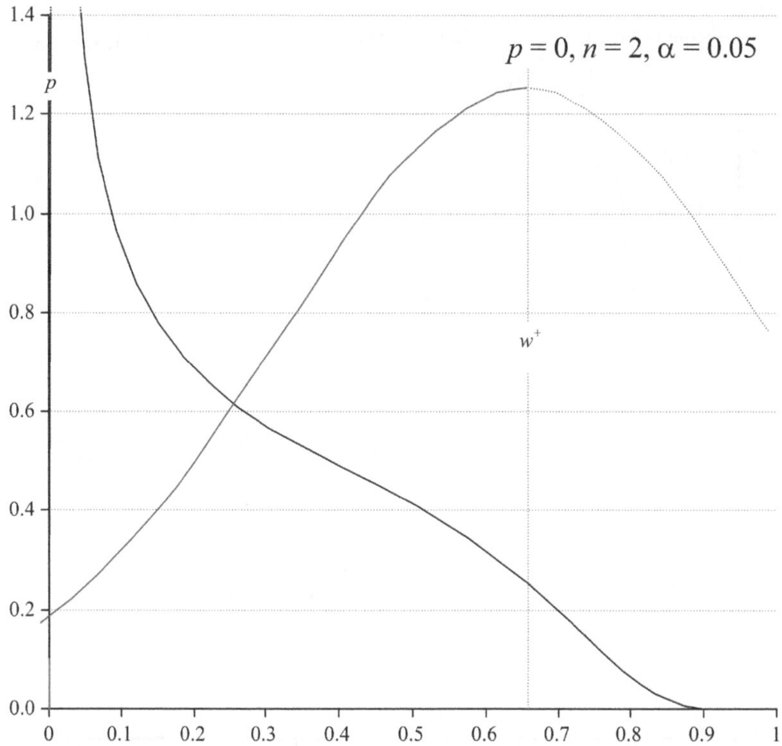

FIGURE 17.9 Wilson plot with undulating gradient decline visible for $p = 0$ and $n = 2$.

It is worth noting at this point that these curves represent rather mathematically abstract extreme distributions! They represent possible values of P when we have $n = 2$ observations and three possible values for p (i.e., $p \in \{0, 0.5, 1\}$).

Second, the most likely value for P in Figure 17.8 is the middle, $p = 0.5$. If we know nothing, there is a 50% chance P is above 0.5, and a 50% chance it is below 0.5. The chance of P being below (or above) any point is *in proportion to the area below* (or above) *that point*. The curve shows that this chance does not decline smoothly.[3]

17.4 Further Perspectives on Wilson Distributions

17.4.1 Percentiles of Wilson Distributions

We can plot percentiles of the two distributions, as in Figure 17.10. A percentile is a fraction of the distribution, so the bottom ten-percentile (or 'decile') is the area under the curve covering a 10% tail area; the next ten-percentile the next area, and so on.

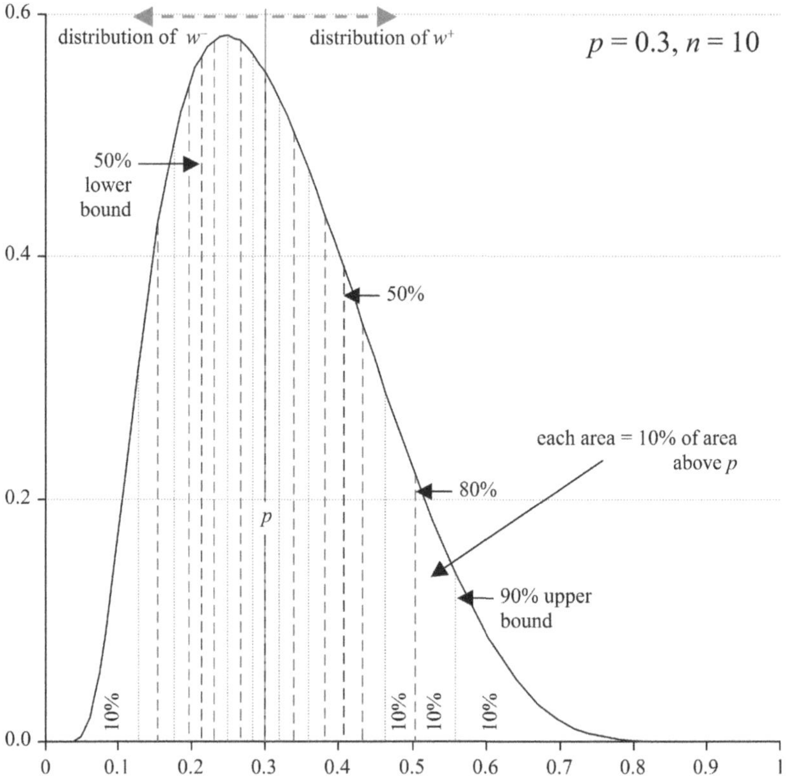

FIGURE 17.10 Ten-percentiles of the Wilson lower and upper distributions for p = 0.3 and n = 10.

Plotting percentiles is a useful way of considering how changes in α impact on the range. Figure 17.10 reveals horizontal positions and tail areas for α = 0.9, 0.8 and so on.

Figure 17.10 contains two distributions, containing 20 ten-percentile areas in total, each equal in area. Each area marked '10%' is of equal area. The fact that areas are equal is not always easy to see, particularly with respect to the tails.

17.4.2 Logit-Wilson Distributions

In Chapter 10, we noted Robert Newcombe's observation (Newcombe, 1998a) that – apart from when p is 0 or 1 – Wilson's score interval is *symmetric* on a logit (inverse logistic) scale. But Newcombe does not comment on the shape of the resulting distribution.

The 'logit-Wilson' regression method introduced in that chapter estimates variance using the Wilson interval on this logit scale. Gauss's method of *least squares regression over variance*, on which our method is based, assumes variance is approximately Normal.

Does *the Wilson distribution on the logit scale resemble a Normal distribution?* We can calculate logit($w^-(\alpha)$) using Equations (20''') and (69):

$$\text{logit}(p) \equiv \ln(p) - (1 - \ln(p)), \tag{69}$$

where 'ln' is the natural logarithm. Figure 17.11 plots the resulting distribution obtained by delta approximation. Half the mean of two heights obtains a unit area of 1:

$$h(\alpha) = \left(\frac{\delta}{\text{logit}(w^-(\alpha)) - \text{logit}(w^-(\alpha - \delta))} + \frac{\delta}{\text{logit}(w^-(\alpha + \delta)) - \text{logit}(w^-(\alpha))}\right) / 4. \tag{112}$$

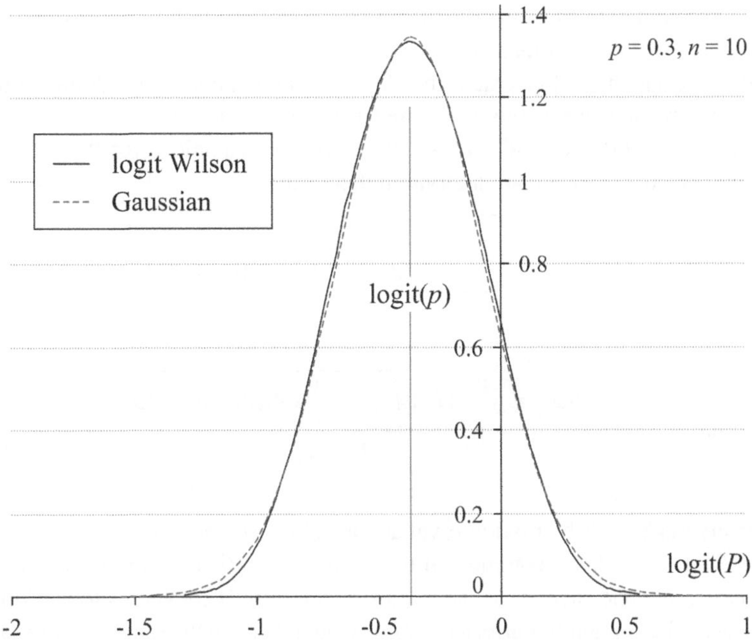

FIGURE 17.11 The logit-Wilson distribution. The Wilson score interval on a logit scale, transformed into a distribution, closely resembles a Gaussian distribution estimated with Equation (113) and $\alpha = 0.5$.

It turns out that, except when p is at boundaries 0 or 1 (which we exclude from fitting), the resulting distribution closely matches a Normal distribution estimated by the following:

$$\textit{mean}\ \mu = \text{logit}(p),$$

$$\textit{standard deviation}\ \sigma = (\text{logit}(p) - \text{logit}(w^-(\alpha))) / z_{\alpha/2}. \quad (113)$$

Figure 17.11 overlays this line with a Gaussian distribution estimated using α = 0.5 in this formula. This approximation improves with increasing centrality and increasing n. Indeed, by experimenting, we find an optimum value for $\alpha = 0.5$, implying we should use this value in regression.

Consequently, we can report that 'logit-Wilson' regression is sound as long as cases where $p = 0$ or 1 are excluded.

17.5 Alternative Distributions

17.5.1 *Continuity-Corrected Wilson Distributions*

The approximation from the discrete Binomial distribution to the Normal introduces an error conventionally mitigated with Yates's (1934) *continuity correction*. See Chapter 6. This widens the Normal interval about P by adding $\frac{1}{2n}$ to the upper bound and subtracting the same term from the lower.

Newcombe (1998a) and Wallis (2013a) present equations for the equivalent continuity-corrected Wilson interval in this form:

$$w_{cc}^- \equiv \max(0, \min(p, \frac{2np + z_{\alpha/2}^2 - \{z_{\alpha/2}\sqrt{z_{\alpha/2}^2 - \frac{1}{n} + 4np(1-p) + (4p-2)} + 1\}}{2(n + z_{\alpha/2}^2)})), \text{ and}$$

$$w_{cc}^+ \equiv \min(1, \max(p, \frac{2np + z_{\alpha/2}^2 + \{z_{\alpha/2}\sqrt{z_{\alpha/2}^2 - \frac{1}{n} + 4np(1-p) - (4p-2)} + 1\}}{2(n + z_{\alpha/2}^2)})). \quad (114)$$

This inverts Yates's Normal interval about P. See Appendix A.

In Section 17.2, we commented that 'the Wilson distribution' was really *two distributions*: one each for w^- and w^+. Equation (20''') converges to a midpoint. However, the continuity-corrected formulae do not obtain the same result for $\alpha = 1$. We cannot use the earlier shortcut, and must calculate intervals and heights separately for w^- and w^+.

Figure 17.12 reveals the effect of the correction on the intervals. As we would anticipate, it causes them to be more conservative (moving them further away from p), at the same time as causing each half-distribution to be compressed even further within the remaining probabilistic range on either side of p.

Each interval starts at $p \pm \frac{1}{2n}$, leaving a region in the middle. What is happening here? It is not part of either distribution. The continuity-corrected Wilson lower bound distribution is the distribution of P *known to be less than p*. The range $(p - \frac{1}{2n}, p)$ is where P is not known to be less than p as a result of Yates's adjustment.[4]

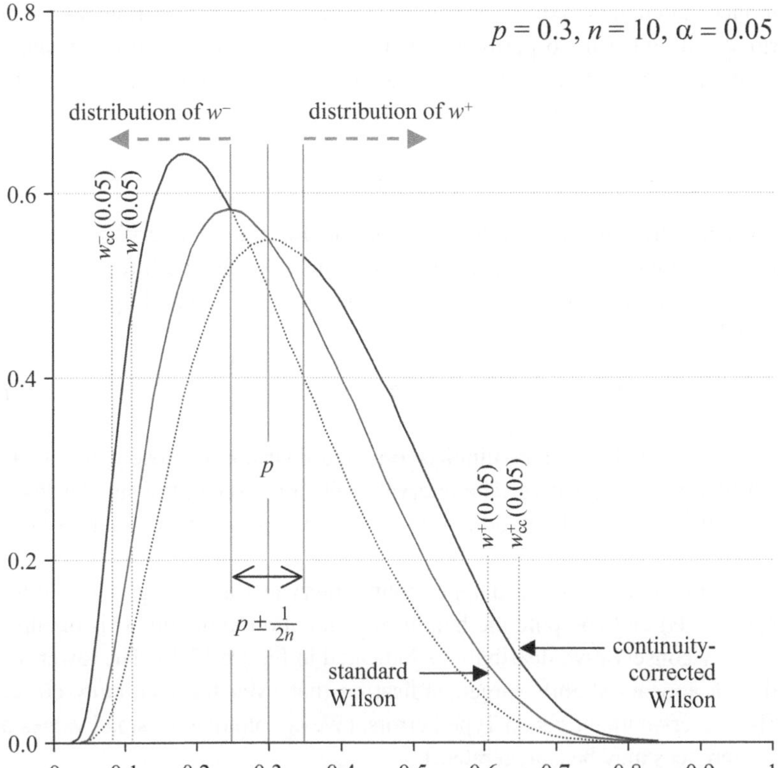

FIGURE 17.12 Uncorrected Wilson distribution (solid line) with continuity-corrected distributions for upper and lower bounds (dashed) and error intervals at $\alpha = 0.05$. By continuing the corrected distributions on the inner side, it is easy to see that the adjusted interval bounds are simply the outer bounds of the Wilson interval for $(p \pm \frac{1}{2n})$.

By continuing the plot, Figure 17.12 also reveals that the adjusted intervals calculated by Equation (114) are in fact Wilson intervals for $(p \pm \frac{1}{2n})$. This observation allows us to derive the following straightforward formula, which we present in this book.

$$w^-_{cc} \equiv \text{WilsonLower}(\max(0, p - \tfrac{1}{2n}), n, \alpha/2)), \text{ and}$$
$$w^+_{cc} \equiv \text{WilsonUpper}(\min(1, p + \tfrac{1}{2n}), n, \alpha/2)). \qquad (36)$$

where WilsonLower and WilsonUpper are functions returning the equivalent uncorrected interval bounds. See also Appendix A.

We have seen that this reformulation is very useful. It separates estimates of variance (calculated in the score interval formula) from the continuity correction term $\frac{1}{2n}$, allowing us to perform principled adjustments for different sampling conditions, for example, for a finite population (see Chapter 8) or random-text sample (see Chapter 16).

17.5.2 Clopper-Pearson Distributions

How does the equivalent p.d.f. distribution for the Clopper-Pearson 'exact' interval compare against this assessment? The lower bound interval for $p = f / n$, b^-, is obtained by finding P where the cumulative Binomial upper bound for P is $\alpha/2$:

$$\text{Find } b^- = P \text{ where } B(f, n; n, P) = \alpha/2. \qquad (39)$$

The result resembles the continuity-corrected distribution closely, but it can be slightly more conservative. The interval omits a region a little smaller than $p \pm \frac{1}{2n}$, slightly closer to the middle of the range. Areas under these curves are also unit areas.

We compute the lower and upper bound intervals for varying values of α (see Appendix B) and compute the height by delta approximation. This obtains the relatively conservative distributions indicated in Figure 17.13. The lower bound tail area appears slightly larger, indicating that even the continuity-corrected Wilson interval might obtain Type I errors. (We are plotting for small values of n, so differences may be exaggerated.)

Wallis (2025) employs delta approximation to plot the p.d.f. distribution of the 'mid-p' confidence interval (see Chapter 8) alongside other intervals.

17.6 Conclusions

The Wilson score interval is a member of a class of confidence intervals characterising expected variation about an observed Binomial proportion, $p \in \boldsymbol{P} = [0, 1]$.

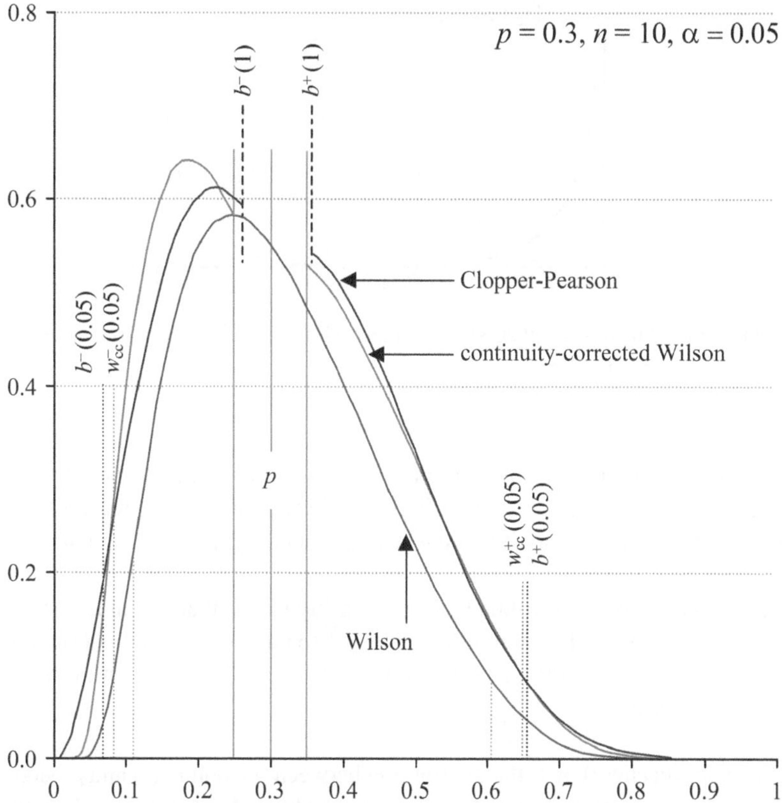

FIGURE 17.13 Twin distributions of Clopper-Pearson intervals compared to the distributions obtained by the Wilson score interval with continuity correction, $p = 0.3$ and $n = 10$.

These intervals also include the Clopper-Pearson interval, calculated by finding roots of the Binomial distribution for a given α, and the Wilson interval with continuity correction. All three behave similarly, with the Clopper-Pearson perhaps being slightly more conservative than the continuity-corrected Wilson interval in Figure 17.13. Wallis (2013a, 2020b) compares their performance empirically.

Aside from where n is very small, distributions computed for Clopper-Pearson bounds using the exact Binomial closely approximate those for continuity-corrected Wilson bounds. Both also reveal that the Wilson 'distribution' is in fact two distributions, one for each bound.

Common to this class of intervals is the fact that they are dramatically affected by boundary conditions at 0 and 1. In Chapter 10, we discussed the logistic curve

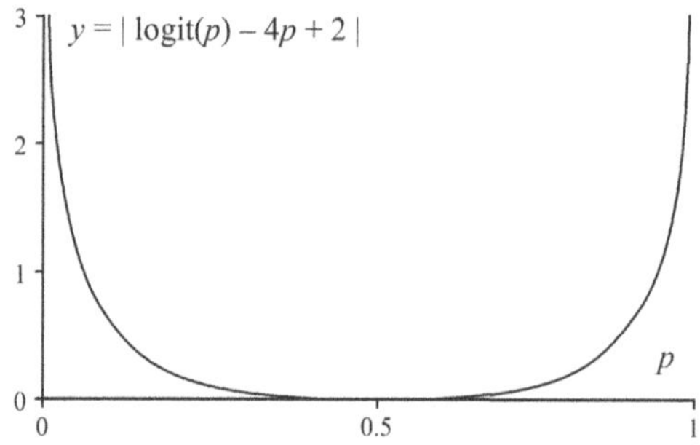

FIGURE 17.14 Absolute logit cross-section, which folds an infinite plane into a probabilistic trench.

at length. We pointed out that the inverse logistic, or 'logit', function maps a probabilistic range p to an unbounded Real dimension y by increasingly compressing the Real space as it approaches the boundary. Figure 17.14 shows the idea.

It is this compression 'folding into probability space' that explains our observations. The Clopper-Pearson plot (Figure 17.13) demonstrates this principle is not limited to the Wilson interval, but arises from the bounded nature of probability space itself:

1. As p approaches 0 or 1, the distribution between the boundary and p becomes increasingly compressed and the curve rises above the mean at p. Meanwhile, the interval on the 'open' side increasingly resembles a decay curve. This explains the curves in Figures 17.5 to 17.7.
2. In Figures 17.8 and 17.9, we examined distributions with small n. This appeared to generate a stranger shape. For $p = 0.5$ and $n = 2$, the distribution is bimodal. A small n causes the distribution to spread over most of the probability range, and the boundaries distort what would otherwise be a declining interval. We see a similar but less dramatic effect for $p = 0$.

The logit transformation of the same bimodal 'wisdom tooth' interval for $p = 0.5$ and $n = 2$ obtains a 'bell curve' approximating to a Normal distribution about 0 (see Figure 17.15). As n increases, the approximation improves, even for skewed p (apart from extremes $p = \{0, 1\}$, which are uncomputable). This observation is support for the logit-Wilson regression method described in Chapter 10.

This 'non-Normal' behaviour is due to the boundaries of the probabilistic scale.

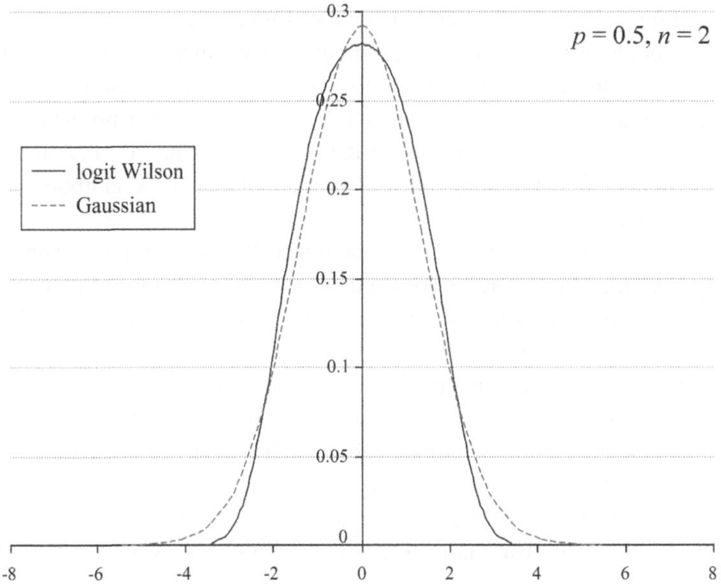

FIGURE 17.15 The logit-Wilson equivalent to Figure 17.8 and its Normal approximation ($\alpha = 0.5$).

We should be careful not to confuse these two formulations:

- **The range of values of *P not significantly different from p*.** This interval definition derives directly from the interval equality principle. It treats the case of P falling above and below p separately. The test is employed for a given value of P where its relative position is known. The intervals discussed in this book use this formulation because it is consistent with statistical testing.
- ;lyh Gilliland and Melfi (2010) discuss different conceptualisations of confidence intervals.

Finally, let us return to a point we made in the Preface. The act of plotting distributions allows us to begin to conceptualise the performance of otherwise dry algebraic formulae.

Statistical variation is not experienced directly. Distributions represent *the aggregated sum of experiences*. Statistical reasoning is therefore necessarily an act of imagination, and we must be careful not to be misled by false expectations.

Thus what we might call the 'bell curve expectation' or 'Normal fallacy' is the ideological predisposition to expect that variation around observations will be Normal and symmetric. The expectation appears in the Wald interval and presentations of 'standard error' for observed proportions or probabilities. It is found in 'bootstrap' intervals, albeit tempered by estimates of skew for sampled Reals. It is reinforced by numerous presentations of statistics. And it is incorrect.

In particular, the expectation is obviously mistaken on a probability scale. Distributions of expected values are often far from Normal. Boundaries exist in other naturally occurring contexts (see Chapter 12), but this assumption is fatally flawed for observed proportions.

The final reason for plotting curves and intervals is to help students understand statistical claims. In Chapter 6, we cited Stahl's (2006) history of early statistics in which he discussed centuries of resistance to statistical reasoning. To bring this chapter to a close, let us return to the 'chicken pox' example in the Preface.

In Figure 17.16, we plot the p.d.f. distribution of the Wilson score interval for $p = 0.25$, $n = 20$ and $\alpha = 0.05$. We can say definitively not just that it is likely the true rate in the population is below 0.5, but that it is even more unlikely to exceed 0.6 or be less than 0.05 – *all on the basis of a mere 20 random people.*

If we now examine the shaded tail area, we can see why chasing smaller error levels becomes a foolish game. If the upper bound, w^+, was 0.6, the tail area

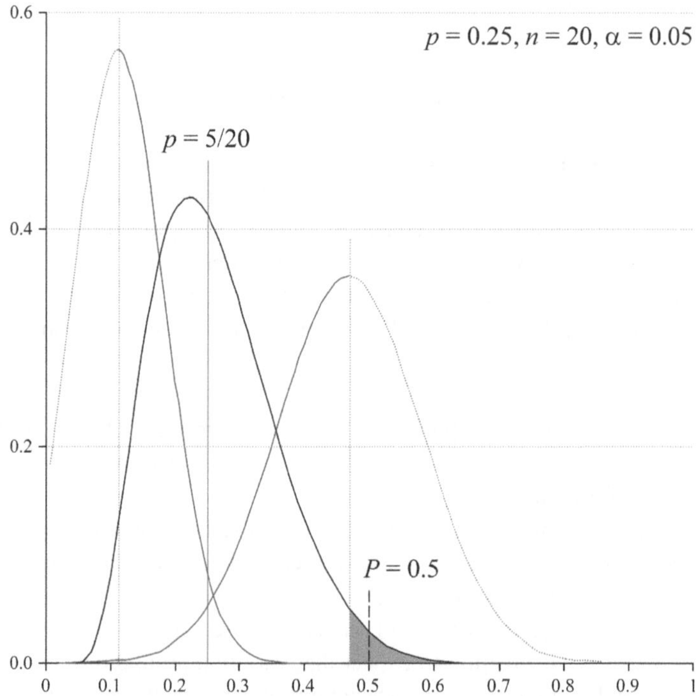

FIGURE 17.16 Wilson and Normal distributions for the 'chicken pox' example.

would be tiny, half of $\alpha = 0.0014$. At 0.7, it is infinitesimal. But the mean p and its Wilson distribution depend on how genuinely random our sampling was in the first place.

Notes

1 A spreadsheet for performing the calculations in this chapter (except the Clopper-Pearson which we compute separately) is available at https://corplingstats.wordpress.com/siclr.
2 It is worth re-emphasising this 'given $P < p$' clause. Despite forming a continuous curve, the upper and lower bound distributions are distinct. The lower bound is premised on $P < p$, whereas the upper assumes that $P > p$.
3 This 'wisdom tooth' distribution also exemplifies the difference between the two different conceptualisations of confidence intervals noted in the conclusion – the non-statistically significant range of P, and the most likely value of P.
4 This is why we decided that the 'DiffCorrect' function in Chapter 14 should set all observed differences falling in the range $p \pm \frac{1}{2n}$ to zero.

18
IN CONCLUSION

In this book, we have tried to demystify *statistical reasoning* in the conduct of corpus linguistics research. We think researchers must be able to understand the analytical steps they make in order to perform sound experimental research and to report and interpret the results of experiments.

The mathematics and logic we have used are not particularly difficult. It is not substantially different from the mathematics used to describe tangible physical variables.

For a researcher, the entire point of a statistical method is to understand the implications of their data. Research concerns the structure of the physical world: in linguistics, the structure of language. By invoking 'statistics' a researcher is trying to predict reliable patterns expressing general linguistic principles rather than describe mere artifacts of their data. Our task was to find ways of rendering statistical assessments *meaningful* and *relevant* to that exploration.

Core to this endeavour was a recognition that what makes inferential statistics difficult to understand is not difficult mathematics. Indeed, many natural phenomena we appreciate daily are mathematically more complex to model. Engineers need calculus.

Our argument has been that inferential statistics is *intangible to us*. Human beings do not experience the world as a distribution of many possible events, but as a sequence of episodes. Even when we experience multiple instances of a phenomenon, our brains can play tricks on us. Memories are faulty; we imagine patterns where none may exist. We miscount alternate cases when events did not happen, fail to measure baselines, and underestimate or overestimate risk.

DOI: 10.4324/9781003622697-24

Reasoning probabilistically requires a level of imagination that may be at times counter-intuitive.

> Do not be put off if you do not understand everything in this book the first time you read it. Everyone finds statistical reasoning difficult, so persevere. Carry out your own research. Plot data with confidence intervals. What do you think your data show? Discuss.

The traditional approach to teaching experimental statistics revolves almost exclusively around significance testing. Distributions are skipped over rapidly, confidence intervals are barely mentioned.

By contrast, in this book, we have concentrated primarily on the concept of a confidence interval. These intervals can be plotted alongside observations, so are immediately tangible. We derived significance tests from confidence intervals rather than the other way around. Even when we considered tests employing χ^2 summation in Chapter 14, we generalised them from simple tests with a single degree of freedom, derived from a confidence interval evaluation.

In Chapter 7, we saw how plotting data with intervals immediately allowed us to identify significant differences in our data without any further steps. Significance testing is secondary to the primary task of plotting data and engaging with a linguistic evaluation of what our results might mean. If we have carried out calculations correctly, the significance test will not contradict the interval assessment, and need only be carried out when intervals partially overlap. We can immediately see what the test is doing, and draw conclusions appropriately.

This allows us to focus more critically on our data. We need to be careful to take care to employ a meaningful baseline, and otherwise engage critically with graphed data.

In particular, we must avoid the trap of interpreting a correlation as evidence for a preferred underlying cause. This mistake is very easy to make. However, in uncontrolled corpus data, an observed effect may be due to multiple underlying causes. If we cannot distinguish these possible causes in our experiment, the right thing to do is to discuss each alternate hypothesis, what they predict, how they might be controlled for and what experiments might potentially refute them.

Crucially, such a discussion is a linguistic, not a statistical one.

This perspective means that regression algorithms for instance, while powerful, are best considered as tools for generalising trends in data, rather than an end in themselves. Multivariate analysis is only as good as the variables in the model. And so on. We do not agree with Briggs (2016) in treating all such methods with suspicion, but we do agree that unless we can engage with data by what he calls 'domain-specific theorising' (linguistic argument), we risk our algorithms ascribing causality where none exists. Algorithms do not 'explain' data.

Along the way, we have solved some problems that have dogged researchers for years. By reconstructing Binomial inferential statistics from the ground up we definitively resolve statistical disputes. Thus, in Chapter 8, we were able to distinguish the performance of different confidence interval estimates, and retire Wald intervals and log-likelihood tests. We could dispense with the 3-sigma rule and Cochran's rule, and use Wilson's and Yates's methods, respectively.

We also showed how confidence intervals can be constructed for multiple observed quantities, allowing us to specify their probable range. In Chapter 9, we demonstrated how a careful application of the 'MOVER' method can be used to derive confidence intervals for properties based on independent Binomial proportions drawn from contingency tables. This means that many effect sizes and other cited quantities are potentially capable of having a closed form confidence interval formula.

In Chapter 10, we showed how the relationship between the logistic function and Wilson interval might be exploited to perform logistic regression efficiently – and discussed the mathematical and conceptual limits of this procedure.

In Chapter 14, we addressed the common error of over-citation of critical values and '*p* scores', and offered instead a range of meta-tests for comparing test results, based on existing tests.

Having surveyed a number of ways we might employ statistical methods to solve research problems in multiple fields, in Chapters 15 and 16 we returned to two important methodological problems that corpus linguists inevitably have to address.

We showed that statistical methods may be used to support the laborious task of manually reviewing sampled data – a necessary and often overlooked step in corpus research. Despite the emphasis in this book on frequencies, proportions, distributions and mathematical models, if our source data are not what we think they are, all statistical generalisation must be in vain! It turns out that we can apply the Binomial statistical model to the task of reviewing examples.

A different application concerns the problem of random-text sampling (a kind of 'cluster sampling'). Corpora are collected as large collections of *texts*, rather than collections of random sentences. Instances drawn from such samples are therefore likely to be more similar than if they were drawn from a genuine random sample. We calculated observed within-text variation and compared it with the variation predicted by a random sampling model, and adjusted estimates of variation in the sample accordingly.

Looking at a single variable over different levels of the text category hierarchy in the ICE-GB corpus, we could see that clustering diverse samples (e.g., speech and writing) were likely to obtain a bimodal or even multimodal distribution. This observation led us to reinforce the argument we made in Chapter 5, that care should be taken in generalising from samples to populations. We cannot legitimately refer to 'American English', 'British English', and so on, but rather an imagined population of 'potential language samples obtained in the same way as the corpus was sampled'. This formulation may sound less satisfactory, but it is more honest!

We can use statistical methods to improve sampling precision and model random sampling. But statistical methods do not turn a poor experimental design into a good one.

This leads us to a final point that brings us back to the start. It is worth reminding ourselves why we are doing this. *Inferential statistics is a necessary part of the scientific method.* Grappling with these problems should be seen as part of the process of becoming a careful, self-critical researcher.

All experiments involve compromises. They obtain a limited sample. They employ approximate methods for extracting data, which (we hope) do not bias the result. Our duty is to try to make the most of what we have, and to be honest in reporting the defects in our research.

There are many types of 'research bias' (for a review, see Harris et al., 2009). Probably the most well-known concerns the non-reporting of non-significant results. Few papers tend to be written saying 'we looked, and there was nothing there'! See Chapter 11. But an allied problem concerns the tendency to gloss over experimental design weaknesses (sometimes called 'design bias'). To end this book, we would make an explicit plea to avoid this.

Reporting defects explicitly may not be popular, but it is essential. Necessary weaknesses in research design restrict the conclusions we may legitimately draw. All experiments represent a compromise. It may be possible for another researcher to improve on our experiment: for example, to employ a controlled laboratory experiment to review the results of a corpus one.

There is no shame in recognising the limits of your data and methodology when you write up your research. On the contrary, it is only through honesty in reporting that science can progress.

APPENDICES

APPENDIX A

The Interval Equality Principle

1 Introduction

In this book, we repeatedly refer to the 'interval equality principle'.

In Chapter 8, we noted that by far the most commonly cited confidence interval formula for an observed proportion (or probability), the Wald interval or 'standard error', fails to observe this principle, and for this reason, is fundamentally incorrect. The result is absurd behaviour (overshoot, zero-width intervals, see Chapter 8) and general imprecision. Newcombe (1998a) comments '[t]hese deficiencies, though well-known to statisticians, are little heeded in leading journals of major areas of application'.

The principle can be simply stated as follows:

when P is at a bound of p, p is at the opposite bound of P.

This statement is an *axiom* – that is, it is a principle that applies to *all* sampling intervals about the true population value P. Indeed, Neyman (1937) emphasises the same principle should apply to intervals on Real scales, such as the confidence interval for Student's t (see Chapter 12), which may need modification for boundaries.

1.1 Axiom

The interval equality principle can be expressed a little more rigorously.

The interval equality principle:

$w^- = P_1 \leftrightarrow E_1^+ = p$ where $P_1 < p$, and

$w^+ = P_2 \leftrightarrow E_2^- = p$ *where* $P_2 > p$,

where P_1 and P_2 are potential positions of P, and E_1^+ and E_2^- are the upper and lower bounds, respectively of P_1 and P_2. Similarly, w^- and w^+ are the sample interval bounds for p.

1.2 Functional Notation

We can also express the same principle with functional notation. Consider a pair of functions defining the lower and upper bounds of a two-tailed sampling interval about P, for sample size n and error level α:

$$E^- = \text{Lower}(P, n, \alpha/2), \text{ and } E^+ = \text{Upper}(P, n, \alpha/2).$$

The interval equality principle states that the equivalent interval about p is obtained from

$$w^- = \text{Upper}^{-1}(p, n, \alpha/2), \text{ and } w^+ = \text{Lower}^{-1}(p, n, \alpha/2).$$

Note that functions are inverted (hence 'Upper^{-1}') and bounds swap ('Lower' becomes 'Upper' and vice versa). For a one-tailed lower bound of p, we might have

$$E^+ = \text{Upper}(P, n, \alpha), \text{ and, correspondingly}$$

$$w^- = \text{Upper}^{-1}(p, n, \alpha).$$

We will refer to the two-tailed interval unless otherwise specified, hence the error level is usually halved.

2 Applications

This axiom, or a version of it, can in fact be applied to any sampling interval. In Chapter 8, we focused on confidence intervals on the probability scale $\boldsymbol{P}$ with parameters p, n and α.

We may compute inverse functions either with an algebraic formula (a 'closed form'), if one is available, or search, if not. Any monotonic function may be inverted by a search procedure. Suppose we want to find the two-tailed upper bound of p, w^+. We use a computer to find P where Lower(P; n, α/2) = p. At this point P will be equal to w^+. See Section 3.

2.1 The Wilson Score Interval

The Wilson interval is the inverse of the Normal sampling interval about P:

$$E^- = \text{GaussLower}(P; n, \alpha/2) = P - z_{\alpha/2} \cdot \sqrt{P(1-P)/n}, \text{ and}$$

$$E^{+} = \text{GaussUpper}(P; n, \alpha/2) = P + z_{\alpha/2} \cdot \sqrt{P(1-P)/n}.$$

The equivalent *confidence* interval about p is obtained from

w^{-} = WilsonLower(p, n, α/2) = GaussUpper^{-1}(p; n, α/2), and

w^{+} = WilsonUpper(p, n, α/2) = GaussLower^{-1}(p; n, α/2).

WilsonLower and WilsonUpper are usually computed directly from the Wilson score interval formula (see Chapter 8):

$$\textit{Wilson score interval}\,(w^{-}, w^{+}) \equiv \frac{p + \dfrac{z_{\alpha/2}^{2}}{2n} \pm z_{\alpha/2}\sqrt{\dfrac{p(1-p)}{n} + \dfrac{z_{\alpha/2}^{2}}{4n^{2}}}}{1 + \dfrac{z_{\alpha/2}^{2}}{n}}$$

Since WilsonLower is equivalent to GaussUpper^{-1}, the Normal z test for a single proportion (or 2×1 χ^2 test) obtains exactly the same result as a test based on the Wilson interval.

2.2 The Wilson Score Interval With Continuity Correction

The continuity-corrected version of each bound is widened, applying the correction thus:

$$E_{cc}^{-} = \text{GaussLowerCC}\,(P; n, \alpha/2) = \text{GaussLower}(P; n, \alpha/2) - \tfrac{1}{2n}, \text{and}$$

$$E_{cc}^{+} = \text{GaussUpperCC}\,(P; n, \alpha/2) = \text{GaussUpper}(P; n, \alpha/2) + \tfrac{1}{2n}.$$

The equivalent interval about p is then obtained from the following:

$$w_{cc}^{-} = \text{GaussUpperCC}^{-1}(p; n, \alpha/2) = \text{WilsonLower}(p - \tfrac{1}{2n}, n, \alpha/2), \text{and}$$

$$w_{cc}^{+} = \text{GaussLowerCC}^{-1}(p; n, \alpha/2) = \text{WilsonUpper}(p + \tfrac{1}{2n}, n, \alpha/2).$$

We can simply employ the same score interval formula to obtain an interval, although we would also wish to restrict this wider interval to the probability scale $\boldsymbol{P}$ = [0, 1]. As previous, the consequence of this derivation is that there is an exact relationship between the continuity-corrected single proportion z test, Yates's 2×1 χ^2 test and this interval.

2.3 Binomial and Clopper-Pearson Intervals

The Binomial interval is a little more complicated. This is for two reasons.

First, p must be an exact fraction of n (i.e., $p = x / n$), where both x and n are natural integers. Second, the cumulative Binomial function $B(x_1, x_2; n, P)$ is applied to find the greatest sum smaller or equal to $\alpha/2$, hence the expression 'max($fn \leq \alpha/2$)':

$$E^- = \text{BinLower}(P; n, \alpha/2) = x / n \text{ where } \max(B(0, x; n, P) \leq \alpha/2), \text{ and}$$

$$E^+ = \text{BinUpper}(P; n, \alpha/2) = x / n \text{ where } \max(B(x, n; n, P) \leq \alpha/2).$$

This obtains a conservative (wider) sampling interval because the source function B is based on a discrete distribution, p is an exact fraction of n, and tail areas need not be equal to $\alpha/2$. See Chapter 6.

The equivalent confidence interval about p is obtained from the Clopper-Pearson interval for $x = p \times n$. Now we can find an exact equality because P may be any rational proportion:

$$b^- = \text{BinUpper}^{-1}(p; n, \alpha/2) = P \text{ where } B(x, n; n, P) = \alpha/2, \text{ and}$$

$$b^+ = \text{BinLower}^{-1}(p; n, \alpha/2) = P \text{ where } B(0, x; n, P) = \alpha/2.$$

As discussed in Chapter 8, we obtain the inverted Binomial by a search procedure to find the value of P where the cumulative Binomial sums to $\alpha/2$. See Appendix B.

For the equivalence to work in both directions, the sampling interval about P must be continuous. The Cumulative Binomial function B is not continuous with p but discrete. On the other hand, since P can be any value, the Clopper-Pearson interval *is* continuous, and exact tail areas may be computed.

Although the equivalence does not hold entirely, the *process* of obtaining the interval for p is still one of inverting the population interval function. A variant of the Clopper-Pearson procedure obtains the 'mid-p' interval. See Chapter 8.

2.4 Log-Likelihood and Other Significance Test Functions

We can invert the log-likelihood function to obtain an interval (see Wallis, 2013a). First, we create an equivalent 2×1 χ^2 contingency table as follows:

$$\mathbf{O} = [np, n(1 - p)], \text{ and } \mathbf{E} = [nP, n(1 - P)].$$

We then employ the chi-square-distributed log-likelihood test formula

$$G^2 \equiv 2\sum o \text{ in}(o / e),$$

where $o \in \mathbf{O}$, $e \in \mathbf{E}$. Finally we employ a search procedure to find P where $G^2 = z_{\alpha/2}^{\ 2}$.

This method can be applied to any arbitrary function representing a significance test, such as a Bayesian function. Wallis (2013a) used this method with Yates's χ^2 test formula rather than the algebraic method in Section 2.2. It obtains the same result.

3 Searching for Interval Bounds With a Computer

To find interval bounds for p, we need to invert the interval formula for P.

At first sight, inverting simple functions appears easy. Every child is taught that the inverse of x^2 is the square root, $\sqrt{x}$. The square root of 9 is 3, and $3^2 = 3 \times 3$ is 9. (Note that in fact there is another value of x that satisfies $x^2 = 9$: *minus* 3. Indeed, the roots of x^2 are properly stated as $\pm\sqrt{x}$.)

But suppose we wanted to find a positive square root of an arbitrary number, say, 10. How could we work it out without using a calculator or computer? (To put it another way, how might a computer work it out?)

We know the integer squares on either side of 10: $3^2 = 9$ and $4^2 = 16$. We also know the square function is *monotonic* for positive numbers. This means that it increases or decreases steadily over its range. So the square root of 10 must fall between 3 and 4. We have to search this range.

A simple 'divide and conquer' binary search method employs an iterative procedure that *converges* on the correct answer by a series of repeated intelligent guesses. There are cleverer methods that converge more quickly, but this method is guaranteed to work with any monotonic function.

Pick halfway (i.e., 3.5) and test that. This gives us $3.5^2 = 12.25$, which is obviously too high. But we have learned something. Since 10 is between 9 and 12.25, the square root of 10 must be between 3 and 3.5. We have immediately eliminated half of the range!

The iterative part is then to say, *let us repeat the 'pick halfway' approach with this lower range.*

So now we examine $3.25^2 = 10.5625$. We are much closer to a solution after only two iterations. Again, this number is too high, and we search the range [3, 3.25], and so on. The next stages give us [3.125, 3.25], [3.125, 3.1875], [3.15625, 3.1875]. We have not yet arrived at a solution, but the range is shrinking, and after six cycles one of the values (3.15625) has an error of less than 0.03. This is what is meant by saying the method 'converges on' a solution. See Figure A1.1.

There are more sophisticated versions of the same procedure employing calculus which converge more quickly, but this method has an important advantage: *it can be employed with any monotonic function or ordered series without further analysis.*

We can use this method to invert the lower bound of an interval for P. Thus to find the lower bound of the Wilson score interval for p by search, we would

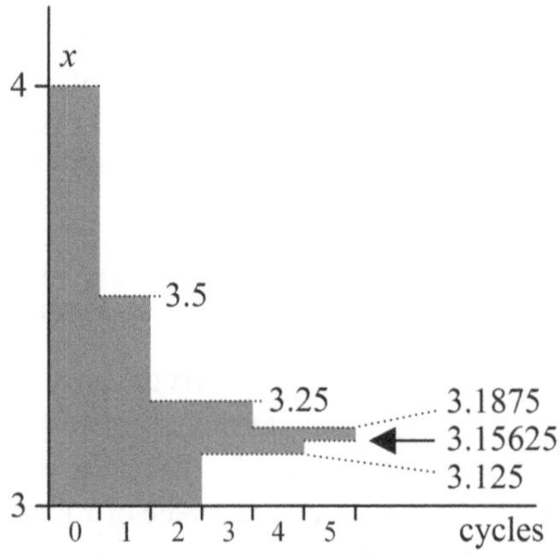

FIGURE A1.1 Sketch of a simple divide and conquer method that converges on $x^2 = 10$.

search for $w^- = \text{GaussUpper}^{-1}(p; n, \alpha/2)$. To search for the lower bound of the Clopper-Pearson interval we search for $b^- = \text{BinUpper}^{-1}(p; n, \alpha/2)$.

The range we need to search is where $P < p$ (i.e., $[0, p]$). We calculate the lower bound of P using $p' = \text{GaussUpper}(P; n, \alpha/2)$ or an equivalent formula (e.g., the Binomial upper bound). We compare desired p and output value p', and repeat until $p = p'$ (or the difference error term is considered 'small enough'). For the Binomial we compare $B(p \times n, n; n, P)$ and the desired tail area $\alpha/2$. See Appendix B.

A variation of the method first selects the midpoint $P = p/2$, and points halfway above and halfway below this midpoint. It takes the value with the smallest error, and reduces the search range by half. If the lower value had the smallest error, the computer searches the lower half of the range. The process repeats with this reduced range until the error is too small to be bothered with.

Searching with Gaussian equations obtains the same result as the Wilson score interval formula, but with more effort! Importantly, since this method works for any monotonic function, we can use it to find intervals where only the generating function is known.

APPENDIX B

Pseudo-Code for Computational Procedures

1 Simple Logistic Regression Algorithm With Logit-Wilson Variance

See Chapter 10. Note that **lP**(x) = logit($p(x)$) and **lVar**(x) (logit variance) are precalculated arrays, calculated in the main function Regress(). See Section 2.4.

Calculating the variance on the basis of a set of observed data, **p**(x), rather than a fitting function, $f(x)$, means that we do not need to keep recomputing variance as $f(x)$ varies. As we saw in Chapter 18, the logit-Wilson distribution for $p(x)$ has a distribution that is extremely close to the Normal distribution, and thus the method of least squares on the logit scale can be said to be robust.

1.1 Calculate Sum of Squared Errors e *for Known* m *and* k

```
function calc_sq_error(m, k)
{
   e = 0
   for x = 0 to total – 1            // cycle over observations
      if (lVar(x))                   // if variance is finite
      {
         diff = m × (x – k) – lP(x)  // y = m(x – k)
         e += diff^2 / lVar(x)       // add squared difference divided by variance
      }
   return e
}
```

1.2 Find Optimum Value of k by Search for Smallest Error e for Gradient m

Input k is used as an initial estimate. We define an 'ACCURACY' level at say 0.000001 (six decimal places) in advance. See also Section 2.2.

```
function find_lsq_k(m, k, &e)                    // &e returns this value
{
   diff = 4, improvement = 1
   e = calc_sq_error(m, k)                       // calculate initial values
   eplus = calc_sq_error(m, k + diff)            // calculate error e for values
   eminus = calc_sq_error(m, k – diff)           // ± a difference in k
   do
   {
      if (eplus < e)                             // pick result with smallest error
      {
         if (eminus < eplus) goto lower
         improvement = e – eplus
         eminus = e; e = eplus                   // go higher
         k = k + diff
         if (improvement ≤ ACCURACY) quit loop and return
         eplus = calc_sq_error(m, k + diff)
      }
      else if (eminus < e)
      {
lower:   improvement = e – eminus
         eplus = e; e = eminus                   // go lower
         k = k – diff
         if (improvement ≤ ACCURACY) quit loop and return
         eminus = calc_sq_error(m, k – diff)
      }
      else                                       // if the middle result is best,
      {                                          // halve the search area
         diff = diff / 2
         if (diff ≤ ACCURACY) quit loop and return
         eplus = calc_sq_error(m, k + diff)
         eminus = calc_sq_error(m, k – diff)
      }
   }
   while ((improvement > ACCURACY) and (diff > ACCURACY))
   return k                                      // also returns e
}
```

1.3 Find Optimum Values of m and k by the Method of Least Squares

```
function find_lsq_m_k(m, &k, &e)
{
   diff = 1; improvement = 1
   k = find_lsq_k(m, k, e)
   kplus = find_lsq_k(m + diff, k, eplus)
   kminus = find_lsq_k(m – diff, k, eminus)
   do                               // eplus, eminus are results for
   {                                // find_lsq_k
      if (eplus < e)                // again, find smallest error
      {
         if (eminus < eplus) goto lower
         improvement = e – eplus
         eminus = e; kminus = k     // go higher
         e = eplus; k = kplus
         m = m + diff
         if (improvement ≤ ACCURACY) quit loop and return
         kplus = find_lsq_k(m + diff, k, eplus)
      }
      else if (eminus < e)
      {
lower:   improvement = e – eminus;
         eplus = e; kplus = k       // go lower
         e = eminus; k = kminus
         m = m – diff
         if (improvement ≤ ACCURACY) quit loop and return
         kminus = find_lsq_k(m – diff, k, eminus)
      }
      else                          // halve search area
      {
         diff = diff / 2
         if (diff ≤ ACCURACY) quit loop and return
         kplus = find_lsq_k(m + diff, k, eplus)
         kminus = find_lsq_k(m – diff, k, eminus)
      }
   }
   while ((improvement > ACCURACY) and (diff > ACCURACY))
   return m                         // also returns k and e
}
```

1.4 Perform Regression

```
function Regress(p, n, total)
{
   for x = 0 to total – 1                    // convert data to a logit scale
   {
      if (p(x) = 0 or 1)
         lP(x) = 0; lVar(x) = 0
      else
      {
         lP(x) = logit(p(x))
         lVar(x) = (logit(p(x)) – logit(WilsonLower(p(x), n(x), α))^2
      }
   }
   m = (lP(first) – lP(last)) / total    // initial estimates
   k = lP(first) / -m
   m = find_lsq_m_k(m, k, e)             // obtain m, k and e
   output m, k and e
}
```

2 Binomial and Fisher Functions

See Chapter 8. Further commentary is at https://corplingstats.wordpress.com/2012/11/20/algorithm-snippets.

2.1 Core Functions

```
function nCr(n, r)                              // combinatorial function
{
   if (n > LIMIT) return -1                     // a limit of 1500 in our C++
   return fact(n) / (fact(r)×fact(n – r))       // factorial array is precalculated
}

function BinP(x, n, P)                          // Binomial function for single
{                                               // value of x out of n
   if (p < 0) or (p > 1) return 0
   if (x = n) and (p = 1) return 1              // calculating 0^0 generates an error
   if (x = 0) and (p = 0) return 1
   if (p = 0.5) return nCr(n, x) / 2^n          // special case
   return nCr(n, x) × P^x × (1 – P)^(n – x)
}
```

Calculate the cumulative Binomial for P, with a 'mid-p' option.

```
function CumBinP(x, n, P)              // sum the Binomial from x to n inclusive
{
   c = 0
   if (MIDP)                           // use a global flag for simplicity
      c = BinP(x, n, P) / 2; x++
   for r = x to n – 1
      c += BinP(r, n, P)
   return c
}
```

```
function Fisher(a, b, c, d)
{
   return  (fact(a+c) / fact(a)) ×     // arranged like this
           (fact(b+d) / fact(b)) ×     // to minimise risk of overflow error
           (fact(a+b) / fact(c)) ×
           (fact(c+d) / fact(d)) / fact(a+b+c+d)
}
```

```
function FisherSum(a, b, c, d)         // sum Fisher scores diagonally
{                                      // towards corner
   p = 0; n1 = a+b; n2 = c+d
   if (a / n1 > c / n2) do
      p += Fisher(a, n1–a, c, n2–c); a++; c –
   while ((a ≤ n1) and (c ≥ 0)
   else do
      p += Fisher(a, n1–a, c, n2–c); a – ; c++
   while (a ≥ 0) and (c ≤ n2))
   return p
}
```

2.2 The Clopper-Pearson Interval

An example interval search procedure. See Appendix A. It attempts to find $B(x, n; n, P) = \alpha/2$, given x and n, by picking halfway points. We can alter the global 'ACCURACY' setting. If we define it at 0.00000001 (8 decimal places), the *function* 'CumBinP' (i.e. $B(x, n; n, P)$) should match $\alpha/2$ at this level. This translates to about 6 decimal places of p.

```
function findBinP(x, n)                  // find P lower bound for p = x / n
{                                        // i.e., p is upper bound of P
   if (x = 0) return 0
   Pplus = x / n; Pminus = 0             // search range from 0 to p
   P = Pplus/2
   a = CumBinP(P, n, x) – α/2
   for i = 0 to 100                      // finite loop:
   {                                     // expected < 30 cycles for 8 decimal places
      if (| a | ≤ ACCURACY) return P
      if (a < 0)
         Pminus = P; P = (P + Pplus)/2
      else
         Pplus = P; P = (P + Pminus)/2
      a = CumBinP(P, n, x) – α/2
   }
   return P
}
```

GLOSSARY

1-tailed An interval or distribution where only one bound is considered. Usually, intervals are two-tailed, and we consider significant variation in both directions. However, a one-tailed model may be employed if variation is only considered in one direction. Wilson intervals become one-tailed at 0 or 1 because the true value of P cannot be outside this range.

3A model A model of corpus linguistic research consisting of three cycles, termed *Annotation, Abstraction* and *Analysis*. See Chapter 1.

3-sigma rule A heuristic used for *Wald intervals*, it says that an interval may only be computed if the observed proportion is 3 or more standard deviations away from 0 and 1. The heuristic is unnecessary in the case of *Wilson score intervals*.

Abstraction In general terms, a process of converting concepts expressed in a more concrete form to another, more abstract one. In the *3A model* of *Corpus Linguistics* (see Chapter 1), the term refers to the process of abstracting individual linguistic items and structures (*linguistic events*) found in an annotated corpus in context, into concepts in the researcher's own framework of *variables* and *hypotheses*, and building a sample dataset, removing them from context. Abstraction is a cycle that includes the reverse process, 'concretisation' (sometimes called *operationalisation*).

Algorithm A complete description of a computational process.

Alternation An alternative expression that a speaker or writer could choose, used in *alternation experiments*. It may be substituted for another expression and plausibly preserve the same referential meaning the speaker/writer intended to convey.

Alternation experiment An experiment where the *dependent variable* (DV) consists of an *alternation set*.

Alternation set A set of alternative linguistic expressions that can replace each other without the meaning changing. See *mutual substitution*.

Alternation studies An *onomasiological* study of variation where the meaning is constant but the form of expression may change. Also termed *variationism*.

Analysis In general terms, a process of reasoning to derive a result, hence *Qualitative Analysis, Quantitative Analysis* or parse analysis, that is, 'analysis of tree structure'. In the *3A model*, the term is used to refer to the highest-level cycle of processing, that is, testing hypotheses against sample datasets using statistical methods.

Annotation A process of assigning meaningful labels to items, sequences and structures drawn from the raw text. Informal annotation may be descriptive labels, such as comments, but formal annotation should follow a system or 'coding scheme' whose labels should be in well-defined relationships (e.g., members of a mutually exclusive set of types, and subsets). In a corpus, it is expected that annotation aims for complete coverage, where every instance of each phenomenon is labelled appropriately. See also the *3A model*.

ANOVA (analysis of variance) A method for analysing variance for Real data building on the *t test*, certain types of ANOVA may be used as a *meta-test* for comparing results of different comparable experiments.

ARCHER (*A Representative Corpus of Historical English Registers*) A *diachronic tagged* corpus of written historical British and American English spanning the period 1600–1999. See www.archer.alc.manchester.ac.uk.

Association Sometimes called 'co-dependence', a bidirectional estimate of the degree to which two variables change in a non-independent way.

Associative For significance tests, a test that does not distinguish between independent and dependent variables and obtains the same result in either direction.

Assumption A statement that is presumed to be true.

Auxiliary assumption In scientific *epistemology*, a statement external to a theory but necessary for it to be applied and evaluated. Auxiliary assumptions might include measurement principles and equipment accuracy, such as the performance of a radio telescope. In linguistics, auxiliary assumptions range from the premise that 'a lexical word is a relevant meaning unit' to a complete grammatical framework. Auxiliary assumptions are often capable of evaluation by other experiments, but are taken as true for the current one.

Axiom A rule or principle of a mathematical system, such as $x \equiv -(-x)$.

Balanced sampling A *heuristic* principle for obtaining a corpus or sample ensuring that a range of different types are obtained using a *sampling frame* specifying the proportions. Sometimes called a 'quota sample'. See Chapter 5.

Baseline The denominator of a Binomial proportion, in simple terms, n in the fraction $p = f / n$. This is the number of opportunities for $p(x \mid \mathbf{X})$ to be measured, $n(\mathbf{X})$ where $\mathbf{X}$ is the set of opportunities. See Chapter 3.

Bernoulli trial A random sample of coin tosses of a given number n.

Bidirectional relationship A relationship between A and B that applies in both directions, that is, from A to B and from B to A, sometimes called a reflexive or *associative* relationship.

Bienaymé formula An axiom that allows independent variances to be summed, very commonly applied in statistics. It is used for computing the *z test for two independent proportions* and the *Newcombe-Wilson interval* as well as *MOVER* methods. The formula is an example of Pythagoras's famous rule for triangles, the idea being that independent variables are considered to vary tangentially (at right angles) to one another.

Bimodal distribution A distribution with two distinct *modes* or peaks.

Binary Based on the number two. Binary numbers are numbers expressed to the base 2 (0, 1, 10, 11, etc.), and a binary choice is two-way (e.g., true or false).

Binomial A model of variation based on a two-way choice, where each item in the sample can, in principle, be either true or false, A or B, 1 or 0, and so on.

Binomial distribution The distribution obtained by repeated sampling of *Binomial samples*. It may be an actual distribution (the result of a series of actual samples) or an ideal or theoretical distribution (the result of a mathematical formula). See Chapter 6.

Binomial function A formula for calculating ideal Binomial distributions from first principles, based on combinatorial mathematics. See Chapters 6 and 8.

Binomial proportion The proportion in a sample (denoted by *p*) or a population (*P*) of the rate of choosing one item out of a pair, where each choice is freely available and independent from the next. We might also say *p* is 'the sample mean' of a set of binary choices. We term *p* the 'observed Binomial proportion' and *P*, the predicted or 'expected' Binomial proportion. It may be translated into a *probability* by imagining the chance of drawing a random individual from the sample or population.

Binomial proportion difference graph A graph for comparing two *Binomial proportions* with *confidence intervals* on both points.

Binomial proportion test A significance test to compare the difference between two Binomial proportions, for example, $p - P$ ('goodness of fit') or $p_1 - p_2$ ('independence of observations'). Goodness of fit tests include the exact *Binomial test*, the *z test for the single proportion* and the *Wilson score interval* test. Independence tests (sometimes termed *homogeneity tests*) include the *Newcombe-Wilson* test. Apart from the Binomial test, other methods employ the *Normal approximation* to the *Binomial distribution*, and *Yates's continuity correction* may be applied to reduce the risk of false positive results (*Type I errors*).

Binomial test An 'exact' test that evaluates the difference between an observed Binomial proportion and a given expected value *P* using the *Binomial function*. We create the *Clopper-Pearson interval* by inverting this test. See Chapter 8.

BNC (*British National Corpus*) A 100 million word *synchronic tagged* corpus was collected in the early 1990s. See www.natcorp.ox.ac.uk. A new spoken and written corpus (BNC-2014) was collected in 2014–2015. See http://corpora.lancs.ac.uk/bnc2014.

Bootstrap interval A popular method that aims to construct confidence intervals by a process of resampling from a given sample. It generates a *Wald interval* when applied to Binomial proportions, which reveals that it is not generating confidence intervals by the *interval equality principle*. For this reason, it should be seen as a last resort. See Chapter 8.

Brown corpus (*A Standard Corpus of Present-Day Edited American English*) The first computer-readable general *corpus* ever collected was a written corpus of American English, collected at Brown University in the 1960s. See https://varieng.helsinki.fi/CoRD/corpora/BROWN.

Brown family of corpora A set of written one million word corpora of English, US and British, based on the Brown corpus. The first corpus was the famous Brown corpus of 1960s US English, *diachronically* repeated with the Frown (Freiburg-Brown) corpus of 1990s US English. These corpora were paralleled *synchronically* by British English equivalents: LOB (Lancaster-Oslo-Bergen) 1960s British English and FLOB (Freiburg-LOB) for the 1990s. Before Brown (B-Brown) and Before LOB (BLOB) have also been compiled for the 1930s.

Case independence In a true random sample, each instance is independent from all other instances in the sample. Corpus samples drawn from a collection of texts typically breach this requirement.

Case interaction The degree to which cases (instances) drawn from a corpus may be co-dependent if they come from the same text. See Chapter 16.

Case study An empirical evaluation of a situation where the conditions, participants, and so on, have already been defined, such as linguistic interventions in defusing a bar-fight, or the effectiveness of a sprinkler system in a fire. We evaluate what happened in a particular case, but there is no control. In corpus research, an examination of a particular text using corpus linguistics techniques is a good example of a case study.

Causal relationship An underlying process between phenomena which explains why one decision appears to affect another. Evidence of a correlation between two events does not allow us to claim that they are causally linked. They could both be separately related to some other factor or process.

Central Limit Theorem The principle that 'the larger the sample, the greater the confidence'. In the Binomial model, as n increases to a limit of infinity, an uncertain observation p tends to become equal to the limit, that is, the population value P.

Chaos A state of dynamic systems that adopt behaviour not predictable by mathematical models, arising when three or more bodies are continuously interacting with each other. As a result, immeasurably tiny differences in initial conditions can lead to different system outcomes over time. For example, linguistic alternation trends that might otherwise adopt a *logistic* curve (a predictable two-body system) may be influenced by other changes (corresponding to a third body) due to *ecological* pressures. See Chapter 10.

Chi-square (χ^2) A type of *contingency test* based on the *Normal approximation* to the *Binomial* or *Multinomial distribution.* There are two main subtypes: *goodness of fit* tests comparing an observed distribution of r frequencies with an expected distribution, and *homogeneity tests* (also called *contingency tests* or independence tests) comparing two Binomial or Multinomial variables in the form of a *contingency table* of $r \times c$ frequencies. See Chapter 8.

Clopper-Pearson interval A confidence interval for the observed *Binomial proportion p*, obtained by finding values of P that satisfy the Binomial formula where the Binomial area for p and the remaining tail area matches a set error level, typically $\alpha/2$. See Chapter 8.

Cluster An inductive concept. Where data are unevenly distributed, we may say they form 'clusters' or notional groups.

Cluster analysis A method for identifying clusters in data. See also *repertory grid analysis.*

Cluster sampling A method where samples are drawn from groups, for example, by obtaining data from randomly sampled families where data from every member of the family are captured. Text sampling is a type of cluster sampling. See Chapter 16.

COCA (*Corpus of Contemporary American English*) A 520+ million word *synchronic tagged* corpus of written and spoken American English. See www.english-corpora.org/coca.

Cochran's rule A heuristic used in *chi-square tests* that says that where cells have an expected frequency smaller than 5, the table should be simplified so that the column or row is collapsed. *Yates's continuity correction* renders it redundant.

COHA (*Corpus of Historical American English*) A 400 million word *diachronic tagged* corpus of written American English spanning 1810–2009. See www.english-corpora.org/coha.

Colligation A string of closely associated words and *wordclass* tags. See also *collocation.*

Collocation A string of closely associated words identified by co-occurrence statistics from a corpus.

Combinatorial function A mathematical formula that counts the number of ways of achieving a particular number, r, of outcomes out of n potential ones, written nCr or $\binom{n}{r}$ and calculated from $n!/(r!(n-r)!)$, where '$n!$' represents the *factorial* of n. The order in which outcomes are found does not matter. For example, $2C1 = 2$ is the number of ways one 'head' can be obtained from two tosses of a fair coin (HT or TH). The *Binomial function* depends on the combinatorial formula See Chapter 6.

Complementation pattern A linguistic term for the pattern of complements that a verb takes in a clause. Sometimes referred to as the 'transitivity' of the verb.

Confidence interval The range of values that are not significantly different from an observation at a given error level α (or, of confidence $1 - \alpha$). This definition is not quite the same as 'the expected range of values of P', although the latter is not an unreasonable way to think about it. See Chapter 17. *Binomial* intervals are defined by the *interval equality principle*, which presumes that the true value P is either above or below p, and tests whether $| P - p |$ is significant at an error level α. Confidence intervals are a visually effective and intuitive method for estimating the reliability of an observation. They should not be confused with *sampling intervals* or *replication intervals*.

Conservative Erring on the side of caution. In statistics, avoiding *Type I errors*, even if it means accepting *Type II errors*. A conservative test will tend to find a result *non-significant* when another more 'radical' test finds it to be *significant*.

Contingency correlation The degree of correlation between two *Binomial* or *Multinomial variables*. Thus, *chi-square* is a 'contingency correlation statistic' and Cramér's ϕ is an *effect size* estimate of the absolute correlation.

Contingency table A table of sample frequencies used for analysis, where each axis represents a different *Binomial* or *Multinomial variable*. Usually these tables have two dimensions, so that variables are compared in a pairwise fashion. One of these variables is called the *Dependent Variable* (DV) and the other the *Independent Variable* (IV).

Contingency test A statistical test for the interdependence between two discrete *Binomial* or *Multinomial variables*. Example contingency tests include the *Fisher 'exact' test*, the *chi-square test* and the *log-likelihood test* for *homogeneity* (independence). *Binomial proportion comparison tests* can be substituted for 2 × 2 tests.

Continuity correction See *Yates's continuity correction*.

Continuous A mathematical term for variables and distributions that have an infinite number of points (a numerical range) rather than finite *discrete* categories. *Real* numbers are continuous, that is, given one point on the distribution, it is always possible to add an infinitesimal amount to find a new point. See also *scale of measurement*.

Controlled experiment An experiment where hypotheses and variables constrain data collection, for example, by 'cueing' participants to ensure they produce the types of linguistic event in which a researcher is interested. Data collection is artificially controlled, which has the benefit in reducing potential sources of variation. However, data may be criticised for being artificial, and great care is needed to ensure that the researcher does not unduly influence participants. Also called a 'laboratory' experiment. See Chapter 2.

Corpus A collected sample of language data. Corpora are typically digital, orthographically transcribed speech or writing and are *annotated*. Typically, corpora are samples of entire sequences or text passages or even whole texts, rather than samples of fragmentary utterances.

Corpus linguistics The study of authentic linguistic data volumes to develop scientific theories about language.

Correlation An observed relationship between two variables which may or may not have an underlying basis. If one variable tends to increase as another decreases, or both change together, the reliability of this tendency is termed the 'degree of correlation'. Correlations can arise for many reasons, of which a causal relationship is only one. Hence, correlations are not causes! See Chapter 2.

Correlation statistic A measure of the degree of correlation between two or more variables. Examples include *chi-square* (a contingency correlation statistic) and *Pearson's* r^2 (a linear correlation statistic).

Cramér's ϕ A bidirectional *effect size* estimate derived from *chi-square*, it is the best estimate of the *associative* population interdependent probability, $p(a \leftrightarrow b)$. See Chapter 13.

Critical value A threshold value used for testing *significant difference*. See also *Normal distribution*.

Cumulative Binomial function The sum of the *Binomial function* over a range, typically from 0 to r or from r to n. See Chapter 8.

Cumulative density function (c.d.f.) The sum of the *probability density function* from the lower bound of a number scale ($-\infty$ or 0, say) to a parameter x. See Chapter 17.

Cumulative Normal distribution A function on a Real number x, obtaining the probabilistic area under the *Normal distribution* curve from $-\infty$ to x. It is *the cumulative density function* for the Normal distribution. See Chapter 17.

DCPSE (*Diachronic Corpus of Present-day Spoken English*) A *diachronic parsed corpus* of over 800,000 words of orthographically transcribed British English data collected between the late 1950s and early 1990s. DCPSE contains texts from the *LLC* and *ICE-GB*, and these texts are fully parsed with the same framework as ICE-GB. See www.ucl.ac.uk/english/dcpse.

Decidability The principle that it is possible to classify a linguistic event into one type or another. It is closely related to *retrievability*, the practical ability to reliably retrieve such events from a *corpus* and gradience (intrinsic category ambiguity or 'fuzziness').

Degree of freedom The minimum number of independent axes of variation, *df*, used as a measure of the complexity of a model, such as a *contingency table*. In particular, 2 × 1 *goodness of fit* and 2 × 2 *homogeneity* tables have one degree of freedom, which means that difference can be visualised in one dimension, with a *confidence interval* expressing the limit of significant difference.

Delta approximation A method for carrying out differentiation in calculus, a delta (δ) is a very small difference between two points over which a curve can be approximated by a straight line. See Chapter 17.

Dependent probability The probability that x is true given y is true, written $p(x \mid y)$. The principle may be extended to variables X, Y: it refers to the degree to which variable X may be predicted by the variable Y.

Dependent Variable (DV) A variable that is investigated for its possible association with one or more *Independent Variables* (IVs). In an experiment to investigate if the value of Y predicted the value of X, X would be the dependent variable.

Descriptive statistics Numbers describing a sample. A 'statistic' is simply a number, such as the size of the sample, n, the number of cases of a particular type, f, and *effect size* ϕ. Contrasted with *inferential statistics*. See Chapter 6.

Diachronic A linguistic term used to refer to a comparison made over time, so 'diachronic change' refers to change over time. Notable diachronic corpora include *A Representative Corpus of Historical English Registers* (ARCHER), the *Corpus of Historical American English* (COHA) and the *Diachronic Corpus of Present-day Spoken English* (DCPSE). Compare with *synchronic*.

Discrete A mathematical term for variables and distributions that take values of distinct units, as opposed to *continuous*. *Binomial*, *Multinomial*, *Ordinal* and *Interval* scales are discrete, as are true fractions (e.g., observed proportions). An observed proportion p will be a true fraction between 0 and 1 and therefore discrete, whereas an expected proportion P could be any rational number in the same range. See also *scale of measurement*.

Distribution In mathematics, an ordered set of numbers, which may be continuous (e.g., the *Normal distribution*) or discrete (e.g., {5, 7, 3.2}). In linguistics, the term 'distribution' refers to the surrounding grammatical pattern of word forms in a which a word or item tends to be found.

Ecological In psychology and linguistics, used to refer to research in which data are obtained from natural environments.

Effect size A traditionally *descriptive statistic* that expresses the degree of effect of the *independent variable* on the *dependent variable*, or the closeness of a *goodness of fit* assessment. In this book we show how *confidence intervals* on effect sizes may be derived, a process that converts them into an inferential statistic and increases their analytic value. See Chapter 13.

Empiricism A philosophical position that emphasises that knowledge is derived by observing the world directly (termed 'empirical observation').

Epistemology The philosophy of knowledge, concerned with 'how we know what we know'.

Error level The allowable rate of error for a statistical evaluation, in this book represented by α. Sometimes confusingly termed a 'p value' in the literature. Significance tests operate by predicting the variation of samples drawn from a population, and use an error level representing the rate at which a sample might fall outside the predicted variation by random chance. In *confidence intervals*, error levels are typically quoted in reverse $(1 - \alpha)$, that is, a 95% confidence interval has a 5% error level.

Expected Binomial proportion A Binomial proportion supplied in advance for the purposes of evaluation (e.g., to compare an observed proportion with 0.5, say) or predicted from some other source, such as a superset of data or previous research.

Expected distribution A set of numbers compared with an *observed distribution* in a *contingency test*, where the set of numbers are predicted by the *null hypothesis*. For example, to test whether an observed distribution $\mathbf{O} = \{10, 20\}$ is consistent with a predicted value of $P = 0.6$, we calculate an expected distribution based on $n = 10 + 20$, scaled by P, $\mathbf{E} = \{0.6 \times 30, 0.4 \times 30\} = \{18, 12\}$.

Experiment An evaluation of a hypothesis against an experimental sample, conventionally considered an attempt to refute a *null hypothesis*. Experiments may be divided into *controlled experiments*, where samples are obtained for the purposes of the experiment in artificially limited conditions, and *natural experiments* where samples are obtained in other ways. Both types have advantages. See Chapter 2.

Experimenter bias A bias or distortion introduced into an experiment due to the experimenter's own actions. Sometimes called 'research bias'. There are a number of different types affecting the design of data collection, which individuals are sampled, the process of collecting data, how participants are guided, and how results are measured or classified.

Exposure rate The rate at which a hearer is likely to be exposed to an item, expressed per word or per multiple of words. A common exposure rate arises from a *per million word baseline*. Exposure rates contain collections of items with diverse meanings and opportunities, and therefore tend to be statistically 'noisy'. See Chapter 3.

External variable A variable external to the text itself, typically representing sociolinguistic aspects of the speaker (gender, age, etc.) or text (genre, topic, date of publication, etc.). Sometimes referred to as 'sociolinguistic' variables in corpus linguistics. We prefer the term 'external' because text-internal variables may also be of sociolinguistic interest.

Factorial The product (multiplication) of an integer series from 1 to n, written as '!'. The function is central to *Binomial* and *Fisher* statistics.

Factual evidence Evidence that a term exists in a sample or corpus. See Chapter 1.

Finite population correction (f.p.c.) An adjustment applied to a confidence interval or test when the population is finite. If the sample represents a substantial subset of the population (5% or more), then it should be applied. The effect of this correction is to reduce the uncertainty of observations and confidence interval widths, and increase test scores.

Fisher 'exact' test A 2×2 contingency test for homogeneity or independence that can be used as a replacement for the 2×2 *chi-square*. See Chapter 8.

Fit/fitness A mathematical term meaning closeness in proximity. See also *goodness of fit test*, *goodness of fit effect size* and *separability test*.

Fitting An algorithm that tries to find a function that has a close match (*fit*, or *fitness*) to data.

Form In linguistics, category labels realising a particular grammatical *function*, such as noun, noun phrase, and so on.

Framing constraint A structural constraint governing optionality, where a primary choice determines the possibility of a secondary choice. In language data, a common type of framing constraint governs the choices available to a speaker or writer. See Chapter 1.

Freedom to vary The principle that an observed proportion may range from 0 to 1 (100%). The property is guaranteed where *mutual substitution* applies, but it may arise in other circumstances. See Chapter 3.

Frequency distribution A distribution (ordered set) of frequency counts.

Frequency evidence Evidence of the total number of a particular type of linguistic event in a sample or corpus. More broadly, frequency evidence is best considered as an ordered set of frequencies (a *frequency distribution*), which can then be translated into proportions (a *probability distribution*). See Chapter 1.

FTF (Fuzzy Tree Fragment) A grammatical model of a potential tree structure, used by *ICECUP* to search a *parsed corpus* for similar tree structures annotating a sentence.

Function In mathematics, a function is an expression defining a relationship between variables, such as add(x, y) $\equiv x + y$. An *inverse function*, written fn^{-1}, rewrites the same relationship so that the output variable swaps places with one of the input variables. It allows us to calculate an input parameter when the result of the original equation is known. In linguistics, a function is the grammatical role performed by a *form* in a particular construction. Functions in a phrase structure grammar might include subject, object, head, and so on.

Gaussian distribution The original name for the *Normal distribution.*

Goodness of fit effect size An *effect size* that obtains a standardised score for the closeness of fit between an *observed* and *expected distribution*, where 0 represents identity and 1, maximal difference.

Goodness of fit test A significance test that evaluates the significant difference between a *Binomial* or *Multinomial observed distribution* with a comparable *expected distribution.* (Despite the name, if the observed and expected distribution fit closely, the result will be non-significant, so the test should really be called a 'badness of fit' test!)

Graceful degradation A concept concerning the robustness of mathematical models, such that if the assumptions of the model are undermined, the model performs worse in proportion to the scale of the breach (it 'gracefully degrades') rather than simply failing completely.

Gradient test A statistical *meta-test* for comparing observed differences in proportions between different tables (e.g., data from different experimental runs) or comparing patterns of effect. See Chapter 14.

Heterogeneity analysis A meta-test for considering whether two datasets may be pooled for the purposes of analysis.

Heuristic An effective but unprincipled rule.

Homogeneity of variance An assessment that the variances of two populations of Interval data are sufficiently comparable for a two sample t test to be legitimately performed.

Homogeneity test A *contingency test* for comparing the interaction between two or more Binomial or Multinomial variables. Also known as an 'independence' test as it evaluates whether the two variables have a correlation.

Hypothesis A proposition about data that may or may not be true. In science, it is generally expected that hypotheses should be 'falsifiable' (or 'testable'), that is, capable of being shown to be false by an experimental evaluation, but the term is occasionally used to refer to speculative statements without a known method of falsification.

ICE (*International Corpus of English*) An international effort that began in the late 1980s to collect corpora of different varieties of English worldwide, from countries where English was the first language or an official second language. Each research team was expected to use the same *sampling frame* to collect data, to ensure comparability between corpora as far as possible. See www.ice-corpora.uzh.ch.

ICECUP 3 (*ICE Corpus Utility Program III*) A research platform designed for exploring *parsed corpora*, developed for the *ICE* project.

ICE-GB (*British Component of the International Corpus of English*) The British English component of *ICE*, collected between 1990 and 1992. ICE-GB is fully parsed using a phrase structure grammar based on Quirk et al. (1985). See www.ucl.ac.uk/english/ice-gb.

Identity matrix A *matrix* of the form $\mathbf{I}$ = [[1, 0], [0, 1]] where all cells are zero except those on the diagonal, which are one. It has the property that any vector multiplied by it is the same as the start. In explaining *Cramér's* ϕ, we observe that where a contingency table has this form, the DV is predicted by the IV in the sample without risk of misclassification. See Chapter 13.

Independence effect size An *effect size* that estimates the degree of correlation between two variables in a *contingency table*. Examples include *Cramér's* ϕ and *Yule's Q*. See Chapter 13.

Independence test A multi-variable *contingency test* also known as a *homogeneity test*.

Independent mutual substitution A type of *mutual substitution* where the referential meaning does not change when substituting one form for another, and therefore the substitution is independent from its context. The forms are considered interchangeable, and we may conceive of the choice as one where the expression of a particular meaning plays no part in the speaker or writer's decision to select one form over another. See Chapter 3.

Independent Variable (IV) A variable that may be changed according to sampling conditions and experimental design, evaluated for its association with a *Dependent Variable* (DV). In an experiment to investigate if the value of Y predicted the value of X, Y would be the independent variable.

Inferential statistics A mathematical method for drawing inferences from a sample to a population. See Chapter 8.

Interaction evidence Evidence that two *linguistic events* are not independent but interact. See Chapter 1.

Internal variable A variable concerning features of *linguistic events* within the text, also sometimes called 'linguistic' variables. Compare with *external variable*.

Interval A continuous set of *Real numbers*, limited by an upper and lower bound. Also known as a range of numbers. For example, the interval [0, 0.5] is the set of all numbers between 0 and 0.5, including both the lower and upper bound. The interval (0, 0.5) is the same set, excluding the bounds. The set of all Real numbers $\mathfrak{R} = [-\infty, +\infty]$ is all (non-imaginary) numbers up to and including plus or minus infinity. See also *confidence interval*.

Interval equality principle A principle for deriving confidence intervals consistently with conventional significance tests. The principle defines the *Wilson score interval* about an observed *Binomial proportion p* from the *Normal interval* based on a population probability P, and other confidence intervals. It says that where observed p is equal to one *bound* of the sampling interval for P, P will be at the opposite bound of the confidence interval for p, that is, the two interval widths are equal. See Chapter 6 and Appendix A.

Inverse function Mathematical functions may be inverted, which means rewriting the function so that one of the input variables becomes an output variable. Suppose we defined $z = \text{add}(x, y) \equiv x + y$. By rearranging the formula, $x = z - y$, so we might invert the function by writing $\text{add}^{-1}(z, y) \equiv z - y$.

iWeb corpus A very very large corpus of English compiled from web pages. Available at www.english-corpora.org/iweb.

Laboratory experiment See *controlled experiment*.

Least squares method A method of *regression* due to Gauss, which sums the squares of the distance between an observation and a function representing a predicted curve or line. The smaller the total sum of squares, the better the *fit*. Unweighted regression is termed *ordinary least squares*.

Lemma The root form of a word without any inflections or derivations (e.g., the root of *children* is child). We follow the convention of using small capital letters to denote lemmas.

Linear regression The process of fitting data to a straight line function, often expressed as $y = f(x) = mx + c$. The variables m and c are manipulated to find the closest fit of the line to data.

Linguistic event The moment or position in a text in which a particular linguistic performance, identified by a single term or structured group of terms (a linguistic *type*), is produced. In corpus linguistics research, every instance in a sample dataset can be considered an *abstracted* linguistic event of a particular type in the corpus.

Linguistic interaction experiment An experimental design investigating the relationship between two or more variables identifying aspects of the same linguistic structure, such as the relationship between adjacent words or structures, terms in a structure, decisions to add optional structure, and so on. Distinguished from experiments that involve text-external variables concerning, for example, sociolinguistic context or characteristics of speakers.

LLC (*London-Lund Corpus*) A spoken British English corpus collected first at the Survey of English Usage in London from the late 1950s to early 1970s, added to with written texts at the University of Lund. This was the first corpus project begun in Europe (after *Brown*) and second in the world. The Survey corpus was the first corpus of spoken data collected. More than two thirds of the spoken Survey corpus is found within *DCPSE*, which is fully parsed.

Logarithm The inverse power function. Where a number $x = b^y$ (b to the power of y), the logarithm to the base b of x, $\log_b(x) = y$. Logarithms (in short: 'logs') can be calculated for any base b greater than 1, such as 2 or 10. An important base is the base of the natural logarithm, e.

Logarithmic scale A scale of measurement, often used for plotting graphs where data are expected to be exponentially distributed. Transforming data to a logarithmic scale turns exponents (powers) to multiples, and renders exponential decay curves as straight lines.

Logic The mathematics of deductive reasoning.

Logistic A *monotonic* function that transforms proportions or probabilities, $p \in \boldsymbol{P}$, into Real numbers, logistic(p) $\in \mathfrak{R}$, generating an 'S'-shaped curve.

Logistic regression The process of fitting data to one or more *logistic* curves. See *regression*. See also Chapter 10.

Logit The inverse of the *logistic* function, also called 'log odds', the logit function transforms Real numbers into probabilities.

Log-likelihood test A logarithmic test that is chi-square distributed, it has some useful mathematical properties that make it highly generalisable. However, it is not a replacement for χ^2 but a different test. See Chapter 8.

Lossy The property of losing information following a mathematical transformation. For example, the absolute value operator, $|x|$, dispenses with the sign of x, which means that positive and negative values of x cannot be distinguished. Non-*monotonic* functions are lossy. *Effect sizes* may reduce multiple degrees of freedom to one.

Lower bound The smallest number in a continuous range or interval.

Mann-Whitney *U* test A significance test for Ordinal data that tests whether the median ranks of two samples are significantly different. See Chapter 12.

Matrix A mathematical term for a multidimensional table of values. A one-dimensional table is termed a *vector*.

Mean The average value of a set of numbers or distribution. The most common type is the *arithmetic mean*, which is simply the sum of the numbers divided by the number in the set. Other types include the geometric mean. See also *median* and *mode*, which are other measures of 'middle values'.

Median The middle value in a distribution, the value where 50% of the data lies above and 50% below. See also *mean* and *mode*.

Meta-test A statistical test for comparing test results or experiments. See Chapter 14.

Methodology The study of method: typically, the method of scientific research.

'Mid-p' Binomial test A variant of the 'exact' Binomial test incorporating the 'mid-p' adjustment. Although the test is not well-known, it is worth recalling when making claims of statistical significance related to the 'mid-p' interval.

'Mid-p' interval A variant of the *Clopper-Pearson interval* in which the Binomial probability of observing a proportion or rate $p = x / n$ is divided in half. Whereas in the Clopper-Pearson interval and *Binomial test*, all of this probability is considered an error, in the 'mid-p' interval, only half is allocated to the tail error. See Chapter 8.

Mode In statistics, the most common value in a distribution (the peak of a curve or sequence). See also *mean* and *median*. A *bimodal distribution* has two peaks. In linguistics, the term 'mode' is also used as shorthand for *mode of delivery* (e.g., speech rather than writing).

Monotonic A property of mathematical functions. A monotonic function has always an upward or downward gradient, that is, $f(x)$ is monotonic if and only if $f(x)$ either increases or decreases as x increases. See Chapter 9.

More test A simple significance test comparing two observed frequency counts that asks *is the larger number significantly greater than the smaller?* It can also be used to compare Binomial proportions in competition. See Chapter 7.

MOVER (method of variance estimate recovery) A method of creating confidence intervals by algebra, it assumes that variance at confidence interval bounds is approximately Normal. Applying the *Bienaymé formula* gives us a general function for the difference of two independent properties provided each has a separate confidence interval. When combined with the Wilson score interval, transformation functions and other axioms, this method allows us to calculate confidence intervals for many properties directly from a formula. See Chapter 9.

Multinomial A *scale of measurement* of simple mutually exclusive categories (e.g., A, B and C).

Mutual substitution In corpus linguistics, the principle that, in a set of forms with the same referential meaning, one form can substitute for another. Subtypes include *independent mutual substitution*, where substitution occurs without changing the meaning of the text, and *mutual substitution with consistent meaning change*, where the form and the meaning change together, but consistently. See Chapter 3.

Mutual substitution with consistent meaning change A type of *mutual substitution* where the replacement of one form with another changes a particular aspect of the meaning of the form, in the same way in every instance, such as to add an explicit progressive aspect to a verb or provide more information about a referent. As a result, the choice of form is also a choice of meaning, and hypotheses that explain variation must take account of this fact. The core referential meaning (the thing referred to) should not change, however. See Chapter 3.

Natural experiment An experiment in which variables are not constrained prior to sampling. Data are collected without the risk of a research hypothesis influencing participants, but participants usually perform different tasks. *Corpus linguistics* consists of natural experiments. Compared to *controlled experiments* where data are collected in pursuit of a particular hypothesis. See Chapter 2.

Newcombe-Wilson difference interval A robust confidence interval for the difference between two *Binomial proportions*, p_1 and p_2, based on the *Wilson score interval*, with or without *Yates's continuity correction*. The interval can be expressed in two forms: (a) as an interval for $d = p_2 - p_1 \in (d^-, d^+)$, where 'significantly different' means the interval excludes zero, and (b) as a zero-based interval, $0 \in (w_d^-, w_d^+)$, where we test if d is within the range. The zero-based interval is quick to calculate and may be a precursor to the interval for d. Transformation is simple: $(d^-, d^+) \equiv (d - w_d^+, d - w_d^-)$. See Chapter 7.

Newcombe-Wilson test A test that employs the Newcombe-Wilson interval to compare whether two *Binomial proportions*, p_1 and p_2, are significantly different. It should be used whenever we consider a potential non-zero difference in expected means, including certain meta-tests. See Chapters 8 and 14.

***n*-gram** A high-frequency string of words of length n obtained from a corpus.

Non-significant A finding of a *significance test* that observed data do not differ from the expected data (predicted by the *null hypothesis*) sufficiently to conclude that the difference is not due to mere random chance.

Normal approximation to the Binomial distribution A mathematical approximation that assumes that the discrete and asymmetric *Binomial distribution* closely matches the continuous and symmetric *Normal distribution*. It is employed by many statistical methods, and it simplifies calculations considerably. See Chapter 6.

Normal distribution A symmetric continuous 'bell curve' distribution, originally termed the *Gaussian distribution*, that assumes that variation between two points is proportional to the square of the distance between them. It is derived from Gauss's method of least squares. Critical values of the standard Normal distribution (where the mean is 0 and standard deviation, 1), represent tail areas of constant area α (for a one-tailed distribution) or $\alpha/2$ (two-tailed). See Chapter 6. It may approximate closely to the *Binomial distribution* and may be substituted for it. Despite the name, however, many distributions are not 'Normal'.

Normal interval A sampling interval based on the *Normal distribution* that may be applied to a population proportion P. It is, however, often erroneously applied as a confidence interval to an observed proportion p, where it is termed the *Wald interval*.

Null hypothesis A *hypothesis* that expresses 'no change' or a null result.

Null hypothesis significance testing (NHST) A procedure for carrying out *statistical tests* to evaluate and reject *null hypotheses*, based on a scientific method due to Karl Popper.

Number scale See *scale of measurement*.

Number theory The logic of different classes of numbers and their relationship. See *scale of measurement*.

Odds A proportion p expressed as the ratio p:$(1 - p)$.

Odds ratio The ratio of two *odds*.

Observed Binomial proportion The fraction of sampled independent choices which are of a single type, represented by lower case p.

Observed distribution An ordered set of numbers observed in a sample.

Onomasiology The study of form change with constant meaning (unlike *semasiology*, which studies variation in the meaning of a single form). In onomasiological variationism, we consider multiple expressions with a single meaning, and the *baseline* represents the opportunity for a particular expression to be uttered. See Chapter 4.

Operationalisation A process of converting a research question into a testable hypothesis, replacing abstract concepts with concrete measurable variables and definitions. In the 3A paradigm, operationalisation is performed in the *abstraction* cycle. See Chapter 1.

Ordinal scale A ranked scale. See *scale of measurement*.

Ordinary Least Squares (OLS) A method of *regression* unweighted by variance.

Orthographic transcription A method of transcribing speech to record every word or part-word uttered. Paraphrasing and omission, which characterise some professional transcriptions, are not permitted. Orthography is the rendering of words into a standard form. Orthographic transcription is not as sophisticated or detailed as phonetic transcription, but it is sufficient for much linguistic research.

Overshoot Exceeding the bounds of a finite set, such as probability $\boldsymbol{P} = [0, 1]$.

Paradigm In science, a distinct set of concepts and principles, marking out an approach to a particular field of inquiry. In linguistic morphology, the term is also used to mean a set of possible inflections.

Parse To create a structured analysis (or 'tree diagram') for a sentence using a particular grammatical framework.

Parsed corpus A *corpus* where every sentence is given a grammatical analysis in the form of a tree diagram. Also called a 'treebank'.

Part-of-speech (POS) See *wordclass* and *wordclass tagger*.

Pearson's contingency coefficient *C* One of the first measures, alongside an adjusted score, C_{adj}, to be proposed for the association between variables in a contingency table. See Chapter 13.

Pearson's r^2 A correlation score used in linear regression for *Real* data (often used for *Interval* or *Ratio* data). The higher the score, the closer the *fitness* and the closer the correlation.

Per million words (pmw) The rate of an item per million words, it is a common type of *exposure rate* used in corpus linguistics.

Percentage difference The difference between the probability of two observations expressed as a proportion of the first. It is an extremely common method for expressing change. See Chapter 7.

Percentile The part of a distribution found within a percentage range. For example, if we partition a distribution into ten-percentiles (termed 'deciles'), we consider the first 10% of the distribution, then the next 10%, and so on. See Chapter 17.

Point test A statistical *meta-test* for comparing observed proportions between different tables. May be extended to cover multiple points at once ('multi-point tests'). See Chapter 14.

Poisson distribution A continuous, asymmetric probability distribution.

Pooled probability estimate A working estimate of P, written $\hat{p}$, calculated by adding up cell frequencies across values of *independent variables* (IVs). In a contingency table where the IV is displayed horizontally and its values form columns, the pooled probability estimate will be simply the row total divided by the grand total, that is, the *prior probability* $p(x)$ where $X = x$ is the value of the dependent variable. The *z test for two proportions drawn from the same population* assumes that the IV does not represent a group of independent populations but random samples from the same population, and thus there is a single mean probability P to estimate. See Chapter 8.

Population The volume of data from which a *sample* may be drawn. *Inferential statistics* draws an inference from the sample to the population. See Chapter 5.

Population proportion The true proportion in the *population*, that is, the actual share of one type out of a choice where that type is available, in the total set of possible data or world at large. In this book, it is represented by upper case P. Unless the population is finite and closed, the population proportion will necessarily be unknown.

POS (*part of speech*) See *wordclass*.

POS tagger See *wordclass tagger*.

Post hoc analysis 'After the fact' analysis performed on data sampled for other purposes. Sometimes referred to as *ex post facto* analysis.

PPCEME (*Penn-Helsinki Parsed Corpus of Early Modern English*) One of a series of *parsed corpora* of historical English available from www.ling.upenn.edu/hist-corpora.

Prior probability The probability of an event y, $p(y)$, prior to a selection x, $p(y \mid x)$. In a contingency table, the prior probability refers to the proportion of the row or column sum (i.e., $p(x)$ or $p(y)$).

Probability A number representing the chance that something may happen. May be derived from a *proportion* of an item within a sample, in which case we reason that the chance that a random selection from the sample will yield that item is the same as that fraction.

Probability density function (p.d.f.) A function obtaining the probability assigned to a Real number x for a probabilistic distribution, such as the *Normal*, *Binomial* or *Wilson distributions*. To obtain the characteristic Gaussian 'bell curve' we plot the probability density function for the Normal distribution over x. See Chapter 17.

Probability distribution A distribution (ordered or continuous set) of *probabilities*.

Probability scale A number that can range from zero to 1 inclusive, often written $\boldsymbol{P} = [0, 1]$.

Probability theory The basics of statistical reasoning, probability theory concerns the mathematics of chance. It is often applied to a closed set, such as a pack of cards. The application to *statistical inference* requires us to reason about how a sample drawn from the population will appear. See Chapter 6.

Proportion A true fraction in the probability range [0, 1].

Qualitative Analysis (QA) A process of developing an annotation scheme by applying it to texts, making distinctions and enumerating types. Usually contrasted to *Quantitative Analysis*, but these may be complementary aspects of the same process. See Chapter 1.

Quantisation A process of converting continuous data into discontinuous data ('quanta') or a set of ordered categories. Examples include converting ages into age ranges, dates into time periods or word counts into 'complexity' categories. Quantisation simplifies data and reduces the amount of information available. Example applications include collapsing time series (see Chapter 12) and plotting frequency distributions of samples (see Chapter 16).

Quantitative Analysis The numerical analysis of data, including statistical analysis.

Quota sampling Another term for *balanced sampling*.

Random sampling A method of obtaining a sample by drawing each instance at random from the next. See Chapters 5 and 16.

Random-text sampling A type of *cluster sampling* where each 'cluster' is a subsample drawn from an independently sourced text. The texts are random, but instances are not. See Chapter 16.

Ratio Another term for 'fraction'. A Ratio scale is a rational number, that is, the fraction of two integers. See also *scale of measurement*.

Real A number that can have any continuous value from minus to plus infinity. It may be written $\mathfrak{R} = [-\infty, \infty]$. See also *scale of measurement*.

Reciprocal One divided by the number, that is, the reciprocal of x is $1/x$.

Reductionism The reduction of complex phenomena to simple explanations. It may be divided into two kinds. 'Experimental reductionism' is a necessary process of simplifying a phenomenon (or the situations in which the phenomenon is detected) to carry out an experiment. 'Philosophical reductionism' (sometimes called 'determinism') is where the apparent success of such simplifications is used to argue that a more complex theory is unnecessary.

Referential meaning The meaning of the underlying concept referred to, for example, the thing, event, attribute or process.

Regression A statistical method for attempting to *fit* data to a general function describing a particular type of line (straight or curved), manipulating parameters of that function until the line has the closest proximity ('fit') to as much of the data as possible. The procedure employs a correlation statistic to estimate this proximity. *Linear regression* matches data against a straight line function, whereas *logistic regression* fits data to a logistic curve.

Repertory grid analysis An exploratory clustering technique, it extracts a cluster tree ('dendrogram') for variables and instances.

Replication The process of repeating an *experiment* with a different sample obtained by the same steps as the original experiment. Thanks to the cost of corpus sampling and the tendency to employ all available data in an initial experiment, true replication is rarely carried out. Repetition, or 'weak replication', is more common. This is where a researcher repeats a corpus experiment on a second, differently sampled corpus. Whereas repeated acts of true replication can tell us about the soundness of the statistical model, should multiple experiments on different corpora obtain distinct results, differences in datasets may explain the results. See Chapter 11.

Replication interval The range of values in which one would expect to find a second observation (e.g., p'), given an initial one (e.g., p), at an error level α. This is wider than a *confidence interval* for p because both observations are uncertain.

Research question A general question motivating a piece of research that may require refinement to be translated into one or more testable *hypotheses*.

Retrievability The principle that a linguistic event may be reliably retrieved from a corpus. Closely related to *decidability*, the ability to classify a linguistic event in the first place.

Risk ratio The ratio of two Binomial proportions.

Root mean square (r.m.s.) The square root of the arithmetic mean of squared terms.

Sample A set of data drawn from a population of possible data. There are several different types of sampling, including random sampling, quota sampling, stratified sampling and cluster sampling. Most corpus data in texts are 'quota samples of cluster samples'.

Sampling distribution The distribution of a property, such as a mean or proportion, when randomly sampled from the population, for example, the *Binomial distribution.*

Sampling frame A set of principles for collecting data.

Sampling interval The predicted range of values of sampled observations of a property obtained from a sampling distribution, such as the *Binomial distribution* of observed proportions p given a population mean P, at an error level α. Not to be confused with a *confidence interval.*

Scale of measurement A term used by number theorists and statisticians to refer to different types of number or category. The simplest scale is simply true or false, called a Binary number or *Binomial* scale. Other scales are *Multinomial* (multiple exclusive categories, e.g., A, B and C), *Ordinal* (ordered categories, e.g., A < B < C), *Interval* (ordered categories with a constant distance between them, such as the integers . . . −1, 0, 1, 2, 3 . . .), *Ratio* (the ratio of two numbers, also known as rational numbers) and *Real* (rational and irrational numbers). See Chapter 2.

Scatter A popular term for the distribution of a sample. See Chapter 6.

S-curve A popular name for the *logistic* curve, that is, the curve obtained by a logistic function. Also known as the 'sigmoid'. See Chapter 10.

Search procedure A computational procedure that solves an equation by a 'brute force' method of trying different solutions and evaluating if they are correct and attempting to converge on the right answer. In this book, the main applications of this kind of procedure are to invert a function or to fit a formula to data. The procedure will converge on a precise answer if the function being inverted is *monotonic*. See Appendices A and B.

Semasiology The study of meaning change of a constant form (in contrast to *onomasiology*). In semasiology, we may use a *baseline* of a particular expression with multiple meanings, but we should also consider each meaning separately in relation to its alternative expressions (i.e., onomasiologically). See Chapter 4.

Separability test A statistical *meta-test* for comparing whether data in one contingency table are significantly different from another table of an identical structure. Includes 'separability of observations' (*point tests* comparing proportions or table cells), 'separability of fit' (comparing χ^2 goodness of fit test results), and 'separability of independence' (*gradient tests* comparing homogeneity or independence χ^2 test results).

Series A mathematical term for an ordered set or *vector*. One of the most famous series in mathematics, {0, 1, 1, 2, 3, 5, 8 . . .}, is called the Fibonacci series. In a series, each position is relevant and the same number may appear more than once. A discrete *distribution* is a type of series.

Set theory The mathematical logic of sets.

Significance A criterion used in *inferential statistics* for evaluating the difference between observed and expected data. Significance is *binary* (true/false), rather than a matter of degree.

Significance test A method for testing a particular proposition about a sample (e.g., an observed difference between two proportions p_1 and p_2) against a model of the sample's expected behaviour, given that samples are likely to vary due to random chance. Different tests evaluate different propositions or *null hypotheses* about the data, and rely on different assumptions and mathematical models about how a statistic drawn from the sample is expected to vary.

Significant A finding from a *significance test* that the difference between observed data and expected data (as predicted by a *null hypothesis*) is greater than a difference expected by mere random chance. If a finding is significant, we can reject the null hypothesis. See Chapter 2.

Significant difference Statistical *significance* is evaluated in terms of differences, for example, between an observed p and predicted P, observed data **O** and expected data **E**, or between two proportions p_1 and p_2. Most *significance tests* are tests of significant differences where the *null hypothesis* is that the difference is zero (or too small to be said to be distinguishable from zero).

Size of effect See *Effect size*.

Spearman's R^2 A ranked order correlation score used in estimating the best line fit (linear regression) for *Ordinal* data. Like Pearson's r^2, from which it is derived, the smaller the score the closer the fit, and therefore the more the two variables x and y can be said to correlate.

Standard deviation A standardised measure of spread that scales a Normal distribution, often written with the symbol s (within-sample spread or 'scatter') or S (the standard deviation of resampled means, 'confidence'). The *variance* is the square of the standard deviation (s^2 or S^2).

Standard error The Normal error interval about an observation. When applied to *Binomial intervals* on the probability scale, another name for the (incorrect) *Wald interval*.

Standardised Normal distribution A *Normal distribution* with *mean* 0 and *standard deviation* 1. See Chapter 17.

Statistical inference A method of making a claim about a population based on a sample drawn from that population.

Stratified sampling A method of obtaining a balanced sample whereby multiple sampling variables divide the data in constant proportions across intersecting sets. See Chapter 5.

Subset test A class of *meta-test* where one table is a subset of another. See Chapter 14.

Survey of English Usage A *corpus linguistics* research group founded by Randolph Quirk.

Synchronic A linguistic term referring to a contrast within a moment in time, as distinct from *diachronic*. Corpora collected as a 'snapshot' within a limited time period may be used for synchronic comparisons. Examples include the *British National Corpus* (BNC), the *International Corpus of English* (ICE) and the *Corpus of Contemporary American English* (COCA).

***t* test (Student's *t* test or Welch's *t* test)** A comparable test to the *z* test, properly for Real data (usually termed on a *Ratio* scale) but sometimes used for *Interval* data. It can be used to compare an observed mean against an expected one (a single-sample test) or two means against each other (a two independent sample test). See Chapter 12.

Tagged corpus A corpus where every word has been given a *wordclass* tag but sentences have not been structurally annotated into tree diagrams (*parsed*).

Tagger A program that assigns category labels to words. Usually these are wordclass tags, hence 'tagger' is typically a shorthand for *wordclass tagger*, but other classifiers, such as semantic taggers, are under development.

Tail area The area under a *probability distribution* from a given *bound x*, to the limit of the potential range, moving away from the *mean*. Thus the lower tail area below the lower bound E^- of a *Normal distribution* about P covers the range $[0, E^-)$.

TIME (*TIME Magazine Corpus*) A 100 million word *diachronic* corpus of American written English derived from the archives of TIME magazine. See www.english-corpora.org/time.

Time series Data where one of the variables (usually an independent variable) is time. Time is to be considered Ordinal at least (if not Interval, Ratio or Real), and so data can be plotted as a series.

Token An instance of a linguistic *type*.

Treebank See *parsed corpus*.

Type In linguistics, an identifiable class of linguistic item (a term or structure). Contrasted with *token*, which refers to the number of items of this class.

Type A, B and C Types of case used to distinguish between two observed forms (A and B) that are *mutually substitutable* and are subject to *alternation*; and a third type, C, which does not substitute for either A or B. Including 'Type C' cases in sets of terms identifying a baseline undermines the *Binomial* or *Multinomial* statistical model used for analysis. See Chapter 3.

Type I errors A false positive evaluation, where a significance test is incorrectly stated to be significant although more accurate methods would report it to be non-significant.

Type II errors A false negative evaluation, where a significance test is incorrectly rated non-significant although more accurate methods would report it to be significant.

Upper bound The largest number in a continuous range or interval.

Variable The conceptualisation of an aspect of a phenomenon such that it can be measured or categorised. Experimental variables are divided into *independent* and *dependent variables*.

Variance The square of the *standard deviation*, often written s^2.

Variation In linguistics, the term is used to refer to discrete alternatives being available or proportions of those alternatives varying.

Variationism An approach to corpus linguistic experimental design where data consist of freely-varying speaker or writer choices. Also referred to as *linguistic choice experiments* and *alternation studies*. The baseline for the purpose of comparison is the opportunity for making a choice of alternative form. See *onomasiology* and *baseline*.

Vector A one dimensional *matrix* or ordered set.

Wald interval A confidence interval obtained by assuming that the sampling variance of an observed Binomial proportion is Normally distributed. This assumption is incorrect. See Chapter 6.

Weight of evidence A concept deriving from the quantity of data supporting an observation, that is, the sample size.

Wilson distribution The probability distribution of values greater than, or less than, an observation p, deriving from the *Wilson score interval*. See Chapter 17.

Wilson interval comparison heuristic A heuristic for quickly comparing two proportions with *Wilson score intervals*. It can also be applied to data points and intervals derived from the Wilson interval provided they are on the same scale, for example, repositioned Newcombe-Wilson intervals or ϕ intervals. The heuristic says that where intervals have no overlap, observations must be significantly different; where one point falls within the interval of the other, they cannot be significantly different. Only where intervals overlap but no points fall in either interval is a significance test required. See Chapter 7.

Wilson score interval An interval for an observed proportion, p, that assumes that samples adopt a *Normal distribution* about the true proportion in the population, P. May be adjusted by *Yates's continuity correction.*

Wilson score test A test for comparing whether a predicted value P falls outside the Wilson score interval for p. It obtains the same result as the equivalent z test for the single proportion.

Wordclass The basic grammatical category of a word, such as noun, verb, adverb, preposition and so on. Sometimes called 'POS' or part-of-speech.

Wordclass tagger A computer program that assigns wordclass labels to words in sentences. Often called a 'POS tagger' or simply 'tagger'. It takes sentences/utterances as input and outputs a sentence where each word is given a wordclass label, proper singular noun, general adjective, and so on. It is one of the most ubiquitous tools in corpus linguistics. A *tagged corpus* is produced by applying a wordclass tagger to a series of plain texts.

Yates's continuity correction An adjustment to the *Normal approximation to the Binomial distribution.* It adjusts for the fact that the *Binomial distribution* is discrete (observations must be of whole numbers or true fractions), whereas the *Normal distribution* is continuous (observations can be any value). It can be applied to the Wilson score interval and thereby, more complex tests based on it, such as the χ^2 test for homogeneity and more complex *meta-tests* (Chapter 14). Applying this adjustment makes tests and intervals slightly more conservative. See Chapters 6 and 8.

Yule's Q A commonly cited *interaction effect size* similar to Cramér's ϕ.

***z* test for the single proportion** A simple test employing the Normal approximation to the Binomial distribution for comparing an observed proportion p with a given expected population proportion P. The test may be calculated with a 2×1 *chi-square goodness of fit test* or a *Wilson score test* and obtain the same result.

***z* test for two independent proportions drawn from independent populations** A test for comparing the difference between two observed *Binomial proportions* p_1 and p_2 drawn from independent populations and an expected difference, $D \neq 0$. The *Newcombe-Wilson test* is the best method for carrying out this test. See Chapter 8.

***z* test for two independent proportions drawn from the same population** A test for comparing the difference between two independently observed *Binomial proportions* p_1 and p_2 to test if they are drawn from the same population. The test is identical to a 2×2 *chi-square homogeneity test*. See Chapter 8.

Zero-width interval An interval of zero width represents a claim that an observation is certain, which can only properly occur if the sample *is* the population! It is produced in error by the *Wald interval* (and other methods related to it) when an observation p is 0 or 1.

REFERENCES

Aarts, B. (2001). Corpus linguistics, Chomsky and fuzzy tree fragments. In C. Mair & M. Hundt (Eds.), *Corpus linguistics and linguistic theory* (pp. 5–13). Amsterdam: Rodopi.

Aarts, B. (2007). *Syntactic gradience: The nature of grammatical indeterminacy*. Oxford: Oxford University Press.

Aarts, B., Close, J. & Wallis, S.A. (2013). Choices over time: Methodological issues in current change. In B. Aarts, J. Close, G. Leech & S.A. Wallis (Eds.), *The verb phrase in English*. Cambridge: Cambridge University Press.

Aarts, B. & Wallis, S.A. (2014). Noun phrase simplicity in spoken English. In L. Veselovská & M. Janebová (Eds.), *Complex visibles out there: Proceedings of the Olomouc linguistics colloquium 2014: Language use and linguistic structure* (pp. 501–511). Olomouc: Palacký University.

Aarts, B., Wallis, S.A. & Bowie, J. (2018). -Ing clauses in spoken English: Structure, usage and recent change. In E. Seoane, C. Acuña-Fariña & I. Palacios-Martínez (Eds.), *Subordination in English: Synchronic and diachronic perspectives* (pp. 129–154). Berlin: De Gruyter.

Abeillé, A. (Ed.). (2003). *Treebanks: Building and using parsed corpora*. Dordrecht: Kluwer.

Alexander, M. (2023). Speech in the British Hansard. In M. Korhonen, H. Kotze & J. Tyrkkö (Eds.), *Exploring language and society with big data: Parliamentary discourse across time and space*. Amsterdam: John Benjamins.

Altman, D.G., Machin, D., Bryant, T.N. & Gardner, M.J. (2000). *Statistics with confidence* (2nd ed.). Bristol: BMJ Books.

Anderson, J.R. (1983). *The architecture of cognition*. Cambridge, MA: Harvard University Press.

Anthony, L. (2023). Common statistics used in corpus linguistics. *Self-Published AntConc Paper*. Retrieved from https://www.laurenceanthony.net/resources/statistics/common_statistics_used_in_corpus_linguistics.pdf

Arppe, A., Gilquin, G., Glynn, D., Hilpert, M. & Zeschel, A. (2010). Cognitive corpus linguistics: Five points of debate on current theory and methodology. *Corpora*, *5* (*1*), 1–27. https://doi.org/10.3366/e1749503210000341

Aston, G. & Burnard, L. (1997). *The BNC handbook: Exploring the British National Corpus with SARA*. Retrieved from http://corpus.leeds.ac.uk/teaching/aston-burnard-bnc.pdf

Baillargeon, R. (1994). How do infants learn about the physical world? *Current Directions in Psychological Science*, *3* (*5*), 133–140. https://doi.org/10.1111/1467-8721.ep10770614

Ball, C.N. (1994). Automatic text analysis: Cautionary tales. *Literary and Linguistic Computing*, *9* (*4*), 295–302. https://doi.org/10.1093/llc/9.4.295

Bauer, L. (1994). *Watching English change: An introduction to the study of linguistic change in standard Englishes in the twentieth century*. London: Longman.

Bendahmane, M., Dubois, A., Raymond, O. & Le Bris, M. (2013). Genetics and genomics of flower initiation and development in roses. *Journal of Experimental Botany*, *64* (*4*), 847–857. https://doi.org/10.1093/jxb/ers387

Berry, G. & Armitage, P. (1995). Mid-*p* confidence intervals: A brief review. *Journal of the Royal Statistical Society Series D (the Statistician)*, *44* (*4*), 417–413. https://doi.org/10.2307/2348891

Biber, D. (1988). *Variation across speech and writing*. Cambridge: Cambridge University Press.

Biber, D. (1993). Representativeness in corpus design. *Literary and Linguistic Computing*, *8* (*4*), 243–257. https://doi.org/10.1093/llc/8.4.243

Biber, D., Johansson, S., Leech, G., Conrad, S. & Finegan, E. (1999). *The Longman grammar of spoken and written English*. London: Longman.

Biber, D. & Reppen, R. (Eds.). (2015). *The Cambridge handbook of English corpus linguistics*. Cambridge: Cambridge University Press.

Bishop, Y.M.M., Fienberg, S.E. & Holland, P.W. (1975). *Discrete multivariate analysis: Theory and practice*. Cambridge, MA: MIT Press.

Böhmová, A., Hajič, J., Hajičová, E. & Hladká, B. (2003). The PDT: A three-level annotation scenario. In A. Abeillé (Ed.), *Treebanks: Building and using parsed corpora* (pp. 103–127). Dordrecht: Kluwer.

Bowie, J. & Wallis, S.A. (2016). The *to*-infinitival perfect: A study of decline. In V. Werner, E. Seoane & C. Suárez-Gómez (Eds.), *Re-assessing the present perfect* (pp. 43–94). Berlin: De Gruyter.

Bowie, J., Wallis, S.A. & Aarts, B. (2013). The perfect in spoken English. In B. Aarts, J. Close, G. Leech & S.A. Wallis (Eds.), *The verb phrase in English*. Cambridge: Cambridge University Press.

Bowie, J., Wallis, S.A. & Aarts, B. (2014). Contemporary change in modal usage in spoken British English: Mapping the impact of 'genre'. In J.I. Marín-Arrese, M. Carretero, J.A. Hita & J. van der Auwera (Eds.), *English modality* (pp. 57–94). Berlin: De Gruyter.

Braithwaite, D.W. & Goldstone, R.L. (2013). Benefits of graphical and symbolic representations for learning and transfer of statistical concepts. In M. Knauff, M. Pauen, N. Sebanz & I. Wachsmuth (Eds.), *Proceedings of the Thirty-Fifth Annual Conference of the Cognitive Science Society* (pp. 1928–1933). Berlin: Cognitive Science Society.

Brezina, V., McEnery, T. & Wattam, S. (2015). Collocations in context: A new perspective on collocation networks. *International Journal of Corpus Linguistics*, *20* (*2*), 139–173. https://doi.org/10.1075/ijcl.20.2.01bre

Brezina, V. & Meyerhoff, M. (2014). Significant or random?: A critical review of sociolinguistic generalisations based on large corpora. *International Journal of Corpus Linguistics*, *19* (*1*), 1–28. https://doi.org/10.1075/ijcl.19.1.01bre

Briggs, W. (2016). *Uncertainty: The soul of modeling, probability and statistics*. New York, NY: Springer.

Brown, L.D., Cai, T. & DasGupta, A. (2001). Interval estimation for a Binomial proportion. *Statistical Science*, *16* (*2*), 101–133. https://doi.org/10.1214/ss/1009213286

Church, K. (2000). Empirical estimates of adaptation: The chance of two Noriegas is closer to $p/2$ than p^2. In *Coling '00: Proceedings of the 18th Conference on Computational Linguistics, July 2000, Saarbrücken, Germany* (Vol. 1, pp. 173–179). Stroudsburg, PA: Association for Computational Linguistics. https://doi.org/10.3115/990820.990847

Clopper, C. & Pearson, E.S. (1934). The use of confidence or fiducial limits illustrated in the case of the Binomial. *Biometrika, 26* (*4*), 404–413. https://doi.org/10.1093/biomet/26.4.404

Cochran, W.G. (1954). Some methods for strengthening the common χ^2 tests. *Biometrics, 10*, 417–451. https://doi.org/10.2307/3001616

Cramér, H. (1946). *Mathematical methods of statistics*. Princeton, NJ: Princeton University Press.

Cribb, V.M. & Rochford, S. (2018). The transcription and representation of spoken political discourse in the UK jouse of commons. *International Journal of English Linguistics, 8* (*2*). https://doi.org/10.5539/ijel.v8n2p1

Cumming, G. (2014). The new statistics: Why and how. *Psychological Science, 25* (*1*), 7–29. https://doi.org/10.1111/j.1745-6924.2008.00079

Davies, M. (2007). *The TIME magazine corpus: 100 million words, 1920s–2000s*. Retrieved from https://corpus.byu.edu/time

Davies, M. (2009). The 385+million word corpus of contemporary American English (1990–2008+): Design, architecture, and linguistic insights. *International Journal of Corpus Linguistics, 14*, 159–190. https://doi.org/10.1075/ijcl.14.2.02dav

Davies, M. (2012). Expanding horizons in historical linguistics with the 400-million word corpus of historical American English. *Corpora, 7* (*2*), 121–157. https://doi.org/10.3366/cor.2012.0024

Denison, D. (2018). That-clauses as complements of verbs or nouns. In E. Seoane, C. Acuña-Fariña & I. Palacios-Martínez (Eds.), *Subordination in English* (pp. 61–84). Berlin: De Gruyter.

Dice, L.R. (1945). Measures of the amount of ecologic association between species. *Ecology, 26*, 297–302. https://doi.org/10.2307/1932409

Dunning, T. (1993). Accurate methods for the statistics of surprise and coincidence. *Computational Linguistics, 19* (*1*), 61–74.

Evert, S. (2004). *The statistics of word co-occurrences: Word pairs and collocations* (Ph.D. thesis). University of Stuttgart.

Gardner, D. & Davies, M. (2007). Pointing out frequent phrasal verbs: A corpus-based analysis. *TESOL Quarterly, 41* (*2*), 339–360. https://doi.org/10.1002/j.1545-7249.2007.tb00062.x

Gelman, A. (2016). What has happened down here is the winds have changed. *Statistical modeling, causal inference and social science*. Retrieved from http://andrewgelman.com/2016/09/21/what-has-happened-down-here-is-the-winds-have-changed

Gelman, A. & Loken, E. (2013). *The garden of forking paths*. Columbia University. Retrieved from www.stat.columbia.edu/~gelman/research/unpublished/p_hacking.pdf

Giardino, V. (2017). Diagrammatic reasoning in mathematics. In L. Magnani & T. Berlotti (Eds.), *Springer handbook of model-based science*. New York, NY: Springer.

Gilliland, D. & Melfi, V. (2010). A note on confidence interval estimation and margin of error. *Journal of Statistics Education, 18* (*1*). https://doi.org/10.1080/10691898.2010.11889474

Gleick, J. (1977). *Chaos: Making a new science*. London: Heineman.

Goldacre, B. (2011, September 9). The statistical error that just keeps on coming. *Guardian*. Retrieved from www.guardian.co.uk/commentisfree/2011/sep/09/bad-science-research-error

Gould, S.J. (1996a). *The mismeasure of man* (2nd ed.). New York, NY: Norton.

Gould, S.J. (1996b). *Life's grandeur*. London: Random House.

Greenbaum, S. (1996a). *The Oxford English grammar*. Oxford: Oxford University Press.
Greenbaum, S. (Ed.). (1996b). *Comparing English worldwide*. Oxford: Clarendon.
Gries, S.Th. (2009). *Quantitative corpus linguistics with R*. New York, NY/London: Routledge.
Gries, S.Th. (2011). Studying syntactic priming in corpora. In D. Schönefeld (Ed.), *Converging evidence*. Amsterdam: John Benjamins.
Gries, S.Th. (2015). The most underused statistical method in corpus linguistics: Multilevel (and mixed-effects) models. *Corpora, 10* (*1*), 95–125. https://doi.org/10.3366/cor.2015.0068
Harris, A.H.S., Reeder, R. & Hyun, J.K. (2009). Common statistical and research design problems in manuscripts submitted to high-impact psychiatry journals: What editors and reviewers want authors to know. *Journal of Psychiatric Research, 43* (*15*), 1231–1234. https://doi.org/10.1016/j.jpsychires.2009.04.007
Harth, E. (1995). *The creative loop: How the brain makes a mind*. London: Penguin.
Hesterberg, T., Moore, D.S., Monaghan, S., Clipson, A., Epstein, R., Craig, B.A. & McCabe, G.P. (2010). Bootstrap methods and permutation tests. Chapter 16 in D.S. Moore, G.P. McCabe & B.A. Craig (Eds.), *Introduction to the practice of statistics* (7th ed.). New York: W. H. Freeman.
Hilbe, J.M. (2009). *Logistic regression models*. Boca Raton, FL: CRC Press.
Hofland, K. & Johansson, S. (1982). *Word frequencies in British and American English*. Bergen: Norwegian Computing Centre for the Humanities/London: Longman.
Huber, M., Nissel, M., Maiwald, P. & Widlitzki, B. (2012). *The Old Bailey Corpus: Spoken English in the 18th and 19th centuries*. Giessen: University of Giessen. Retrieved from www.uni-giessen.de/oldbaileycorpus
Huddleston, R. & Pullum, G.K. (Eds.). (2002). *The Cambridge grammar of the English language*. Cambridge: Cambridge University Press.
Hundt, M. (2004). Animacy, agentivity, and the spread of the progressive in modern English. *English Language and Linguistics, 8* (*1*), 47–69. https://doi.org/10.1017/S1360674304001248
Kanazawa, S. & Vandermassen, G. (2005). Engineers have more sons, nurses have more daughters: An evolutionary psychological extension of Baron-Cohen's extreme male brain theory of autism. *Journal of Theoretical Biology, 233* (*4*), 589–599. https://doi.org/10.1016/j.jtbi.2004.11.009
Keizer, E. (2007). *The English noun phrase: The nature of linguistic categorisation*. Cambridge: Cambridge University Press.
Kelly, G. (1955). *The psychology of personal constructs*. New York, NY: Norton.
Kelly, R., Narayanan, S. & Patel, M. (2017). *Seven rules for spinning analytics straw into golden results*. New York, NY: McKinsey. Retrieved from www.mckinsey.com/business-functions/operations/our-insights/seven-rules-for-spinning-analytics-straw-into-golden-results
King, S. (2002). *On writing*. New York, NY: Pocket Books.
Kroch, A., Santorini, B. & Delfs, L. (2004). *The Penn-Helsinki Parsed Corpus of Early Modern English (PPCEME)* [CD ROM] (1st ed., Release 3). Pennsylvania, MI: Department of Linguistics, University of Pennsylvania. Retrieved from www.ling.upenn.edu/histcorpora/PPCEME-RELEASE-3
Kučera, H. & Francis, W.N. (1967). *Computational analysis of present-day American English*. Providence MA: Brown University Press.
Labov, W. (1966). *The social stratification of English in New York city*. Washington, DC: Centre for Applied Linguistics.
Labov, W. (1972). *Sociolinguistic patterns*. Philadelphia: University of Pennsylvania Press.
Lakatos, I. (1978). *Mathematics, science and epistemology*. Cambridge: Cambridge University Press.

Lavandera, B.R. (1978). Where does the sociolinguistic variable stop? *Language in Society, 7*, 171–182. https://doi.org/10.1017/S0047404500005510

Leech, G. (2011). The modals ARE declining: Reply to Neil Millar's 'modal verbs in TIME: Frequency changes 1923–2006'. *International Journal of Corpus Linguistics, 16 (4)*, 547–564. https://doi.org/10.1075/ijcl.16.4.05lee

Levin, M. (2013). The progressive verb in modern American English. In B. Aarts, J. Close, G. Leech & S.A. Wallis (Eds.), *The verb phrase in English*. Cambridge: Cambridge University Press.

Mair, C. & Leech, G. (2006). Current changes in English syntax. In B. Aarts & A. McMahon (Eds.), *The handbook of English linguistics* (pp. 318–342). Malden, MA: *Blackwell Publishers*.

Marcus, M., Kim, G., Marcinkiewicz, M.A., MacIntyre, R., Bies, M., Ferguson, M., Katz, K. & Schasberger, B. (1994). The Penn Treebank: Annotating predicate argument structure. In *Proceedings of the Human Language Technology Workshop 1994*. San Francisco: Morgan Kaufmann.

Marcus, M., Marcinkiewicz, M.A. & Santorini, B. (1993). Building a large annotated corpus of English: The Penn Treebank. *Computational Linguistics, 19 (2)*, 313–330.

McEnery, T. & Hardie, A. (2012). *Corpus linguistics: Method, theory and practice*. Cambridge: Cambridge University Press.

Millar, N. (2009). Modal verbs in TIME: Frequency changes 1923–2006. *International Journal of Corpus Linguistics, 14 (2)*, 191–220. https://doi.org/10.1075/ijcl.14.2.03mil

Nelson, G., Aarts, B. & Wallis, S.A. (2002). *Exploring natural language: Working with the British component of the international corpus of English*. Amsterdam: John Benjamins.

Nevalainen, T. (2015). Descriptive adequacy of the S-curve model in diachronic studies of language change. In C. Sanchez-Stockhammer (Ed.), *Can we predict language change?* Helsinki: Varieng, University of Helsinki. Retrieved from www.helsinki.fi/varieng/series/volumes/16/nevalainen

Newcombe, R.G. (1998a). Two-sided confidence intervals for the single proportion: Comparison of seven methods. *Statistics in Medicine, 17*, 857–872. https://doi.org/10.1.1.408.7107

Newcombe, R.G. (1998b). Interval estimation for the difference between independent proportions: Comparison of eleven methods. *Statistics in Medicine, 17*, 873–890. https://doi.org/10.1002/(SICI)1097-0258(19980430)17:8<873::AID-SIM779>3.0

Newcombe, R.G. (2020). *Confidence intervals for proportions and related measures of effect size*. Boca Raton, FL: CRC Press.

Newton, I. (1687). *The mathematical principles of natural philosophy* (A. Motte, Trans.). Scotts Valley, CA: Createspace Independent Publishing Platform.

Newton, I. (1730). *Opticks: Or a treatise of the reflections, refractions, inflections and colours of light* (4th ed.). Project Gutenberg. Retrieved from www.gutenberg.org/ebooks/33504

Neyman, J. (1937). Outline of a theory of statistical estimation based on the classical theory of probability. *Philosophical Transactions of the Royal Society of London, Series A: Mathematical and Physical Sciences, 236*, 333–380. https://doi.org/10.1098/rsta.1937.0005

Nieuwenhuis, S., Forstmann, B.U. & Wagenmakers, E.-J. (2011). Erroneous analyses of interactions in neuroscience: A problem of significance. *Nature Neuroscience, 14*, 1105–1107. https://doi.org/10.1038/nn.2886

Oakes, M.P. (1998). *Statistics for corpus linguistics*. Edinburgh: Edinburgh University Press.

O'Keefe, A. & McCarthy, M. (Eds.). (2012). *The Routledge handbook of corpus linguistics*. London/New York, NY: Routledge.

Orne, M.T. (1969). Demand characteristics and the concept of quasi-controls. In R. Rosenthal & R. Rosnow (Eds.), *Artifact in behavioral research* (pp. 143–179). New York, NY: Academic Press. Retrieved from www.sas.upenn.edu/psych/history/orne/orne1969inrosenthalrosnowbc.html

Polya, G. (1945). *How to solve it*. Princeton, NJ: Princeton University Press.

Putnam, H.W. (1981). *Reason, truth and history*. Cambridge: Cambridge University Press.

Quirk, R. (1960). Towards a description of English usage. *Transactions of the Philological Society*, *59*, 40–61. https://doi.org/10.1111/j.1467-968X.1960.tb00308.x

Quirk, R., Greenbaum, S., Leech, G. & Svartvik, J. (1985). *A comprehensive grammar of the English language*. London: Longman.

Rayson, P. (2003). *Matrix: A statistical method and software tool for linguistic analysis through corpus comparison* (Unpublished PhD thesis). Lancaster University, Lancaster, United Kingdom.

Roscoe, J.T. & Byars, J.A. (1971). Sample size restraints commonly imposed on the use of the chi-square statistic. *Journal of the American Statistical Association*, *66*, 755–759. https://doi.org/10.2307/2284224

Roser, M. & Ortiz-Ospina, E. (2018). *Literacy*. Retrieved from https://ourworldindata.org/literacy

Ruxton, G.D. (2006). The unequal variance *t*-test is an underused alternative to student's *t*-test and the Mann-Whitney *U* test. *Behavioral Ecology*, *17*, 688–690. https://doi.org/10.1093/beheco/ark016

Schegloff, E.A. (1993). Reflections on quantification in the study of conversation. *Research on Language and Social Interaction*, *26* (*1*), 99–128. https://doi.org/10.1207/s15327973rlsi2601_5

Schönefeld, D. (Ed.). (2011). *Converging evidence: Methodological and theoretical issues for linguistic research*. Amsterdam: John Benjamins.

Sheskin, D.J. (2011). *Handbook of parametric and nonparametric statistical procedures* (5th ed.). Boca Raton, FL: CRC Press.

Shin, Y. & Raudenbush, S.W. (2013). Efficient analysis of Q-level nested hierarchical general linear models given ignorable missing data. *The International Journal of Biostatistics*, *9* (*1*), 109–133. https://doi.org/10.1515/ijb-2012-0048

Singleton, R.A. & Straits, B.C. (2017). *Approaches to social research*. New York, NY/Oxford: Oxford University Press.

Smith, N. & Leech, G. (2013). Verb structures in twentieth century British English. In B. Aarts, J. Close, G. Leech & S.A. Wallis (Eds.), *The verb phrase in English*. Cambridge: Cambridge University Press.

Smithson, M. (2007). *Confidence intervals*. Thousand Oaks, CA: Sage Press.

Smitterberg, E. (2005). *The progressive in 19th century English: A process of integration*. Amsterdam: Rodopi.

Stahl, S. (2006). The evolution of the normal distribution. *Mathematics Magazine*, *79* (*2*), 96–113. Retrieved from www.maa.org/sites/default/files/pdf/upload_library/22/Allendoerfer/stahl96.pdf

Svartvik, J. (Ed.). (1990). *The London corpus of spoken English: Description and research*. Lund: Lund University Press.

Tognini-Bonelli, E. (2001). *Corpus linguistics at work*. Amsterdam: John Benjamins.

Traugott, E.C. & Heine, B. (Eds.). (1991). *Approaches to grammaticalization*. Amsterdam: John Benjamins.

Tversky, A. & Kahneman, D. (1971). Belief in the law of small numbers. *Psychological Bulletin*, *76* (*2*), 105–110. https://doi.org/10.1037/h0031322

Wallis, S.A. (2007). Annotation, retrieval and experimentation. In A. Meurman-Solin & A.A. Nurmi (Eds.), *Annotating variation and change*. Helsinki: Varieng, University of Helsinki. Retrieved from www.helsinki.fi/varieng/series/volumes/01/wallis

Wallis, S.A. (2008). Searching treebanks and other structured corpora. In A. Lüdeling & M. Kytö (Eds.), *Corpus linguistics: An international handbook* (pp. 738–759). Berlin: Mouton de Gruyter.

Wallis, S.A. (2012a). Measures of association for contingency tables. *corp.ling.stats*. London: Survey of English Usage. Retrieved from https://corplingstats.wordpress.com/2012/04/09/measures-of-association

Wallis, S.A. (2012b). Goodness of fit measures for discrete categorical data. *corp.ling.stats*. London: Survey of English Usage. Retrieved from https://corplingstats.wordpress.com/2012/03/31/gof

Wallis, S.A. (2012c). Freedom to vary and significance tests. *corp.ling.stats*. London: Survey of English Usage. Retrieved from https://corplingstats.wordpress.com/2012/09/30/free-to-vary

Wallis, S.A. (2013a). Binomial confidence intervals and contingency tests. *Journal of Quantitative Linguistics, 20* (*3*), 178–208. https://doi.org/10.1080/09296174.2013.799918

Wallis, S.A. (2013b). *z*-squared: The origin and application of χ^2. *Journal of Quantitative Linguistics, 20* (*4*), 350–378. https://doi.org/10.1080/09296174.2013.830554

Wallis, S.A. (2014). What might a corpus of parsed spoken data tell us about language? In L. Veselovská & M. Janebová (Eds.), *Complex visibles out there: Proceedings of the Olomouc linguistics colloquium 2014: Language use and linguistic structure* (pp. 641–662). Olomouc: Palacký University.

Wallis, S.A. (2019a). Comparing χ^2 tables for separability of distribution and effect: Meta-tests for comparing homogeneity and goodness of fit contingency test outcomes. *Journal of Quantitative Linguistics, 26* (*4*), 330–355. https://doi.org/10.1080/09296174.2018.1496537

Wallis, S.A. (2019b). Investigating the additive probability of repeated language production decisions. *International Journal of Corpus Linguistics, 24* (*4*), 492–525. https://doi.org/10.1075/ijcl.17093.wal

Wallis, S.A. (2019c). Confidence intervals on pairwise ϕ statistics. *corp.ling.stats*. London: Survey of English Usage. Retrieved from https://corplingstats.wordpress.com/2019/12/17/confidence-intervals

Wallis, S.A. (2020a). Grammar and corpus methodology. In B. Aarts, G. Popova & J. Bowie (Eds.), *Oxford handbook of English grammar*. Oxford: Oxford University Press.

Wallis, S.A. (2020b). Further evaluation of Binomial confidence intervals. *corp.ling.stats*. London: Survey of English Usage. (Updated 2025). Retrieved from https://corplingstats.wordpress.com/2020/02/23/further

Wallis, S.A. (2020c). ϕ intervals by inverted Gaussian $S(\phi)$. *corp.ling.stats*. London: Survey of English Usage. Retrieved from https://corplingstats.wordpress.com/2020/02/21/phi-intervals

Wallis, S.A. (2020d). Boundaries in nature. *corp.ling.stats*. London: Survey of English Usage. Retrieved from https://corplingstats.wordpress.com/2020/01/14/boundaries-in-nature

Wallis, S.A. (2021). Evaluating the performance of risk ratio and odds ratio tests. *corp.ling.stats*. London: Survey of English Usage. Retrieved from https://corplingstats.wordpress.com/2021/11/15/evaluating

Wallis, S.A. (2022). The confidence of entropy – and information. *corp.ling.stats*. London: Survey of English Usage. Retrieved from https://corplingstats.wordpress.com/2022/08/08/the-confidence-of-entropy

Wallis, S.A. (2024a). Re-evaluating continuity correction for Wilson intervals. *corp.ling.stats*. London: Survey of English Usage. Retrieved from https://corplingstats.wordpress.com/2024/05/19/re-evaluating

Wallis, S.A. (2024b). Continuity correction for risk ratio and other intervals. *corp.ling.stats*. London: Survey of English Usage. Retrieved from https://corplingstats.wordpress.com/2024/03/02/continuity-correction

Wallis, S.A. (2024c). Confidence intervals for 'common statistics used in corpus linguistics'. *corp.ling.stats*. London: Survey of English Usage. Retrieved from https://corplingstats.wordpress.com/2024/10/29/confidence-intervals

Wallis, S.A. (2024d). The confidence of chi-square. *corp.ling.stats*. London: Survey of English Usage. Retrieved from https://corplingstats.wordpress.com/2024/11/28/the-confidence-of-chi-square

Wallis, S.A. (2025). Plotting the 'mid-p' distribution. *corp.ling.stats*. London: Survey of English Usage. Retrieved from https://corplingstats.wordpress.com/2025/01/26/plotting-mid-p

Wallis, S.A. & Aarts, B. (2007). *Final report to EPSRC: Next generation tools for linguistic research in grammatical treebanks*. London: Survey of English Usage. Retrieved from www.ucl.ac.uk/english/research/survey-english-usage/next-generation-tools-final-report

Wallis, S.A. & Mehl, S. (2022). Comparing baselines for corpus analysis: Research into the *get*-passive in speech and writing. In O. Schützler & J. Schlüter (Eds.), *Data and methods in corpus linguistics: Comparative approaches*. Cambridge: Cambridge University Press.

Wallis, S.A. & Nelson, G. (1997). Syntactic parsing as a knowledge acquisition problem. In E. Plaza & R. Benjamins (Eds.), *Knowledge acquisition, modeling and management: Proceedings of the 10th European knowledge acquisition workshop, Catalonia, Spain* (pp. 285–300). Berlin: Springer-Verlag.

Wallis, S.A. & Nelson, G. (2001). Knowledge discovery in grammatically analysed corpora. *Data Mining and Knowledge Discovery*, *5* (*1*), 307–340.

Wattam, S.M. (2015). *Technological advances in corpus sampling methodology* (Unpublished PhD thesis). Lancaster University, Lancaster, United Kingdom. Retrieved from https://www.proquest.com/openview/26a4791ad32b3442896e362f95d4517d/1

Wilson, E.B. (1927). Probable inference, the law of succession, and statistical inference. *Journal of the American Statistical Association*, *22* (*158*), 209–212. https://doi.org/10.1080/01621459.1927.10502953

Yáñez-Bouza, N. (2011). ARCHER past and present (1990–2010). *ICAME Journal*, *35*, 205–236.

Yates, F. (1934). Contingency tables involving small numbers and the chi-square test. *Journal of the Royal Statistical Society*, *1* (*2*), 217–235. https://doi.org/10.2307/2983604

Yule, G.U. (1944). *The statistical study of literary vocabulary*. Cambridge: Cambridge University Press.

Zar, J.H. (2010). *Biostatistical analysis* (5th ed.). Upper Saddle River, NJ: Prentice Hall.

Zipf, G.K. (1949). *Human behavior and the principle of least effort*. Cambridge, MA: Addison-Wesley.

Zou, G.Y. & Donner, A. (2008). Construction of confidence limits about effect measures: A general approach. *Statistics in Medicine*, *27* (*10*), 1693–1702. https://doi.org/10.1002/sim.3887

INDEX